D1193790

WOMEN AND WAR

WOMEN AND WAR

A Historical Encyclopedia from Antiquity to the Present

VOLUME ONE

BERNARD A. COOK, EDITOR

Santa Barbara, California Denver, Colorado Oxford, England

Library of Congress Cataloging-in-Publication Data is available from the Library of Congress.
ISBN 1-85109-770-8   1-85109-775-9 (e-book)

10 09 08 07 06   10 9 8 7 6 5 4 3 2 1

This book is also available on the World Wide Web as an eBook.
Visit abc-clio.com for details.

ABC-CLIO, Inc.
130 Cremona Drive, P.O. Box 1911
Santa Barbara, California 93116-1911

The acquisitions editor for this title was Alicia Merritt, the project editor was Carla Roberts, the media editor was Ellen Rasmussen, the media manager was Caroline Price, the editorial assistant was Alicia Martinez, the production manager was Don Schmidt, and the manufacturing coordinator was George Smyser.

This book is printed on acid-free paper ♾.
Manufactured in the United States of America

To my children, Bernie and Jennifer;
their spouses, Jen and Bora;
and my grandchildren, Lucy and Emmett

Contents

VOLUME ONE

A

B

C

D

E

F

H

I

J

K

VOLUME TWO

L

M

N

O

P

R

S

T

U

V

W

Y

Z

Foreword

Much of history is shaped by warfare, and women's history is no exception. Across the centuries, noncombatant women have been victims of war, and their multitude of stories have left a sad and enduring legacy. Women's active participation in battle and direct contributions to defense, however, have traditionally been overlooked. Accomplished unofficially, undercover, in disguise, and, until recently, by legislatively limited numbers of participants, women's often obscure activities have been difficult to trace and research and thus have been ignored and forgotten. Within the past twenty years, as military and feminist historians have begun to look more carefully at women in uniform, it has become apparent that historically women have been propelled into ever-increasing military roles by national need.

Limited in the eighteenth and nineteenth centuries to medical and supply-related functions that reflected their societal roles, women served in secret, nursed the wounded, or became involved in the production, collection, and dissemination of food, medicines, clothing, and equipment. Women moved into communications and clerical work at the turn of the century. By 1917, few men possessed these skills, so when the American Expeditionary Force in Europe discovered it needed telephone operators to route commands from headquarters to the front lines and efficient clerks to manage masses of records, the Army recruited women to work under contract. Meanwhile, Army and Navy nurses cared for soldiers and sailors at home and abroad, the influenza epidemic lending increased urgency and importance to their role.

During World War II, a general manpower shortage meant that the nation had to turn to women to serve in widely diverse jobs in both the civilian and military sectors. Servicewomen were assigned not only as nurses and administrators but also to jobs traditionally held by men and became mechanics, truck drivers, and air tower control operators. The function of need even superseded traditional concerns for military women's safety and placed Army nurses on the front lines in North Africa and Anzio and members of the Women's Army Corps in London during the German bombing.

Since then, paralleling women's wider roles in the economic and social sectors of society, servicewomen have entered into a continuously growing array of military occupations, from technical jobs to intelligence, law enforcement, logistics, command, and combat roles. The number of women serving in the Armed Forces has expanded rapidly; women now represent approximately 15 percent of the force. A consequence of this expansion is that women are now an essential part of the force, vital to the mission integrity of a majority of fighting units.

In the recently published memoir of her service in Iraq in 2003, Navy nurse Commander Cheryl Lynn Ruff explained why she wanted to serve with U.S. forces in Iraq: "These guys need us now." In this she speaks for women who served with and in the U.S. Armed Forces across time. Need was the reason that compelled Mary Ann Bickerdyke and Clara Barton to bring food and medicines to soldiers languishing in Army hospitals. Army nurses and female contract surgeons served at casualty clearing stations near the front lines in France and Belgium during World War I because their skills were needed, and Army nurses arrived in North Africa with the invading troops and served under fire at Anzio so that wounded soldiers would receive the best possible medical care. The Navy assigned Lieutenant Commander Bernice Walters, MD, to the hospital ship *Consolation* off the coast of Korea because she was a highly skilled physician anesthetist. The Marine Corps sent Sergeant Barbara Dulinsky to Vietnam because they needed a trained documents manager in Saigon.

During every American war, women sacrificed their lives because they perceived a need and a duty. The roster of their names includes Revolutionary War heroine Jemima Warner, killed by enemy fire during the siege of Quebec, and Civil War Union soldier Rosetta Wakeman who died in disguise during the Louisiana Red River Campaign of 1864. Two Army nurses were among the first U.S. military personnel to die in World War I, and sixteen servicewomen were killed in action during World War II. Army nurse Lieutenant Sharon Lane was killed by an enemy mortar at Chu Lai, Vietnam. Air Force flight nurse Captain Mary Klinker died in the ill-fated Operation Babylift in 1975. As the proportion of women serving in the armed forces grew, so did the numbers of female casualties. Since the beginning of the war in Iraq in 2003, more servicewomen have died from enemy fire than in any past conflict.

Military women's service on the front lines under fire and amid primitive field conditions as well as their deaths in past wars have frequently been overlooked or discounted by military historians, and even some feminist historians, simply because such service did not interest them. Military historians, immersed in battlefield tactics, paid scant attention to women and their activities, and feminist historians were disinclined to write about war. At the Women in Military Service for America Memorial Foundation, our mission is to collect, preserve, and disseminate women's contributions to the defense of the United States. The importance of our efforts was reinforced recently when some politicians questioned how close to the front lines we want our servicewomen assigned and how gender-integrated we want our armed forces to be. During a time when the full extent of women's military roles are being debated, it is essential that we as a nation possess a full and complete understanding of the roles that women have played during times of war throughout the history of the nation.

Historian Bernard Cook of Loyola University has undertaken and brought to fruition the mammoth task of coalescing women's travails during war and their contributions to defense throughout world history. He has included the well known as well as the obscure and missed very few. Readers will quickly realize that the overarching themes of serving because of need and forgotten service remain true no matter which country's history is being studied. This encyclopedia belongs on the reference shelf of every scholar of military history, women's studies, and modern civilizations. May it serve as a starting point for further research in a new and emerging historical field and an inspiration to scholars everywhere.

Judith Lawrence Bellafaire,
Women in Military Service for America Memorial Foundation

Acknowledgments

To my wife, Rosemary, I must express my gratitude for her patience and advice. Her invaluable and tireless assistance proofreading has rendered the book more readable. My secretary, Vicki Horrobin, always demonstrated with this project as with others, cheerful support and extraordinary effort. Victoria McCardel, my student assistant, provided most helpful assistance keeping records, handling correspondence, and doing research. Patricia Doran, the Interlibrary Loan Coordinator at the Loyola University Library, offered her talent and assistance on this project, locating needed books and articles.

I am particularly grateful for the suggestions from many of the contributors to this encyclopedia, who have made it a more comprehensive work. Lee Ann Ghajar and Judith Bellafaire at the Women in Military Service for America Memorial in Arlington, Virginia, were encouraging and most helpful. Britta Granrud, the curator of collections at the Memorial's archives patiently provided me with a wealth of unpublished letters, diaries, memoirs, and photographs.

I am grateful for the talent and effort provided by the professionals at ABC-CLIO. My special thanks to Alicia Merritt, the acquisitions editor, for her encouragement and assistance with all sorts of details; to Carla Roberts, the production editor; to Peter Westwick and Alexander Mikaberidze for their assistance and helpful suggestions; to Ellen Rasmussen for her work in locating illustrations; and to all of the other professionals who helped with this project, including Deborah Lynes and the staff of D&D Editorial Services.

Introduction

This encyclopedia deals with the experiences of women in traditional wars between territorially based armies, but it also approaches war in a much broader sense. It includes the involvement of women in a wide range of organized violence, guerrilla warfare, low-intensity warfare, struggles for national liberation, insurgencies, revolutions, and terrorism. It considers the impact of all sorts of war on women and their role on the home front as well as on the front line. One historian has asserted "women *are* invisible (in history) unless we are looking straight at them" (Rosenhaft 1992, 140). It is hoped that this encyclopedia will contribute to the visibility of women in this unfortunate aspect of the human experience.

War has been a constant plague afflicting humanity. Throughout history, women have been involved in war. Sometimes they were compelled to fight and resist in desperation as their tribes, villages, or towns were under assault. The widow Kenau Hasselaer led the resistance of the women of Haarlem against the besieging Spaniards in 1572–1573 until the city was starved into submission and its defenders massacred. Sometimes a woman would move to the fore to replace male leaders, husbands, fathers, or brothers who had been killed or had failed to provide adequate leadership. Boudicca, who led the Iceni of Britain against the Romans, and Queen Durgautti (Durgawati) of Gurrah (Gondwana) in Hindustan are among the number who fit this category. Trieu Thi Trinh, who led the Vietnamese against the Chinese in 248 and declared, "I wish to ride the tempest, tame the waves, kill the sharks. I want to drive the enemy away to save our people," "merely" rose to the occasion (Bergman 1974, 54).

More frequently and throughout history, women have been the victims of war. They have been forced to grieve slain husbands and children. They have been brutalized and killed. Women have been viewed as property to be seized in war and enslaved. In April 1822, the Turks massacred or enslaved thousands of Greek women on the island of Chios in retaliation for the atrocities perpetrated by Greek insurgents at Tripolitsa. By the time of the rampage of the Turks, which was depicted by Eugene Delacroix in his painting *Massacre of Chios,* was over, the population of the island had been reduced from 120,000 to 30,000. Atrocities against women constantly reoccur in ethnic conflict. Women have been singled out as bearers of the nation. Women were targets of violence in the Bulgarian horrors of 1877 and during the Balkan Wars (1912–1913). Rape has been recurrent in warfare whether or not the warfare was primarily ethnically based. Victorious soldiers felt a right to misuse the women of their conquered foe. Frequently the phenomenon was an act of power, subjecting the enemy, disrupting familial traditions, and inflicting shame on the vanquished—females but also males, who were powerless to protect their women. In World War I, rape and brutality were committed by soldiers of all invading armies—the Germans in the west, the Russians in East Prussia, and even the French when they moved into Alsace (Audoin-Rouzeau and Becker 2002, 34). Stéphane Audoin-Rouzeau and Annette Becker commenting on atrocities committed by

Austro-Hungarian soldiers in Serbia wrote, "facial mutilations, particularly of the eyes, were most frequent, and done to men and women, though women were also the victims of sexual violence and mutilations of the genital organs. Anthropologists of violence have long recorded that such attacks aim at people's most human features, the face and reproductive organs. Women are victimized twice over, as human beings and as future child-bearers, and they are the first whom the invaders want to humiliate" (Audoin-Rouzeau and Becker 2002, 47). The Nazis were single-minded in their desire to wipe out Jewish women to exterminate the Jewish people. Heinrich Himmler, the head of the SS, declared, "How is it with the women and children? I decided to find a clear solution here as well. I did not consider myself justified to exterminate the men—that is, to kill them or have them killed—and allow the avengers of our sons and grandsons in the form of their children to grow up. The difficult decision had to be taken to make this people disappear from the earth" ("Famous Speeches by Heinrich Himmler"). Visibly pregnant women and women with small children were among those selected for immediate gassing on arrival at the death camps.

The dreadful phenomenon of rape in war continued in the twentieth century and into the twenty-first. Wholesale rape was committed by members of the Red Army as it advanced into Germany in 1945, but other Allied forces also raped Germans. Jill Stephenson writes, "foreign troops sometimes regarded Germany's women as part of spoils of war" (Stephenson 2001, 107). Alison Owings writes that U.S., British, and Canadian soldiers "stole, robbed, raped women. It was indescribable" (Owings 1994, 97). French soldiers did the same (Stephenson 2001, 175–176). The rapes committed by the Red Army as it advanced into Germany eclipsed that of the other Allied powers. According to Rita Botwinick, "women were raped without concern or consideration of age or appearance. Many victims felt that the Soviet troops treated such sexual abuse as a victor's justly earned prerogative" (Botwinick 1992, 106). Rape was utilized as a weapon of demoralization in the wars that accompanied the disintegration of the former Yugoslavia during the 1990s. This occurred as well during the twenty-year civil war between the Sudanese government and rebels in the south of the country and was repeated in Sudan during the bloody rampage of the Janjaweed, government-backed militias, against the people of the Dafur region. Amnesty International accused the Janjaweed of using "rape and other forms of sexual violence 'as a weapon of war' to humiliate black African women and girls" (Lacey 2004). Nicholas Kristof, in one of his many moving and graphic reports on the plight of the people of Dafur, wrote of a refugee in Chad who was "pregnant with the baby of one of the twenty Janjaweed raiders who murdered her husband and then gang-raped her." The Janjaweed told her and the women with her, "You are black women, and you are our slaves." One of the women cried and was killed. Another, who survived gang rape, "had her ears partly cut off as an added humiliation" (Kristof 2004).

If women survived war, many found themselves psychologically and economically ravaged by it. Spartan women reputedly told their men to come back with their shields or on them, but most women have been less sanguine about the loss of fathers, husbands, or sons. Although bereaved women have been universal in time and place, the sheer level of bereavement that accompanied the wars of the twentieth century was unprecedented. World War I left behind numbers of widows and orphans, which eclipsed previous conflicts. "In 1920 600,000 widows in France were eligible for state pensions" (Phillips 1996, 136). In addition, women like Vera Brittain survived burdened with the loss of brothers, fiancées, and friends. Of World War I's impact on France, Audoin-Rouzeau and Becker wrote, "two-thirds or even three-quarters of the population were affected directly or indirectly by bereavement or, more accurately, *bereavements*, the intensity of which was much greater than that experienced in peace time. Young people had died violent deaths, having suffered unprecedented mutilations of the body. Their families often did not even have the corpses of their loved ones to honor. So the mourning process was complicated, sometimes impossible, always protracted" (Audoin-Rouzeau and Becker 2002, 8–9). In addition to the pain of loss, many women were fated to live their lives in involuntary solitude. The imbalance between men and women in the age group between 20 and 35 in 1919 was such that many women who desired to marry were unable to find suitable husbands. Roderick Phillips writes, "In Britain more than a quarter of women in the 30 to 34 age group in 1921 had not married, and almost one-fifth of them never did" (Phillips 1996, 139). For many women, the return of a husband was a mixed blessing. Thousands of surviving soldiers were so physically or psychologically impaired that they were economic, physical, and emotional burdens to their wives. According to Phillips, "A million French soldiers were permanently disabled: Of them 125,000 had lost at least one limb and more than 40,000 had been completely or partially blinded" (Phillips 1996, 137).

Apart from the women whom chance, opportunity, or inclination thrust forward into positions of military leadership, those who were compelled to fight by necessity, and the ubiquitous women survivors and victims of war, other women followed and serviced armies.

One writer has referred to camp followers in the vans of the armies of World War II (Stephenson 2001, 107). However, the phenomenon was more common and even a necessity in earlier wars. Women were historically part of the world of camp and train of European armies. The women entrepreneurs who served as *vivandières* or *cantinières,* in addition to providing food and passing out drink on credit during the heat of battle, cooked and did sewing and laundry between engagements. Some were married to soldiers, but many also provided intimate female companionship to soldiers for a price. In the heat of combat, *vivandières* often replaced fallen soldiers from their unit in battle. The legend of Molly Pitcher is a composite of a number of *vivandières* during the American Revolution. A particularly heroic *vivandière* and medic in the Union Army during the American Civil War, Annie Etheridge, was decorated for saving wounded under fire.

Through the Thirty Years' War (1618–1648), the women who followed and serviced armies were largely outside the control of military authorities. Until the time of Louis XIV, private contractors were even used to transport artillery. Like transport, which was integrated into the army, the women, who served as *vivandières* or *cantinières* in armies before supply and medical services were organized in a regular fashion, were increasingly supervised by military authorities in the seventeenth and eighteenth centuries.

In addition to the *vivandières,* women fought, disguised as men, as regular soldiers and sailors. Almost 700 did so in the American Civil War. Women disguised themselves for a number of reasons. Some were desperate to escape oppressive relationships. Some were attracted by pay and rations. Some sought adventure. Some followed lovers, and some were patriots. Fighting disguised as men became more difficult in the late nineteenth century as European armies were regularized and put in standard uniforms and recruits were subjected to more than pro forma physicals. Nonetheless, a number of women disguised as men served in the Russian army in World War I. One, Yasha Bochkareva, distraught over the collapse of discipline in the Russian army, organized the first of several women's battalions. Bochkareva felt that men could be shamed into action by the example of women soldiers. Her hopes were shattered. A British woman, Flora Sandes, openly served as a soldier in the Serbian army during World War I and was promoted to the rank of major.

As armies were put in standard uniform and professionalized, the traditional military roles of women as *vivandières* was largely eliminated. Apart from the few women military leaders, camp followers, *vivandières,* and women disguised as men generally came from lower classes. This changed as armies were professionalized. Women, frequently from the middle class, in accord with Victorian view in Great Britain and the United States of women as succorers, increasingly offered their services as nurses. They served as independent contract labor in the Spanish-American War and as volunteer nurses in the Boer War. In the early twentieth century, women, inspired by the ideology of equality, formed voluntary aid societies. Under the aegis of these, women served as nurses in the Balkan Wars and during World War I. The unprecedented dimensions of World War I led to the mobilization of whole nations in support of the war. Women were recruited for war industries in most belligerent states. Thousands of British women served near the front lines as nurses, ambulance drivers, and mechanics. Thousands of others worked in armament factories and replaced men throughout the workforce. Many of the munitionettes worked with dangerous chemicals. TNT yellowed their skin and won them the sobriquet "canary girls." Although the lives of many were, in all probability, shortened by their exposure to hazardous chemicals, several hundred died during the war due to explosions and other accidents. In one explosion at a factory in the Silvertown area of London, the government admitted that 69 workers were killed and 400 injured, but it was suspected that real total was much greater (Adie 2003, 101).

The war forced Great Britain and the United States not only to organize uniformed nursing components but also to put women in uniform as auxiliaries to the regular male military. Great Britain was the first country to place women in formal military service through the formation of the Women's Auxiliary Army Corps (WAAC), the Women's Royal Air Force (WRAF), and the Women's Royal Naval Service (WRNS, referred to as the Wrens). By the end of the war, 100,000 women had volunteered to serve in these auxiliaries.

Although the British and American auxiliary units were frequently disbanded after the end of the war, they were reactivated or vastly expanded during World War II. Women were again encouraged to replace men in the economy in Great Britain and the United States, where Rosie the Riveter became a symbol for war service on the home front. The front lines of total war during World War II were incredibly far flung. World War II brought the violence of war directly to women, who died in the bombardment of cities from London to Tokyo. In addition to the bombing of Hiroshima and Nagasaki, in July 1945, U.S. planes fire bombed 66 Japanese cities killing as many as 500,000 civilians. On August 6 and 9, Tokyo was fire bombed, and another 100,000 Japanese civilians were incinerated (Boggs 2005, 174). Women were caught up as casualties and combatants in street fighting from Warsaw to Stalingrad. In addition, they were directly involved as voluntary or conscripted combatants to an unprecedented extent. In the Soviet Union, women were utilized to supplement numbers in the Soviet military out of necessity and because of the insistent desire of many. Women saw combat duty in both mixed and all-female units. By the end of 1943, the number of women serving in Soviet armed forces numbered between 800,000 and 1 million, 8 percent of the total strength of the Soviet military. Approximately half of these women served at the front (Cottam 1980, 345). Soviet women served as combat pilots, snipers, tank drivers, and regular soldiers. In addition to women volunteers, 400,000 Soviet women were drafted, of these 100,000 served in air defense units (Cottam 1998, xx). Soviet women also played an important role in the Soviet Resistance movement. By February 1944, 26,707 women were serving with partisan units and constituted 16 percent of partisan strength in Belarus (Cottam 1982, 367; Herspring 1997, 47).

Women served in partisan movements in France, Italy, and Poland as well. It was in Yugoslavia, however, that their role was of particular numerical and symbolic significance: 100,000 women served as soldiers in the National Liberation Army (NLA). Initially 1 out of 10 NLA soldiers were women, but the proportion rose to 1 in 8. In addition, 2 million women were mobilized in the Anti-Fascist Front of Women (AFZ). These women ran local government, provided support to the front fighters, and engaged in sabotage. According to Barbara Jancar, "from 1941 to 1945 8.5 percent of the total female population of Yugoslavia was killed or died" (Jancar 1982, 91). Although 25 percent of the women who joined the NLA died, versus 11 percent for the men, there was an even higher casualty rate among the AFZ (Jancar 1982, 93). The AFZ members were not formally soldiers, but this was a guerrilla war, and the front was elusive. When the Nazis and their allies overran villages, AFZ women fought and were killed or captured. Often capture led to rape, torture, and murder. The casualty rate for female Partisans exceeded that for males. Some have asserted that the higher casualty rate for women fighters resulted from their inexperience. Milovan Djilas, a Communist leader within the Yugoslav resistance asserted, however, that the women, in general, fought more bravely than the men (Djilas 1977, 210). Despite their wartime contribution, after the war women were largely excluded from the Yugoslav military. Nevertheless, according to Barbara Jancar "their political and social emancipation was the product of the military campaign" (Jancar 1982, 92).

The British and the French also officially utilized women in combat during World War II. Of the 400 agents recruited and dispatched to Nazi-occupied Europe by the British Special Operations Executive 39 were women. Women were often used as couriers, who, it was hoped, would be less conspicuous on a bicycle in the French countryside or on a train than a young man. In all, 104 agents, 13 of them women, were killed. Some were killed outright; others were captured, tortured, and then killed (see "Atkins, Vera H.").

Because of the increasing insistence for equal rights and opportunities for women, auxiliaries were not disbanded after the war but were, in fact, integrated into the regular military forces of most developed industrial nations. Women gained the right to serve at sea as ensigns and officers, to fly combat aircraft, and to serve with ground forces short of the front line, not that this makes a great difference in wars of insurgency. The role of women in the Israeli military is perhaps a harbinger of future developments in the military of the industrial democratic states. Women played armed roles in the birth of the Israeli state. During the Arab-Israeli War of 1948, more than 12,000 women served in the Israeli military and 114 died in combat (Gal 1986, 46). After independence, this military tradition continued, although in altered form. Israel is the only state in which women are conscripted. The fear of losing women in combat and opposition from Israel's religious parties led the government to exclude women from combat. There was resentment among women against their second-class status in the military. Lawsuits in the 1990s paved the way toward full participation by women in the Israeli military. By the end of 2001, Israeli women held combat positions in air defense, the air force, and artillery; as combat engineers; and in border patrol units.

If states felt compelled to integrate women into their armed forces to one degree or another, insurgent and guerrilla forces, depending on various cultural restraints, tended to utilize women as logistical support or even as fighters. In Latin America, women were involved in the Cuban Revolution. Celia Sánchez and Melba Hernández participated in Fidel Castro's failed attack on the Moncada Barracks in 1953. They subsequently changed his opinion about allowing women to fight with the guerrillas and, later, to participate in the national military. With a number of other women, they joined him in the mountains after his return from exile. Hernández formed the Mariana Grajales Brigade, a platoon consisting exclusively of women. The fact that women worked and fought alongside their male comrades had a significant impact on their place in the revolutionary movement after its victory. After the revolution, women were not drafted by the Cuban military but could volunteer for any branch and many rose to various levels of command. Elsewhere in Latin America, women since the 1950s have constituted approximately 30 percent of the 50,000 or so participants in armed revolutionary struggle (see "Latin America, Women in Guerrilla Movements").

A Vietnamese saying states, "When the enemy comes, even the women should fight" (Bergman 1974, 32). Vietnamese women have fought successive foreign interlopers—the Chinese, the

French, and the Americans. In 1907, Nguyen Thi Ba, a female innkeeper poisoned 200 French soldiers. In 1931, in Nghe Ahn and Ha Tihn provinces, a guerrilla band of 120 fighters, 40 of whom were women, temporarily drove out local functionaries and established a short-lived soviet. When Nguyen Thi Ngia, a twenty-three-year-old Nghe Tinh guerrilla fighter, was captured, she cut off her tongue to avoid breaking under torture. After the French left Vietnam in 1954, Vietnamese women fought for the South Vietnamese regime but, more significantly, for the North Vietnamese and Viet Cong.

Women played a significant role in the thirty-year-long armed struggle of Eritrea for independence from Ethiopia. By the end of the conflict in 1993, women had constituted 30 percent of Eritrea's approximately 100,000 soldiers (Wax 2004, A4). The Eritrean government attempted to rally its people with images of female soldiers, such as a poster with the legend "Mother Eritrea," which depicted a female fighter with a baby on her back brandishing an AK-47.

If women have so often been victims of violence, they have also proved to be capable of being agents of violence. Women historically have been assassins. Judith killed Assyrian general Holofernes, and Charlotte Corday killed the French revolutionary Jean Paul Marat. With the liberatory ideology unleashed by the French Revolution, however, women have increasingly been involved in revolutionary movements, and when the opposed power seemed impregnable, they have resorted to the weapon of the weak and desperate: terrorism. Women were among the populist terrorists who plotted the assassination of Alexander II in Russia in 1881, and one, Sophia Perovskaya, died on the scaffold for the deed. The execution of Gesia Gelfman was delayed because she was pregnant. She died in prison of peritonitis after giving birth. Women terrorists are an increasing phenomenon even in societies with strictly ascribed sexual differentiation. A woman killed the Indian president Rajiv Gandhi and eighteen others when she blew herself up near him in 1991. Women played a significant role in the Italian Red Brigades and were significant not only as participants in Germany's Red Army Faction but also as its leaders. Christian Lochner, a German antiterrorist, has asserted that women terrorists are more ruthless and dangerous. He said, "For anyone who loves his life, it is a very clever idea to shoot the woman first. From my experience women terrorists have much stronger characters, more power, more energy. There are some examples where a man waited a moment before they [sic] fired, and women shot at once. This is a general phenomenon with terrorists" (MacDonald 1991, xiv). In Muslim Chechnya, Palestine, and Iraq, women have been suicide bombers. They were among the Chechen terrorists at a Moscow theater in October 2002 and at the school at Beslan in 2004.

Reflecting on the pictures of Private First Class Lynndie England of the U.S. National Guard, inside the Abu Ghraib prison in Baghdad, Melissa Sheridan Embser-Herbert wrote, "Just as women have proven themselves capable of leading troops in difficult situations, so they have now shown that they can become vulnerable to the power of a role, the power of wielding power. Images of a woman giving a 'thumbs up' beside a hooded, naked man have highlighted the horrors of war in a way I don't believe would have happened had we seen only more traditional images of men at war. Putting a woman's face on war's brutality has I believe, prompted a depth of discussion that might not otherwise have occurred" (Embser-Herbert 2004, B1 and 4).

—*Bernard A. Cook*

References and Further Reading

Adie, Kate. 2003. *Corsets to Camouflage: Women and War.* Published in association with the Imperial War Museum. London: Hodder and Stoughton.

Audoin-Rouzeau, Stéphane, and Annette Becker. 2002. *14–18 Understanding the Great War.* Translated by Catherine Temerson. New York: Hill and Wang.

Bergman, Arlene. 1974. *Women of Vietnam.* San Francisco: Peoples Press.

Boggs, Carl. 2005. *Imperial Delusions: American Militarism and Endless War.* Lanham, MD: Rowman and Littlefield.

Botwinick, Rita S. 1992. *Winzig, Germany, 1933–1946: The History of a Town under the Third Reich.* Westport, CT: Praeger.

Cottam, Jean. 1980. "Soviet Women in Combat in World War II: The Ground Forces and the Navy." *International Journal of Women's Studies* 3 (July/August 1980) 4: 345–357.

———. 1982. "Soviet Women in Combat in World War II: The Rear Services, Resistance behind Enemy Lines and Military Political Workers." *International Journal of Women's Studies* 5, no. 4 (September/October 1982) 367.

———. 1998. *Women in War and Resistance.* Nepean, Canada: New Military.

Djilas, Milovan.1977. *Wartime.* New York: Harcourt Brace Jovanovitch.

Embser-Herbert, Melissa Sheridan. 2004 "When Women Abuse Power Too." *Washington Post* (May 16): B1, B4.

"Famous Speeches by Heinrich Himmler." On October 6, 1943, Himmler's speech to Gau and Reich chiefs of the party in Posen (Poznan), http://www.scrapbookpages.com/DachauScrapbook/HimmlerSpeeches.html (accessed March 8, 2005).

Gal, Reuven. 1986. *A Portrait of the Israeli Soldier.* Westport, CT: Greenwood.

Herspring, Dale R. 1997. "Women in the Russian Military: A Reluctant Marriage." *Minerva: Quarterly Report on Women in the Military* 15 (summer) 2: 47

Jancar, Barbara. 1982. "Yugoslavia: War of Resistance." In *Female Soldiers—Combatants or Noncombatants? Historical and Contemporary Perspectives,* edited by Nancy Loring Goldman. Westport, CT: Greenwood.

Kristof, Nicholas D. 2004. "Magboula's Brush with Genocide." *New York Times,* June 23.

Lacey, Marc. 2004. "Rape Used as Weapon in Sudan, Group Says." *Times-Picayune* (New Orleans) (July 19).

MacDonald, Eleineen. 1991. *Shoot the Woman First.* New York, Random House.

Owings, Alison. 1994. *Frauen, German Women Recall the Third Reich.* New Brunswick, NJ: Rutgers.

Phillips, Roderick. 1996. *Society, State, and Nation in Twentieth-Century Europe.* Upper Saddle River, NJ: Prentice Hall.

Reiss, Rodolphe Archibald. 1916. *Report upon the Atrocities Committed by the Austro-Hungarian Army during the First Invasion of Serbia.* Translated by F. S. Copeland. London: Simpkin, Marshall, Hamilton, Kent.

Rosenhaft, Eve. 1992. "Women in Modern Germany." In *Modern Germany Reconsidered, 1870–1945,* edited by Gordon Martel. Pages 140–158. London and New York: Routledge.

Stephenson, Jill. 2001. *Women in Nazi Germany/* Harlow, England: Longman/Pearson Educational.

"Vera Atkins, CBE, Légion d'honneur," 64 Baker Street. http://www.64-baker-street.org/also/also_vera_atkins_her_story.html (cited January 10, 2006).

Wax, Emily. 2004. "Respected in Battle, Overlooked at Home: Eritrea's Female Veterans Seek Peacetime Role." *Washington Post* (April 2): A4.

Topic Finder

Combat Units (Female)

Companions

Great Britain, Women in Service during World War I
Great Britain, Women on the Home Front during World War II
Greek Women and War in Antiquity
Iran-Iraq War and Gulf War, Impact on Women of Iraq
Italy, Women in the Resistance during World War II
Italy, Women on the Home Front and in the Services during World War I
Japan, Women and the Home Front, World War II
Korea: Women and the Home Front during World War II
Malta, Women and Wars in
Norway, Resistance Movement during World War II German Occupation, Women and
Roman Women and War
Rosie the Riveter
United States, Home Front during World War I
United States, Home Front during World War II

Impact of War

Civil War, American, and Women
France, World War I, Psychological Impact on French Women
Trauma and Brutalization Unleashed by World War I

Journalists

Chapelle, Dickey
Emerson, Gloria
Fallaci, Oriana
Friang, Brigitte
Gellhorn, Martha
Higgins, Marguerite
Hull, Peggy, pseud.
Journalists, American Women, during World War I
Lederer, Edith
Luce, Clare Boothe
Schuyler, Philippa
Tomara, Sonia
Trotta, Liz
Watts, Jean

Medical Service

Anderson, Louisa Garrett
Australian Army Nursing Service/Royal Australian Army Nursing Corps
Bagot, Lady Theodesia
Barry, James
Barton, Clara
Bennett, Agnes Elizabeth Lloyd
Black, Catherine
Blackwell, Elizabeth
Chisholm, Mairi Lambert
Civil War, American, Women in the Medical Services in the
Conquest, Joan, pseud.
Cornum, Rhonda
Curie, Maria Sklodowska, and the Little Curies
Dix, Dorothea
Etheridge, Anna
Fairchild, Helen
Farmborough, Florence
Furse, Lady Katherine Symonds
Great Britain, Women in Service during World War I
Hamilton, Cicely Marie
Haverfield, Evelina
Hodges, Katherine
Hoge, Jane Currie Blaikie
Hutton, Lady Isabel Galloway
Inglis, Elsie, and the Scottish Women's Hospitals
Kea, Salaria
King, Olive
Livermore, Mary Ashton Rice
Lowther, Barbara
McCarthy, Emma Maud
McDougall, Grace Ashley-Smith
McGee, Anita Newcomb
Medical Specialist Corps, United States Women in Military Service, World War II
Mercy Ship
Nightingale, Florence

Nurses, U.S. Army Nurse Corps in World War I
Nurses, U.S. Army Nurse Corps in World War II
Red Cross of the United States: World War I and World War II
Ross, Ishobel
Sandes, Flora
Smith, Winnie
Stark, Dame Freya
Stobart, Mabel
Tower, Ellen May
Thurstan, Violetta
T'Serclaes, Baroness Elizabeth de
Van Devanter, Lynda
Walker, Mary Edwards
Washington, Marguerite Pat Beauchamp Waddell
Whittle, Reba Zitella

Military Awards

Russia, Women Recipients of the Order of St. George
Soviet Union, Order of Glory, I Class, Soviet Women Recipients
Soviet Union, Order of the Red Banner, Women Recipients
Soviet Union/Russian Federation, Women Heroes of the

Military Leaders

Aishah
Andean Rebellion of the Eighteenth Century
Artemisia of Caria
Azurduy de Padilla, Juana
Boudicca, Queen of the Iceni
Cherokee War Woman
Cleopatra VII, Queen of Egypt
Eleanor of Aquitaine
Fulvia
Gandhi, Indira
Guljamal-Khan(um)
Kurmanjan-Datkha
Matilda of Tuscany
Ward, Nancy
Zenobia, Queen of Palmyra

National Liberation

Andean Rebellion of the Eighteenth Century
Azurduy de Padilla, Juana
Black Sash
Colenso, Harriette
Devlin, Bernadette
First, Heloise Ruth
Fuld, Bracha
Garibaldi, Anita
Gonne, Maud
Islamic Resistance Movements, Women and
Lakshmi Bai and Sepoy Rebellion
Lebrón, Lolita
Mandela, Winnie
Markievicz, Countess Constance
Mau Mau Rebellion, Women in the
Nongqawuse
Philippines, Women during the American Suppression of the Insurrection in
Polish Independent Women's Battalion, Emilia Plater
Ulster, Women during the Troubles in
Wexford Rising, Women of

Nations, War Experience of Women in Various Nations

See Home Front

Native American Warriors/Scouts/Intermediaries

Nonhelema
Ward, Nancy
Winema
Winnemucca, Sarah

Nobel Peace Prize Winners

Balch, Emily Green
Peace People Movement
Suttner, Baroness Bertha Sophie Felicita von
Williams, Jody

Pacifists
McDowell, Mary Stone

Peace Activists
Addams, Jane
Balch, Emily Green
Catt, Carrie Chapman
Curtis, Cathrine
Dilling, Elizabeth
Fonda, Jane
Goldstein, Vida
Hobhouse, Emily
Locke, Elsie
Luxemburg, Rosa
McDowell, Mary Stone
Mead, Lucia Ames
Moore, Eleanor May
Mowlam, Marjorie
Olmsted, Mildred Scott
Onions, Maude
Pankhurst Family: Emmeline, Christabel, E. Sylvia, and Adela Pankhurst Walsh
Peace People Movement
Saumoneau, Louise
Street, Jessie
Suttner, Baroness Bertha Sophie Felicita von
Williams, Jody

Peace Movements
International Congress of Women: Antiwar Protest of Women in World War I
International Manifesto of Women
National Legion of Mothers of America
Peace People Movement
Ulster, Women during the Troubles in
United States, Opposition to U.S. Entry into World War II by Right-Wing American Women
Vietnam, Women in the Buddhist Peace Movement

Photographers
Bonney, Therese
Bourke-White, Margaret
Bubley, Esther
Chapelle, Dickey
Lange, Dorothea
Meiselas, Susan

Pilots
Avenger Field
Baumgartner, Ann
Belik, Vera Luk'ianovna (see Makarova, Tat'iana Petrovna)
Brown, Ruth Humphries
Chamberlain, Margaret Lenora
Cochran, Jacqueline
Dalrymple, Mildred Inks
Fedutenko, Nadezhda Nikiforovna
Fomicheva-Levashova, Klavdiia Iakovlevna
Grizodubova, Valentina Stepanovna
Hobby, Oveta Culp
Johnson, Amy
Leska-Daab, Anna
Lewandowska, Jania
Litviak, Lidiia Vladimirovna
Makarova, Tat'iana Petrovna, and Belik Vera Luk'ianovna
Parrish, Marie O'Dean Bishop
Peake, Felicity
Pilots of the IL-2
Raskova, Marina Mikhailovna
Reitsch, Hanna
Sosnowska-Karpik, Irena
Soviet Union, 46th Taman Guards Bomber Aviation Regiment
Soviet Union, 125th M. M. Raskova Borisov Guards Bomber Aviation
Soviet Union Air Defense, 586th Fighter Aviation Regiment
Tackaberry, Betty Guild
United States, Women's Airforce Service Pilots
United States, Women's Auxiliary Ferrying Squadron
United States, Women's Flying Training Detachment

Sieges
Malta, Women and Wars in
Paris Commune, Women and the

Spies/Secret Agents/Diplomatic Services/Women Accused of Spying
Atkins, Vera
Baissac, Lise de
Baker, E. H.
Bell, Gertrude Margaret Lowthian
Borrel, Andrée
Boyd, Isabelle
Brant, Mary
Cormeau, Yvonne
Cushman, Pauline
Darragh, Lydia
Eriksen, Vera
Granville, Christine, pseud.
Greenhow, Rose O'Neale
Hall, Virginia
Harnack-Fish, Mildred
Khan, Noor Inayat
Kuczynski, Ursula
Martin, Grace, and Moon, Rachel
Mata Hari, pseud.
Moon, Lottie, and Moon, Ginnie
Petit, Gabrielle
Rolfe, Lilian
Rosenberg, Ethel
Rudellat, Yvonne
Sansom, Odette
Schmidt, Kitty
Schulze-Boysen, Libertas
Secord, Laura
Senesh, Hannah
Stark, Dame Freya
Szabo, Violette
Tubman, Harriet
Van Lew, Elizabeth Louise
Wake, Nancy
Witherington, Pearl

Survivors
Brittain, Vera Mary
Scotland: War Widows and Refugees in, 1640s and 1688–1690
Trümmerfrauen

Symbols
Greece, Women and Female Imagery in Greek Warfare
Marianne
Posters, U.S., Images of Women in World War II
Rosie the Riveter
Yugoslavia, Mother and Bride Images of Militant Serbian Nationalism

Terrorists
Baader-Meinhof Gang
Hirsch, Ilse
Islamic Resistance Movements, Women and the
Red Army Faction, West Germany, Women of the
Red Brigades, Italy, Women of the

Vietnam
Baez, Joan Chandos
Fonda, Jane
Gellhorn, Martha
Van Devanter, Lynda
Vietnam, U.S. Women Soldiers in
Vietnam, Women in the Buddhist Peace Movement
Vietnam, Women in War and Resistance before 1954

War Crimes
Armenian Holocaust
Armenian Women Victims of Genocide
Belgium, Women during World War I
Biological Warfare Experimentation, Japanese
Einsatzgruppen
Forced Labor, Nazi Germany
Holocaust and Jewish Women
Lidice Massacre
Nanking, Rape of
Oradour-sur-Glane Massacre
Rape in War
Ravensbrück

War Criminals
Bilien, Valentina

AANS

See Australian Army Nursing Service/Royal Australian Army Nursing Corps

Acquired Immunodeficiency Syndrome

See AIDS, War and the Spread of

Addams, Jane (1860–1935)

Sociologist, social reformer, and pacifist. Jane Addams is probably best remembered as the administrator of a settlement house in Chicago called Hull House and for her effort to improve conditions for racial and ethnic minorities, women, and the poor. She was also an ardent pacifist, however.

Addams, already well known and respected for her work at Hull House and for her support of women's suffrage, developed deep concern about the growing international tension when she traveled to Europe in 1913 as part of the American delegation to the International Suffrage Alliance. In 1914, she became chairman of a pacifist group called the Women's Peace Party, and the following year, she was elected president of the National Peace Federation. Addams called for neutral countries to become involved in continuous mediation in an effort to end hostilities. With her delegates, she visited fourteen countries and spoke personally with many key governmental figures. In 1915, several of her colleagues set sail to Europe on a Norwegian ship dubbed the *Peace Ship*. Addams was ill and did not make the trip, but she was also against the project, fearing the public would regard it negatively. As she had predicted, many Americans labeled the group traitorous.

In 1915, Addams gave a speech at Carnegie Hall in New York in which she stated that many of the young soldiers she had met related being customarily provided with stimulants before advancing with bayonets. The press interpreted her as stating that no American soldier would carry out a bayonet charge unless he was intoxicated, causing a firestorm of protest against her and other pacifists. Despite mounting criticism, Addams continued to protest the war. Nevertheless, in 1917, Herbert Hoover, director of the Department of Food Administration, commissioned her

Jane Addams. (National Archives)

to assist in relief for the hungry, a job she eagerly accepted.

Prior to U.S. involvement in World War I, Addams published *New Ideals of Peace* in 1907 in which she made reference to the work of Leo Tolstoy. Addams published some reflections on her wartime activities in *Women at the Hague* in 1915, *The Long Road of Woman's Memory* in 1916, *Peace and Bread in Times of War* in 1922, and *The Second Twenty Years of Hull House* in 1930. Addams was awarded the Nobel Peace Prize in 1931. Four years later, in 1935, she died of cancer in Chicago. Her funeral service was held at the Hull House.

—Leonard A. Steverson

See also Balch, Emily Green; International Congress of Women: Antiwar Protest of Women in World War I; International Manifesto of Women

References and Further Reading

Levine, Daniel. 1971. *Jane Addams and the Liberal Tradition.* Madison: State Historical Society of Wisconsin.

Linen, James Weber. 1935. *Jane Addams: A Biography.* New York: Appleton-Century.

Afghanistan

Fate of women in Afghanistan under the Taliban regime, which came to power as a result of the armed struggle with the Soviet Union and its Afghan allies and continued to fight the anti-Taliban Northern Alliance until the U.S. invasion of 2001. When the Taliban took control of Afghanistan in 1996, it not only reversed all of the gains that women had made in defining their personal rights and in expanding their professional opportunities, it also engaged in a brutal persecution of women that reflected a deep-seated misogyny. This misogyny likely had its roots in the fact that a large percentage of the generation of Afghani men born during the insurgency against Soviet intervention had been raised in refugee camps in Pakistan, where they had been segregated from women and schooled in especially militant forms of Islamic fundamentalism. Apologists for the Taliban have pointed to the requirements it placed on Afghani men as well, as if there were some sort of underlying equivalency in the conditions under which men and women were expected to live. The most salient demand made on men was the requirement that they grow beards, hardly the equivalent of the wholesale restrictions placed on women.

In an article for *The Australian,* Michael Phillips detailed the abuse of women under the Taliban regime, emphasizing that what might have seemed to be egregious incidents had actually become commonplace occurrences. A group of Taliban dragged one woman from her vehicle and beat her to death for having allowed her bare arm to show while she was driving. Actually, this woman could have been killed simply for being behind the wheel because women were proscribed from driving any sort of vehicle.

Another woman was sentenced to death by stoning for attempting to travel overseas with a man who was neither her husband nor a blood relation. Any hint of extramarital or of premarital contact between men and women provoked a severe response. In one of the more infamous tableaus associated with the Taliban regime, public executions were regularly conducted on the field of the Kabul soccer stadium, and a staple of these events was the execution by gunshot to the back of the head of women accused of adultery.

Indeed, under the Taliban, any man had the right to enforce restrictions on women. That is, any man could, on the spot, beat or even kill a woman for a perceived violation of law or custom. There are stories of women having been whipped by men passing them on the streets because the wind had raised their dresses and had provided a glimpse of their ankles, even though they were wearing heavy, dark stockings.

Beyond the outrageous injustices committed in the name of righteousness, the Taliban simply but brutally reduced the women of Afghanistan to a very circumscribed existence. Before the Taliban had come to power, a large percentage of the professionals in Afghanistan had been women, including some 40 percent of the physicians (*Christian Science Monitor,* November 23, 2001, 10). Although Soviet troops were guilty of atrocities against Afghani women, the Soviet-backed regime did follow the Soviet model in encouraging a progressive attitude toward women's involvement in public life. Women's entry into the professions and other arenas of public life thus became associated, in the eyes of the Islamic insurgents, with the influence of a hated regime. Under the Taliban, women were forbidden to practice any profession. The grimly logical extension of this prohibition was the further proscription of women from any sort of public education.

Moreover, women were forbidden to appear in public unless accompanied by a male relative unless they had covered themselves completely—had covered even their eyes—by wearing the burqa. Even while virtually imprisoned in their homes, women were reminded of their subservient status. To prevent women from being seen without their burqas, the windows of homes were painted. Women were also required to wear soft-soled shoes so that they could not assert their personalities even through their footsteps and so that their footsteps would not provide a reminder to men of their presence.

Women were forbidden to wear any cosmetics, even under the burqa or in the privacy of their own homes. Women could not be photographed, and pictures of women could not be shown in newspapers or periodicals or even displayed within the home. Women were not only banned from making musical recordings, films, and television programs, they were not permitted to listen to music or watch any sort of visual media. This last restriction also applied to men, although the penalties imposed on men who violated it were not as severe or as rigidly imposed as the penalties on female violators.

In this oppressive environment, seeking psychological treatment for depression would have been viewed as an act of defiance rather than a gesture of desperation. In any case, the ban on female physicians and the severe restrictions on the ability of male physicians to provide meaningful diagnoses and care to female patients combined to make even basic medical care unavailable to most Afghani women. For the sizable number of women whose husbands and male relatives had been killed in the countries' prolonged period of conflict, there were no options other than to beg for handouts from the very men who despised them.

To bring this oppression to the attention of the world, expatriate Afghani women formed the Revolutionary Association of the Women of Afghanistan. This group created a documentary record of specific cases of abuse and supported underground efforts to provide Afghani women with at least rudimentary medical care and education. In large part because of their efforts, worldwide opinion was turned against the Taliban, and funding to improve the condition of Afghani women after the defeat of the Taliban came from many quarters.

—Martin Kich

See also Iran-Iraq War and Gulf War, Impact on Women of Iraq; Islamic Resistance Movements, Women and

References and Further Reading

"Afghan Women as Co-Leaders." *Christian Science Monitor,* November 23, 2001: 10.

"Afghanistan: Restrictions on Women Dictated by the Taliban." *Women's International Network News* 27(autumn 2001): 41.

Meier, Andrew. "Stoners." *New Republic,* October 7, 1996: 14–15.

Phillips, Michael. "Taliban Waging War against the Women of Afghanistan." *The Australian,* 27 September 1999: 16.

Spaeth, Anthony, and Alan Pearce. "A Peace That Terrifies." *Time,* October 14, 1996: 62.

"The Road to Koranistan." *The Economist,* 5 October 1996: 21–23.

Agustina de Aragón (née Agustina Zaragoza y Domenech) (1786–1857)

Spanish heroine during the Peninsular War (1808–1814). Emperor Napoleon's attempt to dominate Spain in 1808 was met with an outburst of fierce opposition by Spaniards from all walks of life—men, women, children, churchmen, nobility, civilians, peasants, and soldiers. One of the most spectacular examples of popular resistance occurred during the two French sieges-to-the-death on the city of Zaragoza in 1808 and 1809. It was during the first siege, 15 June to 14 August 1808, when the renowned heroine of Spain's War of Independence, Agustina de Aragón, née Agustina Zaragoza y Domenech, displayed both bravery and temerity against the French besiegers. Agustina became known as *La Astillera* (the Gunner) and *La Defensor de Zaragoza* (the Defender of Zaragoza).

Augustina de Aragón was born on 6 March 1786 in Barcelona of Catalan parents. In 1803, she married Juan Roca Vilaseca, a corporal in the Spanish Artillery. After Roca Vilaseca had fought the French invaders in several battles, he proceeded to Zaragoza. Agustina eventually joined him there. She had acquired a basic knowledge of artillery from her husband, and thus Agustina offered her services to the artillery soldiers. This explains the presence of Agustina at the Portillo Gate battery on the day of the major French onslaught at Zaragoza.

The French siege started on 15 June under the command of Brigadier General Charles

Agustina

LVI.

Her lover sinks—she sheds no ill-timed tear;
Her chief is slain—she fills his fatal post;
Her fellows flee—she checks their base career;
The foe retires—she heads the sallying host:
Who can appease like her a lover's ghost?
Who can avenge so well a leader's fall?
What maid retrieve when man's flushed hope is lost?
Who hang so fiercely on the flying Gaul,
Foiled by a woman's hand, before a battered wall?
—"Childe Harold's Pilgrimage," Lord Byron

The renown of the Maid of Zaragoza (Saragossa) served as an inspiration during the American Civil War.

"The girls, one hundred and three rank and file, each in herself a Joan of Arc or a Maid of Saragossa, have completed their military organization, and are in for the war. They will leave here by steamer for New Orleans on Monday morning. Give them a warm embrace. Hurra [*sic*] for Mississippi!"

—*Natchez Daily Courier* (Mississippi), April 1, 1862, p. 1, c. 2; www.uttyler.edu/vbetts/girls _and_guns.htm.

Lefebvre-Desnoettes. He was superseded by General Jean-Antoine Verdier, who started the attack in earnest on 30 June with a twenty-seven-hour bombardment of Zaragoza. This was a plan for an assault on several of the major fortified gates of the city. At the Portillo Gate, most of the Spanish defenders had been killed or wounded; as a result, the earthworks protecting a twenty-four-pound cannon had been destroyed. Early on 2 July, hundreds of French soldiers launched an offensive on the unmanned Portillo Gate battery. Observing the danger, twenty-two-year-old Agustina rushed forward to the cannon, retrieved the still-burning wick from the hands of a fallen gunner, and fired the cannon loaded with grapeshot at the advancing French column. Her bravery incited the Spanish defenders to continue the attack against the now-retreating French, who suffered five hundred casualties. Agustina's courageous single-handed action and decisiveness had saved the Portillo Gate from falling into the hands of the French. The French soldiers were astounded to encounter women fighting against them. Her reputation spread throughout Spain and Europe. Agustina remained in Zaragoza during the first siege, which the French abandoned in mid-August. During the second siege of 1809, she was involved again in the defense of the city. Agustina was wounded twice during the two sieges. For her remarkable feats of bravery, Agustina was awarded military rank, the privilege to wear a special insignia, and a lifetime pension.

Throughout the remainder of the War of Independence, Agustina de Aragón fought against the French in numerous encounters; she was also present at the sieges of Teruel and Tortosa. When the war ended in 1814, she met King Ferdinand VII on his return to Spain. She later accompanied her husband to various military posts throughout Spain—Barcelona, Segovia, and Valencia. After her husband's death in 1823, Agustina married a doctor from Cobos Mesperuza, and lived in Valencia, Sevilla, and Ceuta. She died in Ceuta on 29 May 1857, at the age of seventy-one and was buried there. The following inscription was etched on her tomb: "Here lie the remains of the illustrious Heroine, whose deeds of valor and virtue in the War of Independence filled the world with admiration." In June 1870 her remains were moved to Zaragoza and interred in the church of Our Lady of Pilar. In her honor, in 1876, King Alfonso XIII bestowed on her widowed husband and his legitimate descendants the title Baron Cobos de Belchite. On 15 June 1909, to commemorate one hundred years since the sieges, King Alfonso again honored the heroine of Zaragoza by his presence when her remains were moved to the parish church of Our Lady of El Portillo.

Agustina de Aragón personified the tenacious and heroic resistance of the Spanish nation against the French armies of Napoleon during the War of Independence. She became the subject of monuments, literary works, songs, philately, and movies. Agustina was also immortalized in paintings, especially that of Francisco de Goya, in the series, "The Disasters of War," with the title, *What Valor!*

—*Gilbert G. Fernandez*

See also Vivandières in the French Army

References and Further Reading

Gomez de Arteche y Moro, Jose. 1868–1903. *Guerra de la Independencia, Historia Militar de España de 1808 a 1814.* 14 vols. Madrid: Imprenta del Deposito de la Guerra.

Lovett, Gabriel. 1965. *Napoleon and the Birth of Modern Spain.* 2 vols. New York: New York University Press, 1965.

Priego Lopez, Juan. 1966–2003. *Guerra de la Independencia 1808–1814.* 8 vols. Madrid: Editorial San Martin.

Rudoff, Raymond. 1974. *War to the Death: The Sieges of Saragossa, 1808–1809.* New York: Macmillan.

AIDS, War and the Spread of

The role of war in the spread of acquired immunodeficiency syndrome (AIDS) and its impact on women. More than 40 million people in the world today are positive for human immunodeficiency virus (HIV), and more than 20 million people have died from AIDS. In sub-Saharan Africa, the majority of HIV-positive people are women, and the trend in almost all nations is for women to represent an increasing proportion of new infections. Since its emergence, the spread of AIDS has been associated with military conflict, which has particularly affected the HIV rate among women (Beyrer 1998, 198–199).

Conflicts tend to spread HIV for a number of reasons (Irwin, Millen, and Fallows 2003, 35–37). Wars may so weaken national governments that they cannot implement AIDS prevention programs. Rural areas or entire sections of a country may be cut off from the government's health authority. For governments struggling to survive, HIV/AIDS may not be a priority, and warfare consumes resources that could otherwise be devoted to health education and programs. For people facing daily risks in a war zone, the long-term dangers of HIV/AIDS may also not be an immediate concern. During warfare the social order tends to collapse, and many women are put in a position in which it is difficult to deny men sex for protection or resources.

Armies at war can also serve to introduce or accelerate the transmission of HIV. In many developing countries, the HIV rate among soldiers is higher than in the general population and may be more than 50 percent in some armies in southern Africa (Irwin, Millen, and Fallows 2003, 36). By the mid-1990s, some army units in Thailand had a 10 percent HIV rate, whereas in Cambodia the rate reached 30 percent (Beyrer 1998, 140, 145). Historically, most soldiers are more likely to visit prostitutes and to have multiple partners (World Bank 1999, 161). The movement of soldiers thus presents opportunities for the transmission of the virus. The first appearance of AIDS in Uganda (the African state most affected by AIDS early in the pandemic) was associated with the Tanzanian invasion that overthrew Idi Amin in 1978–1979. The virus first appeared in the subcounties through which the victorious troops initially traveled (Hooper 2000, 42–51). In civil wars from Colombia to Kosovo, combatants also have used rape as an instrument of terror, which can leave women not only traumatized but also HIV-positive.

The displacement of large numbers of people also creates opportunities for HIV to spread to new groups. From Africa to Southeast Asia, guerrilla groups have turned to trafficking women to support their activities. Soldiers stationed abroad for peacekeeping may have financial resources denied to local communities and have often fueled the sex trade, as has been the case in Kosovo. In Cambodia in the early 1990s, United Nations peacekeepers seem to have contributed to the rapid spread of HIV, which particularly affected women (Beyrer 1998, 63–65). High rates of HIV tend to weaken the state, which may lead to social unrest and exacerbate regional conflicts (Beyrer 1998, 199).

Warfare tends to seal borders. In some instances, this may have helped to isolate nations from the spread of HIV/AIDS. This appears to have been the case in Nicaragua in the 1980s, during which the Nicaraguan contras conducted warfare along its border, without penetrating deep into the country, or challenging the local authority of the state. But such wars are the exception. In most cases, the closing of borders has accelerated the spread of HIV/AIDS. Warfare impedes the ability of UNAIDS and other organizations to acquire accurate information about HIV rates and epidemiology. Danger and chaos also restrict the ability of nongovernmental organizations to educate and pressure governments to act, which has been the case in Burma and the Democratic Republic of the Congo. For this reason in many developing nations at war, it is difficult to obtain good information about HIV rates among women, although it is clear that they are heavily affected.

—Shawn Smallman

See also Rape in War

References and Further Reading

Beyrer, Chris. 1998. *War in the Blood: Sex, Politics and AIDS in Southeast Asia.* New York: Zed.

Hooper, Edward. 2000. *The River: A Journey to the Source of HIV and AIDS.* New York: Little, Brown.

Irwin, Alexander, Joyce Millen, and Dorothy Fallows. 2003. *Global AIDS: Myths and Facts.* Cambridge, MA: South End.

World Bank. 1999. *Confronting AIDS: Public Priorities in a Global Epidemic.* New York: Oxford University.

AISHAH (AISHA) (CA. 614–678)

Wife of the Prophet Muhammad. Daughter of Abu Bakr of Mecca, Aishah belonged to the Bani Tamim clan of the tribe of the Quraysh. Aishah is said to have accepted Islam when she was still young and followed her family to Ethiopia around 615, where some early Muslims immigrated seeking refuge from persecution. After returning to Mecca, Aishah was betrothed to Muhammad and is usually described as his favorite wife. After Muhammad's death in 632, Aishah's father, Abu Bakr, became the first caliph, an event that eventually divided the Muslim community because a small group of Muslims believed that Muhammad's son-in-law Ali should have been chosen to lead. Abu Bakr's reign proved short, and he was succeeded by Umar in 634 and Uthman in 644. In the meantime, Aishah lived in Medina and made several pilgrimages to Mecca. After Uthman was killed in 656, Aishah ventured into political struggle for power against Ali and raised a small army, which confronted Ali's troops outside the city of Basra. Aishah personally directed her forces from the back of a camel, but the battle, known as the Battle of the Camel, ended in a crushing defeat for her. She was captured and sent to Medina under military escort, where she lived a retired life until she died in approximately 678. Aishah's legacy was, and still is, hotly debated by the Sunni and Shia Muslim scholars. Two events in the early life of this woman, who was married at age nine and widowed at eighteen, became topics of interpretation and debate. The first was the accusation of adultery levied against her in 627 when she was fourteen years old. Although she was declared innocent by divine revelation, she has never been completely vindicated. Later scholars unfavorably compared her to Muhammad's first wife Khadija ("the best of Muslim women") and his daughter Fatima ("pure"). She thus has served the aims of Muslim men who wanted to cultivate the idea that women are the ultimate source of temptation and to whom Aishah represented the force of female sexuality that had to be feared and restrained. The second and even more consequential event was the Battle of the Camel, which served as a proof for arguments against political rights for Muslim women because of concern that they could do only harm to the political and social order.

—Alexander Mikaberidze

See also Islamic Resistance Movements, Women and; Zenobia, Queen of Palmyra

References and Further Reading

Abbott, Nabia. 1942. *Aishah, the Beloved of Mohammed.* Chicago: University of Chicago Press.

Keddie, Nikki, and Beth Baron. 1991. *Women in Middle Eastern History: Shifting Boundaries in Sex and Gender*. New Haven, CT: Yale University Press.

Spellberg, D. 1994. *Politics, Gender, and the Islamic Past: The Legacy of 'A'isha Bint Abi Bakr.* New York: Columbia University Press.

Alexandra, Czarina of Russia (1872–1918)

Czarina of Russia at the time of World War I and the Russian Revolution. Alexandra of Hesse-Darmstarmstadt, a German noblewoman, became empress (czarina) of Russia upon her marriage to the newly installed monarch, Nicholas II, in April 1894. Unpopular both at the imperial court and among the wider public, her influence during World War I played an important role in the decline of political stability within her adopted country. Following the outbreak of revolution in March 1917, Alexandra and her husband were forced from power. They were held captive by the new provisional government and, after a second revolution in November 1917, by the Bolshevik forces led by V. I. Lenin. As White (antirevolutionary) forces neared the Siberian city where they were confined in the summer of 1918, Alexandra, her husband, their children, and the members of their immediate entourage were executed on Lenin's order.

A strikingly beautiful woman, Alexandra suffered from a variety of physical and psychological ailments, including a weak heart. After her marriage to Nicholas, the empress quickly gave birth to four daughters; her failure to produce a son and heir to the throne frustrated her until ten years after her wedding. She was then crushed to learn that the boy, Alexis, was afflicted with hemophilia. Alexandra had long been prone to mystical religious feelings and attracted to religious charlatans. Starting in 1907, Alexandra fell under the influence of Rasputin, a dissolute, self-proclaimed holy man who seemed able to ease her son's suffering. Alexandra's apparent domination by Rasputin led to widespread and salacious rumors of a sexual liaison between the two.

The outbreak of World War I heightened Alexandra's influence. Although the empress's German origins intensified public hostility toward her, Nicholas's departure for the fighting front in the late summer of 1915 made Alexandra the key figure in the Russian monarchy. At the urging of Rasputin, she resisted political re-

Russian Czarina Alexandra Fyodorovna. (Bettmann/Corbis)

forms such as giving more power to the Duma, Russia's representative assembly, and arranged the dismissal of capable government leaders such as the war minister, Andrei Polivanov. She also arranged the appointment of incompetent protégés of Rasputin, including Russia's new prime minister, Boris Stürmer, in January 1916. Alexandra ignored warnings that appointing a top official with a German name would be a grave provocation for the Russian public in the midst of a bitter war.

As Russia's wartime difficulties grew, Alexandra became increasingly determined to serve as a bastion of monarchial strength, even trying to influence the strategy of the Russian army. In the winter of 1916–1917, as starvation spread in the country's cities and the army was wracked by desertion, she insisted that the basic loyalty of Russia's peasant population would overcome such difficulties.

The outbreak of revolution in March 1917 led to the collapse of the monarchy as Nicholas abdicated and the imperial family was imprisoned. No foreign government would offer them sanctuary, and the former royalty, their children, and a few servants were subjected to increasingly harsh conditions of captivity. They were dispatched to western Siberia shortly before Lenin and the Bolsheviks took power in November 1917. Rescue seemed possible when civil war broke out and forces sympathetic to the czar approached Ekaterinburg where he and his family and servants were held. Late on the night of 16 July 1918, however, Alexandra and the rest of her family were shot.

—Neil M. Heyman

See also Russian Revolution and Women

References and Further Reading

Carrère d'Encausse, Hélène. 2000. *Nicholas II: The Interrupted Transition.* Translated from the French by George Holoch. New York: Holmes and Meier.

Erickson, Carolly. 2001. *Alexandra: The Last Empress.* New York: St. Martin's.

King, Greg. 1994. *The Last Empress: The Life and Times of Alexandra Fedorovna, Tsarina of Russia.* New York: Birch Lanes.

Massie, Robert. 1995. *The Romanovs: The Final Chapter.* New York: Random House.

Algeria, Women in the War of National Liberation

The role of women in the Algerian people's armed struggle for independence waged against the French from 1954 until 1962. The French held on to Algeria more tenaciously than Vietnam because they regarded it to be an integral part of France and approximately 1 million French colons resided there. On the Algerian side, women played a decisive role in the national liberation struggle. "The mobilization of a large segment of the population, particularly women, was a determining element in the victory" (Amrane 1982, 124). This was especially remarkable considering the traditional lives that most Algerian women led. They were excluded from the public sphere. They were almost entirely deprived of access to education; they were not allowed to vote; and they played no leading role in Algerian political parties. Nevertheless, during the war of liberation, they struggled "at the side of men, and rendered invaluable assistance and support to them" (Amrane 1982, 125). The women militants, like the majority of the Muslim population, were predominantly rural, and they operated in the countryside. Those more directly involved served as nurses; transported arms; or provided shelter, support, and information to fighters. A larger segment of Muslim women sympathized with the militants and provided assistance to those who directly assisted them. "[W]omen kept the network of male soldiers mobile, alive and protected" (Ladewig 2000, 247).

"The French realized that the participation of women in the war kept alive an organizationally and militarily overwhelmed resistance movement" (Ladewig 2000, 246). The French attempted to use Algerian women as their tool to break down traditional Algerian society. They promoted "unveiling" and trumpeted their opposition to patriarchal society. However, their effort failed. Algerian women coalesced behind the cause of national liberation. "Algerian women never envisioned female liberation as being a necessary component of national liberation" (Ladewig 2000, 246). Rather, in their struggle to liberate themselves from French colonial subjection, they reaffirmed their cultural distinctiveness. The veil, which could be put aside at will, proved a valuable tool during the struggle, enabling Algerian women to assume diverse identities at will. This was particularly valuable during the 1957 Battle of Algiers, during which the aid and action of militant women was essential.

Although on one level the French attempted to depict themselves as liberators of women, many Algerian women experienced violence perpetrated by the French during the war of liberation. "Many women were beaten, raped, and even tortured within their own homes" (Amrane 1982, 127). The fear of sexual violation by French soldiers motivated many young Algerian women, with the blessing of their families, to join the guerrilla resistance, the Army of National Liberation (ANL). Women aged between thirty-one and fifty-one, however, participated at a proportionately higher rate in the ANL resistance (Amrane 1982, 127). Nevertheless, it was exceptionally rare for a woman to be an actual fighter, for there were more men willing to fight than there were arms. Most women who joined the ANL were relegated to the "feminine" functions of nursing and cooking.

Women, because they roused less suspicion, did commit acts of terrorism, but this was extremely rare. Perhaps 2 percent of the women militants (Amrane 1982, 132) planted bombs, assisted in assassinations, or committed assassinations. Ladewig asserts that less than seventy women "directly worked with explosives or carried arms" (Ladewig 2000, 247). French courts condemned six women terrorists to death, but pardoned them because of their sex.

Frantz Fanon created a myth of the Algerian woman who liberated herself by participating in the struggle for national liberation on an equal basis with Algerian men (Helie-Lucas 1988, 175). After Algeria gained its independence in 1962, discrimination on the basis of sex was outlawed by the constitution. There was a dramatic increase in educational opportunities for females, and females were admitted to engineering, medical, and flight training in the national People's Army. Nevertheless, despite the expectations of Fanon, women remained largely relegated to traditional roles and their participation in politics and the economy remained limited.

—*Bernard Cook*

See also Rape in War

References and Further Reading

Amrane, Djamila. 1982. "Algeria: Anti-Colonial War." In *Female Soldier-Combatants or Noncombatants: Historical and Contemporary Perspectives,* edited by Nancy Loring Goldman, translated by Richard Stites, 123–135. Westport, CT: Greenwood.

Helie-Lucas, Marie-Aimee. 1988. "The Role of Women during the Algerian Liberation Struggle and After." In *Women and the Military System,* edited by Eva Isakson, 171–189. New York: Harvester Wheatsheaf.

Horne, Alistar. 1977. *The Savage War of Peace: Algeria 1954–1962.* London: Penguin.

Ladewig, Nicole F. 2000. "Between Worlds: Algerian Women in Conflict." In *A Soldier and a Woman: Sexual Integration in the Military,* edited by Gerard J. DeGroot and Corinna Peniston-Bird, 240–255. Harlow, England: Pearson Education.

Allen, Eliza (b. 1826)

Female volunteer who, disguised as a man, fought with the U.S. Army in the Mexican War of 1846–1848. Eliza Allen was born on January 27, 1826, in Eastport, Maine, where she enjoyed a life of comfort on the family estate. Trouble between Allen and her parents began after a man named Billings moved from Canada into the vicinity of Eastport. Billings was a poor man who worked as a day laborer to support his large family. His eldest son, William, also a day laborer, was frequently employed by Allen's father. Eliza and William Billings fell in love. After many secret meetings, Eliza pledged her troth to William despite knowing her parents would not approve of marriage to a man beneath their social status. Informed of the couple's intentions, the Allens forbade Eliza to see William. Eliza was told that if she pursued the relationship, she would be disinherited and turned out of the family mansion.

Allen received word that Billings was leaving Maine to restore harmony to the Allen family. Billings joined a volunteer company to fight in the Mexican War. Allen had read accounts of Deborah Sampson in the American Revolution and Lucy Brewer in the War of 1812 disguising themselves as men. Thanks to family wealth, she had enough personal money to go in search of Billings. She left home, cut her hair, dressed in men's clothing, and caught a ship to Portland. Using the name George Mead as her alias, she found an officer who would muster her without any formal examination. Allen then sailed with her company to join General Zachary Taylor's forces in Texas.

In March 1847, Allen participated in General Winfield Scott's spectacular landing of nearly 10,000 troops in the Mexican port city of Veracruz. Scott successfully carried out the largest amphibious attack in history to that date, but Mexican guerrilla fighters consistently harassed his troops as they advanced toward Mexico City. Allen received a severe cut to her left arm from a Mexican sword at the battle of Cerro Gordo. There she was also reunited with her beloved Billings, who was also wounded in the battle. Remaining behind with the sick and wounded, Allen and Billings entered the Mexican capital after Scott had taken possession of it. Allen, who did not reveal herself to Billings, was quartered with him in a private house during the U.S. occupation. After a peace treaty was signed, Allen and her fellow Americans sailed to New York City, where they were discharged.

Billings and his mates soon lost their military pay gambling. They took work as crewmembers aboard a ship to California, where they would pay off their passage prospecting for gold. In pursuit of Billings, Allen also boarded a ship bound for California. In the Strait of Magellan, Allen's ship rescued Billings and his shipwrecked companions. Still disguised as a man, Allen panned for gold in California. After regaining funds, the group of former volunteers sailed from San Francisco to Boston, arriving in September 1849. Allen then revealed her true identity to Billings, and the couple was eventually married with the consent of Allen's parents. Allen described her experiences in her 1851 memoir, *The Female Volunteer; or the Life, and Wonderful Adventures of Miss Eliza Allen, A Young Lady of Eastport, Maine,* a highly emotional plea and warning to parents to allow children to choose their own spouses.

—*David M. Carletta*

See also Borginis, Sarah

References and Further Reading

Allen, Eliza. 1851. *The Female Volunteer; or the Life, and Wonderful Adventures of Miss Eliza Allen, A Young Lady of Eastport, Maine.* Ohio: H. M. Rulison.

Amazons

Greek legends of Amazons, warrior women who lived beyond the borders of civilization and inverted normal gender roles. According to legend, this tribe of female warriors was descended from Ares, Greek god of war, and the nymph Harmonia. They were devotees of Artemis, goddess of the hunt. The first mention of the Amazons appears in Homer's *Iliad,* which tells that they assisted the Trojans in the Trojan War. Accounts of Amazons usually placed them even further back in a mythic past, and only the legends of Alexander the Great place them in historical time. The historian Arrian reports an account in which Alexander met Amazons, but adds that he does not believe it.

Most often, legends place the Amazons on the southeastern shore of the Black Sea, but as the Greeks explored and settled that region, the tales situated the Amazons still farther away, in Scythia or even North Africa, beyond civilization. There may have been a historic core to the legends of Amazons: archaeologists have discovered that in one Scythian tribe, which Herodotus called the Sauromatians, women hunted and fought alongside their men, and weapons have been discovered in their tombs. The legend was popular in Greece, however, as an exotic example of the "barbarous" world where all natural human law was overthrown.

The historian Strabo tells that the Amazons were an exclusively female tribe. They reproduced by visiting their neighbors each year and engaging in promiscuous sex. When the children were born, the women kept the female infants, but sent the males back to their fathers. This in itself is an inversion of normal Greek practice, which valued male children over females. Diodorus presents an even more inverted picture, one that was probably deeply shocking to Greco-Roman audiences. He tells that the Amazons did indeed live with men, but men who served as househusbands while the women were warriors, hunters, and rulers. The Amazons preserved this reverse gender discrimination, according to Diodorus, by dislocating the legs of their boy children, crippling them for life. Later writers depict Amazons even abandoning the nurture of their female children. Some authors write that, to keep their breasts from growing, the Amazons fed their daughters mares' milk instead of breast-feeding them. More radically, later authors produced a spurious etymology for *a-mazon,* which can be interpreted as "without a breast." They report that the Amazons cut off or cauterized the right breasts of young girls, so they would not be discommoded when drawing a bow.

In legend, the Amazons are always gloriously defeated. Heracles defeated and killed the Amazon queen Hippolyta. The hero Theseus later married her sister Antiope, leading to an Amazonian invasion of Athens that was only repelled after a desperate struggle—the Athenian victory over the Amazons was carved on the shield of the great statue of Athena Parthenos on the Acropolis. Similarly, Queen Penthesilea brought her army to help Troy but was killed by Achilles in battle. Achilles falling hopelessly in love with Penthesilea as she died was a popular image in art. A recurrent theme was that the Amazon warriors were wild and had to be tamed by Greek men, who were endowed with the superior gift of reason. The ultimate purpose of these tales was to reinforce Greek ideas of gender, not to overturn them.

Fascination with Amazons—with the *possibility* that women could fight and triumph in the men's world of the battlefield—continues to the present, as attested by Wonder Woman and Zena the Warrior Princess. Legends of the Amazons have also been used to explain fighting women in other cultures, and it is thus that the Amazon River in Brazil got its name after explorers saw women fighting there alongside men.

—Phyllis G. Jestice

See also Greek Women and War in Antiquity

References and Further Reading

Lefkowitz, Mary. 1986. *Women in Greek Myth.* Baltimore: Johns Hopkins University Press.

Tyrrell, William B. 1984. *Amazons: A Study in Athenian Myth-Making.* Baltimore: Johns Hopkins University Press.

American Revolution, Role of Women in the

Women's roles during the Revolutionary War in America between 1776 and 1783. Americans declared independence from Britain in 1776, and the British sent troops to the colonies to quell the revolt. Patriots (Americans who supported the Revolution) fought against the British and colonial loyalists (Americas who did not want independence from Britain). During the war, some women helped the patriots, and others sided with the loyalists. Some women, although not loyalists themselves, were affected by their husbands' loyalty to Britain, which jeopardized their safety during the war. The same was true for women whose husbands were patriots.

Throughout the war, many women maintained the household economy (i.e., they tended to farm work and family businesses) and protected their property while husbands and male relatives were at war. The wartime role of these women was to maintain such activities until the men returned home. In addition, both the British and American armies had women camp followers, who lived in the camps, helping out with chores. Some women even enlisted in the American Continental Army disguised as men, although this was illegal. The army's medical units included women who served as nurses. Women further supported the effort by feeding and providing clothing for the soldiers. Some loyalist women passed information about American troops to the British, and women could be accused of being spies or sympathizers simply by giving sanctuary to British soldiers in their homes. Married women faced property confiscation if their husbands were loyalists. Rape was another reality women faced during wartime when either army occupied an area. In Connecticut and New Jersey, rape and gang rape occurred. It became a symbol of power for the victorious side, with women the victims of this practice.

On January 1, 1776, the Continental Army began recruiting to build up its infantry, rifle, and artillery regiments, which included more than 20,000 men. If a woman wanted to enlist, she did so illegally by disguising herself as a man. For example, Deborah Sampson used the name Robert Shurtleff to enlist. It was not until she was wounded in battle and consequently undressed by a doctor that her true identity was discovered. However, her brave and patriotic behavior received compliments rather than punishment. A few women went onto the battlefield with their husbands or took their husbands' places after they were killed on the battlefield. For instance, Mary Hays fired artillery cannons against the British and stayed with her husband, a gunner, during the war. Margaret Corbin took over her husband's cannon when her husband was killed by enemy fire. The army allowed women to stay with their husbands, fathers, or sons mainly because some men might not have joined the regiments if their women were not

Women intelligence riders from South Carolina during the Revolutionary War intercepting dispatches. (Bettmann/Corbis)

allowed to go with them. Some women brought their children with them as well.

At first women camp followers were seen as a burden for the troops, but later even George Washington, commander in chief of the Continental Army, would see the value of women in the camps. They could cook and do laundry. They could also serve as nurses, although their status was low among the hospital staff, and their main duties were custodial. Nurses were also paid poorly because their work was not seen as skilled employment. Female nurses could, however, free up men from taking care of the wounded, allowing more men to fight for the army. In 1777, a Continental Army Medical Corp requirement indicated that every one hundred wounded needed one matron and ten female nurses. The nurses took nonmedical direction from the matron, who supervised the hospital and distributed medicine under the supervision of a surgeon. Women were involved in other activities at camps and battle sites as well; they molded bullets, carried water and gunpowder, and assisted at the cannons, for example.

Although women were seen as nonofficial auxiliaries, they did draw rations from the army; children who accompanied them received a half ration. When food supplies were tight, women and children used up part of the rations, which the soldiers desperately needed. Nonetheless, women did have their function in the army, and their tasks were valuable, especially because men were not adept at chores such as cleaning and mending and washing clothes.

At the start of the Revolution, the British army limited the number of women accompanying its troops to one woman for every ten men, but this ratio later increased. The Continental Army did not set a quota for the ratio of men to women in the regiments because this would force some refugee women to leave the camps when the army needed them to take care of various tasks.

In general, women's participation in combat depended on whether men were available to fight the enemy. As men left home to join the army, few, if any, were left to defend the towns and villages. Thus, many women defended their communities from the British by joining local militia groups or serving as guards. They dressed in men's clothing and armed themselves with muskets or pitchforks.

Other women were left behind after their husbands left for Britain or joined the British loyalists, and the wives of loyalists were regarded as enemies. Because married women were not considered independent from their husbands and did not have property rights, the leaders of the American Revolution seized the property and personal belongings of women married to loyalists; this included items such as carriages, jewels, clothes, and furniture. Loyalists' wives were eventually allowed to leave or were expelled by the patriots. When a woman's husband sided and served with the British, she automatically fell under suspicion of treason. If she wrote to her husband at all, she was considered a traitor. Mobs threatened women who were suspected of helping the British. Women who actually did so certainly risked their lives. In New Jersey, the penalty for treason was death. Nevertheless, the first time a woman was convicted, she only had to pay a fine of three hundred pounds and serve one year in prison. If convicted a second time, she would receive the death penalty, and no reprieve would be granted.

In Pennsylvania, New Jersey, Maryland, and Virginia, some women helped to raise funds for the Continental Army. General Washington worried that giving money to soldiers directly was not a good idea and suggested that the women instead give the funds to the government. The women refused, and Washington then suggested they provide shirts to the soldiers instead of cash. The women agreed and used the money to buy linen to make clothing for the troops.

During the war, approximately 20,000 women served in various capacities with the Continental Army. A few hundred more were enlisted in various local and state units (Gunderson 1996, 164).

—*Edy M. Parsons*

See also Corbin, Margaret Cochrane; Fulton, Sarah Bradlee; Greene, Catherine Littlefield; Ludington, Sybil; Martin, Grace, and Martin, Rachel; Molly Pitcher; Samson, Deborah; Washington, Martha Dandridge Custis; Zane, Elizabeth

References and Further Reading

Bohrer, Melissa Lukeman. 2003. *Glory, Passion, and Principle: The Story of Eight Remarkable Women at the Core of the American Revolution.* New York: Atria Books.

DePauw, Linda Grant. 1981. "Women in Combat." *Armed Forces and Society* 7 (2): 220–225.

Evans, Elizabeth. 1975. *Weathering the Storm: Women of the American Revolution.* New York: Charles Scribner's Sons.

Gundersen, Joan R. 1996. *To Be Useful to the World: Women in Revolutionary America, 1740–1790.* New York: Twayne.

Kerber, Linda K. 1980. *Women of the Republic: Intellect and Ideology in Revolutionary America.* Chapel Hill: University of North Carolina.

Andean Rebellion of the Eighteenth Century

Role of women in eighteenth-century Andean rebellions against the Spanish. The eighteenth century in the Andes has been called the age of Andean rebellion. Starting in 1730 with a rebellion in Cochabamba, the era was marked by numerous localized village revolts, insurrections, and protests, culminating in the firestorm of the Great Rebellion of 1780–1782. This violent upheaval in southern Peru and territories in present-day Bolivia and northern Chile, according to probably exaggerated contemporary estimates, left more than 100,000 dead. The rebellion comprised two large insurgencies, which gradually merged during the first half of 1781: the Túpac Amaru uprising in southern Peru and the Túpac Catari uprising in Charcas (present-day Bolivia). Women played a central role in the Great Rebellion, as both protagonists and victims. The participation of rebel women in these insurgencies often stemmed from their insertion into the kinship network of a male insurgent leader, but they led as well as followed, and some acted entirely of their own volition. That they were able to do so owed much to the remarkable relative freedom that rural, especially indigenous, women enjoyed in eighteenth-century rural Andean society.

After two centuries of colonial rule, Andean women of the eighteenth century, despite legal provisions that ostensibly circumscribed their freedom of action, were deeply enmeshed in all areas of economic and social life. Restrictions bore more heavily on elite Hispanic women than on their indigenous or mixed-race counterparts. The exceptions to this rule were female slaves, as distinct from free blacks; the conditions in which the slaves lived ranged from poor to appalling. Yet here, too, ways were found to navigate legal prohibitions to one's own advantage. Domestic slaves, particularly those in urban areas, often enjoyed a fair measure of de facto liberty, at least in comparison to their counterparts on rural haciendas and coastal plantations, whose living conditions were often dire.

Women immersed themselves fully in productive and commercial endeavors, despite ostensibly being severely restricted by law from the freedom to work in a trade or to engage in commerce. Marriage, of course, was the most viable way of life for women of the time, but numerous middle- and lower-class Hispanic women earned their daily bread as market traders or tailors, by making and renting festive costumes, by conducting long-distance commerce, and as petty *rentières* and money lenders. Among the upper tiers of society, not a few women held sway over family haciendas and estancia operations; others ran textile manufactories both large and small. From surviving notarized testaments, it is evident that many such women accumulated impressive fortunes and exercised de facto influence, both over their extended families and within colonial society.

Away from the cities, rural women, especially indigenous women, appear to have had fewer constraints. It was among the overwhelmingly more numerous indigenous population that women came to exercise an influence that took them to war in roles ranging from leaders (*cacicas*, or female chiefs) to camp followers (*rabanas*). Rural areas, however far-flung, did have strong links to the cities; members of the indigenous communities realized that cities offered a chance to market their produce and a place where they might find work. It was the city that provided an opportunity for women to become wage earners. This was not a woman's individual decision, but a collective community, or at least familial, strategy to earn money for taxes and to obtain merchandise and foodstuff otherwise unavailable through subsistence farming and village markets. Urban domestic service in the coastal cities depended heavily on slave or free black workers, but in the highland cities such as La Paz and Cuzco, indigenous servants were the norm; young indigenous servant women, in particular, were ubiquitous in urban households. Indigenous and mixed-race women (*castas, mestizas, mulattas, cholas, pardas*) had a salient presence in late colonial protests, whether violent or peaceful.

In both cities and the country, indigenous and caste women shared the general malaise that led to the outbreak of the Great Rebellion of 1780–1782 in the southern Andes. Three women in particular stood out as leaders in 1780–1781: Micaela Bastidas, wife of José Gabriel Túpac Amaru; Bartolina Sisa, wife of Túpac Catari; and Túpac Catari's sister, Gregoria Apasa, who upon becoming the consort (*amante*) of Andrés Túpac Amaru, helped to unify the two insurgencies following the capture and execution of her brother. These three consorts were more than the "women behind the throne." They played an active role that perhaps owed more to indigenous understandings of shared familial or clan responsibilities than to European notions of patriarchal leadership. In rural society, female authority was more pronounced among the upper tiers of indigenous society, manifest in the widespread phenomenon of female incumbency of the indigenous chieftainships (*cacicazgos*). These were the *cacicas,* whose authority spanned the full gamut of functions associated with this office. Their authority ranged from sole responsibility or shared responsibility with their spouses to nominal responsibility in which the woman inherited the office from a relative, the duties of which were performed thenceforth by her husband.

The most prominent of these three figures was Micaela Bastidas. At times, she appears to have directed rebel operations and to have had a better sense of military priorities than her husband, whose undoubted charisma was not always matched by a clear strategic vision or a recognition of the need to take urgent action to forestall looming military and logistical crises. Bastidas, on the contrary, combined strategic clarity with a heightened sense of urgency. Her demonstrated ability as a military planner and staff officer was superior to that of her husband. Moreover, Bastidas was reputed to have been fiercer than her husband, issuing threats to the fainthearted and ordering reprisals against deserters, peninsular Spaniards (*chapetones*), and even creoles (*españoles*), although she herself had been registered as a Creole (*española*) at her baptism. It was alleged that her orders and threats led to the death of many *chapetones* and Creoles in the provinces. She employed a mixture of menace and persuasion in forging and maintaining alliances and allegiances, oversaw prisoners and their interrogation, and directed recruiting efforts once the rebellion had commenced. She also made rebel loyalists and her "favorites" officeholders (*caciques, alcaldes*) in many highland villages. Bastidas received aid from her kinswomen, among whom Cecilia Túpac Amaru and Marcela Castro are the best known. She ruled with an iron hand at the rebel headquarters in Tungasuca while her husband was on expeditions. She sent written orders to the provinces, organized logistics, and even reprimanded her spouse over his lack of urgency and inability to understand the ebb and flow of the fortunes of war. Bastidas combined decisiveness in command with a clear appreciation of strategic and tactical considerations; her grasp of details was as assured as her astute appreciation of the strategic imperatives.

Bartolina Sisa did not exercise control over rebel partisans to nearly such a degree as did Bastidas, but she did accompany her husband and his army in battle. Indeed, her husband similarly lacked the stature of Túpac Amaru, such that Catari needed to shore up his own uncertain authority by invoking Amaru's name. Nevertheless, Bartolina Sisa remained at the center of operations in upper Peru. In particular, she helped form, organize, and direct the *catarista* army. Gregoria Apasa, however, surpassed Sisa's achievements and leadership status, and her role from mid-1781 was more akin to that of Bastidas in the northern movement. By that time, José Gabriel had been captured and executed, and his nephew Andrés (Mendigure) Túpac Amaru had taken effective control of the greater insurgency. His personal liaison with Túpac Catari's sister facilitated the union of the two movements. Their relationship was part political, part personal, and it is impossible to ascertain precisely the extent to which Andrés and Gregoria shared power. Clearly, however, she played a major role in the combined operations of the joint insurgency. In a notorious incident, when rebel forces took the town of Sorata, she and Andrés jointly sat in judgment of the captives, many of whom were summarily executed.

Gregoria Apasa became popularly known as queen (*reina*) of the southern insurgency. Micaela Bastidas was deferred to variously as *la cacica, señora gobernadora,* or simply "wife of the rebel." There was, however, tacit recognition of her de facto regal status: Túpac Catari called himself viceroy and his wife *vicereine,* thereby acknowledging the sovereignty of José Gabriel Túpac Amaru; Micaela was thus implicitly regarded as queen, in contrast to Bartolina's *vicereine.* Titles were important within indigenous society; rank lent elite authority. This held true for both women and men. Micaela derived her authority from José Gabriel's status as Inca. There were, however, other women who collaborated closely during the rebellion whose elite status sprang from their high birth or innate talents. The *cacica* of the towns of Acos and Acomayo, Tomasa Tito Condemaita, led the Indians within her chiefdom to the field of battle. The *cacica* of Combapata, Catalina Salas Pachacuti, was of noble Incan lineage; her husband was Ramón Moscoso, who derived his local authority from her inherited office and who was the cousin of the powerful bishop of Cuzco. Therefore, Doña Catalina enjoyed an elite status in both town and country. We know less about a third rebel *cacica,* Francisca Herrera, who nevertheless is perhaps the most interesting of these three: she is also described as a *beata,* or holy woman. This intriguing aside hints at a religious wellspring of female political authority in rural areas.

There is similar testimony in two later movements: in Lircay (Huancavelica) in 1811 and in Ocongate in the Cuzco region in 1814–1815. During the former, which was a localized messianic revolt, the charismatic authority of the leader was said to derive from his mother, an alleged sorceress (*bruja*); in the latter case, a major indigenous insurgency within the 1814 so-called revolution of the fatherland, the wife of the principal insurgent was also said to be a *bruja.* In any event, religious praxis and political authority were probably indivisible within native Andean society, and political authority in the colonial Andes encompassed the principle that a woman or a man might hold political office, either separately or jointly.

It was therefore right and proper that female leaders such as Bastidas, Sisa, Apasa, and Tito Condemaita should be tried for treason and related crimes; they could hardly expect a plea of mitigation, based on compulsion from their spouses, to succeed. It followed ineluctably that they would be found guilty, and the penalty for treason was death. Because of their culpability, many women died, because the death penalty was judged appropriate to their crimes. What was not consonant with due legal process, however, was the horrific manner of their execution. A few details will suffice: Bastidas's tongue was cut out, and she was then garroted. Because of the slenderness of her neck, this method was unsuccessful, and the two official executioners tied ropes around her neck, which each pulled, all the while punching her stomach and breasts until she died. Apasa was paraded with a crown made of nails, and Sisa was ritually humiliated in a similar manner. The corpses of all three were decapitated and dismembered, with their heads, arms, and hands placed on pikes at select villages throughout the southern highlands. If under prevailing legal norms they deserved death, the manner of their execution was unwarranted—and is resented to the present day by Peruvians and Bolivians. Today these women are venerated as martyrs and heroines in the struggle for freedom from Spanish tyranny.

—*David Cahill*

See also Latin America, Women in Guerrilla Movements in; Peru: Shining Path

References and Further Reading

Campbell, Leon. "Women and the Great Rebellion in Peru, 1780–1783," *The Americas* 42, no. 2 (1985):163–196.

Martín, Luis. 1983. *Daughters of the Conquistadores: Women of the Viceroyalty of Peru.* Dallas, TX: Southern Methodist University Press.

Silverblatt, Irene. 1987. *Moon, Sun, and Witches: Gender Ideologies and Class in Inca and Colonial Peru.* Princeton: Princeton University Press.

Socolow, Susan Migden. 2000. *The Women of Colonial Latin America.* Cambridge, England: Cambridge University Press.

Stavig, Ward. 1999. *The World of Túpac Amaru: Conflict, Community, and Identity in Colonial Peru.* Lincoln: University of Nebraska Press.

Thomson, Sinclair. 2002. *We Alone Will Rule: Native Andean Politics in the Age of Insurgency.* Madison: University of Wisconsin.

Anderson, Louisa Garrett (1873–1943)

Cofounder of the British Women's Hospital Corps (WHC) during World War I. Dr. Louisa Garrett Anderson, surgeon and militant suffragette, was born at Aldeburgh, Suffolk, on July 28, 1873, to Elizabeth Garrett Anderson, first female doctor in Britain, and James G. S. Anderson, a shipping magnate. She graduated from London School of Medicine for Women in 1897. Louisa then began private practice. Unlike her mother, Louisa Garrett Anderson did not face opposition to her medical education. By the beginning of the twentieth century, the right of women in Britain to study medicine and enter private practice was accepted. Nevertheless, subtle discrimination remained. The women of Britain had to struggle for emancipation, and Louisa took a leading part in this struggle.

Louisa Anderson was a militant suffragette and joined the Women's Social and Political Union (WSPU) in 1906. The organization demanded voting rights for women. Its members utilized illegal methods when their demand was rejected by Parliament in 1906. In 1912, Anderson was arrested in one violent incident when shops were attacked and stones thrown at the prime minister's residence, 10 Downing Street. At the outbreak of World War I, the suffragettes demanded the right to serve the nation. Anderson along with a fellow doctor and suffragette, Flora Murray, established the Women's Hospital Corps (WHC) in September 1914. Anderson was the chief surgeon of the corps between 1914 and 1918. Because there was still considerable opposition in the British War Office to using the services of female surgeons, both went to work for the French Red Cross. They set up military hospitals for the French army in Paris and Wimereux. The War Office then recognized the work they were doing and asked the WHC to manage the Endell Street Military Hospital in London, which was staffed completely by women—from its top surgeon to the cooks. Anderson's mother, Elizabeth Garrett Anderson, also worked at the hospital. She and the other women doctors experimented with new treatments and gained a high level of medical experience. The hospital functioned until 1919 and treated 26,000 patients.

The efforts of Anderson and the other suffragettes were vindicated when British women gained the right to vote in 1918. Anderson, who did not marry, wrote medical articles after the war and in 1939 authored a biography of her mother. Anderson died on November 15, 1943, and was buried near her home at Paul End.

—Patit Paban Mishra

See also Inglis, Elsie, and the Scottish Women's Hospitals; Stobart, Mabel

References and Further Reading

Leneman, Leah. 1994. *In the Service of Life: The Story of Elsie Inglis and the Scottish Women's Hospitals.* Edinburgh: Mercat.

Stobart, Mabel Annie Boulton. 1935. *Miracles and Adventures: An Autobiography.* London: Rider and Co.

Arab-Israeli Wars

The impact on women of the wars fought between the Israelis and Arabs since the proclamation of an independent Jewish state in 1948. During any national emergency, such as a war, women's traditional roles in society are usually altered to meet the needs of the population in crisis. The Arab-Israeli conflict is no exception. For more than fifty years, Israeli and Palestinian women have fought with knives, guns, and bombs; they have formed clubs and associations to achieve peace; and they have fought against the traditional gender roles in Jewish and Arab societies. In other words, Palestinian and Israeli women have been fighting a multifront war: against each other, against those who wage war, and against their traditional roles in society.

Gender itself has been an important element of the conflict. For example, the Israeli prime minister, David Ben-Gurion, called on Jewish women to have at least four children each and stated that to do so was their duty and obligation to the newly established Jewish state. For Israeli women who had ten or more children, Ben-Gurion bestowed the title "heroine mothers" and distributed monetary awards. Palestinian women were considered to be the "mothers of the nation," and it would be through their reproductive prowess that the continued expression of a Palestinian reality would live on (Sharoni 1995, 34–35). For both Arabs and Jews, motherhood is seen as the highest expression of nationalism, sometimes referred to as "patriotic wombs" (Kandiyoti 1996, 91).

During the Great Revolt of 1936–1939, Palestinian women provided food, water, medical attention, and shelter for countless Palestinian guerillas, and they smuggled weapons through British checkpoints. During the Intifada (the Palestinian "uprising"; 1987–1993) Palestinian women threw stones, marched in protest, burned tires, and acted as field medics to the injured. Most recently, some Palestinian women have become suicide bombers. On January 27, 2002, Wafa Idris became the first Palestinian woman to do so. One month later, Darine

Abu Aisha, an undergraduate at the Al-Najah University in Nablus, blew herself up at an Israeli army checkpoint.

Israeli women must serve two years in the military, yet the vast majority of Jewish women perform what are described as traditional womanly roles as they fulfill their obligations to the state in such positions as clerks, secretaries, typists, kitchen workers, and entertaining the male troops. The rest are loaned out to various Israeli government agencies to work as teachers, nurse's aides, and other traditional womanly jobs (Sharoni 1995, 39). Israeli women in the military belong to a gender-specific organization called the Women's Corp, referred to as *chen* in Hebrew, which translates as "charm and grace" (Sharoni 1995, 46). As Rachel Persico, who spent two years in the Israeli military, points out, "women are the auxiliary force." When the October War began in 1973, all women, civilians and those in the military, were evacuated from the conflict zone (Kandiyoti 1996, 117).

The Palestinian Women's Union was the first all-woman Palestinian group and it was established in 1921 primarily to demonstrate against Jewish immigration and to halt Palestinian prisoners from being tortured by the British governing authority. The Arab Women's Congress called on Arab women to form women's groups throughout the country to fight politically against increased Jewish immigration in particular and the British Mandate in general (Sharoni 1995, 59).

Between the establishment of Israel in 1948 and the 1967 War, or the Six-Day War, Palestinian women continued to establish political organizations, such as the General Union of Palestinian Women in 1964. Yet increasing pressures from the governments of Jordan, Egypt, and Syria as well as the continued occupation resulted in a rather stunted political front. Nonetheless, Palestinian women found spaces for themselves in such political organizations as the Palestinian Women's Association (1964), which sent delegates to attend the Palestine National Council in Jerusalem in 1965. Their work in the West Bank, however, was officially terminated in 1965 when King Hussein of Jordan declared that all organizations tied to the Palestine Liberation Organization (PLO) be officially disbanded (Sharoni 1995, 61–62).

When the Intifada broke out in 1983, numerous Jewish women's organizations emerged such as Women in Black, Israeli Women against Occupation, Peace Quilt, Women for Women Political Prisoners, and Women's Peace Net. Holding signs on Jerusalem street corners that read "Stop the Occupation" in Arabic, English, and Hebrew, the Women in Black endured verbal abuse and curses from others Jews, some with their own signs that read "The Women in Black Are Longing for Auschwitz" and "The Women in Black—A Knife in the Back of a Nation" (Emmett 1996, 23 and 33).

Palestinian women, for the most part, did not articulate a collective response to the Israeli occupation during the Intifada in part because of the fight for control of the leadership of the Intifada that was taking place between the PLO and a relatively new group, the Islamic Resistance Movement, or Hamas. Nevertheless, it was during the Intifada that Jewish and Arab women first began on a massive scale to work together to bring an end to the Arab-Israeli conflict. For example, in 1989, Israeli and Palestinian women met in Brussels. At this meeting, the binational group decided on three principles: (1) Israel needed to deal with the actual representatives of the Palestinian people, (2) resolution to the conflict would only come from negotiations, and (3) there must be mutual recognition of peace and self-determination. In other words, these women embraced the two-state solution before any official representative of the Israelis, Palestinians, or Americans (Sela and Ma'oz 1997, 215).

Palestinian and Israeli women also fought to alleviate the social, economic, and political problems that Arab and Jewish women suffered as a direct result of the decades-long Arab-Israeli conflict. In the 1970s, Palestinian women's organizations once again flourished as a result of increased Palestinian economic, social, and political pressure against the govern-

Three young women from the suicide bomber unit of the Al-Aqsa Martyrs' Brigade, Gaza Strip, 2004. (Jean Chung/Corbis)

ment of Israel. Educated women who had been born after the establishment of Israel or who grew up in areas under Israeli occupation formed the Women's Work Committee (WWC) in 1978. The WWC first worked to identify the needs of Palestinian women under occupation, including educational resources and social services such as providing help against abusive spouses. Initially, the WWC was not affiliated with any Palestinian national movement, such as the PLO. When, however, some leaders of the WWC voted to join a rival PLO faction, the Democratic Front for the Liberation of Palestine, the WWC fractured as the women decided to join up with other groups of varying political platforms (Sharoni 1995, 66).

During the Intifada, Palestinian women, such as the novelist Sahar Khalifeh, established Women's Centers to help teach and train Palestinian women to read, write, and become involved in women's issues that transcended the violence of the Arab-Israeli conflict. After the Intifada, Palestinian women continued to develop new organizations to meet the needs of the vast majority of Palestinian women who were in need of basic education and social services; however, those organizations split over disagreements of political ideology (Sharoni 1995, 83). In other words, the Arab-Israeli conflict transcended most Palestinian women's efforts to maintain a unified Palestinian women's organization.

Jewish women who were disappointed at being assigned what were considered "traditional" womanly roles in the developing social, political, and economic strategies of Jewish communities in Palestine founded the Women's Workers' Movement (WWM) in 1911. These women emphasized their equality with Jewish men and called for men to recognize their important roles in developing their new society (Sharoni 1995, 91–92). Gender took a backseat to nationalism, and in 1930, the WWM became the Organization of Working Mothers; it brought legitimacy to gendered roles in society (Sharoni 1995, 93).

Between the establishment of Israel in 1948 and the 1967 War, the state limited Israeli women's groups to serving the needs of an increasingly militarized, nationalized, and Zionist program. In other words, women's goals, ideas, and pursuits were subjected to official government interference through which Israeli women's roles in society were limited to what the state believed to be their natural or traditional roles, such as raising children, cooking, and cleaning (Sharoni 1995, 96). After the 1967 War, Israeli women's groups typically embraced ideas and positions that were already widespread or popular among the Jewish population, for example, a Jewish women's group called the Women of the First Circle protested in the 1970s against Israeli withdraw from the territories occupied as a result of the 1967 War. Israel's first woman prime minister, Golda Meir, despised feminism. She referred to feminists as "those crazy women who burn their bras and go around all disheveled and hate men" (Sharoni 1995, 98–99).

Arab and Jewish women have also worked to bring peace to the region. Israeli women founded the Women's Party in 1977 as both a political entity and as a mechanism to shed light on the plight of Israeli women and to link the problems that women in Israel faced to the larger Arab-Israeli conflict (Sharoni 1995, 104). Women against the Invasion of Lebanon and Parents against Silence were formed against the backdrop of the 1982 Israeli invasion of Lebanon. Both groups articulated a political message and sought the immediate end of the Israeli occupation of Lebanon. Although these and other Jewish women's groups disbanded after the Israeli army officially began its withdrawal from Lebanon in 1985, the Israeli invasion of Lebanon spurred the creation of new, permanent, and more militant Jewish women's groups that continue to oppose the Arab-Israeli conflict and women's traditional roles in Israeli society (Sharoni 1995, 108).

—Jim Ross-Nazzal

See also Islamic Resistance Movements, Women and; Israeli Military, Women in the

References and Further Reading

Emmett, Ayala. 1996. *Our Sisters' Promised Land: Women, Politics, and Israeli-Palestinian Coexistence.* Ann Arbor: University of Michigan.

Joseph, Suad, ed. 2000. *Gender and Citizenship in the Middle East.* Syracuse, NY: Syracuse University.

Kandiyoti, Deniz, ed. 1996. *Gendering the Middle East.* Syracuse, NY: Syracuse University.

Sela, Avraham, and Moshe Ma'oz, eds. 1997. *The PLO and Israel: From Armed Conflict to Political Solution, 1964–1994.* New York: St. Martin's Press.

Sharoni, Simona. 1995. *Gender and the Israeli-Palestinian Conflict: The Politics of Women's Resistance.* Syracuse, NY: Syracuse University.

Victor, Barbara. 2003. *Army of Roses: Inside the World of Palestinian Women Suicide Bombers.* New York: Rodale.

Argentina, Dirty War against Civilians

The impact on women of the military crackdown and paramilitary assault against dissidents and suspected leftists in Argentina from 1975 to 1983. Argentina's Dirty War has become synonymous with a ruthless dictatorship, repression of civil society, systematic disappearance, and murder. It began on March 24, 1976, when Isabel Perón, the first woman president in the Western Hemisphere, was overthrown by a military junta. Isabel was the third wife of Argentina's notorious leader Juan Perón, who was president from 1946 until he was overthrown by a coup in 1955. When he returned to Argentina in 1973 as president after eighteen years of exile, Isabel arrived as his wife and vice-president. The left-of-center Peronist supporters assumed that Perón would return Argentina back to its glory days. Instead, the right prevailed; the elderly Perón was no longer the champion of the *descamisados* (workers). Since 1970, Peronist guerrillas, Movimiento Peronista Montoñeros, had engaged in economic sabotage, which led to a military crackdown that weakened the organization by 1974. On July 1, 1974, Juan Perón died, leaving the inexperienced Isabel as president. The following year, she was kidnapped and eventually overthrown in a bloodless coup led by General Jorge Rafael Videla, Admiral Emilio Eduardo Massera, and Brigadier Ramón Agosti, who formed a military junta to govern the country.

In the wake of the coup, the military junta began to suppress popular expression and civil liberties. The junta suspended the Congress and removed judges from all branches of the judiciary. Besides its attack on the institutions that governed and preserved civil society, the junta turned its attention to its "enemies." Using concepts of just war, the junta saw itself as the savior of Western civilization. The weakened guerrilla organizations, such as the Montoñeros, were targets, but so, too, were civilians who were viewed as accomplices or subversives. Any organization or person who opposed the regime became suspect.

The campaign against "subversives" resulted in the displacement, disappearance, torture, and murder of thousands and the terrorizing of a nation. The "disappeared" included union leaders; junior high, high school, and college students; opposition party members; journalists; doctors; priests and nuns; laypeople; lawyers; military conscripts; artists; professionals; and workers. The purpose of disappearance was to terrorize the people into submission to the junta. Women, like men, were targets. Although asserting themselves to be protectors of traditional values, the junta and the military, who "disappeared" women, used rape or the threat of rape to further terrorize women. From the terror, though, emerged feminine voices of resistance that resonate in Argentine society to this day.

As so-called protectors of Western civilization and traditional values, the military junta confronted a confounding adversary: the Mothers of the Plaza de Mayo, the mothers of the disappeared. Women who lost their children and spouses sought their loved ones at the Ministry of Interior, which was controlled by the junta. Finding little help and at times jeopardizing their children's friends and acquaintances by filing reports, the grieving mothers came to know one another. In 1977, fourteen mothers began to meet in the Plaza de Mayo. From 1977, the Mothers gathered in the Plaza de Mayo every Thursday at 3:30 demanding the return of their children. Despite the traditional values espoused by the junta, the mothers were attacked, disappeared, and murdered. Even so, others continued to demand the return of their children.

The emergence of the Mothers and their continued existence challenged and continues to challenge Argentine leaders and political processes. Although the Mothers were instrumental in the toppling of the regime, they continue to ensure that the past is not repeated. They challenged the amnesty given the military leaders by Argentine president Saúl Menem (1989–1999) in 1990, which reversed President Raúl Alfonsín's (1983–1989) prosecution and imprisonment of eight military leaders of the Dirty War. Although Videla could not be prosecuted for the charges absolved by Menem, the Mothers, working with other human rights organizations, pushed for him to be tried for new charges: the kidnapping of children and pregnant women and illegal adoption. The Mothers continue to be a viable human rights organization and political influence in Argentina.

—Elaine Carey

See also Argentina, Mothers of the Plaza de Mayo

References and Further Reading

Bouvard, Marguerite Guzman. 1994. *Revolutionizing Motherhood: The Mothers of the Plaza de Mayo.* Wilmington, DE: Scholarly Resources.

Fisher, Jo. 1990. *Mothers of the Disappeared.* Boston: South End Press.

Partnoy, Alicia. 1988. *The Little School: Tales of Disappearance and Survival.* San Francisco: Midnight Editions.

Argentina, Mothers of the Plaza de Mayo

Mothers during the Argentine dictatorship of 1976–1983 searching for their children who had been abducted by the military. The Mothers of the Plaza de Mayo (Madres de Plaza de Mayo) developed into a unique women's movement of nonviolent resistance to tyranny.

The repression carried out by the Argentine military, which seized power on March 24, 1976, developed into a state terrorist plan targeting civilians. Men and women of all ages were abducted by security forces in clandestine operations and taken to one of the 360 hidden detention centers in the country. Usually tortured, victims were often killed in extrajudicial executions and buried in collective, unmarked graves or thrown to the sea from airplanes while still alive. Almost 10,000 people are officially reported as *desaparecidos* ("disappeared"), although human rights organizations estimate the real figure reaches 30,000.

Driven by anguish about the unknown fate of their children, the mothers of the disappeared—together with other relatives and human rights supporters—stood as the only civilian resistance to the military. Their denunciations contributed to the international discrediting of the regime and eventually to its fall. The Mothers of Plaza de Mayo did not manage to find their children. Instead, they provided a model of resistance against authoritarian dictatorship and greatly contributed to the reconstruction of Argentine civil society.

The mothers of the disappeared had met each other while trying to determine the whereabouts of their sons and daughters. As the mothers realized that abductions of their children followed similar patterns that amounted to a systematic plan, they decided to act together, uniting their efforts and making one claim out of their many personal sufferings. Because the higher authorities refused to grant them an audience, they gathered in front of the seat of the government at the Plaza de Mayo.

When they first demonstrated on April 30, 1977, there were only fourteen mothers. Ignored by passersby in central Buenos Aires and unacknowledged by the local press, they kept meeting every week, defying police intimidation. As policemen ordered them to keep moving, hoping to get them away from the square, the mothers began to walk in twos around the pyramid in the center of the Plaza de Mayo. Thus began their tradition of circling around this monument. They also began to wear white scarves, originally their children's diapers, as a way of recognizing each other in public. Although branded by the military as terrorists or madwomen, they were generally middle-class housewives without any previous political experience. They gradually acquired consciousness of their resources and skills and increasingly politicized their action. The enormous risk these women took is illustrated by the fact that some of the Mothers themselves disappeared. Among them was the first president of the movement, Azucena Villaflor de Devicenzi, as well as two French nuns who supported the group, who were abducted after a church meeting in December 1977. Despite this, their movement soon counted some 150 members and had grown to comprise several thousand by the end of the dictatorship in 1983.

The prohibition and persecution of political parties, social organizations, and workers' unions had left the victims and their relatives in a situation of helplessness and isolation. Fear of state terrorism on one side and public indifference or even mild complicity with the military by broad sectors of Argentine society on the other left the Mothers standing alone against the regime. In the early phase of the movement, their only support came from a few engaged human rights activists and foreign journalists, who helped to make their struggle known abroad. Commitment to human rights by some U.S. State Department officials in the Carter administration, together with pressure exerted by exiled Argentines and a growing international network of humanitarian help, contributed to reverse the isolation of the Mothers. The visit of the Inter-American Commission on Human Rights (IACHR) in September 1979 backed their credibility by registering thousands of reports of serious human rights violations. The Mothers received further international recognition when the Nobel Peace Prize was awarded to Argentine pacifist Adolfo Perez Esquivel in 1980. In his acceptance speech, he mentioned the Mothers of the Plaza de Mayo.

Even if they had evidence of their children's murders, the Mothers of Plaza de Mayo refused to consider them dead as long as the state did not account for and take responsibility for their deaths. When the military passed a law declaring all disappeared dead in 1979, they refused its benefits and insisted in calling their children *desaparecidos*. Together with other human rights organizations, the Mothers of Plaza de Mayo played a decisive role during the transition to democracy in Argentina, managing to place the problem of the missing persons on the agenda of the newly elected government. They were disappointed, however, that the trial of the military chiefs in 1985, ordered by President Raúl Alfonsín (1983–1989), dealt with only the senior members of the junta and did not divulge information about what happened to their children. The Mothers of Plaza de Mayo transformed themselves into a political group seeking a just and fair-minded society, maintaining their claim of justice for the military's crimes while adopting a broader definition of their plea for human rights.

Internal dissent about their role in post-dictatorship Argentina led in 1986 to the split of the Mothers of Plaza de Mayo into two groups. The groups differed in their willingness to cooperate with the state, in their involvement in wider social or political causes, and in the way they wished the disappeared to be commemorated or even defined. The Asociación Madres de Plaza de Mayo (Association of the Mothers of Plaza de Mayo) led by the charismatic Hebe Pastor de Bonafini, was opposed to the search for and identification of the corpses of the missing; it rejected any cooperation with the state. Considering themselves "revolutionary mothers," members of the Asociación thought commemoration should consist of appropriating the political goals of their children and fighting for the ideals of social justice. They founded the Universidad Popular de las Madres (Popular University of the Mothers), where courses such as popular education, history, and political thought were taught.

The other group, Madres de Plaza de Mayo—Línea Fundadora (Founding Line), also stress the singularity of the category of the *desaparecido* but accepted a wider range of commemorative practices, including individual memorials. They cooperated with other human rights organizations and with official institutions in the identification of corpses and former detention centers and were active in the projected creation of a Museo del Nunca Más (the Never Again Museum) as well as the construction of a memorial including the names of all the disappeared. Both groups continue to demonstrate every Thursday at 3.30 P.M. in the Plaza de Mayo.

The struggle of the Mothers of Plaza de Mayo has been recognized worldwide as a leading example of pacific resistance to dictatorship and has had a significant moral impact in Argentine society. Among feminist scholars, however, there is controversy about the extent to which the Mothers of Plaza de Mayo meant to challenge patriarchal structures (Taylor 1997, 193–207). Some authors think that their struggle, although worthwhile and encouraging for other oppressed women, was based on a traditional understanding of motherhood and reinforced the role of women as suffering, self-sacrificing housewives, leaving the patriarchal values of Argentine society intact. Other authors, such as Marguerite Bouvard (1994), think instead that these women called into question the very notion of motherhood, politicizing its otherwise merely biological definition. The Mothers of Plaza de Mayo consider themselves born by their own children, that is, that through searching for them, they were born anew into political consciousness. They decided to "socialize" their motherhood, stating that every disappeared person is the child of every mother. Such conceptualizations, according to Bouvard, go beyond all traditional definitions and revolutionize the notion of motherhood.

The original group also led to the formation of the Grandmothers of Plaza de Mayo, made up of women who had not only children but also grandchildren among the missing. They started demonstrating together with the other mothers but soon discovered that they shared the more specific goal of finding their abducted grandchildren. These children had been kidnapped with their parents or were born in captivity in clandestine detention centers, where their pregnant mothers were kept alive until delivery and killed shortly after giving birth. These infants were given up for adoption, often to families of military or police personnel, and because their true identities were hidden from them, they grew up not knowing their past. The Grandmothers of Plaza de Mayo dedicated themselves to the investigation of their whereabouts, the use of DNA testing to find their kin, and the restitution of their identity. By 2004, 79 out of an estimated 500 kidnapped children, who were now young adults, had been identified, and most were able to recover their true history and establish contact with their biological families.

—Estela Schindel

See also Argentina, Dirty War against Civilians

References and Further Reading

Arditti, Rita. 1999. *Searching for Life. The Grandmothers of the Plaza de Mayo and the Disappeared Children of Argentina.* Berkeley: University of California Press.

Bouvard, Marguerite Guzmán. 1994. *Revolutionizing Motherhood. The Mothers of the Plaza de Mayo.* Wilmington, DE: Scholarly Resources.

Fisher, Jo. 1989. *Mothers of the Disappeared.* Boston: South End Press.

Navarro, Marysa. 1989. "The Personal Is Political: Las Madres de Plaza de Mayo." In *Power and Popular Protest: Latin American Social Movements,* edited by Susan Eckstein, 241–258. Berkeley: University of California Press.

Taylor, Diane. 1997. *Disappearing Acts: Spectacles of Gender and Nationalism in Argentina's Dirty War.* Durham, NC: Duke.

Armenian Holocaust

Deliberate effort to eliminate the Ottoman Empire's Armenian minority during World War I. Estimates for the number of people who perished in the ensuing genocide vary, but perhaps 1.5 million of the 2 million Armenians living in the Ottoman Empire died. One million were killed or died between 1915 and 1918, and another half million died as the Turkey of Mustafa Kemal "sought to free herself of foreign occupation and expel minorities" (Melson 2004, 122).

The Ottoman Empire's violence against the Armenian minority predated World War I. Between 1894 and 1896, Sultan Abdul-Hamid launched a series of attacks on his Armenian subjects. Although between 100,000 and 300,000 predominantly male Armenians were killed, the purpose was not to eliminate the Armenian minority but to cow it into submission.

The campaign during World War I was different. The Young Turks (the Committee of Union and Progress) had seized power in 1908. The

Press Reports of Armenian Holocaust

"500,000 Armenians Said to Have Perished": A New York Times *Report*

"Reports reaching Washington indicate that about 500,000 Armenians have been slaughtered or lost their lives as a result of the Turkish deportation order and the resulting war of extinction. Turkish authorities drove the Gregorian Armenians out of their homes, ordered them to proceed to distant towns in the direction of Bagdad [*sic*], which could only be reached by crossing long stretches of desert. During the exodus of Armenians across the deserts they have been fallen upon by Kurds and slaughtered, but some of the Armenian women and girls, in considerable numbers, have been carried off into captivity by the Kurds."

—*New York Times,* September 24, 1915, p. 2.

"Says Extinction Menaces Armenia": A New York Times *Report*

"Dr. M. Simbad Gabriel, President of the Armenian General Progressive Association in the United States told a TIMES reporter last night that no American could possibly conceive of the atrocities which the Turks had perpetrated on the Christian Armenians. He said that from correspondence he had received from Nubar Pasha, the diplomatic representative in Paris of the Katholikos or head of [the Armenian Church] the number of Armenians put to death as more than 450,000, while 600,000 others had been driven from their homes to wander among the villages of Asia Minor all these out of a population of 1,500,000.

" 'We in America can't begin to realize the extent of this reign of terror,' says Dr. Gabriel, 'because Armenians in Turkey are not allowed to write, nor even to converse with each other of what we are undergoing at the hands of the Turks. . . .

" 'I was talking to an Armenian woman two or three days ago,' he continued, 'who had come from Constantinople last month with her three children. Beseeching me not to reveal her name, lest vengeance be visited upon her husband, who is still in Constantinople, she told me of horrors that made my blood run cold. One morning twenty of her friends were taken out by the Turks and hanged in cold blood, for no other reason than that they were suspected of being unfriendly to the Turkish cause. This is but an example of what the Armenian in Turkey who has not been exiled wakes every morning to fear.'

"The doctor said that greed, religion, and politics all combined to induce the Turks to massacre the Armenians. The Government was always behind every massacre, and the people were acting under orders.

" 'When the bugle blows in the morning,' he said, 'Turks rush fiercely to the work of killing the Christians and plundering them of their wealth. When it stops in the evening, or in two or three days, the shooting and stabbing stop just as suddenly then as it began. The people obey their orders like soldiers.

" 'The dead are really the happiest,' he continued. 'The living are forced to leave their homes and wander in an alien country amid a hostile population. They are allowed as a food ration by the Government only half a pound of grain a day. The youngest and strongest of the men are forced into the army but not to fight. They are not armed and have to do all the trench digging and the supply carrying for the Turkish soldiers. Do you blame them that they do not favor their country's cause?'. . .

" 'What has occurred during the last few months in Cilicia and Armenia is unbelievable,' he writes. 'It is nothing more or less than the annihilation of a whole people.'

(continues)

Press Reports of Armenian Holocaust (continued)

"A letter from Constantinople says that Armenians in all the cities and villages of Cilicia have been exiled to the desert regions south of Aleppo. 'They have not been allowed to carry any of their possessions with them,' the letter goes on, 'and Moslems are occupying the lands and houses left vacant.' . . .

"'The villages in the vilayets of Van and Bitlis have been pillaged and the population put to the sword. . . . Christian martyrdom has at no time assumed such colossal proportions; and if the neutral powers, especially the United States of America, do not intercede, there will be very few left of the million and a half of the Christian Armenians in the Turkish Empire.'"

—*New York Times,* September 25, 1915, p. 3.

hope of the Young Turks of saving the empire by liberal reform foundered as Turkey continued to lose territory and population in the Italo-Turkish and Balkan Wars. The Young Turks then embraced ardent and exclusivist Turkish nationalism. As non-Turks and non-Muslims, the Armenians became a particular concern when the Ottoman Empire went to war with Russia in 1914. The Armenians, who were Christian, were concentrated in eastern Anatolia next to Russia. Other Armenians lived across the border in Russia. They were regarded as potential subversives and as an impediment to the creation of a Pan-Turkic state, which would extend eastward to China.

The 1915 genocidal campaign targeted the entire Armenian population of the Ottoman Empire. Turkey would be ethnically cleansed of this minority; the cultural heritage of the alien minority would be erased and its wealth confiscated. The thousands of Armenians in the Ottoman army were placed in labor battalions where they perished from exhaustion or were shot. Most male Armenians were then removed from towns and villages and shot. The remaining Armenians, the elderly, women, and children were brutally marched toward the Syrian Desert near Aleppo. Few on the death marches reached the supposed destination. Thousands died from exposure and starvation. Untold others were killed, often after rape and torture by killing squads (Teshkilat-I Makhsusiye), composed of released convicts and by Turkish and Kurdish peasants manipulated into a murderous anti-Armenian frenzy. Some individuals survived physically through enslavement or adoption or as involuntary sex slaves.

Armenians living in European Turkey were shipped across the Sea of Marmara. Once in Anatolia, they and other Armenians living near rail lines were packed into cattle cars for shipment to the desert concentration camps, where most perished due to starvation and thirst. Those who survived the ordeal joined other Armenians who had fled Turkey earlier and formed the Armenian diaspora in the West.

—*Bernard Cook*

See also Armenian Women Victims of Genocide; Smyrna Tragedy, Continuing Ordeal for Women Survivors of

References and Further Reading

Melson, Robert. 2004. "The Armenian Genocide." In *Defining the Horrific: Readings on Genocide and Holocaust in the Twentieth Century,* edited by William L. Hewitt, 119–127. Upper Saddle River, NJ: Pearson/Prentice Hall.

———. 1995. *Revolution and Genocide: On the Origins of the Armenian Genocide and the Holocaust.* Chicago: University of Chicago.

Suny, Robert. 1983. *Armenia in the Twentieth Century.* Chino, CA: Scholars Press.

Armenian Women Victims of Genocide

Female victims of the mass killing of Armenians by the Ottoman government (1915–1923) and their behavior in the killing fields. Armenian male leaders were arrested and killed; younger and able-bodied men were mostly rounded up and segregated in labor camps or murdered outright. As a result of this strategic approach, women, children, and the elderly were left unprotected and were easy targets. The women had to face tragic choices in their decision to live or die. Their ordeal in many cases was shaped by their gender because they endured sexual attacks, abduction, and dreadfully traumatic childbirth along deportation routes. The lot of women who were "rescued" (most of the time not with an altruistic motivation but for egotistic reasons) or abducted and forcibly converted to Islam was no better. Their experience as concubines in Moslem households was additionally burdened by their lifelong compunction for the compromise they had made. Unfortunately, their life stories are not recorded, and their image as victims of genocide remains obscure.

Mayr Hayastan (Mother Armenia)—the homeland ravaged and ruined under the yoke of foreign rulers—and female martyrs of Christianity became revered archetypes in the collective memory of the Armenian people, influencing the image of female victims of national catastrophes throughout time. Another view stemmed from the secularist nineteenth-century emancipation movement. National liberation was the goal and armed struggle the means to achieve it. Patriotism, aspiration for freedom, and acts of self-defense and retaliation were encouraged. In this context, the response of the Armenian woman to the victimization of son or husband deviated from the traditional response. She did not console herself with the vision of her beloved rising to heaven and embracing immortality as a reward for his sacrifice. Her words of sorrow projected a rebellious spirit against the Turk and also against God, who allowed the atrocity to happen. She did not expect God to avenge her son's murder, but she entrusted it to the "valiant men of Armenia" (Damadian 1917, 277–278). She was encouraged by her dying son not to weep but to be proud because his deed is a sacrifice to the altar of freedom. Even lullabies were fashioned to encourage heroism for the sake of Armenia (Patkanian 1917, 75–76).

The massacres of Ottoman Armenians from 1894 through 1896 (a precursor to the 1915 genocide) were such a catastrophe that traditional concepts shaping outlooks and responses to trauma were put to the test. An unnamed old woman, the lyrical hero of Daniel Varuzhan's *Hayhoyank* (Curse), stands above the crowd of wretched survivors of a mass slaughter and, raising her clenched fists toward the sky, curses God for what befell the Armenian nation. She questions God's judgment, protesting His indifference toward the persecution of a people who faithfully worshipped Him and sacrificed their lives for Him. Varuzhan's *Jarde* (The Carnage) remains closer to ancient archetypes. Mother Armenia weeps not over the ruined land, but because her friends, meaning the European powers, abandoned her. She does not lament the loss of her sons but their servitude. Siamanto's *Pare* (The Dance) is the poet's artistic rendering of a German missionary's testimony. She had helplessly watched the Turks round up young women and force them to dance naked. Then they had poured kerosene on them and set them on fire.

The horrors of genocide permeate the entire literary legacy of Suren Partevian, who depicts the traumatic experience of the Armenian women victims of the massacres of 1894–1896 and praises their "unbelievable interfusing of patience, endurance, docility, and superhuman tolerance for pain and suffering" (Partevian, 1911). In many ways, however, their behavior displays the collapse of moral order, the irreversible impact of the catastrophe on the human psyche. If they miraculously survive, they will come out of their forced predicament demoralized and tainted, incapable of building a new, healthy, and normal life.

In Partevian's narratives of the massacres and deportations of 1915, women are more sophisticated and heroic. Siranush is an educated woman. She can realistically judge the Turkish-Armenian relationship and see the imminent catastrophe. She is entrapped in the cunning intrigues of her Turkish admirer who arranges the arrest of her husband to abduct her. She surrenders herself to him to save the life of her young son. Soon after she arranges her son's escape, however, she commits suicide to put an end to her defiled existence. Partevian's *Anmah botse* (The Undying Flame, 1917) and *Dzaine hnchets* (The Sound Echoed, 1916) were published jointly in a single volume in 1917. Princess Sonia Asaturof, a Russified Armenian woman, lives a lavish life in Tbilisi but is suddenly sensitized to the Armenian plight and joins the Armenian volunteers fighting the Turks. Zaruhi also joins the volunteers and fights the Turks disguised as a man. These heroines symbolize Partevian's perception of women's role in the Armenian armed struggle. Resistance does not necessarily connote taking arms and fighting the assailant. It is also the strong determination to survive against all odds to tell the world about Turkish inhumanity and unparalleled atrocities.

Zapel Esayan records the Armenian massacres in Cilicia in 1909. At times, she portrays female victims as embodiments of cowardice and self-centered drives, ready to sacrifice anything for the sake of mere survival. At other times, they appear as symbols of courage and endurance. "We survived, but we will soon die. That is all right. But will our sufferings serve a purpose? Is there hope of deliverance for our nation?" She suffers, but only her doleful eyes and occasional shivering betray the consuming pain in her mutilated body (Esayan 1957, 57). The traditional catharsis is rejected. The only solace is the hope for a better future for Armenians. Another woman, whose son was killed defending the city, tearfully vows, "If the Turks attack us again, our sons will be on the ramparts to fight and die on the ramparts" (Esayan 1957, 20).

Henry Morgenthau, the U.S. ambassador to the Ottoman Empire, records horrifying scenes of pillage, rape, and murder and the brutalities of the gendarmes accompanying the caravans of the deportees. "They even prodded pregnant women with bayonets; if one, as frequently happened, gave birth along the road, she was immediately forced to get up and rejoin the marchers. . . . Kurds would sweep down from their mountain homes. Rushing up to the young girls, they would lift their veils and carry the pretty ones off to the hills. . . . Turkish roughs would fall upon the women, leaving them sometimes dead from their experiences or sometimes ravingly insane." Women often committed suicide to save their honor by jumping into the river, their children in their arms. Morgenthau writes, "There were women who held up their babies to strangers, begging them to save them from their tormentors, and failing this, they would throw them into wells or leave them behind bushes, that at least they might die undisturbed. Behind was left a small army of girls, who had been sold as slaves—frequently for a medjidie, or about eighty cents—and who, after serving the brutal purposes of their purchasers, were forced to live lives of prostitution" (Morgenthau 1919, 315–317).

The brutality led to the collapse of religious, cultural, and traditional values. Aram Antonian reports instances of cannibalism in the desert of Der-El-Zor. After months of dehumanizing, incapacitating suffering, the wretched deportees come face-to-face with a choice between death and survival. They must either starve to death or eat the corpses of their own children who had died of starvation. A famine-stricken girl is lying in the desert sand with her helpless mother at her side. The girl smells meat cooking nearby. "Mother, go ask some for me. I cannot go on anymore." The mother returns empty-handed. "They didn't give you a piece?" the girl asks. "When I die, mother, you eat my flesh alone; share it with no one" (Antonian 1977, 116–117).

Lusik's last son's body is pulled out of the raging waters of Euphrates. The scene of her gradual loss of sense and reason surpasses any description of motherly love. She showers the body with warm kisses; then, in a violent fit of madness, she sinks her teeth deep into her son's neck and the dark blood gushes out, painting the woman's face with the deadly color. Then she collapses unconscious, her teeth still clenched on the boy's neck, the blood oozing from the wound drop by drop, running into the desert sand, and tracing sinister configurations as though to record this horrifying scene (Antonian 1921, 66).

Life was a prolonged agony in the Armenian concentration camp in Meskeneh, and Antonian, an inmate of that same camp, tried to record this agony as close to the incommunicable reality as he could. An old woman fought with another deportee. They grappled with each other in the mud, shouted, and cursed. The man grabbed the old woman's hair and knocked her down, rubbing her face in the mud. The skirmish continued for a while; then the man stood up victorious. But why had she started the ridiculous fight? The man was able to bribe the undertakers to remove the body of his daughter from his tent. The old woman had no money, and the undertakers refused to take her grandson's body away. "Leave your dead outside, like others do," they told her. She begged them to carry the corpse away to make room for her last grandchild burning with fever. He, too, the last survivor of the family, had come down with typhus. The old woman, left with a rotting corpse and a dying child, in a nearly maddened state, attacked the man, another victim of that same tragedy. Femininity, moral standards, human dignity, and normal patterns of behavior had long lost their meaning (Antonian 1921, 134).

These women are the collective embodiment of all victims in modern times, subjected to the most unthinkable human suffering. They were not always the typical heroines who transcended torture and pain. At times, in their prolonged agony, they suffered physical and moral exhaustion and gave in. At other times, they fell, like unknown soldiers, holding up the dignity of their gender and the pride of their nation.

—*Rubina Peroomian*

See also Armenian Holocaust; Smyrna Tragedy, Continuing Ordeal for Women Survivors of

References and Further Reading

Antonian, Aram. [1921] 1977. *Mets vochire* [The great crime]; 2nd ed. Reprint, Beirut: Ghukas Karapetian.

Dadrian, Vahakn N. 1995. *The History of the Armenian Genocide.* Providence, RI, and Oxford: Berghahn.

Damadian, Mihran. [1917] 1978. "The Lament of Martyred Smbat's Mother." In *Armenian Poems,* translated by Alice Stone Blackwell. Reprint, Delmar, NY: Caravan.

Esayan, Zapel. 1957. *Averaknerun mej* [Amid the ruins]. Beirut: Etvan.

Hovannisian, Richard G., ed. 2003. *Looking Backward, Moving Forward: Confronting the Armenian Genocide.* New Brunswick, NJ/London: Transaction.

Morgenthau, Henry. [1919] 1975. *Ambassador Morgenthau's Story.* Reprint, Plandome, NY: New Age.

Partevian, Suren. 1911. *Hayuhin* [The Armenian woman]. Constantinople: P. Palents.

———. 1917. *Anmah botse* [The undying flame]/*Dzaine hnchets* [The sound echoed]. Alexandria, Egypt: Aram Stepanian.

Patkanian, Rapael. [1917] 1978. "Lullaby." In *Armenian Poems,* edited by Alice Stone Blackwell. Reprint, Delmar, NY: Caravan.

Peroomian, Rubina. 1993. *Literary Responses to Catastrophe: A Comparison of the Armenian and The Jewish Experience.* Atlanta, GA: Scholars.

Artemisia of Caria

Admiral in the fleet of the Persian emperor Xerxes; reputedly the first female admiral. Artemisia, daughter of Lygdamis, was the ruler of Caria in southwest Asia Minor in the second half of the fifth century B.C. As a vassal of the Persian Empire, she provided a contingent of five fighting ships when Xerxes I invaded Greece in 480 B.C. Unusually, Artemisia decided to command the ships herself instead of appointing a male deputy; thus, she is the first known female admiral.

The Greek historian Herodotus, himself from the Carian city of Halicarnassus and in a good position to get information, was deeply impressed by Artemisia's role in the invasion of Greece, for which he is the sole source. He tells that her ships proved their worth by capturing a Greek scouting trireme. Despite the Persian fleet's large numerical superiority, however, Artemisia advised Xerxes against meeting the allied Greek fleet at Salamis. Her advice was overridden but, in hindsight, was clearly prophetic: through a combination of trickery, luck, and intimate knowledge of the sea around Salamis, the Greeks defeated the Persian fleet. In particular, the Persian fleet especially displayed tactical weakness by advancing in tightly packed lines of ships that proved to be unmaneuverable during the battle. After the tide of battle had turned, Artemisia found that her way of escape was blocked by another contingent of Persian ships. Thinking fast, she ordered her ship turned and rammed one of her own allies—the Greek ships that had been pursuing her thus thought she was on their side and left her alone. Ironically, Xerxes, watching from land, also saw Artemisia's ship fiercely attacking but did not realize that it was one of his own vessels that was being destroyed. He is said to have exclaimed admiringly at the sight of Artemisia's boldness: "My men have turned into women, my women into men" (Herodotus 1972, 8: 88). Luckily there were no survivors of the ship Artemisia sunk to accuse her. It is also fortunate that Artemisia was not captured by the Greeks, who resented the fact that a woman was bearing arms against them and had offered an enormous reward of 10,000 drachmae for anyone who captured her alive.

After the Battle of Salamis, Artemisia advised Xerxes to retreat from Greece, and this time he listened to her advice. As a further sign of his trust in her, Xerxes entrusted those of his children who had gone on the expedition to her care for the return to Asia Minor. After this, Artemisia vanishes from the historical record.

—Phyllis G. Jestice

See also Greek Women and War in Antiquity; Helen of Troy; Spartan Women

References and Further Reading

Green, Peter. 1996. *The Greco-Persian Wars.* Berkeley: University of California.

Herodotus. 1972. *The Histories,* rev. ed., translated by Aubrey de Sélincourt. Harmondsworth, England: Penguin.

ASHWARI, HANAN (1946–)

The highest-ranking woman member of the Palestinian movement, official spokesperson of the Palestinian delegation to the Middle East Peace Process (1991–1993). Hanan Ashwari is known for her staunch defense of Palestinian rights, her dedication to human rights, and her commitment to the emancipation of women.

Born a Christian in Palestine in 1946, before the creation of the state of Israel deprived her family and her people of their homes and their rights, Ahswari was educated in a Quaker school in Ramallah, now part of the West Bank. Like many Palestinian families, her parents taught her the history of her country. Her father also encouraged her to pursue an education and taught her that equality is women's right (Ashwari 1995, 47).

She became a political activist following Israel's annexation of the West Bank, the Golan Heights, and the Sinai during the 1967 War (the Six-Day War). At that time she was studying English literature at the American University in Beirut, Lebanon. After obtaining her degree, she was unable to return home to Ramallah because Israel forbade Palestinians who were outside the country in 1967 to come back. Offered a scholarship at the University of Virginia, she obtained her doctorate in English literature there. In 1973, Israel allowed Palestinians families to reunite, and she returned to Ramallah, where she taught English and became the head of the English Department at Ber Zeit University. In her dual role as professor and activist, she participated in student demonstrations against the Israeli occupation of Palestine and their abuse of Palestinian rights, an activity for which the Israelis jailed her for a brief period. She also found time to form a feminist study group with other women and to speak out in defense of women's rights.

Ashwari's dual commitment to peace and women's rights led her to work with Israeli women who also supported Palestinian rights. In 1988, she participated in a women's conference in Belgium that brought Israeli and Palestinian women together for dialogue. That same year, she appeared on Ted Koppel's *Nightline,* along with other Palestinians and Israelis, to participate in a town meeting on the Palestinian-Israeli conflict. Recognizing the political importance of Palestine to peoples in the Middle East, U.S. Secretary of State James Baker attempted to engineer peace between Palestinians and Israelis following the Gulf War. Hanan Ashwari and other Palestinians met with Baker during the eight months that led up to the 1991 Arab-Israeli Peace Conference in Madrid. She was instrumental in projecting a positive image of the Palestinian people and dispelling an image that equated them with terrorists. Following the disclosure of the Palestine Liberation Organization Chairman Yasser Arafat and Israeli Prime Minister Yitzak Rabin's behind-the-scenes formulation of the 1993 Oslo Accords, Ashwari temporarily withdrew from official politics.

Later she established the Palestinian Independent Commission for the Occupied Territories to help build institutions "as an essential component of the reconstruction of a nation" (Ashwari 1995, 15). She served as minister of higher education and research for the Palestinian Authority from 1996 until her 1998 resignation in protest against corruption within the Palestinian government and against Arafat's leadership. Since that time, she has dedicated herself to a just peace and a humanitarian solution to the Israeli-Palestinian conflict through the Palestinian Initiative for the Promotion of Global Dialogue and Democracy.

—*Margaret Power*

See also Arab-Israeli Wars; Islamic Resistance Movements, Women and

References and Further Reading

Ashwari, Hanan. 1995. *This Side of Peace.* New York: Touchstone Book.

Bouvard, Marguerite Guzman. 1996. "Hanan Mikhail Ashwari." In *Women Reshaping Human Rights.* Wilmington, DE: Scholarly Resources, 1996.

Ashwell, Lena Margaret Pocock (1872–1957)

Actress, playwright, feminist, and suffragette who organized a network of entertainers with the Young Men's Christian Association (YMCA) for allied troops at various fronts during World War I and received the Order of the British Empire for her contributions.

Lena Margaret Pocock was born aboard a ship, the *Wellesley,* on the River Tyne in England on March 13, 1872. She was raised and educated in Canada and then studied music in Switzerland and at the Royal Academy of Music in London. Her voice proved inadequate, and she turned to the theater, first as an actress using Ashwell as a stage name and then as an administrator. In 1908, she married the royal obstetrician, Sir Henry Simpson. Ashwell cofounded the Women's Emergency Corps (WEC) with fellow members of the Actresses' Franchise League (AFL). The WEC provided industrial training and organized a registry of qualified women who wanted to contribute to the wartime efforts.

In 1914, Ashwell began organizing traveling companies to perform at military bases in Britain with the AFL. She coordinated companies of professional actors with the YMCA Concert Parties, which toured the fronts performing for the troops beginning in February 1915. Because these companies consisted mostly of women, Ashwell encouraged soldiers to volunteer to perform the male roles in their plays.

Ashwell raised more than £100,000 to fund entertainment tours for the troops by hosting special matinees at the London Coliseum, Chelsea Palace, and Lyric Theatres. She also organized entertainment for military families and soldiers within England. In 1918, Ashwell took over the Palace Theatre in Winchester, which was located near several military hospitals and bases. Ashwell's company performed for nearby soldiers, including prisoners of war.

By 1918, Ashwell had twenty-five companies at the fronts. Her companies performed for troops in France, Malta, Egypt, and Palestine. The companies remained at the front after the war's end to entertain soldiers still overseas.

Ashwell inspired the creation of the Entertainment National Service Association (ENSA), a government-funded organization that provided entertainment for the troops during World War II. She returned from retirement in 1939 to organize theatrical parties in France on behalf of ENSA. She died in London on March 13, 1957.

—*Barbara Penny Kanner*

See also Great Britain, Women in Service in World War I; Young Men's Christian Organization, World War I

References and Further Reading

Ashwell, Lena.1936. *Myself a Player.* Plymouth, UK: Michael Joseph LTD.

Kanner, Barbara Penny. 1997. *Women in Context.* New York: G. K. Hall.

Atkins, Vera H. (1908–2000)

Intelligence officer in Great Britain's secret service during the World War II. Vera Atkins was born Vera Maria Rosenberg in Bucharest, Romania, on June 16, 1908. Her family moved to England in 1933, and she adopted her mother's last name. She attended finishing school in Lausanne, Switzerland, and studied modern languages at the University of Paris (Sorbonne). When Germany invaded France in 1940, Atkins returned to Britain and joined the Women's Auxiliary Air Force (WAAF) . She worked as a secretary in the France or "F" section of the British Special Operations Executive. Colonel Maurice Buckmaster, the head of "F" section, recognized her ability and promoted her to an intelligence officer and made her his assistant. In that position, she directed covert operations, working with the Resistance in German-occupied France. She recruited, trained, and dispatched more than 400 agents, the "Buckmasters," to France, among whom 39 were women. Women were often used as couriers, who, it was hoped, would be less conspicuous on a bicycle in the French countryside or on a train than a young man. Atkins personally stood on the runway to see off each agent to be parachuted into occupied France. More than 100 of her agents were lost. Some were killed outright; others were captured, tortured, and then killed. Of the 104 dead agents, 13 were women. Among those lost were Yolande Beekman, Madeleine Damerment, Vera Leigh, Sonya Olschanezky, Elaine Plewman, Diana Rowden, and Violette Szabo. Odette Sansom was tortured but survived. Atkins, who is thought to have inspired Ian Fleming's "Miss Moneypenny" of the 007 series, personally undertook the task of scouring concentration camp records and interviewing Nazi concentration personnel and staff officers to discover what had happened to her lost agents and to bring their killers to trial. In a three-month period, aided by a temporary commission as a WAAF squadron commander and an appointment from the War Office to the War Crimes Investigation Unit in the British Zone of occupation in Germany, she accomplished her task. Atkins subsequently lived alone in a cottage on the coast at Winchelsea from which, on a clear day, she could see the French coast. In

1987, she was honored by President François Mitterrand as a commandant of the Legion of Honor. She died on June 24, 2000.

—*Bernard Cook*

See also Beekman, Yolande; Damerment, Madeleine; France, Resistance during World War II, Women and; Khan, Noor Inayat; Leigh, Vera; Olschanezky, Sonya; Plewman, Elaine; Rowden, Diana; Sansom, Odette; Szabo, Violette

References and Further Reading

Helm, Sarah. 2005. *A Life of Secrets: The Story of Vera Atkins and the Lost Agents of SOE.* London: Little, Brown.

Martin, Douglas. "Vera Atkins, 92, Spymaster for British Dies." *The New York Times,* June 27, 2000.

Stevenson, William. 2005. *Spymistress: The Secret Life of Vera Atkins.* New York: Arcade Publishing.

"Vera Atkins, CBE, Légion d'honneur," 64 Baker Steet. http://www.64-baker-street.org/also/also_vera_atkins_her_story.html (accessed January 10, 2006).

"Vera Atkins," Women of the Special Operations Executive, http://www.64–baker–street.org/text_version/also/also_vera_atkins_obituary_2_txt.html (accessed September 23, 2004).

Atomic Bomb, World War II

See Hiroshima, Nagasaki, and Women

Aubrac, Lucie (b. 1912)

Member of the French resistance during World War II. Lucie Aubrac was born in 1912, the daughter of wine growers in Burgundy. She attended the Sorbonne, earning a degree in history. Returning from study in the United States, she married Raymond Aubrac in 1938. When war broke out, she joined the communist wing of the Resistance in Lyon. She founded Liberation-Sud with her husband and worked on and helped distribute its illegal newspaper, *Libération.* Her duties also included leading an armed group that freed jailed resistance members. For safekeeping, her infant son was in other people's care and, by summer of 1940, in a children's home. When her husband was arrested in May 1940, she boldly threatened the French prosecutor with reprisals, and he was released. Raymond Aubrac was arrested again in June 1940 in Caluire at a meeting of leaders that included Jean Moulin. This sweep, under the direction of Klaus Barbie, was disastrously successful, but at first, the Germans seemed unaware of the identities of some captives, including Raymond Aubrac and Moulin. Lucie Aubrac, now pregnant, disguised herself as the mistress of the arrested "Claude Ermelin" (aka Raymond Aubrac) to convince an influential German officer that the prisoner should be made to marry her. They were able to meet frequently to work out the "marriage" details. The ruse enabled the armed group she led to free Raymond Aubrac and two others while they were in transit. Moulin and others were tortured and killed, although the details of this remain unclear. The Germans sought both Aubracs, and they escaped to England with their son. The Aubracs' baby girl was born two days after their arrival. With the liberation of France, Aubrac served as a delegate to the provisional government and resumed her teaching career. She later opposed France's role during the Algerian War of Independence.

Disputes have arisen since the end of the war over who betrayed the Caluire meeting; resistance members at the time pointed to Rene Hardy, but this has never been proved. Gerard Chauvy implicated the Aubracs in his *Aubrac: Lyon 1943,* but the couple successfully sued him.

—*Page Delano*

See also Borrel, Andrée; Fourcade, Marie-Madeleine; Hall, Virginia; Moreau-Evrard,

Emilienne; Souliè, Geneviève; Tillion, Germaine; Wake, Nancy; Witherington, Pearl

References and Further Reading

Aubrac, Lucie. 1993. *Outwitting the Gestapo* (English translation of *Ils partiront dans l'ivresse,* 1984). Lincoln: University of Nebraska Press.

Diamond, Hanna, and Claire Gorrara. 2001. "The Aubrac Controversy." *History Today* 51 no. 3 (March): 26.

Gorrara, C. 1995. "Reviewing Gender and Resistance: The Case of Lucie Aubrac." In *The Liberation of France: Image and Event,* edited by H. R. Kedward and N. Wood, 143–155. Oxford, England: Berg.

Weitz, Margaret Collins. 1995. *Sisters in the Resistance.* New York: J. Wiley.

Women officers in the Australian Armed Forces. (Time Life Pictures/Getty Images)

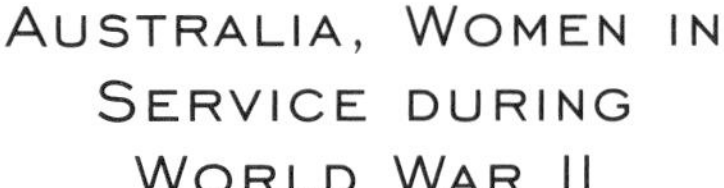

Australia, Women in Service during World War II

Role of Australian women during World War II. During World War II, Australian women played a broader and more active role in the war effort than they had in World War I. The Australian Army Nursing Service served abroad as it had done in World War I. In addition, Voluntary Aids Detachments (VADs) were set up to provide needed service in Australia. The women's services of the Australian army, navy, and air force were initially organized to provide radio operators. By June 1941, voluntary aides, who had been mobilized into special Australian Army Voluntary Aid Detachments, were permitted to volunteer for service in North Africa. By December 1941, the Australian Army Medical Women's Service was formed from VADs working in military hospitals. Fifty thousand women enlisted for the various Australian female military services, and in 1945 the number serving was forty-two thousand.

Some 3,600 women of the Australian Women's Army Service (AWAS) were assigned to antiaircraft searchlights and costal defense batteries. Japanese mini-submarines entered Sydney Harbour in 1942, and there was concern about both naval and air attacks. The women assigned to air and coastal defense did everything except load and fire weapons. Colonel Sybil Irving, the controller of AWAS, did not believe that women should actually fire the guns. In her opinion, because women would one day be mothers, they would not wish to have the death of another woman's son on their conscience.

In addition, women played an essential role in the labor market depleted by male conscription. A developing manpower shortage in 1941 led to the formation of a women's Land Army to provide rural labor. Developing shortages in industry, commerce, munitions work, and food processing led to an extension of the program into the other sectors and the introduction of compulsion. Without the contribution of its women workers, Australia could not have contributed to the Allied war effort as it did. In 1942, Australia conscripted women who did not have dependents for war work, and they were not allowed to change jobs without permission of a government commission. The number of women employed in Australian industry peaked at 710,000 in 1943.

—*Bernard Cook*

See also Australian Army Nursing Service/Royal Australian Army Nursing Corps; Bullwinkel, Vivian

References and Further Reading

Harvey, Joyce. 2002. *A.W.A.S. in the Australia Women's Army Service, 1942–1945: A Personal Narrative in Retrospect as told to Harvey J. Pierce.* Perth, Australia: Pearce.

Jeffrey, Betty. 1998. *White Coolies.* Tellamarine, Australia: Bolinda.

Scott, Jean. 1996. *Girls with Grit: Memories of the Australian Women's Land Army.* St. Leonards, Australia: Allen and Unwin.

Simons, Jessie Elizabeth. 1985. *In Japanese Hands: Australian Nurses as POWs.* Melbourne: Heinemann.

Australian Army Nursing Service (AANS)/Royal Australian Army Nursing Corps (RAANC)

Australia's military nursing service. The first military nursing service in Australia, the Army Nursing Service, was established in New South Wales in May 1899, and army nurses sailed for the Boer War in South Africa with the second contingent of the New South Wales Medical Corps. In July 1902, the Australian Army Nursing Service Reserve was organized to provide trained nurses for Australia's military in the event of war.

New recruits joined reservists in the expanded Australian Army Nursing Service (AANS) of World War I. Nurses of the AANS served in Egypt and aboard hospital ships during the Gallipoli campaign, on the western front, on the Salonika front, and in Mesopotamia and Palestine. During the war, 2,139 nurses served abroad, and a further 423 served in military hospitals in Australia; 29 died while serving ("Australian Army Nursing Service [AANS]" 1995, 62). Nurses of the AANS had the nominal rank of officers without the pay or privileges of army officers. The pay of the nurses was little more than that of a corporal, but unlike corporals the nurses had to pay for their food and laundry. Nurses of the AANS were subjected to strict regulations and supervision. They could not drink alcohol or wear lipstick while wearing their uniforms and were required to wear their inappropriate heavy uniforms with starched collars even while working in the heat of Egypt.

During World War II, the service, which had reverted to reserve status after World War I, was reactivated. The professional nurses were now given the full rank of military officers with all of the duties and privileges attached to it. They served in Africa, Europe, and the Middle East as well as in the Pacific theater. Seventy-one nurses died as a result of hostilities, forty-one of them in Malaya ("Australian Army Nursing Service [AANS]" 1995, 62). In 1942, sixty-five Australian army nurses were evacuated from Malaya shortly before Singapore fell to the Japanese. Two days later, the Japanese bombed and sank their ship. Fifty-three of the nurses survived, but twenty-one of these were killed when they reached the shore; the remaining were taken prisoner and remained in Japanese prisons until the end of the war.

In July 1949, the AANS was incorporated into the regular Australian Army as the Royal AANS (RAANS), and in February 1951,

RAANS and the Australian Army Medical Women's Service were combined in the new Royal Australian Army Nursing Corps (RAANC). Companies of the RAANC were formed in each command of the Australian Army. RAANC nurses were stationed in Malaya in 1955 during the guerrilla war against communist insurgents and remained in Malaysia until 1971. They were also stationed in Papua New Guinea in 1966 and were dispatched to Vietnam in 1967 with the 8th Field Ambulance and then the 1st Australian Field Hospital. The last of the forty-three RAANC nurses was withdrawn from Phouc Tuy in 1971. During the 1991 Gulf War, RAANC nurses served on the U.S. medical support ship *Comfort*.

As of 1970, nurses who married were allowed to continue their service in the RAANC. Subsequently, married women were allowed to join the RAANC. In 1975, nurses who had children were allowed to remain in the service. The first male nurse was admitted in 1972. In 1988, RAANC nurses were required to carry sidearms when on duty in theaters of combat. The same year, all other ranks were transferred to the Royal Australian Army Medical Corps, and the RAANC became the preserve of nurse-officers.

—Bernard Cook

See also Bullwinkel, Vivian

References and Further Reading

"Australian Army Nursing Service (AANS)." 1995. In *The Oxford Companion to Australian Military History*, edited by Peter Dennis, Jeffrey Grey, Ewan Morris, and Robin Prior, with John Connor, 61–62. Melbourne: Oxford University Press.

Bassett, Jan. 1992. *Guns and Brooches: Australian Army Nursing from the Boer War to the Gulf War.* Melbourne: Oxford University Press.

"Royal Australian Army Nursing Corps (RAANC)." 1995. In *The Oxford Companion to Australian Military History*, edited by Peter Dennis, Jeffrey Grey, Ewan Morris, and Robin Prior, with John Connor, 513. Melbourne: Oxford University Press.

Avenger Field

The first and largest all-female air base in U.S. history. Located outside Sweetwater, Texas, Avenger Field most notably served as the training site for the Women Airforce Service Pilots (WASP) from March 1943 to December 1944. It was later used to train male pilots and housed several Cold War defense units.

Originally christened the Sweetwater Municipal Airport, the airfield opened on August 10, 1929. It survived the Depression era thanks to a construction project sponsored by the Works Progress Administration (WPA). In 1940, the town of Sweetwater voted to allow the federal government to use the airport as a training facility.

On April 1, 1942, the Plosser-Prince Air Academy leased the six-hundred-acre site for $1 a year as part of President Roosevelt's Lend-Lease program to train British pilots of the Eagle Squadron of the Royal Air Force. The Sweetwater newspaper held a contest to give the airport a new name, thus Sweetwater Municipal Airport became Avenger Field on May 14, 1942. The first and only group of British cadets arrived in May 1942 and graduated three months later.

Beginning with Class 43-W-5, WASP training was transferred from Houston to Sweetwater in March 1943 while men were still using the base. The men then moved elsewhere, and Avenger Field served only female pilots for the next twenty-one months. In all, fourteen WASP classes graduated from Avenger Field before the program was disbanded in December 1944. After the women pilots left, Avenger Field was used to train fighter pilots for the remainder of World War II.

Although few buildings associated with the WASP program at Avenger Field remain standing, there is evidence that the women pilots were once there. The wishing well, into which each female pilot was thrown following her first solo flight, still stands, along with two Texas granite walls later erected that bear the names of each WASP to come through training. The thirty-eight WASPs who died are identified by gold stars. WASP veterans occasionally held their reunions on Avenger Field, and an educational organization called *Wings across America* has proposed building a WASP museum on the site.

—*Rebekah Crowe*

See also United States, Women Airforce Service Pilots; United States, Women's Auxiliary Ferrying Squadron; United States, Women's Flying Training Detachment

References and Further Reading

Alexander, Thomas E. 2000. *The Stars Were Big and Bright: The US AAF and Texas During World War II.* Austin, TX: Eakin.

WASP-WWII Museum, http://www.waspwwii.org/museum (accessed on March 21, 2004).

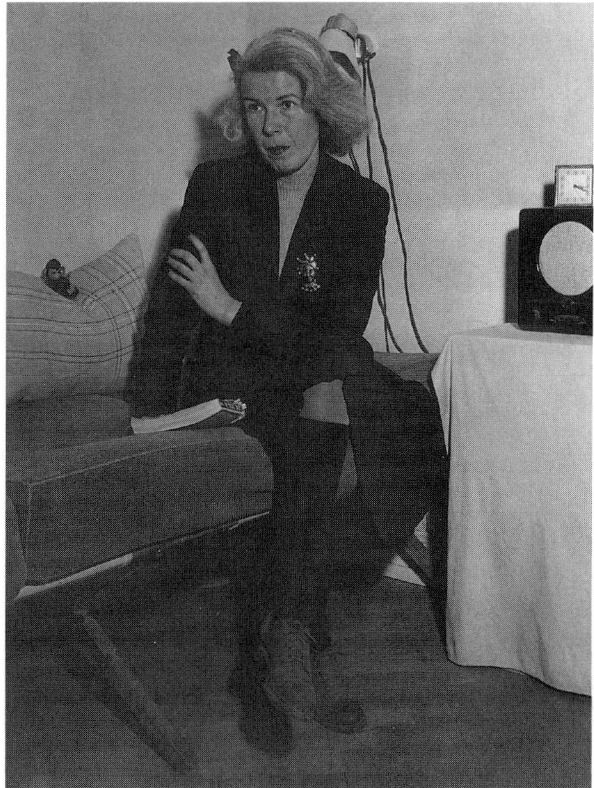

Mildred Elizabeth Gillars in a prison cell in Germany, 1947. (National Archives)

"Axis Sally" (Mildred Elizabeth Gillars) (1901–1988)

Commentator on Radio Berlin who broadcast German propaganda to Allied troops during World War II. Mildred Elizabeth Gillars was born in Portland, Maine. Her mother divorced her father, Vincent Sisk, when the young girl was seven, and married Robert Bruce Gillars, who adopted her. Mildred Gillars studied drama at Ohio Wesleyan University but left before graduating. Unsuccessful as an actress, in 1933 she went first to Algiers and then to Germany. In Germany, she taught English at a Berlitz Language School. In 1940, she was employed as an announcer on "Bremen Sender," part of *Rundfunk,* the German Radio Service. Her passport was confiscated by a U.S. vice-consul in the spring of 1941. Max Otto Koischwitz, an official in the German Foreign Office with whom she was romantically involved, persuaded Gillars to join him on broadcasts beamed to U.S. soldiers. With some reluctance, she agreed and was transferred to the main German Radio Service station, Radio Berlin. There she aired shows with Koischwitz and her own shows, *Home Sweet Home, Midge-at-the-Mike,* and *Medical Reports.* The American soldiers to whom she directed her defeatist appeals nicknamed her *Axis Sally.* When Gillars found out that a competitor using that name was broadcasting from Rome, she used her influence to have the imposter yanked from the air.

The Americans detained Gillars briefly in 1945, but in 1948, she was brought back to the United States and tried. After a six-week trial, Gillars was convicted of treason on March 10, 1949, and sentenced to ten to thirty years imprisonment. In prison, Gillars converted to Catholicism, and, upon her release on parole in 1961, she taught music at a Catholic school in Columbus, Ohio. She also resumed her own education and earned a degree in speech from Ohio Wesleyan in 1973. She died on June 25, 1988.

—Bernard Cook

See also "Lady Haw Haw"; "Tokyo Rose"

References and Further Reading

Edwards, John Carver. 1991. *Berlin Calling: American Broadcasters in Service to the Third Reich.* New York: Praeger.

Harper, Dale. 1995. "Axis Sally: American-born Axis Sally made propaganda broadcasts for Radio Berlin in Hitler's Germany." *World War II Magazine* (November 1995), http://womenshistory.about.com/library/prm/blaxissally1.htm (accessed October 29, 2003).

Azurduy de Padilla, Juana (1781–1862)

Heroine of the South American struggle for independence from Spain. Juana Azurduy de Padilla was born in Chuquisaca (now Sucre, Bolivia) in the Viceroyalty of Río de la Plata in 1781. Chuquisaca was the seat of the Audencia of Charcas, an important colonial court. The city was also residence to the wealthy owners of mines in nearby Potosí, South America's greatest source of silver. After being educated in a convent to become a nun, Azurduy renounced a religious vocation in 1805 to marry a soldier, Manuel Ascencio Padilla, with whom she had five children.

Chuquisaca was the first city in colonial Spanish America to experience political unrest as a result of the 1808 French invasion of the Iberian Peninsula and the Spanish king Ferdinand VII's forced abdication on orders of Napoleon Bonaparte. In Buenos Aires, the vice regal capital of Río de la Plata, the independence struggle against Spain began in 1810. The United Provinces of Río de la Plata was created. It consisted of the modern states of Argentina, Uruguay, Paraguay, and southern Bolivia, which was called Upper Peru during the colonial era. After joining the patriotic forces of Upper Peru, the Padillas recruited soldiers and organized and commanded battalions.

The numerous incursions of liberating Argentine forces from the south during the more than fifteen years of fighting for independence devastated the Upper Peruvian countryside. Small enclaves independent of Spanish colonial rule called *republiquetas* (little republics) were formed in Upper Peru to keep the cause alive. The patriots also strengthened their resolve by aligning with Cumbay, Upper Peru's most important leader of the Chiriguano people. The Padillas shared power and combat in their *republiqueta* until Manuel's death in 1816. Thereafter, Juana withdrew to the city of Salta in what is now northwest Argentina. There she became a valued fighter with the local independence leader, Martín Güemes, who had been elected governor by Salta's municipal council the previous year. After recognizing Azurduy's military and leadership skills, Güemes secured permission from Juan Martín Pueyrredón, supreme director of the United Provinces, to make Azurduy a lieutenant colonel in the rebel army with all the rights and privileges of that rank without regard to her sex. Azurduy's reputation was further acknowledged when General Manuel Belgrano, commander of the Army of the North and creator of the blue and white banner that became the Argentine national flag, bestowed the sword of an officer on her.

Upper Peruvian patriots declared independence in 1825 and named their new country Bolivia, in honor of Simón Bolívar, the foremost leader of Spanish American independence. Azurduy retired to her birthplace, renamed Sucre in honor of Marshal Antonio José de Sucre, the first constitutional president of Bolivia. Azurduy's first four children had contracted malarial fever and died even before their father's death in the Battle of Viloma. Azurduy lived out life quietly with her fifth child, Luisa, until her death in 1862. Today the town and province of Azurduy bear tribute to Bolivia's most famous heroine of independence. In 1903, the Bolivian Congress changed the name of Pomabamba to Villa Azurduy. The municipality of Azurduy was created in 1917.

—David M. Carletta

See also Andean Rebellion of the Eighteenth Century; Latin America, Women in Guerrilla Movements in

References and Further Reading

Joaquín, Gantier. 1980. *Doña Azurduy de Padilla.* 3d ed. La Paz, Bolivia: Editoria y Libería Icthus.

Urquidi , José Macedo. 1918. *Bolivianas Ilustres*. La Paz, Bolivia: Escuela Tipográfica Salesiana.

B

Baader-Meinhof Gang

Terrorist group in Germany in the 1960s and 1970s. Baader-Meinhof Gang was the name given by the international press to the West German Red Army Faction (RAF). The name Baader-Meinhof was taken from the names of leading members Andreas Baader (1943–1977) and Ulrike Meinhof (1934–1976). In 1967, Baader and his friend Gudrun Ensslin, a member of the German Socialist Student Organization (SDS), were active in radical student politics at the Free University of Berlin.

At night on April 2, 1968, Ensslin, Baader, Horst Söhnlein, and Thorwald Proll firebombed two Frankfurt department stores. All four were arrested, convicted of arson, and sent to prison. Released on appeal, Baader and Ensslin fled to the Middle East, where they received training from the Popular Front for the Liberation of Palestine. Baader returned to Germany and was arrested, and then, on May 14, 1970, in a dramatic and violent jailbreak, he was freed by Ulrike Meinhof, Irene Goergens, and Ingrid Shubert.

Meinhof was born in Oldenburg, Lower Saxony, on October 7, 1934. She was strongly influenced by her foster mother, Professor Renate Riemeck, who was a widely known activist. Riemeck was a historian, Christian-pacifist, socialist, and an advocate for the West German extra-parliamentary opposition to the coalition between the Social Democrats and Christian Democrats in the mid-1960s. Meinhof, who had studied psychology and pedagogy, joined the SDS and participated in protests against atomic weapons. In 1960, she moved to Hamburg where she became the editor of the left-wing student monthly *konkret.* Like her mother, she was active within the External Parliamentary Opposition (APO, Ausserparlamentarische Opposition), but became increasingly radical and convinced that violence was the key to revolution. When the APO failed to achieve the objective of radical reform, Meinhof and other radical intellectuals joined with Baader and those responsible for arson in Frankfurt.

Meinhof produced the group's first manifesto, *The Concept of the Urban Guerilla.* Marxist-Leninist in ideology, it borrowed heavily from South American Carlos Marighella's theories of urban guerilla warfare. Its goal was to push the government into repressive opposition that would reveal its latent fascism. Meinhof's theory was that urban warfare would be in the antifascist tradition of the resistance in World War II and that it would awaken the working masses.

In 1970 and 1971, Meinhof, Ensslin, Baader, and other members of the RAF robbed a number of banks. They also engaged in several running gun battles with the police in the streets of German cities. In May 1972, the RAF launched a "people's war." They claimed their action was military support for the "liberation struggle of the Vietnamese people." They bombed a number of prominent targets including the Fifth United States Army Corps headquarters in Frankfurt and the U.S. Army Headquarters Europe (USAREUP) in Heidelberg. Nearly two dozen people were injured and four U.S. soldiers were killed.

The German police launched a massive manhunt. Eventually Ensslin, Meinhof, Baader, and other leaders were arrested. The Baader-Meinhof trial lasted from May 21, 1975, until April 28, 1977. They were sentenced to life imprisonment for murder, arson, robbery, and other charges. To prevent their escape, they were put into solitary confinement in the Stammheim prison. On May 8, 1976, Meinhof hanged herself in her cell.

In the autumn of 1977, remaining members of the RAF conducted a number of operations designed to free Ensslin, Baader, and the others. They kidnapped several German industrialists and hijacked a Lufthansa jet. A German government operation freed the plane's hostages, and Germany refused to negotiate the release of the imprisoned RAF leaders. On the night of October 18, 1977, Baader and Jan-Carl Raspe used pistols hidden in their cells to shoot themselves. Ensslin hung herself. Irmgard Moeller failed in her suicide attempt with a table knife. The members of the RAF were predominantly women from middle-class backgrounds. Among them were Ingrid Jakobsmeier, Birgit Hogefeld, Brigitte Asdonk, Brigitte Mohnhaupt, Irene Goergens, Ingrid Shubert (who committed suicide on November 13, 1977), Margrit Schiller, Illse Stachowiak, Christa Eckes, Ingrid Jakob Meier, Barbara Ernst, Beate Sturm, Susanne Albrecht, Christine Duemlein, Monika Helbing, and Eva Sybille Haule-Frimpong.

—Andrew Jackson Waskey

See also Red Army Faction, West Germany, Women of the

References and Further Reading

Becker, Jillian.1978. *Hitler's Children: The Story of the Baader-Meinhof Terrorist Gang.* New York: Panther.

Horchem, Hans Josef. 1974. *West Germany's Red Army Anarchists.* London: Institute for the Study of Conflict.

Laqueur, Walter. 1978. *Terrorism Reader: A Historical Anthology.* New York: New American Library.

Baez, Joan Chandos (1941–)

American folk singer and antiwar activist. Joan Baez, who experienced the height of her popularity in the 1960s and 1970s, successfully combined her musical career with a philosophy of nonviolence and anti–Vietnam War activism. Her views on nonviolence were the result of her Quaker upbringing by her parents Joan Bridge and the physicist and antinuclear activist Albert V. Baez, as well as the influence of Ira Sandperl, a Gandhi scholar, and Martin Luther King, Jr.

Baez started her singing career during the folk revival movement of the late 1950s. The political ferment of the early 1960s and the socially critical topical songs, especially those written by Bob Dylan, urged her to combine music with activism. She was first drawn to civil rights protest in the South, taking part in acts of civil disobedience. Baez first expanded her range of protest to the nuclear arms race, and when the debate over the U.S. intervention in Vietnam emerged, she declared herself a conscientious objector, withholding taxes that would pay for the war. For ten years, beginning in 1964, she refused to pay a large portion of her income tax .

Baez increased her use of music to oppose the expanding war. After performing in 1965 at the Easter March, the first major antiwar demonstration in Washington, D.C., and at the "Sing-In for Peace in Vietnam" in Carnegie Hall in 1966, Baez took the antiwar cause overseas.

Joan Baez, American folk singer, in performance at an Anti–Vietnam War demonstration in Trafalgar Square, London, 1965. (Sally Soames/The Observer/Getty Images)

Government agencies, including the Federal Bureau of Investigation and Central Intelligence Agency, followed her movements and attempted to silence her; she was also censured by various mainstream media and conservative organizations.

Baez's pacifist ideology was based on Gandhi's principle of sanctity of life, which states that no person has the right to kill or harm another person, and noble objectives or notions such as enemy cannot justify violent acts. Her goal was a nonviolent revolution to create a world of peace, love, and equality. In 1965, her founding of the Institute for the Study of Nonviolence in Carmel, California, evidenced her commitment to peace. She financed the school and became involved in its mission of teaching nonviolence. In 1967, she became active in Resistance, an organization that opposed the draft. After picketing and confronting authorities at the Armed Forces Induction Center in Oakland, California, both the singer and her mother were jailed for forty-five days.

The political commentary she incorporated into her concerts persuaded young men to hand her their draft cards on stage. A poster Resistance issued in 1968 photographed Baez together with her sisters under the caption "GIRLS SAY YES to boys who say NO." Although the poster's message enraged feminists, Baez argued that women should share a responsibility for peace. Baez married David V. Harris, founder of Resistance and himself a draft resister, in 1968. Soon after their marriage, he was arrested. They were divorced shortly after his release in 1971.

Baez and Coretta Scott King, together with Women Strike for Peace, organized the antiwar demonstration Ring around the Congress in 1972. The culmination for Baez's antiwar effort was her trip to Hanoi, Vietnam, at the end of that year. While visiting Hanoi, she witnessed the United States' Christmas bombing aerial attack. Baez wrote the antiwar song "Where Are You Now, My Son?" after witnessing the destruction and suffering the war caused.

Since the U.S. withdrawal from Vietnam, Baez's activism has focused mainly on human rights with Amnesty International and the organization known as Humanistas, which she founded in 1979.

—Avital H. Bloch

See also Fonda, Jane

References and Further Reading

Baez, Joan. 1987. *And a Voice to Sing With: A Memoir.* New York: Summit.

DeBenedetti, Charles. 1990. *An American Ordeal: The Antiwar Movement of the Vietnam War.* Syracuse, NY: Syracuse University.

Fuss, Charles J. 1996. *Joan Baez: A Bio-Bibliography.* Westport, CT: Greenwood.

Bagot, Lady Theodosia (1865–1940)

Member of the Church Army (CA) who was instrumental in organizing several war hospitals during the Boer War and World War I. Lady Theodosia Bagot's service was recognized with several medals including the South Africa Medal, the 1914 Star, and the Medal of Queen Elizabeth of Belgium.

In October 1899, Dr. George Stoker inspired Lady Bagot to begin a voluntary mobile hospital unit for the war effort in South Africa. After soliciting funds for the unit, she established Portland Hospital at Bloemfontein, South Africa, which operated until August 1900. Although she had little nursing experience at the beginning of this war, she was soon assisting in every aspect of the hospital and came to enjoy her work in the surgical wards.

At the start of World War I, Lady Bagot began organizing a CA hospital for the British war effort. Her hospital unit left for France on September 12, 1914, and established itself at Caen under the auspices of the French Red Cross. She split her time between the CA hospital and nearby railway sheds where she tended wounded solders, often until the early hours of the morning.

In January 1915, Lady Bagot left the CA Hospital at Caen to establish the Hospital of Friendship in Adinkerke, Belgium. She and her staff worked under constant bombardment, yet according to her fellow war worker, Sarah Macnaughtan, her hospital was happy and serene. In 1917, the hospital was forced to evacuate, and Lady Bagot returned to London to establish Charmy's, a CA club for ex-servicemen.

—Barbara Penny Kanner

See also Hobhouse, Emily

References and Further Reading

Bagot, Theodosia. 1901. *Shadows of the War.* London: E. Arnold.

Macnaughtan, Sarah. 1919. *My War Experiences.* London: John Murray.

Bailey, Anne Trotter (ca. 1742–1825)

Pioneer heroine of border warfare in the Kanawha Valley in what is now West Virginia, immortalized in an 1861 poem, "Anne Bailey's Ride" by Charles Robb. Born Anne Hennis in Liverpool, England, around the year 1742, Bailey went to live with relatives in the colony of Virginia after her parents died in 1761. In 1765, after the French and Indian War, she married a local settler, Richard Trotter, from

Staunton in the Shenandoah Valley. The couple had one son, William.

The onrush of new settlers to the western portions of the Appalachian Mountains inevitably led to clashes with the Native American inhabitants. In an effort to quell the fighting, Virginia governor John Murray Lord Dunmore organized a border militia in 1774, and Richard Trotter enlisted. On October 10, 1774, in what is sometimes referred to as the first battle of the American Revolution, Trotter was killed at Point Pleasant. The Virginia militia successfully subdued Shawnee leader Cornstalk and his tribe, and a Native American alliance with the British was averted.

Trotter's death forever changed Anne's life. Leaving her seven-year-old son to the care of others, Anne "became a skilled frontier scout, horsewoman, hunter, messenger, and storyteller, wearing buckskins, carrying hatchet, knife and long rifle" (Hoffman). During the American Revolution, she aided the cause of the new nation by drumming up support for General George Washington's Continental Army. She often rode alone from one recruiting station to another, from the Potomac River to the Roanoke, later boasting, "I always carried an ax and auger, and I would chop as well as any man" (Cammarata). A valuable frontier messenger for the colonial forces, she frequently traveled the 160-mile route between Fort Savannah (now Lewisburg) and Fort Randolph at Point Pleasant.

After the American Revolution, Trotter met and married John Bailey, a border leader and member of the Rangers, a group of frontier scouts. In 1788, Bailey was assigned to Fort Clenendin (now Charleston). Settler and Native American conflicts had been reignited as more and more settlers were pushing their way westward into Kentucky and Ohio.

Anne continued her duties as a scout and messenger for the fort, warning the soldiers and nearby settlers of Indian movements. Her most famous ride, commemorated in the poem by Robb, took place in 1791. Word had been sent from Point Pleasant to Fort Clenendin that a large-scale Indian attack was about to take place. At the time, the fort was low on ammunition. Anne rode 100 miles across wilderness trails to Lewisburg to obtain gunpowder. Riding day and night, as legend has it, Anne raced up the Kanawha Valley to the Greenbriar Mountains, where she secured the gunpowder and an extra horse to carry it back to the fort. The soldiers were able to repulse the attackers the following morning after she returned. Local folklore has it that her ride to Lewisburg was the most daring feat recorded in the annals of what was then considered the frontier West.

Anne, also known as Mad Anne (the Native Americans believed she was possessed by an evil spirit) and the White Squaw of Kanawha, continued her scouting duties until 1795 when the Greenville Treaty ended the Indian Wars. After John Bailey died in 1802, she went to live with her son and became a storyteller and trader. In 1817, they moved across the Ohio River to Gallia County, Ohio. She died peacefully on November 22, 1825.

—Charles F. Howlett

See also American Revolution, Role of Women in the; Duston, Hannah

References and Further Reading

Cammarata, Kathy. "Won't You Come Home Anne Bailey?" http://www.ohiou.edu/southeastohio/marchives (accessed July 22, 2005).

Case, Fred M. 1944. *Anne Bailey.* Charleston, WV: Telfords, 1944.

Hall, Grace McCartney. 1955–1956. "Anne Bailey in West Virginia Tradition." *West Virginia Historical Quarterly Magazine* 17: 22–85.

Hoffman, Jean. "'Mad' Anne Bailey," http://freepages.genealogy.rootsweb.com (accessed July 22, 2005).

Lewis, Virgil Anson. 1891. *Life and Times of Anne Bailey: The Pioneer Heroine of the Great Kanawha Valley.* Charleston, WV: Butler.

Poffenbarger, Livia Simpson. 1907. *Anne Bailey: Thrilling Adventures of the Heroine of the Kanawha Valley.* Point Pleasant, WV: L.S. Poffenbarger, 1907 (private printing).

Royall, Anne. 1826. *Sketches of History, Life and Manners in the United States.* New Haven, CT: Anne Royall, 1826 (private printing).

Baissac, Lise de (1905–2004)

British operative during World War II. Lise Baissac was born on May 11, 1905, to well-to-do French parents settled in Mauritius. With her brother Claude de Baissac (b. 1907), she went to Paris in 1920 to study. After the German invasion of France in 1940, she went to London, where she worked as an assistant in a shop. Both she and her brother joined the Special Operations Executive (SOE). Baissac had basic training under the First Aid Nursing Yeomanry (FANY) and was assigned the task of helping the French Resistance movement.

Baissac, under the code name of "Odile," and Andrée Borrel became the first female agents to be parachuted into France. The first attempt had failed because of adverse weather conditions, and they landed in the Loire Valley on September 24, 1942, on their second attempt. Baissac's task was to liaison between various networks such as "Prosper," "Scientist," and "Bricklayer." From her base at Poitiers, she had to go either to Paris or to her brother's home in Bordeaux to send and receive important messages. She formed a new circuit called "Artist" for helping agents. Masquerading as a widow named Madame Irene Brisse who had come to Poitiers for a tranquil life, Baissac lived near the Gestapo headquarters and was even cordial with the Gestapo chief. The Gestapo did not suspect Baissac, and with her charm and dexterity, she performed her mission well. Without a wireless set, she traveled by bicycle for her task. After the Gestapo penetrated spying networks and apprehended Borrel and others, Baissac and her brother were flown back to Britain in August 1943.

Baissac could not return to France right away because she broke her legs while training new agents. Only in April 1944 was she able to parachute again to France with the code name "Marguerite." Her liaison with the "Pimento" circuit was tense because of political differences, and Baissac joined her brother in Normandy, where his circuit, "Scientist," was engaged in arming the resistance groups and preparing groundwork for D-day. She also went to Paris to induct new agents. After receiving a message informing her of D-day, she made her way through hostile territory on bicycle, avoiding the Gestapo and returned to Normandy.

Baissac actively took part in attacks and often covered 40 miles a day on a bicycle with explosives and arms for resistance groups. Lucky to survive, Baissac returned to Britain in September 1944. She joined the parade on the VE day and was received by Queen Elizabeth at Buckingham Palace. She was named Member of British Empire, and the French Government made her a chevalier de la Legion d'Honneur and awarded her the Croix de Guerre.

After the war, Baissac worked for the BBC and then married her childhood sweetheart Henri Villameur, an artist and interior decorator. The Valençay SOE Memorial, inaugurated on May 6, 1991, in the Indre department of France was a tribute to her and other operatives. She died on March 29, 2004, in her apartment at Marseilles.

—*Patit Paban Mishra*

See also Borrel, Andrée; Rudellat, Yvonne

References and Further Reading

Binney, Marcus. 2002.*The Women Who Lived for Danger, the Women Agents of SOE in the Second World War.* London: Hodder and Stoughton General.

Foot, MRD. 1984. *SOE: The Special Operations Executive 1940–46.* Westport, CT: Greenwood.

Kramer, Rita. 1995. *Flames in the Field: The Story of Four SOE Agents in Occupied France.* London: Michael Joseph.

Baker, E. H. (Mrs.) (n.d.)

Union spy during the American Civil War. Mrs. Baker successfully delivered intelligence about undersea vessels being developed by the Confederacy in the race for naval technologic superiority during the American Civil War.

Mrs. E. H. Baker had been employed by Allan Pinkerton's detective agency in Chicago prior to being dispatched as a spy to Richmond, Virginia, in November 1861. Pinkerton was General George McClellan's secret service chief and had learned that the Confederates were developing torpedoes and submarine vessels in response to the Union blockade. Pinkerton believed that Richmond's Tredegar Iron Works was the leading producer of this technology, and he sent Mrs. Baker to investigate.

Baker had once lived in Richmond and was acquainted with a captain in the Confederate navy. He took Baker to an exhibition along the James River of a submarine vessel intended for use against the Union fleet blocking the river's mouth. She recorded her observation of the submarine vessel that attached a floating magazine to the side of a ship. Baker watched as the submarine backed away and detonated the charge, sinking the ship in a large explosion.

Atwater also gave Baker a tour of Tredegar Iron Works, where she saw a much larger undersea vessel being produced, one she said was a larger version of the submarine used in the demonstration. Baker promptly returned north and reported her findings to Pinkerton, who then duly informed General McClellan.

There is some speculation about what Baker saw. The submarine she saw demonstrated was likely that designed by William Cheeney, and the larger vessel at Tredegar might in fact have been a larger model. The armor plating for the CSS *Virginia* (also known as the *Merrimack*) was being produced at this time as well. Pinkerton claims that Baker's intelligence thwarted a submarine attack on the USS *Minnesota* in Hampton Roads, which captured a Confederate submarine using grappling hooks, although the capture took place a month prior to the time that Pinkerton reported that Baker was in Richmond.

—*Kristen L. Rouse*

See also Civil War, American, and Women; Civil War, American, Women Combatants during the

References and Further Reading

Coski, John M. 1996. *Capital Navy: The Men, Ships, and Operations of the James River Squadron.* Campbell, CA: Savas Woodbury.

Pinkerton, Allan. 1883.*The Spy of the Rebellion; Being a True History of the Spy System of the United States Army during the Late Rebellion.* New York: G. W. Carleton.

Balch, Emily Green (1867–1961)

Awarded the Nobel Peace Prize in 1946. Emily Balch was born into a prosperous Boston family on January 8, 1867. She was a member of the first graduating class at Bryn Mawr College and continued her studies in sociology and economics at Harvard, as well as in Paris, Chicago, and Berlin. Her active involvement in social reform led to her friendship and collaboration with Jane Addams. Balch's concern for the plight of Slavic immigrants to the United States led to her 1910 study, *Our Slavic Fellow Citizens.* She became a full professor at Wellesley College in 1913 and chair of its Department of Sociology and Economics. Although she had devoted herself intellectually and practically to issues of social justice and women's rights, with the outbreak of World War I, Balch decided that her prime work in life would be the promotion of peace. She was as devoted to this cause as she had been to social reform—to the detriment of her personal life. She served as a delegate to the International Congress of Women at the Hague in 1915 and was a founder of the Women's International Committee for Permanent Peace, which became the Women's International League for Peace and Freedom (WILPF). She participated in the Neutral Conference for Continuous Mediation in Stockholm sponsored by Henry Ford. She spoke and wrote opposing entry into the war by the United States. Because of her peace activity, Wellesley's board refused to approve additional leave and dismissed her.

Emily Greene Balch. (Library of Congress)

Balch attended the 1919 conference of the International Congress of Women in Zurich and agreed to become secretary of its Geneva-based Women's International League for Peace and Freedom (WILPF). She left that position when the league experienced financial difficulty in 1922 but assumed it again in 1934 for a year and a half without compensation. She was an early critic of the Versailles Treaty that ended World War I. Between the wars, she participated in League of Nations programs related to peace and international cooperation and served on a WILPF commission investigating conditions in Haiti under U.S. occupation. The plight of the victims of Nazism led Balch to alter her pacifism in favor of a forceful defense of human rights. Nevertheless, she continued to emphasize internationalism and cooperation. After receiving the Nobel Prize, which she donated to the WILPF, Balch continued to serve the league in an honorary capacity. During her last years, she lived in a retirement home with limited economic resources.

—Bernard Cook

See also Addams, Jane; International Congress of Women: Antiwar Protest of Women in World War I; International Manifesto of Women

References and Further Reading

Balch, Emily Green. 1918. *Approaches to the Great Settlement.* Introduction by Norman Angell. New York: Husbach.

Balch, Emily Green, Jane Addams, and Alice Hamilton. 1915. *Women at the Hague: The International Congress of Women and Its Results.* New York: Macmillan.

Randall, John Herman. 1946. *Emily Greene Balch of New England: Citizen of the World.* Washington, DC: Women's International League for Peace and Freedom.

Balkan Wars

Two wars fought in the Balkans in 1912 and 1913. In the first, which began on October 17, 1912, Bulgaria, Greece, Montenegro, and Serbia, hoping to take advantage of Turkish weakness following the victory of Italy in Tripolitania in 1911–1912, fought the Ottoman Empire and surprisingly drove the Turks back almost to Constantinople. However, the allies immediately were at odds over the distribution of the unexpected gains. A second war, which began on June 29, 1913, pitted Bulgaria against its old allies, Turkey and Romania, and in the end they took advantage of Bulgaria's vulnerability. In both wars ethnic hostility led to atrocities against civilians. This was particularly true in the contested area of Macedonia.

In 1913, the Carnegie Foundation commissioned an inquiry into the causes, character, and results of the Balkan Wars. The commission reported that the wars were rooted in pas-

Incidents of Ethnic Violence during the Balkan Wars Reported by the Carnegie Commission

"[I]n the final result [of the Macedonian uprising against the Turks in 1903], 200 villages ruined by Turkish vengeance, 12,000 houses burned, 3,000 women outraged, 4,700 inhabitants slain and 71,000 without a roof. . . . The burning of villages and the exodus of the defeated population is a normal and traditional incident of all Balkan wars and insurrections. It is the habit of all these peoples. What they have suffered themselves, they inflict in turn upon others. . . . Donchev, a notoriously cruel [Macedonian] guerilla chief['s] . . . band massacred [Turkish] women and children. . . . While marching through Gumurjina, the [Macedonian] legion saw the dead bodies of about fifty murdered Bulgarian peasants. The dead body of a woman was hanging from a tree, and another with a young baby lay dead on the ground with their eyes gouged out [by the Turks]. . . . [R]aces whose minds have been molded for centuries by the law of reprisal and the practice of vengeance, tend to a common level of degradation. . . . Women and children to a number of over a hundred were massacred in a single house, and the slaughter was carried out with every conceivable circumstance of barbarity. . . . Deny that your enemies are men [human], and presently you will treat them as vermin. . . . [A]ll the Balkan races have grown up amid Turkish models of warfare. Folk-songs, history and oral tradition in the Balkans uniformly speak of war as a process which includes rape and pillage, devastation and massacre. . . . In the villages of Pichman, Ouroun-Béglé and Mavro, the Greeks . . . outraged more than 400 women. . . . A woman of Haskovo described how her little child was thrown up in the air by a Turkish soldier who caught it on the point of his bayonette . . . three young women threw themselves into a well after their fiancés were shot . . . the Turkish soldiers went down into the well and dragged the girls out. Two of them were dead; the third had a broken leg; despite her agony she was outraged by two Turks. . . . [T]he Greeks and Turks spared none from little girls of twelve up to an old woman of ninety. . . . On September 20 . . . in all of these villages the Servians committed acts of horrible massacre and outrage on women, children, and old people. . . . In Has-Keuï . . . all the [Bulgarian] women were collected in a spacious barn and the [Turkish] soldiers banqueted for twenty-four hours, outraging all the women from eight to seventy-five. . . . At Kolibia a young girl, pursued by a soldier, fell from a window . . . while her body was still breathing the soldier assaulted her. . . . The Turks are fleeing before the Christians, the Bulgarians before the Greeks and the Turks, the Greeks and the Turks before the Bulgarians, the Albanians before the Servians and the Bulgarians. . . . Widespread and almost universal maltreatment of women and girls by the soldiers of the . . . nations has left behind moral consequences which cannot be estimated."

— *The Other Balkan Wars: A 1913 Carnegie Endowment Inquiry in Retrospect with a New Introduction and Reflection on the Present Conflict by George F. Kennan.* Washington, DC: Carnegie Endowment for International Peace, 1993, Pages 34, 73, 74, 76, 78, 80, 95, 108, 131, 132, 154, 267.

sion, race antagonism, and desire for national aggrandizement. Ethnic violence was not new to the Balkans. Present atrocities as well as memories of past atrocities evoked reprisals. During the wars of 1911 and 1912, competing national ambitions fueled by antipathy for and fear of rival nationalities led to acts of unrestrained brutality, the victims of which were women and children as well as men.

—*Bernard Cook*

See also Armenian Holocaust; Bulgarian Horrors

References and Further Reading

Carnegie Endowment for International Peace, 1993 [originally published 1914]. *The Other Balkan Wars: A 1913 Carnegie Endowment Inquiry in Retrospect with a New Introduction and Reflection on the Present Conflict by George F. Kennan.* Washington, DC: Carnegie Endowment for International Peace.

Ballestrem-Solf, Countess Lagi (ca. 1919–1955)

Member and cofounder of the Solf tea parties, which brought together anti-Nazi intellectuals and helped Jews obtain hiding places and falsified passports to escape the Third Reich. Lagi Countess Ballestrem-Solf was the daughter of Wilhelm Solf (1862–1936), an opponent of national socialism and ambassador to Japan under the Weimar Republic. The countess spent the early and mid-1930s living in Shanghai, China, where she aided several Jewish refugees who had escaped to Asia. The Gestapo learned of her activities and questioned her upon her return to Berlin in 1938. When she was released, both she and her mother, Johanna (1887–1954), began work in Germany, hiding Jewish families in their apartment and planning escape routes to other parts of Europe for them. The Gestapo, however, caught several of these Jews, who then implicated the Solfs in helping them to escape; consequently, the German police increased their surveillance of the women and began tapping their phone lines.

Undaunted, the countess and her mother continued to resist the Nazi regime by holding tea parties, which were actually secret meetings aimed at organizing anti-Nazi intellectuals. The members of these meetings, known as the Solf Circle, were prominent members of society, including Otto Keip, a high-ranking official in the Foreign Office; Father Erxleben, a well-known Jesuit priest; Countess Hanna von Bredow, the granddaughter of Bismarck; Albrecht von Bernstorff, a diplomat, banker, and Rhodes Scholar; and Elisabeth von Thadden, head of a respected girls' school near Heidelberg.

On September 10, 1943, von Thadden brought a new guest with her to the tea party, the Swiss Dr. Reckzeh, who unbeknownst to von Thadden was working as an undercover Gestapo agent. When the group's anti-Nazi sentiments became clear to Reckzeh, he reported the members to the Gestapo, who four months later, on January 12, 1944, arrested each of the tea-party guests. The countess and her mother were held for two days and eventually transferred to the Ravensbrück concentration camp, where they underwent sleep deprivation, starvation diets, and other intense interrogation methods.

Between 1944 and 1945, all of the members of the Solf Circle were executed for their political activities, except for the countess and her mother. On February 3, 1945, the two were being tried by the Berlin People's Court when a U.S. bombing raid occurred. The prisoners were rushed to their cells by the court's guards, but the president of the court, Roland Freisler, was killed in the raid when a bomb made a direct hit on the building, and the Solfs' file was destroyed. The women were rescheduled to be tried in the same court on April 27, but by that time the Russians had invaded Berlin. As a result, the countess and her mother, who were previously facing death sentences, were released. The war ended in Europe two weeks later.

—*Tricia Jenkins*

See also Von Thadden, Elizabeth

References and Further Reading

Boehm, Eric. 2003. *We Survived: Fourteen Stories of the Hidden and Hunted in Nazi Germany.* Boulder, CO: Westview Press.

Shirer, William. 1990. *The Rise and Fall of the Third Reich.* New York: Simon and Schuster.

Dr. James Barry: The Woman Who Served as a British Military Surgeon

"An incident is just now being discussed in military circles so extraordinary that, were not the truth capable of being vouched for by official authority, the narration would certainly be deemed incredible. Our officers quartered at the Cape between 15 and 20 years ago may remember a certain Dr Barry attached to the medical staff there, and enjoying a reputation for considerable skill in his profession, especially for firmness, decision and rapidity in difficult operations. The gentleman had entered the army in 1813, had passed, of course, through the grades of assistant surgeon and surgeon in various regiments, and had served as such in various quarters of the globe. His professional acquirements had procured for him promotion to the staff at the Cape. About 1840 he became promoted to be medical inspector, and was transferred to Malta. He proceeded from Malta to Corfu where he was quartered for many years. He . . . died about a month ago, and upon his death was discovered to be a woman. The motives that occasioned and the time when commenced this singular deception are both shrouded in mystery. But thus it stands as an indisputable fact, that a woman was for 40 years an officer in the British service, and fought one duel and had sought many more, had pursued a legitimate medical education, and received a regular diploma, and had acquired almost a celebrity for skill as a surgical operator."

—*Manchester Guardian,* August 21, 1865.
From "Theses Alive! at Edinburg University Library."
http://www.thesesalive.ac.uk/ta_exemplary_theses.shtml (accessed March 3, 2006).

"He was clever and agreeable, save for the drawback of a most quarrelsome temper, and an inordinate addiction to argument, which perpetually brought the former peculiarity into play. He was excessively plain, of feeble proportions, and laboured under the imperfection of a ludicrously squeaking voice. Any natural 'chaffing' with regard to these, however, especially roused his ire, but was at length discontinued on his 'calling out' a persevering offender, and shooting him through the lungs. About 1840 he was promoted to be medical inspector, and was transferred to Malta. There he was equally distinguished by his skill and by his pugnacious propensities, the latter becoming so inconveniently developed upon the slightest difference of opinion with him, that at last no notice was allowed to be taken of his fits of temper."

—*Malta Times and United Service Gazette,* September 7, 1865.
From Savona-Ventura, C. "Dr James Barry: An Enigmatic Army Medical Doctor,"
http://www.geocities.com/hotsprings/2615/medhist/barry.html (accessed April 20, 2005).

Barry, James Miranda (1795–1865)

An inspector general in the British Army Medical Corps. James Miranda Barry, a woman who posed as a man, was born in London around 1795. She earned a doctorate in medicine from the University of Edinburgh in 1812. Although disguised as a man, she was the first woman to graduate from a medical school in the United Kingdom. Barry passed the Army Medical Board examination and became a hospital assistant with the British army. She was posted to the Cape of Good Hope as assistant surgeon in 1816, to Mauritius in 1828, and to Jamaica in 1831.

In 1835, Barry was assigned to St. Helena as principal medical officer. There she became involved in dispute with the island's administrators and was arrested and sent back to England. After being demoted to staff surgeon, she was sent back to the West Indies. There she successfully devoted herself to the improvement of the conditions of the soldiers and was promoted to principal medical officer. In 1845, she returned to England after a bout with yellow fever. During that illness, a colleague discovered her true sex, but he was sworn to secrecy and maintained his silence. In 1846, Barry was sent to Malta as the principal medical officer. She served there and at Corfu until 1857.

Barry was a contentious character confident in her own expertise gained through long experience. Although personally generous with her time and resources, she was intolerant of colleagues whose expertise and diagnoses fell short of her standards. At Malta as elsewhere, she demanded better sanitary conditions and food for the men in the ranks, whose health was her concern. As a result of her efforts during a cholera epidemic in 1850, she was promoted to deputy inspector general of hospitals and posted to Corfu. There she supervised the care of sick and wounded soldiers from the Crimean campaign. In 1857, she was promoted to inspector general of hospitals and posted to Canada. On December 7, 1858, she was promoted to inspector general, a rank equivalent to that of major general. In 1859, after a bout of influenza, she was declared unfit for service and returned to England. She died in London on July 26, 1865. She had ordered that she be buried without an autopsy, but during the preparation of her body for burial, her sex was finally discovered.

—*Bernard Cook*

See also Great Britain, Women in Service in the Seventeenth, Eighteenth, and Early Nineteenth Centuries

References and Further Reading

Rae, I. 1958. *The Strange Story of Dr. James Barry, Army Surgeon, Inspector-general of Hospitals, Discovered on Death to Be a Woman.* London: Longmans.

Savona-Ventura, C. "Dr. James Barry: An Enigmatic Army Medical Doctor," http://www.geocities.com/hotsprings/2615/medhist/barry.html (accessed April 20, 2005).

Barton, Clara (1821–1912)

American battlefield nurse, founder of the American Red Cross. Born on December 25, 1821, in North Oxford, Massachusetts, Clara Barton was the youngest child of Captain Stephen and Sarah Stone Barton. Raised by doting elder siblings, Barton was a precocious learner and became an excellent marksman and rider. In the 1840s, however, these skills did not offer career prospects beyond school teaching, which Barton pursued in Massachusetts and New Jersey until 1850, when she founded a public school in New Jersey, only to be removed to make way for a male principal. Until the outbreak of the Civil War, Barton worked in a Republican patronage job as a clerk in the U.S. Patent Office, one of only four women employed by the federal government before 1862.

Barton became involved in the Civil War when she saw how badly friends and relatives in the 6th Massachusetts Regiment fared without medical supplies or food after being hurt in the Baltimore riots. Using her own salary and calling on a wide network of women's organizations in Massachusetts, Barton assembled a warehouse of goods that she began distributing to troops on the battlefield. Encouraged by her dying father, who urged her to take action as a respectable lady, Barton used her connections in Washington, D.C., to receive permission from the War Office to accompany the Army of the Potomac. From the battles of Culpepper Court House to Bull Run, Sharpsburg, Fredericksburg, and Antietam, Barton became the "angel of the battlefield," often the only person organizing care for the wounded and doling out food, blankets, and comfort. Ironically, having won acclaim for working under fire on the battlefield, Barton made it possible for women like Dorothea Dix and her Sanitary Commission nurses to cross gender barriers and work with the army, yet she found herself excluded from their activities.

Barton was present at the siege of Charleston in April 1863, where she developed a deep antipathy for slavery and an appreciation for feminists

Clara Barton, Civil War Nurse

"In my feeble estimation, General McClellan, with all his laurels, sinks into insignificance beside the true heroine of the age, the angel of the battlefield."

— Dr. James Dunn,
Surgeon at Antietam Battlefield.

Letter from Clara Barton to Her Cousin

Head Quarters 2nd Div.
9th Army Corps-Army of the Potomac
Camp near Falmouth, Va.
December 12th, 1862 – 2 o'clock A.M.
My dear Cousin Vira:

Five minutes time with you; and God only knows what those five minutes might be worth to the many-doomed thousands sleeping around me.

It is the night before a battle. The enemy, Fredericksburg, and its mighty entrenchments lie before us, the river between—at tomorrow's dawn our troops will assay to cross, and the guns of the enemy will sweep those frail bridges at every breath.

The moon is shining through the soft haze with a brightness almost prophetic. For the last half hour I have stood alone in the awful stillness of its glimmering light gazing upon the strange sad scene around me striving to say, "Thy will Oh God be done."

The camp fires blaze with unwanted brightness, the sentry's tread is still but quick—the acres of little shelter tents are dark and still as death, no wonder for us as I gazed sorrowfully upon them. I thought I could almost hear the slow flap of the grim messenger's wings, as one by one he sought and selected his victims for the morning. Sleep weary one, sleep and rest for tomorrow's toil. Oh! Sleep and visit in dreams once more the loved ones nestling at home. They may yet live to dream of you, cold lifeless and bloody, but this dream soldier is thy last, paint it brightly, dream it well. Oh northern mothers wives and sisters, all unconscious of the hour, would to Heaven that I could bear for you the concentrated woe which is so soon to follow, would that Christ would teach my soul a prayer that would plead to the Father for grace sufficient for you, God pity and strengthen you every one.

Mine are not the only waking hours, the light yet burns brightly in our kind hearted General's tent where he pens what may be a last farewell to his wife and children and thinks sadly of his fated men.

Already the roll of the moving artillery is sounded in my ears. The battle draws near and I must catch one hour's sleep for tomorrow's labor.

Good night near cousin and Heaven grant you strength for your more peaceful and less terrible, but not less weary days than mine.

Yours in love,
Clara

—"Clara Barton"
http://americancivilwar.com/women/cb.html
(accessed May 7, 2005).

Clara Barton. (National Archives)

and abolitionists such as Frances Gage who were educating former slaves. Barton took particular pride in the all-black 54th Massachusetts Regiment and saw to the treatment of many black soldiers who otherwise would have been ignored. Barton was a master letter writer and crafted clever appeals to the women of the North, assuring them of the importance of their donations of medical supplies for wounded soldiers. She was also a dedicated Republican, who publicly supported Abraham Lincoln and his execution of the war. While in South Carolina, Barton carried on a discreet affair with married Lt. Colonel John Ellsworth, but this was not known until long after her death.

As the war ended, Barton took up the cause of finding and identifying missing and dead soldiers, securing a $15,000 appropriation from Congress to carry out her work. She led a party to Andersonville Prison in Georgia, where she located more than 13,000 dead prisoners and collected evidence later used to convict Andersonville's camp administrator, Henry Wirz. After a successful national lecture tour, Barton sailed for Europe to recuperate in 1869. While there, she learned of both the Geneva Convention and the International Red Cross, whose activities she witnessed on the battlefields of the Franco-Prussian War in 1870. Upon returning to the United States, she lobbied tirelessly for the United States to join the Geneva Convention, which happened in 1882. She also founded the American Red Cross, serving as its first president from 1881 to 1904. While in charge, she extended the charge of the organization into disaster relief in peacetime, and led Red Cross volunteers on both the battlefields of the Spanish-American War and the battered aftermath of the Galveston Flood in 1900.

Barton retired from the Red Cross in 1904 and died at her home in Glen Echo, Maryland, on April 12, 1912.

—Margaret Sankey

See also Dix, Dorothea; Nurses, U.S. Army Nurse Corps in World War I

References and Further Reading

Boyleston, Helen. 1955. *Clara Barton: Founder of the American Red Cross.* New York: Random House.

Burton, David H. 1995. *Clara Barton: In the Service of Humanity.* Westport, CT: Greenwood.

Oates, Stephen. 1994.*Woman of Valor: Clara Barton and the Civil War.* New York: Free Press.

Baseden, Yvonne (b. 1922)

Wireless operator parachuted into France as a British Special Operations Executive (SOE) operative during World War II and later imprisoned in the Ravensbrück concentration camp. Yvonne Baseden was one of many women who parachuted into France to work with the French resistance. Baseden began her career in Britain with the WAAF (Women's Auxiliary Air Force), and because of her foreign language skills, she was recruited to the SOE. Baseden transmitted wireless information regarding the delivery and parachuting of supplies in the Dôle region of France before being captured by the Gestapo.

Baseden began her service in the WAAF as an airwoman clerk at age eighteen. Stationed at Kenley in 1941, Baseden helped teach French pilots technical English. She was born and raised in Paris by her French mother and English father and was therefore ideal for work in wartime France. Baseden became the assistant section officer in Intelligence and later worked for the Directorate of Allied Air Co-operation and Foreign Liaison. She was accepted into the Special Operations Executive in 1943 and was trained as a wireless operator. Baseden, whose code name was Odette, was parachuted into France on March 19, 1944, near Toulouse and served as a wireless operator in a cheese factory in the Dôle region. Baseden worked on a resistance circuit called Scholar along the Swiss border. In June 1944, after the Allied landings, Baseden and her associates faced increased danger. The Germans were becoming more alarmed about the resistance movement and the damage it was creating to German infrastructure. On June 26, 1944, the Gestapo discovered Baseden's safe house, and she and her associates were arrested. Baseden was taken to Dijon, questioned, and held in solitary confinement until August 1944, at which point she was sent to Saarbrück concentration camp. Facing interrogation by the Gestapo, Baseden was believed to be a French helper, not an English spy, because of her fluent French and apparent ignorance of any important information; the Gestapo did not suspect that she was integral to the safe delivery of supplies to the French Resistance. Baseden was transferred to Ravensbrück concentration camp in Germany; during her time at Ravensbrück, she contracted tuberculosis and because of this was to be sent to Belsen concentration camp. A friend intervened, however, and on April 28, 1945, Baseden and others were traded by the Swedish Red Cross for German prisoners and released from Ravensbrück. Baseden returned to Britain and is an example of the significant roles of women in the war effort against the Axis powers during World War II.

—J. Lyndsey Rago

See also Atkins, Vera H.; Ravensbrück

References and Further Reading

Escott, Beryl E. 1991. *Mission Improbable: A Salute to the RAF Women of SOE in Wartime France.* Somerset, England: Patrick Stephens.

Miller, Russell. 2002. *Behind the Lines: The Oral History of Special Operations in World War II.* New York: St. Martin's Press.

"The WAAF Agents—Yvonne Baseden," 64 Baker Street, http://www.64-baker-street.org/text_version/agents/agent_waaf_yvonne_baseden_txt.html (accessed December 30, 2004).

Battalion, Emilia Plater

See Polish Independent Women's Battalion, Emilia Plater

Baumgartner, Ann (b. 1918)

The first American woman to fly a jet aircraft. Ann Baumgartner was born in August 1918 in Augusta, Georgia, while her father served with U.S. forces in France. She grew up in New Jersey and graduated from Smith College with a degree in biology.

Baumgartner and her mother were visiting family in England at the outbreak of World War II. She learned to fly in 1940 and began training as a Women Airforce Service Pilot (WASP) in early 1943 at the Houston (Texas) Municipal Airport. A temporary illness sent her home midway through her WASP training. She was able to return and finish her training at Avenger Field near Sweetwater, Texas, graduating with class 43-W-5 in September 1943. She was then assigned to Camp Davis, North Carolina, a base notorious for its poor treatment of the women stationed there and the site of several accidents in which WASP were killed. There, as part of a tow-target squadron, she flew planes trailing cloth targets for target practice from the ground.

In February 1944, Baumgartner moved temporarily to Wright Field near Dayton, Ohio, to test high-altitude, low-temperature equipment for WASP and other female pilots. She helped design a female attachment to the relief tube that allowed pilots to urinate in flight. Baumgartner transferred permanently to Wright Field the next month when she reported to the Fighter Flight Test (FFT) Branch to test a variety of airplanes. For a few weeks, she even flew for the Bomber Flight Test (BFT) Branch. When she returned to the FFT Branch, Baumgartner became the first American woman to pilot an airplane powered by jet propulsion, the top-secret YP-59A, on October 14, 1944.

Orville Wright, who visited Wright Field often, is said to have enjoyed his conversations with Baumgartner. She met her husband, Bill Carl, at Wright Field where he was an aeronautical engineer serving as the liaison officer between the National Advisory Committee for Aeronautics (NACA) and Wright Field. His conceptual design, which Baumgartner helped test, of two P-51 Mustang fighters connected into one aircraft became the XP-82, the "fastest prop-driven fighter . . . with the longest range" (Carl 1999, 105). The WASP was disbanded in December 1944, and they married in May 1945.

When the National Air and Space Museum opened in Washington, D.C., in 1976, the Flight Testing Gallery exhibit included the XP-59A, the first plane powered by jet propulsion, and recognized Baumgartner as the first woman to fly a jet, although the plane she flew was the YP-59A. In 1992, Baumgartner gave a lecture with General Laurence Craigie, the first U.S. Air Force pilot to fly a jet, at the National Air and Space Museum to celebrate fifty years of jet flight. In March 2001, she was inducted into the Women in Aviation International Pioneer Hall of Fame.

—*Rebekah Crowe*

See also United States, Women's Airforce Service Pilots

References and Further Reading

Carl, Ann B. 1999. *A WASP among Eagles.* Washington, DC: Smithsonian Institution Press.

Beatty, Bessie (1886–1947)

War correspondent during World War I and the Russian Revolution. Bessie Beatty grew up in Southern California and began her career at the *Los Angeles Herald* while still in college, eventually becoming the drama critic and editor of the women's pages. From Southern California, she moved to Nevada, living in a cabin near the gold mines and writing a book, *Who's Who in Nevada: Brief Sketches of Men Who Are Making History in the Sagebrush State.* For the next ten years, she worked as a correspondent for *The San Francisco Bulletin.* In April 1917, Beatty was headed for an assignment in Asia when the United States entered World War I. Beatty traveled to Japan, then on to China, followed by a twelve-day trip on the Trans-Siberian Express to Petrograd, Russia. From Petrograd, she traveled south to the eastern front, where she wrote that she had gotten within 150 yards of the trenches. Beatty, along with U.S. writer and war correspondent Rheta Childe Dorr, met with the Women's Battalion of Death, interviewing its leader Marie Bochkareva. In 1918, Beatty had articles published in *Asia, Century, Outlook,* and *Woman's Home Companion.* She returned to the United States to write a book about her experiences, *The Red Heart of Russia,* which was followed by a lecture tour around the country. In 1921, Beatty traveled back to Russia with the intent to spend nine weeks there. Instead, she stayed for nine months and interviewed both Vladimir Lenin and Leon Trotsky, sending stories home to the *San Francisco Bulletin.* Upon her return to the United States, Beatty became the editor of *McCall's Magazine.* She later worked for other magazines, broadcast on radio, and supported charitable causes for veterans. Beatty died in 1947.

—*Katherine Burger Johnson*

See also Bochkareva, Mariya; Russian Revolution and Women

References and Further Reading

Beatty, Bessie. 1918. *The Red Heart of Russia.* New York: Century.

Edwards, Julia. 1988. *Women of the World: The Great Foreign Correspondents.* New York: Ivy Books.

Emery, Michael. 1995. *On the Front Lines: Following America's Foreign Correspondents across the Twentieth Century.* Washington, DC: American University Press.

Higonnet, Margaret R. 1999. *Lines of Fire: Women Writers of World War I.* New York: Plume.

Paneth, Donald. 1983. *The Encyclopedia of American Journalism.* New York: Facts on File.

Ross, Ishbel. 1936. *Ladies of the Press: The Story of Women in Journalism by an Insider.* New York: Harper and Bros.

Beekman, Yolande (1911–1944)

British secret agent during World War II. Yolande Elsa Maria Unternährer, the daughter of a Swiss businessman, was born in Paris in 1911. Her family moved to London when she was a child. She was educated in England and Switzerland. Her French and German were as impeccable as her English.

At the beginning of World War II, she joined the Women's Auxiliary Air Force and became a radio operator. After training, she was posted to several flight command stations. Her language skills and her expertise with the wireless attracted the interest of the British Special Operations Executive (SOE) when she volunteered. Her training for work in France began in February 1943. In August of that year, she married Jaap Beekman, a sergeant in the Dutch army, and the following month, on September 18, she was flown to a site near Tours in German occupied France. In France, Beekman, known by the codenames Yvonne (Foot 1984, 466) or Mariette (Women of the SOE), worked in the north of the Aisne department as a wireless operator for the Musician network, headed by the Canadian Gustave Biéler. In addition to her communications work, Beekman was armed and present at twenty parachute drops of weapons and supplies. One of their team members described Beekman and Biéler as "both of the finest stuff imaginable" (Foot 1966, 268). Her mother described her as "a gentle, quiet, self-effacing child with a core of steel" (Women of the SOE).

Beekman made the fatal mistake of transmitting messages from the same location, on the same wavelength, at the same hour, on the same three days of the week for months. Using a direction finder, the Germans located the transmission site. Beekman and Biéler were arrested at the Café Moulin Brulé in St. Quentin on January 13, 1944. Apparently she and Biéler had decided, contrary to their training, that it was safer to send messages from a well-hidden transmitter than to risk seeking another secure house and moving the transmitter there. Foot (1966, 106) also blames London for not introducing changing schedules of transmission earlier. An informant from the Prosper network in Paris, however, broken through torture, might well have provided the information, which led to their capture (Women of the SOE).

After undergoing torture at the Gestapo headquarters in St. Quentin, Beekman was taken to the Fresnes prison in Paris and subjected to additional brutal interrogation. Despite repeated brutalization, she never revealed information to her captors. In May, she was transferred with seven other female agents to the Karlsruhe civil prison. On September 10, 1944, on the direct order of Ernest Kaltenbrunner, the head of the SS Security Office, Beekman was transferred with Madeleine Damerment, Noor Inayat Khan, and Eliane Plewman to Dachau. There, on September 11, 1944, the day after their arrival, the four agents were told to kneel down. Kneeling in pairs and holding hands, they were executed with shots to the back of the neck.

Beekman was posthumously awarded the Croix de Guerre. Her name is inscribed on the SOE Runnymede Memorial and on the Valençay SOE memorial in France.

—Bernard Cook

See also Atkins, Vera H.; Damerment, Madeleine; Khan, Noor Inayat; Plewman, Eliane

References and Further Reading

Foot, M. R. D. [1966] 1984. *SOE in France: An Account of the Work of the British Special Operations Executive 1940–1944.* Reprint, Frederick, MD: University Publications of America.

"The WAAF Agents—Yolande Beekman," The Women of the Special Operations Executive, http://www.64-baker-street.org/agents/agent_waaf_yolande_beekman.html (accessed September 29, 2004).

"Yolande Beekman," Spartacus Web, http://www.spartacus.schoolnet.co.uk/SOEbeekman.htm (accessed September 29, 2004).

Belgium, Women during World War I

The fate of women during the German invasion of Belgium in 1914 and the subsequent occupation of the country by Germany until 1918. In

The German Attack on the Civilians of Louvain (Leuven) in August 1914

Report of Hugh Gibson, Secretary of the American Legation in Brussels, on His Visit to Louvain (Leuven) during the German Violence against Civilians of That City

"[W]e began to see more ghastly sights—poor civilians lying where they had been shot down as they ran—men and women—one old patriarch lying on his back in the sun, his great white beard nearly hiding his swollen face. . . .

"In harmony with the policy of terrorising the population, the Germans have trained them to throw up their hands as soon as any one comes in sight, in order to prove that they are unarmed and defenseless. And the way they do it, the abject fear that is evident, shows that failure to comply with the rule is not lightly punished.

"Our worst experience of this was when in coming around a corner we came upon a little girl of about seven, carrying a canary in a cage. As soon as she saw us, she threw up her hands and cried out something we did not understand. Thinking that she wanted to stop us with a warning of some sort, we put on the brakes and drew up beside her. Then she burst out crying with fear, and we saw that she was in terror of her life. We called out to reassure her, but she turned and ran like a hunted animal.

"It was hard to see the fear of others—townspeople, peasants, priests, and feeble old nuns who dropped their bundles and threw up their hands, their eyes starting with fear. The whole thing was a nightmare."

—Gibson, Hugh. 1917. *A Journal from Our Legation in Belgium by Hugh Gibson, Secretary of the American Legation in Brussels.* Garden City, NY: Doubleday, Pages 158 and 170.

Brand Whitlock, the U.S. Minister to Belgium, on the German Action in Louvain and One Incident at Dinant

"The number of citizens of Louvain slain was 210, of both sexes and all ages, from infants of three months to persons of eighty years. Several thousand were taken prisoner; over 600, of which 100 were women and children, were deported to Germany.

" . . . the people were held there [at Dinant], evidently as a screen, while the Germans began to construct a temporary bridge over the river. The French were on the other side, and now and then they shot at the soldiers working there. The Germans . . . sent a citizen of Dinant, one of the prisoners, across the river to inform the French that unless they ceased firing the civilians would be shot. . . . But a few stray bullets still sped across the river. Then was committed the atrocious crime. The prisoners were massed together, nearly ninety of them—old men and young, women, girls and boys, little children, and babies in mothers' arms. A platoon was called up, the colonel in command gave the word to fire, and the grey soldiers in cold blood shot down those ninety persons as they stood huddled together. Among them were twelve children under the age of six years, six of whom were little babies whose mothers, as they stood up to face their pitiless murderers, held them in their arms."

—Brand Whitlock.
1919. *Belgium: A Personal Narrative.*
New York: D. Appleton, Pages 178 and 203.

A Belgian Account of German Violence against Civilians in Herve and Mélen-la-Bouxhe

"On the 8th of August, about 10 o'clock in the morning, some fresh troops arrived, who immediately began to fire in every direction. They burned the railway station, as well as the house of Mme. Christophe, who was asphyxiated, with her daughter. Seeing that the fire was reaching her house, a neighbour, Mme. Hendrickx, rushed into the street, a crucifix in her hand; she was immediately shot down. After this, other murders took place; houses were sacked and burned; forty persons, of whom five were women, were assassinated; the town was pillaged from end to end, and more than 300 houses were burned.

" . . . At Mélen-la-Bouxhe the victims were no fewer than 120. Entire families were exterminated, on the 5th and 8th of August, by German troops infuriated by the resistance of the forts [at Liège]. Among the victims were old men of eighty years and children of five or six. One young girl, Marguerite W—, was sacrificed to the lust of twenty soldiers before she was shot beside her father and mother."

—Commandant De Gerlache de Gomery.
1918. *Belgium in War Time.*
Translated by Bernard Mall. New York: George H. Doran, Pages 48–49.

the summer of 1914, as the Germans prepared to set their Schlieffen Plan in motion, they had hoped that Belgium would not resist. It did, and the German response was brutal. The Germans took male and female hostages and at times used them as human shields. People—including a number of women—suspected of being guerrillas, of committing acts of sabotage, or of providing support to Belgian soldiers were executed summarily. In response to resistance or perceived resistance, houses, villages, and parts of towns were put to the torch. Ordinary German soldiers undoubtedly believed that Belgian civilians were firing on them and inflicting casualties.

American cartoon of Germany holding Belgium, "What Will You Give for Her?" (Bettmann/Corbis)

The execution of hostages and reprisals against hostages was ordered or condoned by the German military in an effort to cow the civilian population of Belgium. In the largest killing of civilians, between 150 and 200 male civilians were executed on August 23 in Leffe near Dinant. Altogether, the Germans killed approximately 5,500 Belgian civilians. Women were among the number, but the majority were undoubtedly men. There were also reports of an array of individual acts of brutality against women and children. Although the diaries of German soldiers disclose fearful brutalities (Horne and Kramer 1994, 7, 11, 22), British propaganda exaggerated the number and character of German atrocities.

According to Arnold J. Toynbee "the destruction of Louvain (today Leuven) was the greatest organized outrage which the Germans committed in the course of their invasion of Belgium and France" (Toynbee 1917, 88). On the evening of August 25, German soldiers in Leuven were in a high state of tension, and many were inebriated. There was fighting in nearby Mechelen, where the Belgians were conducting a counterblow against the invading Germans. Artillery fire from the battle was clearly audible in Leuven. German troops billeted near the train station apparently mistook new arrivals for Belgians and opened fire. The Germans in the street thought that they were being fired on by Belgians. An orgy of arson and killing followed: 2,441 houses were burned, and 2,722 were looted; 251 civilians were killed; and 831 civilians, women as well as men, were temporarily deported to an internment camp in Germany.

Under German occupation, Belgian women and children suffered. The Germans imposed heavy war contributions on the Belgians and resorted to widespread requisitioning, sometimes with inadequate compensation but often with none. The Germans curtailed U.S. relief to Belgian civilians in May 1916 because they believed that it was hampering their effort to lure Belgian workers to Germany to bolster the depleted German workforce. Between October 1916 and February 1917, the Germans forcibly deported approximately 120,000 Belgians to work in Germany. In general, the war was a time of hunger and hardship.

—Bernard Cook

See also Cavell, Edith Louisa; Petit, Gabrielle; Stobart, Mable

References and Further Reading

Cook, Bernard A. 2002. *Belgium: A History.* New York: Peter Lang.

Horne, John, and Alan Kramer 1914. "German 'Atrocities' and Franco-German Opinion, 1914: The Evidence of German Soldiers' Diaries." *Journal of Modern History* 66 (March): 1–33.

Toynbee, Arnold J. 1917. *German Terror in Belgium: An Historical Record.* New York: George H. Doran.

BELIK, VERA LUK'IANOVNA (1921–1944)

See Makarova, Tat'iana Petrovna, and Belik, Vera Luk'ianovna

BELL, GERTRUDE MARGARET LOWTHIAN (1868–1926)

British intelligence agent in the Middle East during and after World War I, political officer of the British army, author, and amateur archaeologist. Gertrude Bell advocated self-rule for the Arabs and played a decisive role in developing the postwar Mesopotamian state of Iraq.

Gertrude Margaret Lowthian Bell was born in Washington Hall, Durham County, England, on July 14, 1868. After homeschooling, she attended Lady Margaret Hall at Oxford. She was the first woman to obtain first-class honors at Oxford. Bell's fluent Arabic and her experiences in Arabia and other parts of the Middle East on archaeological expeditions would have seemed to give her a unique level of expertise of immense value to the British government during World War I, but initially the Middle East was considered too dangerous for women. Instead, she traced missing soldiers for the Red Cross in London and Boulogne, France, until November 1915, when she left for Cairo.

Bell's knowledge of Arabia indeed proved invaluable to the British Intelligence and influenced Britain's decision to support the Arab revolt against the Turks. Bell possessed unpublished maps that she had made herself during her travels. These maps helped the British army move across uncharted territory toward Baghdad. In Basra (now in Iraq), Bell gathered firsthand information from locals. She knew many of the leaders of the nomadic tribes personally and encouraged the British to foster local support among the Arabs.

When the British occupied Baghdad in 1917, she was assigned to the city and given the post of Oriental secretary by Sir Percy Cox. She served as the intermediary between the British and the Mesopotamian people. Bell also worked in Delhi, facilitating communications between the Arab Bureau at Cairo and Indian officials. With her political ally and friend T. E. Lawrence, she represented Mesopotamia at the Paris Peace Conference.

In 1921, Bell was the only woman attending the Cairo Conference, where Winston Churchill agreed to an Arab government in Iraq with Faisal, Bell's personal pick, as king. Bell's friendships and connections helped secure prominent Iraqis for government posts and the job of drawing Iraq's borders.

Bell authored several books including *Persian Pictures, Desert and the Sown, Amurath to Amurath,* and a white paper, *Review of the Civil Administration of Mesopotamia.* She lived in Baghdad until her death.

—Barbara Penny Kanner

See also Great Britain, Women in Service during World War I

References and Further Reading

Wallach, Janet. 1996. *Desert Queen.* New York: Doubleday.

BENNETT, AGNES ELIZABETH LLOYD (1872–1960)

Australian doctor, who headed the 7th Medical Unit, Scottish Women's Hospitals in World War I. Agnes Elizabeth Lloyd Bennett was born on June 24, 1872, at Neutral Bay, New South Wales, to Amelia Hays and William Christopher Bennett. She, her sister, and her mother left for Great Britain in 1878 because her mother believed that she would receive a better education there. Agnes attended school at Cheltenham and Dulwich. After her mother died of smallpox in 1881, Agnes returned to Australia and received a bachelor of science degree in 1884 from the University of Sydney with honors in biology and geology. Despite her excellent academic credentials, she faced many impediments because of her gender. She went to Britain to study medicine and graduated in 1899 from the College of Medicine for Women, University of Edinburgh. In 1911, after completing her thesis on breast-feeding, she received the degree of doctor of medicine. She worked in private practice in Sydney from 1901 to 1904 and in Wellington, New Zealand, from 1905 to 1908 despite prejudice against women doctors.

From 1908 until 1936, she served as the chief medical officer at St. Helen's maternity hospital in Wellington. During that period, she accepted various assignments all over the world and received accolades for her service to the medical profession. She was commanding officer of the 7th Medical Unit, Scottish Women's Hospitals for Foreign Service. Bennett was put in charge of a wing of Scottish Women's Hospitals in Serbia (1916–1917) and performed her duties amid the harsh and dangerous environment of World War I on the Serbian front. She was forced to leave in 1917 after contracting malaria. She was subsequently decorated with the Order of St. Sava of Serbia and the Cross of Honor of the Serbian Red Cross. She recovered sufficiently to work in Glasgow during the influenza epidemic of 1918 and then returned to New Zealand. She was the first president of the Wellington branch of the International Federation of University Women in 1923. At St. Helen's Hospital, she reduced maternal and infant mortality rates by applying new methods, and by 1936, New Zealand had one of the lowest rates of maternal and infant mortality in the whole world, largely due to her efforts.

During World War II, Bennett organized the Women's War Service Auxiliary in Wellington and gave lecture tours in New Zealand on sex education for service women. She also worked with the Women's Voluntary Services for Civil Defense in the United Kingdom. While serving at Chatham Islands in 1947, she was awarded the Order of the British Empire. Bennett devoted her life to the betterment of humankind with special emphasis on amelioration of women's lives; she did not marry. She died in Wellington on November 27, 1960.

—Patit Paban Mishra

See also Inglis, Elsie, and the Scottish Women's Hospitals

References and Further Reading

"Agnes Elizabeth Lloyd Bennett." 1960. *The Press* (Christchurch, NZ), December 10.

Manson, Cecil, and Celia Manson. 1960. *Doctor Agnes Bennett.* London: Michael Joseph.

Bilien, Valentina (n.d.)

German convicted of war crimes following World War II. Bilien was an ethnic German who had been married to a Russian and taught school in Russia. She sought refuge in Germany in February 1944. There she was appointed by Heinrich Gerike to administer a children's home at Velpke, a village near Helmstedt. The home housed children of Polish women forced to work on German farms. The mothers were compelled to hand over their children when they were four months old. Under Bilien, who was eventually assisted by four young Polish and Russian female forced-laborers, the infants were deprived of sufficient nourishment, and within months, eighty of them had died. After the war, a British military court in Brunswick tried Gerike, Bilien, and six others associated with the Velpke children's home. Gerike and Georg Hessling were sentenced to death. Bilien, the only woman to be tried, was sentenced to fifteen years imprisonment.

—Bernard Cook

See also Grese, Irma; Koch, Ilse; Plavsic, Biljana

References and Further Reading

The United Nations War Crimes Commission. 1948. *Law-Reports of Trials of War Criminals.* Volume VII. London: HMSO.

"Trial of Heinrich Gerike and Seven Others (The Velpke Children's Home Case)," Stuart Stein's Web site, http://www.ess.uwe.ac.uk/WCC/velpke.htm (accessed April 19, 2005).

Biological Warfare Experimentation, Japanese

Japanese use of men and women in the testing of biological weapons. Before and during World War II, the Japanese military pursued a vigorous program to develop biological weapons. The use of humans as experimental subjects facilitated the development of these weapons and new drugs. The program, headed by Dr. Shiro Ishii who became a lieutenant general, took place at various sites in Manchuria after 1934.

Human experimentation was regarded as an essential part of the program. It enabled the researchers to test the results of their work. The Japanese secret police, the Kenpeitai, provided Dr. Ishii's team with Chinese and Russians, both soldiers and civilians. To optimize the testing, the human guinea pigs were male and female, young and old. Prisoners were injected with various pathogens and then observed. Some had their blood replaced with horse plasma. Prisoners were vivisected. To experiment with techniques for reviving frozen subjects, prisoners were sprayed with water in freezing prison courtyards until their limbs froze. Flamethrowers were used to inflict terrible burns for burn experimentation. Bombs containing pathogens were dropped on the Anta testing ground where prisoners had been chained to stakes to test their reaction. At the Pingfan complex, 24 kilometers south of Harbin, an estimated 3,000 males and females were murdered with approximately 500 to 600 prisoners suffering ghastly deaths yearly (Swanger 2004, 183).

In the middle of 1945, the Pingfan testing complex was destroyed to prevent it from falling into enemy hands, and the surviving prisoners were all murdered. The Russians executed some of the perpetrators whom they had captured. The U.S. government, however, protected Ishii and many of his colleagues and used the results of the Japanese testing for its own biological warfare program.

—Bernard Cook

See also China, Women on the Home Front in World War II

References and Further Reading

Harris, Sheldon H. 2002. *Factories of Death: Japanese Biological Warfare, 1932–1945, and the American Cover-Up.* Revised ed. New York: Routledge.

Swanger, Andrew J. 2004. "Japanese Scientists Conducted Biological Research Experiments on Human Subjects in the Isolated Region of Manchuria." In *Defining the Horrific: Readings on Genocide and Holocaust in the Twentieth Century,* edited by William L. Hewitt, 180–184. Upper Saddle River, NJ: Pearson/Prentice Hall.

Black, Catherine (b. 1883)

Professional nurse who volunteered for Queen Alexandra's Imperial Military Nursing Service (QAIMNS) during World War I. She went to France in 1916 and worked at several hospitals and clearing stations until the end of the war. She was appointed private nurse to King George V.

Black was on the private nursing staff of the London Hospital when the war broke out. She volunteered for QAIMNS and was sent to the Cambridge Hospital in Aldershot, England. In the fall of 1916, she was assigned to the No. 7 Hospital in St. Omer, England, where she treated shell-shocked officers. She was moved to the casualty clearing station at Poperinghe, Belgium, to replace a nurse who had been killed there, then to the 41st Stationary Hospital in Sailly-Lorette, where she was in charge of treating self-inflicted wounds.

In March 1918, the 41st Stationary Hospital was ordered to join the Allied retreat. Catherine and a fellow nurse came upon a group of abandoned wounded soldiers, and they assembled a makeshift hospital. Afterward, Black was sent to the No. 5 General Hospital at Rouen and then to various other clearing stations until the end of the war.

—*Barbara Penny Kanner*

See also Great Britain, Women in Service during World War I; Inglis, Elsie, and the Scottish Women's Hospitals; Stobart, Mabel

References and Further Reading

Black, Catherine. 1939. *King's Nurse—Beggar's Nurse.* London: Hurst and Blackett.

Kanner, Barbara Penny. 1997. *Women in Context.* New York: G. K. Hall.

Black Sash

White, liberal, women's human rights organization in South Africa that opposed the apartheid regime and provided free legal and other aid to black South Africans. Six women—Jean Sinclair, Ruth Foley, Elizabeth McLaren, Tertia Pybus, Jean Bosazza, and Helen Newton-Thompson—originally formed the Women's Defence of the Constitution League in 1955 in reaction to a proposed Senate Bill that would have removed colored (mixed-race) voters from the common voters role. They organized 20,000 women across the country against the bill, and at one rally a black sash draped across a symbolic replica of the constitution gave the organization its name.

Although they lost this battle, the women continued to organize, officially adopting the name Black Sash in 1956. It then became the practice for members to hold protest "stands" (standing silently in front of Parliament, courts, and other symbols of apartheid injustice), each wearing a black sash. During the apartheid era, women led the way in resisting many race-related restrictions, particularly the pass laws. These required Blacks to carry so-called books of life, which documented where they lived and worked and that permitted them to be in whites-only areas. The Black Sash led the struggle against such laws, establishing pass-law advice centers in many cities, monitoring pass-law courts, and providing bail and free legal assistance to pass-law violators. The advice centers also handled other problems relating to employer-employee problems, work compensation, unemployment insurance, inferior education, and pensions. Black Sash members, using a variety of nonviolent methods including petitions, protests, marches, and vigils, also fought against the broader, harsher aspects of the apartheid system such as forced removals, indefinite detention without trial, and the death penalty. The organization also used well-documented press releases and publications to report on the extent of the discrimination, inequality, human suffering, hardship, and poverty that apartheid legislation was causing and to protest against these laws. Black Sash members sought to raise white South Africans' awareness of apartheid abuses, to play on white consciences by keeping the issues continually before the public, and to replace white complacency and apathy with action.

Black Sash members were frequently arrested, held in detention, kept under surveillance, and harassed, particularly during the darkest days of apartheid rule in the 1960s and 1970s. Black Sash worked with a number of other organizations, including the Federation of South African Women, the End Conscription Campaign, and particularly the United Democratic Front to fight apartheid. After Nelson Mandela's release from prison in 1990 and the legalization of political parties, the Black Sash helped prepare for a peaceful transition to a new democratic nation by sponsoring debates, advising on the new constitution, and engaging in extensive voter education campaigns. After the 1994 elections, the Black Sash was transformed into a professional nongovernmental organization, with a national director and board of trustees, overseen by the

Black Sash Trust. The focus remains on the socioeconomic rights of the poorest and most vulnerable sectors of South African society.

—*Roger B. Beck*

See also First, Heloise Ruth; Mandela, Winnie

References and Further Reading

Michelman, Cherry. 1975. *The Black Sash of South Africa.* New York: Oxford University Press.

Spink, Kathryn. 1991. *Black Sash: The Beginning of a Bridge in South Africa.* London: Methuen.

Blackwell, Elizabeth (1821–1910)

Pioneer woman physician, who worked as an administrator with the U.S. Sanitary Commission during the American Civil War, providing medical assistance to the wounded and sick. Elizabeth Blackwell was born in Bristol, England, the third daughter in a large, closely knit family. In 1832, when she was eleven, her family immigrated to New York and later moved to Ohio. A dying friend suggested that Elizabeth enter the field of medicine. Although she was initially opposed to the idea, the possibility of becoming a physician gradually appealed to her, especially when she was continually told that a female entering the male-dominated field was an outlandish plan.

Blackwell obtained teaching positions in North and South Carolina, but she continued her independent study of medicine, reading medical books provided to her by local physicians. In 1847, she moved to Philadelphia with the intention of entering medical school, but male administrators were unsympathetic. Rejected by medical schools in both Philadelphia and New York City, she was eventually accepted at Geneva University in rural western New York.

After graduation Blackwell worked with patients at an almshouse in Philadelphia where she learned much about epidemiology. From 1841 to 1851 she continued her studies in Europe where she met and became friends with Florence Nightingale. Blackwell returned to New York in 1851 and adopted an Irish immigrant child whom she nicknamed Kitty. When the Civil War began, medical assistance was needed for the massive number of wounded soldiers; to meet this end, Blackwell helped create the Women's Central Association of Relief. In addition to the relief organization, she and her sister Emily, also a physician, worked with the U.S. Sanitary Commission during the war.

In 1868, Blackwell and her sister founded the Women's Medical College of the New York Infirmary. She returned to England in 1869 where she started the London School of Medicine. There she served as a professor of gynecology from 1875 until 1907. She died three years later in England.

—*Leonard A. Steverson*

See also Barton, Clara; Civil War, American, and Women; Dix, Dorothea; Nightingale, Florence

References and Further Reading

Blackwell, Elizabeth. 1895. *Work in Opening the Medical Profession to Women.* London: Longmans, Green.

Wilson, Dorothy Clarke. 1970. *Lone Woman: The Story of Elizabeth Blackwell, the First Woman Doctor.* Boston: Little, Brown.

Blanche of Castile (1188–1252)

Queen of France, regent for Louis IX, and expert at military logistics. Blanche of Castile (1188–1252) was one of the greatest rulers of France; historians have commented that by right she should be listed as one of the *kings* of France because she was so much more than simply a queen consort. Blanche's career was extraordinary and provides evidence of women's roles in medieval war not only in the making of treaties between states and in support from the home front but also in the much rarer form of active planning and directing of military campaigns.

Blanche was a Spanish princess, the daughter of Alfonso VIII of Castile and Eleanor, a daughter of Henry II of England. In 1200, she was married to Louis, heir to the French throne, as one of the terms in a treaty between the French and English (she was dowered with lands that had been contested between the two kings). Little more is known of her until 1216, when she began to display the firm, resourceful personality that won her fame. In that year, Prince Louis invaded England at the invitation of rebellious English barons, claiming the throne of England in Blanche's name. Blanche was her husband's chief supporter. She established herself at Calais, where she organized two fleets and an army for the invasion. Although the campaign failed, Blanche's own position as head of logistics had been beyond reproach.

It is unclear what role Blanche played during her husband Louis VIII's brief (1223–1226) rule; queen consorts were not expected to be politically active in this period. However, Louis died young, and left Blanche as regent and guardian of their twelve-year-old son Louis IX (later canonized as St. Louis). The situation was dangerous. The nobles of France had deeply resented Philip II Augustus's strong rule (1180–1223) and further despised Blanche as a woman and a foreigner. A league of barons was established in 1226 to seize the regency from Blanche and generally weaken royal authority. Blanche responded so vigorously, showing her talent for military organization by raising an effective army and engaging in adroit diplomacy, that the league dissolved. The nobles of Poitou went on to make an alliance with the English against Blanche's regency, but she fought down this combined English-Poitevin attack in 1230.

From 1248 until her death at the end of 1252, Blanche served France as regent a second time when her son Louis IX decided to go on crusade despite Blanche's strong disapproval. She succeeded in keeping peace in France and yet again showed her talent for logistics, channeling ever more men and money to the East to support Louis's ruinously expensive and ultimately disastrously defeated venture. She died before her son's return, worn out by her efforts to provide the logistical support for a war that stretched France's resources to their limits.

—Phyllis G. Jestice

See also Eleanor of Aquitaine

References and Further Reading:

Pernoud, Régine. 1975. *Blanche of Castile.* New York: Coward, McCann and Geoghegan.

Bochkareva, Maria (Mariya or Yasha) (b. 1889)

Commander of the Russian Women's Battalion of Death. Maria (Yasha) Bochkareva was born in Nikolsko, Siberia. She was physically abused by her alcoholic peasant father. At age fifteen, she married Afansi Bochkareva, who also abused her. She left him and her job as a construction worker and worked on a river steamer. Her second husband, Yakov Buk, was also violent. In 1914, Maria left him and was allowed to join the Russian 25th Reserve Battalion as a woman soldier. She was wounded twice and awarded three times for her bravery.

In May 1917, she was able to persuade Alexander Kerensky, then minister of defense of the provisional Russian government, to allow her to form a women's battalion. She reputedly said, "If the men refuse to fight for their country, we will show them what the women can do!" (Farmborough 1975, 299). She was able to recruit 2,000 women. There were young women from prominent families and university students swept away by patriotic emotion, and perhaps sometimes "drawn to battle through personal sorrow or failure in love" (Stites 1978, 297). Some of these became officers, but after

Maria Bochkareva

Yasha Bochkareva's Dream

"I had a vision. I saw millions of Russian soldiers rise in an invincible advance after I and my three hundred women had disappeared into No Man's Land on the way to the German trenches. Surely, the men would be shamed at the sight of their sisters going into battle. Surely the front would awake and rush forward like one man, to be followed by the powerful armies of the rear. No force on earth could withstand the irresistible momentum of fourteen million Russian soldiers.... I felt that Russia's manhood was ready to follow the Battalion and strike the final blow for the salvation of the country. It was an illusion and my disenchantment was not very long delayed."

—Maria L. Bochkareva with Don Levine.
Yashka: My Life as a Peasant Officer and Exile.
New York: Frederick A. Stokes, 1919, Pages 207 and 191.

Bochkareva culled the ranks and drove away most of her recruits with her draconian discipline, only 300, predominantly peasant women, remained. Those who remained were instructed by men from the Volhynia Regiment. Before shipping to the front, the battalion was praised by the British suffragette turned patriot Emmeline Pankhurst.

The battalion, bolstered by officers and rank-and-file male volunteers, fought credibly in the July offensive, driving through three German trench lines. Bochkareva thought, "Surely, the men would be shamed at the sight of their sisters going into battle. Surely, the front would awake and rush forward like one man" (Bochkareva 1919, 207). To her dismay, the battalion was left in the lurch by all-male units, who refused orders to support its attack. Some of her own unit and their reinforcements faltered. During the fighting, Bochkareva discovered one of her women making love with a Russian male soldier. She ran the woman through with a bayonet, but the man escaped before she could kill him (Bochkareva 1919, 217). The women were forced to fall back to avoid encirclement and suffered staggering casualties, between 109 and 210 of its 300 soldiers (Stites 1978, 297), including Bochkareva, who was wounded. After recovering, she was attacked and almost lynched by disgruntled male onlookers when she attempted to impose discipline on a women's unit in Moscow. She returned to the front and her unit, but defeatism was rampant. Her effort to shame men into fighting led to insults and threats. Finally, twenty of her soldiers were lynched by defeatist men (Bochkareva 1919, 256). At that point, Bochkareva dissolved her unit.

Asked by an old officer acquaintance to confer with General Lavr Kornilov, she went to an area in the south where Kornilov and the Bolsheviks were fighting. Captured by the Bolsheviks, she narrowly escaped execution. Through luck, being recognized as a soldier who had saved wounded soldiers on the battlefield at great personal danger, and the help of acquaintances, she was released. She was able to make her way to Vladivostok, and on April 18, 1918, she was transported to the United States on a U.S. ship. There she told her story, which was turned into a book by Isaac Don Levine. She left the United States in July and returned via England to Archangel, Russia. There she disappeared in 1919.

The 135 women soldiers stationed in the Winter Palace in Petrograd at the time of the October Revolution are frequently identified as members of the Women's Battalion of Death. They were not part of Bochkareva's unit, but a

Commandant Maria Bochkareva, leader of the Russian military's Women's Death Battalion. (Duncan-Clark, S. J., Pictorial History of the Great War, *The John A. Hertel Co., Toronto, 1919)*

company from a women's battalion formed in Petrograd after Bochkareva disbanded her unit and left the front. They were almost the sole defenders of Kerensky's Provisional Government against the Bolsheviks. Kerensky left the women soldiers and young male cadets to fight while he escaped in an automobile commandeered from the U.S. embassy. His effort to rouse reinforcements failed, and the company of women left their barricades and surrendered. The women were taken to various barracks for the night. They were insulted and beaten; three were raped, and one committed suicide. Despite wild rumors, there was no massacre and no mass rape. The next day, the women were marched to the Finland station and sent to their barracks, after which they disbanded.

—Bernard Cook

See also Russia, Women in the Armed Forces

References and Further Reading

Bochkareva, Maria L., with Don Levine. 1919. *Yashka: My Life as a Peasant Officer and Exile.* New York: Frederick A. Stokes.

Daniels, Robert V. 1967. *Red October: The Bolshevik Revolution of 1917.* New York: Charles Scribner's Sons.

Farmborough, Florence. 1975. *With the Armies of the Tsar: A Nurse at the Russian Front 1914–18.* New York: Stein and Day.

Stites, Richard. 1978. *The Women's Liberation Movement in Russia: Feminism, Nihilism, and Bolshevism, 1860–1930.* Princeton, NJ: Princeton University.

BONNEY, THERESE (1894–1978)

War photographer. The first correspondent to capture the coming of the Russo-Finnish War in 1939 and the only woman photographer on the Finnish and Western Fronts during the major part of the fighting, Bonney's photos of the aftermath of World War II lead to the founding of UNICEF.

Bonney was born in Syracuse, New York, in 1894 but spent most of her youth in California. After graduating from the University of California, she earned a master's degree in romance languages at Harvard. In the midst of studying for her Ph.D. at Columbia, she moved to Paris to study at the Sorbonne, where in 1921 she was the tenth American and fourth woman to earn a Ph.D.

She launched the European branch of the American Red Cross's Correspondence Exchange between European and American children, hoping to foster cultural relationship between the two continents. While lecturing and touring Europe, she wrote for newspapers and magazines in the United States, France, and England. Finding it impossible to locate appropriate images to accompany her articles, she established the Bonney Service, the first U.S. illustrated press service in Europe, which supplied images for newspapers and periodicals in thirty-three countries.

Before World War II, Bonney organized several photography exhibits in Europe and the United States and coauthored guide and cooking books with her sister, Louise Bonney Leicester. On the pretext of shooting photos of the Finland's preparations for the Olympics Games, Bonney scooped the Russo-Finnish War and was decorated with the highest honor of Finland, the White Rose. Sometime after 1940, she was involved in a secret mission in Finland for the Office of Strategic Services. Leaving Finland in 1940, she returned to France, where she worked with the American Red Cross and Anne Morgan's section of the American Friends of France and helped evacuate refugees. At the time of the German invasion, she was the only foreign correspondent at the Battle of the Meuse and made the most complete record of the Battle of France.

Returning to the United States, she exhibited her war photos at the Library of Congress. The Carnegie Corporation granted her money to return to Europe to comment on the war's aftermath. In 1943, Bonney published a shocking book, *Europe's Children,* which documented the ravages of the war on children. With her lens, Bonney's images horrified Americans and Europeans alike in a manner that words could not. Making her home in Paris after the war, she wrote a column for the French daily *Le Figaro* and translated French plays that were produced on Broadway. For her bravery and humanitarian efforts, the French government awarded her the Croix de Guerre in 1941.

—*Rebecca Tolley-Stokes*

See also Bubley, Esther; Chapelle, Dickey; Lange, Dorothea; Meiselas, Susan; Red Cross of the United States: World War I and World War II

References and Further Reading

Kolosek, Lisa Schlansker. 2002. *The Invention of Chic: Therese Bonney and Paris Moderne.* New York: Thames and Hudson.

"Therese Bonney." 1944. In *Current Biography,* 51–54. New York: H. Wilson.

Borden, Mary (1886–1968)

American writer and nurse who wrote about her nursing experiences in World Wars I and II. Mary Borden, the daughter of a wealthy businessman, was born in Chicago. She began her nursing career in France working for the French Red Cross in 1914. At her own expense, Borden equipped and ran a mobile surgical hospital along the French-Swiss border. For her medical effort, she was awarded the Croix de Guerre by the French government. In March 1918, she married Edward Spears, the head of the British Military Mission in France.

After the war, she turned to writing. She published a novel, *Flamingo,* in 1928. She then wrote about her experiences in the war in her 1929 book, *The Forbidden Zone.* The tone of *Forbidden Zone* is pessimistic, and the accounts in her collection are to be taken as interpretations of events rather than factual reports. Borden's writing employed modernist styles, including free movement between fiction, poetry, and prose. Her narrator downplays her own achievements and abilities.

In Borden's writing, "No Man's Land" is inhabited by a select few women. Accounts written by nurses like Borden refuted the idea that only soldiers could write an authoritative account of the war. Scholars praised Borden's writing as brilliant and as a form of important historical documentation. Borden's work is typical of the chaotic influence of the war's new technology and of the experimental art employed by women out of a desire to be innovative. In "Conspiracy," one of the essays in *Forbidden Zone,* Borden argues that the war changed the balance between male and female, with women suddenly holding power at the expense of men. Nurses were partly guilty for causing pain and breaking men's bodies, a symbol of the fragmentation evident in modernist literature. Women were stripped of their own identity and forced to take on one that was more akin to that of an animal. Men were literally emasculated, and she often uses the metaphor of X-rays peering into their bodies.

In 1940, Borden returned to nursing creating a mobile hospital in France. Her 1946 *Journey down a Blind Alley,* considered to be her autobiography, described her work without supplies in a casino that had been converted into a hospital and her work at the frontline. She explored the political difficulties that came with her status as the wife of a British official and revealed her growing frustration with the French, whom she accused of collaborating with the Germans. She also attacked the personal ambition, marketing, and hypocrisy of the medical profession. Finally, U.S. volunteers received her scorn. She derided them as merely in the war out of curiosity and "sensation seeking."

—*Laura Finger*

See also Nurses, United States Army Nurse Corps in World War I

References and Further Reading

Higonnet, Margaret R. 2001. *Nurses at the Front: Writing the Wounds of the Great War.* Boston: Northeastern University Press.

Smith, Angela K. 2000. *The Second Battlefield: Women, Modernism and the First World War.* New York: Manchester University Press.

Borginis, Sarah (1812–1886)

American heroine in the Mexican War (1846–1848). Sarah Borginis was born in Clay County, Missouri, in 1812. Married to a soldier by 1840, she worked for the U.S. Army as a laundress. Her duties included washing clothes and cooking for officers, as well as caring for the sick and wounded. Strong, athletic, and graceful, she stood over six feet tall with an hourglass figure. Borginis's striking appearance brought her much attention. Her nickname, the Great Western, was inspired by the largest steamer afloat in its day.

Anticipating trouble in 1845 over the U.S. annexation of Texas, President James K. Polk authorized General Zachary Taylor to assemble the largest number of military troops since the Revolutionary War. Borginis and her husband joined Taylor's forces in Corpus Christi, Texas. Borginis, who idolized Taylor, was outspokenly confident in the general's leadership ability. When orders came from Washington for Taylor's forces to move into Mexico, Sarah drove her donkey cart full of supplies south with great skill. On the Rio Grande River opposite Matamoras, Mexico, Taylor hurriedly constructed Fort Texas. After the war officially began, Taylor maneuvered to protect his supply base, leaving Major Jacob Brown in charge of the fort and its 500 inhabitants. In May 1846, the Mexicans laid siege to Fort Texas for seven days. Borginis frequently exposed herself to danger as she served meals, dressed wounds, and loaded rifles. Brown was killed before Taylor returned to save Fort Texas, which was renamed Fort Brown in his honor.

Borginis achieved national attention when word of her courage and composure under attack appeared in U.S. newspapers. The Great Western became a notable part of western lore as the heroine of Fort Brown. Borginis maintained her reputation accompanying Taylor's forces in several battles. After her first husband was killed in combat, she had several other male companions and husbands. Borginis, a woman of great business acumen despite being able neither to read nor write, managed two hotels, both called the American House, in the Mexican cities of Saltillo and Monterrey. The hotels provided soldiers with entertainment, food, lodging, liquor, and women.

The war's end in early 1848 coincided with the discovery of gold in California. Borginis eventually moved to what became El Paso, Texas, where federal troops were ordered to protect westward migrating Americans. Borginis is remembered as El Paso's first Anglo female resident, as well as its first madam. After a few years in El Paso, Borginis headed west with a new man, Albert Bowman, a European immigrant and Mexican War veteran. They settled in Fort Yuma, Arizona, where Borginis, Yuma's first Anglo female resident, started a business cooking and cleaning for officers while her husband pursued mining. Soon she was running a restaurant, bar, boarding house, and brothel across from the fort. Her final years were spent managing her various businesses in Arizona, most of them in Yuma. Borginis, the only woman laid to rest in Fort Yuma's cemetery, was buried with full military honors in 1866. Her body and others there were reinterred at San Francisco National Cemetery, where her gravestone is marked Sarah A. Bowman.

—David M. Carletta

See also Allen, Eliza

References and Further Reading

Sandwich, Brian. 1921. *The Great Western: Legendary Lady of the Southwest.* El Paso, TX: Texas Western.

Borrel, Andrée (1919–1944)

British secret agent during World War II. André Borrel was born outside Paris on November 18, 1919, to working-class parents. She imbued the socialist sentiments prevalent in her class and left school when she was fourteen to become a seamstress. She moved to Paris in 1933 and took a job as a shop assistant. During her free time, she was an avid hiker and cyclist, pastimes that would later serve her well. At the beginning of the war, she moved to Toulon. She trained as a nurse with the Red Cross and attended wounded French soldiers. Following the fall of France in June 1940, Borrel and her friend, Maurice Dufour, joined a Resistance group, which helped downed Allied airmen escape France. When the group was uncovered, Borrel and Dufour made their way to Portugal, where she was able to find employment with the Free French Propaganda Office of the British Embassy. In April 1942, she went to England. The Gaullists in England were suspicious of her because of her socialist sympathies. After interrogation to determine whether she might be a secret agent of the Nazis, Borrel was cleared to join the British Special Operations Executive (SOE). Bearing the code name Denise, Borrel parachuted into France with Lise de Baissac on September 24, 1942. She was assigned as a courier to the Prosper network led by Francis Suttill. Foot (1984, 156) judged Borrel, Madeleine Damerment, and Nancy Wake "three of F section's best couriers." Borrel proved herself much more than a courier. Her left-wing political outlook was useful among the workers of Paris's Red Belt suburbs. She became an organizer, trainer, and active participant in sabotage operations. By March 1943, she had risen to second in command in "Prosper." Suttill said, "Everyone who has come into contact with her in her work agrees with myself that she is the best of us all" (Foot 1984, 257).

On June 23, 1943, Borrel, Suttill, and Gilbert Norman, their radio operator and the other key figure in Prosper, were arrested. After interrogation at the hands of the Gestapo during which "she treated them [the interrogators] with fearless contempt throughout" (Foot 1984, 316), Borrel was held in the Fresnes prison in Paris. On May 13, 1944, she was sent from Fresnes with seven other captured British women agents to the Karlsruhe civil prison in Germany. On July 6, 1944, on the direct order of Ernest Kaltenbrunner, the head of the SS Security Office, Borrel, Sonia Olschanezky, Vera Leigh, and Diana Rowden were moved to the Natzweiler-Struthof concentration camp. The day of their arrival, the women were ordered to undress in front of a camp doctor. They refused, but, when told that they were to be inoculated against typhus, bared their arms and were injected with phenol. They fell into a stupor and were put directly into a crematorium. As the last was being shoved into the oven, she regained consciousness and resisted but was nevertheless burned alive. A watercolor of Borrel and her three companions executed by Brian Stonehouse, an SOE agent who as a prisoner had witnessed their arrival at Natzweiler-Struthof, has a place of honor in the Special Forces Club in London.

—Bernard Cook

See also Atkins, Vera H.; Leigh, Vera; Olschanezky, Sonya; Rowden, Diana

References and Further Reading

"Andrée Borrel," Spartacus Web, http://www.spartacus.schoolnet.co.uk/SOEborrel.htm (accessed September 30, 2004).

Foot, M. R. D. [1966] 1984. *SOE in France: An Account of the Work of the British Special Operations Executive 1940–1944*. Reprint, Frederick, MD: University Publications of America.

Kramer, Rita. 1995. *Flames in the Field: The Stories of Four SOE Agents in Occupied France*. New York: Viking Penguin.

Nicholas, Elizabeth. 1958. *Death Be Not Proud*. London: Cresset.

"The FANY Agents—Andrée Borrel," The Women of the Special Operations Executive, http://www.64-baker-street.org/agents/agent_fany_andrée_borrel.html (accessed September 28, 2004).

Boudicca, Queen of the Iceni (d. ca. 60–61)

Leader of a massive rebellion against Roman rule of Britain. The Romans had previously antagonized the Iceni, long-standing clients of Rome, by demanding that they disarm while Rome conquered Wales. This was further aggravated by the demands of the nearby military colony constructed at Colchester (Camulodunum) and the sudden death of Prasutagus in the year 59. Boudicca, who probably married him around 43–45, had two daughters and seems to have inherited the chieftaincy of the Iceni. A Roman observer later described her as very tall, red haired, and wearing the torque and armor of an Iceni war leader. The Roman procurator for the area, Catus Decianus, demanded that the Iceni honor a legacy by Prasutagus to Rome, which left the emperor Nero half of the Iceni lands and property. This will was probably a forgery, made to convert previous gifts to the Iceni into a loan, which was being repaid. When Boudicca refused to comply, a Roman force invaded the royal compound, flogged Boudicca and raped her two daughters, then declared the Iceni royal family stripped of its land.

This insult to Boudicca and her tribe could not be ignored, and other Celtic Britons rallied to them, including rogue elements of the Catuvellauni and Dobrunni, and the full body of the Trinovantes, Coritani, Durotriges, and Brigantes. The fury of the Celts only increased when they learned that the Roman general Suetonius had massacred druids on the sacred island of Anglesey. In response, the Celts attacked Colchester, sacking the town and killing its inhabitants. When a relief force under Petilius Cerealis from the IX Legion attempted to come from Lincoln to help them, they were attacked and defeated in a separate battle in the fens. Boudicca is credited with leading the Celts at both battles, although they occurred too closely together for this to be possible. Notified in Wales, Suetonius raced to London, only to learn that he could get no help from the II Augusta Legion at Gloucester and that the civil administrators in London, including Catus Decianus had fled to Gaul. With no options, he returned to meet his infantry marching from Wales, abandoning London to Boudicca's swelling army, which attacked and burned it to the ground, looting and displaying the severed heads of the Roman inhabitants.

Despite overwhelming success, Boudicca's army was racing the clock. Leadership of this large tribal force was fragmented; supplies were dwindling; and the tribes had fought all summer rather than sow their crops. Although she still had superior numbers, Boudicca sought a decisive battle, maneuvering to meet Suetonius somewhere between the towns of Wall and Tourchester. Although the Celts may have outnumbered them handily, Roman discipline and use of the

Celtic Queen Boudicca, who led Britons in rebellion against the Romans during the first century A.D. *(Library of Congress)*

terrain allowed Suetonius to hold off the Celts and, even though the numbers are probably exaggerated, may have killed 80,000 while losing only 400 Roman legionaries. Boudicca could expect no clemency from Rome after the atrocities committed at London and left the battlefield for Iceni lands, where she died shortly after the battle, although from wounds or self-administered poison is not known. She was buried secretly, probably with a royal horde of gold.

In the aggressive Romanization of the tribes that followed, Boudicca faded from importance, surfacing again in British history when Elizabethan scholars rediscovered Tacitus and Suetonius, and she quickly became a favorite martial and nationalistic model for Elizabeth I of England and a subject for John Fletcher's drama and for John Milton. Victorian fascination for Boudicca centered on her maternal role, emphasized by Tennyson's "Boudicca," which inspired Prince Albert to push for a statue of Boudicca and her daughters, finally erected on the Thames embankment in 1902. Most recently, Margaret Thatcher was frequently caricatured as Boudicca during the Falkland War.

—Margaret Sankey

See also Artemisia of Caria; Zenobia, Queen of Palmyra

References and Further Reading

Cotterell, Leonard. 1958. *The Great Invasion*. New York: Coward-McCann.

Dudley, Donald, and Graham Wilister. 1962. *The Rebellion of Boudicca*. New York: Barnes and Noble.

Bourke-White, Margaret (1904–1971)

The first accredited American woman war correspondent and the first woman correspondent to accompany an aerial bombing mission. Born June 14, 1904, in New York, Margaret Bourke-White gained her photography skills from her father and funded her college tuition by taking photographs, eventually casting aside her plans of becoming a biologist. A pioneer in the new field of photojournalism and an original staff photographer for *LIFE* magazine, Margaret Bourke-White captured the likenesses of the leading political figures of her time. She and her second husband, Erskine Caldwell, a southern novelist, were the only foreign journalists in the Soviet Union when the Germans invaded that summer. A decade earlier, she had made a trip to Russia and collected her photographs and reminiscences in *Eyes on Russia* (1931). Those contacts and her reputation garnered her special privileges during the early days of the war. She evaded the military ban on civilian cameras and was eventually the only foreigner with photographic privileges, although the censorship she endured made her work impossible. She scooped other journalists during the summer and fall of 1941, and her articles received prominent treatment in *LIFE*.

After the attack on Pearl Harbor on December 7, 1941, Bourke-White felt it was her patriotic duty to lend her skills to the fight. She was accredited to the U.S. Air Force as a correspondent in 1942. She survived a torpedo attack on her way to Algiers to cover the fighting in North Africa. On January 22, 1943, she became the first woman correspondent to accompany a bombing mission. Flying in the 97th Bomb Group's *Little Bill*, a B-17, on it way to destroy an airfield at El Aouina near Tunis, Bourke-White shot photographs of the crewmen at their posts and the *Peggy Dee*, another B-17, beside them. She claimed that she was too busy shooting photographs to be frightened. She accompanied the U.S. 5th Army in Italy. In 1945, Bourke-White accompanied General George Patton when he liberated Buchenwald.

Bourke-White published three books recounting her experiences on the various European fronts during World War II: *Shooting the Russian War* (1942), *"Purple Heart Valley," A Combat Chronicle of the War in Italy* (1944), and *"Dear Fatherland, Rest Quietly," A Report on the Collapse of Hitler's "Thousand Years"* (1946).

In the spring of 1952, Bourke-White went to Korea as a correspondent accredited to the United Nations. She felt that journalists had neglected an essential topic: the Korean people. Roaming through central Korea, she documented the activities of Communist guerrillas, and before she had finished, there was a price on her head. In 1958, she was diagnosed with Parkinson's disease. She died in Darien, Connecticut, on August 27, 1971.

—Rebecca Tolley-Stokes

See also Chapelle, Dickey; Emerson, Gloria; Gellhorn, Martha; Higgins, Marguerite; Lederer, Edie; Luce, Claire Boothe

References and Further Reading

Bourke-White, Margaret. 1963. *Portrait of Myself.* New York: Simon and Schuster.

Bower, Ursula Graham (1914–1988)

World War II jungle fighter. Ursula Violet Graham Bower was born in 1914 in England. She attended school at Roedean, but the Depression kept her from attending Oxford. In 1937, she went to Manipur in the extreme northeastern corner of India along the border with Burma (now Arundachal Pradesh on the border with Myanmar) where she took photographs of the Zemi Naga people. They had only recently given up headhunting. One group of Nagas decided she was the reincarnation of the prophetess Gaidiliu and worshipped her as a goddess.

After the start of World War II, Ursula joined the Women's Auxiliary Corps (India)—WAC(I). In March 1942, she recruited a team of Naga volunteers to be jungle scouts. In August 1942, Colonel Rawdon Wright, who had retired from the Assam Rifles years before, gave Bower valuable military assistance. Unfortunately Wright died from an injury and the strain of age after three weeks. Bower was able to gain weapons and supplies. She then set the Naga to work gathering intelligence on the Japanese. She was aided by a Naga named Namkia who served as her assistant and bodyguard.

"Bower's Force," as it was known, of Nagas was one of the V forces that were part of the 14th British Army fighting in the Forgotten War. In May 1944, the Japanese offensive advanced to the center of Nagaland but was stopped at the Battles of Kohima and Imphal. Ursula found herself in the frontline between two armies. Her V Force fought so effectively that the Japanese put a price on her head.

Bower engaged in patrolling and treating the wounded before sending them to the rear. Rescued British pilots called her the Naga Queen. Americans called her the Jungle Queen, which was the name used in a U.S. comic strip about her (*True Comics,* winter 1945). Her favorite weapon was a Sten gun.

Bower's Naga Watch and Ward mission ended in November of 1944 because the Japanese threat had retreated. She was then assigned to training troops in jungle survival and warfare. In May 1945, Ursula married Lieutenant Colonel F. N. Betts, with whom she would later have two daughters, Trina and Alison. That same year, she was awarded the Lawrence of Arabia Memorial Media by the Royal Society for Asian Affairs (formerly the Royal Central Asian Society). She was made a Member of the Order of the British Empire (MBE) for her wartime work.

In 1950, Ursula received a doctorate in anthropology from the University of London. In 1960, she began aiding the Nagas who were being suppressed by the Indian government. Ursula's husband died in 1973, and she died on November 12, 1988.

—Andrew Jackson Waskey

See also Lakshimi Bai

References and Further Reading

Bower, Ursula Graham. 1950. *Naga Path.* London: John Murray, 1950.

———. 1950. *Drums behind the Hill.* New York: William Morrow.

———. 1953. *The Hidden Land.* London: John Murray.

Thompson, Julian. 1998. *The Imperial War Museum Book of War behind Enemy Lines.* London: Sidgwick and Jackson.

Boyd, Isabelle (Belle) (1843–1900)

Confederate spy during the American Civil War. Born to Mary Rebecca Glenn and Reed Boyd on May 9, 1843, in Martinsburg, Virginia (now West Virginia), Belle Boyd became one of the Confederacy's most active and well-known female spies. Boyd's success as a Civil War spy resulted in part from her ability to use her femininity to escape detection and punishment. Belle Boyd's early support of the Confederacy came in the form of traditional female roles. She served as a nurse and raised money for the Confederacy, and she organized groups of women to visit Southern troops. Approximately a week after shooting and possibly killing a Northern soldier who broke into her house, Boyd began her career as a Confederate spy. As a spy, Boyd played on her femininity to gather information. After gleaning details from federal soldiers through flirtatious conversations, she passed information on Union troop movements and plans to Confederate officials.

Marriage of a Confederate Heroine

"On the 25th [August, 1864], a most interesting ceremony of marriage took place at the church of St. James, Piccadilly, London. The bridegroom, Lt. Samuel Wilde Hardinge, who is about 30 years of age, was an officer in the United States navy, holding the rank of Lt. on board the American war steamer *Connactacu*. The lady, who is about the same age as the gallant bridegroom, was the daughter of Gen. Boyde, of the army of the Southern States, who lately expired in prison, having been made a prisoner by the Federals. The lady's career is full of the most eventful, heroic, and romantic features. Her father, who possessed vast estates in Virginia [and] early embraced the cause of Southern independence ... was soon entrusted with command, obtaining the rank of general. His daughter, the bride, enthusiastically embraced the cause, followed her father to the field and accompanied him throughout his campaign with the celebrated 'Stonewall' Jackson, and on two occasions, heroically, as a modern Joan of Arc led on the troops to battle. She was, however in a skirmish captured, and made prisoner, and conveyed to Washington where she was imprisoned. Here she remained 13 months, when she was exchanged for Gen. Cochrane, who had been made prisoner by the Confederates. On her return to the South, she went on board the *Greyhound* Confederate steamer which was captured by the Federal steamer *Connactacu* while running the blockade. Lt. Hardinge was sent on board the *Greyhound* as a prizemaster, with his young heroine as a prisoner. The result was that they mutually became enamoured and escaped together from the ship, and found their way to this country, the bride having succeeded in withdrawing her lover from his allegiance to the United States flag, and enlisted his sympathies and support for the South. It is the intention of Lt. Hardinge with his bride to leave this country at the latter end of Sept. to run the blockade and enter the service of the Southern States. The marriage cortege was comparatively private, being confined to the bridesmaid and two or three lady friends, the bridegroom being attended by a number of American gentlemen connected with the South. After the conclusion of the ceremony the parties repaired to the Brunswick Hotel Jermyn street, where the bridegroom has resided since his sojourn in this country, and partook of an elegant dejeuner."

—*Bellville Countryman* (Texas), November 1, 1864, p. 1.
"Women Soldiers, Spies, and Vivandieres,"
http://www.ultyl.edu/vbetts/women_soldiers.htm (accessed March 4, 2006).

Boyd most often shared information with two prominent Confederate generals, P. G. T. Beauregard and Thomas Stonewall Jackson. These two commanders used Boyd as a courier, and she repeatedly carried information, supplies, and weapons successfully across enemy lines. In the spring of 1862, after delivering information to Jackson as he launched an offensive in the Shenandoah Valley, Boyd's part in this successful campaign was discovered. Consequently, Union forces arrested her on July 29, 1862, and held her in Washington's Old Capitol prison for the next month. In June 1863, she was again arrested for her role as a spy and imprisoned in Washington's Carroll Prison. After contracting typhoid, Boyd was released in December 1863 and banished to the South. Union officials hoped this was the end of her espionage career.

The arrests did not deter Boyd. In May 1864, she boarded a blockade-runner headed toward England to deliver Confederate dispatches. Before the mission could be carried out, Union forces captured Boyd's ship and placed her under arrest. In Boston, Boyd escaped from federal custody. She fled first to Canada and then England. Union officials held Ensign Samuel Wylde Hardinge, Jr., the officer in command of the captured ship, responsible for Boyd's escape. Hardinge followed Boyd to

Belle Boyd, Confederate spy during the American Civil War. (National Archives)

England where they married in August and later had a daughter. He died soon after that. From England, Boyd published her memoirs, *Belle Boyd in Camp and Prison* (1865) in her continuing effort to recruit support for the Confederacy.

After the Civil War, Boyd pursued a stage career, with most of her performances centered on her activities as a Confederate spy. In the 1880s, Boyd lectured throughout the United States about her wartime activities, stressing the importance of national unity and reunion. Her speeches became especially popular among Union veterans. Belle Boyd died of a heart attack on June 11, 1900.

—*Lisa Tendrich Frank*

See also Civil War, American, and Women; Civil War, American, Women Combatants during the

References and Further Reading

Boyd, Belle. [1865] 1968. *Belle Boyd in Camp and Prison, Written by Herself.* Edited by Curtis Carroll Davis. Reprint, New York: Thomas Yoseloff.

Leonard, Elizabeth D. 1999. *All the Daring of the Soldier: Women of the Civil War Armies.* New York: W. W. Norton.

BRANT, MARY (MOLLY) (CA. 1735–1796)

Native American Loyalist during the American Revolution. Mary or Koñwatsi-tsiaiéñni was the oldest surviving child of Margaret, a Mohawk from Canajoharie Castle, New York (along the Mohawk River). Mary, sometimes called Molly, was baptized as an infant by an Anglican missionary at Fort Hunter in 1735. Margaret's last marriage to Brant Canagaraduncka (also called Niklaus Brant) in 1753 provided the surname by which all of her children, including Mary, became known. Mary received a mission school education and could read and write in English. She came of age during the French and Indian War. In 1754, Mary was part of a delegation of Mohawk who traveled to Philadelphia to discuss issues related to land fraud.

Mary's father hosted Sir William Johnson, a very wealthy trader who often served as a British Indian agent. In 1759, Molly Brant bore Sir William Johnson a child. Johnson's sexual relationships with influential Mohawk women had been a key to his trading success. He also had had a long-standing relationship with his housekeeper, Catherine Weissenberg, whom he married shortly before her death in 1759.

Over the next fifteen years, Mary and Johnson had eight children, and she served as hostess and housekeeper for his large and complex household. When Johnson died in 1754, his will provided for her and her children. A powerful clan matron in her own right, Mary retired to Canajoharie and opened a trading business.

Mary Brant risked all with her strong support of the British during the American Revolution. She sheltered Loyalists and passed information to the British during the British invasion in 1777. The runner she sent warning the British of an approaching American force allowed the British to surprise and defeat the Americans at Oriskany. After the battle, Mary, her children, her mother, and servants fled to Niagara. The rebels confiscated her property. She moved from Niagara to Montreal in 1779 but spent part of the bitter winter of 1779–1780 at Fort Haldimand on Carlton Island. Throughout these years, she was a major force in keeping most Iroquois loyal to the British, including the several thousand Mohawk refugees who had sought shelter near the British forts. At the end of the war, she settled on lands provided as compensation from the British Loyalist Claims Commission and received a £100 annual pension. She remained devoted to the British, the Mohawk, and the Anglican Church and was buried in the churchyard at Kingston, Ontario, in 1796.

—*Joan R. Gundersen*

See also American Revolution, Role of Women in the

References and Further Reading

Gundersen, Joan. 1996. *To Be Useful to the World: Women in Revolutionary America, 1740–1790,* New York: Twayne.

Kelsay, Isabel Thompson. 1984. *Joseph Brant, 1743–1807: Man of Two Worlds.* Syracuse, NY: Syracuse University.

McKenna, Katherine M. J. 2000. "Mary Brant: (Konwatsi 'tsiaienni Degonwadonti) 'Miss Molly,' Feminist Role Model or Mohawk Princess?" In *The Human Traditions in the American Revolution,* edited by Nancy L. Rhoden and Ian K. Steele. Wilmington, DE: Scholarly Resources.

Braun, Eva (1912–1945)

Hitler's companion with whom he committed suicide shortly after their marriage on April 30, 1945. Eva Braun was born on February 7, 1912, in Munich. Hitler met her in 1929 through his photographer, Heinrich Hoffmann, with whom she worked as an assistant. Hitler was impressed by her attempted suicides in 1932 and 1935, which had the perhaps intended effect of attracting his attention and admiration. His career had been shaken by the suicide of his beloved niece, Gele Rabaul, on September 18, 1931.

Braun, who never joined the Nazi Party, was a shadow figure. In 1935, Braun moved into Hitler's villa at Berchtesgaden. Although Hitler's inner circle knew her, she and her position were unknown to the German public. Hitler believed that his appeal to German women required him to project the image of a powerful and all-consumed bachelor. On April 15, 1945, Braun went to Berlin to be with Hitler. At the end, Hitler gratified Braun's desire that their relationship be legally recognized. In his political testament, Hitler wrote, "I have decided to take as my wife the girl who after long years of faithful friendship entered this city, already almost besieged, of her own free will, in order to share my fate with me" (Fest 1973, 746). They were married in the underground bunker in the chancellery garden as the Russians closed in. After a celebration with cake and champagne the two retired to their private quarters where they committed suicide. Robert Waite asserts that Hitler trusted no one but Eva and asked her to execute the coup de grace with a pistol after he took the cyanide capsule his aides provided (Waite 1977, 508–515). Eva then took poison. As Hitler had ordered, their bodies were taken above ground and set afire with gasoline. Because of the ferocity of the Russian bombardment, the cremation was incomplete, and the Russians found

Eva Braun dines with Adolf Hitler. (National Archives)

their charred cadavers when they occupied the chancellery grounds.

—*Bernard Cook*

See also Petacci, Clara

References and Further Reading

Fest, Joachim C. 1973. *Hitler.* Translated from the German by Richard and Clara Wilson. New York: Harcourt Brace Jovanovich.

Gun, Nerin E. 1968. *Eva Braun: Hitler's Mistress.* New York: Meredith.

Waite, Robert G. L. 1977. *Adolf Hitler: The Psychopathic God.* New York: New American Library.

BRAUNSTEINER, HERMINE (1920–1999)

Nazi concentration camp guard and the first person accused of war crimes to be extradited from the United States. From 1941 to 1942, Hermine Braunsteiner was a guard at the Ravensbrück concentration camp for women. In 1943, she was transferred to the Maidanek death camp in Poland. She was convicted by an Austrian court of infanticide and murder in 1949 and sentenced to three years imprisonment. Upon her release, an Austrian court gave her immunity from future prosecution in Austria. She married an American, Russell Ryan, in

1959, and moved to New York City. In 1963, she became a U.S. citizen, but Simon Wiesenthal, director of the Federation of Jewish Victims of the Nazi Regime, accused her of war crimes and pressed the U.S. Immigration and Naturalization Service to deport her. She was accused of brutally kicking prisoners, even kicking them to death, a crime that gained her notoriety as the Mare (Graham, 1981). Survivors stated that she had thrown children by their hair onto trucks bound for the gas chamber and personally supervised the hanging of a young woman who had aggravated her (Maeder 2001). In 1971, Braunsteiner was stripped of her U.S. citizenship because she had not indicated that she had been a concentration camp guard. A German court issued a warrant for her arrest, and Braunsteiner was extradited in 1973. In Germany, she was tried with another woman, Hildegard Lächert, and seven men in the Majdanek Trial, which lasted for five years, the longest of West Germany's war crime trials. Braunsteiner was sentenced to life imprisonment. Lächert, whom witnesses referred to as Bloody Brigitta (Graham 1981), was sentenced to twelve years. Six males received lesser terms, and one was acquitted.

—Bernard Cook

See also Grese, Irma; Koch, Ilse

References and Further Reading

Graham, Bradley. 1981. "Eight Are Sentenced for Nazi Crimes," *Washington Post,* July 1, 1981, p. A1.

Maeder, Jay. 2001. "The Nazi Next Door." *Daily News* (New York), September 6, p. 37.

Bray, Linda (1960–)

First American woman soldier to command troops in battle. When the U.S. military entered Panama in December 1989 during Operation Just Cause, Captain Linda Bray became the first female to lead U.S. troops in battle. Her leadership became a catalyst for controversy over the role of women in the U.S. armed forces.

Captain Bray commanded the 988th Military Police Company in Fort Benning, Georgia. In charge of three simultaneous missions, 29-year-old Bray commanded more than 100 troops, 2 two-and-a-half ton trucks, and 12 Humvees. Her orders included securing a suspected stronghold of the Panamanian Defense Forces (PDF). Designated as a military dog kennel, intelligence reports estimated that 12 to 30 members of the PDF were inside.

On December 20, 1989, Captain Bray positioned members of the 988th Military Police Company outside the kennel and called for the surrender of PDF forces inside. They refused, and the anticipated routine mission turned into a three-hour, infantry-style firefight. When they crashed through the kennel gate to secure the area, Captain Bray's troops discovered a mini-arsenal, including more than a dozen AK-47s, M-16 assault rifles, cases of fragmentation grenades, and thousands of rounds of ammunition. Forty military cots, a cache of Cuban money, and spare uniforms suggested that the dog kennel served as barracks for Special Operations troops. Three PDF soldiers were killed and one taken prisoner. There were no U.S. casualties. Later, Bray estimated that twelve of the fifteen women under her command had been in combat.

The invasion of Panama was the largest deployment of U.S. troops since Vietnam, and approximately 800, or 4 percent, of the 18,400-member force were women. Those assigned to helicopters and ground troops served under fire, yet in 1989, military exclusion policies prohibited women's assignment to combat positions. The army's Direct Combat Probability Coding (DCPC) system, established in 1983, rated each assignment along a continuum. Jobs with low probability of enemy contact were on one end, and those of high probability were on the other—and closed to women.

By definition, military police units such as Captain Bray's were designated to perform tactical operations at the rear of a battlefield. Even though they were combat-ready, their mission was classified as noncombatant. The 988th's assault on the dog kennel shifted the boundaries between noncombat and combat missions. News coverage of the action brought these issues of women in combat into the public forum.

Congresswoman Patricia Schroeder (D-Colorado), then a member of the House Armed Services Committee, immediately called for legislation to open up all jobs in the army to women, pointing out that combat-exclusion policies failed to keep women out of combat while restricting women's careers. Controversy about the role of Linda Bray in the battle and the role of women in war flew in the press, Congress, the Department of Defense, and among the public; Captain Bray swirled at the epicenter. She requested and received an official discharge from the army in April 1991. No policy changes concerning women's role in the U.S. Armed Forces occurred as a direct result of Operation Just Cause.

—Lee Ann Ghajar

See also Gulf War, Women and the

References and Further Reading

Franke, Linda Bird. 1997. *Ground Zero: The Gender Wars in the Military.* New York: Simon and Schuster.

Brewer, Lucy (b. ca. 1793)

By her own account, the first woman U.S. Marine. Born in the late 1700s, on a farm 40 miles outside Boston, Massachusetts, Lucy Brewer supposedly disguised herself as a man and served in the U.S. Marine Corps during the War of 1812, serving on the USS *Constitution.* As a sixteen year old, a trader's son seduced her. Leaving her family, she journeyed to Boston, seeking anonymity and sanctuary for herself and her unborn child. When she could not secure employment, she found lodging at a brothel. After the death of her newborn daughter, Brewer apparently assumed the life of a prostitute. After three years, according to her accounts, she learned about cross-dressing. In male attire, she experienced complete freedom as George Baker and was able to ignore female gender roles of nineteenth-century U.S. society. That she enlisted in the U.S. Marines during the War of 1812 and served with patriotic distinction during three sea battles aboard the USS *Constitution* is a legend. The U.S. Marines regard Brewer's claim as a colorful story. She recounted her supposed adventure in *The Female Marine; or, Adventures of Miss Lucy Brewer.* She also used the pseudonym Louisa Baker in some of her writings. According to her account, she returned home after her maritime exploits, redeemed and welcomed back into her family. She eventually married, becoming what nineteenth-century respectability dictated for women.

Whether or not Lucy Brewer actually served in the United States Marines, the fact that she was able to experience male freedom and follow her own ambitions is phenomenal. Brewer never displayed remorse for those years of her life when she dressed as a man. She only showed repentance for her life as a prostitute.

—Deanne Nuwer

See also Civil War, American, Women Combatants during the; Great Britain, Women in Service in the Seventeenth, Eighteenth, and Early Nineteenth Centuries; Edmonds, Sarah Emma; Samson, Deborah

References and Further Reading

Cohen, Daniel A., ed. 1997. *The Female Marine and Related Works: Narratives of Cross-Dressing and Urban Vice in America's Early Republic.* Amherst: University of Massachusetts Press.

West, Lucy Brewer. 1966. *The Female Marine; or, Adventures of Miss Lucy Brewer who served three years on board the U.S. frigate* Constitution *during the late war with Great Britain.* 4th ed. Cambridge, MA: Da Capo Press.

Brion, Hélène (1882–1962)

French pacifist, tried for her active opposition to World War I. On November 18, 1917, over three years after the beginning of World War I, the front page of the newspaper *Le Matin* announced to the French people that a traitor had been lurking in their midst. The accused was Hélène Brion, a nursery schoolteacher from the Parisian suburbs. The author of the article claimed Brion to be well known for "the violence of her anti-patriotic feelings." The paper accused her of being an advocate of birth control, a defeatist, an anarchist, and a spy. Other papers also took an avid interest in this unusual woman, following the story from her arrest to her trial four months later, as Hélène Brion became the first French woman tried by a military tribunal in France (*Le Matin,* November 18, 1917).

Pacifism was the cause for which Brion was arrested, but it was neither her first nor her only passion. Prior to 1914, Brion dedicated much of her free time to working-class and feminist causes. She helped run an orphanage for poor children, and she was an active member of the socialist party and of the National Federation of Teachers' Unions. As devoted as she was to working-class politics, Brion also maintained that full equality between the sexes was an absolute prerequisite to a just society. Her beliefs led her to join a number of feminist organizations and, in 1916, to publish a brief treatise titled *La Voie féministe* (The Feminist Path).

When war erupted in 1914, Brion initially responded by helping to start a soup kitchen in her community. She also agreed to head the national teachers' union as the male leadership was called up for duty. At this early date and with German troops entrenched on French soil, Brion saw the war as a necessary act of self-defense. A year later, however, the justice of the war appeared less clear, and Brion became an outspoken advocate of an immediate, negotiated peace. Brion began sending pacifist propaganda to fellow teachers and to soldiers at the frontlines, activities that eventually led to her arrest.

Although she was to stand trial for pacifism, Brion's sex and her feminist commitment never ceased to be an issue in the case. *Le Matin* printed a picture of the accused with the caption, "Hélène Brion in Masculine Clothing." Another paper described Brion as she appeared at her trial: "A small man's hat placed devilishly on her blond hair, tied in back without any attempt to please, a loose lavaliere, a jacket which strangely resembles a man's coat, definitely a somewhat masculine and neglected ensemble" (*La Voix nationale,* March, 25, 1918). Clearly, it was not Brion's pacifism alone that raised questions about her loyalty to the nation. Journalists cast her as a dangerous "New Woman," whose unconventionality was as dangerous to the nation as her ideas.

The press was not alone, however, in making gender an important issue. Brion saw to it that her trial, which opened on March 25, 1918, would serve as a soapbox not only for the pacifism for which she was arrested but also for the feminism that defined all of her political and social engagement. "I am an enemy of war because I am a feminist," Brion explained. "War is the triumph of brutal force; feminism can only triumph by moral force and intellectual worth" (*La Revue des causes cèlébres, politiques et criminelles,* May 2, 1918, 153). Prominent feminists and socialists also spoke in her defense, and the trial garnered Brion widespread sympathy among war-weary compatriots. Ultimately, the judges returned a mixed verdict. Brion was found guilty, but the court suspended her sentence, effectively setting her free.

The end of the trial marked the end of Hélène Brion's active public life. From the 1920s to the end of her life in 1962, Brion turned her intellectual and rhetorical talent to another purpose: the research and writing of a massive feminist encyclopedia. To the end of her days, Brion remained devoted to the feminist principles and cause that had animated the turbulent actions of her younger years.

—Mona L. Siegel

See also Addams, Jane; Balch, Emily Green; Catt, Carrie Chapman; Curtis, Cathrine; Dilling, Elizabeth; Fonda, Jane; Goldstein, Vida

References and Further Reading

"La Propagande dèfaitiste. Une Institutrice arretée."1917. *Le Matin,* November 18.

"Les Procès de trahison. Le Procès Hélène Brion et Mouflard devant le Premier Conseil de Guerre." 1918. *La Revue des causes célèbres, politiques et criminelles,* 5 (May 2): 152–154.

Sant'Andrea, N. 1918. "Le Procès d'Hélène Brion devant le 3e Conseil de guerre." *La Voix nationale,* March 25.

Brittain, Vera Mary (1893–1970)

British survivor and author. Vera Brittain is best known for her "generational" autobiography of World War I: *Testament of Youth* (1933). Dedicated to the memory of her fiancé, Roland Leighton and her brother Edward Brittain, the autobiography traces her journey from what she called her "provincial young ladyhood"; to World War I when she nursed in England, Malta, and France and watched as, one by one, her closest male companions were killed; through to a postwar commitment to the politics of pacifism. *Testament of Youth* is unusual in its integration of the generational experience with the woman's voice. Drawing on her own wartime diaries and letters exchanged between her and her male counterparts, Brittain successfully created a work that was an elegy to those who had died in the war and at the same time legitimized the woman's war experience both as the waiting and grieving woman and as the war worker.

Vera Mary Brittain was born in Newcastle-under-Lyme, Staffordshire, England, on December 29, 1893. At school she encountered the suffrage movement and was especially influenced by Olive Schreiner's *Women and Labour.* Unwilling to accept the dull routine laid out for the provincial upper-middle-class woman, she worked for and won an exhibition to Somerville College at Oxford. She fully expected to go to Oxford in the autumn of 1914 with her brother Edward and his friend Roland Leighton, but the war intervened, with both Edward and Roland joining up. Although Brittain found undergraduate life at Somerville stimulating, the presence of the war increasingly intruded, particularly after Leighton, with whom she had fallen in love, went to the front in April 1915.

At the end of her first year, determined to come as close as possible to the war experience of her male counterparts, Brittain began training as a VAD (Voluntary Aid Detachment) nurse, first in Buxton and then at the First London General, where she started to realize the horror of war through the wounds of the men she nursed. During Roland Leighton's leave in August 1915, the two became engaged, but Leighton was killed on the western front on December 23, 1915, the day before he was due home on leave. His death left Brittain desolate, and she only gradually recovered some of her former energy and interest in life after she was sent to Malta to nurse in September 1916. In the spring of 1917, however, two more close male friends were killed. Brittain returned home but requested to be sent to France when Edward, who had been wounded in 1916, went back to the front later in the year. In France, she nursed through the German push in the spring of 1918. She would later date her commitment to pacifism to this period when, nursing German prisoners, she recognized the absurdity of her nursing them when only days before her brother had been trying to kill them. In July 1918, her brother was killed in Italy, a final blow after the physical and emotional misery of the war and one from which she would never recover.

After the war, she returned to Oxford, burdened by a legacy of grief and emotional exhaustion from the war. Friendship with the writer Winifred Holtby aided in restoring her equilibrium, and after graduating, the two shared a flat in London where Brittain committed herself to international relations and pacifism through the

League of Nations and Canon "Dick" Sheppard's Peace Pledge Union. With the publication of *Testament of Youth* in 1933, she became much sought after as a lecturer and journalist, and she continued to work on fiction. Her novel *Honourable Estate,* which deals extensively with World War I and its aftermath, was published in 1936. Holtby's death in 1935 was necessarily a severe blow to Brittain, who had only just begun to let go of the ghosts from her wartime past.

Throughout World War II, Brittain maintained her pacifism in the face of much criticism and even ostracism. She published the ongoing *Letters to Peace Lovers* throughout the war, during which she lived mostly in London, and she was outspoken in her revulsion at Britain's blanket bombing of German cities. She continued to lecture and write and to work for international peace almost until her death on March 29, 1970.

Renewed interest in Brittain's life and work was stimulated by a television series based on *Testament of Youth,* broadcast in 1979, closely followed by Alan Bishop's edition of Brittain's World War I diaries (*Chronicle of Youth,* 1981). Further editions of Brittain's diaries (*Chronicle of Friendship,* 1986; *Wartime Chronicles,* 1986) reveal an interesting commentary on Europe and Britain in the 1930s, including a visit to Hitler's Germany and a day-by-day account of life in London during the blitz and throughout the war years.

—*Carol Acton*

See also Great Britain, Women, Social Impact of World War I on

References and Further Reading

Berry, Paul, and Mark Bostridge. 1995. *Vera Brittain: A Life.* London: Chatto and Windus.

Bishop, Alan, and Mark Bostridge, eds. 1998. *Letters from a Lost Generation: First World War Letters of Vera Brittain and Four Friends.* London: Little, Brown.

Brittain, Vera. [1933] 1978. *Testament of Youth.* Reprint, London: Virago.

———. [1936] 2000. *Honourable Estate.* Reprint, London: Virago.

———. 1981. *Chronicle of Youth.* Edited by Alan Bishop. London: Victor Gollancz.

———. 1986. *Chronicle of Friendship: Vera Brittain's Diaries of the Thirties.* Edited by Alan Bishop. London: Victor Gollancz.

———. 1986. *Wartime Chronicle: Vera Brittain's Diary 1939–1945.* Edited by Alan Bishop. London: Victor Gollancz.

Gorham, Deborah, 1996. *Vera Brittain: A Feminist Life.* Oxford, England: Blackwell.

Brown, Mary-Agnes (1902–1998)

Officer in the U.S. Women's Army Corps. Mary-Agnes Brown served as executive officer (1943–1944) to Colonel Oveta Culp Hobby, director of the Women's Army Corps (WAC), and as WAC staff director in the Southwest Pacific Area (1944–1945). She was awarded the Legion of Merit. A lawyer for the Veterans Administration, she joined the Women's Army Auxiliary Corps in 1942 and advanced to top leadership positions. She was among the first women officers promoted to the ranks of major and lieutenant colonel in the WAC during World War II. Once the war ended, Lieutenant Colonel Brown served as advisor to Veterans Administration head General Omar N. Bradley on matters pertaining to women veterans.

Born on February 13, 1902, in Washington, D.C., Mary-Agnes Brown was a graduate of George Washington University, where she also earned two law degrees. In 1919, she began a longtime career in veterans-related issues when she worked as a clerk for a predecessor agency of the Veterans Administration. She served as executive secretary to the medical director of the Veterans Bureau (1921–1931) and as an attorney for the Veterans Administration (1931–1941). Brown coedited *Federal Laws Relating to Veterans of Wars of the United States (Annotated) August 1, 1932* and *Supplement 1: July 21, 1932 to January 1, 1937* (U.S. Government Printing Office 1932, 1937).

In September 1942, she graduated from Officer Candidate School at the WAAC Training Center at Fort Des Moines, Iowa. Brown served as public relations officer for the Third Service Command and as Women's Auxiliary Army Corps staff director for the Eighth Service Command (1942–1943) before she assumed her position as executive officer to Director Hobby in Washington, D.C. Colonel Hobby appointed Lieutenant Colonel Brown as WAC staff director in the Southwest Pacific Area, and in mid-March 1944, she arrived in Australia to prepare for the arrival of the first contingent of members of the WAC in May. There she confronted a lack of adequate clothing and supplies, as well as resistance from male officers to recognizing WAC officers' authority over enlisted women. Several years later, Brown wrote, "In my opinion the service of WAC members was essential to the success of Army operations in New Guinea and the Philippines. I deplore the failure of those immediately over the Staff Director . . . to accept my recommendations on procedures to assure the well-being of WAC personnel, but the WAC mission was accomplished in spite of these and other obstacles and at not too great a sacrifice" (Treadwell 1954, 461).

After the war, she returned to work at the Veterans Administration as head of the women's division (1945–1946), as chief of the legislative projects division (1946–1948), and as a member of the Board of Veterans Appeals (1949–1959).

On May 28, 1952, she married Dr. Gordon Lewis Groover, who had practiced medicine in Savannah, Georgia, before working at the Veterans Administration in Washington, D.C. Mary-Agnes Brown Groover died on July 22, 1998, in Washington, D.C., and is buried at Arlington National Cemetery.

—*Sharon Ritenour Stevens*

See also Hobby, Oveta Culp

References and Further Reading:

Morden, Bettie J. 1990. *The Women's Army Corps, 1945–1978.* Washington: U.S. Government Printing Office.

Treadwell, Mattie E. 1954. *The Women's Army Corps,* a volume in the *United States Army in World War II.* Washington, DC: U.S. Government Printing Office.

Brown, Ruth Humphries (1920–)

Women's Air Force Service (WASP) pilot. Born November 11, 1920, the daughter of pilot Albert Humphries, Brown flew across the nation on her father's small yet plush passenger plane. Her only recollections of this childhood experience are of the nausea she suffered during every flight. Brown's dreams while a student at Farmington Preparatory School in Connecticut were not of becoming a pilot but of performing in the theatre. World War II created the need for female pilots, however, and Brown, always adventurous, viewed participation in the WASP as an exciting option. In 1943, she began flight training in Denver, Colorado, logging thirty-five hours of flight time and receiving her private pilot's license before applying for admission to the WASP. After passing flight tests and a thorough physical, Brown reported for WASP training on July 5, 1943, in Sweetwater, Texas. After obtaining flight experience in the PT-19, BT-13, and the AT-6, Brown graduated with forty-eight other women on December 17, 1943. She then received additional training at instrument school in Orlando, Florida, from January to May 1944. Brown was sent to Childress Air Force Base (Texas) for two months, where she flew bombardier missions at low altitudes to test the accuracy of the AT-11. Brown and other members of the WASP astonished their male counterparts with their skill at hitting ground targets, often with more success than the male pilots. As the summer of 1944 came to an end, Brown was transferred to a gunnery school in Harlingen, Texas, where she flew targets from her B-26 for shooting practice. Such a perilous assignment would frighten most pilots, but Brown's bold nature made her the perfect candidate for the job. By October 1944, Brown grew tired of small towns in Texas and obtained a transfer to March Air Force Base in California, where she served as squadron leader until December when the WASP was deactivated. Brown would only fly once more after leaving the WASP.

Two weeks later, Brown returned to Denver where she opened The Smuggler, a small but successful gift shop. On September 13, 1947, she married former PT boat Captain David R. C. Brown.

—*Amanda Gibbens*

See also United States, Women's Airforce Service Pilots

References and Further Reading

Brown, Ruth Humphries. Interview. September 12, 2000 with Deanie Parrish. Aspen, Colorado. Wings across America Project and the WASP WWII Museum, Sweetwater, Texas, http://www.wasp-wwii.org/wings/information.htm (accessed November 18, 2004).

Bruskina, Masha (1924–1941)

Jewish nurse from Minsk executed by the Nazis during World War II for assisting Soviet soldiers to escape from Nazi-occupied territories. Masha Bruskina was hung along with two male comrades in the first and best photographically documented public execution of partisans in the occupied Soviet Union. Born into a Jewish family in Minsk, Masha was incarcerated in the Minsk ghetto shortly after the German occupation of Belorussia. She escaped by adopting her mother's last name, which was not distinctively Jewish, and by bleaching her hair. She volunteered as a nurse in a local hospital for Soviet prisoners of war (POWs) where she joined one of the first partisan cells formed in Nazi-occupied Soviet territories. Her role as a partisan was to smuggle medicines, civilian clothing, and false documents to captured Soviet soldiers to facilitate their escape. She occasionally supplemented these supplies with leaflets describing the situation at the front. The actual process of escape was then arranged by male members of the partisan cell. During World War II, the proportion of women in Soviet partisan cells averaged no more than 2 to 5 percent, and women who participated in the partisan movement generally functioned like Bruskina as messengers and distributors of information and supplies. Hence, Bruskina was a typical representative of women's participation in the Soviet underground World War II resistance, although the majority of partisan women did not become involved until 1943 and 1944.

On October 14, 1941, a POW informed on Bruskina and other members of the cell. This led to her prompt arrest and execution on October 26. At the time of her hanging, a Lithuanian photographer, who collaborated with the Germans, documented every step of the execution, taking seven pictures. These photographs were made public at the war's end and were displayed in museums around the world. Two out of the three people in the photographs were immediately identified as Volodia Shcherbachevich and Kirill Trus, both members of the early partisan movement in Minsk. The young woman in the photographs, however, remained unidentified until the investigation in 1968 discovered that "the unknown girl" was Masha Bruskina. Soviet authorities, however, refused to recognize the identity of this woman or to award her a medal for heroism posthumously.

Many believed that the refusal of the Soviet authorities to honor or recognize Bruskina's heroism was prompted by her Jewishness, and her image was subsequently appropriated as a symbol of the anti-Jewish policies of the Soviet regime. In the 1990s, several historians argued that Bruskina's early date of execution was likely the reason she was denied recognition. Her heroic deed could not be allowed to overshadow or precede that of the renowned Soviet, and Russian, partisan girl, Zoya Kosmodemianskaia, who was executed two months after Bruskina and immediately became a symbol of Russian women's resistance to the Nazi occupation. The heroism of Masha Bruskina remains widely unrecognized.

—Irina Mukhina

See also Soviet Union, Women in the Armed Forces (1917–1991)

References and Further Reading

Arkadiev, Lev, and Ada Dikhtiar. 1987. "The Unknown Girl: A Documentary Story." *Yiddish Writers' Almanac.* 1: 161–204.

Tec, Nechama, and Daniel Weiss. 1997. "A Historical Injustice: The Case of Masha Bruskina." *Holocaust and Genocide Studies* 11, no. 3: 366–377.

Bubley, Esther (1921–1998)

Photographer who gained fame during World War II for her pictures depicting the lives of U.S. civilians during wartime. The interest of Esther Bubley was the home front aspects of war. She is probably best remembered for the photographs she took on a bus trip across country showing civilian life during this period.

Bubley was born in Wisconsin to Russian Jewish immigrants and developed an early love of photography. She graduated from art school in Minnesota and in the early 1940s found her way to New York City, working for a short time with the popular magazine *Vogue.* She later moved to Washington, D.C., with the hope of working with Roy Stryker, the head of the Office of War Information (OWI). Stryker was well known as an artist and mentor of many young photographers, and Bubley wanted to learn the trade from this greatly admired figure. Stryker hired Bubley as a lab technician in his office. During her free hours, she began taking pictures of people around the capital. These photographs impressed Stryker, and he decided to give her some assignments because of her potential as a photojournalist.

Bubley did not possess a driver's license, so her ability to travel was limited, and she was passed over for some assignments. When an assignment to photograph people for a story on wartime transportation materialized, she was selected for the task. Bubley toured the United States on crowded Greyhound buses, taking pictures of the riders, the drivers, and sites in the cities, towns, and rural areas she visited. Her subjects included passengers who were tourists, salespersons, youngsters, family members of soldiers, and the servicemen themselves. The bus drivers were interesting subjects also and were depicted as promiscuous but always concerned about the safety of the passengers. Her pictures were effective in providing a feeling of what life was like for civilians during the war. Viewers of these photographs can sense feelings of displacement, fatigue, and concern, as well as a perception of isolation because the roads were empty due to wartime gas and tire rations.

In 1943, Stryker resigned from the Office of War Information and asked his prize student to join him at his new job at Standard Oil. In 1947, she photographed another cross-county bus tour under the guidance of her mentor. Bubley's fame grew as she continued to produce photo essays for popular magazines. She is best remembered, however, for the bus stories and her portrayal of the life of Texas oil workers. The demand for photojournalists waned in the 1960s, and Bubley married and settled down in New York City. She became an avid gardener and began publishing books on plants and animals in the 1960s and 1970s. Esther Bubley died in 1998.

—Leonard A. Steverson

See also Bonney, Therese; Chapelle, Dickey; Lange, Dorothea; Meiselas, Susan

References and Further Reading

Fleischhauer, Carl, and Brannan, Beverly W. 1988. *Documenting America, 1935–1943*. Berkeley: University of California.

Library of Congress. 1995. *Women Come to the Home Front: Journalists, Photographers, and Broadcasters during World War II*. Washington, DC: Library of Congress.

Yochelson, Bonnie. "Esther Bubley, Photojournalist: Biographical Sketch," http://estherbubley.com/bio_main.htm (accessed October 25, 2004).

Buch, Eva Maria (1921–1943)

German opponent of the Nazis. Eva-Maria Buch, who was born in Berlin on January 31, 1921, received a Catholic education from the Ursuline nuns and studied linguistics at Humboldt University. She worked as an assistant at the university and at a secondhand bookstore. At the bookstore, she met William Guddorf, who introduced her to the Red Orchestra (Rote Kappelle) Communist-oriented resistance group led by Harro Schulze-Boysen and Arvid and Mildred Harnack. After her arrest on October 10, 1942, Buch courageously insisted that she had written an appeal in French to forced laborers, calling on them to sabotage the weapons on which they were working. She was sentenced to death by a Nazi court, which asserted that she combined the deviousness of a Catholic with the hostility of a Communist. Hitler personally rejected the appeal of her parents for clemency. She was executed at the Plötzensee prison on August 5, 1943.

—Bernard Cook

See also Harnack-Fish, Mildred; Schulze-Boysen, Libertas

References and Further Reading

Brysac, Shareen Blair. 2000. *Resisting Hitler: Mildred Harnack and the Red Orchestra: The Life and Death of an American Woman in Nazi Germany.* New York: Oxford University Press.

Bulgaria, Women and World War II

Service of Bulgarian women during the World War II. Bulgaria joined the Anti-Comintern League but did not declare war against the Soviet Union. As Soviet forces approached Bulgaria in 1944, conservative elements in the country attempted to withdraw from the war. The Soviet Union declared war on Bulgaria, however, and demanded that the country surrender. Bulgaria's exit from the war was followed by attacks from the German army on Bulgarian territory and troops. The Bulgaria declaration of war on Germany was popular among the Bulgarian people. A great number of volunteers formed the National Guard, a company of which was attached to every regiment of the army. Former partisans, concentration camp inmates, and men and women aged eighteen to forty-five volunteered. Traditionally, according to Bulgarian law, women were not supposed to enter the military. Nevertheless, a great number of mainly young women applied. Most were supposed to go to medical and communication units. Among the women who volunteered was Nedialka Kocheva. She was given the task of recruiting volunteers in her village. At first she had no success. Then she wrote her name at the top of the list, and this inspired many of her fellow villagers to volunteer.

The new pro-Allied government proclaimed the slogan: "Everything for the Front, Everything for the Victory!" The nation was totally mobilized. The Women's Section of the Fatherland Front called on all Bulgarian women to devote their intellectual and physical effort to support Bulgaria's soldiers. Under the leadership of the Bulgarian National Women's Union, which had about 250,000 members, and, after November 1944, the Central Committee of the Assisting Organization, which was also a women's organization, Bulgarian women were mobilized to assist the country's fighters. At factories and in towns and villages, women cared for the people going to war and for their families. Women prepared clothes and food packages for the soldiers. The country was turned into a big working camp, where the women were the main productive force.

The activity of the Bulgarian People's Women's Union on behalf of the army during World War II received recognition at the International Women's Congress, held in Paris on November 26, 1945. The congress was informed that Bulgarian women volunteers, despite harsh economic conditions, devoted an aggregate of 12,076 unpaid working days to projects for soldiers, 900 for wounded and sick soldiers, and 940 for Yugoslav child refugees.

—Dimitre Minchev

See also Norway, Resistance Movement during World War II, Women and; Poland, Resistance during World War II, Women and

Bulgarian Horrors

Brutal attacks against Bulgarian civilians by Turkish irregulars in 1876. At the end of April 1876, the accumulated mass of exactions, exploitation, and humiliation imposed on the Bulgarian people by the Turks produced a desperate rising. Inspired by an insurrection in Bosnia and hoping for redress rather than independence, a few Bulgarians, educated and inspired by the ideas and movements of the nineteenth century, planned a rising. The leaders belatedly realized the futility of their plans. The Bulgarians were without arms and lacked preparation. Although the leaders attempted to abort their plans, word did not reach all of the desperate people whom they had inspired. In the district of Silven, a group of almost sixty men rallied. There was practically no response around Turnovo. There was none in the district of Vratsa, other than a small band of rebels, led by Hristo Botev, who had hijacked an Austrian boat on the Danube. After advancing about 20 kilometers from the river, they were surrounded and slaughtered by Turkish irregulars. Elsewhere the results were worse. Georgi Benkovski and his followers had won over the men in a number of villages around Philippopolis (today Plovdiv). A hundred or so rebels, some with old muskets, but most with clubs, headed for the Balkan Mountains to the northeast of Sofia. The Turkish authorities were alerted and the band of rebels was crushed. Those not killed were imprisoned. At Panagurishta, Benkovski had persuaded a young woman, Raina, a school mistress and the daughter of a priest, to ride a horse in a procession and carry a flag, which she had embroidered with a Bulgarian lion and the words "Freedom or Death." After the Turks had taken the young woman prisoner, they derided her as "The Queen of the Bulgarians."

Aziz Pasha, the governor of Philippopolis realized that the situation was under control. His moderation cost him his job. Irregular companies of Turkish vigilantes, Bashi-Bazouks, were formed, and the new governor, Abdul Hamid Pasha, gave them free rein. They left a trail of blood and horror. Sixty to seventy villages were burned. The current estimates of the number of Bulgarians slaughtered runs from 25,000 to 100,000. Although the exact number of the dead will never be known, atrocities can be specified with precision. In Batak, 200 women and children were burned alive in a school. There Achmed Aga's Bashi-Bazouks slaughtered as many as 5,000

Bulgarian Horrors

"Panagurishta (Otluk-kui) was attacked by a force of regular troops, together with Bashi-Bazouks, on the 11th of May. Apparently no message to surrender was sent. After a slight opposition on the part of the insurgents the town was taken. Many of the inhabitants fled, but about 3,000 were massacred, the most of them being women and children. Of these about 400 belonged to the town of Panagurishta, and the others to nine neighbouring villages, the inhabitants of which had taken refuge there. Four hundred buildings, including the bazaar and the largest and best houses, were burned. Both churches were completely destroyed, and almost leveled to the ground. In one an old man was violated on the altar, and afterwards burned alive. Two of the schools were burned, the third—looking like a private house—escaped. From the numerous statements made to me, hardly a woman in the town escaped violation and brutal treatment. The ruffians attacked children of eight and old women of eighty, sparing neither age nor sex. Old men had their eyes torn out and their limbs cut off, and were then left to die, unless some more charitably disposed man gave them the final thrust. Pregnant women were ripped opened and the unborn babes carried triumphantly on the points of bayonets and sabers, while little children were made to bear the dripping heads of their comrades. This scene of rapine, lust, and murder was continued for three days, when the survivors were made to bury the bodies of the dead. The perpetrators of these atrocities were chiefly regular troops commanded by Hafiz Pacha. The Turks claim and the villagers admit the death of fourteen Mussulmans, two of whom were women who were killed with arms in their hands during a conflict with a party that refused to surrender to the insurgents.

"While pillage reigned supreme at Koprishtitsa, and lust at Panagurishta, at Batak the Turks seems to have no stronger passion than the thirst for blood. This village surrendered without firing a shot, after a promise of safety, to the Bashi-Bazouks, under the command of Ahmed Aga, of Burutina, a chief of the rural police. Despite his promise, the few arms once surrendered, Ahmed Aga ordered the destruction of the village and the indiscriminate slaughter of the inhabitants, about a hundred young

Bulgarians—men, women, and children. From the region of Philippopolis to Sofia, women and children were raped, tortured, and murdered. Bashi-Bazouks bragged about beheading children, whose bodies momentarily flailed about like decapitated chickens.

This orgy of violence, brought to the attention of the West by journalist Januarius MacGahan and diplomat Eugene Schuyler, both American, generated foreign pressure on the Ottoman government to reform. When the reforms proved stillborn, the Russians intervened. The Russian defeat of Turkey in 1877–1878 led to the formation of an independent Bulgaria.

—Bernard Cook

See also Armenian Holocaust; East Timor, Abuse of Women during War; Germany, Armed Forces, World War II Atrocities of; Herero of Namibia, Repression of the; Lidice Massacre; Oradour-sur-Glane Massacre; Rwanda: Women and the Genocide; Smyrna Tragedy, Continuing Ordeal for Women Survivors of the; Sudan, Women and Civil War in

References and Further Reading

Crampton, R. J. 1997. *A Concise History of Bulgaria.* New York: Cambridge University.

girls being reserved to satisfy the lust of the conqueror before they too should be killed. I saw their bones, some with the flesh still clinging to them, in the hollow on the hill side, where the dogs were gnawing them. Not a house is now standing in the midst of this lovely valley. The saw mills—for the town had a large trade in timber and sawn boards—which lined the rapid little river, are all burned, and of the 8,000 inhabitants not 2,000 are known to survive. Fully 5,000 persons, a very large proportion of them women and children, perished here, and their bones whiten the ruins, or their putrid bodies infect the air. The sight of Batak is enough to verify all that has been said about the acts of the Turks in repressing the Bulgarian insurrection. And yet I saw it three months after the massacre. On every side were human bones, skulls, ribs, and even complete skeletons, heads of girls still adorned with braids of long hair, bones of children, skeletons still encased in clothing. Here was a house the floor of which was white with the ashes and charred bones of thirty persons burned alive there. Here was the spot where the village notable Trandafil was spitted on a pike and then roasted, and where he is now buried; there was a foul hole full of decomposing bodies, here a mill dam filled with swollen corpses; here the school house, where 200 women and children who had taken refuge there were burned alive, and here the church and churchyard, where fully a thousand half-decayed forms were still to be seen, filling the enclosure in a heap several feet high, arms, feet, and heads protruding from the stones which had vainly been thrown there to hide them, and poisoning all the air."

—Eugene Schuyler, "Preliminary Report,"
in *The Turkish Atrocities in Bulgaria: Letters of the Special Commissioner of the "Daily News,"*
J. A. Macgahan, Esq. With an Introduction and Mr. Schuyler's Preliminary Report.
London: Bradbury, Agnew, 1876, Pages 89–94.
Also to be found as an attachment to *No. 106, United States Legation,*
Constantinople November 21, 1876, Mr. Maynard to the Secretary of State,
Subject: The Bulgarian Tragedy Mr. Schuyler's Report.
National Archives, Washington, D.C., M46, roll 31.

MacGahan, J. A., and Eugene Schuyler. 1876. *The Turkish Atrocities in Bulgaria: Letters of the Special Commissioner of the Daily News, J. A. MacGahan, Esq. with an introduction and Mr. Schuyler's Special Report.* London: Bradbury, Agnew.

Bullwinkel, Vivian (1915–2000)

Nurse who enlisted in the Australian Army Nursing Service (AANS) during World War II, the sole survivor of the Banka Island Massacre, when almost ninety nurses and soldiers were shot and bayoneted by the Imperial Japanese Army following the fall of Singapore in 1942.

Vivian Bullwinkel enlisted with the AANS in 1941 and later that year she embarked for Singapore, eventually being assigned to the 13th Australian General Hospital in Johore Bahru, Malaya. Following the invasion by the Japanese in December 1941, the nurses were among those evacuated to Singapore, but this was to provide only temporary safety in the face of the Japanese Imperial Army's relentless march south. By the third week of January 1942, alarmed at the progress of the enemy, Colonel

A. Derham repeatedly requested that Major General H. Gordon Bennett evacuate the AANS. His requests were denied. Finally, a matter of days before the Japanese commenced an aerial assault on Singapore, orders were given to evacuate the nurses (Goodman 1988, 151). Bullwinkel and sixty-four of her colleagues boarded the *Vyner Brooke,* which was already seriously overloaded prior to their embarkation. When it left the port of Singapore, more than 300 people were on board, mostly civilian women and children. Two days after sailing, the small ship was spotted by Japanese aircraft, which fired on the vessel, eventually sinking it. The seamen and nurses loaded as many of the civilians as they could into the few seaworthy lifeboats. Those who could not be accommodated left the sinking vessel relying on life jackets, makeshift rafts, and their swimming skills to reach land.

Twelve of the nurses drowned. Thirty-one of the nurses who survived the sinking reached the shore and almost immediately became prisoners of war. Bullwinkel and twenty-one of her colleagues, plus scores of the women and children, found themselves on the shore of Banka Island at Radji Beach. British soldiers who had survived the sinking of their ship soon joined them. When it became clear that it was only a matter of time before those who remained on Radji Beach would also be captured, they decided to surrender voluntarily. A naval officer went to contact the Japanese base at Muntok, the civilians began to walk to the nearest village, and the soldiers and nurses waited along with the wounded for the arrival of the Japanese. When the Japanese soldiers arrived at Radji Beach, the British and Australian servicemen and women expected to become POWs. Instead, the Japanese marched half of the British and Australian servicemen further along the beach, out of sight of the remainder of the group, reappearing almost immediately to collect the rest of the men. According to Bullwinkel, the Japanese soldiers "came back and cleaned their rifles and bayonets in front of us" a short while later, leaving no doubt as to what had happened to the servicemen (Bassett 1992, 140). But the fate of the twenty-two members of the AANS was also sealed. The Japanese ordered them to form a line and march into the sea, whereupon the nurses were machinegunned. All but Bullwinkel died; she feigned death until the Japanese left the area and then struggled back to shore to hide. Eventually she met up with a British soldier who had also survived the massacre, although he was later to die of his wounds. They managed to escape detection for more than a week before finally being captured by the Japanese and made POWs. Bullwinkel was reunited with the thirty-one nurses who had survived the original sinking and been captured earlier by the Japanese, although eight died while incarcerated. At war's end, Bullwinkel and her remaining colleagues returned to Australia. For her wartime bravery and subsequent peacetime work as a nursing professional, Bullwinkel was awarded a number of honors, including the Officer of the Order of Australia, Member of the British Empire, Associate of the Royal Red Cross, Efficiency Decoration, and the Florence Nightingale Medal.

—*Susan R. Allan*

See also Australia, Women in Service during World War II; Australian Army Nursing Service/Royal Australian Army Nursing Corps

References and Further Reading

Bassett, Jan. 1992. *Guns and Brooches: Australian Army Nursing: From the Boer War to the Gulf War.* Oxford, England: Oxford University Press.

Goodman, Rupert. 1988. *Our War Nurses: The History of the Royal Australian Army Nursing Corps 1902–1988.* Bowen Hills, Australia: Boolarong.

Kenny, Catherine. 1986. *Captives: Australian Army Nurses in Japanese Prisoner Camps.* St. Lucia, Australia: University Queensland Press.

Bunke, Tamara (1937–1967)

Revolutionary who died fighting in Bolivia. Tamara Bunke was born on November 19, 1937, in Buenos Aires (Argentina) to German parents who had emigrated from Nazi Germany. In 1952, her parents returned to the Communist German Democratic Republic (East Germany), where Bunke joined the Communist youth movement. From that point, it is difficult to establish the political and personal development of young Tamara, because her life was later widely used for Communist propaganda purposes and was posthumously streamlined to fit the image of a Communist heroine. The official history asserts that Tamara met the revolutionary Che Guevara when he visited East Berlin, and the Spanish-speaking Bunke served as a translator during his talks with representatives of the East German Communist government. She decided to join Che Guevara in his revolutionary activities, but it is unclear whether she also became his mistress. After training in Cuba, she went to Bolivia, and following clandestine activities, she joined an armed partisan group. Cuban and Eastern bloc media began to celebrate Bunke as "Tania la guerrillera" by the mid-1960s. She was depicted as a young European Communist joining the people of the Third World in their struggle for liberation from capitalism and imperialism. On August 31, 1967, Tamara Bunke was killed either in combat with Bolivian government troops or after being captured. She was celebrated as the female Che Guevara. Her grave has not yet been found. Up to the collapse of the German Democratic Republic in 1989–1990, more than 200 schools, factories, and other facilities had been named after Bunke. The Bunke cult did not reach the level of Che Guevara's; nevertheless, the story of a young woman engaging in and perishing in revolutionary combat inspired many young people not only in former Eastern bloc countries with their all-dominant state propaganda, but also in the West. Recent research on the life and death of Tamara Bunke has been overshadowed by court injunctions. The mother of Tamara Bunke took legal action against a book claiming that Tamara Bunke was not only an idealistic freedom fighter but had strong links to the East German and other Eastern bloc security services.

—*Oliver Benjamin Hemmerle*

See also Latin America, Women in Guerrilla Movements in

References and Further Reading

Panitz, Eberhard. 2000. *Tamara Bunke. Mit Che Guevara in Bolivien.* Berlin: GNN.

Rojas, Marta.1993 *Tania, guerrillera heroica.* Buenos Aires, Argentina: Cedeno.

Zapata, Jose A. Friedl. 1997. *Tania. Die Frau, die Che Guevara liebte.* Berlin: Aufbau.

Byck, Muriel (1918–1944)

Radio operator who parachuted into France with Britain's Special Operations Executive (SOE) during World War II. Muriel Byck is representative of the many women who were integral to the fight against the Nazis in France during World War II. Byck joined the SOE through the Women's Auxiliary Air Force in Britain, where, like many other women, her ability to speak fluent French allowed her to be of great use to the French Resistance. Byck translated and sent messages to London regarding recruits to the resistance and also worked as a courier. She died in 1944 in France of meningitis.

Byck was born in the London borough of Ealing on June 4, 1918, of French Jewish parents who were British citizens; she also spoke Russian and spent time in Germany. She joined the Women's Auxiliary Air Force in December 1942, working with the First Aid Nursing Yeomanry and the records office. In July 1943, Byck was recruited by the SOE because of her grasp of the French language and was parachuted into France in April 1944 under the code names "Michele" and "Violette." Byck worked as a radio operator in the Resistance circuit known as "Ventriloquist" under Philippe de Vomécourt in the Loire and Cher area. She translated messages into ciphers and tapped them into Morse code; she also received messages from London and deciphered them. Byck trained local wireless operator recruits and transferred recruiting information to London. She also served as a courier when necessary, delivering or receiving messages for the Resistance. Byck moved daily to and from four wireless receivers to avoid discovery by the Gestapo. She narrowly escaped capture when a German spy discovered her at work in her safe house in April 1944, but Byck was quickly transferred to a new location under the guise of recuperating from an illness. In early May, London and the Resistance circuit bombed the German ammunition supply in Michenon, and the explosions physically and psychologically traumatized Byck. She was transferred to numerous safe houses, but she never recovered; Byck contracted meningitis as a child and hid this fact from the SOE, but she contracted the disease again while in France and was taken to the hospital. The hospital staff could have informed the Gestapo, but the nuns at the hospital where she was taken did not do so. Byck died of meningitis on May 23, 1944. She was originally buried under a false name, and Vomécourt was almost arrested by the Gestapo at her funeral. Byck's grave was later moved to the War Cemetery at Pornic for British lost in the war effort. Like other female participants in the war effort, Byck is honored in several war memorials in England and is commemorated in the town of Romorantin, France, where she was originally buried.

—J. Lyndsey Rago

See also Atkins, Vera H.; Khan, Noor Inayat; Sansom, Odette; Witherington, Pearl

References and Further Reading

Escott, Beryl E. 1991. *Mission Improbable: A Salute to the RAF Women of SOE in Wartime France.* Somerset, England: Patrick Stephens Limited.

"The FANY Agents—Daughter of Yael: Yvonne Baseden," 64 Baker Street, http://www.64-bakerstreet.org/text_version/agents/agent_fany_muriel_ byck_yael_txt.html (accessed December 30, 2004).

C

Campaign for Nuclear Disarmament (CND) and the Greenham Common Women

The involvement of women in anti–nuclear weapon protests in the United Kingdom. The Campaign for Nuclear Disarmament (CND), founded in January 1958, soon achieved fame as one of Britain's largest extra-parliamentary protest movements. Women have played an important role in the CND since its earliest days. The organization went into decline in the mid-1960s, only to revive during the early 1980s as a result of renewed Cold War tensions. In 1981, a group of women organized the Greenham Common Peace Camp to protest against the introduction of cruise missiles to Britain.

Britain detonated its first hydrogen bomb in 1957. Both major political parties, the governing Conservatives and the opposition Labour party, agreed on the need for an independent British nuclear capability. Nonetheless, the intensification of the Cold War, the steady buildup of nuclear stockpiles, and the continuous testing of nuclear devices in the late 1950s alarmed many in Britain. The emergence of the CND in 1958 reflected the opposition in Britain to nuclear escalation. The CND attracted a number of prominent British intellectuals, including philosopher Bertrand Russell (who became the first president of the CND) and author Doris Lessing. Canon John Collins became the chairman, and Peggy Duff, who had been active in an earlier, smaller antinuclear organization, became the organizing secretary. The objective of the CND was to "ban the bomb" worldwide. The first step would be British unilateral nuclear disarmament and the declaration of a neutral foreign policy. The CND was mainly a middle-class movement that initially favored lobbying politicians of the two major parties. The CND had some success in 1960 when the Labour party membership adopted a unilateral disarmament resolution at its annual party conference. That decision was reversed one year later, however. The activity of the CND that gained the most public notice was an annual Easter weekend protest march from Trafalgar Square in London to Aldermaston in Berkshire, home of the British Atomic Energy Authority's main research center. These marches, which covered a 50-mile route over 4 days, attracted between 50,000 to 150,000 supporters during the peak years of 1960 to 1963 (Byrne 1988, 45).

Some in the CND became impatient with the slow progress of the movement and left to join groups that advocated nonviolent civil disobedience. The rapid reduction of East-West hostility following the near miss of the Cuban Missile Crisis of 1962 seemed to indicate that the great powers had learned a lesson. The CND declined in strength in the late 1960s as activists turned their attention to campaigning against the Vietnam War.

Cold War tensions escalated again in the late 1970s and early 1980s, and the CND gained renewed support. The North Atlantic Treaty Organization's (NATO) December 1979 decision to station U.S. cruise missiles and Pershing II intermediate missiles in Britain prompted one of the most celebrated episodes of social protest in modern British history, the Greenham Commons women's peace camp. Greenham Common was a U.S. air base slated to receive cruise missiles. In September 1981, "Women for Life on Earth," a group of thirty-six, marched from Cardiff and set up camp outside the main gate of the Greenham Common air base. Supporters soon joined in increasingly large numbers. In February 1982, camp members voted to become a women-only movement. The Greenham protestors endured harsh weather, police harassment, arrests, attempted evictions, and occasional outbreaks of violence. In December 1982, an estimated 30,000 women joined hands around the base perimeter in an "embrace the base" protest. The CND broke with its traditional lobbying tactics and extended support to the protestors. In April 1983, 70,000 CND supporters formed a human chain that linked Greenham with Aldermaston and Burghfield, site of another nuclear base. In December of that year, 50,000 women encircled the Greenham base holding mirrors. The women protestors maintained a continual presence at Greenham Common, with some staying for only a short time and others for many months. The international situation relaxed in the late 1980s as the Cold War wound down, and in August 1989, NATO started withdrawing the cruise missiles from Greenham Common following signature of the Intermediate Nuclear Forces Treaty two years earlier. The last missile left in 1991. The base was returned to civilian ownership in 1997. A small group of protestors stayed on until 2000, however, demonstrating against Britain's nuclear arsenal.

—Paul W. Doerr

See also Peace People Movement; Ulster, Women during the Troubles in; Vietnam, Women in the Buddhist Peace Movement

References and Further Reading

Byrne, Paul. 1988. *The Campaign for Nuclear Disarmament.* London: Croom Helm.

Junor, Beth, ed. 1995. *Greenham Common Women's Peace Camp: A History of Non-Violent Resistance, 1984–1995.* London: Working Press.

Liddington, Jill. 1991. *The Road to Greenham Common: Feminism and Anti-Militarism in Britain Since 1820.* Syracuse, NY: Syracuse University Press.

Taylor, Richard. 1988. *Against the Bomb: The British Peace Movement, 1958–1965.* Oxford, England: Clarendon.

Cannan, May Wedderburn (1893–1973)

World War I poet and memoirist. May Wedderburn Cannan was the second daughter of Charles Cannan, dean of Trinity College, Oxford, and his wife Mary, née Wedderburn. During the war, May Cannan was a member of the Voluntary Aid Detachment and worked at the Clarendon Press, which produced pamphlets and books for the government's propaganda bureau. The four weeks she spent in France as a canteen worker form the basis of one of her finest poems, "Rouen." Her first volume of poetry, *In War Time,* was published in 1917. She was working for British Intelligence, MI5, in Paris when the armistice was declared. May Cannan was engaged to her childhood friend, Major Bevil Quiller-Couch, son of Arthur Quiller-Couch ("Q"), professor of English literature at Cambridge. Their happiness was short-lived, for although Bevil survived the war, he died in the influenza epidemic in 1919. Cannan's grief inspired some of the most poignant poems of the war, including "When the Vision Dies." She published two more collections, *The Splendid Days* (1919) and *The House of Hope* (1923). *The Lonely Generation,* her fictionalized memoir, appeared in 1934. She died in 1973.

Unlike Vera Brittain, May Cannan did not ascribe to the idea that World War I was a futile waste of a generation. Her posthumously published autobiography, *Grey Ghosts and Voices* (1976) is an evocative portrait of her Oxford childhood and a moving account of her experience of war and its aftermath.

—*Jane Potter*

See also Brittain, Vera Mary

References and Further Reading

Cannan, May Wedderburn. 1976. *Grey Ghosts and Voices.* Kineton, England: Roundwood.

Fyfe, Charlotte. 2000. *The Tears of War.* Wiltshire, England: Cavalier Books.

Cantinières

See Vivandières in the French Army

Catt, Carrie Chapman (née Clinton Lane) (1859–1947)

Women's suffrage and peace activist. Carrie Chapman Catt played a critical role in the passage in the United States of the Nineteenth Amendment to the U.S. Constitution that granted women the right to vote. As the president of the National American Women's Suffrage Association (NAWSA), she lobbied Congress to enfranchise women at the same time the United States faced world war. Despite pacifist leanings, Catt tied women's suffrage to patriotism and supported U.S. participation in World War I.

Carrie Clinton Lane was born in Ripon, Wisconsin, on January 9, 1859, and at the age of seven years moved with her family to Charles City, Iowa. She entered Iowa Agricultural College in 1877 and was the only woman graduate in the class of 1880. After college, she worked as a teacher and served as the superintendent of schools in Mason City, Iowa. In 1885, she resigned her post to marry Leo Chapman, editor of the *Mason City Republican.* Their marriage ended with his death from typhoid fever. She later married George Catt, a former college classmate.

Catt joined the Women's Christian Temperance Union and launched her career as a social reformer and suffragist. Between 1895 and 1899, she served the Iowa Woman Suffrage Association, where she quickly made a name for herself and worked on a number of state suffrage referenda with Susan B. Anthony, the president of NAWSA. In 1900, Catt was handpicked by the retiring Anthony to take over the leadership of NAWSA, where she served as president from 1900 to 1904 and again from 1915 to 1920. In between these years, she worked toward international suffrage, and in 1915, she helped found the Women's Peace Party.

In 1915, the suffrage movement divided over the defection of younger, more radical members led by Alice Paul. Catt agreed to return as the president of NAWSA, and in 1916 she presented her "Winning Plan." With this plan, NAWSA became a single-issue group, focused on suffrage to the exclusion of other reform efforts. The organization abandoned the state-by-state approach and concentrated on winning a federal amendment. Despite criticism from other organizations, Catt believed that women's patriotism would be rewarded if the NAWSA endorsed United States involvement in the war. In vindication of her approach, Congress ratified the Nineteenth Amendment in 1919.

Following the suffrage victory, Catt continued to encourage female political participation through the Women's League of Voters (WLV) and she campaigned for world peace. Through the WLV, she promoted U.S. support of the League of Nations, and in 1924, she founded the National Council for the Cause and Cure for War (1924–1948) to promote peace and to influence the U.S. government to embrace internationalism. During World War II, she worked to save German Jews from the Nazis. She formed the Protestant Committee of Non-Jewish Women against the Persecution of the Jews in Germany and served on the Women's Action Committee for Victory and Lasting Peace. Catt retired from public life in 1941 when she was honored with the Chi Omega Achievement Award at the White House. She died in New Rochelle, New York, on March 9, 1947.

—Danelle Moon

See also Livermore, Mary Ashton Rice

References and Further Reading

Van Voris, Jacqueline. 1987. *Carrie Chapman Catt: A Public Life.* New York: The Feminist Press.

Edith Cavell. (Duncan-Clark, S. J., Pictorial History of the Great War, *The John A. Hertel Co., Toronto, 1919)*

CAVELL, EDITH LOUISA (1865–1915)

British nurse executed by the Germans during World War I. Edith Cavell was born on December 4, 1865, in Swardeston, England. After studying nursing at London's Fever Hospital, she dedicated herself to the service of poor children. In 1907, she was hired as an administrator and teacher at the École Belge d'Infirmieres Diplomées (The Belgian School for Certified Nurses) in Brussels. When the Germans occupied the city during World War I, Cavell was also administering St. Giles Hospital. On August 4, 1915, she and others were arrested for hiding Belgian, British, and French soldiers and assisting them to escape. Cavill did not deny the charges. In fact, she had helped nearly 200 soldiers elude the Germans. She and seven members of the clandestine network, including Elizabeth Thuliez, were sentenced to death by firing squad. Despite appeals of the neutral U.S. and Spanish governments, Cavell's sentence was carried out on October 12, 1915. Before her execution, Cavell declared to the chaplain, Stirling Gahan, "I know now that patriotism is not enough. I must have no hatred and no bitterness towards anyone" (Grey 1961, 181). Besides Cavell, only Philippe Baucq was executed. The sentences of the others were commuted to hard labor.

The execution of Nurse Cavell was exploited by British wartime propaganda, despite her obvious guilt, as a manifestation of German barbarity. After the war, her remains were brought back to Britain with much ceremony. After a funeral at Westminster Cathedral, they were interred in Norwich Cathedral.

—Bernard Cook

The Execution of Miss Edith Cavell

An Account by Hugh Gibson, Secretary of the American Legation in Brussels

"It seems that Miss Cavell was prosecuted for having helped English and French soldiers, as well as Belgian young men, to cross the frontier into Holland in order that they might get over to England. She had made a signed statement admitting the truth of these charges and had further made public acknowledgment in court. She frankly admitted that not only had she helped the soldiers to cross the frontier but that some of them had written her from England thanking her for her assistance. This last admission made the case more serious for her because if it had been proven only that she had helped men to cross the frontier into Holland, she could have been sentenced only for a violation of the passport regulations, and not for the 'crime' of assisting soldiers to reach a country at war with Germany.

" . . . Last night Mr. Gahan [an Anglican priest] got a pass and was admitted to see Miss Cavell shortly before she was taken out and shot. He said she was calm and prepared and faced the ordeal without a tremor. She was a tiny thing that looked as though she could be blown away with a breath, but she had a great spirit. She told Mr. Gahan that soldiers had come to her and asked to be helped to the frontier; that knowing the risks they ran and the risks she took, she had helped them. She said she had nothing to regret, no complaint to make, and that if she had it all to do over again, she would change nothing. And most pathetic of all was her statement that she thanked God for the six weeks she had passed in prison—the nearest approach to rest she had known for years.

"They partook together of the Holy Communion, and she who had so little need of preparation was prepared for death. She was free from resentment and said: 'I realise that patriotism is not enough. I must have no hatred or bitterness toward any one.'

"She was taken out and shot before daybreak.

"She was denied the support of her own clergyman at the end, but a German military chaplain stayed with her and gave her burial within the precincts of the prison. He did not conceal his admiration and said: 'She was courageous to the end. She professed her Christian faith and said that she was glad to die for her country. She died like a heroine.' "

—Gibson, Hugh. 1917.
A Journal from Our Legation in Belgium, by Hugh Gibson
Secretary of the American Legation in Brussels.
Garden City, NY: Doubleday,
Pages, 347–348, 360.

See also Belgium during World War I, Women in; Mati Hari, pseud.

References and Further Reading

Grey, Elizabeth. 1961. *Story of Nurse Edith Cavell.* Boston: Houghton Mifflin.

Ryder, Rowland. 1975. *Edith Cavell.* London: Hamilton.

Chalbur, Vera de Cottani de

See Eriksen, Vera

Chamberlain (Tamblin), Margaret Lenora (1918–)

One of the first women to pilot U.S. military aircraft in the Women's Airforce Service Pilots (WASP) program. Part American Indian, Margaret Chamberlain was born in Vinita, Oklahoma, where her father was born two decades earlier on the Indian reservation. After graduating from Centenary College in Shreveport, Louisiana, Chamberlain enrolled in a Civilian Pilot Training course sponsored at her alma mater. Chamberlain first soloed in a J-3 Piper Cub in 1941 and with seventy hours under her belt became a WASP in April 1944. During her training, she flew PT-19s, PT-17s, BT-13s, and AT-6s. On April 22, 1944, Chamberlain received her first orders to report to Love Field in Dallas, Texas, one of the four main military ferrying bases. At Love Field, she served as a ferry pilot along with more than ninety other WASPs at the base. Her ferrying assignments included piloting new aircraft from the factories to bases across the country, taking airplanes from one base to another, and flying planes to a salvage site when they became too dilapidated to be flown. Often the women piloted planes their male counterparts refused to fly, and such was the case with Chamberlain as a ferry pilot in Dallas. She received advanced instrument training to prepare her to instruct pilots to fly in inclement weather. At her final base assignment, Perrin Army Air Base in Sherman, Texas, Chamberlain served as an instrument instructor on BT-13s. She stayed at Perrin until the WASP was disbanded in December 1944. The military leaders at the base gave the women a full review and allowed them to choose their own pilot and plane to fly them home instead of making them pay their way.

Following her service as a WASP, she completed an extensive program to obtain her instructor's rating, allowing her to teach others to fly. A few years later, she joined the American Red Cross and lived in Korea, Burma, Indonesia, and Canada before retiring to Arizona.

—*Caressa Lattimore*

See also United States, Women's Airforce Service Pilots

References and Further Reading

Chamberlain (Tamblin), Margaret Lenora. Interview. Wings across America and the WASP WWII Museum, Sweetwater, Texas, http://www.wasp-wwii.org/wings/information.htm (accessed November 18, 2004).

Chapelle, Dickey (aka Georgia Lou Meyer, G. L. Meyer) (1919–1965)

Award-winning journalist and photographer who was one of the first women reporters in the United States to report on combat situations from the front lines of the battlefield. Georgia Lou Meyer was born in suburban Milwaukee, Wisconsin, in 1919. She was a youngster with immense energy and a fixation for airplanes. When she was fourteen, she submitted an article on flying to the U.S. Air Service magazine under the name G. L. Meyer; the article was published, probably because the editor thought she was male. This article began the career of the person who would eventually become known as Dickey Meyer and, after her marriage, Dickey Chapelle.

Dickey Meyer entered the Massachusetts Institute of Technology, but her love for being around airplanes outweighed her scholastic efforts. After failing college, she became a press release agent for local air shows in Florida and Cuba. She later moved to Manhattan and married Tony Chapelle, a World War I navy photographer from whom she learned the art of photography. Shortly before the outbreak of World War II, Dickey Chapelle wrote two books for the government, *Needed: Women in Government Service* and *Needed: Women in Aviation.* These books reflected the government's need for women in the upcoming war effort but continued to reflect gender biases.

When World War II began, Dickey was assigned as a correspondent and photographer to a U.S. Marine unit with which she saw battle activity firsthand. She returned to the United States as staff photographer for *Seventeen* magazine. Chapelle later left that magazine and began work as a photographer for relief agencies in Europe, India, and the Middle East.

Chapelle eventually separated from her husband, whom she learned was already married when he married her. She wrote articles on the marines and began work as a public relations officer with the Research Institute of America with which she wrote about and photographed the marines in Lebanon during political disturbances in that country. She also was assigned to Cuba to cover the nation's growing civil unrest and subsequent revolution.

Chapelle became a celebrity and was a guest on popular television shows of the era. She published another government book along with an autobiography titled *What's a Woman Doing Here? A Reporter's Report on Herself.* When the Vietnam War began, Chapelle was there, despite injuries suffered while parachuting and in a jeep accident. In 1962, as a result of her coverage of the war in Vietnam, she became the second woman to win the George Polk award. In 1965, Chapelle became the first American female journalist killed in action. For her efforts, she received a marine color guard at her funeral, a rarity for a civilian. A year later, a monument was erected in her honor in Chu Lai, South Vietnam.

—Leonard A. Steverson

See also Bonney, Therese; Bubley, Esther; Lange, Dorothea; Meiselas, Susan

References and Further Reading

Chapelle, Dickey. 1962. *What's a Women Doing Here? A Reporter's Report on Herself.* New York: William Morrow.

Ostroff, Roberta. 1992. *Fire in the Wind: The Life of Dickey Chapelle.* New York: Ballantine.

Chechnya, Impact on Women of Wars in

The impact of the Russo-Chechen wars on women. Since 1994, Chechnya has experienced two destructive wars. Indeed, the wars have triggered a transformation of gender roles. If female Chechen suicide bombers, who made their first appearance in 2000, embodied a new involvement of women in the war and terror, they only represent a small fraction of the Chechen female population. They, however, do reflect the societal changes brought about by war.

In 1991, the small North Caucasian Republic of Chechnya unilaterally declared its independence from the nascent Russian Federation. After two and a half years of political and economic pressures and negotiation, President Boris Yeltsin's Russian administration decided to launch a military campaign. Lasting from December 1994 to August 1996, the war, according to various estimates, caused between 50,000 and 100,000 deaths (Cherkasov 2004, 7–8). In the aftermath of the conflict, a problematic political situation prevailed and new tensions appeared between the two former belligerents. At the same time, the persisting tensions significantly strengthened the Chechen's opposition to Aslan Maskhadov, the newly elected Chechen president. An open conflict arose between the moderate Chechen president and the warlords who converted to radical Islam. By 1997, Chechnya was plagued by anarchical lawlessness.

On October 1, 1999, the Russian armed forces launched a second campaign in Chechnya as a result of two events. In August 1999, the radical warlord Shamil Basayev led an invasion of neighboring Dagestan, a constituent republic of the Russian Federation, with the aim of creating an independent Islamic north Caucasian state. Then in September, the bombing of three apartment buildings killed 300 people in Moscow and southern Russia. The Russian government blamed the attacks on Chechnya and argued that Chechen terrorism justified Russian military action. The military operations quickly turned into a tremendously destructive war. In

A woman, one of fifty armed Chechens who seized a crowded Moscow theater in October 2002, poses with a pistol somewhere inside the theater in this image from a Russian television station. Some of the women claimed to be widows of ethnic Chechen insurgents. (*AP Photo/NTV Russian Channel*)

2003, after a referendum managed by the Russians, the Chechen Republic adopted a new constitution and organized a contested election that led to the nomination of a pro-Russian Chechen president. Russia subsequently claimed that the situation was improving, but, by early 2005, it remains dramatically unchanged.

From the start of the first war, the Chechen civilian population has endured harsh conditions and extreme violence on a daily basis (Tishkov, 2004). The first conflict produced many documented atrocities against civilians, but the second has proved to be even more violent. The Russian armed forces have introduced new tactics, called mop-up or cleansing operations (*zachistka*) during which widespread human rights abuses are committed. At the same time, the Chechen resistance radicalized and some rebel groups have developed new strategies based on terror.

Throughout the Russo-Chechen wars, violence has primarily targeted men who are suspected of being fighters or of having links with pro-separatist or Islamist groups. They have been subjected to arbitrary arrest and detention in the filtration camps. They have frequently been tortured, if not executed. The violence, however, has never spared women. Although Chechen women rarely complain or openly express their sufferings, they have been undergoing two main types of violence. War first brought symbolic violence. Chechen women have been living in extreme precariousness and an insecure environment since the beginning of warfare. Many of them have lost one or several relatives who were either killed or abducted. Extrajudicial killings, illegal reprisals, arbitrary arrests, disappearances, torture, and looting have been pervasive. A ruined Chechnya has become a no man's land where total impunity dominates. Many women have also experienced physical violence. As in other wars, rape of women has been part of the war in Chechnya. These sexual crimes are certainly underreported but are presumed to widely occur, particularly during nighttime raids and mop-up operations. Rape is extremely shameful in the traditional Chechen Muslim context. A woman who experiences sexual assault brings dishonor on her family and could be repudiated and even killed in the name of family honor.

This insecure and extremely violent context has been a catalyst for social changes. Indeed, it has had strong effects on gender roles within the Chechen society. In Chechen society, women are assigned the roles of housekeeper and guardian of ancestral traditions. On one hand, men typically insist on the central role of women in society, yet on the other, the men always relegate them to a subordinate position. Under the Soviet regime, women were granted better access to education. Hence, many of them played new roles in education, medicine, and commerce. Since the 1957 return of the Chechens from the deportation inflicted on them by Stalin, however, identity tensions arose between traditional representations and social injunctions and the effective roles women were playing within the society. These tensions were heightened after Dzhokhar Dudayaev, the first proseparatist president of Chechnya, encouraged a return to tradition. Even though this political move proved to have little impact on the private sphere, it aroused new frustrations for women, who were excluded from all public and political affairs.

The first war, in such a context, represented a turning point. While men took up arms to fight the Russian army, women became wholly responsible for their families. They became deeply involved in small commercial activities, selling on local markets either their own products or the merchandise that they had bought in the neighboring Ingushetia. Women relied on their traditional image of harmlessness to go through checkpoints and to cross the frontiers. Such trips were indeed hazardous; although the women may commonly have aroused less suspicion than men, they had to deal with the hostile soldiers' attitudes, the widespread practice of extortion at checkpoints, and the risk of being kidnapped and raped.

This image of harmlessness has also served other purposes. Since the first war, women have played the role of negotiators or intermediaries with the Russian soldiers. For instance, they have bought the release of their relatives from the filtration camps or obtained the corpse of a relative for a fee. Since 2003, they have protested in the streets against arrests and arbitrary disappearances and denounced the inertia of the local pro-Russian Chechen administration. It seems that these demonstrations have not been spontaneous but have been encouraged by either opponents to the Chechen pro-Russian government or human rights activists. Women may thus become a de facto political force and assume a traditional male social role. This evolution has, of course, taken place in other wars, but it appears to be particularly significant in the Chechen case.

Far from being passive actors, Chechen women took an active part in the war. Those who fight represent an insignificant minority. Much more common is their support of the fighters. They have provided fighters with information, materials, and arms, as well as food and medical care. Since the first suicide attack was carried out by a woman in June 2000, however, the perception of the role of women in the Russo-Chechen war deeply changed. This act symbolized two concomitant evolutions. Suicide terrorism marks the radicalization of some rebel groups and the importation of new tactics. These attacks have become more numerous than other types of terrorism, and women have committed more than 50 percent of them. Since 2000, about 42 women have become martyrs (*Shahidki*), although no exact figures exist.

Female suicide bombers, while having their own personal histories, show some common characteristics (Juzik 2003, 161–168; Reuter 2004, 19). Most were young, educated Chechen women coming from a middle-class or privileged social milieu. All were directly or indirectly affected by the wars and lost at least one relative. Finally, only a few have links with Islamist groups. Three of the Chechen female suicide bombers were arrested before committing attacks. Their testimonies have to be viewed cautiously because they have been distorted and instrumentalized by both parties to their own purposes.

The Russians have interpreted the onset of suicide attacks as a sign of an Al Qaeda presence in Chechnya and suspect the existence of "*Shahidki* battalions." For some experts, women who fall into the hands of extremists are blackmailed after having been kidnapped, drugged, and raped; according to this view, they have been indoctrinated and forced to become suicide bombers to avoid dishonor. The Chechens, on the other hand, offer another explanation; according to them, the involvement of women shows the commitment of the whole nation to fighting the Russian invaders. Women commit suicide bombing on their own because of despair or to avenge their killed or abducted relatives. This version gave birth to the black widows myth, a term referring to the female members of the commando that took hostage the audience in Moscow's Dubrovka theatre in October 2002.

All these interpretations are ideologically biased. To understand fully the commitment of these women, a distinction should be made between individual motivations and collective strategies. A strong correlation can be seen between the Russian mop-up operations and the rise of female suicide attacks. Hence, extreme personal commitment could be explained in most cases by motives of revenge and despair (Reuters 2004, 4). In July 2001, Sveta Tsagaroeva killed the military commandant responsible for the death of her husband and brother. Vengeance could have led her to suicide terrorism. In some other cases, religion may have played a more decisive role. Khava Barayeva had strong connections to the Islamist milieu; she was the niece of Arbi Barayev, the radical Chechen warlord killed in 1999, and the sister of Movsar Barayev, head of the Moscow commando. Individual motivations evidently vary.

Suicide terrorism must also be considered in light of a larger strategy that some of the rebel groups adopt. Indeed, the organizational dimension of Chechen terrorism is revealed by the targets of the suicide-bombing operations, which were first directed against military and political objectives, well before hitting civilians, and the logistic required for large-scale hostage-takings (the Moscow theatre and the school in Beslan in September 2004). This moreover suggests that while the involved groups claim to belong to radical Islam, religion assumes an instrumental role in most cases. Chechen terrorist attacks are part of a local conflict. The Chechen field commanders who are behind these attacks, although indisputably influenced by the *Jihadi* mercenaries who came to Chechnya during the first war and after, have not extended their agenda to a more global struggle against Infidels. Even the most radical leaders, such as Shamil Basayaev or Movladi Udugov, who both rely on the Islamist symbols and rhetoric make the independence of Chechnya and the retreat of the Russian armed forces from North Caucasus their sole objectives. Those facts strongly undermine the Russian thesis. Suicide bombings appear in this regard as a worrying sign of the radicalization of Chechen society (Larzillière 2003, 162). Political violence and the strong social uncertainties provoked by the conflict make women more vulnerable or more desperate, so that they have become a new military and psychological arm in the hands of radical warlords.

Some songs and poems celebrate the female suicide bombers and praise them for their devotion to the nation. It seems, however, that suicide terrorism rouses indignation and revulsion within the Chechen society. Notwithstanding the incomprehension and the disgust they incite, female suicide bombers symbolize the social transformations engendered by war.

—*Aurélie Campana*

See also Rape in War

References and Further Reading

Cherkasov, Alexander. 2004. "Book of Numbers. Book of Losses. Doomsday Book. Demography, population Losses and Migration in the Armed Conflict Area, Chechnya," Moscow, February 2004, http://eng.kavkaz.memo.ru/analyticstext/enganalytics/id/645415.html (accessed June 7, 2004).

German, Tracey. 2003. *Russia's Chechen War.* London and New York: Routledge Curzon.

Juzik, Julija. 2003. *La fidanzate di Allah. Volti e destini delle kamikaze cecene* [Allah's fiancées. Portraits and destinies of the Chechen suicide bombers]. Rome: Manifestolibri.

Larzillière, Pénélope. 2003. "Tchétchénie: le Jihad territorialisé" [Chechnya: territorialized Jihad]. *Critique Internationale* 20: 151–164.

Reuter, John. 2004. *Chechnya's Suicide Bombers: Desperate, Devout or Deceived?* The American Committee for Peace in Chechnya, http://www.peaceinchechnya.org/reports.htm (accessed September 23, 2004).

Tishkov, Valery 2004. *Chechnya: Life in a War-Torn Society.* Berkeley and Los Angeles: University of California Press.

Cherokee War Woman

Title given to Cherokee Indian women who were mothers or wives of great warriors or to those who distinguished themselves in time of war by wisdom or in deed. The title bestowed on these women varied. *Ghighau* can be translated as "Beloved Woman." In the form *Agigaue,* it is translated as "War Woman."

The position of War Woman arose out of the social and governmental structure of the Cherokee. The social system of the Cherokee was matrilineal. Marriage was exogamous, or outside of the clan. Women held the property, and a man would move to his wife's home after marriage. A child was born into one of the seven Cherokee clans—Deer, Wolf, Bird, Wild Potato, Paint, Blue, or Long Hair—would trace descent through the mother's kin in her clan.

To accommodate the clan system the Cherokee lived in compact villages. Council houses were built to accommodate representatives of the seven clans. Government was dual with a peace government (White) and a war government (Red). The War Woman would be a member of the Red government or war council.

The Cherokee War Woman had several functions. She was responsible for preparing the Black Drink that was used in a purification ritual by the warriors preparing for battle. She could also declare the fate of captives and prisoners who were taken in times of war.

The most famous of the Cherokee War Women was Nancy Ward, whose Cherokee name was *Nanye-hi*. Another important War Woman was Maggie Axe Wachacha, who was a healer, teacher, and leader. Cuhtalatah is cited in the Wahnenauhi manuscript for distinguishing herself in battle.

Two other War Women were Cornblossom and Standing Fern. They were part of the Thunderbolt Cherokees who lived on the Cumberland Plateau. Cornblossom's son was the war chief Peter Troxell. Cornblossom, daughter of War Chief Thunderbolt, and Standing Fern were planning to relocate with other traditionalist Cherokee to the Sequatchie Valley just west of Chattanooga, Tennessee. They and a number of children were killed in the Great Cherokee Children Massacre at Ywahoo Falls in southeastern Kentucky on August 10, 1810, by Americanizing Cherokee from the Free State of Franklin in Western North Carolina, led by Big Tooth Gregory.

Until recently, the title of War Woman was not used among the Cherokees of either the Eastern (North Carolina) or the Oklahoma Bands after the Trail of Tears. Joyce Dugan, principal chief of the Eastern Band of Cherokees in North Carolina, however, was given the title of War Woman in 1995.

—*Andrew Jackson Waskey*

See also Wake, Nancy

References and Additional Reading

Hatley, Thomas. "Nancy Ward: The Last Beloved Woman of the Cherokees." *Tennessee Historical Quarterly* 21 (1962): 354–364.

Swan, Patricia A. "Maggie Axe Wachacha, Beloved Woman of the Cherokees." *Now and Then: The Appalachian Magazine* 3 (1986, autumn) 3.

China, Women and the Communist Revolution

The role of women in the revolutionary struggle in China. The Chinese Communist revolutionary period lasted from the mid-1920s until the founding of the People's Republic of China in 1949 during which time the successes of the Chinese Communist Party (CCP) depended in part on the political participation of women. The party embraced gender equality as a theoretical maxim and devoted considerable resources to cultivating women's allegiance in the civil war against the Nationalist Chinese.

The CCP was founded in 1920, when post–World War I upheavals presaged a radical break with China's tradition-bound past. With its large foreign communities and vibrant industrial economy, the city of Shanghai became an early focus of Communist activism in China. Shanghai's small female working class and foreign-influenced feminist elite both gravitated toward the newly introduced Communist ideology. Despite Communism's apparently egalitarian stance, male Communists dominated the party, and a handful of female activists struggled for inclusion. These included Wang Huiwu, who argued against China's paternalistic tradition of arranged marriages and who, in 1921, organized the earliest women's program endorsed by the CCP. In the northern Chinese city of Tianjin, another feminist leader, Deng Yingchao, became a prominent pamphleteer, leader of the city's Women's Rights League, and editor of the *Women's Daily* newspaper. In late 1923, Deng married Zhou Enlai, a rising Communist leader and future premier of the People's Republic of China. By 1925, Deng emerged as a party leader in her own right, and she remained an influential force on women's issues through the 1960s.

Efforts to develop a broader base of support among women workers in urban centers such as Shanghai and Tianjin faced formidable obstacles, including resistance within the party's overwhelmingly male leadership. The party's 1925 Resolution on the Labor Movement, for example, downplayed the revolutionary potential of women factory workers, and party discipline required even fervent feminist activists to minimize their recruitment of female laborers. In February 1925, however, when female mill workers in Shanghai went on strike because experienced workers were fired in favor of lower paid trainees, party policy changed. Sympathy strikes spread throughout China's coastal cities, and the party quickly endorsed and tried to guide the strike movement. A new Women's Bureau was organized, but its female leader, Xiang Jiangyu, was ostracized by male party officials, and the bureau became a vehicle for Nationalist, rather than Communist, activities.

During the First United Front Period (1925–1927) of cooperation between the fledgling CCP and the growing Nationalist Party (Guomindang or Kuomingtang [KMT]) led by Jiang Jieshi (Chiang Kaishek), an unprecedented political mobilization of both urban and rural women took place. As the CCP-KMT alliance fought against China's many warlord armies, women provided such services as cooking, nursing, and intelligence gathering. A special all-women propaganda team of more than 100 members was organized by the KMT Women's Bureau in Guangxi province, and scores of women's associations were organized as the joint CCP-KMT Northern Expedition moved northward through central China. The Communists renewed their independent organizing work, targeting female peasants and urban workers. Soong Quingling, the U.S.-educated widow of revered nationalist leader Sun Yatsen, promoted women's emancipation, organized feminist women's groups, and helped change local laws in the regional capital of Wuhan city, where marriage, property, and civil rights were extended to women. The CCP's radical actions soon provoked a violent break with the stronger Nationalists, who decimated urban Communist networks in eastern and southern China. As the CCP slowly rebuilt its popular support during the 1930s under Mao Zedong, its focus shifted from urban to rural recruitment, including the women of China's huge peasant class.

While the Nationalist government dominated China's major coastal cities and fought the warlords of northern China, it also tried to eliminate the Communist movement. In 1934, to escape encirclement by Nationalist troops, some 100,000 Communists, including at least 1,000 women, began a perilous, yearlong trek through central China. Pursued by Nationalist armies, the Communists suffered heavy losses during the Long March. Settling in remote Shensi province, the survivors revitalized the outlawed party by gaining support from the agricultural peasants. New programs attracted their support, including a land-to-the-tiller campaign that redistributed agricultural lands from landlords to poor farmers. This movement helped rebuild CCP political power and popular appeal. Paternalistic landholding patterns meant that women benefited little from the program, but in the accompanying propaganda campaigns, the Communists enlisted thousands of young women, many of whom were former employees of local landlords who could reveal the landlords' political "crimes." These women increasingly found permanent roles as party propagandists, helping to launch the land reform movement and staffing the growing Communist Party bureaucracy. Later, these propaganda specialists helped to organize troupes of female speakers, actresses, singers, and musicians who gave politically oriented performances to peasant audiences.

The Nationalists bore the primary burden of the war against Japan's invading forces during the late 1930s and early 1940s, but the Communists, concentrated in remote provincial border regions, consolidated their own bases of support. Priority was assigned to creating large-scale party, military, and economic organizations with manpower drawn from the local peasantry. Women's organizations were vital to the Communists' successes in this period. Women farmed on a larger scale, while female administrators directed production programs in the agricultural, textile, and other industries, allowing male managers and employees to take up military duties. Meanwhile, at the leadership level, three women joined the policy-setting Party Central Committee in 1945, and the China Liberated Areas Women's Federation was organized to enlist more women in the Communist movement.

In the long-running civil war between the Communists and Nationalists that flared again in 1947, women played a key role in the Communists' mobilization programs. Huge manpower drafts by both armies caused industrial and food production to drop, but only the Communists actively encouraged women to make up the shortfall. Communist women's groups focused on maintaining morale and enhancing women's status within the family and the Communist movement, even as party cadres escalated their demands for more output. The Communist leadership was forced to recognize the central importance of women's support in maintaining production. Land redistribution campaigns, which were seldom directly beneficial to women, were scaled back, and women's issues, including expanded property rights, received greater attention at party meetings.

During 1949, the Communists achieved a final victory over the Nationalists, and party interest shifted toward integrating all classes of Chinese women into the new Communist-led state. General policies for this process were outlined at the First Congress of Women in March-April 1949, and several senior female revolutionists were given prominent, if not always powerful, positions in the new government. Furthermore, the international significance of women's participation in the Chinese revolution was highlighted at the December 1949 Asian Women's Conference held in Beijing. At this meeting, 165 female delegates from fourteen Asian countries heard how they might follow the Chinese revolutionary model by enlisting women in Communist-led political and guerrilla movements.

—*Laura M. Calkins*

See also French Revolution, Impact of War on Women's Protest during the; German Revolution of 1918–1919; Russian Revolution and Women

References and Further Reading

Chesneaux, Jean. 1968. *The Chinese Labor Movement, 1919–1927*. Stanford, CA: Stanford University Press.

Davin, Delia. 1976. *Woman-work: Women and the Party in Revolutionary China*. London: Clarendon.

Gilmartin, Christina Kelley. 1995. *Engendering the Chinese Revolution: Radical Women, Communist Politics, and Mass Movements in the 1920s*. Berkeley: University of California.

Johnson, Kay Ann. 1983. *Women, the Family, and Peasant Revolution in China*. Chicago: University of Chicago Press.

China, Women on the Home Front in World War II

The experience of women in China during World War II. China's long wartime experience was punctuated by extremely violent attacks against civilians, including women, by Japanese military forces. The brutality of Japanese troops deepened Chinese women's nationalism and fueled their demands for personal, political, and civil rights and for representation. Vast numbers of women enrolled in a variety of auxiliary assistance and armed resistance movements led by independent warlords and sects as well as by the much larger Chinese Communist and Nationalist Parties.

China's experience of World War II is variously dated from 1931, when Japanese forces occupied Manchuria, or from 1937, when Japan's troops seized control of the principal cities of Beijing, Shanghai, and Nanjing (Nanking). Popular anti-Japanese sentiments predate these main-force military incursions, however, and as early as 1927, Chinese women were instrumental in the success of long-running anti-Japanese consumer boycotts.

Japan's creation of a puppet government in Manchuria in 1932 was followed in 1935 by military operations in northern China, and in 1937 Japan embarked upon an all-out invasion of eastern China. The Japanese advance forced the Nationalist government under Jiang Jieshi (Chiang Kaishek) to abandon its capital at Nanjing in late 1937 in favor of Chongqing (Chungking) in remote Sichuan province. As early as Japan's July 1937 attack on Beijing, small networks of women in coastal Chinese cities began organizing to provide nursing and food services to Chinese Nationalist troops. During the battle for Shanghai in September and October 1937, some 2,000 women residents of the city enrolled in emergency nursing courses. Other women who supported the rival Chinese Communist Party (CCP) joined its small guerrilla detachments as propagandists or communications specialists; a handful also acted as spies, providing information on both Japanese and Nationalist troop movements to Communist leaders in China's interior.

In Japanese-occupied areas, China's relatively new personal and civil rights laws were abandoned in favor of martial law—or of no law at all. The often anarchic conditions that accompanied the advance of Japanese troops placed women at high risk for kidnapping, rape, and murder. Japanese servicemen were trained to view the Chinese as subhuman, and Chinese women were particularly reviled. Virtually as a matter of course, at least before 1938, Japanese troops systematically captured, raped, and often killed as many Chinese women as they found in their paths. In Chinese Communist–run areas, especially in northern China, Japan's troops employed particularly brutal "pacification" methods to quell and control civilian populations, including widespread use of rape as a weapon of intimidation. The most well known of the many attacks on civilian Chinese women occurred in the former capital of Nanjing in late December 1937, when tens of thousands of civilians were viciously raped and killed, in an episode known as the rape of Nanjing. Estimates of the total number of casualties vary widely, with some Western and Chinese Communist sources suggesting as many as 400,000 Chinese civilian and military victims; Japanese sources offer considerably lower figures (Masaaki 2000, 70–71).

Whatever the actual scale of the brutalities at Nanjing, the incidents gained international notoriety and profoundly accelerated the political mobilization of Chinese women against the Japanese invaders. As a result, in 1938, the Nationalist Chinese government made its first major effort to attract women's support by convening a conference to establish a Women's Advisory Committee. This committee centralized control over many wartime initiatives, including providing food for Nationalist troops, aiding wounded soldiers, and raising funds for orphanages. The committee's funds and scope were limited, however. Well-organized female Communists, including party leader Deng Yingchao, turned the committee's efforts toward recruiting rural women as auxiliaries for the Communists'

Women's Defense Corps training at Canton, China, 1938. (Hulton-Deutsch Collection/Corbis)

armed guerrilla forces. The Nationalists, fearing that social disturbances might accompany the growth of feminism, soon returned to endorsing conservative positions on women's issues, particularly on the proper roles for women in the anti-Japanese resistance. In 1941, the Nationalists issued directives instructing women to have more children and to limit their concerns to family issues, leaving politics and the prosecution of the war to men.

The Chinese Communist Party, on the other hand, actively sought to mobilize women throughout the war, especially peasants in the rural areas of China's interior provinces. Several pro-Communist, women-only paramilitary organizations were formed under Communist leadership to promote women's self-defense activities against the invading Japanese. These included the Hunan War Service Corps, the Yunnan Women's Battlefield Service Unit, the Guangxi Province Women's Brigade, and the Northwest Women's Battlefield Group, the last of which was headed by female propaganda expert and feminist leader Ding Ling.

Even the Communists, however, did not always fully address the security concerns of those peasant women directly confronted by the unpredictable actions of Japanese troops. In October 1941, an armed revolt against local Communist authorities occurred in Shanxi province, led by a sect known as the Li Gua Dao (Salvationist Sect of the Goddess from the Southern Sea). At least 10 percent of this millennial group's members were women, who joined chiefly because the sect's emphasis on mutual self-defense seemed to offer protection against Japanese troops who had moved through the area several times during 1940–1941 (Goodman 1997). Local Communist militia units quelled the uprising, but party cadres investigated the cult's popular appeal, especially to women. Local policies were changed to provide more resources to the Communists' own Women's National Salvation Association, an organization that supported paramilitary training for women and the formation of anti-Japanese resistance cells in the villages under Communist control.

The Japanese military itself was also affected by the international scandal over the rape of Nanjing. The indiscipline of its troops caused tremendous embarrassment to the Japanese Imperial Army's officer corps. To prevent a recurrence, Japanese leaders decided in 1938 to expand the existing system of officially sponsored brothels, known colloquially as comfort stations, to occupied mainland China. At these stations, Japanese soldiers were given sexual access to women. The number of women involved remains uncertain. An official report on Japan's 21st Army stationed in Guangzhou (Canton) indicated that some 1,000 women were made available to that unit's 40,000 men. In the Shanghai area, the so-called comfort women received army rations and worked under the direct supervision of Japanese military officials. Some of the comfort women were Japanese and Korean, but many were Chinese, recruited or kidnapped from poor families. Special discriminatory practices, including lower pay or no pay at all, were the rule for Chinese comfort women.

Chinese women's resistance to the Japanese occupiers was an important theme in public discussion, popular literature, and films. After the fall of Shanghai, Japanese troops occupied only part of the city until 1942, allowing many elements of the city's prewar public culture to flourish, including filmmaking. One of this period's most popular movies, *Hua Mulan Joins the Army* (1939), portrayed a traditional Chinese story about a young woman who, disguised as a man, takes her father's place in China's conscript army to fight a foreign invasion force. The self-assured star of the film, Chen Yunshang, infused the role with defiant patriotism and her portrayal of a female warrior became a symbolic heroine for China's wartime female filmgoers.

—Laura M. Calkins

See also Biological Warfare Experimentation, Japanese; China to 1911, Women Warriors in; Korea: Comfort Women; Nanking, Rape of

References and Further Reading

Fogel, Joshua, ed. 2000. *The Nanjing Massacre in History and Historiography.* Berkeley: University of California Press.

Goodman, David S. G. 1997. "The Licheng Rebellion of 1941: Class, Gender and Leadership in the Sino-Japanese War." *Modern China* 23, no. 2 (April): 216–245.

Hicks, George. 1996. "The 'Comfort Women.'" In *The Japanese Wartime Empire, 1931–1945,* edited by Peter Duus, Ramon H. Myers, and Mark R. Peattie, 305–323. Princeton, NJ: Princeton University Press.

Massaki, Tanaka. 2000. *What Really Happened in Nanking: The Refutation of a Common Myth.* Tokyo: Seka Shuppan.

Soong, Ching-ling. 1952. *The Struggle for New China.* Peking: Foreign Languages Press, 1952.

China to 1911, Women Warriors in

Exceptional women, who were warriors, bandits, and rebels in Imperial China. Ancient China has handed down many legends and stories of women war leaders and warriors. China's most celebrated woman warrior was the legendary Hua Mulan or Fa Mu Lan, who in the fifth century A.D. reputedly took the place of her conscripted but ill father. According to Chinese legend, Hua Mulan, with her hair cut short and wearing her father's armor, fought for ten years with valor without her sex being discovered. Tradition lauds her for preserving her chastity and desiring nothing but to cast off her armor and return home. Her exploits are touted in the traditional Chinese "Mulan Play" and, more recently, in an animated Disney movie.

Women are remembered in Chinese history as defenders of the castles in which they resided and as bodyguards to the masters whom they served. Women served as military leaders as well. The Tang Empress Wu Chao (684–704) had learned martial arts as a child. She avenged her murdered father and seized the throne. She then directed an ongoing war with Korea to a successful conclusion. During the Sung Dynasty (960–1126), Liu Chin Ting, a sixteen-year-old Tartar, led her people's resistance against rival clans and then against the emperor himself. Her forces defeated and captured General Chun Pao, sent by the emperor to pacify the Tartars. Liu Chin Ting ordered Chun Pao executed, but her admiration for his courage grew into love. She pardoned him and then married him. For the emperor, Chun Pao's marriage to an imperial enemy was treasonous. To gain pardon from the emperor for her husband's betrayal, Liu Chin Ting went over to the side of the emperor. As a general with Chun Pao as her second, she successfully commanded Sung armies for thirty years. Liu Chin Ting was not the only woman military commander of the Sung. Mu Guiying served as a Sung commander in chief.

During the Ming dynasty (1368–1644), Ch'in Liang-Yu fought along side her husband Ma Sian-cheng. Before his death, she had been appointed commander of a division, and after his death she succeeded him as commander. During the Ming dynasty, women fought in the armies of the empire and among rebels. Women played a key role in the nationalist White Lotus Society. There had been women bandits in China, such as Nie Yin-Niang, who, schooled in the martial arts as a girl by a nun, became a Chinese counterpart to the later Western Robin Hood. During the Manchu period, Hsi Kai Ching was the chief of an immense pirate fleet. Unable to subdue her, the Chinese government persuaded her to retire with a pardon and a rich bribe.

At the end of the imperial period, Ch'iu Chin joined the Nationalist movement of Sun Yat-sen at its inception in 1904. As principal of the Ta-t'ung School of Physical Culture in Shao-hsing, she trained her students for struggle against the corrupt imperial regime. In 1907, when she was thirty-two, she was arrested, tortured, and beheaded. After the empire fell in 1911, Ch'iu Chin was given a hero's burial by the new Chinese republic.

—Bernard Cook

See also China, Women and the Communist Revolution; India to 1857, Women Warriors in; Vietnam, Women in the War and Resistance before 1954

References and Further Reading

Ayscough, Florence. 1975. *Chinese Women.* New York: Da Capo.

Jones, David E. 1997. *Women Warriors: A History.* Washington, DC: Brassey's.

Chisholm, Mairi Lambert (1896–1981)

First aid worker and ambulance driver during World War I. Mairi Chisholm and Elizabeth "Elsie" Knocker (who later married for a short time a Belgian pilot and became known as the Baroness de T'Serclaes) ran a first aid post near the front. They were the only two women officially allowed to work at the Belgian lines. Chisholm and Knocker were decorated by the Belgians as Knights of Leopold II and by the British with Military Medals and the Order of St. John of Jerusalem.

At the start of the war, Chisholm, who came from a wealthy Scottish family, rode her motorcycle to London and volunteered as a motorcycle dispatcher with the Women's Emergency Corps. Another dispatcher, Elsie Knocker, whom Chisholm had met at motorcycle races, recruited Chisholm to join her in Hector Munro's Ambulance Corps. The corps was sponsored by the Belgian Red Cross and began work overseas in September 1914.

The hectic ambulance work, in which many of the wounded were dead on arrival or soon after, inspired Knocker to establish a first aid post near the front lines to treat men for shock to improve their chances of surviving the traumatic journey to the base hospitals. Despite Munro's disapproval of women living in close vicinity to soldiers, Chisholm and Knocker left the ambulance corps to establish their post in a cellar in Pervyse in late November 1914.

Chisholm and Knocker experienced immense difficulties when living on the front lines, including lack of supplies and funds as well as their cellar house being temporarily overrun by the Germans. Despite these obstacles, they ventured into the trenches to rescue wounded and provide them with medical care; the Germans agreed not to target them if they wore their nurse's veils.

The Two, as they were known among the Allied troops in Belgium, continued their work until they were affected by a gas attack in 1917, which forced them to return to England for their health. Chisholm briefly joined the British Women's Royal Air Force (WRAF) and after the war raced cars until the effects of her gassing forced her to give up strenuous activity.

—Barbara Penny Kanner

See also: Great Britain, Women in Service in World War I; T'Serclaes, Baroness Elizabeth de

References and Further Reading

Mitton, G. E. 1917. *The Cellar-House of Pervyse; a Tale of Uncommon Things, from the Journals and Letters of the Baroness T'Serclaes and Mairi Chisholm.* London: A. and C. Black.

CHURCHILL, JENNIE (1854–1921)

Mother of Winston Churchill and war-service volunteer. Jennie Churchill was the daughter of Leonard Jerome, a New York financier and sportsman, and his wife Clara. Much of her youth was spent in France, until she, her sisters, and mother left there for England as a result of the fall of the Second Empire in 1871. At age nineteen, she met Lord Randolph Churchill, second son of the duke of Marlborough, on a visit to the yachting center at Cowes and became engaged to him three days later. Their marriage followed. In November 1874, their first child, Winston, was born prematurely, and he was followed by a second son, Jack.

Lively and beautiful, Churchill swiftly became part of the social world and had a number of affairs as her husband's meteoric political career was torpedoed by a wrongheaded resignation and his health by the effects of the tertiary stage of syphilis. She later married two other men, both far younger than herself.

Revered by but distant from Winston, they became closer after Lord Randolph's death in 1896. Using her social and political connections, she greatly assisted him in the furtherance of his military and journalist career, especially his participation in Horatio Herbert Kitchener's drive against the Mahdi in the Sudan in 1898, which ended in the Battle of Omdurman and Winston's famous cavalry charge.

In 1899, Winston went to South Africa as a soldier and journalist in the war against the Boers, and her younger son, Jack, enlisted in the army. Jennie Churchill gained a great deal of attention by leading the effort to bring the hospital ship *Maine,* sponsored by a group of American women and named after the battleship sunk in Havana Harbor in Cuba, to Durban. Jennie took charge, and a number of troops were treated or evacuated, including her son Jack.

During World War I, Jennie again became an active volunteer. She entertained troops on the piano, served meals to soldiers, helped with convalescent homes, and raised money for an American's Women's War Hospital. She also became head matron of a hospital at Lancaster Gate. In addition, she edited a book, *Women's War Work,* and contributed in numerous other ways. Finally, she had to worry about her son Jack, who was fighting, as well as about the fate of Winston, whose career seemed greatly damaged as a result of the disasterous execution of the campaign against Turkey in 1915 at the Dardenelles, which was his brainchild.

—*Marc L. Schwarz*

See also: Great Britain, Women in Service during World War I

References and Additional Reading

Leslie, Anita. 1969. *Lady Randolph Churchill.* New York: Scribner's Sons.

Martin, Ralph. 1969–1971. *Jennie: The Life of Lady Randolph Churchill.* 2 Vols. Englewood Cliffs, NJ: Prentice Hall.

Civil War, American, and Women

Women across the United States took on active—and often new—roles during the American Civil War. They encouraged men to enlist, organized and worked in aid societies, spied on the enemy, worked as nurses and in factories, ran farms and households, and fought as soldiers. By the end of the hostilities in 1865, the war and emancipation had transformed the lives of women.

Women proved vital to both the Union and Confederate war efforts. At times, women urged family members to enlist, and when their men left to fight, they managed their families' homes, farms, businesses, and plantations. They also took jobs outside the home. Through their work in aid societies and factories as well as on farms, white women became major suppliers of food, uniforms, and other goods in both the Union and Confederacy. During the first few weeks of the war, women formed more than 20,000 aid societies. Most towns had their own aid societies that provided local soldiers with socks, undergarments, shirts, gloves, blankets, shoes, handkerchiefs, scarves, bandages, and food. As the war lengthened, supplies were sent where needed and not only to local regiments. Women in rural areas where there were no organized societies often worked as individuals to supply the troops.

Many white women also planned and attended bazaars, fairs, concerts, raffles, and dances to raise money for army supplies. These events, although invaluable to the causes they supported, faced resistance from some men in both regions as "unladylike." Nevertheless, women ran public fundraisers throughout the war. They often justified their participation and behavior by stressing the important services they offered to the men at the front.

During the Civil War thousands of white women became nurses, an occupation that had traditionally been filled by men. In the North approximately 20,000 women served as nurses. The Women's Central Relief Association and the U.S. Sanitary Commission coordinated, enlisted, and oversaw white women's relief work, including their duties as nurses. Both of these organizations helped women participate in the war while restricting them to the domestic spheres. They also shielded women from the horrors of the battlefield. Other women refused to conform to such restrictions and worked directly on the battlefields.

Without a centralized organization, relief work and nursing in the Confederacy remained local throughout the war. Southern women set up makeshift hospitals in homes, churches, town halls, and railway stations, as they took on the care of the wounded as best they could. As Southern towns became battlefields, many white women unwittingly became frontline nurses. Unlike their Northern counterparts, they could not be shielded from the horrors of the battlefield.

Although nursing was often seen as a natural outgrowth of women's nurturing natures, some women crossed the boundaries of womanhood

Confederate Female Volunteer

Mrs. Laura J. Williams of Arkansas

"Among the registered enemies of the United States government who have been recently sent across the lines from New Orleans, there is now in Jackson, Mississippi, a lady whose adventures place her in the ranks of the Mollie Pitchers of the present revolution. At the breaking out of the war Mrs. Laura J. Williams was a resident of Arkansas. Like most of the women of the South, her whole soul was enlisted in the struggle for independence. Her husband was a Northern man by birth and education, and a strong Union man. After Arkansas seceded from the Union he went to Connecticut, he said, to see his relations and settle up some business. Mrs. Williams suspected his purpose and finally she received information that he had joined the Yankee army. The Jackson Mississippian gives the rest of her history:

"She disguised herself in a Confederate uniform, and adopting the name of 'Henry Benford,' she proceeded to Texas, where she raised and equipped an independent company and went to Virginia with it as 1st Lieutenant. She was in the battle of Leesburg and several skirmishes, but finally, her sex having been discovered by the surgeon of the regiment—the 5th Texas Volunteers, to which the company had been attached—she returned to her home in Arkansas. After remaining there a short time she proceeded to Corinth, and was in the battle of Shiloh, where she displayed great coolness and courage. She saw her father on the field, but, of course, he did not recognize her and she did not make herself known to him. In the second day's fighting she was wounded in the head, and was ordered to the rear. She wrote to her father, and then came on down to Grenada, where she waited for some time, but never saw or heard from him.

"She then visited New Orleans, was taken sick, and while sick the city was captured. On recovery she retired to the coast, where she employed herself in carrying communications and assisting parties to run the blockade with drugs and cloths for uniforms. She was informed on by a negro and arrested and brought before Gen. Butler. She made her appearance before Gen. B. in a Southern homespun dress. She refused to take the oath—told him she gloried in being a rebel—had fought side by side with Southern men for Southern rights, and if she ever lived to see 'Dixie' she would do it again. Butler denounced her as the most incorrigible she rebel he had ever met with. By order of the Beast she was placed in confinement, where she remained three months. Some time after her release she was arrested for carrying on 'contraband correspondence,' and kept in a dungeon fourteen days on bread and water, at the expiration of which time she was placed in the State Prison as a dangerous enemy. Her husband, it so happened, was a Lieutenant in the 13th Conn. regiment, and on duty as provost guard in the city. He accidentally found her out and asked if she wanted to see him. She sent him word she never wanted to see him so long as he wore the Yankee uniform. But he forced himself upon her, tried to persuade her to take the oath, and get a release, when he said he would resign and take her to his relations in Connecticut. She indignantly spurned his proposition, and he left her to her fate. When Gen. Banks assumed command he released a great many prisoners, but kept her in confinement until the 17th of May last, when she was sent across the lines to Meadesville with the registered enemies.

" . . . [S]he has attached herself to the medical staff of a brigade now in this city [Jackson, Mississippi], and will render all the assistance in her power to the wounded in the approaching struggle for possession of the great Valley of the Mississippi."

—*Savannah Republican* (Georgia), June 30, 1863, p. 1.
http://www.uttyl.edu/vbetts/women_soldiers.htm
(accessed January 22, 2006).

by dressing as men and enlisting as soldiers. Scholars have documented hundreds of women who donned military uniforms to fight during the Civil War. Some fought alongside male family members, and others enlisted on their own. Often female soldiers' true identity was only revealed when they were injured or killed in battle. As a result, there is no way to calculate accurately the number of women who served in the Civil War armies.

Other women worked as spies during the Civil War. Because white women were rarely searched when they passed through enemy lines, they easily smuggled information, guns, medicine, and other valuable items under their skirts, in their shoes, or in the elaborate hairstyles of the day. Because of the secretive nature of the work, it is impossible to determine an accurate count of female spies. Some left written accounts of their wartime work, however. Confederate spy Belle Boyd and Union spy Sarah Emma Edmonds published accounts of their successes and experiences during the Civil War. African American women also served as spies during the war. Harriet Tubman, who escaped from slavery in the 1840s and served as a conductor on the Underground Railroad, continued to lead slaves to freedom during the war and alerted slaves to the location of Union troops.

Slave women also took an active role in the American Civil War. They found ways to escape from slavery, protect their children, and reunite with family members. The arrival of Union troops provided black women, especially those in the Upper South, the opportunity to run toward freedom with their children and reunite with other loved ones. With emancipation, whether claimed or granted, the lives of African American women changed dramatically.

For many women, the war demanded that they find work outside of the home to support their families. Some found work in occupations that had been open to them in antebellum America as maids, laundresses, seamstresses, and boardinghouse keepers. Those who lived in towns and cities also found work in factories, often helping to produce war-related materiel such as minié balls, paper cartridges, percussion caps, fuses, and shells. Other women became teachers, both for the children on the home front and the freed people in the South. Union and Confederate women also found positions as government workers. Finally, the Civil War promoted the growth of prostitution in U.S. cities.

Not all white women supported the war. In the South, food shortages, inflation, and government policies provoked bread riots in several Confederate cities in 1863. In Richmond, more than 1,000 women looted shops for food and other necessities. The Northern home front experienced similar problems. In New York City, poorer men and women protested the loopholes of the 1863 Draft Law that allowed wealthy men to buy out or hire a substitute to escape conscription. Although the riot began to end draft exemptions, it degenerated into racial violence. After six days of rioting, hundreds of women were arrested and convicted for their participation.

—*Lisa Tendrich Frank*

See also Boyd, Isabelle; Civil War, American, Women Combatants during the; Clayton, Frances; Dix, Dorothea; Edmonds, Sarah Emma; Livermore, Mary Ashton Rice; Moon, Lottie, and Moon, Ginnie; Stowe, Harriet Beecher; Tubman, Harriet; Walker, Mary Edwards

References and Further Reading

Edwards, Laura F. 2000. *Scarlett Doesn't Live Here Anymore: Southern Women in the Civil War Era.* Urbana: University of Illinois Press.

Leonard, Elizabeth D. 1994. *Yankee Women: Gender Battles in the Civil War.* New York: W. W. Norton.

Schwalm, Leslie A. 1997. *A Hard Fight for We: Women's Transition from Slavery to Freedom in South Carolina.* Urbana: University of Illinois Press.

Civil War, American, Women Combatants during the

Women served as combatants in both the Union and Confederate Armies. Throughout the American Civil War, hundreds of women pretended to be men to allow them to serve as soldiers and sailors in the Union and Confederate armies and navies. It is impossible to document the exact number of women who disguised themselves as men to enlist in the military and then effectively carried out their roles as soldiers. Historians can only track down those "unsuccessful" women whose sex was discovered and reported. Those who successfully mustered in as men and remained incognito throughout their service remain men on the military rolls as well as in the history books.

Although most women took on home-front roles during the Civil War, many refused to remain at home as the men of their families marched off to war. At least several hundred passed themselves off as men and reported to enlisting officers as new recruits. They bound their breasts, cut their hair, donned masculine clothing, took up smoking, gambled, and otherwise tried to look and act like men. Some female soldiers were cross-dressers before the war, making their decision to act like men and become soldiers less dramatic. For all of these women, cursory and harried medical exams at their enlistment allowed them to hide their sex and qualify for military service.

When women joined the army, they did so in contexts and for reasons similar to male soldiers. Some women joined the Union or Confederate militaries with the knowledge of their husbands, brothers, or fathers. A few even served alongside members of their family. Others enlisted without their family's knowledge or approval. Female soldiers cited reasons that were similar to those of men for joining the military. They justified their decision to enlist by pointing to their patriotism, abolitionist or proslavery sentiments, desire for vengeance or adventure, or need for money. Many joined the military to escape a bad home situation.

Once in the army, all soldiers, male and female, dealt with the everyday difficulties of military life. They had to survive training, camp life, and the general risks of the battlefield. Female combatants were promoted, captured, injured, and killed in the line of duty. In addition to these general wartime experiences, female combatants lived with a constant fear that their identities would be detected. They knew the dangers of discovery and worked daily to hide their sex. They found ways to change clothes, bathe, deal with menstruation, lie about their backgrounds, and otherwise elude discovery. A fear of exposure led many female soldiers to resist medical care unless it was absolutely necessary.

Despite their desire to avoid detection, the identities of hundreds of female soldiers were uncovered during the war. This unmasking often occurred after female combatants were injured, sick, captured, or killed. In these situations, close examination and treatment by medical personnel inevitably resulted in the discovery of their sex. In addition, a few women's sexual identities were discovered when they became pregnant or gave birth. Other women had their identities revealed during more mundane activities such as changing clothes or dealing with menstruation. Still others unwittingly gave themselves away when their feminine behavior or appearance led to suspicions and then accusations by fellow soldiers. In these instances, a lack of an Adam's apple, an unusually high voice, or a beardless face eventually led to their inability to pass as a man.

Women whose sex was discovered in active duty were typically discharged from service and immediately sent home. After their discharge, some determined female combatants reenlisted in other units and continued to fight until they were discovered again. Discharge was not the only punishment for female soldiers. Army officials could also arrest and jail those soldiers discovered to be women—and often did so. In addition, instead of punishing female combatants

Women Combatants in the American Civil War

A Confederate Woman Soldier

"Among the strange, heroic and self sacrificing acts of woman in this struggle for our independence, we have heard of none which exceeds the bravery displayed and hardships endured by the subject of this notice, Mrs. Amy Clarke. Mrs. Clarke volunteered with her husband as a private, fought through the battles of Shiloh, where Mr. Clarke was killed—she performing the rites of burial with her own hands. She then continued with Bragg's army in Kentucky, fighting in the ranks as a common soldier, until she was twice wounded—once in the ankle and then in the breast, when she fell a prisoner into the hands of the Yankees. Her sex was discovered by the Federals, and she was regularly paroled as a prisoner of war, but they did not permit her to return until she had donned female apparel."

—*Southern Confederacy* (Atlanta), January 11, 1863, p. 3.
http://www.uttyl.edu/vbetts/southern_confederacy.htm
(accessed January 22, 2006).

Woman Appointed Major

"Governor Yates has paid a rather unusual but well merited compliment to Mrs. Reynolds, wife of Lieut. Reynolds, of Co. A, 17th Illinois, and a resident of this city. Mrs. Reynolds has accompanied her husband through the greater part of the campaign through which the 17th has passed, sharing with him the dangers of a soldier's life. She was present at the battle of Pittsburg Landing, and like a ministering angel, attended to the wants of as many of the wounded and dying soldiers as she could, thus winning the gratitude and esteem of the brave fellows by whom she was surrounded.

"Gov. Yates, hearing of her heroic and praiseworthy conduct, presented her with a commission as Major in the army, the document conferring the well-merited honor being made out with all due formality, and having attached the great seal of the State. Probably no lady in America will ever again have such a distinguished military honor conferred upon her. Mrs. Reynolds is now in this city, and leaves to join her regiment in a day or two."

— *Dubuque Herald,* May 1, 1862, p. 2.
http://www.uttyl.edu/vbetts/women_soldiers.htm
(accessed January 22, 2006).

Female Soldiers in the Union Army of the West

"A Pennsylvania girl, who has been serving as a soldier in the Army of the West for ten months, says that she has discovered a great many females among the soldiers, one of whom is now a Lieutenant. She has assisted in burying three female soldiers at different times, whose sex was unknown to any one but herself."

— *Peoria Morning Mail* (Illinois), May 16, 1863, p. 1.
http://www.uttyl.edu/vbetts/women_soldiers.htm
(accessed January 22, 2006).

by sending them out of the army, some officials reassigned the female combatants to perform feminine duties as regimental laundresses, cooks, and seamstress.

After the war, some female combatants maintained their wartime identities and received pensions for their service. Most did not and instead returned to their lives as nineteenth-century women.

—*Lisa Tendrich Frank*

See also Clayton, Frances; Deavers, Brigette; Etheridge, Anna

References and Further Reading

Blanton, DeAnne, and Lauren M. Cook. 2002. *They Fought Like Demons: Women Soldiers in the American Civil War.* Baton Rouge: Louisiana State University Press.

Leonard, Elizabeth D. 1999. *All the Daring of the Soldier: Women of the Civil War Armies.* New York: W. W. Norton.

Civil War, American, Women in the Medical Services in the

Nurses during the American Civil War (1861–1865). The Civil War gave women a chance to leave the domestic sphere and enter the public sphere; it provided them with paid work and built their self-confidence, and they thrived on the satisfaction and feeling of accomplishment they received. Their work also helped make nursing more acceptable as a career for women and led to the establishment of more nursing schools.

There was much hostility directed at female nurses, from family members and husbands who believed women belonged at home and from male doctors, surgeons, and officers who often resented the presence of female nurses and their frequent challenges to male authority. Many people believed it was an indecent environment because the male patients were often undressed. Women were also thought to be too weak physically and emotionally to endure the rigors of nursing.

The term *nurse* was used much more broadly than it is now. Although some nurses did help surgeons with amputations and other operations or helped clean and dress wounds, many did little actual medical work. The majority of the time, nurses prepared and distributed food, administered medicines, washed laundry, provided comfort and company for the wounded, changed bedding, and bathed patients. They also did much of the cleaning and helped distribute supplies.

Somewhere between 2,000 and 10,000 women worked as nurses during the Civil War. Nurses in the North worked under the auspices of either Superintendent of Women Nurses Dorothea Lynde Dix (1802–1887) or the Sanitary Commission (including more than 600 nuns from twelve orders). Still others were independent volunteers, many of whom had followed husbands or other family members to the camps. Union nurses were better organized than Confederate nurses because there was no equivalent to Dix or the Sanitary Commission in the South. In fact, Confederate female nurses were not given official status until 1862. The majority of nurses, North and South, were untrained and working class. African American women comprised 10 percent of the Union's female relief workers. Some volunteered, others were paid workers, and some were runaway slaves who worked in exchange for the relative safety of Union hospitals and camps. Nurses who worked under Dix in the North were paid forty cents a day.

Nursing could be dangerous work. Nurses were often under enemy fire and exposed to life-threatening diseases. The work was also taxing both mentally and physically given the long hours, scanty rations, and unsanitary conditions. In 1892, some of the surviving nurses were compensated through the Army Nurses' Pension Act. Only nurses who had official records or some proof that they had served for more than six months were eligible to collect a pension, however, and then only if they were not already collecting a widow's pension.

Mary Ann Ball Bickerdyke (1817–1901) was one of the most famous of the Union nurses, known particularly for her resourcefulness, dogged personality, and calico dresses. Nicknamed Mother Bickerdyke and the Cyclone in Calico, she was both a force to contend with and a favorite with wounded soldiers. She battled administrators, officers, surgeons, and anyone else to protect the rights of soldiers, and she had several incompetents dismissed. It is said that Major General William T. Sherman once claimed that she outranked even him. She was born July 19, 1817, in Knox County, Ohio. In 1847, she married Robert Bickerdyke. They had three children, but one died in infancy. She was widowed in 1859. In March 1861, the townspeople of Galesburg, Illinois (where she then resided) chose her to accompany $500 worth of supplies they had donated to an army camp in Cairo, Illinois, where Galesburg men were stationed. When she arrived at the camp in June, the conditions she found horrified her. She immediately set to cleaning and organizing the makeshift hospital and feeding and clothing the patients. Following the Battle of Shiloh, she worked as a field agent for the Sanitary Commission. Bickerdyke was assigned to Ulysses S. Grant's army and then William T. Sherman's forces. She worked at nineteen battles, often on the front line. She was particularly talented at obtaining and distributing supplies, building hospitals, and establishing mobile laundries and kitchens. She was known to search the battlefields at night with a lantern, worried that there might be wounded left among the dead. She did not resign from the commission until the last Illinois soldier was discharged in May 1866. She then helped veterans and nurses obtain pensions and continued welfare work throughout the United States. She died November 8, 1901, in Bunker Hill, Kansas. In 1943, a hospital ship was named in her honor.

Sally Louisa Tompkins (1833–1916) was a well-known Confederate nurse and the only woman commissioned into the Confederate Army. She was nicknamed Captain Sally, Dearest of Captains, and the Little Lady with the Milk-White Hands. She was born into wealth and privilege, November 9, 1833, in Matthews County, Virginia, to Colonel Christopher Tompkins and Maria Patterson Tompkins. After the death of her father, she moved to Richmond. She never married. Following the first Battle of Bull Run, the Confederate government asked for help caring for the wounded. Tompkins asked a friend, Judge John Robertson, if he would donate his home. He agreed, and she turned the house into a hospital, naming it after him. Robertson Hospital opened August 1, 1861. She used her inheritance to run it. What makes Tompkins particularly noteworthy is the level of care that patients received at her hospital. She was militant about cleanliness. Of the more than 1,300 wounded who were sent to Robertson Hospital, only 73 died. Her 94 percent survival rate was unparalleled in both North and South. It is even more impressive given the fact that some of the worst cases were sent to her because of her good record. She was commissioned an unassigned captain in the cavalry on September 9, 1861. Some private hospitals had been overcharging the Confederate government, so a regulation was passed that all hospitals were to be run by military personnel. Tompkins protested this, and given her excellent record, President Jefferson Davis bent the rules and made her an officer. The hospital closed in June of 1865, but she continued her charity work, including work with veterans, until her fortune had been exhausted. She died July 25, 1916, in the Confederate Women's Home in Richmond and was buried with military honors in Matthews County.

Mary Edwards Walker (1832–1919) served as both a nurse and a physician for the Union Army during the Civil War. She was the first female surgeon in the U.S. Army and the only woman in the Civil War to receive the Congressional Medal of Honor. She was born November 26, 1832, in Oswego, New York. Her father, Alvah, was an abolitionist, farmer, teacher, and doctor. He encouraged her to pursue her dreams. She became one of the first female doctors in the United States when she graduated from Syracuse Medical College. In 1855, dressed in men's clothes (as she would be for most of her life), she married Doctor Albert Miller. The two opened a practice together in Rome, New York, that eventually closed given the reticence of most people to go to a female doctor. She and her husband began a ten-year separation in 1859, which finally culminated in divorce. She volunteered her medical expertise following the Battle of Bull Run. When her commission was turned down, she became a nurse until she was finally made an assistant surgeon to the 52nd Ohio Infantry, although without military rank. She served at the Patent Office Hospital in Washington, D.C., and as a field surgeon on the front lines. Following the Battle of Chickamauga, she was captured and imprisoned in Richmond. She remained there from April 10, 1864, until August 12, 1864. Upon her release, she continued her work as a physician. After the war, President Johnson awarded her the Congressional Medal of Honor, and she worked as a writer and lecturer on temperance, dress reform, and women's rights. In 1917, Congress rescinded her Medal, and those of more than 900 others, to make it more prestigious. She refused to return it and continued to wear the medal until her death in Oswego on February 21, 1919. In 1977, President Jimmy Carter reinstated it, and in 1982, she was honored on a postage stamp.

—*Paula K. Hinton*

See also Barton, Clara; Civil War, American, and Women; Dix, Dorothea; Livermore, Mary Ashton Rice; Walker, Mary Edwards

References and Further Reading

Donahue, M. Patricia. 1985. *Nursing, the Finest Art: An Illustrated History.* Illustrations edited and compiled by Patricia A. Russac. St. Louis, MO: C. V. Mosby.

Haerman, Keppel. 1996. *Dearest of Captains: A Biography of Sally Louisa Tompkins.* Whitestone, VA: Brandylane.

Maggiano, Ron. 2002. "Captain Sally Tompkins: Angel of the Confederacy." *OAH Magazine of History* 16 (2002, winter).

Robbins, Peggy. 1979. "General Grant's Calico General." *American History Illustrated* 14 (1979) 1: 4–7, 43–48.

Roberts, Joan I., and Thetis M. Group. 1995. *Feminism and Nursing: An Historical Perspective on Power, Status, and Political Activism in the Nursing Profession.* Westport, CT: Praeger.

Schultz, Jane E. 1994. "Race, Gender, and Bureaucracy: Civil War Army Nurses and the Pension Bureau." *Journal of Women's History* 6 (1994) 2: 45–69.

Clayton, Frances (n.d.)

An enlisted soldier in the American Civil War, who altered her appearance and gender-specific conduct to assume a male role. The Boston Public Library possesses a startling pair of photographs showing Frances Clayton in both uniform and hoop skirts, yet, like many female soldiers of the era, the historical record yields little about her. Available sources are filled with contradictions; the National Archives states she served with Missouri Volunteers, whereas the Library of Congress lists her with a Minnesota regiment. She is said to have fought with artillery or infantry, although the photograph shows her dressed as a cavalry trooper. Additionally, she may appear as Frances Clalin or Lalin.

Frances Clayton enlisted with her husband and successfully disguised her gender. She served in the western theater under General William Starke Rosencrans, where she was wounded in combat. Her husband was marching in the front rank at Stone's River, several paces ahead of her, when he was hit and instantly killed. She continued the charge with the unit, stepping over her husband's body to keep her place in formation. Several Minnesota infantry regiments fought at Stone's River, as well as two

Missouri artillery regiments, and Clayton may have participated with any of them.

Clayton remained with her unit following her husband's death. Noted as a fine horseman, excellent swordsman, and good fighter, she carried herself in a soldierly manner and performed all the tasks of the men in the field. Whether standing guard or doing picket duty, she acquitted herself well and never raised suspicions about her true identity. She was badly wounded in the battle for Fort Donelson in February 1863 and discharged after her convalescence. Several newspapers covered her return home in 1863. She claimed to have lost her papers and valuables when she was robbed by Confederate guerrillas on the way home.

Clayton was tall and plain, and she adopted masculine social characteristics to enhance her appearance as a private soldier. She drank alcohol, used tobacco, and altered her speech patterns to include profanity as a means of concealing her sex. By altering the culturally constructed patterns of her gender, she was able to maintain her position as a man until medical necessity required a revelation. There is no available record of her life after the war.

—Dawn Ottevaere

See also Civil War, American, Women Conbatants during the

References and Further Reading

Blanton, DeAnne. "Women Soldiers of the Civil War." *Prologue* 25, no. 1 (1993, spring), http://www.archives.gov/publications/prologue/1993/spring/women-in-the-civil-war-1.html (accessed January 30, 2005).

Blanton, DeAnne, and Lauren M. Cook. 2002. *They Fought Like Demons: Women Soldiers in the American Civil War.* Baton Rouge: Louisiana State University Press.

Hall, Richard. 1993. *Patriots in Disguise: Women Warriors of the Civil War.* New York: Paragon House.

Library of Congress. "Women in the Union Armies," http://memory.loc.gov/learn/features/timeline/civilwar/northwar/women.html (accessed January 30, 2005).

Middleton, Lee. 1993. *Hearts of Fire: Soldier Women of the Civil War.* Franklin, NC: Genealogy Publishing.

Tsui, Barbara. 2003. *She Went to the Field: Women Soldiers of the Civil War.* Guilford, CT: TwoDot.

Cleopatra VII, Queen of Egypt (69–30 B.C.)

Egyptian queen. Queen Cleopatra VII of Egypt is a rare example of a ruling queen who raised armies and conducted wars, although she does not appear to have led her troops in person. She was the daughter of King Ptolemy XII, who when he died in 51 B.C. willed his throne to his son Ptolemy XIII (age ten) and his daughter Cleopatra (age seventeen), who then married in typical Ptolemaic fashion.

Ptolemy's advisors feared the charming, intelligent Cleopatra and soon drove her from Egypt. She responded by raising an army against her brother. The Roman dictator Julius Caesar attempted to mediate between the two, but Ptolemy refused to cooperate, and Caesar's and Cleopatra's troops together defeated and killed Ptolemy. Cleopatra was then wed to her youngest brother (Ptolemy XIV) but soon became Caesar's lover.

Cleopatra's liaison with Caesar strengthened her precarious position as the last independent ruler of the Mediterranean world. This need to protect Egypt also led her, after Caesar's death, to begin an affair with the Roman general Mark Antony, who had gained control of the eastern Roman provinces. Antony returned to Rome for a time, but his relationship with Cleopatra began afresh in 37 B.C. In 32, he went so far as to marry Cleopatra, who had borne him three children. To do so, Antony had to divorce his Roman wife Octavia, the sister of his arch-rival Octavian (the future Augustus Caesar).

Octavian naturally saw his sister's divorce as a personal insult and seized the opportunity to declare war on both Antony and Cleopatra. It was a war over who would rule the Roman world, but Octavian's skilful propaganda caused many to regard it as a struggle specifically against Cleopatra—an unnatural woman who exercised a thoroughly un-Roman dominance over Antony. The resources of Egypt made it possible for Cleopatra to provide a large squadron of ships to the struggle and also to provide the wages for much of Antony's army. She did not command troops in battle but did act unusually for the age by insisting on being with the army and fleet during the campaign.

Octavian's admiral succeeded in trapping Cleopatra's and Antony's combined fleet at Actium on the west coast of Greece. They finally attempted a desperate breakout in September of 31 B.C. Cleopatra's squadron sailed straight for the open Mediterranean, leaving Antony's contingents to fight, and Antony soon broke loose and followed her. A legend perhaps begun by Octavian himself tells that Cleopatra lost her nerve and ran, while the besotted Antony abandoned his command to follow. This story is not plausible. Because all accounts agree that Cleopatra's ships had their masts and sails aboard, her flight must have been intended from the beginning, apparently in the hope of getting the war chest to Egypt so her party could regroup and continue the fight from there. Octavian's army pursued Cleopatra and Antony to Egypt, where both soon committed suicide to avoid falling into his hands.

—Phyllis G. Jestice

See also Fulvia; Helen of Troy; Roman Women and War; Zenobia, Queen of Palmyra

References and Further Reading

Pomeroy, Sarah B. 1984. *Women in Hellenistic Egypt: From Alexander to Cleopatra.* New York: Schocken.

Walker, Susan, and Peter Higgs, eds. 2001. *Cleopatra of Egypt: From History to Myth.* Princeton, NJ: Princeton University Press.

CND

See Campaign for Nuclear Disarmament and the Greenham Common Women

Cochran, Jacqueline (ca. 1906–1980)

Director of women's flight training, later of women pilots, for the U.S. military during World War II. Highly respected and an award-winning test pilot in her own right, Jacqueline Cochran first suggested the idea of female military pilots to Eleanor Roosevelt in 1939. For Cochran, every woman pilot serving in a training or ferrying capacity freed a male pilot for combat. Although the suggestion did not win immediate support from the U.S. government, Cochran continued to lobby for a women's pilot training program. In June 1941, she became the first woman to ferry a bomber across the North Atlantic. By late 1941, inspired by British female ferry pilots, she recruited twenty-four American women to join her in Britain's Air Ferrying Command. Returning to the United States in late 1942, Cochran was appointed director of the Women's Flying Training Detachment (WFTD), a paramilitary group. The WFTD merged with the Women's Air Ferrying Squadron (WAFS), headed by Nancy Love, in July 1943, forming the Women's Airforce Service Pilots (WASP). General Henry "Hap" Arnold appointed Cochran to the general staff of the U.S. Army Air Forces as director of the WASP.

Against great opposition, Cochran worked constantly to keep her female pilots above reproach and rumor. She personally interviewed each applicant and chose only those who would reflect well on her leadership and her program. She recruited few ethnic minority women and no African Americans because she feared controversy over race would doom her fragile program. Even though the women were considered civilians employed by the military, Cochran insisted that her recruits undergo army military training and live under military regulations. She also secured for the WASPs their own training facilities in Sweetwater, Texas, and arranged for clothing designer Bergdorf Goodman to create WASP uniforms that fit her sense of style.

Full military status for the WASP appeared imminent by the end of the war, but support for the program remained limited. Cochran's insistence that the WASP should not be absorbed into the Women's Army Corps (WAC), and active lobbying against the program from out-of-work male pilots afraid of being sent to the front, sealed the fate of the organization. Even after the WASP were disbanded in 1944 Cochran remained dedicated to the idea of women military pilots. She also supported plans for an air force separate from the army.

Cochran received numerous awards for her contributions to the war effort, including the U.S. Distinguished Service medal in 1945, the French Legion of Honor in 1949, and the Distinguished Flying Cross with two oak leaf clusters in 1969, along with citations for civilian service and recruitment. In 1975, the Air Force Academy honored her as the first woman with a permanent display. Cochran remained supportive of the women pilots, hosting WASP reunions at her ranch until her death in 1980.

—Rebekah Crowe

See also United States Women's Airforce Service Pilots

References and Further References

Cochran, Jacqueline, and Maryann Bucknum Brinley. 1987. *Jackie Cochran: An Autobiography.* New York: Bantam.

Douglas, Deborah G. 1990. *United States Women in Aviation: 1940–1985.* Smithsonian Studies in Air and Space No. 7. Washington, DC: Smithsonian Institution.

Colenso, Harriette (1847–1932)

British evangelical humanitarian, eldest child of the famous Anglican bishop, John William Colenso, and tireless advocate of and campaigner for civil and human rights for the Zulu people in their struggle against British imperialism and colonial injustice. Harriette accompanied her family to South Africa in 1852 when her father came to establish a new diocese in Natal. She spent much of her youth and adult life on the family homestead and mission station, Bishoptowe, east of Pietermaritzburg, and became fluent in Zulu. Support for her father's and her own causes filled her life with controversy. Soon after his arrival in Natal, Bishop Colenso angered not only the local settler population by siding with the Zulu but also Church of England clergy and lay believers by questioning biblical truth, for which he was excommunicated. Harriette served as her father's secretary; because of the guidance and support she gave him, the Zulu called her *Udlwedlwe* (the staff).

In the early 1870s, she aided her father in his defense of the Hlubi chief Langalibalele; through her petitions to the imperial government, she had his banishment on Robben Island relocated to a farm in the Cape. She also helped her father with his writings, particularly his *Digest of Zulu Affairs.* During the Zulu War (1879) and its aftermath, the Colensos defended the Zulu king Cetshwayo. After her father's death in 1883 and the king's death the following year, Harriette took it upon herself to protect the new king, Dinuzulu, from attempts by British imperial authorities to break up the Zulu kingdom and reduce the king's royal powers. She believed the king held the Zulu together as a people and that the loyalty paid him by the lesser chiefs and the commoners gave them a united front to resist outsiders. In 1888, the British colonial authorities banished Dinuzulu to St. Helena on trumped-up charges. Harriette spent the next ten years traveling between Natal, St. Helena, and London, writing, speaking, petitioning, and meeting with British officials to gain his release and to protest imperial exploitation of Zulu lands and people. She also wrote withering public critiques of the arch-imperialist Cecil Rhodes and his South African Company. Through her efforts, Dinuzulu was allowed to return to the Cape in 1898. After Bambatha's Rebellion in 1906, the king was arrested again on spurious charges, and Harriette again took up his defense, only to see him sentenced to prison where he died in 1913.

The Church Properties Act of 1910 forced Harriette and her family off of Bishoptowe. She and her sister Agnes lived the remainder of their lives near Pietermaritzburg and carried on missionary work until they died in relative obscurity in 1932.

—*Roger B. Beck*

See also First, Heloise Ruth; Hobhouse, Emily; Mandela, Winnie; Mau Mau Rebellion, Women in the; Nongqawuse

References and Further Reading

Guy, Jeff. 1979. *The Destruction of the Zulu Kingdom. The Civil War in Zululand, 1879–1884*. London: Longman.

———. 1983. *The Heretic. A Study of the Life of J. W. Colenso*. Johannesburg, South Africa: Ravan Press.

———. 2002. *View across the River. Harriette Colenso and the Zulu Struggle against Imperialism*. Charlottesville: University of Virginia.

Marks, Shula. 1963. "Harriette Colenso and the Zulus, 1874–1913." *Journal of African History* 4, no. 3: 403–11.

Rees, W., ed. 1958. *Colenso Letters from Natal*. Pietermaritzburg, South Africa: Shuter and Shooter.

Colombia, Women and Political Violence in

Impact on women of the lengthy political violence in Colombia. Corruption, social inequality, class antagonism, U.S. Cold War policies, and drug trafficking are the sources of the political violence that has haunted Colombia since the 1940s. The continued civil war has led to hundreds of thousands of dead and displaced.

Colombia's civil war can be traced back to what is commonly referred to as *La Violencia* (the violence). *La Violencia* emerged in part due to an election that took place in 1945 ensuring conservative rule; however, midyear elections gave liberals a majority in the Colombian Congress. In 1947, workers' strikes led to political violence and economic sabotage. When liberal populist leader Jorge Eliécer Gaitán led a popular movement in Bogotá demanding that the president restore order, he was targeted for death. Two months later, Gaitán was assassinated, thus ushering in *La Violencia*. Liberal supporters formed guerrilla groups to engage in armed conflict. Under siege, ruling elites, while trying to maintain the status quo in the urban centers and in the countryside, destroyed the urban populist movement. In the countryside, Communists formed peasant self-defense groups. That, in turn, led to the establishment of paramilitaries funded by landowners and conservatives. With the emergence of guerrilla groups that closely identified with the left, the anti-Marxist liberals joined the conservatives to share power under the National Front in 1958, thus ensuring a complete monopoly of power by elites.

From *La Violencia* one of the first and most successful guerrilla movements emerged, the Revolutionary Armed Forces of Colombia (Fuerzas Armadas Revolucionarios de Colombia, FARC) formed by Manuel Marulanda and Jacobo Arenas. FARC has direct ties to the peasant land movements and Communist insurgency of the 1940s. With the formation of the National Front, FARC was joined by other organizations that took up arms against the political repression of the National Front. The National Liberation Army, the ELN (Ejército de Liberación Nacional), was organized in the mid-1960s by Fabio Vazquez and Colombian

Priest Camilo Torres. Both groups, FARC and ELN, embraced Che Guevara's method of insurrectionary armed enclaves. In the mid-1970s, the FARC, ELN, and other groups were joined by the April 19 Movement (M-19), which emerged as a result of the political corruption that took place during the 1970 presidential election. In that election, the National Popular Alliance (Alianza Nacional Popular, ANAPO) candidate, Gustavo Rojas Pinilla, a populist, was defrauded.

Because of the continued social unrest, women have played roles in all sides of the conflict. In M-19, young women could identity with Rojas Pinilla's daughter María Eugenia Rojas de Moreno. Rojas de Moreno took over ANAPO upon the death of her father in 1975. Although she has attempted to disassociate herself and ANAPO from M-19, the two remained tied. One of the founders of M-19 was an ANAPO senator, Carlos Toledo Plata. In the ELN, Catholic women also came to the revolution through a linkage between a religiously motivated desire for social justice and the social revolutionary movement. A number of ELN leaders and activists have been priests. In an interview with Colombian journalist Patricia Lara Saliver, an ELN member whose nom de guerre was Doña Margarita, the revolutionary explained that she was introduced to the ELN by a priest who had created a youth club that introduced young people to revolutionary ideas. When he was arrested, she received a one-word message from him: "ENLIST" (Lara Saliver 2000).

As women became combatants, certain rules were established by the guerrilla groups. FARC leaders have attempted to address the issues of gender. Like their counterparts in other parts of Latin America, they asserted on one hand that "guerrillas are like angels, they have not gender"; on the other hand, the FARC confronted sexism and family issues. The FARC commanders, male and female, insisted that women take birth control pills to ensure they would not become pregnant. To the FARC, the struggle was no place for children. FARC women who had children, however, whether before or after they join the struggle, had to find care for them. Olga Luciá Marín, a FARC commander, had a child with her FARC *compañero* (companion). She spent a year with the baby but then returned to the struggle. Like other female combatants, Marín argued that the struggle was to make a better world not only for her child, but also for all children (Lara Saliver 2000, 114).

By 2000, women accounted for one-third of FARC combatants. They joined the guerrillas for many reasons, but many reported that joining the guerrillas was their only option in a country whose economy and society is plagued by continued violence. Because of Colombia's tradition of a division of labor by gender, FARC commanders had to train men to accept the women as their equals. FARC issued specific guidelines calling for an end to discrimination against women (see www.farcep.org).

Paula Rodriguez, a member of the Fuerzas Armadas Revolucionarios de Colombia (FARC), checks a taxi near San Vincente del Caguan Airport, 1999.
(Tore Bergsaker/Sygma/Corbis)

The ongoing civil war and the intervention of the United States in its War on Drugs have ensured that all Colombian women have experienced violence. Civilian men, women, and children are caught between the guerrillas, the military, the paramilitaries, and the drug traffickers. Many women have lost family members or have been displaced by the violence. Even those from wealthy and politically connected families are not immune to violence. As a senator and during her presidential campaign in 2002, Ingrid Betancourt challenged the status quo arguing that there must be reform at all levels of the Colombian government. While running for president, she was allegedly kidnapped in 2002 by the FARC and remains in captivity.

—Elaine Carey

See also Latin America, Women in Guerrilla Movements in

References and Further Reading

Betancourt, Ingrid. 2002. *Until Death Do Us Part: My Struggle to Reclaim Colombia.* New York: HarperCollins.

Dudley, Steven. 2004. *Walking Ghosts: Murder and Guerrilla Politics in Colombia.* New York: Routledge.

FARC-EP Web site: www.farcep.org (accessed August 20, 2004).

Lara Saliver, Patricia. 2000. *Las mujeres en la guerra.* Bogotá: Editorial Plantea.

Conquest, Joan, pseud. (Mary Eliza Louise Gripper Martin-Nicholson) (1876–1941)

British novelist and nurse who volunteered with the British Red Cross in World War I. She served in Belgium, Russia, and France until she fell ill in 1916 and returned to Britain. She received the 1914 Star for her work.

Conquest arrived in Brussels, Belgium, with a contingent of nurses on August 20, 1914, the same day as German occupying troops. Cut off from British mail and news, she was separated from her fellow nurses and sent to a military hospital where, because of her fluent German, she was given charge over the German wounded. On October 6, 1914, the Germans sent all British nurses in Brussels back to England via Denmark. In Copenhagen, Conquest and three other nurses, including Violetta Thurstan, decided to offer their services to the Russian Red Cross rather than return to England.

After working briefly at a hospital in Petrograd, Russia, Conquest was assigned to the No. 1 Red Cross Military Hospital in Warsaw, Poland, which she found crowded and disorganized despite the steadfastness of the women doctors. Conquest returned to England for a brief period before she was reposted to a typhoid hospital in France, where she served until 1916.

—Barbara Penny Kanner

See also Great Britain, Women in Service during World War I; Thurstan, Violetta

References and Further Reading

Conquest, Joan. 1937. *Strange Beds: Life Story of Love, Thrills and Adventure.* London: Jarrolds.

Kanner, Barbara Penny. 1997. *Women in Context.* New York: G. K. Hall.

Martin-Nicholson, Mary. 1916. *My Experiences on Three Fronts.* London, George Allen and Unwin.

Conscientious Objectors in the United States during World War II, Women and

American women whose husbands were conscientious objectors during World War II. During World War II a number of men and women identified themselves as conscientious objectors opposing the war due to both religious and nonreligious reasons. During the war there were 100,000 men who claimed conscientious objector status. The U.S. conscription law of 1940 exempted persons who could not participate in war because of their religious beliefs from combatant duties. The Selective Training and Service Act of 1940 created the Civilian Public Service (CPS), which offered a noncombatant work for conscientious objectors during the war. Conscientious objectors also worked in health care agencies, mental hospitals, and other civilian facilities. For those who did not object to taking noncombatant duties in the military forces—around 25,000 people—positions were found in military units. Some women followed their husbands or fiancés to the CPS camps. The men's status as conscientious objectors affected the lives of these women. Some women also opposed the war, so they supported their loved ones' decision. Many wives of the conscientious objectors who had decided not to follow their husbands maintained their relationships through letters. Some wives of the conscientious objectors brought their children with them to live near the CPS camps. These women had to find jobs in the communities around the CPS camps or ask for financial aid from their relatives and friends. Sometimes their husbands could find them jobs in their CPS camps. Between 1943 and 1946, a few hundred college women who were peace activists joined male conscientious objectors working in state psychiatric institutions.

The National Service Board for Religious Objectors (NSBRO) ran the CPS camps. The conscientious objector was assigned an eighteen-month tour of service, which was regarded as equal to the time a man was required to serve in the armed forces. The conscientious objectors who were assigned to the CPS camps worked without pay. About 12,000 men accepted CPS assignments. Between 1943 and 1945, the U.S. government also opened camps which were independent from the NSBRO, which was religious in its orientation.

In 1942, Congress passed the Servicemen's Dependents Allowance Act, which allowed the wives of those conscientious objectors who worked in CPS camps to receive a family allowance and obstetric care. Financial hardship pushed some conscientious objectors' wives to ask their husbands for a reclassification from CPS to noncombatant or even combatant status. The change of status could help them qualify for additional government benefits. The financial difficulty also caused some conscientious objectors' wives to divorce their husbands because of the lack of financial support.

Some female pacifists wanted to share the experience with the male conscientious objectors. These women chose to work in some peace-oriented church groups and could be assigned to CPS camps. They often studied at liberal arts colleges that were affiliated with the peace churches. They were recruited to the CPS program and worked side by side with the conscientious objectors. Before 1943, CPS openings for women were limited to dietitians, nurses, matrons, or secretaries. By 1943, more college women who identified themselves as conscientious objectors wanted to work in CPS sites; therefore, they pressed for more openings.

In 1944, three peace churches including the Mennonites, Brethren, and Society of Friends, raised funds to help the dependents of conscientious objectors as long as they demonstrated that they needed financial support. NSBRO also offered assistance to the wives of the conscientious objectors. Some branches of the Women's International League for Peace and Freedom also joined NSBRO to provide aid to the wives of the conscientious objectors.

After the end of the war, the U.S. government did not demobilize conscientious objectors at CPS camps immediately. The process of demobilization lasted until 1947.

—Edy M. Parsons

See also Balch, Emily Green; International Congress of Women: Antiwar Protest of Women in World War I; International Manifesto of Women

References and Further Reading

Anderson, Richard C. 1994. *Peace Was in Their Hearts: Conscientious Objectors in World War II.* Watsonville, CA: Correlan.

Eller, Cynthia. 1991. *Conscientious Objectors and the Second World War: Moral and Religious Arguments in Support of Pacifism.* New York: Praeger.

Goossen, Rachel Waltner. 1997. *Against the Good War: Conscientious Objection and Gender on the American Home Front, 1941–1947.* Chapel Hill: The University of North Carolina.

Corbin, Margaret Cochrane (1751–1800)

The first woman awarded a pension by Congress for her service in the Revolution. Born in Franklin County, Pennsylvania, Margaret and her brother were raised by an uncle after Indians killed her father, Robert Cochrane, and took their mother captive. Margaret married Virginian John Corbin about 1772.

John Corbin enlisted in 1776 in Thomas Porter's First Company of Pennsylvania Artillery. Margaret accompanied him, probably serving as a regimental woman, who received half-rations in exchange for cooking, washing, or hauling water to the gun crews. On November 16, 1776, Porter's Company took part in the unsuccessful defense of Fort Washington again a much larger Hessian army. John Corbin was killed and Margaret took his place on the gun. Margaret Corbin was among the 2,818 Americans taken prisoner. Badly wounded by grape shot that mangled her left side and completely disabled her arm, Corbin's survival as a prisoner of war is surprising.

The Pennsylvania Supreme Council awarded her $30 relief on June 29, 1779, and recommended action to the Congressional Board of War because her ration allowance was inadequate. Congress voted her a half-pay pension on July 6, 1779. Corbin also was immediately assigned to the Corps of Invalids, created in 1777, to put to garrison work at West Point soldiers too injured for combat. In 1780, the Board of War increased her annual compensation to include a suit of clothes. In 1782, she married another invalid soldier (name unknown) and successfully had her pension increased to full rations including an allowance for spirits. Corbin received a regular discharge from the Invalid Corps in April 1783.

After discharge, "Captain Molly" remained in the West Point area until at least 1789. She was cared for in a private home while receiving supplies from the fort commissary. Although legend says she died in Pennsylvania in 1800, the grave authenticated as Corbin's was in Highland Falls, New York. In 1926, her remains were moved to West Point where a monument marks her grave.

—Joan R. Gundersen

See also American Revolution, Role of Women in the; Molly Pitcher; Samson, Deborah

References and Further Reading

Hall, Edward H. 1943. *Margaret Corbin: Heroine of the Battle of Fort Washington, November 16, 1776.* New York: American Scenic and Historic Preservation Society.

Parker, Amella C. 1926. "Revolutionary Heroine Interred in West Point Cemetery." *Daughters of the American Revolution Magazine* (June): 347–352.

Teipe, Emily J. "Will the Real Molly Pitcher Please Stand Up?" *Prologue* XXXI (1999): 118–126.

Ward, Harry. 1999. *The War for Independence and the Transformation of American Society.* London: UCL Press.

Wensyl, James W. 1981. "Captain Molly." *Army* 31 (November): 48–53.

Cormeau, Yvonne (1909–1988)

British special agent during World War II. Yvonne Cormeau was one of the first female radio operators assigned by the British Special Operatives Executive (SOE), Section F, to work with the French Resistance movement. Using the code names Annette, Fairy, and Sarafan, she began work near Bordeaux but then operated with the Armagnac Battalion, a large group of fighters, under the command of the French Colonel Parisot. As the battalion moved throughout the southwest region of France before the liberation of Paris, Cormeau was wounded.

Cormeau was born Beatrice Yvonne Biesterfeld in Shanghai in 1909 to British parents. Her father was a consular official and moved his family to France, Belgium, and Switzerland. She had married, given birth to a daughter, and was leading a quiet life in London when the war broke out. Her husband, Charles Edouard Emile Cormeau, was killed in 1940 when their London apartment was destroyed in a German bombing raid. Their daughter escaped, having been sent to the country for safety. Cormeau joined the Women's Auxiliary Air Force in 1941 and began her training as a radio operator in August 1943. Cormeau served 13 months in the field and sent over 400 messages. By limiting her transmissions to only 15 to 20 minutes and a strategy of frequent relocation, Cormeau was able to avoid detection by the Germans. For her war service, she was appointed a Member of the British Empire (MBE) and was awarded the Croix de Guerre (Gold) and Medaille Combattant Volontaire de la Resistance. She died in England in 1988.

—*Pamela Lee Gray*

See also Atkins, Vera H.

References and Further Reading

Rossister, Margaret L.1986. *Women in the Resistance.* New York: Praeger.

Sweets, John F. 1976. *The Politics of Resistance in France, 1940–1944.* De Kalb: Northern Illinois University Press.

Cornum, Rhonda (1955–)

Female prisoner of war (POW) during the Gulf War of 1991. Rhonda Cornum, U.S. Army flight surgeon with the rank of major, became one of two American military women taken POW in Iraq during Operation Desert Storm of the Gulf War. Cornum had earned a Ph.D. in nutrition and biochemistry at Cornell University, joining the army in 1978 to work at the Letterman Army Institute of Research in San Francisco. In 1982, she entered the Uniformed Services University medical school in Washington, D.C., and earned her M.D. in 1986. As a wife and mother, Cornum became a focal point of national debate on the role of women in combat.

On January 12, 1991, the U.S. Congress had authorized the use of military force to drive Iraqi troops out of Kuwait following Iraq's failure to respond to United Nations Security Council Resolution 678 ordering this withdrawal. The war became the largest deployment of women to a combat theater: more than 40,000 were sent (Holm 1992, 469).

A flight surgeon for the army's 2–229th Attack Helicopter Battalion attached to the 101st Airborne division, Major Cornum was charged with the medical care of more than 300 soldiers. During attack missions, her job as the battalion flight surgeon required her to fly behind Apache attack helicopters, prepared to provide emergency medical care and rescue if the helicopters were shot down. On February 27, 2001, one day before the official cessation of hostilities, Cornum received assignment as flight surgeon aboard a Black Hawk helicopter on a search-and-rescue mission for a downed F-16 pilot. Her Black Hawk was shot down over Iraqi territory.

Five members of the eight-person crew died in the crash; the remaining, including Cornum, were taken prisoner.

Cornum had two broken arms, a bullet wound in the right shoulder, a broken, infected finger, and ligament tears in both knees. As a prisoner of war, she was interrogated, and an Iraqi guard sexually molested her. Their eyes covered as they were moved among various locations in Iraq, Cornum and fellow POWs from the helicopter crash discovered that the pilot they were charged with rescuing was also a POW. He identified himself and announced cessation of hostilities to a busload of blindfolded POWs, over the protests of their Iraqi captors. Prior to Cornum's release, an Iraqi surgeon performed an operation to align and set the bones in her arms temporarily until she could obtain definitive surgery and medical care at home.

Major Cornum was repatriated to friendly forces March 6, 2001, with other POWs. She received the Distinguished Flying Cross and Purple Heart for her actions in Operation Desert Storm.

—Lee Ann Ghajar

See also Whittle, Reba Zitella

References and Further Reading

Cornum, Rhonda, as told to Peter Copeland. 1992. *She Went to War: The Rhonda Cornum Story.* Novato, CA: Presidio Press.

Holm, Jeanne. 1992. *Women in the Military: An Unfinished Revolution.* Revised ed. Novato, CA: Presidio Press.

Craig, May (1889–1975)

American war correspondent. Elisabeth May Adams attended George Washington University School of Nursing and then married Donald A. Craig, head of the Washington bureau for the *New York Herald.* A freak car accident changed her life. The car in which her husband was traveling, following President Warren Harding's motorcade, plunged off a cliff near Denver, Colorado, killing the driver and leaving Donald gravely injured and unable to work. Hesitantly at first, his young wife began to file political items, and gradually, May Craig became one of the leading female political correspondents in Washington. By the 1930s, she was penning a column called "Inside Washington" for the Gannett newspaper chain. During the New Deal years, fond male colleagues called her Quoddy, in reference to her advocacy of the Passamaquoddy power project in Maine. She became one of the few women accredited for President Franklin Roosevelt's press conferences.

When First Lady Eleanor Roosevelt breathed fresh life into Washington, among her innovations was holding press conferences at which only female reporters were allowed. A dismissive male press corps derided these women as "the incense burners," but Craig became one of Eleanor Roosevelt's inner circle of reporters. A suffragist, Craig had participated in a women's suffrage parade on the eve of Woodrow Wilson's inauguration in 1913. She ardently advocated women's rights, but her stance was strictly that of liberal feminism; she felt and said emphatically that equality demanded that male reporters should be allowed access to Mrs. Roosevelt's press conferences. Joseph Alsop observed that he never thought of May Craig as a woman. Instead, to him, she was a reporter.

Craig's insistence on gender fairness continued into the war years when she served on the five-woman committee to credential reporters who could attend Eleanor Roosevelt's press conferences after demand had swollen attendance. Her insistence on absolute fairness later led her to advocate successfully the barring of two long-time female veterans of the first lady's press conferences from asking questions because they had taken war jobs with the government. May Craig feared planted questions and opposed "any hint of government propaganda" (Beasley 1987, 154). Advocating for her sex, she filed a protest in 1944 as president of the Women's National Press Club, when female White House reporters were barred from the annual dinner of the Correspondents' Association.

During World War II, May Craig filed stories from Europe, reporting on buzz bomb raids in London, the progress of the Normandy campaign, and the liberation of Paris. In the Cold War years, she flew in the Berlin Airlift and covered truce talks in Korea. It was a point of pride that in 1949 she was the first woman allowed on a battleship at sea. Late in her career,, she noted wryly that "Bloody Mary of England once said that when she died they would find 'Calais' graven on her heart. When I die, there will be the word 'facilities,' so often has it been used to prevent me from doing what men reporters do" (Library of Congress n.d.).

In her later years, Craig enthusiastically covered the rise and career of Maine's Margaret Chase Smith. Craig was always noted for her personal charm and attractiveness, as well as what one fellow correspondent called her "mind as sharp as cider vinegar and as retentive as a lobster trap" (Marzolf 1977, 59). She died in 1975.

—*Pamela Tyler*

See also Roosevelt, Eleanor

References and Further Reading

Beasley, Maureen. 1987. *Eleanor Roosevelt and the Media: A Public Quest for Self Fulfillment.* Urbana: University of Illinois Press.

Library of Congress. n.d. "May Craig," Women Come to the Front: Journalists, Photographers, and Broadcasters During World War II, http://www.loc.gov/exhibits/wcf/wcf0014.html (accessed May 3, 2005).

Marzolf, Marion. 1977. *Up from the Footnote: A History of Women Journalists.* New York: Hastings House.

Ross, Ishbel. 1936. *Ladies of the Press.* New York: Harper and Bros.

Crusades, Women and the

Camp followers, combatants, vivandières, leaders, and tenders of home property during the Crusades. The crusades—medieval European attempts to conquer and control Jerusalem and its surrounding territory—were the largest and longest military endeavor of the Middle Ages. Between 1096 and 1400, well over a million European men, women, and children "took the cross," vowing to reach Jerusalem or die in the attempt. Besides the Holy Land crusades, there were holy wars against Muslim rulers of Spain, non-Christian Slavs, heretics in southern France, and, increasingly, the enemies of the papacy. Although women only bore weapons in the direst emergencies, they still played interesting roles in these conflicts because of the nature of crusading itself.

In the Middle Ages, the only women who normally accompanied troops were camp followers, but a crusade was a holy war and the reward for participation was remission of all penalties for sin. At a more mundane level, a Holy Land crusade could last for years, a long time for families to be separated. Thus, when the First Crusade was preached in November 1095, wives, daughters, and even nuns joined the cause. Pope Urban II tried to dissuade women from going without the permission of their legal guardians but recognized their right to participate. Because the crusade was a holy endeavor, attempts were made, especially on the First Crusade (1096–1099), to drive the prostitutes from camp and even to prevent sexual encounters between married couples. Still, the women played a useful role dealing with supplies, nursing the sick and injured—and of course providing sex.

The largest role played by a crusading woman was that of Eleanor of Aquitaine, queen of France and participant with her husband Louis VII in the Second Crusade (1147–1148). Eleanor went as spokesperson for the contingent of soldiers from her province of Aquitaine, who otherwise would not have been represented in military councils. Her command position was considered so outrageous that imaginative chroniclers later decided that she and her female attendants must have dressed up as Amazons and that Eleanor must have behaved scandalously with her uncle the prince of Antioch. The truth of the matter seems to be that Eleanor disagreed with Louis on the conduct of the war (which was a miserable failure), and he exerted his husbandly rights by placing her under restraint. Arabic reports of the Third Crusade (1189–1192) also tell of female Europeans taking part in battles. These tales should not be taken at face value; the Arabic authors were eager to show how barbarous the westerners were, and to Muslims as to medieval Europeans, warrior women were the height of barbarity. The only certain cases of women participating in crusading battles are when they were in besieged cities or castles; the Albigensian crusade commander Simon de Montfort was killed by a stone shot by a woman during a siege. As always in premodern war the women of the losing side could expect rape or worse; one crusade chronicler commends the good Christian soldiers for not raping Muslim women but only killing them.

Because of the length of an average crusade, the role of women left behind was particularly important. Women controlled estates in their husbands' absence and acted diplomatically for their distant spouses. Queen Blanche of Castile even served as regent of France while her son Louis IX was off on the first of his two crusades and had to raise his ransom when he was captured.

—*Phyllis G. Jestice*

See also Blanche of Castile; Eleanor of Aquitaine

References and Further Reading

Fulcher of Chartres. 1969. *A History of the Expedition to Jerusalem, 1095–1127.* Translated by Frances Ryan. Knoxville: University of Tennessee Press.

Nicholson, Helen. 1997. "Women on the Third Crusade." *Journal of Medieval History* 23: 335–349.

Owen, D. D. R. 1993. *Eleanor of Aquitaine: Queen and Legend.* Oxford, England: Blackwell.

Cuban Revolution, Women in the

Part played by women in the Cuban Revolution. The role and position of women in Cuba has changed drastically for the better as a direct result of their participation in the Revolution in 1959. Earlier suffragist and feminist activity prepared women to organize and provide crucial support for the rebel forces throughout nearly a decade of insurrection. When Fidel Castro and Che Guevara returned from exile in what would be the beginning of their charge to victory, a surprising number of women joined the guerrilla troops in the Sierra Maestra. The persuasive powers of a few key women convinced Castro and Guevara that women could serve the revolution by bearing arms in addition to attending to the more domestic tasks of war. Although the ideological platform of the revolution already included the goal of eliminating racial, economic, and gender discrimination, the heroic efforts of the Mariana Grajales Brigade and women involved in espionage and grassroots organizing underscored the legitimacy of gender equality. During and since the revolution, fighting women such as Celia Sánchez and Haydée Santamaría have been all but canonized, and Cuba's leading actresses have positively portrayed guerrilla fighters in films such as *Manuela.* To the present, women have continued to serve in the police and the military both at home and in revolutionary efforts abroad, especially in Central America and Africa. Nevertheless, despite their historical and ongoing contributions to the success of the revolution, no women have been promoted to the highest government or military positions.

Over the course of history, Cuban women have faced the rigidly dividing and codifying gender and sex roles in Hispanic society. In the years between independence (1898) and the revolution, feminist groups and activists made many strides in the battle for equality, but for the most part, woman's place was still assumed to be in the home. The most accepted symbol for a strong woman was still that of the self-sacrificing mother, like the historical icon Mariana Grajales, who heroically surrendered her sons to die fighting for Cuban independence (Smith and Padula 1996, 11). The Club Femenino, founded in 1917, organized Cuba's first National Women's Congress in 1923, where women with higher socioeconomic status debated a wide range of topics including employment, sexuality, and the vote. In the late twenties and early thirties, women attended the university in Havana, became involved in labor unions, and joined the Communist Party. In the 1940s, Fulgencio Batista sponsored a new constitution that instituted some political changes favorable to women. Feminist initiatives seemed to have reached a plateau by the early fifties, however, and Batista's 1952 military coup brought a more conservative agenda, the tightening of controls, and a ubiquitous military presence.

Women Cuban rebel soldiers wave on arrival in Havana, Cuba, 1959. (Lester Cole/Corbis)

When Fidel Castro began to challenge Batista's administration, women from the middle and upper classes utilized their skills in organizing, writing, and networking to support his efforts. They were joined by women from all stations, who, according to Margaret Randall, made the difference in Fidel Castro's revolutionary drive. She asserts that thousands were "selling war bonds and producing rebel uniforms, taking part in propaganda work, participating in action and sabotage units in the cities, transporting arms, and fighting in the mountains" (Randall 1981, 22). Female support for Fidel Castro's July 26 Movement was originally culled from the Women's Martí Civic Front, headed by feminist activist Carmen Castro Porta. The Revolutionary Women's Union (UFR), organized in 1959 by communist activists Elena Gil, Clementina Serra, and Rosario Fernández, began an extensive campaign of door-to-door recruitment and fundraising (Smith and Padula 1996, 34).

According to Che Guevara, women would constitute a necessary part of the revolutionary corps. He writes that women are capable of doing virtually every task that a man can do, including bearing arms and firing upon the enemy if need be, and that due to perceptions of female fragility, women could serve especially well in espionage and transmission of messages, supplies, and even arms. Nonetheless, the Argentine guerrilla ends his famous essay extolling the particularly "feminine" virtues that will also benefit the revolution, including women's ability to sew, cook palatable meals, and compassionately care for the wounded or despairing soldier (Guevara 1972, 131–33). In this way the Cuban women were thrust into a double duty role that resembles the contradictory and difficult expectations of women in any modern and developed nation.

As point of fact, it was Celia Sánchez and Melba Hernández who ultimately changed Fidel Castro's opinion about allowing women into the offensive ranks of the guerrillas, and later the national military (Smith and Padula 1996, 24). Sánchez and Hernández took part in Fidel's abortive attack on the Moncada Barracks in 1953. They kept the home fires burning during their leader's exile and then, along with numerous other women, rejoined him in the mountains on his return. Hernández formed the Mariana Grajales Brigade, the first all-women platoon, who found themselves the subjects of great adulation after the triumph of the revolution. As Guevara had envisioned, women worked and fought alongside their male comrades, guaranteeing their place in the evolving hierarchy of the revolution.

Fighting as guerrillas, women had proved their efficacy in battle, a sure influence on Cuba's current armed forces, which contains thousands of women at varying levels of command. Although women do not participate in the draft, both voluntary service and enlistment into any branch of the service are options. Women have been key in numerous campaigns, both on the island and in foreign operations in Angola, Ethiopia, and Nicaragua. Not surprisingly, the principal women who have maintained political power over the last five decades were also key players in the insurrection (Randall 1981, 22).

On a less optimistic note, studies instigated by the Federation of Cuban Women (FMC) suggest that decades after the Cuban Revolution, the original objectives in terms of gender equality have not yet been realized. The suicides of revolutionary heroines Celia Sánchez and Haydée Santamaría were a blow to the image of women's progress on the island, as are statistics on women's involvement at the highest levels of policy making and government.

—Sara E. Cooper

See also Grajales Coelho, Mariana; Hernández Rodríguez del Rey, Melba; Latin America, Women in Guerrilla Movements in; Sánchez Manduley, Celia; Santamaría Cuadrado, Haydée

References and Further Reading

Cortázar, Octavio, et al., director. 1975. *Con las mujeres cubanas.* Havana: ICAIC.

Guevara, Ernesto (Che). 1972. "El papel de la mujer." In *Ernesto Che Guevara: Escritos y discursos,* edited by Juan J. Soto and Pedro Alvarez Tabío, 131–133. Havana: Instituto Cubano del Libro.

Maloof, Judy, ed. and trans. 1999. *Voices of Resistance: Testimonies of Cuban and Chilean Women.* Lexington: University of Kentucky Press.

Randall, Margaret. 1981. *Women in Cuba—Twenty Years Later.* New York: Smyrna.

Solás, Humberto, director. 1968. *Lucía.* Havana: ICAIC.

———, director. 1962. *Manuela.* Havana: ICAIC.

Smith, Lois M., and Alfred Padula. 1996. *Sex and Revolution: Women in Socialist Cuba.* New York: Oxford University Press.

Stone, Elizabeth, ed. 1981. *Women and the Cuban Revolution.* New York: Pathfinder.

Tetreault, Mary Ann, ed. 1994. *Women and Revolution in Africa, Asia, and the New World.* Columbia: University of South Carolina Press.

Curie, Maria Sklodowska (Madame Curie) (1867–1934), and the Little Curies

Contribution of Madame Curie to the care of France's war-wounded during World War I. Best known for her early-twentieth-century discovery of radium and its radioactive properties, Madame Maria Curie used her knowledge to help the French in World War I with the invention of portable X-ray machines, or Little Curies.

Born Manya Sklodowska in Warsaw, Poland, Curie broke boundaries in both science and gender when in 1903 she became the first woman to receive a Nobel Prize. Although the prize was given to her in conjunction with her husband, Pierre Curie, and A. Henri Becquerel, Madame Curie was not one to ride the coattails of others.

A dedicated and creative chemist, she won her own Nobel Prize in 1911 for the discovery of radium. Curie's second award made her the first person, man or woman, to win two Nobel Prizes. Coincidentally, it was her work leading up to the discovery of radium and its practical uses, rather than her many honors, that had the biggest impact on the people of France and the history of World War I.

During the course of her research on radium and radiation in France, Curie became familiar with the work of the German physicist Wilhelm Roentgen. In 1895, Roentgen discovered a new form of radiation that created transparent images on photographic paper, or X-rays. Curie believed that X-rays held numerous possibilities for modern medicine, but more specifically, she saw their value in terms of wartime medicine.

Curie felt that X-ray technology could aid military doctors in locating bullets and shrapnel hidden in the bodies of wounded soldiers. Yet because of the relative infancy of X-ray technology in 1914, most of the available X-ray machines were still located in research laboratories rather than hospitals. Curie used her influence and power of persuasion with the scientific community to arrange for all of the available X-ray machines in French laboratories to be moved to various hospitals. By the end of the war, she had helped set up 200 permanent X-ray stations throughout France. Curie was still concerned with the well-being of the soldiers being treated on the front lines. She knew that it was not always possible to transport wounded men to a hospital before operating, so she sought to provide the field surgeons with a more feasible alternative.

In response to the particular nature of wartime medicine, Curie developed the first transportable X-ray machine. The Petite Curies (Little Curies) were ordinary cars that had been outfitted with X-ray equipment and a generator. The car's engine was used to power the generator, which in turn powered the X-ray machine. In fact, the cars and the technology behind them were so unique that at first the French army refused to take Curie seriously. It was not until military doctors on the front lines realized the lifesaving potential of Curie's invention that military leaders agreed to use the device.

Curie through her elite connections raised enough money to purchase and equip a small fleet of twenty cars. Because of the lack of trained radiographers, Curie and her teenage daughter, Irene, accompanied the trucks to the front lines. She and Irene ran machines themselves until they were able to properly train members of the military medical corps to take over the controls. By 1916, Curie was training women to work as radiological assistants to further aid doctors in the treatment of the wounded. It is impossible to tell exactly how many lives were saved by Madame Curie's efforts, but it is safe to assume that thousands of soldiers benefited from X-rays and the Little Curies.

—*Catherine D. Griffis*

See also Inglis, Elsie, and the Scottish Women's Hospitals; T'Serclaes, Baroness Elizabeth de

References and Further Reading

Curie, Eva. 2001. *Madame Curie: A Biography.* Translated from French by Vincent Sheean, edited by Da Capo Press. New York: Doubleday and Company.

Goldsmith, Barbara. 2004. *Obsessive Genius: The Inner World of Marie Curie.* New York: W. W. Norton.

Curtis, Cathrine (1918–1955)

American isolationist who fused feminism with conservatism. Cathrine Curtis was distinguished by energy, charisma, combativeness, and a talent for organization. She was a prominent figure in the mothers' movement, a right-wing women's coalition that sought to keep the United States out of World War II, and a leader of two of its principal organizations, the National Legion of Mothers of America and the Women's National Committee to Keep the U.S. Out of War.

Born to rich parents in Albany, New York, Curtis profited as a stock speculator during her teenage years. Later, she owned a citrus farm in Arizona and acted in Hollywood movies. In 1934, a New York City radio station began to air her program, which advocated women's financial independence and legal equality. After her program was canceled because of her strident criticism of the New Deal, she founded a nonprofit organization, the Women Investors Research Institute, which combined anti–New Deal economic conservatism with women's rights. By 1939, the institute numbered 300,000 women members. Curtis became a well-known foe of the Roosevelt administration on many issues. Increasingly, her pronouncements encouraged anti-Semitism and notions of vast global conspiracies involving Jews, Communists, and European nations.

Convinced that Roosevelt was leading the nation into war, she founded the Women's National Committee to Keep the U.S. Out of War in September 1939. One of the committee's most visible charter members, aviator Laura Ingalls, made promotional flights and speeches on behalf of isolationism and dropped peace pamphlets written by Curtis over the White House. Ingalls would later be convicted of acting as a Nazi agent.

Curtis cultivated allies in the Senate and House of Representatives, who invited her to address congressional committees with her views on U.S. neutrality. Although childless, she prominently employed maternal arguments in her case against war. Curtis also held that when a nation is at war, the interests of women, including concern for their children, are inevitably sacrificed to the needs of the state. She asserted that Great Britain planned to reincorporate the United States into its empire under cover of World War II. Germany, she claimed, posed no threat. In April 1941, Curtis wrote and circulated an antiwar Mothers' Day petition, which stated that war resulted from the exclusion of women in political decision making. She was usually able to attract tens of thousands of signatures from a large constituency of American women.

After Pearl Harbor the Women's National Committee to Keep the U.S. Out of War disbanded. Still, Curtis continued to denounce administration policies. Her Women Investors Institute focused on combating restrictions on the domestic economy, such as rationing and price controls. In the postwar era, Curtis attempted to remain an outspoken public figure, attacking the United Nations, the Truman Doctrine, the Marshall Plan, and the civil rights movement. Her influence declined rapidly, however, and her views appeared increasingly out of step with the times.

—*Glen Jeansonne and David Luhrssen*

See also Dilling, Elizabeth; National Legion of Mothers of America

References and Further Reading

Jeansonne, Glen. 1996. *Women of the Far Right.* Chicago: University of Chicago.

Cushman, Pauline (1833–1893)

Union spy during the American Civil War. Famous for both her antebellum acting career and her role as a spy for the United States during the American Civil War, Pauline Cushman was born in New Orleans in 1833 but spent most of her childhood in Michigan. As a spy for the Union, Cushman employed her talents for both verbal and physical disguises.

Pauline Cushman, Union Spy

"Shelbyville, June 18th.

". . . Forrest's forces on Friday last went in pursuit of a woman to whom suspicion had been attached. She had reached the Yankee pickets in front of Franklin when they came in sight, but on they dashed, driving in the Yankees and capturing their 'booty.' She proved to be a Miss Cushman, a theatre actress, claiming relationship with the celebrated Charlotte, and had upon her person plans and drawings of our fortifications, and the disposition made of the latter. It is said that she was a crinoline scout for McClellan in Virginia, and performed valuable services. Her fine talents are, doubtless, occupied at present time in planning an escape from Columbia, where she is under guard. . . ."

—*Savannah Republican,* June 22, 1863, p. 2.
http://www.uttyl.edu/vbetts/women_soldiers.htm
(accessed January 22, 2006).

"It is stated that Major Pauline Cushman called on President Lincoln a few days ago, in proper female attire, and preferred her claim for five months of back pay which had been refused her in the West after being wounded and her sex discovered. The President wrote a note to the Paymaster-General, saying that as she had received her pay the greater part of the time, he could see no reason why she was not entitled to the remainder, and therefore directed the payment of the balance."

—*Nashville Dispatch,* September 29, 1864, p. 1.
http://www.uttyl.edu/vbetts/women_soldiers.htm
(accessed January 22, 2006).

Cushman's espionage career began in Louisville, Kentucky, in 1863. During a performance at Wood's Theater, a group of Confederate officers dared Cushman to offer a toast in Jefferson Davis's honor. Cushman took this challenge and an unusual idea to the city's Union provost marshal, Colonel Moore, suggesting that she offer the proposed toast and convince Confederates in Louisville that she supported their cause. Doing so, Cushman continued, would allow her to carry out activities on behalf of the Union without discovery. The provost marshal agreed, providing Cushman would take an oath of loyalty to the United States. She took the oath. At her performance the next evening, Cushman offered praise of Davis and the Confederacy to her shocked audience. The Northern theater company expelled her and sent her to Nashville. Once in occupied Nashville, Cushman reported to the Union's chief of army police to get her instructions.

In Nashville Cushman cultivated her reputation as an ardent secessionist and Confederate. This image allowed her inside access to valuable details about Confederate fortifications and operations. As part of her intelligence operations, Cushman also made lists of people who harbored what she considered dangerous anti-Union sentiments. She passed this list, as well as the names of local Confederate spies, on to Union officials. In addition, she served as a federal courier, moving information through Kentucky, Tennessee, Georgia, Alabama, and Mississippi. Cushman successfully passed through enemy lines, using her acting skills, disguises, and the enemy's assumption that she supported the Confederacy. The Union army valued Cushman's assistance and awarded her an honorary military commission.

Pauline Cushman. (National Archives)

Cushman's activities on behalf of the Union did not go unnoticed. Late in the spring of 1863, Confederate General John Hunt Morgan arrested Cushman on suspicion of espionage. After questioning Cushman, General Nathan Bedford Forrest gave her a death sentence. The hanging was not carried out, perhaps because it was interrupted by the sudden arrival of Union troops. The publicity surrounding Cushman's arrest by Morgan, however, brought her espionage activities to a halt.

After the Civil War Cushman went on a speaking tour. In addition, a biography celebrating Cushman's role on behalf of the United States was published in 1865. Pauline Cushman died on December 2, 1893, from an overdose of morphine. Local Civil War veterans gave her a full military burial.

—*Lisa Tendrich Frank*

See also Baker, E. H.; Civil War, American, and Women

References and Further Reading

Leonard, Elizabeth D. 1999. *All the Daring of the Soldier: Women of the Civil War Armies.* New York: W. W. Norton.

Sarmiento, F. L. 1865. *Life of Pauline Cushman.* Philadelphia: John E. Potter.

D

Dahomey, Women Warriors

Female warriors of the Kingdom of Dahomey in West Africa. Enemies of Dahomey described its women warriors as frenzied cannibals, Europeans called them Amazons, and the people of Dahomey knew them as *ahosi,* or wives of the king, or *mino,* "our mothers." Initially these women of the palace served as the king's guard. They fought for the kingdom as early as the beginning of the eighteenth century and, under the rule of Gezo (1818–1858), they became full-fledged warriors. By the mid-nineteenth century, their numbers averaged from 4,000 to 5,000, although some estimates went higher (Law 1993, 251). Gezo's reign was characterized by constant warfare and slave trading, and his fear of a coup d'etat made him rely on women as his personal and political protectors.

The women warriors of Dahomey were exalted in Fon (Dahomey's dominant ethnic group) society. Fon society allowed for this development because, although it was certainly male dominated, there were some arenas that allowed women a surprising amount of power. In all aspects of the national government and military, there were parallel positions for men and women, such as the king to the queen mother.

Both Fon and non-Fon women served in the military. In Dahomey, fathers brought their daughters to the palace, and only the tallest and strongest were selected. The bulk of the ranks entered Dahomey's military either as slaves or prisoners of war. These women were not ethnically Fon, but their status as foreigners in the palace and lack of kin in the area facilitated their complete allegiance to the king, making them well-suited for their positions. All the Amazons lived in the king's palace where men could not reside.

Visitors to the kingdom, especially Victorian Europeans, found the arrangement of the palace and the status of its female guards fascinating, and they recorded their impressions of the king and the women of the palace. Europeans were intrigued by the celibacy that most of these women practiced. As *ahosi,* they were permitted to have sex with no one but the king (although very few actually did), and adultery carried the death penalty. The threat of capital punishment did not deter all lovers, and when discovered, both the woman and her paramour would be executed. Contrary to popular mythology, there is evidence of neither clitoredectomy nor cannibalism, and reports of widespread lesbianism were created by the imaginations of European visitors to the kingdom. The women were supposed to

An engraving entitled Armed Women with the King at Their Head *by Francis Chesham (1749–1806). Published in* The History of Dahomey *by Archibald Dalzel in 1793. (Historical Picture Archive/Corbis)*

channel the energy of their libidos into energy on the battlefield.

By all accounts, the female warriors were fierce no matter who the adversary or with what they fought. Firearms replaced less efficient bows and poisoned arrows. The women were usually outfitted with muskets that they fired from their shoulders. They also carried rope to tie up prisoners, along with gunpowder, cartridges, and short swords. Some carried razors from 18 inches to 3 feet in length that snapped into covers; they used these to take body parts as trophies.

The Amazons fought to subdue the enemy, to take prisoners, and to protect the king. Initially, the king was surrounded by his royal female guard in the front and at the center of the army, and the women and king were buttressed by male soldiers. After King Agaja was injured, however, the kings continued to go on campaigns, but they stayed to the rear of the action, still surrounded by Amazons. These women were the elite of the elite. Other women warriors and their male counterparts wended their way silently through forests and high grasses to participate in the surprise attacks favored by Dahomey. Women warriors did not fight in units with men but had their own corresponding units and fought in the same battles; women's units were commanded by women.

The dress of the Amazons did not easily distinguish them as women. Even in the palace and on military parade, they wore sleeveless, kilt-length tunics and shorts. In the palace, their uniforms were blue and white striped, and on campaign they wore brown. Each unit sported its own hairstyle. Contrary to popular belief, they left both breasts intact.

The women underwent intense physical training accompanied by education in their traditions, use of weapons, gymnastics, and all they needed to know to be outstanding warriors. Because of their training and positions in Dahomey, the *ahosi* had a much greater degree of autonomy than other women in the kingdom. The Amazons disdained "women's work." They spent some of their leisure time drinking alcohol, dancing, and singing songs proclaiming that the men would stay in Dahomey planting crops while they would defeat and eviscerate their prisoners.

In 1851, Dahomey attacked the town of Abekuta after many counselors, including women of the palace, had advised the king against it. It ended in a crushing defeat for Dahomey, and nearly 2,000 women warriors, half their original number, perished. Years of warfare had weakened the kingdom and as French troops encroached, the Dahomey fought them off to the best of its ability. Considering the outdated weapons with which they fought, Dahomian forces inflicted considerable casualties but were unable to save the kingdom.

In fighting both Africans and Europeans, the Amazons raised the hackles of their adversaries because they were women. Legend says that when the men of Abekuta discovered that they fought women and that some of their ranks had been killed by the women warriors, their shame drove them to fight twice as hard to defeat the invaders. The French recounted stories that the Amazons drank themselves into drunken frenzies before battles. Some European men said that these women were hideously ugly, and others reported that they were beautiful. Commander Terrillon called them harpies, while many of his men greatly enjoyed watching defeated Amazons bathe in a nearby pond, insisting that they were some of the loveliest women in the world (Markouis 1974, 253; Mercer 1964, 177).

The arrival of the French ended the once-strong kingdom of Dahomey, and the corps of women warriors disbanded. Some would marry (although some suffered from low fertility rates); many others refused to wed, declaring no desire to ever be subordinate to men. These women—who gained such respect, who were feared and revered—could not reconcile themselves to returning to a life in which, for reasons of gender, status, origin, or all of these, they could never again be part of society's elite.

—*Jacqueline Woodfork*

See also Amazons

References and Further Reading

Alpern, Stanley B. 1998. *Amazons of Black Sparta: The Women Warriors of Dahomey.* New York: New York University.

Bay, Edna G. 1998. *Wives of the Leopard: Gender, Politics, and Culture in the Kingdom of Dahomey.* Charlottesville: University of Virginia.

Law, Robin. 1993. "The 'Amazons' of Dahomey." *Paideuma* 39 (1993): 245–260.

Markouis, Thomas Constantine. 1974. Warfare and society in the Kingdom of Dahomey: 1818–1894. Ph.D. diss., Boston University.

Mercer, Charles. 1964. *The Foreign Legion: The Vivid History of a Military Tradition.* London: Arthur Barker.

Dalrymple, Mildred Inks Davidson (1920–)

Pilot Mildred "Millie" Inks was born in Austin, Texas, and grew up on a ranch in Llano. When she was a child, her grandfather rented a plane and took her and four other grandchildren for a flight over his ranch. Eventually four grandchildren became pilots. Later she flew with her first husband, Bill Davidson, after he received his pilot's license. She studied at Texas State College for Women in Denton and earned a degree in journalism at the University of Texas, Austin.

While her husband was serving with the Air Corps in World War II, Millie worked as a secretary for the adjutant general's office in Austin. After Davidson was shot down over the North Sea, Millie and a co-worker, Kay McBride D'Arezzo, whose husband was missing in action, took flying lessons to qualify for the Women Airforce Service Pilots (WASP) training program. Millie said, "After Bill was killed, I had to do something. I couldn't just stay in the Adjutant General's department typing. I wanted to get this war over with" (Weigand 2002). After she and D'Arezzo had each logged thirty-five hours of piloting, they qualified for WASP training. On November 5, 1943, they entered the program at Avenger Field, Sweetwater, Texas. At the end of a prolonged training flight, Millie and another pilot, who were late, narrowly missed being part of a collision that killed one of her classmates.

On May 23, 1944, Millie was one of the fifty-two trainees to graduate out of the ninety-four who had entered with her. Following graduation, she worked at the Eastern Training Command at Maxwell Field in Montgomery, Alabama, as a utility pilot and an engineering test pilot, whose task was to fly and test planes after they had been repaired. She said that her "commanding officer, Colonel [Robert L.] Thomas, had no bias against women and he desperately needed pilots" (Weigand 2002). In addition to testing repaired aircraft, she flew officers from Montgomery to assignments all over the eastern United States and ferried planes, including B-17 bombers, from Montgomery to other fields. In all she logged 900 hours in the cockpit.

After the WASP program was deactivated on December 20, 1944, she married Edwin Dalrymple, a colonel. He later became an FBI agent, and they lived in various parts of the country. In addition to raising their three children, Millie Dalrymple worked at an ad agency and an insurance company, served in the Texas state legislature, and was a teacher. In her spare time she played competitive tennis and did volunteer work.

—Bernard Cook

See also United States, Military Service of Women in World War II; United States, Women Airforce Service Pilots; United States, Women's Auxiliary Ferrying Squadron; United States, Women's Flying Training Detachment

References and Further Reading

"Dalrymple, Mildred Davidson," WASP Oral History Project. Oral History Interview, March 1, 1996. Interviewed by Dawn Letson, the Woman's Collection, Texas Woman's University, Denton, Texas.

"Mildred Dalrymple—See and Hear," WASP Site. http://wasp-wwii.org/wasp/seenhear.htm (accessed February 10, 2006).

Van Ryzin, Jeanne Claire. 2003. "For Millie Dalrymple and Other Women, Answering World War II's Call to Arms Led to the Cockpit." *Austin American-Statesman* (Texas), January 11, 2003: E1.

Weigand, Cindy. 2002. "Yankee Doodle Gals of World War II," *Texas Co-op Power,* June 2002 issue. http://www.texas-ec.org/publications/texascooppower/archive/602wasp.aspx (accessed February 10, 2006).

Damerment, Madeleine (1917–1944)

Participant in the French Resistance and a member of the British secret service in World War II. Madeleine Zoe Damerment was born in Lille, France, on November 11, 1917. Her family joined the Resistance after the Germans defeated France in 1940. Damerment worked as an assistant to Michael Trotobas with the PAT escape line, a group set up by Albert Guerisse, a Belgian army doctor, to help downed Allied airmen escape to England. Andrée Borel and Nancy Wake were also members of this group. When a traitor divulged particulars about the group in 1942, Damerment was forced to make her way to Spain. There she was temporarily detained at a camp near Bilbao. After her release, she reached England where Damerment volunteered to work for the British Special Operations Executive (SOE). After training, she and two other agents were parachuted into France near Chartres on February 28, 1944. Damerment, described as unassuming and "brave and gentle" (Women of the SOE n.d.), was to join the Bricklayer network as a courier. The agents' plans had been betrayed to the Germans, however, who were awaiting their arrival. Arrested as she landed, Damerment was taken to Gestapo headquarters in Paris and interrogated and tortured.

On May 12, Damerment was transferred with seven other captured female agents to the Karlsruhe civil prison. On September 10, 1944, on the direct order of Ernest Kaltenbrunner, the head of the SS Security Office, she was transferred with Yolande Beekman, Noor Inayat Khan, and Eliane Plewman to Dachau. There, on September 11, 1944, the day after their arrival, they were shot.

Damerment was posthumously awarded the Legion of Honor, the Croix de Guerre, and the Médaille combatant de la Résistance. Her name is inscribed on the SOE Runnymede Memorial and on the Valençay SOE Memorial in France.

—*Bernard Cook*

See also Atkins, Vera H.; Beekman, Yolande; Borrel, Andrée; Khan, Noor Inayat, Plewman, Eliane; Wake, Nancy

References and Further Reading

"Madeleine Damerment," Spartacus Web, http://www.spartacus.schoolnet.co.uk/SOEdamerment.htm (accessed September 29, 2004).

Foot, M. R. D. 1984 [1966]. *SOE in France: An Account of the Work of the British Special Operations Executive 1940–1944*. Frederick, MD: University Publications of America.

"The FANY Agents—Madeleine Damerment," The Women of the Special Operations Executive, http://www.64-baker-street.org/agents/agent_fany_madeline_damerment.html (accessed September 29, 2004).

D'Aquino, Iva Ikuko Toguri

See "Tokyo Rose"

Darragh, Lydia (1729–1789)

American Revolutionary patriot. In the winter of 1777, the British army commanded by Lord William Howe occupied Philadelphia after fighting General George Washington's smaller force. Howe settled his headquarters into a Second Street townhouse and became the neighbor to William and Lydia Darragh, members of the Society of Friends. Lydia Barrington Darragh was born in Dublin, Ireland, in 1729 and married William Darragh, a teacher. In 1765, the couple immigrated to Philadelphia. A year after her arrival, Darragh advertised her services making grave clothes and other burial needs. In addition to caring for her large family, she built a career as a midwife, nurse, and mortician.

When the British occupied Philadelphia, the Darraghs decided to remain in the city and sent two of their children to the country. A son, Charles, was stationed with the Continental Army at Whitemarsh, a camp about eight miles away. Life in Philadelphia meant accommodating the British officers who commandeered a room in the house for staff meetings. On December 2, an officer informed Lydia Darragh of an eight o'clock meeting at her house and demanded that her family be asleep by that time. Surprised by this request, she agreed, and the family went to their rooms. Fired with curiosity, Lydia slid into a closet and listened through the thin wall. The officers planned to dispatch a large force for Whitemarsh in two days. Understanding that surprise attack meant the Americans' destruction, Darragh resolved to warn General Washington. Without telling her family of her purpose, she arose early the next day and applied for permission to leave the city and buy flour.

Dropping her sack at the mill, Darragh started toward the Rising Sun Tavern located north of the city. She met a passing horseman who happened to be a friend and an American officer, Lieutenant Colonel Thomas Craig. Darragh walked with Craig as she explained Howe's plan and exacted a promise of secrecy. Craig escorted Darragh to a house for food and rest before he rushed to camp with the vital intelligence. Darragh returned to the mill, picked up her flour, and walked home.

The British army marched out as intended only to meet with fully prepared soldiers. Repulsed by Washington, Howe's contingent returned to Philadelphia and Washington moved to Valley Forge. Because it was clear that their plans had been betrayed, British officers closely questioned Darragh about the meeting at her house. She replied confidently that her family was in bed and unaware of these plans.

Lydia's story survived through family history and was first published in 1827. A different account emerged when the private diary of Elias Boudinot, Washington's chief intelligence officer, appeared. According to Boudinot, a little old lady approached him with a pocketbook at the Rising Sun Tavern. Boudinot searched the pocketbook and found a rolled slip of paper with Howe's plans. It is thought that Lydia Darragh may have wanted to make sure that her information would be taken into account and made sure that it got to Boudinot. Overall, with little contemporary documentation, the popular tale remains contested by historians.

—*Lisa Porter*

See also American Revolution, Role of Women in the

References and Further Reading

Claghorn, Charles. 1991. *Women Patriots of the American Revolution: A Biographical Dictionary.* Metuchen, NJ, and London: Scarecrow.

Somerville, Mollie. 1974. *Women and the American Revolution.* n.p.: Daughters of the American Revolution.

Dawidson (Draenger), Justina (1917–1943)

Anti-Nazi underground activist. Justina (Gusta) Dawidson Draenger was born in Krakow, Poland. From her teens, she was attracted to Zionism and became a leading member of the Akiba movement established in 1901 for the defense of the Jewish people. She married Shimon Draenger, a leader of Akiba and editor of a Zionist weekly. Justina and Shimon were determined to respond to the brutality of Nazis.

In 1940, the Akiba leaders, including Shimon Draenger and Aaron Libeskind, considered armed resistance to defend the Jewish community, and they amalgamated different splinter groups of the Jewish anti-Nazi movement into the Jewish Warring Organization of Pioneer Youth (JWOPY). Justina arranged fake IDs, and Akiba was able to arrange for some Jews to escape from German-controlled Poland. On December 22, 1942, in a major operation, Akiba launched a grenade attack on coffee shops where German officers frequented. The Nazi officers were killed, and military trucks were destroyed. The operatives were betrayed by collaborators, however. Shimon was arrested on January 8, 1943. Justina surrendered to the Gestapo to suffer the fate of her husband and was sent to Montelupich prison. An ordeal of inhuman treatment, beating, and torture began. Some of the leaders of Akiba were executed in the Plaszow camp, and others were sent to Auschwitz. Between February and April of 1943, Justina wrote her diary titled, *Yomana shel Justina* (*Justina's Diary*), a saga of the bravery of Jewish resistance fighters. Her memoirs were written amid intense mental and physical brutality on toilet papers and hidden in the doorpost of her cell. The couple managed to escape from the prison on April 29, 1943. They resumed resistance activities, carrying out hit-and-run tactics on German targets from a bunker in Wisnicz Forest near Bochnia. Justina and her husband even went to Warsaw with forged papers to buy a typewriter. Wide contacts were established to distribute their journal, *The Warrior Pioneer,* which attempted to lift the spirit of the

Jewish people. The last issue was printed on October 1, 1943.

Because of German pursuit of the resisters in Wisnicz Forest, Justina and Shimon went to Krakow towards the end of October 1943. While attempting to escape to Hungary in November 1943, the Germans caught and executed the couple. The heroic deeds of Justina and other members of the Jewish resistance in Nazi-occupied Poland were a testimony to Jewish armed resistance against Nazi repression.

—Patit Paban Mishra

See also Holocaust and Jewish Women

References and Further Reading

Dawidson, Justina. 1996. *Justyna's Narrative.* Amherst: University of Massachusetts Press.

Latour, Anny. 1981. *The Jewish Resistance in France, 1940–1944.* New York: Schocken.

De Jongh, Andrée (Dédée) (1916–)

Belgian Resistance leader during World War II. Andrée (Dédée) de Jongh was born in Schaerbeek, Belgium in 1916. She dropped out of high school because of her distaste for mathematics, but later trained as a nurse. Dédée was working as a commercial artist in Malmédy when Belgium was invaded in May 1940. Inspired by the activity of Edith Clavell during World War I, de Jongh volunteered to serve as a nurse for wounded soldiers. After the surrender of Belgium on May 28 she moved to Brussels. With her father, Frederic de Jongh, a headmaster, and her older sister, Micheline (Michou), she organized the so-called Comet Line to shuttle British soldiers who had evaded capture at Dunkirk and downed Allied airmen through France to Spain and back to England. She set up safe houses and provided the men with civilian clothes and false identity cards. Dédée and her father were anticlerical and liberal, but they were able to recruit a broad spectrum of devoted helpers, including Elvire de Greef (Tante Go), who headed the southwest sector of the Comet Line. Assisted by local guides, Dédée (Nadine) personally crossed the Pyrenees 20 times, assisting a total of 118 escapees (Rossiter 1986, 56). She marched the servicemen at night and encouraged them by her endurance. Colonel Claude Dansey of MI6 lauded her "courage, tenacity and powers of personal endurance" (Rossiter 1986, 56). It is estimated that the Comet Line assisted in returning approximately 800 Allied servicemen to Britain.

In June 1943 Frederic de Jongh was arrested at Brussel's Gare du Nord. After interrogation by the Gestapo he was executed. Andrée de Jongh was arrested in January 1944 and sent to the women's concentration camp at Ravensbrück. She survived her imprisonment and subsequently worked at a hospital for lepers in Ethiopia. Andrée, her sister, Micheline, and Elvire de Greef were awarded the George Medal by the British and received the Medal of Freedom from the United States.

—Bernard Cook

See also Clavell, Edith; Petit, Gabrielle; Schaft, Joanna

References and Further Reading

Rossiter, Margaret. 1986. *Women in the Resistance.* New York: Praeger.

Spartacus Web. "Andrée de Jongh." http://www.spartacus.schoolnet.co.uk/FRjonghl.htm (accessed September 30, 2004).

De Pizan, Christine (1364–ca. 1430)

Author of a late medieval military handbook. Christine de Pizan was one of the most important European writers of the late Middle Ages, notable as probably the first woman who lived by the pen. While most famous for her "feminist" works (such as the *Book of the City of Ladies*) in which she made a spirited attack on male misogyny, Christine was also an avid French nationalist during the Hundred Years' War against England (1337–1453). She wrote two important works on medieval warfare, the *Book of Deeds of Arms and of Chivalry* (ca. 1410) and a praise poem about Joan of Arc, written in 1429 when Joan was still alive, in which Christine hails the Maid of Orléans as the savior of France.

Christine's extraordinary life was made possible because her father, a court astrologer to King Charles V of France, gave his daughter a classical education comparable to that of noble boys of her time. Her husband, the scholar Étienne du Castel, further encouraged Christine's erudite tastes. Étienne died around 1390, however, leaving Christine nearly destitute with several children to support. She decided to make a living by writing, soon attracting noble patrons and a large circle of admirers.

In her works Christine displays a deep and insightful knowledge of medieval warfare. This is especially true of the *Livre des faitz d'armes, ci de chevalerie (Book of Deeds of Arms and of Chivalry),* intended as a textbook for noblemen on how to wage war. It was published anonymously, because Christine believed her contemporaries would despise the work if they knew the author was a woman. This book, in the French vernacular of her time, is essentially a compilation of treatises on warfare, relying especially on the classical Roman author Vegetius. Christine was selective, however, organizing her texts into a comprehensive work on warfare and carefully explaining which practices were still in use and which were obsolete. The *Deeds of Arms* offers a level of general moral instruction—war should only be waged to defend the kingdom, not for revenge or because of grudges—but also includes much useful information on the strategy, tactics, and technology of medieval war, clearly based on information received from men with battlefield experience. One of the notable features of the treatise is that Christine provides one of the few contemporary accounts of the use of artillery in war.

The *Deeds of Arms* became popular in Christine's lifetime and continued to be so throughout the fifteenth century. By the mid-1400s it could be found in the libraries of leading French commanders. It was also one of the earliest books to be printed. A French edition appeared in 1488, and in 1489 William Caxton published an English translation made at the request of King Henry VII. Until recently modern military historians have largely ignored the work, but a 1999 translation makes it likely that the book's obscurity has reached an end.

—*Phyllis G. Jestice*

See also Joan of Arc

References and Further Reading

De Pizan, Christine. 1999. *Book of Deeds of Arms and of Chivalry.* Trans. Sumner Willard; edited by Charity Willard. University Park: Pennsylvania State University Press.

Willard, Charity. 1984. *Christine de Pizan: Her Life and Works.* New York: Persea Books.

Deavers, Bridget (b. 1839)

Union soldier in the American Civil War. Born in Ireland about 1839, Bridget Deavers immigrated to the United States about 1849 and fought with the Union army during the Civil War. Known as Michigan Bridget, she rode with the First Michigan Cavalry during 1864 and 1865 but may have joined earlier. Deavers, who also appears in historical records as Irish Biddy, Divers, Devers, or Devens, served in battle as a vivandière, never disguising her gender. Some Victorian-era accounts indicate that she followed her husband into the army, but neither federal nor state records list a man of the same name on the cavalry rosters. As a working-class immigrant, she may have had a common-law spouse, but she has not been positively linked to any male patron. Her independence and status as a female member of the unit make her somewhat unique among women who fought in the Civil War.

Deavers was about twenty-six years old during her wartime service. She was small, weathered, and ruddy. She lived with the men and slept on the ground in the field, assuming all the tasks and hardships of the soldiers. Although she performed many traditional female roles in caring for the troops, she also fought alongside the men and had several horses shot from under her. During battles, she filled the ranks when men fell and acquitted herself well under fire and on campaign. She is mentioned in the contemporary accounts of several women, including Mrs. M. M. Husband, Rebecca Usher, and Mrs. Charlotte McKay. She was often sighted at City Point Hospital in Virginia; both the nurses and military staff there held a high opinion of her capabilities as a battlefield medic.

Described by the people who knew her as fearless, brave, heroic, enthusiastic, and compassionate, her actions on campaign at Five Forks exemplify her dedication to the men of the Michigan Brigade. During battle, the colonel was wounded and a captain killed in action. Deavers assisted the colonel to the rear and accompanied him to City Point Hospital before returning to the front. When she discovered the captain had been left on the field, she rode fifteen miles, identified the body, and tied it to her horse. Traveling several more miles she found a coffin and shipped the remains back to Michigan by rail. Many soldiers had been left without care on the battlefield, so Deavers notified the command of her regiment. She was furnished with ambulances to retrieve the wounded, traveling through Confederate territory with a single orderly to retrieve the men of her unit. Deavers encouraged more nurses to travel to the battlefields, but they were reluctant to defy convention and the general orders that kept them confined to specific areas. In response, Deavers claimed that she could not be stopped as she had General Sheridan's support in her efforts.

Bridget Deavers followed her cavalry unit out west to fight Indians at the end of the Civil War. She disappeared in 1865, although numerous accounts verify that she accompanied the unit to Texas. There is no record of her death.

—Dawn Ottevaere

See also Civil War, American, Women Combatants during the

References and Further Reading

Brocket, L. P., and Mary C. Vaughn. [1867] 1993. *Women at War.* Facsimile of the first edition. Stamford, CT: Longmeadow.

Hall, Richard. 1993. *Patriots in Disguise: Women Warriors of the Civil War.* New York: Paragon House.

Massey, Mary Elizabeth. 1994. *Women in the Civil War.* 1966. Reprinted with Introduction by Jean V. Berlin. Lincoln: University of Nebraska Press.

Middleton, Lee. 1993. *Hearts of Fire: Soldier Women of the Civil War.* Franklin, NC: Genealogy Publishing Service.

Moore, Frank. 1867. *Women of the War: Their Heroism and Sacrifice.* Hartford, CT: S. S. Scranton.

Delano, Jane Arminda (1862–1919)

Superintendent of the Army Nurse Corps (ANC), 1909–1912, and founding chair of the American Red Cross (ARC) Nursing Service. Jane Arminda Delano was born in Schuyler County, New York, in 1862. She taught school before attending Bellevue Hospital Training School for Nurses, where she graduated in 1886. In 1888, she went to Florida to be superintendent of nurses during a yellow fever epidemic. Next Delano went to Arizona to nurse copper miners suffering with typhoid. In 1891, she moved to Philadelphia to be superintendent of Nurses at the University of Pennsylvania Hospital School of Nursing. She then served as superintendent at New York City's House of Refuge on Randall's Island. During the Spanish-American

Jane Arminda Delano. (Library of Congress)

War, she began her long association with the ARC by joining the New York Chapter. In 1902, she became superintendent at the Bellevue Hospital.

In 1908, Delano accepted the positions of president of the American Nurses Association and chair of the Board of Directors of the *American Journal of Nursing*. In 1909, she became chair of the ARC Nursing Service and superintendent of the ANC. She served in the office of the Surgeon General from 1909 to 1912, and her efforts kept the ANC viable. From 1912 on, she concentrated strictly on ARC work. Delano deserves much of the credit for the recruiting of more than 21,000 army nurses who served in World War I.

After the armistice, Delano went to France on an inspection tour and became ill with an ear infection. She died April 15, 1919, and was buried in Savenay, France. She was posthumously awarded the Distinguished Service Medal, and in 1920, her body was exhumed and moved to Arlington National Cemetery.

—*Katherine Burger Johnson*

See also Nurses, United States Army Nurse Corps in World War I; Stimson, Julia Catherine

References and Further Reading

Jane A. Delano: A Biography. 1950. Washington, DC: American National Red Cross.

Detzer, Dorothy (1893–1981)

Peace lobbyist. Radicalized by her war relief work with the American Friends Service Committee in Vienna and Russia after World War I, Dorothy Detzer became a committed pacifist and launched a twenty-year career as the National Executive Secretary of the U.S. Section of the Women's International League for Peace and Freedom (WILPF), where she lobbied for disarmament and economic justice.

Born in 1893, Detzer spent her youth in Fort Wayne, Indiana. After graduating from high school, she traveled to the Far East rather than attend college. She returned to the United States and pursued social work at Jane Addam's settlement house (Hull House) in Chicago. After World War I, she joined the American Friends Service Committee and traveled to Vienna and Russia to provide hunger relief. The starvation and economic devastation she witnessed, combined with the tragic death of her twin brother, who died from mustard gas poisoning, led her to pursue peace work.

In 1924, despite her youth and limited experience, she was hired as the executive secretary of the U.S. section of WILPF to direct the organization's lobbying campaign to promote peace through disarmament legislation and economic justice. She became a quick study on foreign policy and the political process, and she used her connections with grassroots organizations to pressure legislators and the executive branch to promote U.S. neutrality, disarmament, and Good Neighbor policies.

As a lobbyist, she influenced numerous legislative investigations, including the munitions inquiry launched by Senator Gerald P. Nye to investigate allegations that U.S. bankers and arms manufacturers instigated World War I for profit. The investigation and resulting conclusions of the Nye Commission reinforced U.S. neutrality while Europe slid toward war. Detzer also played a key role in promoting anticolonial foreign relations with Africa and Central America, including the withdrawal of U.S. forces from Nicaragua. She believed that disarmament and self-determination could guarantee peace, and she strongly supported the League of Nations and formation of the World Court.

Peace organizations asserted tremendous power during the interwar years, both separately and together. WILPF relied on coalition building to promote peace through cooperation and collaboration with other groups such as the National Council for the Prevention of War, National Committee on the Cause and Cure of War, National Association for the Advancement of Colored People, National Peace Conference, League of Nations Association, and Emergency Peace Campaign. Together these organizations had a significant impact on U.S. foreign policy during the interwar years.

In 1944, Detzer retired from WILPF and subsequently wrote her memoir, *Appointment on the Hill*. She married Ludwell Denny and worked as a freelance foreign correspondent for several years before retiring in Monterey, California. She died in 1981.

—Danelle Moon

See also Addams, Jane; Olmstead, Mildred Scott

References and Further Reading

Foster, Carrie A. 1995. *The Women and the Warriors: The U.S. Section of the Women's International League for Peace and Freedom*. New York: Syracuse University Press.

Jeffreys-Jones, Rhodri. 1995. *Changing Differences: Women and the Shaping of American Foreign Policy, 1917–1994*. Piscataway, NJ: Rutgers University Press.

Deuell, Henrietta Eleanor Goodnough

See Hull, Peggy

Devlin, Bernadette (1947–)

Irish civil rights activist and opponent of the British presence in Northern Ireland. Bernadette Devlin (MacAliskey) was born in Cookstown, County Tyrone, Northern Ireland. As a student at Queen's University in Belfast, she took part in the marches of the Northern Civil Rights Association in 1968 and 1969. In August 1969, Devlin was arrested when Catholics erected barricades in Derry to protect their neighborhood. She was convicted of incitement to riot and sentenced to six months in prison. She was a founder of People's Democracy and, as one of the party's candidates, was elected to the Parliament of the United Kingdom in 1969; she served as an member of Parliament until 1974. She was to be one of the speakers at the antiinternment rally in Derry on January 30, 1972, which was attacked by the British 1st Parachute Regiment at the cost of thirteen dead protestors. At Westminster, when the British home secretary, Reginald Maulding, claimed that the soldiers had fired in self-defense, she called him a liar and hit him. In 1975, she was a founder of the Irish Republican Socialist party. In 1980–1981 she served H-Block Committee, set up to support Republican prisoners seeking to win the status of political prisoner through hunger strikes. On January 17, 1985, she and her husband were shot and seriously wounded in their home by a Loyalist death squad. After recovering, she still spoke out on political issues but was not affiliated with any major group. She was critical of the peace process, which led to the Good Friday Accords in 1999. In February 2003, she was stopped when she attempted to enter the United States on holiday and deported as a security threat.

—Bernard Cook

See also Farrell, Mairead; Mowlam, Marjorie; Peace People Movement; Ulster, Women during the Troubles in

References and Further Reading

McAliskey, Bernadette Devlin. 1994. *On the Irish Freedom Struggle.* London: Pathfinder.

Target, George William. 1975. *The Story of Bernadette Devlin.* London: Hodder and Stoughton.

Dietrich, Marlene (1901–1992)

German American actress and war volunteer for the Allies. Marlene Dietrich (originally Maria Magdalene von Losch) was born in Berlin, Germany. Her father, a policeman, died, and her stepfather was killed while serving in World War I. She later entered the world of the German theatre in the creative years of the postwar Weimar Republic. Dietrich received attention as a singer and dancer but she achieved greatest acclaim for her film roles, particularly as Lola in *The Blue Angel* (1930). In 1923, she married Rudolph Sieber, with whom she had a daughter, Maria.

In 1930, Dietrich was invited to Hollywood and remained there, returning to Europe and Germany only occasionally. It became clear that she was unsympathetic to the Nazi dictatorship because of its censorship and anti-Semitism. In 1936, she refused the offer of Joseph Goebbels to return to Germany to make a film. She was offered £50,000 and promised that criticism of her by the German press would cease. Instead, she starred in the Hollywood production *Destry Rides Again.* In 1939, much to the consternation of the Nazis, she became a U.S. citizen.

During World War II, Dietrich was an enthusiastic supporter of the Allied cause, and in 1944–1945, she achieved legendary status, beginning with her work at the Stage Door Canteen and culminating in memorable tours entertaining the troops. This action she saw as affirming her patriotism, and, more mundanely, it came at a time when her film career had fallen on hard times. Dietrich, accompanied by a troupe that featured Danny Thomas as comedian and manager, began her tour in Algiers. She then traveled through Italy and Western Europe, and even Germany. Dietrich gained special access to the army through individuals such as General George Patton, with whom she established a close relationship, and General James Gavin of the 82nd Airborne, with whom she was on intimate terms. Working in all sorts of weather and ready to perform in any circumstance, Dietrich established a tremendous rapport with her soldier audiences, as she sang, played the musical saw, and exhibited the beautiful legs for which she was especially known. She also visited with wounded German prisoners of war and broadcast from London to Germany. In tribute to her efforts on behalf of the troops, Dietrich was presented the Medal of Freedom, the highest civilian honor, November 18, 1947, by General Maxwell Taylor at West Point.

—Marc L. Schwarz

References and Further Reading

Riva, Maria. 1993. *Marlene Dietrich.* New York: Alfred Knopf.

Spoto, Donald. 1992. *Blue Angel.* New York. Doubleday.

Dilling, Elizabeth (1894–1966)

A leading figure in the mothers' movement, the largely right-wing coalition of women's groups opposed to U.S. involvement in World War II. Dilling was born to a prosperous Chicago family on April 19, 1894. She became the most important woman of the U.S. far right in the 1930s, gaining notoriety as an anti-Communist crusader who laced her speeches with accusations about Communist influence in the United States and invectives against Franklin Roosevelt and the New Deal. Her numerous pamphlets were widely circulated. Foreshadowing a common practice during the McCarthy era, Dilling catalogued organizations and persons she accused of promoting Communism. By 1941, her book-length index of alleged Communists, *The Red Network,* had gone through eight printings. Dilling was so notorious that Sinclair Lewis based a character on her in his novel about American fascism, *It Can't Happen Here.*

When World War II began in 1939, Dilling was part of a national network of anti-Semitics, anti-Communists, and Nazi sympathizers such as Father Charles Coughlin, Reverend Gerald L. K. Smith, Reverend Gerald Winrod, and William Dudley Pelley. Material generated by Nazi organizations in Germany to inspire race hatred and exploit dissatisfaction in the United States found its way into Dilling's publications. She spoke at rallies hosted by the leading U.S. Nazi organization, the German-American Bund, and had traveled to Germany, pronouncing the country as flourishing under Hitler.

Dilling called for appeasing Germany; she blamed the war on Jews and Communists and accused the Roosevelt administration of being controlled by Jewish Communists. She made common cause with the mothers' movement, spearheaded by the National Legion of Mothers of America (NLMA), which numbered several million women. After the Lend-Lease Bill to aid Great Britain passed the House of Representatives in February 1941, Dilling launched the Mothers Crusade to Defeat H.R. 1776 to lobby the Senate against Lend-Lease. Working closely with Dilling's Mothers Crusade were other isolationist groups, including the NLMA, the America First Committee, and the Daughters of the American Revolution. Dilling coordinated marches and protests by women in Washington, D.C., against Lend-Lease and was arrested for disorderly conduct on Capitol Hill. The Lend-Lease Act passed despite the efforts of the isolationists.

After Pearl Harbor, Dilling resisted wartime rationing and denounced the Allies. In July 1942, a grand jury indicted twenty-eight extreme rightists, including Dilling, for conspiring to cause insubordination in the military, largely for distributing virulent isolationist propaganda. In 1944, she was also charged with conspiring to overthrow the government with the aid of Nazi agents. The sedition trial hinged on free speech issues, with Dilling's supporters in Congress accusing the Roosevelt administration of trying to silence political foes. The government's case was vague and lacking evidence. In 1946, a federal judge dismissed the charges.

Dilling spent the remainder of her life publishing broadsides against the North Atlantic Treaty Organization, foreign aid, the income tax, racial mixing, the fluoridation of water, the Vietnam War, and the war on poverty. She had long been dismissed as a crank before her death in 1966, although some of her literature continues to be cited in right-wing circles.

—Glen Jeansonne and David Luhrssen

See also Curtis, Cathrine; National Legion of Mothers of America

References and Further Reading

Jeansonne, Glen. 1996. *Women of the Far Right.* Chicago: University of Chicago.

Dix, Dorothea (1802–1887)

The first U.S. superintendent of nurses. Dorothea Dix was born in Hampden, Maine, into a chaotic family. Her minister father had drinking and emotional problems, and her mother became bedridden with severe headaches when Dorothea was still young. As a result, Dorothea was frequently sent to spend time with her wealthy grandmother in Boston, and at age twelve, due to her father's increasing religious fanaticism and erratic behavior, she was sent to live with her grandmother. While still young, Dix became a teacher of small children. In 1824, she published a book, recommending equal education for both sexes.

Dix, a budding social reformer, was moved by the deplorable conditions of the mentally ill and began a crusade to improve their lives. She was able to convince Massachusetts legislators to provide more humane and effective services for the mentally ill and construct new hospitals. Her devotion to helping disabled people led to social activism on behalf of the blind and the imprisoned.

At the outbreak of the American Civil War, Dix and some volunteer nurses went to the War Department and offered assistance to the injured Union soldiers. The secretary of war commissioned her as the first superintendent of U.S. army nurses, the first such office of its kind. In her new position, she organized the training and activities of the volunteer nursing corps, a duty for which she drew on her administrative experience with mental hospitals. Dix was an autocratic leader but possessed much care and concern for the nurses under her supervision and the soldiers under her care.

Dorothea Lynde Dix (Library of Congress)

Likening herself to Florence Nightingale, she worked tirelessly in her position, but her persistence and unyielding style frequently caused some friction with military leaders and surgeons. Probably because of this friction with the military leadership, her post was abolished. This did not discourage her efforts, however. She continued volunteer work at makeshift hospitals until the end of the war. After the war, she assisted soldiers and their families and then returned to her work with mental patients, widows, and orphaned children.

—*Leonard A. Steverson*

See also Livermore, Mary Ashton Rice; Nightingale, Florence; Nurses, United States Army Nurse Corps in World War I

References and Further Reading

Brown, Thomas. 1998. *Dorothea Dix: New England Reformer.* Cambridge, MA: Harvard University Press.

Gollaher, David. 1995. *Voice for the Mad: The Life of Dorothea Dix.* New York: Free Press.
Marshall, Helen E. [1967] 1937. *Dorothea Dix: Forgotten Samaritan.* New York: Russell and Russell.

Douglas-Pennant, Violet (1869–1945)

Head of the British Women's Royal Air Force (WRAF) in World War I. Born in 1869, Violet Blanche Douglas-Pennant was the sixth daughter of the second Lord Penrhyn. As a young adult, she joined the Conservative Party and was active in Welsh affairs. Her particular interests were social change and educational progress. She became an active supporter of the Workers' Educational Association, and in 1911, she was appointed the National Health Insurance Commissioner for Wales. This post reflected her committee experience and public influence, and she received a salary of £1,000 a year, an unusually high figure for a woman in the early twentieth century (Izzard 1969, 184).

When Great Britain entered World War I, Douglas-Pennant shifted her attention toward war work. She helped to establish several female ancillary organizations, including the Women's Army Auxiliary Corp (WAAC) and the Women's Royal Navy Service (WRNS). In the spring of 1918, she became involved with the formation of the WRAF and was named its commandant. Communications between the WRAF and the Royal Air Force were poor, and Douglas-Pennant found her organization lacking supplies, staff, and authority. These difficulties were compounded by personality clashes among her staff and with other auxiliary leaders—namely, Dame Katharine Furse, head of the WRNS. Rumors and innuendos swirled about Douglas-Pennant's ability and suitability to lead, with the most vicious attacking her mental stability, personal life, and character. Finally, six weeks into her tenure, Sir William Weir, Secretary of State for Air, called for an inquest.

The resulting report was highly critical of Douglas-Pennant and led to her eventual dismissal by August 1918. Helen Gwynne-Vaughan replaced her as commandant, and Douglas-Pennant prepared for a full parliamentary investigation of the WRAF under her leadership. This inquiry came to a humiliating conclusion in late 1919, as the House of Lords agreed with the Air Ministry's management of the situation. Now branded "a woman of unreliable temperament," the scandal colored the remainder of her life, and any public contributions she had made before the war faded in the wake of the inquest (Izzard 1969, 213). Douglas-Pennant died in October 1945.

—*Rachel Finley-Bowman*

See also Furse, Lady Katherine Symonds; Great Britain: Women in Service during World War I; Gwynne-Vaughn, Helen

References and Further Reading

Izzard, Molly. 1969. *A Heroine in Her Time: A Life of Dame Helen Gwynne-Vaughan, 1879–1967.* London: Macmillan.

Draenger, Justina

See Dawidson, Justina

Dromgoole, Will Allen (1860–1934)

American newspaper writer and naval reserve officer who reported on domestic base operations during World War I. Dromgoole was born in Murfreesboro, Tennessee, and studied law with her father. Because Tennessee legal restrictions prevented her from practicing law, she turned to writing and stints as an engrossing clerk with the Tennessee legislature. Dromgoole edited and contributed to *Will Allen's Journal: A Literary Society Weekly*, published in Nashville for several years. In 1900, Dromgoole became literary editor for the *Nashville Banner*, writing book reviews and weekly features. Dromgoole's sentimental work and tales of natives in the Tennessee countryside invoked a feeling of familiarity with her readers and gave her credibility with the average reader. Her works were most widely read in the South, and she was named Poet Laureate of Tennessee and of the Poetry Society of the South.

Dromgoole was one of the first women to volunteer for service when the United States entered World War I in 1917. She entered the navy as a yeomanry warrant officer, becoming the first woman from Tennessee to do so, and she is often credited with being the first American woman to serve in that capacity. Lauding her achievement, the *Nashville Banner* praised her as holding the highest honor the United States military would bestow upon a woman at the time. Dromgoole spent most of her time stationed on shore duty at the naval base in Norfolk, Virginia. While in Virginia, Dromgoole was sent on recruiting cruises along the coasts of Virginia, Maryland, and North Carolina. One three-month tour took her to the area of Virginia's famous Lost Colony. While touring the area, Dromgoole used the opportunity to report on the folkways and history of the area interspersed with her daily reports of life for soldiers stationed stateside.

The *Banner* credited Dromgoole as being the only publicity woman working for the navy during World War I. She was notable for using her considerable public image to report firsthand on conditions for the average solider stationed stateside during the war. She worked as a makeshift base librarian, living in a small white shack that consisted of a one-room canteen, a one-room library, and her living space of two rooms. She selected books for soldiers stationed abroad. During her service, she served as the director of the base's YMCA, which was famous for having its own picture show. She also successfully sold government insurance.

After the war, Dromgoole returned to her role as writer, producing thirteen books, 8,000 poems, an operetta, numerous nonfiction articles, and more than 5,000 newspaper articles.

—*Laura Finger*

See also Journalists, American Women, during World War I

References and Further Reading:

Lyday-Lee, Kathy. 1980. "Will Allen Dromgoole: Forgotten Pioneer of Tennessee Mountain Fiction." *University of Mississippi Studies in English* 1, New Series (1980): 71–81.

———. 1992. "Will Allen Dromgoole: A Biographical Sketch." *Tennessee Historical Quarterly* 51 (summer):107–112.

———. 1998. "Will Allen Dromgoole." In *The Tennessee Encyclopedia of History and Culture,* edited by Carroll Van West, 259–260. Nashville: Tennessee Historical Society.

Durova, Nadezhda Andreyevna (1783–1866)

Russian soldier during the Napoleonic Wars. Nadezhda Andreyevna Durova was born to a minor official's family in the Vyatka *gubernia* of Russia. In 1801, she married Vasily Chernov, a local official in Sarapul, and had a daughter the following year. The marriage soon ended, however, when Durova met a Cossack officer and decided to enlist in the army. She disguised herself as a nobleman named Aleksandr Andreyevich Aleksandrov and joined the Polish Horse Uhlan Regiment. She took part in the 1807 campaign in Poland, fighting at Guttstadt, Heilsberg, and Friedland, where she was promoted to ensign in the Mariupol Hussar Regiment. She was wounded in one of the skirmishes, however, and her deception was revealed. Nevertheless, Emperor Alexander commended her for her valor and allowed her to remain in the army.

In 1812, Durova served with the Lithuanian Uhlan Regiment, fighting at Smolensk, Kolotsk, and Borodino, where she suffered a minor leg wound. In September–December 1812 she served on Kutuzov's staff, and the following year, she participated in the sieges of Modlin and Hamburg. In 1816, after the war, she retired with a rank of staff *rotmistr* and returned to her family in Sarapul. Durova is the only known female officer of the Russian army during the Napoleonic Wars. She wrote interesting and vivid military recollections titled *Kavalerist Devitsa* (Cavalry Maiden).

—Alexander Mikaberidze

See also Agustina of Aragón; Engel, Regula; Russia, Women in the Armed Forces (1700–1917)

References and Further Reading

Durova, Nadezhda. 1988. *The Cavalry Maiden: Journals of a Russian Officer in the Napoleonic Wars.* Translated by Mary Fleming Zirin. Bloomington: Indiana University Press.

Mikaberidze, Alexander. 2004. *The Russian Officer Corps in the Revolutionary and Napoleonic Wars, 1795–1815.* New York: Savas Beatie.

Duston, Hannah (1657–1736)

American frontier woman. At the end of the seventeenth century, Hannah Duston, a Puritan settler of Haverhill, Massachusetts, who escaped from Indian captivity during King William's War (1689–1698), was the most famous woman in New England. She was considered by many to be an American Amazon because of the circumstances of her capture and escape from Indian captivity. On March 15, 1697, just a few days after giving birth to Martha, her eighth child, Indians raided Duston's village. The Indians, identified in various accounts as Mohawks or Eastern or Western Abenakis, entered Duston's home, removing her, the infant Martha, and Mary Neff, a woman from the village serving as Duston's nurse. Thomas Duston, Hannah's husband, witnessed the abduction, but at her entreaty led the other children to safety.

The next day, after the Indians killed or captured forty of the town's inhabitants and set Duston's home aflame, Duston, Martha, and Neff were marched toward Canada. Martha was wrested away from her mother and killed instantly when her head was crushed against a tree.

About two weeks later, after a 100-mile trek in the snow without shoes or adequate clothing, Duston arrived at a small island at the junction of the Merrimack and Contoocook Rivers, a few miles north of present-day Concord, New Hampshire. Duston's captors placed her in the custody of an Indian family who were Roman Catholic converts. Already in the household was another English captive, Samuel Lennardson.

On March 30, 1697, just before dawn, Duston, along with Neff and Lennardson, stole the family's hatchets and killed ten family members, six of whom were children. The threat of being stripped, scourged, and forced to run the gauntlet prompted Duston's actions. With Neff's assistance, Duston killed nine of the Indians, and Lennardson killed one. As proof of her deed, Duston scalped her victims using techniques Lennardson had learned from their captors. She then led Neff and Lennardson downstream in an appropriated Indian canoe.

Upon safely reaching Haverhill a few days later, Duston appeared at the General Court in Boston with her husband and requested a bounty for the scalps. Duston received £25, while Neff and Lennardson each received £12 and 10 shillings.

Duston's actions, lauded by Cotton Mather, were exonerated because they were fueled by the death of her own child and her victims were Catholic. In 1836, Nathaniel Hawthorne decried Duston's violence as symptomatic of Puritan brutality against Native Americans, but in nineteenth-century New England Duston was revered and monumentalized as an archetypal pioneer heroine. A monument erected at Duston Island, New Hampshire, on June 17, 1874, the first public monument in the United States erected in honor of a woman, depicts Duston with a tomahawk in one hand, scalps in another. Another monument to Duston was erected in Haverhill on November 25, 1879.

—*Rebecca Tolley-Stokes*

See also Frontier Soldiers, U.S., Wives of; Nonhelema; Ward, Nancy; Winema; Winnemucca, Sarah

References and Further Reading

Levernier, James A. 1998. "Hannah Duston." In *Dictionary of Literary Biography,* Vol. 200, *American Women Prose Writers to 1820,* 107–112. Detroit, MI: Gale Research.

McKinley, Allida Shuman. 1999. "Hannah Duston." In *American National Biography,* 170–171. New York: Oxford University Press.

Weis, Ann-Marie. 1998. "The Murderous Mother and the Solicitous Father: Violence, Jacksonian Family Values, and Hannah Duston's Captivity." *American Studies International* 36, no. 1: 46–65.

E

Earley, Charity Adams (1918–2002)

Commander of the only all-black U.S. Women's Army Corps (WAC) unit that served overseas during World War II. At a time when a segregated military provided few opportunities for African Americans, Charity Adams Earley achieved the rank of lieutenant colonel, the highest attainable rank for women in the army except the WAC director. Earley remained in the WAC until March 26, 1946.

Throughout her military experience, Earley confronted personal and institutional racial prejudice and discrimination—both latent and overt—that was endemic to a segregated military in a segregated society. "I had been raised in the South," she wrote in her biography, *One Women's Army,* "and I knew there was no such thing as separate but equal" (Adams 1989, 60). She also experienced the reluctance of military men to accept women into a man's army. Her service in the WAC became emblematic of many of the firsts achieved by women and by African Americans during World War II.

Charity Adams grew up in Columbia, South Carolina. Her father was a minister in the A.M.E. (African Methodist Episcopal) Church and a scholar who was fluent in Greek and Hebrew. Her mother was a teacher. Earley graduated from Wilberforce University, an African American Episcopal school in Wilberforce, Ohio. She was attending graduate school at Ohio State when she joined the Women's Army Auxiliary Corps (WAAC) in 1942 and entered the first Officer's Candidate Class (OCS) at Fort Des Moines, Iowa. (In 1943, Congress removed auxiliary status and the WAAC became the Women's Army Corps [WAC], an official branch of the army.) She was among the twenty-nine black women chosen to fulfill the 10 percent quota the army allotted to African Americans. After graduation from OCS, she served as company commander for the Basic Training Company at Fort Des Moines, training African American recruits.

Racial issues loomed throughout the nation and the U.S. Armed Forces during World War II. The African American press was among the loudest voices calling for an end to segregation, and its efforts for equality included a campaign to send African American WACs overseas. Early in 1945, Charity Adams received orders to report to Birmingham, England, and assumed command of the 6888th Central Postal Directory in March. In May 1945, the unit transferred to Rouen, France. Called the Six-Triple-Eight, the battalion consisted of 824 enlisted women and 31 officers at its peak strength.

Under Earley's leadership, the Six-Triple-Eight assumed responsibility for redirecting mail to the estimated 7 million U.S. military, paramilitary, and civilian support personnel in the European theatre of operations (ETO). Under Earley's direction, the battalion broke all records for redirecting mail. They censored correspondence, repackaged undeliverable items, and developed record-keeping and tracking systems to trace the movements of personnel whose addresses could change two to three times weekly as they moved from combat zone to combat zone. The Six-Triple-Eight moved almost 200,000 letters and packages daily, living up to the motto, "No mail; low morale."

After her army years, Earley earned a master's degree in vocational psychology from Ohio State University and continued postgraduate work at the University of Zurich and at the Jungian Institute of Analytical Psychology in Zurich, Switzerland. She served as a college professor and dean and remained active in community affairs after her marriage and the birth of her children.

—Lee Ann Ghajar

See also United States, Military Service of Women in World War II; United States, Women's Army Auxiliary Corps

References and Further Reading

Earley, Charity Adams. 1989. *One Woman's Army: A Black Officer Remembers the WAC*. College Station: Texas A&M University Press.

Papers of Charity Adams Earley, 1928–2002 (bulk 1942–2002), Library of Congress.

East Timor, Abuse of Women during War

Abuse of women by Indonesian forces during the struggle for independence in Timor. In the early stages of the more than quarter-century-long insurrection that led to the independence of East Timor from Indonesia, rape was used primarily as a weapon against individual women detained under suspicion of being rebels or of being sympathetic to the rebel cause. In several instances, relatives of men prominent in the independence movement were detained and tortured to provoke those rebel leaders to reveal their whereabouts. The torments endured by the women in these families often included repeated rapes.

As the conflict became intensified in the late 1990s, rape became part of the strategy of the Indonesian military and of the paramilitary militia recruited as an ostensible alternative to the independence movement. In interviews conducted during the Human Rights Commission's investigation of atrocities committed during the conflict, the head of the Indonesian forces in East Timor, Brigadier-General Tono Suratman, admitted that both the regular military and the militia forces were encouraged to use rape as a weapon of intimidation (Powell 2001, 20). These forces sought to terrorize the population of East Timor into submission, to make the population associate the struggle for independence with an almost anarchic level of violence.

Moreover, as East Timorese men left their villages to join the rebel forces based in the highlands, the progovernment militias began to target pointedly the families the men had left behind. The women and girls were raped to undermine the morale of the rebel forces by making their husbands, fathers, and sons feel derelict for having left them vulnerable to such predatory attacks. The rapes also served as a warning to those men who had not yet left their villages for the highland camps of the rebels.

Initially established in response to the large numbers of refugees fleeing the conflict, the refugee camps in West Timor eventually became, in effect, relocation camps as the military and the militias sought forcibly to clear areas of East Timor in which there were high levels of rebel activity. The majority of the refugees were women, children, and the elderly. Frequently, the military and militias used the refugee camps as informal brothels, forcing large numbers of the women and girls into sexual slavery.

Ironically, when these women and girls were permitted to return to East Timor, many—and especially those who had become pregnant as a result of the rapes—were subsequently stigmatized and traumatized by their victimization. They became painful reminders not only of the costs of independence but of the ineffectualness of the independence movement in shielding the most vulnerable noncombatants among its own population. Thus, in the patriarchal society of East Timor, the stigma attached to the victims of rape—the suggestion that they have been somehow complicit in their victimization, if only because they have endured it to survive—not only persisted in the aftermath of the conflict but also was even reinforced. Writing for *The Weekend Australian,* Sian Powell has reported that the women forced into sex slavery have often resorted to describing themselves as *isteri simpanan,* or "kept wives," to euphemize their victimization and soften its stigma (Powell 2001, 20).

The threat of rape became such a widespread preoccupation among the East Timorese population that as the conflict gradually subsided, the militias were able to create distrust of the United Nations peacekeepers by spreading rumors that they, too, were taking advantage of the chaotic conditions and indiscriminately raping women and girls.

Kirsty Sword Gusmao, the Australian-born wife of East Timor's first president, Xanana Gusmao, has emerged as a vocal advocate of women shunned simply because they were raped during the war. She has tried to move public opinion in the new nation toward a more reasonable view of these women as representative figures in the difficult struggle for independence. In the process, individual women such as Juliana dos Santos, who was in her midteens when she was coerced into sex slavery in a refugee camp, have been presented as exemplary figures of stoic fortitude and undaunted perseverance.

—Martin Kich

See also Rape in War

References and Further Reading

Ansley, Greg. 1999. "Militia Reign of Terror Engulfs West." *The New Zealand Herald,* November 22.

O'Kane, Maggie. 2001. "Return of the Revolutionaries: The Conflict May Be Over, But for the Women of East Timor, There Is Another Battle to Be Won." *The Guardian,* January15: 8.

Powell, Sian. 2001. "Rape: Just Another Weapon of War." *The Weekend Australian,* March 10: 20.

Shanks, David. "Overcoming Trauma Part of the Agenda Facing the New East Timor." 2000. *The Irish Times,* January: 14.

Edmonds, Sarah Emma (1841–1898)

American Civil War combatant. Born and raised on a farm in New Brunswick, Canada, in 1841, Sarah Emma Edmonds came to the United States in 1860 posing as a man, Franklin Thompson. As Thompson, she served in the Union army for two years.

Edmonds enlisted on May 17, 1861, as Thompson in Company F of the Second Michigan Infantry in the Union Army. Her male identity went unquestioned. During her service, Edmonds served as a male nurse in the regimental hospital, witnessing the horrors of injuries arising from modern weaponry and outdated battle tactics. She would also become the regiment's postmaster and then its mail carrier. Her first combat experience came at the Battle of Bull Run in July 1861. Edmonds emerged uninjured. She and her regiment continued to fight with George McClellan's Army of the Potomac in 1862.

While in Lebanon, Kentucky, in April 1863, Edmonds deserted from the army. She later excused her desertion as necessary to avoid being discovered as a woman. Afterward, Edmonds traveled to Ohio and resumed her female identity. In June 1863, she began work as a female nurse under the supervision of the U.S. Christian Commission in Union hospitals.

Edmonds wrote a memoir, which she later admitted contained fictionalized versions of her wartime experiences. First published in 1864 as *Unsexed; or, The Female Soldier,* the book was reissued in 1865 as *Nurse and Spy in the Union Army.* After revealing herself to her former comrades in arms, her fellow soldiers testified to her valor as a soldier. In July 1884, Congress granted Edmonds her pension for her service as Thompson and formally deleted the charge of desertion from Thompson's military record.

Edmonds died on September 5, 1898. She was buried with full military honors in Houston's Washington Cemetery.

—*Lisa Tendrich Frank*

See also Civil War, American, and Women; Civil War, American, Women Combatants during the

References and Further Reading

Blanton, DeAnne, and Lauren M. Cook. 2002. *They Fought Like Demons: Women Soldiers in the American Civil War.* Baton Rouge: Louisiana State University.

Edmonds, S. Emma E. 1865. *Nurse and Spy in the Union Army.* Hartford, CT: W. S. Williams.

Leonard, Elizabeth D. 1999. *All the Daring of the Soldier: Women of the Civil War Armies.* New York: W. W. Norton.

Einsatzgruppen (Special Action Groups)

Nazi mobile killing units, literally attack or operational groups, assigned the task of murdering Jews in occupied portions of the Soviet Union. Einsatzgruppen (special action groups) with the assistance of local militias killed an estimated 1.4 million Jews—women, children, as well as men (Hilberg 1967, 256). To this total must be added unknown numbers of Roma (Gypsies), suspected communist operatives, and partisans, and others.

Einsatzgruppen had operated in Poland during the invasion of September 1939, but their targets were Polish priests and other members of the intelligentsia. The Einsatzgruppen of 1941 were new units, however, formed and trained for mass murder on Soviet territory. They operated independently of the regular army, which nevertheless provided logistical support to the Einsatzgruppen. Their personnel was drawn from the ranks of the SS: the Security Service (SD), the Order Police (Sipo), the Criminal Police, the Gestapo, the Waffen-SS, and police reserve battalions. The Einsatzgruppen ultimately received its orders from Heinrich Himmler and his second in command, Reinhard Heydrich. At Nuremberg, SS General Erich von dem Bach-Zelewski stated, "The principal task was the annihilation of the Jews, gypsies, and political commissars" (Taylor 1992, 259).

Four groups, A, B, C, and D, were formed to follow the North, Central, and South Army groups and the 11th Army into the Soviet Union. Each of these consisted of 600 to 1,000 men divided into 4 or 5 companies of Einsatzkommandos (operational commandos) or Sonderkommandos (special commandos). A typical action involved marching the residents of villages to pits dug by prisoners of war or to an area where the victims themselves would dig their own pits. The victims would be forced to strip, driven into the pits, and shot, or they would be shot on the edge of the pits so that the corpses would fall into the mass grave. When hard alcohol proved insufficient to numb the murderers, who were repeatedly ordered to shoot women and children, the SS experimented with special gas wagons, which used carbon monoxide to asphyxiate victims packed into vans. These killing operations thus provided a precedent for the gas chambers of the death camps.

One of the most infamous of the mass killings of the Einsatzgruppen occurred at the Babi Yar

Nazi Shutzstaffel Einsatzgruppen (SS mobile killing squads) line up Jews to execute them before a ditch, Babi Yar Massacre, Ukraine, 1941. (Hulton Archive/Getty Images)

ravine outside Kiev. There Sonderkommando 4a of Einsatzgruppen C, commanded by Paul Blobel, shot 33,771 Jewish men, women, and children on September 29–30, 1941.

—*Bernard Cook*

See also Holocaust and Jewish Women

References and Further Reading

Edeiken, Yale F. "An Introduction to the EINSATZGRUPPEN," The Holocaust History Project, http://www.holocaust-history.org /intro-einsatz/ (accessed February 5, 2004).

Hilberg, Raur. 1967. *The Destruction of the European Jews.* Chicago: Quadrangle.

Spector, Shmuel. 1990. "Einsatzgruppen." In *Encyclopedia of the Holocaust,* 433–439. New York: Macmillan.

Taylor, Telford. 1992. *The Anatomy of the Nuremberg Trials: A Personal Memoir.* New York: Knopf.

El Salvador, Women and the Civil Strife in

Impact of civil war in El Salvador on women. The civil war in El Salvador lasted from the mid-1970s to 1992, with much of the fiercest fighting taking place in the 1980s. Revolutionary forces led by the Farabundo Martí National Liberation Front (Frente Farabundo Martí para la Liberación Nacional, FMLN) battled the U.S.-backed military governments that ruled the country. Women played active roles in both the FMLN and the mass organizations that emerged during this time.

The FMLN was formed in 1980 when five leftist guerrilla groups merged. By the late 1980s, the FMLN controlled regions of El Salvador and established locally run governments. The FMLN opposed the lack of participatory democracy that characterized the country and the abysmal living conditions in which the majority of Salvadorans lived. For example, in the 1970s, more than 40 percent of the rural population was landless, and 60 percent of Salvadoran children died before age 5. According to a 1988 study, 2 million Salvadorans out of a population of 5 million lived in extreme poverty (Golden 1991).

The poverty directly affected many Salvadoran women, who were primarily responsible for taking care of their families. In some of the poor neighborhoods in San Salvador, the capital, women headed 40 percent of the households in the 1970s, a figure that rose perhaps as high as 70 percent by the late 1980s (New American Press 1989). Many Salvadoran women became politically active through their involvement in the Christian Base Communities (CBCs) that spread through poor urban and rural areas in the late 1960s and 1970s. The philosophy of the CBCs reflected the changes then taking place in the Catholic Church throughout Latin America. Calling for a preferential option for the poor following the 1968 Catholic Conference in Medellin, Colombia, much of the work of the church focused on seeking social justice for the poor and marginalized. Women played an important role in the CBCs; they learned to read, discussed theological interpretations of the Bible, presided over meetings, and assumed leadership positions. These activities offered them concrete organizational experience, a new role for themselves as community leaders, and an identity that extended beyond the four walls of their homes (Golden 1991).

In the 1970s, women joined mass organizations that worked to alleviate poverty and obtain a higher standard of living for the population. One of the most significant of these groups was ANDES, the teacher's organization headed by Melida Anaya Montes. Montes subsequently became the second in command of one of the five organizations that made up the FMLN. Women also formed their own organizations that operated in conjunction with the various organizations that made up the FMLN. One of the first groups was AMES, the Association of Salvadoran Women, which formed in 1978. In the FMLN-run parts of the country, AMES participated in organizing the local governments, set up child care and health care projects, worked in food production, and helped to defend the area (Golden 1991). The military government targeted these groups, along with the other mass organizations that worked with the FMLN. Between 1979 and 1981 the U.S.-financed military disappeared and/or murdered tens of thousands of Salvadorans in an effort to eliminate opposition (New Americas Press 1989). As a result, many of the women (and men) active in the public movement went underground, fearful that their continued public activity signified a death sentence.

While some women continued their mass work clandestinely, others fled the cities and towns and joined the FMLN. During the 1980s, the FMLN distinguished itself by having a large percentage of women combatants; women made up 29 percent of the fighting forces and 36 percent of the political personnel. Women occupied positions at all levels within the FMLN. They were military and political commanders; they operated radios, became demolition experts, conducted political education classes, offered logistical support, carried out propaganda actions, and practiced battlefield medicine (New Americas Press 1989; Hipsher 2001). Women planned and fought in many of the major military operations carried out by the FMLN.

Women's participation in the FMLN and mass organizations, combined with the need to involve greater numbers of women in the struggle against the government, led to increased attention to and questioning of gender roles. AMES, for example, supported the collectivization of activities such as child rearing and food preparation to allow more women to join the political struggle. It also encouraged men to cook, clean, and take care of the children when female members of their families were conducting political or military activities that took them away from home and their daily chores. The main motivation behind these changes, however, was to enhance the ability of the population to fight the government, not to challenge male domination.

As in most war situations, women were frequently the victims of rape by the military. Captured activists were often subjected to savage torture. In a book published after her release from jail, Ana Guadalupe Martínez, a FMLN leader, recounts the abuse she experienced while she was imprisoned and tortured by the Salvadoran military. The Salvadoran military applied electric shocks to the most sensitive parts of her body, beat her repeatedly, and raped her (Martínez 1980).

In 1992, the FMLN and the military government signed the peace accords that effectively ended the war. The accords, however, made no mention of women's needs or demands. Dissatisfied with the lack of recognition they received and drawing on the political experience they had gained during the civil war, some women formed their own autonomous organizations in the 1990s to address the specific needs and concerns of women (Hipsher 2001).

—*Margaret Power*

See also Latin America, Women in Guerrilla Movements in

References and Further Reading

Golden, Renny. 1991. *The Hour of the Poor, the Hour of the Women.* New York: Crossroad.

Hipsher, Patricia. 2001. "Right and Left-Wing Women in Post-Revolutionary El Salvador." In *Radical Women in Latin America, Left and Right,* 133–164. University Park: Pennsylvania State University Press.

Martínez, Ana Guadalupe. 1980. *The Secret Prisons of El Salvador.* Culiacán, Mexico: Universidad Autónoma de Sinaloa.

New American Press, ed. 1989. *A Dream Compels Us: Voices of Salvadorian Women.* Boston: South End Press.

Eleanor of Aquitaine (ca. 1122–1204)

Medieval political and military figure. Duchess Eleanor of Aquitaine was the only child of William X of Aquitaine and his wife Aenor. She became one of the most powerful and controversial figures of medieval Europe thanks to her position as heir of Aquitaine, which gave her a power base that was almost unheard of for a medieval woman.

Eleanor's father died in 1137, and for her protection from predatory nobles, a marriage was arranged almost immediately with Louis VII, who soon after became king of France. Their marriage was difficult because the high-spirited southern Eleanor had little in common with her husband; her behavior was widely criticized. A more important issue of contention was rule of Eleanor's duchy of Aquitaine, a task that automatically fell to her husband but in which she wanted a say.

The desire or need to represent her Aquitainian subjects led Eleanor to the most controversial action of her career: when her husband vowed in 1147 to go on the Second Crusade, Eleanor did as well. She took part in the crusade as the lord of the Aquitainian contingent; without a spokesperson at the crusade councils, they would have had little standing, and apparently the Aquitainian knights had held back from joining the crusade for that reason. Medieval chroniclers, eager to vilify an excessively manly woman, told that Eleanor set out on crusade garbed as an Amazon, with 300 ladies similarly dressed—this story is highly unlikely. Eleanor left daily command of her troops to a man but did indeed play an active role in councils. This caused trouble because she was blamed for choosing a poor campsite, leaving the army open to a devastating Turkish raid. She also argued policy independently, siding with her uncle (and perhaps lover) Raymond of Antioch against her husband and urging that the army's objective ought to be recovery of the principality of

Edessa. Louis retaliated by having her carried off by force. In the end, the crusaders made a pathetically misguided attack on Damascus and returned home without accomplishing anything but the estrangement of Eleanor and Louis.

Eleanor's marriage to Louis was annulled in 1152, and within six weeks she married Henry of Anjou, the future Henry II of England. Again, Aquitaine proved to be a contentious issue. Henry wanted to exert greater control; Eleanor wanted one of her younger sons to inherit the duchy, securing its future independence. With her support, three of Eleanor's sons rebelled against Henry in 1173–1174. Their uprising was soon suppressed, and Eleanor was captured while trying to join her sons. She was imprisoned for the next fifteen years, until her son Richard I came to the throne.

Richard spent most of his reign away from England on the Third Crusade and fighting on the Continent. Eleanor played an important role in controlling England, especially against her youngest son, John. When Richard was captured by the duke of Austria while returning from crusade, it was Eleanor who negotiated and raised his ransom.

Thus, while Eleanor did not bear arms or command troops, her life was much closer to warfare than that of most medieval women. Her life demonstrates the need for an heiress in feudal society to take on male roles and also how little the male-ruled society of her time accepted such a situation.

—*Phyllis G. Jestice*

See also Crusades, Women and the

References and Further Reading

Meade, Marion. 1991. *Eleanor of Aquitaine.* London: Penguin.

Weir, Alison. 2001. *Eleanor of Aquitaine: A Life.* New York: Ballantine.

Emerson, Gloria (1929–)

American journalist and novelist. In covering conflicts in Africa, Ireland, Vietnam, Central America, and the Middle East, Gloria Emerson often focused on the physical and psychological traumas wrought by war on combatants and civilians while simultaneously describing acts of courage and compassion. Rather than concentrating on military aspects, Emerson often detailed war's effects on children, families, and populations that received little attention elsewhere.

After beginning her career as a lifestyle reporter for the *New York Times,* Emerson in 1968 began to focus primarily on war. Her coverage of the Nigerian Civil War described the plight of civilians, especially children, university students and members of the Ibo tribe, and the bitterness of Biafrans living in London over Britain's support for Nigeria. During this period, Emerson also reported on the motivations of Protestants in Northern Ireland.

Emerson is best known for coverage of the Vietnam War from 1970 through 1972 for which she received the George Polk Award. Her portraits of the French and Vietnamese middle class, Vietnamese youth, U.S. civilians, soldiers in the South Vietnamese army, and Viet Cong prisoners illustrated that the war had a significant impact beyond American military casualties. These experiences provided the basis for her first book, *Winners and Losers.* A chronicle of the war's physical, psychological, and cultural impact on both Americans and Vietnamese, *Winners and Losers* surveyed the diverse and complex attitudes toward U.S. involvement in Vietnam held by those who fought in or lived through the war as well as those in the United States who had supported or opposed it. Despite having won the 1977 National Book Award for nonfiction, Emerson suggested that her descriptions of the trauma of Vietnam were insufficient.

As a professor of journalism, columnist, and speaker, Emerson reflected on her experiences and spoke against what she believed was a mythology of violent masculinity that glorified war in U.S. culture. She explored this topic in

Some American Men. Her coverage of the Middle East, Central America, and Algeria resulted in two books, *Gaza: A Year in the Intifada* , which explores the impact of the Israeli-Palestinian conflict on Palestinians, and *Loving Graham Greene,* her first novel, which takes place during the Algerian civil war.

—*David Kieran*

See also Chapelle, Dickey; Gellhorn, Martha; Higgins, Marguerite; Hull, Peggy, pseud.; Lederer, Edie; Luce, Claire Boothe; Schuyler, Philippa; Tomara, Sonia; Trotta, Liz; Watts, Jean

References and Further Reading

Emerson, Gloria. 1976. *Winners and Losers: Battles, Retreats, Gains, Losses and Ruins from a Long War.* New York: Random House.

Emilia Plater Independent Women's Battalion

See Polish Independent Women's Battalion, Emilia Plater

Emslie, Isabel

See Hutton, Lady Idabel Galloway

Engel, Regula (1761–1853)

Woman combatant in the armies of Napoleon. Daughter of a Swiss mercenary from Zurich, Regula ran away from her family at thirteen, and in 1778, she married Florian Engel von Langwies, a sergeant major in the French army. By 1789, she had seven children, but during the French Revolution, her husband, who served in a Swiss unit in Paris, was arrested. She appealed to Maximilian Robespierre and impressed him enough to gain her husband's release. She then followed her husband to Italy in 1796–1797 and Egypt in 1798–1799. According to her memoirs, she chatted with General Napoleon Bonaparte on the ship sailing to Egypt. Pregnant during the voyage, she gave birth to twins in Alexandria, and they were baptized by Napoleon himself. She claims that she wore an officer's uniform during the campaigns and took part in actions. Returning to France, she and her sons took part in the 1800 campaign in which her two sons (Johann age twenty and Rudolph age twenty-one) were killed at Marengo; her son-in-law was also killed, and on hearing of his death, Engel's daughter died as well. In 1805, Regula followed her husband to Austerlitz, where, although pregnant, she took part in action and was slashed with a saber (the child, Joseph, was born in January 1806 and died at Waterloo in 1815). In 1808, Engel served in Spain, where another son, Conrad (age seventeen), was captured by the Spaniards and nailed to a tree to die. In 1809, she was pregnant with her twentieth child but took part in the operations in Bavaria and was captured by the Austrians near Regensburg. She gave birth to a child in captivity. Fortunately for her, Engel did not take part in the disastrous campaign in Russia in 1812 and subsequent battles in Germany and France. She did welcome Napoleon's return in 1815, however. At Waterloo, she fought alongside French troops and was shot in the neck and bayoneted in the side. Her husband was killed before her eyes, and her son was shot in the head. Engel survived this ordeal and later spent years looking for her surviving children. One of her sons, Caspar, immigrated to the United States, and Engel traveled to New Orleans. She arrived on January 6, 1817, only to find that her son had died of yellow fever three days before. Engel spent the rest of her life in Zurich, where she died on June 25, 1853, at the age of ninety-two.

—*Alexander Mikaberidze*

See also Durova, Nadezhda Andreyevna

References and Further Reading

Engel, Regula, 1977. *Frau Oberst Engel: von Cairo bis New York, von Elba bis Waterloo: Memoiren einer Amazone aus napoleonischer Zeit* [The wife of Officer Engel: From Cairo to New York, from Elba to Waterloo: memoirs of an Amazon from the time of Napoleon]. Zurich: Artemis-Verlag.

Eriksen, Vera (aka Vera de Cottani de Chalbur) (b. 1912)

German secret agent during World War II. Vera Staritzka was born in Siberia on December 12, 1912. Her adoptive parents, the Eriksens, took her to Denmark after the Russian Revolution, and she eventually ended up in Paris dancing at the Folies Bergeres. In 1930, she married Count Sergei Ignatieff, who was involved in White Russian intrigues but disappeared in Russia in the mid-1930s. He apparently introduced Vera to the world of espionage and drugs. In the mid-1930s, after Vera's relationship with Ignatieff had soured, she was recruited by the German Intelligence Service (Abwehr). In 1937, she married a German Abwehr officer, Hans Friedrich von Wedel, an aristocrat who had persuaded her to become a German agent. He naturally lied about her ethnic background. The couple was sent to England to establish links with people in high levels of society sympathetic to Germany. In England, she had a child, the subject of much speculation regarding its paternity. The child was placed in an orphanage, and, after von Wedel died in an auto accident in the first part of 1940, Vera was transferred to Norway. There she became part of a team of spies who were to be landed in Britain. The team was to be headed by Vera's current lover, Hilmar Dierks. Dierks was killed in an automobile accident the day before the launching of the mission, however, and it was delayed until the night of September 29, when Vera and two other spies were flown to the northeast coast of Scotland in a flying boat. They then set out in a rubber dinghy. Because of their distance from the shore and the rough water, they threw their bicycles overboard before reaching the shore of the Moray Firth between Buckie and Port Gordon. There they separated. Vera and Francois de Deeker made their way to the station at Port Gibson. Their behavior roused the suspicion of a porter and the stationmaster, who telephoned the police, and the pair was arrested. Vera claimed to be Vera de Cottani de Chalbur, the niece of an elderly Italian countess who lived in Kensington. Their collaborator, Werner Heinrich Walti, had more success. He had boarded a train but was arrested at the Waverley Station in Edinburgh. The two men were tried, convicted, and executed. Vera, for her part, escaped both trial and execution. Some claim that the father of her English-born son was an Englishman of influence; others claim that Vera turned and provided useful information to the British. The latter seems probable in light of Vera's subsequent disappearance. Vera was sent back to Germany after the end of the war, and, in true undercover fashion, she vanished.

—Bernard Cook

See also Kuczynski, Ursula; Schmidt, Kitty

References and Further Reading

"Nazi Spy's Love Child Linked to Reprieve." 2000. *The Herald* (Glasgow). October 26: 13.

"Vera Eriksen," German Spies, http://rgu-swim.rgu.ac.uk/history/German%20spies.htm (accessed October 25, 2003).

Wells, Matt. 1999. "Tragic Past Turned a Russian Ballerina into a Reluctant Spy." *The Scotsman,* January 27: 3.

Eritrea, Women and the Struggle for Independence of

Role of women in the thirty-year armed struggle of Eritrea for independence from Ethiopia. By the end of the conflict in 1993, women comprised 30 percent of Eritrea's approximately 100,000 soldiers (Wax 2004, A1). The government used images of female soldiers to rally the Eritrean people. One government poster with the legend of "Mother Eritrea" depicted a female fighter with a baby on her back brandishing an AK-47. When fighting broke out again between Ethiopia and Eritrea in 1998 because of a border dispute, women again constituted a sizeable component of the Eritrean fighting force. In that conflict, which lasted until December 12, 2000, it is estimated that a quarter of the Eritrean fighters were women (Jenkins 1999).

After Eritrea won its independence on May 24, 1993, women were rewarded with legal guarantees, including the right to own property, to initiate divorce, and to gain custody of children. Thirty percent of the seats in the Eritrean parliament were set aside for women. One of independent Eritrea's leading political figures, Fawzia Hashim, the minister of justice, had gained prominence as a fighter during the war of independence. The independence war and the subsequent border war had a devastating impact upon Eritrea, however. More than 550,000 people were displaced and reduced to desperate conditions. The 30-year struggle left the countryside planted with 150,000 to 200,000 land mines. The death toll left 30 percent of Eritrean

Young female soldier of the Eritrean Liberation Front, Eritrea, 1975. (Patrick Chauvel/Sygma/Corbis)

families headed by women. In addition, some former fighters complained that their individuality was respected more when they were fighters than when they returned to a civilian life dominated by traditional patriarchal values.

—*Bernard Cook*

See also Algeria, Women in the War of National Liberation; Mandela, Winnie; Mau Mau Rebellion, Women in the; Sudan, Women and the Civil War in

References and Further Reading

"Ethiopia/Eritrea War," http://www.globalsecurity.org/military/world/war/eritrea.htm (accessed April 19, 2004).

Jenkins, Cathy. 1999. "Battle in the Horn," BBC News, July 22, http://news.bbc.co.uk/1/hi/special_report/1999/07/99/battle_in_the_horn/396183.stm (accessed April 19, 2004).

Matthews, Jenny. 2003. "In a Sea of Troubles." *The Guardian* (London), March 8: 32.

Wax, Emily. 2004. "Respected in Battle, Overlooked at Home: Eritrea's Female Veterans Seek Peacetime Role." *The Washington Post,* April 2: A1.

ESKIMO SCOUTS

Women serving in the U.S. Alaska Territorial Guard (ATG). In 1941 during World War II, the United States faced the prospect of an enemy invasion of the territory of Alaska, an area comprising a half million square miles. U.S. military authorities did not have the forces necessary to defend the nation's longest coastline and Alaska's resource-rich interior. Their solution was to create an unorganized militia called the Alaska Territorial Guard. Alaskan Native women would be among the first recruits for this new armed force for the Arctic.

The ATG's mission was to defend Alaska and provide intelligence on any enemy coastal or espionage operations. Alaska at that time was sparsely settled. Any invasion would likely come in remote areas, and thus military authorities wanted recruits who lived in these areas and could survive easily in the harsh Arctic conditions. Throughout 1942 and 1943, Major Marvin R. "Muktuk" Marston of the U.S. Army Air Corps traveled by dogsled, boat, and airplane throughout Alaskan Native villages to recruit volunteers for the Guard.

At the time, there were few white settlers in the remote Arctic coastal areas; most of the rural population consisted of Native Alaskans. As they enrolled in the Alaska Territorial Guard, they became known as the Eskimo Scouts. During World War II, approximately 3,000 Native Alaskans in western Alaska served in Eskimo Scout units. Both male and female recruits were accepted. Although there are no records of exactly how many women served in the units, surviving documents from the war show that their numbers were significant. For example, about thirty women signed up for the unit in Kotzebue (a small city in Western Alaska) and were issued rifles.

Perhaps the most famous World War II woman Eskimo Scout was Laura Beltz Wright of Haycock, Alaska, a Native Alaskan woman who shot forty-nine out of fifty bull's eyes during marksmanship training, giving her the best score in her company. In addition to women who trained with rifles, other women and even children served as auxiliaries in Eskimo Scout units, serving food, helping with transportation, and operating radios.

The Eskimo Scout women continued to serve even after World War II ended. In 1949, as Alaska became a state, men who had served in the Alaska Territorial Guard were encouraged to join the new Alaska National Guard. The small unit organization and the coastal patrolling function of the Eskimo Scout units of World War II were preserved in the new Alaska Guard units, whose Cold War mission was to monitor the Alaska coastline for evidence of Russian activities. Although women were not formally allowed to join the units, they continued to accompany the men on scouting missions and to participate in training.

For several decades, the women were not given pay and benefits, despite participating on a regular basis. On October 1, 1971, however, women were officially permitted to join the Army National Guard, and the Alaska National Guard trained the first of its official Eskimo Scout women at Camp Carroll in Fort Richardson, Alaska. The women received official recognition of their service. By 1980, there were about sixty women assigned to Eskimo Scout units throughout Western Alaska.

In 2000, the Pentagon decided that it was no longer feasible to allow women to belong to the Eskimo Scouts, which were being retrained and reorganized to participate as infantry units with the prospect of worldwide combat deployment. The remaining Eskimo Scout women were reassigned to noncombat units, ending a proud tradition of service and an unusual episode in U.S. military history.

—Margaret D, Stock

See also United States, Home Front during World War II; United States, Military Service of Women in World War II

References and Further Reading

Marston, Muktuk. 1969. *Men of the Tundra; Eskimos at War.* Introduction by Ernest Gruening and epilogue by C. F. Necrason. New York: October House.

Salisbury, C. A. 1992. *Soldiers of the Mists; Minutemen of the Alaska Frontier.* Introduction by Major General John W. Schaeffer. Missoula, MT: Pictorial Histories.

Espín Guillois, Vilma (1930–)

Cuban revolutionary. Vilma Espín Guillois was born in 1930 in Santiago de Cuba, the largest urban center in the rustic eastern provinces of Cuba. Although Espín was a member of the Cuban elite, she grew up seeing firsthand the deprivation and scarcity in rural Cuba, one of the factors that influenced her early and sustained participation in the revolutionary process. She organized protests against Fulgencio Batista's coup with other students at the Universidad de Oriente, where she graduated with a degree in industrial chemical engineering. After additional studies at the Massachusetts Institute of Technology in the United States, she practiced engineering in Cuba for several years as a cover for her clandestine activities. After supporting the failed attack by Fidel Castro on the Moncada Barracks on July 26, 1953, she served in the Frank País underground, carrying messages to the exiled Castro in Mexico (Rodríguez Calderón 1992). In April 1957, she was named the July 26 Movement coordinator in the eastern provinces, where she also participated in the Revolutionary National Movement, Oriente National Action, and Revolutionary National Action (Shnookal 1992). When Espín's undercover persona, "Deborah," became too well known, it became necessary for her to leave behind her professional life, at which time she joined the guerrilla fighters in the mountains outside of Santiago. Known as Marianela, she bore arms with the Second Eastern Guerilla Front during the1959 Cuban Revolution, where she met her future husband Raúl Castro (Rodríguez Calderón 1992). Vilma Espín's experience in the trenches and proven ideological commitment to social justice and economic restructuring, in addition to her standing as sister-in-law of Fidel Castro, allowed her to become perhaps the most influential woman in postrevolutionary Cuba. President of the Federation of Cuban Women since its inception in 1960, Espín also has occupied key positions on the Cuban Communist Party's Central Committee, the Political Bureau, and the Council of State, where she worked to achieve full equality and rights for women.

—Sara E. Cooper

See also Cuban Revolution, Women in the

References and Further Reading

Brenner, Philip, et al. 1989. *The Cuba Reader.* New York: Grove.

Rodríguez Calderón, Mirta. 1992. "This Is a Battle of the Advance Guard, Requiring Valiant Combatants." In *Cuban Women Confront the Future: Three Decades after the Revolution,* edited by Deborah Shnookal, 35–52. Melbourne, Australia: Ocean Press.

Shnookal, Deborah, ed. 1992. *Cuban Women Confront the Future: Three Decades after the Revolution* (Collected interviews of Vilma Espín). Melbourne, Australia: Ocean Press.

Stone, Elizabeth, ed. 1981. *Women and the Cuban Revolution.* New York: Pathfinder.

Etheridge, Anna (1839 or 1844–1913)

American Civil War medic. Anna Blair was born on May 3 near Detroit, Michigan, but the year of her birth is uncertain; both 1839 and 1844 are cited. She moved to Wisconsin as a child, living a comfortable life as the daughter of a merchant farmer. She later married James Etheridge and returned to Detroit at the outbreak of the Civil War. As the Michigan Volunteer Infantry was mustered, there was a general need for the auxiliary support of nurses and laundresses. Anna Etheridge joined the 2nd Michigan Infantry as a daughter of the regiment, assuming the duties of a battlefield medic. Although many women initially responded to the call for volunteers, only two other women served with the 2nd Michigan for a significant time, nurse Jane Hinsdale and a disguised soldier, Sarah Emma Edmonds, who was known as Franklin Thompson. James Etheridge also enlisted and appears on the roster of the regiment.

Anna accompanied the unit to Washington, D.C., in May 1861 and participated in the battle of Blackburn's Ford, Virginia, in July. She served on the front lines, delivering water and first aid to the wounded on the battlefield during her first engagement with the enemy. She followed the 2nd Michigan on campaign, seeing combat at First Bull Run and nursing the sick in camp.

During the Battle of Williamsburg, Anna gained the attention of General Phil Kearny, who commended her work. Later, while treating the wounded at Second Bull Run, a soldier was hit and killed by artillery fire during her ministrations. General Kearny again commended her courage and promised her a horse and the rank of sergeant. Kearny was killed before she received the rank, but the regiment did provide a horse. Anna subsequently had two animals shot from under her. She was often seen riding through the lines, receiving cheers from the men, who called her Gentle Annie. In one incident, she incited the entrenched troops to cheer, giving away their position to the Confederates and drawing fire. In 1863, Anna received the Kearny Cross for courage.

Anna preferred to remain with the Army of the Potomac and moved from the 2nd Michigan to the 3rd and 5th Michigan Infantry. She was present at Fredericksburg and Chancellorsville, where she was wounded in the hand. In July 1863, she was seen in the Peach Orchard at Gettysburg and at the Third Corps Hospital. When General Ulysses S. Grant gained control of the Army of the Potomac in 1864, he ordered all women to rear echelon hospitals. Anna served at City Point, Virginia, and on hospital ships, although she also spent time with her unit in the field. She was mustered out with her regiment in 1865.

It is unclear what became of James Etheridge, but after the war, Anna married Connecticut infantry veteran Charles Hooks. He was disabled, and she worked for the Treasury Department until she was unfairly dismissed in 1878 so that another person could be hired. Many men from her regiments wrote on her behalf, but she could not reclaim her employment. She applied for a wartime service pension in 1886 and received the stipend in 1887. Anna Etheridge died on January 23, 1913, in Georgetown and was buried at Arlington Cemetery.

—Dawn Ottevaere

See also Civil War, American, and Women; Civil War, American, Women Combatants during the

References and Further Reading

Brocket, L. P., and Mary C. Vaughn. [1867] 1993. *Women at War.* A facsimile of the first edition. Stamford, CT: Longmeadow Press.

Hall, Richard. 1993. *Patriots in Disguise: Women Warriors of the Civil War.* New York: Paragon House.

Massey, Mary Elizabeth. 1966. *Women in the Civil War.* Reprinted with introduction by Jean V. Berlin. Lincoln: University of Nebraska Press.

Michigan Adjutant General. 1988. *Record Second Michigan Infantry, Civil War, 1861–1865.* Reprint, Detroit, MI: Detroit Publishing Company.

Michigan Soldiers and Sailors Alphabetical Index. Detroit, MI: Detroit Publishing Company, 1984.

Middleton, Lee. *Hearts of Fire: Soldier Women of the Civil War.* Franklin, NC: Genealogy Publishing Service, 1993.

Moore, Frank. 1867. *Women of the War: Their Heroism and Sacrifice.* Hartford: S. S. Scranton and Company.

F

Fairchild, Helen (1884–1918)

The first American nurse to die while serving at the front in World War I. She served with the American Expeditionary Forces from May 1917 until her death in France in January 1918. Born in Milton, Pennsylvania, in 1884, Helen grew up in a well-to-do farm family with three sisters and four brothers and graduated from the Pennsylvania Hospital nursing school in 1913. She was among a preparedness medical team from Pennsylvania Hospital in Philadelphia who had pledged to the Red Cross to mobilize in the Army Reserve Corps in time of war. On Sunday, May 2, 1917, three weeks after the United States officially entered World War I, the twenty-three physicians and sixty-four nurses of her unit, Base Hospital Number 10, received orders to mobilize and prepare for departure to France. On May 19, 1917, the unit sailed to LeTreport, a fishing village on the Normandy coast to relieve the staff of the British-run, 2,000-bed General Hospital 16 (renamed Pennsylvania Base Hospital 10).

On July 22, 1917, five days after arrival at LeTreport, Helen Fairchild was sent on the first team with two physicians and an orderly to work at the front in Belgium near Passchendaele at Casualty Clearing Station Number 4. Casualty Clearing Stations were mobile units that served as the first step in the chain of medical evacuation from the front lines. Subjected to regular bombing attacks, the medical staff slept under the floor of their tents in shallow dugouts covered with a hinged section of the tent floor lined with a piece of sheet iron. "We . . . wade through mud to and from the operating room where we stand in mud higher than our ankles," she wrote to her family (Fairchild collection).

Fairchild served in Station 4 during the third battle of Ypres, often working twelve to sixteen hours daily in the operating room. Internal and external blisters from mustard gas accounted for many of the wounded, and medical personnel as well became ill from vapors clinging to their clothing. Despite their grueling work, Helen later wrote, "it really has been surprising to me that the various hospitals are as well-fitted up as they are and that the men are gotten off the field so rapidly after being wounded" (Fairchild collection).

Casualty Clearing Station 4 temporarily closed August 17, 1917, a day of the heaviest of bombing and gassing to that point. Helen evacuated to Base Hospital 10. In early October, she became ill, suffering from severe abdominal

Helen Fairchild. (Courtesy Helen Fairchild's niece, Nelle Fairchild Hefty Rote)

pains. Her condition slowly progressed to jaundice and anemia. She requested exploratory surgery for suspected ulcers, lapsed into a coma following the operation, and died on January 18, 1918. According to autopsy reports, her death resulted from "acute yellow atrophy of the liver" and chloroform poison. Later medical analysis concluded that exposure to mustard gas through patient's clothing probably exacerbated her condition.

She was buried with full military honors in a small cemetery at LeTreport and later removed to Somme American Cemetery and Memorial at Bony, France.

—*Lee Ann Ghajar*

See also Nurses, U.S. Army Nurse Corps in World War I

References and Further Reading

Helen Fairchild Collection. Donated by Nelle F. Rote. Arlington, VA: Women in Military Service for America Memorial Foundation.

Hoeber, Paul B. 1921. *Pennsylvania Hospital Unit in the Great War.* New York: Paul B. Hoeber.

Stimson, Julia. 1918. *Finding Themselves.* New York: Macmillan.

Falklands War and Thatcher, Margaret (1925–)

War fought under the leadership of British Prime Minister Margaret Thatcher between Britain and Argentina from April to June 1982 following the Argentine occupation of the Falklands or Malvinas Islands in the southern Atlantic. The islands had been settled by the British in the nineteenth century, but Argentina had never relinquished its claim to the territory. Although the United Kingdom did not allow female members of the British military to participate in the battle zone, the leader of Britain during the war was the country's first female prime minister, Margaret Thatcher (1925–). The war also saw the appointment of Linda Kitson as Britain's first female official war artist. Kitson, selected by an Imperial War Museum committee, sailed with the British armada, was on the islands during the fighting, and produced 400 drawings that captured the experiences of the British combatants.

The war resulted from multiple miscalculations. The Argentine government did not believe that Britain would fight to retain the islands. It underestimated Thatcher. Thatcher's government for its part failed to make it clear to the Argentine government that it would fight to retain control of the islands. Thatcher's response to the Argentine occupation reinforced her image as the "Iron Maiden." She led Britain in war, declaring, "Defeat—I do not know the meaning of the word!" (Tucker 2001, 364). Later she asserted that "the Falklands victory put the Great back in Britain" (Wegs 1991, 307).

Thatcher, the leader of Britain's Conservative Party, had become prime minister in 1979. The unemployment and cuts in services that initially accompanied Thatcher's efforts to dismantle the British welfare state had produced an adverse reaction among the British electorate. The war stirred British patriotic feeling and enabled Thatcher to demonstrate her forceful leadership during wartime. Spencer Tucker argues that "lost in the euphoria of victory was her failure to avoid the war" (Tucker 2001, 364). Thatcher capitalized on the euphoria by calling a parliamentary election following Britain's June victory. Although the Conservatives only received 42 percent of the vote, they won an overwhelming majority of the seats in the House of Commons and kept Thatcher at the helm of the country. She became Britain's longest serving prime minister in the twentieth century. Thatcher served as prime minister until November 1990 when opposition within the Conservative leadership to her governing style and her attitude toward the strengthening of the European Community forced her resignation.

—*Bernard Cook*

References and Further Reading

Ogden, Chris. 1990. *Maggie: An Intimate Portrait of a Woman in Power.* New York: Simon and Schuster.

Saywell, Shelly. 1985. *Women in War: First-Hand Accounts from World War II to El Salvador.* New York: Viking Penguin.

Tucker, Spencer. 2001. "Falklands War." In *Europe since 1945: An Encyclopedia,* edited by Bernard Cook, 362–364. New York: Garland.

Wegs, J. Robert. 1991. *Europe since 1945: A Concise History.* 3d ed. New York: St. Martin's Press.

Young, Hugo. 1990. *The Iron Lady: A Biography of Margaret Thatcher.* New York: Noonday.

Fallaci, Oriana (1930–)

Italian novelist and journalist, best known for her skills as an uncompromising political interviewer. Her style has been referred to as both controversial and abrasive.

Oriana Fallaci was born in Florence, Italy, on June 29, 1930. Her father, Edoardo, was a member of a liberal underground movement that opposed Benito Mussolini's rise to power. He was jailed and tortured during the Nazi occupation of Florence but was later released. Following her father's example, Oriana became a member of the Corps of Volunteers for Freedom, actively fighting the Nazis by the time she was ten. At age sixteen, Oriana made the decision to become a writer. Her writing, both as novelist and journalist, reflects the social and political atmosphere in Italy before her birth and during her childhood.

Oriana's professional career began when she was hired to write a crime column in an Italian daily paper. She quickly became one of the country's first successful female journalists, developing an interviewing style that is uniquely her own, boldly asking aggressive questions, highlighting the abuse of power by officials, and writing with subjectivity. She has interviewed such political notables as Henry Kissinger, the Ayatollah Khomeini, Indira Gandhi, Yasser Arafat, the Shah of Iran, Golda Meir, Muammar Muhammad al-Gaddafi, and Deng Xiaoping.

Fallaci, who said, "I am obsessed by the uselessness and the stupidity and the cruelty and the folly of the war" (Bibliography Resource Center n.d.), wrote *Nothing, and So Be It* on the Vietnam War and the novel *Inshallah,* which deals with Italian troops in Lebanon after U.S. and French troops had becomes targets of suicide truck bombs.

—*Joann M. Ross*

See also Friang, Brigette; Trotta, Liz

References and Further Reading

Arico, Santo L. 1998. *Oriana Fallaci: The Woman and the Myth.* Carbondale: Southern Illinois University Press.

Franks, Laura. 1981. "Behind the Fallaci Image." *Saturday Review* 8: 18–22.

Levy, Elizabeth. 1975. *By-Lines: Profiles in Investigative Journalism.* New York: Four Winds Press.

"Oriana Fallaci," Bibliography Resource Center, n.d., http://www.giselle.com /oriana.html (cited June 2, 2004).

Farmborough, Florence (1887–1980)

Nurse with the Russian army during World War I. Florence Farmborough, who was born and raised in the country in Buckinghamshire, moved from Britain to Russia in 1908. After two years in Kiev, she moved to Moscow and tutored the daughters of a surgeon, Dr. Pavel Sergeievich Usov, until the outbreak of World War I. She volunteered to train as a nurse at a hospital for wounded soldiers founded by Princess Golitsin. Dr. Usov had joined the staff of the hospital, and he persuaded the princess to accept his two daughters and Farmborough as voluntary aids. After six months training, Farmborough was certified as a qualified Red Cross nurse. Usov, who insisted that one of his daughters was too frail and the other too young, intervened again on behalf of Farmborough. She was accepted as a nurse by a frontline surgical unit. She witnessed the great retreat of 1915, the Brusilov offensive of 1916, and the collapse of morale in the Russian army as the country sank into revolution. During the fall of 1916, Farmborough suffered a life-threatening fever. She returned to the front after a lengthy recuperation only to learn of the death of her elderly father in England. In March 1918, following the Treaty of Brest-Litovsk, which ended the war between Russia and Germany, Farmborough, with a group of English citizens and other foreign refugees, crossed Russia via the Trans-Siberian Railway to Vladivostok. There they boarded a ship sent by U.S. President Woodrow Wilson to transport Allied refugees to San Francisco. From San Francisco, Farmborough made her way back to her home in England.

In 1926, Farmborough became a lecturer at the University of Valencia. During the Spanish Civil War, she made broadcasts in English from Salamanca in favor of General Francisco Franco and the Nationalists whom she admired as "the saviour of Spain and of European Civilisation." She decried "the disease of Bolshevism" and expressed her revulsion at "the stamp of bestiality and uncouthness on the face of those who had no religion and no God" (Farmborough 1938, 8, 4, 33).

She returned to England after the beginning of World War II. Her memoir, *With the Armies of the Tsar: A Nurse at the Russian Front in War and Revolution,* based on her wartime diary, was published in 1974. Her diary vividly recounts the demoralizing shortages that often afflicted the Russian forces and the suffering of the wounded as well as her own experiences at the front. She died in 1980.

—*Bernard Cook*

See also Russia, Women in the Armed Forces (1700–1917)

FLORENCE FARMBOROUGH, MEDICAL VOLUNTEER IN RUSSIA DURING WORLD WAR I

August 1914

"We are very raw recruits, and it's not surprising that we sometimes wince, even shrink into the background, when an unusually ugly wound is bared for dressing, or when a man's cry of anguish follows an awkward attempt to alleviate an excruciating pain. It is, however, astonishing how quickly even a raw recruit can grow accustomed, though never hardened, to the sight and sound of constant suffering."

April 20, 1915

"A soldier was lying in a corner, breathing heavily, but otherwise quiet. It was his turn now; I went and knelt down on the straw at his side. His left leg and side were saturated with blood. I began to rip up the trouser-leg, clotted blood and filth flowing over my gloved hands. He turned dull, uncomprehending eyes toward me and I went on ripping the cloth up to his waist. I pushed the clothes back and saw a pulp, a mere mass of smashed body from the ribs downwards; the stomach and abdomen were completely crushed and his left leg was hanging to the pulped body by only a few shreds of flesh. I heard a stifled groan at my side and, glancing round, I saw the priest with his hands across his eyes turn and walk heavily across the room towards the door. The soldier's dull eyes were still looking at me and his lips moved. But no words came. What it cost me to turn away without aiding him, I cannot describe, but we could not waste time and material on hopeless cases. . . ."

July 1915

" . . . [O]ne hears, one feels, but in a numb, apathetic sort of way—as though all the edge of reality had been smoothed away . . ."

—Florence Farmborough.
With the Armies of the Tsar: A Nurse at the Russian Front in War and Revolution, 1914–1918.
New York: Cooper Square, 2000, Pages 22, 41–42, 101–102.
With permission of the publisher.

References and Further Reading

Farmborough, Florence. 1938. *Life and People in National Spain.* London: Sheed and Ward.

———. 1979. *Russian Album, 1908–1918.* Edited by John Jolliffe. Salisbury, England: Michael Russell.

———. 2000. *With the Armies of the Tsar: A Nurse at the Russian Front in War and Revolution, 1914–1918.* New York: Cooper Square.

FARRELL, MAIREAD (1957–1988)

Irish political radical who actively supported the republican campaign and women's rights. Mairead Farrell is best remembered for her coordination of prison protests and hunger strikes and her revelations regarding life under British rule. She died in March 1988, reportedly murdered by the British Army's Special Air Services (SAS) in Gibraltar.

Farrell was born in Belfast in August 1957. The youngest of six children, she gained an intense interest in politics and the republican cause during her adolescence, witnessing the British army's occupation of Belfast in 1969. At age fourteen, frustrated by the constant curfews, crackdowns, and coercion related to martial law, she joined the Irish Republican Army (IRA), the militant republican armed group that fought a war of terror to drive the British from Northern Ireland. Her membership in the Provisionals remained casual until at sixteen she began undertaking more formal duties, such as scouting and transporting weapons. These duties quickly expanded to active militant service, and by 1976, Farrell was arrested for conspiracy and possession of explosives. She was sentenced to fourteen and half years in the Armagh Women's Prison.

At Armagh, Farrell led demonstrations against the government's decision to refuse convicted members of the IRA special status as prisoners of war. She balked at the government's perception of them as criminals and organized her fellow inmates into hunger strikes and "dirty protests," protests characterized by the refusal to bathe and the smearing of excrement and menstrual blood on cell walls. When she was set free in 1986, after almost eleven years of internment, she studied political science and economics at Queens University and remained active in political work, giving lectures and attending meetings on various republican and feminist causes.

Despite these new interests and at least the appearance of more legitimate means of protest, Farrell never abandoned the IRA. In fact, her militant activities resumed almost immediately upon her release from jail. She became one of the organization's top operatives by the late 1980s, a distinction that would put her life decidedly at risk. Yet she seemed almost resigned to that risk, stating in an interview that "You have to be realistic. You realize that ultimately, you're either going to be dead or end up in jail. It's either one or the other. You're not going to run forever" (Eckert 1999, 22).

Her eerie premonition became reality in 1988 when she and two of her IRA colleagues, Daniel McCann and Sean Savage, were killed by an SAS unit in Gibraltar. Unarmed, the three were ambushed, and Farrell, only thirty-one, was reportedly shot eight times. Her death brought controversy and inquiry, ultimately fostering a hearing by the European Court of Human Rights in 1995. The court ruled that the Gibraltar Three, as they came to be known, were unlawfully killed in breach of Article 2 of the European Convention on Human Rights. The British government had violated their "right to live" by using "unreasonable force" (Eckert 1999, 284).

—Rachel Finley-Bowman

See also Devlin, Bernadette; Ulster, Women during the Troubles in

References and Further Reading

Eckert, Nicholas. 1999. *Fatal Encounter.* Dublin: Poolbeg.

Fawcett, Millicent (1847–1929)

Feminist supporter of Great Britain during the Boer and First World Wars. Millicent Fawcett was born Millicent Garrett in Aldeburgh, Suffolk, England, in 1847 into a family that operated a pawnshop. Before Millicent entered her teens, the family had purchased a successful coal-mining firm and could afford to send her and her two sisters to private schools for their education. When her older sister, Elizabeth Garrett (Anderson), attended medical school in London, Millicent and her sister Louise went to speeches by advocates of equal rights for women. Millicent was impressed and inspired by the ideas of John Stuart Mill, and this motivated her to become a leader in the women's movement. Millicent also fell in love with and married Henry Fawcett, a member of Parliament. When he died in 1884, Millicent devoted herself

Millicent Garrett Fawcett. (Library of Congress)

full time to the cause of female suffrage. She was not a radical feminist but believed that women could fulfill their "female roles" better if they were given the right to vote. She supported the causes of safe working conditions and increased pay for women workers and worked against the female slave trade. She strenuously advocated the right of women to receive quality education and attend college. Her major contribution to the women's movement was her ability to organize and mediate between factions of the movement at a time when it splintered into many directions. She served as president of the National Union of Women's Suffrage Societies (NUWSS) from 1897 to 1919.

Great Britain's involvement in the Boer War created a special role for Fawcett because of her prominence in the women's movement. She supported the government's involvement in the war, and, to counter the devastating revelations made by Emily Hobhouse of inhumane conditions and death in British concentration camps, Fawcett was appointed to lead a commission to investigate conditions of women and children in British prisoner of war and internment camps in South Africa. To the consternation of the British government, the commission largely corroborated the accusations of Hobhouse. During World War I, Fawcett championed support for Great Britain's cause as president of the NUWSS. Her repeated refrain was "Let us show ourselves worthy of citizenship, whether our claim to it be recognized or not" (Adie 2003, 36).

Fawcett wrote about her life experiences in *The Women's Victory* (1919) and *What I Remember* (1924). She was awarded the Grand Cross, Order of the British Empire, in 1925 for her work and was later made a dame of the British Empire.

—*Pamela Lee Gray*

See also Great Britain, Women in Service during World War I; Hobhouse, Emily

References and Further Reading

Adie, Kate. 2003. *Corsets to Camouflage: Women and War.* London: Hodder and Stoughton.

Pugh, Martin. 1992. *Women and the Women's Movement in Britain, 1914–1959.* Basinstoke, England: Macmillan.

Rubenstein, David. 1991. *A Different World for Women: The Life of Millicent Garrett Fawcett.* Athens: Ohio University Press, 1991.

Fedutenko, Nadezhda Nikiforovna (1915–1978)

Soviet dive bomber squadron commander of World War II. Guards Major Nadezhda Nikiforovna Fedutenko occasionally led her entire air division onto major targets.

Nadezhda Fedutenko. (V nebe frontovom *[In the Sky Above the Front]. 1971. 2nd edition. Edited by M. A. Kazarinova et al. Moscow: Molodaia Gvardiia)*

Fedutenko served in the 125th M.M. Raskova Borisov Guards Dive Bomber Regiment. In her teens, she was active in an aircraft modeling club, and in 1935, she qualified both as a pilot and parachuting instructor upon graduating from the Tambov School for Civil Aviation Pilots. Having mastered several types of aircraft, Fedutenko flew passengers and cargo by day and night. In action from the beginning of the hostilities with the Kiev (now Kyiv) Special Civil Aviation Group on the South-Western Front, she flew the R-5, usually at a low level and without an escort, delivering ammunition, equipment, food, and medical supplies. Also, she was charged with evacuating the wounded from enemy-held areas, transporting members of the general staff, and reconnoitering.

She had accumulated several thousand flying hours prior to enlisting in her wing, which flew twin-engine, medium-range Pe-2 dive bombers and was one of the three women's aviation units to emerge from Air Group No. 122 formed by Marina Raskova, a prominent navigator-pilot. Fedutenko took part in her wing's first operational mission on January 28, 1943, over Stalingrad and flew twice that day with an experienced men's squadron. On her second sortie, she led a flight into battle. With each mission, her proficiency increased. Her squadron flew more than 500 missions (1943–1945) in support of Soviet ground troops on the Southern, Don, North-Caucasus, Western, 3rd Belorussian, and 1st Baltic Fronts, defying antiaircraft fire and repelling fierce enemy fighter attacks.

One of her most memorable missions occurred on September 2, 1943, when she replaced her deputy divisional leader after he was shot down. With her navigator, Antonina Zubkova, she led fifty-four aircraft onto a target, a fortified area near El'nia, enabling friendly troops in this sector to go on the offensive. On August 18, 1945, she was awarded the highest Soviet military decoration, Hero of the Soviet Union. She was also the recipient of the orders of Lenin, Red Banner (twice), and Patriotic War I Class, as well as many medals. In 1946, Fedutenko was demobilized and transferred to the reserves.

—Kazimiera J. Cottam

See also Soviet Union, 125th M. M. Raskova Borisov Guards Bomber Aviation Regiment; Soviet Union/Russian Federation, Women Heroes of the

References and Further Reading

Cottam, Kazimiera J. 1998. *Women in War and Resistance.* Nepean, Canada: New Military.

———. 2003. "Fedutenko, Nadezhda Nikiforovna." In *Amazons to Fighter Pilots,* Vol. 1, edited by Reina Pennington, 168–169. Westport, CT: Greenwood.

Fernig, Félicité (1770–1841), and Fernig, Théophile (1775–1819)

Patriotic women warriors during the French Revolution. The Fernig sisters were born in Mortague, a city near the Franco-Belgian border. Their family and especially their father, an old veteran, were concerned with the revolutionary war occurring during 1792. Felicité and Théophile, sharing their family concerns, were worried by the growing rumors of defections in the French army in the area. Consequently, in May 1792, the Fernig sisters decided to wear men's clothing and joined the soldiers in Maulde. Quickly recognized as women, their courage and the significant role they played in battle made the soldiers overlook their gender. General Dumouriez, in charge of the Belgian campaign, upon hearing about these sisters and wishing to profit from their notoriety, invited them to join his force. In fact, the action of the Fernig sisters soon became known in Paris in the National Convention and among the public. As warriors, Félicité and Théophile also took part in the crucial battle of Valmy on September 20, 1792, and served under the command of Louis-Philippe d'Orléans, who was later to become King Louis-Philippe. Félicité and Théophile subsequently participated in the battles of Jemmapes, Anderecht, and Nerwinden.

On April 1793, however, the Fernig sisters followed the treasonous action of Dumouriez and joined the Austrian army with him. In her memoirs, Théophile, reports: "Accustomed to obeying him, to respecting him (he called us his children [. . .]), we believed what he was telling us" (Bonhomme 1873, 91). The sisters soon realized what was really happening and left Dumouriez's side to fight for the revolutionary Republic. It was too late. The National Convention already considered them to be his accomplices. The Fernig sisters fled to Belgium and sought for many years to obtain the right to return to France, which was only granted in 1801. Nevertheless, they returned to Brussels, where they both died.

The notoriety the Fernig sisters acquired in France is impressive. They inspired many women to fight for the nation in different ways. The sisters were mentioned in a proposal for a women's battalion project (Dupont 179[?], 2–3). Olympe de Gouges, the well-known revolutionary and feminist author, also celebrated Félicité and Théophile's actions in her piece about Dumouriez's victories. One should note, however, that the Fernig sisters were female warriors among many others. In fact, thousands of women joined the revolutionary forces until a decree was promulgated on April 30, 1793, officially calling for women to leave the army. Disobeying the orders, many remained.

—Eve-Marie Lampron

See also French Revolution, Impact of War on Women's Protest during the

References and Further Reading

Bonhomme, Honoré. 1873. *Correspondance inédite de Mademoiselle Théophile Fernig.* Paris: Firmin-Didot.

Dupont, Manette. 179[?]. *Départ de 900 citoyennes de Paris qui se sont enrôlées, déguisées en hommes, pour partir aux frontières.* Paris: Impr. de Guilhemat.

Lamartine, Alphonse. 1849–1850. *History of the Girondists; or, Personal Memoirs of the Patriots of the French Revolution.* Translated by H. T. Ryde. London: H. G. Bohn.

Fernig Sisters

See Fernig, Félicité, and Fernig, Théophile

58th Fighter Aviation Regiment

See Soviet Union Air Defense, 58th Fighter Aviation Regiment

Finland, Lotta Svärd

Finnish women's auxiliary corps. At the height of its activities, which date from 1922 to 1944, Lotta Svärd had some 200,000 members and a highly developed nationwide organization that combined work in vocational, religious, and ideological education; in social service; in home-front civil defense; and in various forms of battlefield support. The organization was affiliated with the reserve of the Finnish Defense Forces, the Civil Guards, and during the severe manpower shortages of the Russo-Finnish wars of 1939–1940 and 1941–1944, it came to play a crucial part in the Finnish war effort. Its name refers to a fictional character, Lotta Svärd, in J. L. Runeberg's *Tales of Ensign Stål* (1848), who went to the front during the Finnish War of 1808–1809 to feed and care for soldiers fighting the Russians.

The origins of the Lotta Svärd lay in the women's volunteer groups of the victorious White side of the Finnish civil war of 1918. Because the organization always stood for the bourgeois, Protestant, and antisocialist ideologies of the Whites, until the outbreak of the Winter War of 1939–1940, it remained deeply suspect in the eyes of the Finnish left. This suspicion was increased after 1927, when the Lotta Svärd was called on to assist the White Civil Guards to protect the Lutheran religion, home, and country and to elevate patriotism and civic-mindedness in general. Additional duties of the Lotta Svärd included the manufacture and maintenance of military uniforms, commissary duties in the Defence Forces, recruitment and fund-raising, as well as the upkeep of cemeteries for war dead and aid to war invalids, widows, and orphans. Whether undertaken in peacetime or in war, all this was voluntary, unpaid work.

During the Winter War with the Soviet Union, Lotta members were not allowed into combat, but they did take up tasks in air raid and naval defense and in military communications, as well as in the supply, maintenance, and production of military clothes and equipment, in running a total of eight field hospitals, and in managing the relocation and care of a half a million evacuees from the lost territories of eastern Finland. Up to 3,000 Lotta members served in antiaircraft defense during the war, many of them on the Karelian Isthmus. Forty-nine Lottas were killed in that war. During the War of 1941–1944, the organization was even more deeply involved in battlefield support, and it has been estimated that the activities of its so-called battlefield-Lottas freed up to a division of men for battlefield duties. Their constantly increasing involvement in battlefield support meant that by the end of the war the Lotta organization had suffered 113 battlefield-related deaths and 661 casualties.

Two women of the Finnish Lotta Svärd read from books, 1942. The purpose of the Lotta Svärd, a volunteer organization made up of Finnish women, was to boost national morale and support the civil guard. (Hulton-Deutsch Collection/Corbis)

Labeled a fascist organization by the Soviet Union, the Lotta Svärd was abolished by the

Soviet-dominated Control Commission that oversaw the pacification of Finland between the Finnish surrender of September 1944 and the Paris Peace Treaty of 1947. Lotta Svärd's ideological values were later nurtured by a heritage association, the Lotta Svärd Perinneliitto [Heritage Association], and some of its social functions by the new women's social service organization, Naisten Huoltosäätiö [Finnish Women's Welfare Association], but after 1944, no actual women's auxiliary corps existed in Finland.

—*Markku Ruotsila*

See also Finland, Women in the Winter War

References and Further Reading

Ollila, Aino 1996."Women's Voluntary Associations in Finland during the 1920s and 1930s." *Scandinavian Journal of History* 20: 97–107.

Olsson, Pia 1995. "'Learn to Love Your Country and Its People': From Lotta Ideology to Action." In *Encountering Ethnicities: Ethnological Aspects on Ethnicity, Identity and Migration,* edited by Teppo Korhonen. Helsinki: SKS.

FINLAND, WOMEN IN THE WINTER WAR

Women's organizations played a crucial role in assisting the Finnish Defense Forces during the 105 days of warfare that constituted the Russo-Finnish Winter War of 1939–1940. Finnish women were not allowed to take part in combat, but in addition to their extensive home-front tasks, they did assume many ancillary battlefield duties. Forty-nine women auxiliaries were nevertheless killed in battle during the war. This mass voluntary participation in the war effort by women from all social groups contributed to the legendary spirit of the Winter War in which a nation was exceptionally unified and determined against a much more powerful invader.

The most significant contribution of Finnish women to the war effort was by the Lotta Svärd organization, a legally constituted women's auxiliary corps that was affiliated with the Finnish reserve, the Civil Guards. Among other tasks, the Lotta Svärd members operated field hospitals; oversaw the production, supply, and maintenance of military clothes and other equipment; allocated relief to fatherless families and evacuees; and participated in air raid and naval defense.

On the home front, the Lotta Svärd's activities were supplemented by those of various women's societies in the churches, in business, and in agriculture as well as in the cooperative movement, the labor unions, and the socialist political organizations. Until the outbreak of the war, the latter had viewed the right-wing Lotta organization with deep suspicion, but animosities were put aside for the duration of the war, and these widely different groups cooperated in running most local bomb shelters and home guard units. They also set up joint advisory centers for those dislocated, impoverished, or otherwise injured by the war. During the war, all state assistance to war widows, orphans, and evacuees was channeled through these joint women's organizations. Few foreign imports of foodstuff or other necessities reached Finland during the war, and it further devolved on the women's groups to teach methods of conserving foodstuff using substitutes, and enhancing agricultural production. A joint agency for recruiting and allocating women for industrial work was created by thirty-six of these groups, and the agency successfully filled a large part of jobs previously held by men in the armaments industry, hospitals, and the postal services.

It has been estimated that the activities of the women's volunteer groups made it possible during the Winter War for at least a division worth of men who would otherwise have been needed in the industries and in municipal services on the home front to go to the battlefield. In view of the massive superiority in manpower that the Soviet armies enjoyed, this service of Finnish women was of material importance to the persistence of the Finnish war effort. It was also a turning point in the role that women were to play in Finnish society, for although they had enjoyed full and equal political rights since 1905, it was only through their industrial and municipal activities during the Winter War that Finnish women established themselves in all areas of the social, economic, and industrial life of the nation. Their services were applauded as crucial by the commander in chief, Field-Marshal Carl Gustav Mannerheim and were deeply appreciated by the nation at large, thus providing Finnish women with that new moral authority that sustained their presence, in unprecedented numbers, in postwar politics.

—*Markku Ruotsila*

See also Finland, Lotta Svärd

References and Further Reading

Koskimies, Airi, and Rafael Koskimies. 1964. *Suomen lotta.* Helsinki: Weilin and Göös.

Saraste, Erja. 1999. "Tuntemattomien naisten sota." In *Talvisodan pikkujättiläinen,* edited by Jari Leskinen and Antti Juutilainen, 756–769. Porvoo: Werner Söderström Oy.

First, Heloise Ruth (1925–1982)

Writer, teacher, and political activist against racism, economic exploitation, and the South African apartheid regime. Born to émigré parents from the Baltics who were founders of the South African Communist Party (SACP), Ruth First joined the SACP while studying at Witwatersrand University. In her early twenties, she assisted black miners in the African Mine Strike of 1946, supported the Indian Passive Resistance campaign, and edited various radical journals and newspapers. From 1947, she published a series of exposés that uncovered the harsh conditions experienced by Africans on labor farms and other influential articles on migrant labor, bus boycotts, the women's antipass campaign, and urban slums. In 1949, she married Joe Slovo, a labor organizer, lawyer, and fellow Communist, with whom she had three children. One daughter, Shawn, wrote the movie script for *A World Apart,* a life of Ruth First and her family, and another daughter, Gillian, based her novel, *Ties of Blood,* on the Slovo family.

The Assassination of Ruth First

"Our Comrade Ruth First was killed by a letter bomb on Tuesday, August 17th, in the office of Mozambique's Centre for African Studies. With her were the Centre's director, Aquino de Braganca, a lecturer at the Centre, Bridget O'Laughlin, and a visiting ANC activist, Pallo Jordan. All were injured. All were victims of the spawning South African state terrorism, which is spreading like a blood-poison throughout southern Africa. Ruth's murder is the latest—but surely not the last—in that long trail of murder and assassination which South Africa has made into its first line of defence of apartheid."

—Obituary in *Sechaba,* October 1982, http://www.sacp.org.za/biographies/rfirst2.html.

"On Tuesday, 17th August, Ruth First was killed by a letter bomb in Maputo, Mozambique, to become another martyr in this long and bitter struggle for liberation. Her death had been fashioned in the macabre hearts of the Pretoria madmen who had long realised that she was a tireless and committed fighter and revolutionary in the true sense of the word; a writer of consummate skill gifted with a rare, incisive vision who combined her craft and energy to actively combat the unspeakably evil South African system."

—Obituary in *Mayibuye,* http://www.sacp.org.za/biographies/rfirst1.html.

First and Slovo were among 156 people, including Nelson Mandela and Walter Sisulu, who were arrested and then acquitted in the famous 1956 Treason Trial. After authoring a book in 1963 revealing the injustices perpetrated on the people of Namibia under South African rule, First was banned from journalism and then detained for 117 days, most of it served in solitary confinement. First and her family moved to London in 1964.

While in England, First edited the works of several important antiapartheid figures, including Nelson Mandela's *No Easy Walk to Freedom,* and also wrote a number of significant studies of her own. She traveled widely, including visits to the Soviet Union, China, and several countries in Africa, experiences about which she later wrote. She also taught courses on the sociology of underdevelopment at the University of Durham, England.

In 1977, First accepted a post as professor at the Centre for African Studies at the Eduardo Mondlane University in Maputo, Mozambique. There she organized a team of researchers investigating migrant labor, particularly on the South African gold mines. On August 17, 1982, First was killed by a letter bomb sent by the South African security forces. She was buried in Maputo alongside other victims of the brutal apartheid regime.

—*Roger B. Beck*

See also Mandela, Winnie

References and Further Reading

First, Ruth. 1982. *One Hundred and Seventeen Days: An Account of Confinement and Interrogation under the South African 90-Day Detention Law.* 2d ed. Harmondsworth, England: Penguin.

Marks, Shula. 1983. "Ruth First: A Tribute." *Journal of Southern African Studies* 10, no. 1 (October): 123–128.

Pinnock, Don. 1995. *Ruth First.* They Fought for Freedom series. Cape Town, South Africa: Maskew Miller Longman.

"Ruth First—Memorial Issue." 1982. *Review of African Political Economy* 9 no. 25 (winter).

Williams, Gavin P. 1982. "Ruth First: A Preliminary Bibliography." *Review of African Political Economy* 9 (winter): 54–64.

Wolpe, AnnMarie. 1983. "Tribute to Ruth First." *Feminist Review* 13 (spring): 3–4.

Fittko, Lisa (1909–2005)

Anti-Nazi resister. Lisa Fittko, a German Jewish leftist, joined the antifascist German resistance movement to oppose the Nazis. After she escaped from Nazi Germany with her husband, Hans, she eventually settled in southern France, from where she helped other refugees make their way across the Pyrenees to the relative safety of Spain. From France, she and her husband Hans made their way to Cuba and then to the United States, where she now lives.

Lisa Ekstein was born to a middle-class Jewish family in Uzhgorod in the Ruthenian sector of the Austro-Hungarian Empire. As a child she lived in Budapest and Vienna. After World War I, her family moved to Berlin, and she grew up there during the politically and culturally tumultuous 1920s. While in secondary school she became active in a communist organization, the Socialist Students League, and once the Nazis took power, she committed herself to defeating them, protesting the Nazis through leaflets and demonstrations. As she told her parents, "Now everything depends on beating fascism—I can't waste any time with university and pleasant living" (Fittko 1991, 2–3). In 1933, when the Gestapo appeared close to arresting her for her antifascist actitivities, she went to Prague, where she met her future husband, Hans Fittko.

They went to Paris in 1938, where they aided refugees from Hitler's Germany. After the Nazis invaded France in 1940, she made her way to southern France, where the Vichy government interned her at Gurs, a women's camp for enemy aliens. Realizing how dangerous it was for her to remain in the camp, she managed to escape and rejoin her husband. Hans Fittko was not Jewish, but he was a leftist and opponent of the Nazis, which made him a target of the Gestapo as well (Fittko, 1995).

They made their way to the port city of Marseilles, hoping to leave France by boat. Their efforts were unsuccessful, in part because Fittko lacked the papers she needed to make good her escape. While waiting for the papers, Lisa Fittko agreed to help smuggle other refugees over the Pyrenees into Spain. She worked with the North American Varian Fry, who set up a network to help get resistance fighters and Jews out of Europe. Fittko managed to save at least 100 people by leading them over the mountains into Spain.

In September 1940, Fittko guided the eminent German philosopher Walter Benjamin over the escape route to Spain. Benjamin carried a heavy black briefcase with him that contained his last manuscript throughout the steep ascent over the high mountains, a trip that Fittko (1991) describes in her book *Escape through the Pyrenees.* Unfortunately, the Spanish border guards captured Benjamin and, according to Fittko, he committed suicide rather than allow them to send him back to France (Fittko, 1991).

In 1950, she moved to Chicago, where she spoke about her experiences and was active in the peace movement. In 1986, the Federal Republic of Germany awarded her the Distinguished Service Medal, First Class. At the acceptance ceremony she said, "Are awards like this only for individuals? Shouldn't this be, first and foremost, an occasion for recognizing the Resistance movement as a whole? The Resistance struggle against a criminal regime must be accorded its rightful place in our history, so that a new generation can believe in itself and in its future" (Fittko, 1995, 160).

—*Margaret Power*

See also Buch, Eva Maria

References and Further Reading

Fittko, Lisa. 1991. *Escape through the Pyrenees.* Evanston, IL: Northwestern University.

———. 1995. *Solidarity and Treason. Resistance and Exile, 1933–1930.* Evanston, IL: Northwestern University.

Fomicheva-Levashova, Klavdiia Iakovlevna (1917–1958)

Soviet air squadron commander. Guards Lieutenant-Colonel Klavdiia Iakovlevna Fomicheva served in the 125th "M. M. Raskova" Borisov Guards Bomber Aviation Regiment, which flew medium-range Petliakov (Pe-2) bombers. Initially a flight and deputy squadron commander, Fomicheva assumed command of No. 2 squadron after her superior, Evgeniia Timofeeva, became deputy of Major V. V. Markov, who had replaced Marina Raskova as commanding officer after the latter's accidental death on January 4, 1943.

Employed at the Moscow Regional Office of the State Bank, Fomicheva took gliding lessons sponsored by her employer. As one of the best glider pilots in her group, she was encouraged to pursue flying training and in 1938 became full-time instructor at Reutovsky Flying Club of the Moscow Region.

In January 1943, she flew her first two missions with an experienced men's squadron in the most crucial sector of the Stalingrad Front. Skilled in evasive actions, target approach in formation, flying straight on a bomb run, and clearing targets, she thoroughly trained her subordinates. All her well-trained aircrews survived the fierce fighting over the Kuban area of North Caucasus. On June 2, 1943, Fomicheva's squadron, abandoned by its fighter escort, engaged eight enemy fighters and shot down four. Its performance was held up by the air force commander in chief as an example for the entire Soviet bomber aviation to follow.

On September 17, 1943, during the stubborn fighting near Smolensk, Fomicheva was shot down and put out of action until early 1944. Brought down again on June 23, 1944, at the beginning of the Belorussian offensive, she was back in action with her navigator, Galina Dzhunkovskaia, by August 28, 1944. She especially distinguished herself in the stubborn fighting for the Baltic and East Prussia. Altogether, Fomicheva flew fifty-five operational missions and was credited with shooting down eleven enemy aircraft in group combat (Cottam 2003, 172).

Awarded the prestigious Hero of the Soviet Union on August 18, 1945, Fomicheva was also presented with the orders of Lenin, Red Banner (twice), and Red Star, as well as many medals. She took part in the Victory Parade on Moscow's Red Square on June 24, 1945. Employed for four years as a flying instructor at the air force academy, she was grounded due to deteriorating health and taught air tactics at the Military Aviation School for Pilots in Borisoglebsk. She died prematurely from an illness related to her wartime injuries. At her grave at the Novodevich'e Cemetery, a tiny aircraft soars above the white marble obelisk. Underneath there is an epitaph: "Though you have died, you will live forever as an inspiration to those who are bold and strong in spirit!" (Maxim Gorky's *Pesnia o sokole* [The Falcon Song]).

—*Kazimiera J. Cottam*

See also Soviet Union, 125th M. M. Raskova Borisov Guards Bomber Aviation Regiment; Soviet Union/Russian Federation, Women Heroes of the

References and Further Reading

Cottam, Kazimiera J. 1998. *Women in War and Resistance.* Nepean, Canada: New Military.

———. 2003. "Fomicheva-Levashova, Klavdiia Iakovlevna." In *Amazons to Fighter Pilots,* Vol. 1, edited by Reina Pennington, 171–172. Westport, CT: Greenwood.

Fonda, Jane (1937–)

American actress, born in 1937, who was a leading critic of U.S. involvement in the Vietnam War. Reflecting on her life in 1997, Jane Fonda, daughter of actor Henry Fonda, compiled a film portrait of the various personae in her productive life. Looking for a defining theme, she asked, "Am I simply a chameleon that changes color according to the times and the men in my life?" (Braunstein 2001). In an attempt to find and be herself, she successfully escaped the Lady Jane image of her privileged childhood. Later in life, she embraced the Workout Queen image that projected physical and emotional health, and she then described herself as content with her life as a single woman with her newfound Christian faith. But this immensely talented and complex creative woman has been unable to distance herself from a moment of antiwar activism that led to accusations of treason in the 1970s.

Fonda's prodigious talent and willingness to defy convention placed her in the cultural vanguard of the 1960s and 1970s. She was among the first American film actresses to perform nude in Paris; her trip to Hanoi in 1972 and the speeches she gave there transcended the radicalism of most antiwar celebrities; she capitalized on the U.S. fitness craze in the 1980s; and her current dedication to education, women's issues, and personal faith place her in the mainstream of American values in the conservative twenty-first century. Nevertheless, Fonda has been unable to transcend the "Hanoi Jane" label ascribed to her by many Americans.

Fonda's work with her husband, director Roger Vadim, in the 1960s projected an image of uninhibited sexuality. In the campy comedy *Barbarella* (1968), Fonda played a "five star double-rated astronautical aviatrix" who wore outlandish costumes and Nancy Sinatra go-go boots. Director Vadim called the film "a kind of sexual Alice in Wonderland of the future" (Guthmann 1996).

By 1968, Fonda was beginning to tire of "the world of Roger Vadim, with my blond hair and falsies" (Guthmann 1996). Realizing that her marriage to Vadim was disintegrating, Fonda returned to the United States. She had been out of touch with politics for most of her life, but the civil rights, antiwar, and countercultural movements awakened her political interests. Energized by a new relationship with activist Tom Hayden, she jumped into her new role as energetically as any Method actor. Fonda was drawn to radical politics. She accepted uncritically the verities of the antiwar movement, along with those of the American Indian Movement and the Black Panther Party.

In February 1971, Fonda supported the Winter Soldier Investigation sponsored by Vietnam Veterans Against the War in which veterans testified in Detroit regarding wartime atrocities and war crimes. As the summer approached, Fonda joined forces with *Klute* costar Donald Sutherland, singers Holly Near and Country Joe McDonald, writer Jules Feiffer, and director Mike Nichols to produce a satirical antiwar revue at the Haymarket Square GI Coffeehouse in Fayetteville, North Carolina, just outside of Fort Bragg. The show was called FTA, "Fox Trot Alpha," "Free the Army," "Fun, Travel, and Adventure" (the satirical name of a GI antiwar newspaper published at Fort Knox, Kentucky).

Even before Fonda's involvement in the FTA shows, she provided financial support to the Indochina Peace Campaign (after which she would later name her film production company, IPC). The group also raised funds and support for the United Farm Workers and the presidential campaign of George McGovern. But it was Fonda's trip to Vietnam that earned her the hatred of many Americans.

In July 1972, Fonda traveled to North Vietnam to create a documentary film about the everyday realities of the war in the city of Hanoi. She also filmed craters and bomb damage to dikes, damage that the U.S. government had denied existed. She thus crossed the line from protest and antiwar activism to activities that drew the attention of the State Department and prowar veterans groups, just as her domestic appearances and speeches had already attracted the attention of the FBI. United States citizens were not permitted to travel to Vietnam, and Fonda's arrival in Hanoi from Moscow saw her wearing pajama-like clothing similar to that worn by the Viet Cong. Fonda's documentary contradicted official U.S. government pronouncements. In the eyes of her critics, her activities in Hanoi provided aid and comfort to an enemy of the United States.

The start of a new decade, 1980 was the year of Ronald Reagan and a "get government off our backs" rejection of both the liberalism of the late 1960s and the hedonistic self-absorption of the latter part of the 1970s. Reagan ran on a platform that promised a return by the United States to preeminent political and military leadership in the world, and his wife, Nancy, promised a return of elegance and alcohol to White House parties. The self-reliance, with the implication that there would be no government help to rely on, of Nancy Reagan's "Just Say NO" solution to the problem of drugs in U.S. society also ushered in new political and personal priorities. Government and society were there to help those who helped themselves, and Jane Fonda was in the forefront of the newest self-help crusade.

Fonda's persona mutated in the self-help 1980s into that of the workout queen. With the advent of the new millennium, Fonda embraced a new identity as a born-again Christian. Nevertheless, despite her noteworthy philanthropic activity, particularly on behalf of causes to benefit the lives of women and girls, Fonda has been unable to shake the negative Hanoi Jane image that many still hold.

—Barbara L. Tischler

See also Baez, Joan; Vietnam, U.S. Women Soldiers in

References and Further Reading

Andersen, Timothy P. 1990. *Citizen Jane: The Turbulent Life of Jane Fonda.* 1990. New York: Henry Holt.

Braunstein, Peter. 2001. "Ms. America: Why Jane Fonda Is a Mirror of the Past Forty Years." *American Heritage Magazine* (July–August 2001), http://www.americanheritage.com/AMHER/2001/05msamerica.shtml (accessed November 1, 2004).

Guthmann, Edward. 1996. "1968 Barbarella Is a Romp with a Babe." *San Francisco Chronicle*, September 13, D17.

Holzer, Henry Mark, and Erika Holzer. 2002. *Aid and Comfort: Jane Fonda in North Vietnam*. New York: McFarland.

Forced Labor, Nazi Germany

People in German-occupied Europe were compelled to work in Germany. Between 1941 and 1945, between 10 and 12 million people were forced to leave their homes and were transported to work in Germany (Stephenson 2001, 121–124). In August 1944, women constituted one-third—1.9 million—of the 5.7 million foreign forced laborers in Germany (Herbert 1997, 296). With its male workforce depleted by conscription and unwilling to compel its own women, who employed many strategies to avoid unpleasant labor, to do industrial or agricultural work, the Nazi regime was dependent on foreign labor. Women from Western Europe were not normally compelled to work in Germany, although many volunteered to do so. This was not the case with Eastern European women, who were forcibly removed to Germany and, after the ordeal of transportation, were subjected to harsh conditions and grinding exploitation. Women from Eastern Europe, predominantly from Soviet territory, constituted 87 percent of foreign female workers in Germany (Herbert 1997, 296). Western European female workers were paid wages, could rent rooms, and were free. Eastern European women, assigned to industry, were housed in barracks and were under police control. If they became pregnant, they might be forced to submit to abortion or were forced to work until delivery and to return to work immediately. Children with supposedly Aryan characteristics were placed in the *Lebensborn* program to be raised as Germans. Others were warehoused in institutions where they usually perished from neglect and malnutrition. Eastern European women often suffered sexual abuse. Some were forced into prostitution to service the bordellos established for foreign workers. Women workers assigned to agriculture, particularly in southern Germany, often fared better than those in the cities.

—*Bernard Cook*

See also Holocaust and Jewish Women

References and Further Reading

Herbert, Ulrich. 1997. *Hitler's Foreign Workers: Enforced Foreign Labor in Germany under the Third Reich*. Cambridge, England: Cambridge University.

Homze, Edward L. 1967. *Foreign Labor in Nazi Germany*. Princeton, NJ: Princeton University.

Stephenson, Jill. 2001. *Women in Nazi Germany*. Harlow, England: Pearson Education.

46th Tuman Guards Bomber Aviation Regiment

See Soviet Union, 46th Tuman Guards Bomber Aviation Regiment

Fourcade, Marie-Madeleine (1900–1989)

Leader of a French Resistance network during World War II. In the late 1930s, Marie-Madeleine Fourcade was working as a general secretary for a magazine publishing company run by a World War I hero, Commandant Georges Loustaunau-Lacau. With Loustaunau-Lacau, Fourcade founded one of the first Resistance networks in France, Alliance, called Noah's Ark by the Germans because each agent had an animal's name. Fourcade was "Hedgehog."

In 1941, Loustaunau-Lacau, code-named Navarre, was arrested. Fourcade, code-named PoZ/ 55, then ran the organization. From Pau, she sent agents throughout the country. She organized intelligence networks throughout France, including the ports and major cities. Fourcade's 3,000 agents sent information to the British concerning movements of coastal defense boats, supply ships, and submarines in the Atlantic. They even provided a map of the coastline indicating German deployments just before the 1944 D-Day invasion.

Impressed with the work of Fourcade and her agents, the British sent her a wireless operator in August 1941. Unfortunately, this particular operator turned out to be a double agent. Fourcade and a number of her agents were arrested. She was able to escape from the Gestapo and fled France for Switzerland with her two children. She resumed her Resistance work, however, rescuing downed British airmen and sending them back to England. Fearing Fourcade's arrest and possible execution, in July 1943, the British MI6 organization decided that Fourcade should move to England. From a house in Chelsea, she was able to assist with the reorganization of the secret services in France, and her agents were able to obtain German military papers for the Allies. She returned to France (Provence) for a mission in August 1944.

In May 1945, she went to a number of detention camps looking for survivors of her network. She lost 438 of her 3,000 agents during the course of the war.

After the war, the French government awarded her the Legion of Honor, the Medal of the Resistance with Rosette, and the Croix de Guerre. The British Secret Service considered Fourcade's Noah's Ark to be the most effective independent information service in occupied France. They awarded her the Order of the British Empire in recognition of her contributions.

—*Leigh Whaley*

See also Aubrac, Lucie; Borrel, Andrée; France, Resistance during World War II, Women and; Hall, Virginia; Moreau-Evrard, Emilienne; Souliè, Geneviève; Tillion, Germaine; Wake, Nancy; Witherington, Pearl

References and Further Reading

Fourcade, Marie-Madeleine. 1974. *Noah's Ark.* Translated from the French by Kenneth Morgan. Preface by Commander Kenneth Cohen. New York: E. P. Dutton.

France, Resistance during World War II, Women and

Role of women in organized opposition to the German occupiers of France and the Vichy Regime during World War II. The French Resistance, in which women played an integral role, consisted of various forms of opposition to Nazi and pro-Nazi rule in occupied and Vichy France during World War II.

The lightning advance of German air and ground forces through the French countryside during the spring of 1940 led to a quickly demoralized French nation. An armistice with Germany on June 22, 1940, split France into occupied and unoccupied zones. The unoccupied zone was run by Marshal Henri Phillipe Pétain from the French resort town of Vichy and became a collaborationist regime that partnered closely with Nazi Germany. Resistance against collaborationist Vichy France and Nazi Germany was advocated by General Charles de Gaulle of the Free French forces in England. Resistance groups sprang up in the occupied and unoccupied zones and these organizations relied on the efforts not only of men but also of women to subvert Nazi and Vichy activities.

Resistance against the Nazis and their collaborators took many forms. Besides armed combat, resisters collected and disseminated information and resistance-oriented news; they protected and hid fugitives and downed Allied pilots; and they obtained and transported messages, weapons, and news, planted explosives, assassinated Nazi officials, and provided support and logistical services. Women from all social, religious, and political affiliations became involved in the various activities of the resistance groups. These women, like men, joined the resistance for various reasons including their patriotic or political views, religious or ethical principles, or even due to a desire for adventure.

Women were warmly welcomed into most French Resistance organizations, and in many activities women were considered preferable to men because women "had the best disguise: they were women!" (Schwartz 1989, 131). Women drew little suspicion because they were considered to be politically insignificant and, therefore, harmless. In fact, women often used their gender to their advantage by flirting and otherwise using "feminine wiles" to create a sense of innocence that fooled the enemy. France Pejot, for example, escaped two militiamen by insisting on providing the men with coffee. As the coffee "brewed," she ran down the back stairs and made her escape (Weitz 1995, 252–253). Clara Malraux also used her femininity as a tool when she undertook missions where she socialized with German soldiers to determine if any were demoralized or discouraged enough to be recruited to help the Resistance (Weitz 1995, 128).

Women were heavily involved in courier and clandestine news activities. Most couriers in the Resistance were women because men aroused too much suspicion. Women were entrusted with transporting extremely sensitive information that if found by the Nazis or their collaborators could have meant arrest, interrogation, and even death for the captured courier. Using the ubiquitous bicycle, couriers such as Dr. Geneviève Congy transported intelligence messages, including maps indicating military deployments, to heads of various resistance units (Weitz 1995, 78).

Although not traditionally considered "resistance," social support services for resisters and refugees were imperative activities that were overwhelmingly performed by women. Women in these roles supplied fighters with ration cards and supplied food to people in refugee camps (Poznanski 1998, 238 and 242). They also risked their lives to rescue others. Marianne Cohn, for example, led a group of Jewish women to the Spanish border before the Nazis killed her (Weitz 1995, 172). Many social service activities became formalized within resistance movements. Berty Albrecht, for example, "conceived of and organized formal social services for Combat," a major resistance organization, which other resistance organizations soon followed (Weitz 1995, 177).

It was unusual for a woman in the French Resistance to be a leader, although there are a few exceptions. Berty Albrecht is one example. She was in charge of the social services section of Combat, and she also produced the organization's first newsletter. Lucie Aubrac helped found the Libération-Sud movement and Marie-Madeleine Fourcade, the only woman to head an entire network, commanded the three thousand strong British-backed Alliance network.

Leadership, however, was rare for women. Even more uncommon were women participants in assassinations, sabotage, and armed combat. However, female participants in armed resistance did exist. Jeanne Bohec, for example, blew up a major rail line in preparation for the Allied landings in Normandy (Weitz 1995, 154). Another female resister, code named "Claude," was assigned to assassinate a "notorious member of the Gestapo." Claude walked into a Parisian restaurant frequented by German officers, flirted with the Nazi officer she was assigned to kill, dined with him, persuaded him to join her in a pre-arranged taxi, and then in the back of the taxi shot him point blank and fulfilled her mission (Schwartz 1989, 130). Full-time female fighters were extremely rare, but they nevertheless existed (Schwartz 1989, 129). There were

Women members of the maquis display the rifles and pistols they used to fight the Nazi garrison in Marseille before the entry of Allied troops, 1944. (Bettmann/Corbis)

even a few all-women groups that focused on combat missions. One such group specialized in placing grenades under German trucks (Poznanski 1998, 242). These women fought in and sometimes commanded co-ed units. Georgette Gérard, for example, became one of only two known women who led maquis (fighting) units (Weitz 1995, 151). Another woman, Madeleine Riffaud, commanded a Parisian guerrilla team when she was only nineteen years old (Schwartz 1989, 129). Women in combat and leadership roles were thought of more as "honorary men" than they were as women performing male-specific roles (Schwartz 1989, 138). In this way it was possible for traditionalist Frenchmen to reconcile women performing male-identified roles. Anna Pouzache, for example, was a liaison agent who frequently camped with maquis men. When one new arrival questioned a woman belonging to the maquis, a fellow partisan sprang to Pouzache's defense saying, "It's not a woman, it's Anna" (Schwartz 1989, 136).

The impact of the French Resistance on female participants was varied. Although many female resisters lived with constant fear and had to postpone their lives and schooling during the occupation, resistance activities provided women with an unheard-of freedom that was unavailable to them prior to the war. They traveled alone, spent days and nights away from home, and worked in places otherwise forbidden. Their experiences in the Resistance provided women with newfound confidence and assurance in their capabilities.

—*Tracey J. Axelrod*

See also Aubrac, Lucie; Borrel, Andrée; Fourcade, Marie-Madeleine; Hall, Virginia; Moreau-Evrard, Emilienne; Souliè, Geneviève; Tillion, Germaine; Wake, Nancy; Witherington, Pearl

References and Further Reading

Lande, D. A. 2000. *Resistance! Occupied Europe and its Defiance of Hitler.* Osceola,WI: MBI Publishing Company.

Poznanski, Renée. 1998. "Women in the French-Jewish Underground: Shield-Bearers of the Resistance?" Pp. 234–252 in *Women in the Holocaust.* Edited by Dalia Ofer and Lenore J. Weitzman. New Haven: Yale University Press.

Schwartz, Paula. 1989. "Partisanes and Gender Politics in Vichy France." *French Historical Studies* 16, 1: 126–151.

Weitz, Margaret Collins. 1995. *Sisters in the Resistance: How Women Fought to Free France 1940–1945.* New York: John Wiley and Sons.

France, Revolution of 1848

The participation of women in the revolutionary events in Paris between the February 1848 upheaval and the six bloody June Days. The oppressed positions of Parisian women both as women and as workers influenced their participation in these events.

Revolutionary movements in many European capitals in 1848 encouraged women's involvement in republican, democratic socialist, and feminist activities. In France, the end to restrictions on the press and the right to assembly encouraged women's political involvement. This was especially true in Paris, where the Second Republic had been declared in February. Women participated in the revolt that overthrew King Louis Philippe and demanded inclusion in political and economic changes. In March, Eugénie Niboyet (1799–1883) published the first feminist daily political newspaper, *Voix des femmes* (Voice of Women), and women associated with this publication created a club called Société de la *Voix des femmes* (Society of the *Voice of Women*).

Clubs relevant to women and the challenges they faced in society abounded, with the most radical being the Vesuvians, made up of young, unmarried, poorly paid workers. Representing themselves as volcanically powerful, they demanded not only equality but also women's participation in the military and for men and women to dress the same. Equality in marriage—including sharing of household chores—formed part of their platform. Many of those supporting changes for women disavowed that shouting, riots, or masculine attire should be employed to that end. Those associated with the *Voix des femmes* disapproved of some of the Vesuvians' ideas and tactics, including street demonstrations and wearing masculine clothing and bloomers.

Something that militant women could agree on was the franchise. Although many women felt suffrage would not guarantee equality, the republic's declaration of universal male suffrage prior to April elections forced women to respond. Pauline Roland (1805–1852) tried to vote in local elections in Boussac but officials barred her from doing so. On March 16 in Paris, women presented a petition requesting political and social rights equal to those of men. On March 22, members from the Comité des Droits de la Femme (Committee of the Rights of Woman) met with a member of the provisional government, Armand Marrast. He deferred, however, arguing that the soon-to-be elected National Assembly, not a provisional government, should respond. On April 6, Niboyet, as editor of the *Voix des femmes,* called for George

Sand to be elected to the Constituent Assembly, although Sand disavowed any interest or association with Niboyet's group. Every effort women made to gain suffrage met at best with minimal verbal acceptance from men. After the Second Republic's new assembly had been elected, a proposal on women's suffrage was defeated 899 to 1.

With conservatives feeling validated by the April elections, men bent on destroying the Société de la *Voix des femmes* attempted to inundate its meeting on May 11. The club's members responded by denying men entrance; after June 4, when a similar event occurred, the women demanded a double entry fee for men. Police then permanently shut down the club. This created a split among women regarding the means of advancing their efforts. Worker and feminist Jeanne Deroin (1805–1894) left the club, founding the *Politique des femmes* (Women's Politics), and the *Voix des femmes* published its last edition in June.

Women as workers faced particular discrimination despite their contributions to the national economy—and the profits of producers. By 1848, one-quarter of the wood gilders in Paris were women; female upholstery workers made up half of that trade. Overall, in 1848, about 40 percent of the Parisian manufacturing workforce was female. Women received less than half men's wages. Although women workers were not generally involved in the earlier feminist or socialist agitation, the outlook of some workingwomen in 1848 was affected by their discrimination as both women and women workers. Though often underrepresented in feminist efforts, some workingwomen asserted themselves. Désirée Gay (1810–c.1890) and Suzanne Voilquin (1801–1876/7) aligned with Deroin and gave voice to working women's social interests.

Désirée Gay had been part of the government's national workshop programs, created to solve the rampant unemployment in France. The Luxembourg Commission, overseeing this effort, had unceremoniously excluded women from the formulation of commission decisions and the administration of national workshops. Despite the efforts of Gay, the government of the republic removed her as a workshop director, threatening that if workshop workers protested the point, it would close the workshop all together.

And, indeed, on June 22 the conservative republican government closed all of the workshops, sparking six days of street fighting. The "bloody June Days" resulted in the death of 1,500 to 3,000 rebelling workers; the arrest of 15,000; and the deportation of 4,000.

The June Days revealed the conflict in interests between the masses of poor workers of Paris and the conservative republic. They also bracketed the place of women in the social conflict. Women filled frontline and supply line positions during the six days of the June insurrection. Historian David Barry wrote that for some the supply line role was an extension of women's carrying a husband's tools or lunch to the workshop. Police and military archives reveal the military participation of women, as well as what the Republican government thought about their participation. Shoelace-maker, Geneviève Boulanger stood guard in a rebel area, distinguishing herself in the fighting. Some women went door-to-door, collecting food or supplies to aid the defense. In one case, Marie-Madeleine Cheron made neighbors give her cutlery to be melted for bullets. Others threatened "cowardly" men with death if they did not serve on the barricades. Shoemaker Marie Goyon put up mattresses in windows, aiding the efforts of anti-government snipers. Other women hid ammunition in mattresses and their clothing. As they had in the 1790s and would again in 1871 at the start of the Paris Commune, some women announced the arrival of government troops. Thérèse Calayon, a dressmaker and prostitute, roused her neighborhood to defense by ringing the bells of Saint Severin church.

Though the battles of the June Days were relatively brief, women found many ways to serve in military roles. Flourishing red flags and otherwise associating themselves with the revolution led women to their deaths—or to later arrest. The bodies of women fell behind barricades and elsewhere. Furniture finisher Elisa Debeurgrave was arrested with her hands and face black with gunpowder near Place de la Bastille on June 26. Harking back to the first French Revolution, sixty-four-year-old widow Anne Goussery pressed her neighbors to burn down the house of a wallpaper manufacturer. In doing so she reminded her audience that the same fate had awaited another manufacturer of the same product in 1789, when he rejected the demands of his workers. The results of women's participation in the fighting led to swift repression against them. A writer in *Voix des femmes* echoed earlier feminist, Flora Tristan (1803–1844), "In the Republic of 1848, which has for its mission the abolition of privilege, there still exist pariahs, and these pariahs will be [women]!"

In addition to arrests and deaths, on June 28 the republic's assembly declared that the participation of women in political clubs was illegal. This silenced women's vocal political expression and later legislation forced Deroin's *Politique des femmes* to change its name to *Opinion des femmes* (Opinion of Women). The change in title indicates that women could not associate themselves with anything "political." Previously, she had managed to scrape together the funds to keep the newspaper open and paid the government "caution money," indicating her willingness to lose her deposit should she prove subversive. Deroin's attempt to hold political office failed, marking a dead-end to women's political activity for the time being. An attempt to resuscitate the worker cooperative movement found Deroin and Roland imprisoned in 1850. Ongoing harassment of workers' organizations followed, and with Louis Napoleon's coup d'état of December 1851 repression further limited democratic social changes, including those for women. Niboyet, Deroin, Voilquin, Gay, Tristan, and Roland were all either dead or in exile by the end of 1852.

A new Republic in February 1848 had again provided women an opportunity to express their desires for equality, with some, like the Vesuvians, arguing that military performance and attire similar to that of men could create that equality. With the June Days, some women simply made their "argument" for worker and gender equality by asserting their presence in military events and on barricades. The repression that followed indicates the goals of women—and women-as-workers—expressed in events from February through June 1848 would not be realized anytime soon. However, some of women retained memories of their military roles in the June Days, which would again ignite in the spring of 1871 during the Paris Commune.

—Pamela J. Stewart

See also French Revolution, Impact of War on Women's Protest during the; Paris Commune, Women and the; Sicilian Revolutions of 1820 and 1848, Women and the

References and Further Reading

Barry, David. 2000. "Community, Tradition, and Memory Among Rebel Working-Class Women of Paris, 1830, 1848, 1871," in *European Review of History,* 7, 2: 261–276.

DeGroat, Judith A. 1997. "The Public Nature of Women's Work: Definitions and Debates during the Revolution of 1848," in *French Historical Studies,* 20, 1: 31–47.

Moses, Claire Goldberg. 1984. *French Feminism in the Nineteenth Century.* Albany: SUNY Press.

Strumingher, Laura S. 1987. "The Vésuviennes: Images of Women Warriors in 1848 and Their Significance for French History," in *History of European Ideas,* 8, 4–5: 451–488.

France, Wars of Religion

A series of religious and political conflicts between groups of Protestants and Catholics in France between 1562 and 1629. Religious dissent and reform movements had swept through

Europe in the early sixteenth century, destroying the unity of the Latin Christian church. French kings employed repressive measures beginning in the 1530s, causing reformers such as John Calvin to flee. Divisions hardened between groups who were increasingly known as Catholics and Protestants. Urban and elite women were crucial in the spread of Protestantism, converting their husbands and sons. By the 1550s probably almost a tenth of France's population and a third of its nobles had become Protestant, most of them practicing Calvinism. This religious minority increasingly demanded legal protections for their religious practices, while many Catholics felt that Protestants polluted their communities at a time when everyone saw religion as public. The religious divisions deepened after King Henri II died in 1559, leading to the outbreak of religious warfare in 1562.

Two French queens played important roles in directing policy and organizing warfare during the French Wars of Religion. French law stipulated that only males could rule the kingdom, but allowed for women to head temporary regency governments to manage the country on behalf of kings too young to govern. Queen Catherine de Medici, wife of Henri II, acted as regent for her three sons, all of whom died as young men. Through three decades of continuing succession crises and religious conflicts, Catherine attempted to manage religious conflicts and negotiate peace in France. However, she maintained firm support for Catholicism and approved a preemptive strike against Calvinist leaders in 1572 when she feared that they were plotting to take over Paris, resulting in the infamous Saint Bartholomew's Day Massacre. Later, Marie de Medici acted as regent after her husband, king Henri IV, was assassinated in 1610. Both of these queens wielded considerable power as regents, but also faced serious challenges by nobles and royal officials who contested the authority that they exercised on behalf of their sons.

Women of all social backgrounds were directly involved in all phases of the French Wars of Religion, participating directly in reform movements, pious activities, and religious conflict. Noblewomen often managed family estates, defended chateaux, and engaged in political activity while their husbands were fighting. Female family members of noblemen who were captured often had to raise money and negotiate for their ransom. In remote rural areas peasant women could shape the religious destinies of their villages. Urban women were often entangled in struggles for control of religious sites and civic spaces in religiously divided areas of France. When armies besieged cities, women within the walls helped to defend their communities, assisting in religious, medical, and logistical activities. Besieged women could even take up arms and participate directly in combat.

The French Wars of Religion embroiled women and other non-combatants in brutal civil warfare and horrifying atrocities. Armies routinely intimidated women as they extracted contributions and pillaged communities. Women often suffered physical and sexual violence, especially in mixed-religious areas where fighting frequently erupted. Soldiers and civic guards raped, mutilated, and killed women during orgies of religious massacres or when cities were sacked.

—*Brian Sandberg*

See also Peasants' War; Scotland: War Widows and Refugees in, 1640s and 1688–1690

References and Further Reading

Holt, Mack P. 1995. *The French Wars of Religion, 1562–1629*. Cambridge: Cambridge University Press.

Neuschel, Kristen B. 1996. "Noblewomen and War in Sixteenth-Century France." Pp. 124–144 in *Changing Identities in Early Modern France*. Edited by Michael Wolfe. Durham, NC: Duke University Press.

Sandberg, Brian. 2004. "'Generous Amazons Came to the Breach': Besieged Women in the French Wars of Religion," *Gender and History* 16 (November): 654–688.

France, World War I, Psychological Impact on French Women

Psychological burden of the war on French women. Few French women were able to escape the psychological repercussions of World War I. As their men departed for battle, women were left with the stresses of tending to the farm or joining the industrial workforce to make ends meet. Through the war, hundreds of thousands of women were forced to cope with the sadness of losing a loved one.

The departure of husbands and sons for the front has often been portrayed as a sort of celebration, in which women proudly sent off young warriors and men eagerly embarked on a great masculine adventure. In truth, however, mobilization caused more agitation and nervousness than enthusiasm. Although most soldiers and their families thought the war would be over quickly, as the Franco-Prussian War had been, that assumption did not allay concerns. Women worried not only about their husbands' safety, but also about their own well-being and their ability to provide for their families.

On the home front, women faced difficult decisions and stressful tasks. In what was a predominantly agrarian society, many French women were left to run the farm. Along with children and the elderly, women finished the harvest of 1914, but they hoped that their men would be home before the next season. At first, separation allowances paid to households whose men had gone to war helped families to survive and maintained morale. Over the course of the long war, however, economic tensions increased. The rising cost of living drove some women out of the fields and into jobs at factories. Women substituted for men in civilian industries and helped to expand the workforce in war manufacturing. Economic frustrations continued to escalate, however, and in 1917, those frustrations drove many men and women workers to strike (Becker 1985).

With the exception of Red Cross nurses, few French women had a direct role to play in the war zone. Nevertheless, many women, especially those in northeastern France, experienced the war firsthand. Within the invaded territory, rumors abounded of German atrocities, including mutilation, rape, deportation, and forced labor (Darrow 2000). Anxious women behind the approaching front lines were forced to choose between remaining with their homes and protecting themselves and their children by journeying toward the country's interior.

Those who chose to flee packed up their family and what few belongings they could manage, and either crammed onto trains or lined congested roads. The exodus brought its own travails. For a small number of women, the physical and psychological strains of the journey were unbearable. Mademoiselle D., a seventeen-year-old from northeastern France, left her town with family and other townspeople in August 1914. During the long journey toward Paris, one family member began to suffer convulsions; other members of the group were crushed by a train. By the time Mademoiselle D. reached the capital, the stresses and strains of the war and the flight from the front had overtaken her. She was taken to a psychiatric facility, where she was excited and incoherent, with severe mood swings and flights of ideas. Committed to a mental asylum, her condition gradually improved only after months of rest (Imianitoff 1917, 57–59).

For evacuees of the invaded territory, France's capital turned out to be no safe haven. Air raid sirens frequently sent Parisians scrambling to safety in cellars and underground metro stations and brought civilians directly in contact with the war. Most French women avoided artillery barrages, but few eluded the grief produced by losing a loved one. As of 1920, the war had produced more than 600,000 French widows, plus more than 750,000 fatherless children and more than 1.3 million bereaved parents (Smith, Audoin-Rouzeau, and Becker 2003, 70). Added to these numbers should also be the millions of extended family members and friends who were touched by grief (Audoin-Rouzeau and Becker 2002). During the war, the black clothes of mourning were ubiquitous.

Widows were supposed to suffer stoically, but for some, hearing the news that their spouse had given his life for the country was an incapacitating blow. One thirty-one-year-old widow was picked up by police near a lake in 1915 as she contemplated suicide. Her husband had been killed in action a few months earlier. Taken to a medical facility, her doctors found her suffering from profound depression, despair, and anxiety. She admitted that had not eaten in a week. "Since I didn't have the will to drown myself, I had decided to let myself die from hunger" (Imianitoff 1917, 92–93). Attempts at suicide were certainly rare reactions to the loss of loved ones, but the story reminds us that civilians were in no way immune to the psychological strains of the war.

—*Gregory M. Thomas*

See also France, World War I, Women and the Home Front

References and Further Reading

Audoin-Rouzeau, Stéphane, and Annette Becker. 2002. *14–18: Understanding the Great War.* Translated by Catherine Temerson. New York: Hill and Wang.

Becker, Jean-Jacques. 1985. *The Great War and the French People.* Translated by Arnold Pomerans. Dover, NH: Berg.

Darrow, Margaret H. 2000. *French Women and the First World War: War Stories of the Home Front.* New York: Berg.

Fridenson, Patrick, ed. 1992. *The French Home Front, 1914–1918.* Translated by Bruce Little and Helen McPhail. Providence, RI: Berg.

Imianitoff (née Ourison), Mme. [S]. 1917. Contribution à l'étude du rôle des emotions dans la genèse des psychoses [Contribution to the study of emotions in the genesis of psychosis]. Thesis for the Paris Faculty of Medicine.

Prost, Antoine. 1977. *Les anciens combattants et la société française 1914–1939* [Veterans and French society]. 3 vols. Paris: Presses de la Fondation nationale des sciences politiques.

Smith, Leonard V., Stéphane Audoin-Rouzeau, and Annette Becker. 2003. *France and the Great War, 1914–1918.* Cambridge, England: Cambridge.

France, World War I, Women and the Home Front

New roles imposed upon women in France by World War I. The mobilization of France's military age males created an unprecedented demand for women to work in heavy industry, while women in the countryside took up the burden of running many of the nation's small farms and filled local political posts. Numbers of women flocked to wartime nursing, and some took up the novel role of *marraines de guerre,* "godmothers" supporting frontline soldiers as pen pals. In a country whose population had long stagnated, French women became the target of an intense campaign to produce more children.

The scope of the conflict placed civilians of both sexes in jeopardy. French women suffered through the bombardment of Paris from the air and from long-range artillery. Some were maimed or even paid with their lives as a consequence of accidents in the country's munitions factories. Others endured four years of German occupation in the ten districts of northeastern France that the enemy had conquered in 1914.

However, the shifts the war brought to the patterns of women's lives had only limited long-term effects. Political efforts to reward the nation's women with the right to vote in return for their contribution to the war effort failed. Women's entry into governing posts in the countryside ended with the conclusion of the conflict. Almost all the new positions in the workforce that had opened to women were restored to men who had served in the military. The proportion of women in the work force declined with the close of the war.

Millions of Frenchwomen were already in the work force before World War I. Although the conflict brought them new economic opportunities in the country's factories, such openings appeared only after a period of hardship. The outbreak of the war and the ensuing mobilization shut down many of the traditional sources of employment such as domestic service, clothing shops, and parts of the textile industry. Never-

Women workers in a French war plant, 1916. (Hulton-Deutsch Collection/Corbis)

theless, even without government action to open positions for them, women entered the metal trades in large numbers by the start of 1915. The growing realization that the war would be a prolonged one, and, in particular, the huge casualties resulting from the Battle of Verdun in 1916 pushed the government to widen employment opportunities for women. By November 1918 unemployment for most women had disappeared as they entered wartime industry. In some metalworking plants four out of every five workers were women (Downs 1995, 41).

Nevertheless, many of those women faced continuing discrimination. Women and men were given separate working areas in many factories. At first men received higher wages for doing tasks nearly identical to those of women in the same plants. Employers often claimed that women did not need to earn as much as men since men worked to support a family whereas women lacked such responsibilities. Complex tasks were broken down into simple steps and divided among teams of women workers. Thus, women could be identified as unskilled rather than skilled members of the work force.

Pressure from the Ministry of Munitions diminished the wage differential between female and male workers, and a wave of strikes by women workers in the spring of 1917 likewise helped women to gain pay equal to men. Nonetheless, French society showed its ambivalence toward the new *munitionettes* in numerous ways. Stories circulated describing how they used their new wages to indulge in luxurious foods like chicken and chocolate. Moreover, they supposedly employed their newfound freedom to drink and engage in sexual adventure. In the harshest canard thrown at such women, they were accused of enjoying the war so much that they hoped it would continue indefinitely.

A more pressing concern for female workers was the set of dangers that came with factory work. War production meant exposure to toxic chemicals, dangerous machinery, and explosives. Over one hundred women were killed in a single accidental explosion in a plant near Paris (Heyman 2002, 216). For much of the war's duration pre-1914 safety regulations were brushed aside in the interest of accelerating arms production.

Civilian women played a direct role in the war effort by working for the military. By 1917, 120,000 women held jobs with the military as drivers, office workers, telephone operators, laundresses, and cooks (Darrow 2000, 255). Women could often fill such positions while living in their home, and their efforts freed men to take positions at the front.

The government appealed directly to the women of rural France in August 1914 to help bring in the harvest. From this point on, farmwomen, who had normally tended the fields as helpers for their men, found they had to tend the land alone. For many the burden of farming with the assistance of only very young and very old men proved too great. Shortages of draft animals and fertilizer made food production more difficult as the war proceeded. Hardship for France's farmwomen led to declining food production and sometimes even abandoned farmsteads. But a shortage of men in the countryside provided a few women with new responsibilities in government. In some rural communities women took posts as municipal councilors and mayors.

Starting in the spring of 1915 some women in unoccupied France volunteered for the role of "war godmothers," *marraines de guerre*. The occupation of ten French departments meant that thousands of French soldiers could have no contact with home. To provide the moral support these men, so called "war orphans," could not receive from their families, women in unoccupied areas became pen pals and a welcoming presence away from the battle front when the soldiers received leave

Many women took training as nurses from the Red Cross, the majority of them, middle class women who did not need to worry about the need to support their families. This marked a significant change in the practices of the French army. The French military had been hesitant to employ female nurses up to the years immediately preceding 1914. Only one hundred military nurses were on duty when the war broke out. But 63,000 newly qualified Red Cross nurses staffed 1480 auxiliary hospitals outside the war zone, and, in the spring of 1917, some were permitted to volunteer for service close to the front (Darrow 2000, 137–141).

Concern about the size of France's population, evident among politicians and intellectuals for decades before 1914, grew into a potent pronatalist movement during the wartime years. The absence of men for duty at the front brought the birthrate to an all time low in 1915 and 1916. Frenchwomen were urged to produce babies to fill the population gap brought on by the conflict's huge casualty lists. Proponents of wartime motherhood often described pregnancy and childbirth as the female equivalent of the soldier's service at the front.

The expanded presence of women in French factories combined with pronatalism in diverse ways. Some experts warned of the dangers such work posed for women's bodies and their unborn children and urged that pregnant women workers be sent home. Others sought improvements in factory life for women and mothers, such as private rooms where women could nurse their children. The government agreed with the latter position, and helped pregnant women and nursing mothers to continue in the workforce. In August 1917 factories were required to provide facilities like nurseries to ease the burden placed on working women. Women welfare supervisors were assigned to French factories with the primary task of protecting the health of females of childbearing age.

In the 12 percent of French territory occupied by the Germans two million French women faced multiple intrusions on their lives. The initial invasion brought a wave of rape and pillage. Thereafter, the shortage of food and fuel became a daily torment. Some food entered the zone through the efforts of Herbert Hoover's relief organization, but it provided only one meal a day. Those in the occupied zone had to demolish their wooden houses stick by stick for fuel. Restrictions on travel within the occupied zone as well as rigid curfews added to their burden. In a telling example of German power over the female population, German occupation authorities forcibly mobilized 8,000 women to help with the harvest in 1916. Middle class women were billeted with females of dubious reputation, and all were subjected to humiliating public physical examinations (Darrow 2000, 117–119; Becker 1996, 635–636).

The most direct danger for women came from enemy attacks, which modern weapons now made possible against civilians behind the fighting front. Paris was first bombed in September 1914, and German airplanes and zeppelins returned regularly. Starting in March 1918 a long-range cannon located seventy-five miles northeast of the city fired shells into Paris killing hundreds of civilians. Living in cities closer to the front like Soissons exposed French women to aerial and artillery bombardments from both sides.

Although millions of women supported the war effort with their labors, women sometimes took a prominent role opposing the continuation of the conflict. Strikes rocked French industry in the spring of 1917, with women making up the majority of those who abandoned their workplaces. Their rhetoric called not only for improvement in working conditions but also for an end to the conflict. One prominent woman, the schoolteacher and union leader Hélène Brion, was arrested in November 1917 and charged with "defeatism." Tried during late March 1918, a tense moment when the Germans were mounting their final offensive on the western front, she was found guilty and sentenced to three years imprisonment.

Despite the vast changes war had brought to France's women, the postwar period saw only limited shifts in their political and economic status. The question of voting rights for women had emerged during the war, since the contribution of women to the war effort seemed to call for an appropriate reward. Some suggested giving the vote to women who had lost husbands in the conflict so that the family could retain its voting influence. In the end no change took place. The Chamber of Deputies approved awarding the franchise to women in 1919 by an overwhelming vote, but the French Senate successfully blocked the measure. One salient argument for opponents of woman's suffrage was the view that French women were too prone to follow the dictates of the Roman Catholic Church. Another argument focused on the need for women to concentrate on child bearing rather than politics in the post-war period. French women received the right to vote only in 1944.

Moreover, women lost most of the new positions in the labor force they had occupied during the wartime years. Where women were hired back after 1918, the differential between the wages they and male workers received widened beyond the gap existing during the war years.

—*Neil M. Heyman*

See also Brion, Hélène; France, World War I, Psychological Impact on French Women; Mata Hari, pseud.

References and Further Reading

Becker, Annette, 1996. "Life in an Occupied Zone: Lille, Roubaix, Tourcoing." Pp. 630–641 in *Facing Armageddon: The First World War Experience.* Edited by Hugh Cecil and Peter H. Liddle. London: Leo Cooper.

Darrow, Margaret H. 2000. *French Women and the First World War: War Stories of the Homefront.* Oxford: Berg.

Downs, Laura Lee. 1995. *Manufacturing Inequality: Gender Division in the French And British Metalworking Industries, 1914–1939.* Ithaca. NY: Cornell.

Grayzel, Susan R. 1999. *Women's Identities at War: Gender, Motherhood, and Politics in Britain and France during the First World War.* Chapel Hill: University of North Carolina.

Heyman, Neil M. 2002. *Daily Life during World War I.* Wesport, CT: Greenwood.

Higonnet, Margaret Randolph, et al., eds. 1987. *Behind the Lines: Gender and the Two World Wars.* New Haven, CT: Yale University.

McPhail, Helen. 1999. *The Long Silence: Civilian Life under the German Occupation of Northern France, 1914–1918.* London: I. B. Tauris.

Roberts, Mary Louise. 1994. *Civilization without Sexes: Reconstructing Gender in Postwar France, 1917–1927.* Chicago: University of Chicago.

Wall, Richard, and Jay Winter, eds. 1988. *The Upheaval of War: Family, Work and Welfare in Europe, 1914–1918.* Cambridge, England: Cambridge University Press.

Winter, Jay, and Jean-Louis Robert, eds. 1997. *Capital Cities at War: Paris, London, Berlin, 1914–1918.* Cambridge, England: Cambridge University.

France, World War II, Women and the Home Front

Important consequences of World War II on the lives of French women. The war impacted the lives of French women in every conceivable way, from work to the domestic front. With the fall of France in June 1940, many women had lost husbands and loved ones, and were forced to take control of their own lives. In addition, the new government of Vichy inaugurated a moral revolution, which deeply affected women.

Women in France worked in virtually every sphere of the economy. They were mobilized in 1939 after the outbreak of war to work in factories to contribute to the war effort and to replace the men who had gone off to the front. Before the fall of France the major employer of women was the state, in particular the Ministry of Defense. Wives of soldiers were given priority for employment because their families were left without a breadwinner. A law passed on February 29, 1940, made female labor in certain professions, administrations, and companies obligatory for the duration of the hostilities (Diamond 1999, 30). Women, both skilled and unskilled, were employed in large numbers in armament factories throughout the country. While the armaments industry flourished, that of textiles deteriorated, putting female textile workers into the ranks of the unemployed. However, new jobs were created for women in other sectors of the economy. These included replacing men in the postal service.

With the fall of France in June 1940, the country entered a period of chaos. The country was divided into two zones: the Vichy administered center and southeast and the occupied zone in the north and along the Atlantic controlled by the Germans. Defense industries were closed and unemployment levels rose. Immediately following the fall of France, the new Vichy regime implemented a campaign to strengthen the family and increase the birth rate. The *femme au foyer* or mistress of the home was glorified. "Work, Family and Nation," the Vichy slogan, which replaced the revolutionary motto of "Liberty, Equality and Fraternity," took on special meaning for women. Domestic Revolution is a term employed by one scholar describing the National Revolution, which was implemented by the Vichy government in 1940. France's declining birth rate was held to be both a symptom and a cause of national decadence. Because of their vanity, selfishness, loose morals, and consumerism, women were held to be partially responsible for the defeat. They had neglected their most important role of wife and mother. To be a woman meant to be a wife, a mother, and a teacher. The institutionalization of the female role as a mother took place on May 31, 1942, when an official Mothers Day became a national holiday. Posters extolled the virtues of motherhood. These included duty and sacrifice (Pollard 1998, 45–48).

Gender roles were clearly demarcated at a young age. Both male and female identities were reconstructed. From 1942, young girls were taught domestic skills at school in order to prepare them for their future role as wives and mothers while boys were given physical education. Professional training for girls at the youth centers included learning how to sew and other household tasks while boys were sent to work camps to prepare for war. In spite of the official ideology of the *femme au foyer,* the realities of war and occupation made it difficult to enforce.

With male unemployment spiraling and the new ideology ubiquitous, women were laid off from their places of employment, but were given several months pay. New legislation, which underscored official Vichy ideology of fatherland, work, and family was implemented. This was the Married Women's Work act passed on October 11, 1940. Married women were no longer permitted to work outside the home if their spouses could provide for the family. The retirement age for women was set at fifty (Diamond 1999, 32–33). However, as war demands on the economy grew throughout the autumn and winter of 1940–1941, the government decided to abandon the new legislation and replace it with yet another law on September 12, 1942. The government argued that due to new circumstances the Married Women's Work act would have to be cancelled. Married women were now permitted to work in all sections of the economy where they were needed. Labor shortages were serious enough to introduce emergency measures to employ more women. Teenagers aged fourteen to nineteen were also employed. Women were even taken on in the police force. Vichy established a special *Corps des Surveillantes Auxiliares* (Corps of Auxiliary Inspectors) of women. In fact, by the time the Germans occupied the entire country in November of 1942, there was a severe shortage of male workers.

Although the Catholic Church in France voiced its disapproval of women working for the Germans, this did not prevent the Vichy government from passing legislation in February and March, 1944, which specified that women from ages eighteen to forty-five, both single and married without children could work near their homes and that work previously done by men could now be carried out by women (Diamond 1999, 37). Women worked in various capacities for the Germans: as cleaners, housekeepers, cooks, and laundresses. Others worked as secretaries, translators, and telephone operators. Due to the fact that they were well paid, much better than those working for the French, most women who worked for the Germans did so without compulsion (Burrin 1995, 288). Women who worked for the Germans also received perks such as access to German cafeterias and goods unavailable to most French people (Cobb 1983, 105).

Women also were employed by the Germans in the entertainment industry during the war. They worked in the theater, ballet, opera, and nightclubs. Edith Piaf is a famous example of a singer working in this business. Some worked in France, while others went on tour to Germany. More women worked for the Germans in the northern zone.

Numbers of women practicing prostitution rose notably during the war. Both the Germans and the Vichy government attempted to regulate the profession: the tolerated brothel of the past acquired official status and was considered like any other business. No Jews or Blacks could be prostitutes and condom use was enforced to protect the Germans from disease. One expert, citing German authorities, maintains that 80,000 to 100,000 women in Paris were engaged in this trade and that 5,000 to 6,000 women carried a bilingual card. Soldiers would receive a card indicating the name of the brothel, the date of the meeting, and the name of the woman. Most women, however, worked on the streets. Figures of 100,000 on the streets to 2,000 in brothels are cited for Paris in 1940 (Burrin 1995, 210–211).

No discussion of women and work during the war would be complete without mentioning agriculture. Similar to their predecessors in World War I, wives once again took over the family farm when their husbands went off to war. However, their burden was often lessened with the help of neighbors, male relatives and villagers too old to serve in the army, and refugees. Peasant women were the epitome of the ideal Vichy woman.

Women in all walks of life, whether they remained at home or were in the labor force, still had to worry about feeding their families and carrying out the chores in the household. Food and other necessities were rationed from September 1940. Women were issued ration cards and were forced to stand in long queues each day to obtain provisions. As necessities became scarcer and women increasingly frustrated, they began to protest in front of town halls and prefect offices for more bread and milk for their families.

Childcare was also an important concern for women, particularly those who worked outside the home. Day care facilities, which had been in existence before the war, continued during the war, but these were limited. For the most part, women had to rely on personal arrangements with relatives to take care of children.

—Leigh Whaley

See also France, Resistance during World War II, Women and

References and Further Reading

Burin, Philippe. 1995. *La France l'heure Allemande 1940–1944*. [France in the German Period]. Paris: Seuil.

Cobb, Richard. 1983. *French and Germans, Germans and French: A Personal Interpretation of France and Two Occupations, 1914–1918/1940–1944*. Hanover, NH: Brandeis University Press by University Press of New England.

Diamond, Hanna. 1999. *Women and the Second World War in France: Choices and Constraints*. London and New York: Longman.

Muel-Dreyfus, Francine. 2001. *Vichy and the Eternal Feminine*. Translated from the French by Kathleen A. Johnson. Durham and London: Duke University.

Pollard, Miranda.1998. *Reign of Virtue: Mobilizing Gender in Vichy France*. Chicago: University of Chicago.

Frank, Anne (1929–1945)

Jewish girl who perished in the Holocaust. Annelies Marie "Anne" Frank was a Jewish girl who wrote a diary about her experiences while hiding with her family from the Nazis during World War II. Anne was born on June 12, 1929, in Frankfurt, Germany. When she was four years old, Hitler became dictator of Germany. Her father, Otto, a banker, chose to take Anne, her sister Margot, who was three years older, and her mother, Edith, to the Netherlands.

During World War II the Germans invaded the Netherlands and instituted anti-Semitic regulations there. Jews were banned from going to the movies, libraries, museums, and many other public places. As a way of controlling their movements, Jews were not allowed to use bicycles or cars. Also, for identification purposes, Jews were required to wear a yellow six-pointed Star of David. Furthermore, non-Jewish people were discouraged from associating with Jewish people. Anne, for example, was segregated in an all-Jewish school.

On June 12, 1942, Anne's thirteenth birthday, her father gave her a diary, which she named "Kitty." Anne kept a personal record of events in her diary between 1942 and 1945. Otto had prepared a hiding place for his family in an annex to a warehouse on Prinsengracht. Consequently, when the Germans announced that all Jews would be sent to work camps, Otto put his plan into action. Life in hiding was difficult. The family had to keep complete silence during the day for fear of being heard by workers. Living conditions became even more strained after Hermann and Auguste van Pels and their son Peter came to live in the annex, and were joined a few months later by Fritz Pfeffer, a friend of the Frank family.

At great risk, Victor Kugler, the owner of the warehouse, built a false bookcase to cover the entrance to the annex. Also at great risk, Miep Gies, on a daily basis, used forged ration coupons to buy food for the hideaways. However, on August 4, 1944, the Gestapo, following an anonymous tip, found the secret annex and arrested all eight occupants. Gies found Anne's diary and put it in a safe place. The Frank family was sent to Auschwitz-Birkenau (where Edith died). Anne and Margot were separated from their parents and were eventually sent to Bergen-Belsen where they both died of typhus shortly before the liberation of the camp. Only Otto survived.

After the war Otto published an abridged version of Anne's diary in 1947. Since that time, millions of copies have been sold, and it has been translated into at least fifty-five languages. It has also been adapted into award winning plays and motion pictures. In 1995 an English "definitive edition" of the diary was published. However, in 1998, five previously unknown pages of the diary were discovered, which document some of the Franks' marital problems.

—*Rolando Avila*

See also Holocaust and Jewish Women

References and Further Reading

Frank, Otto H., and Mirjam Pressler, eds. 1995. *The Diary of a Young Girl: The Definitive Edition.* New York: Doubleday.

Gies, Miep, and Alison Gold. 1987. *Anne Frank Remembered: The Story of the Woman Who Helped to Hide the Frank Family.* New York: Simon and Schuster.

Lindwer, Willy. 1992. *The Last Seven Months of Anne Frank.* New York: Anchor.

French Revolution (1789–1799), Impact of War on Women's Protest during the

The impact of the issue of war on women during the French Revolution (1789–1799). During the French Revolution the issue of war led to the radicalization of women's claims to political participation but also led to the repression of this participation.

The era of the revolutionary wars began in 1792. The first of a long list of declarations of war occurred on April 20, 1792. These wars were mainly caused by a desire to propagate the principles of the French Revolution and were linked to the threat of invasion by European monarchs afraid of the new regime. The decision to declare the country in danger on July 11, 1792, calling on each patriot citizen to help to protect the nation, increased the feeling of urgency.

Women's political demands in this period were linked to the evolution of the Revolution itself. In the years 1792–1793, the main claims were made during the debate surrounding the war, with the right to bear arms being the most important issue. On March 6, 1792, a delegation of women presented a petition signed by 300 Parisian women to the National Assembly. Pauline Leon, a chocolate merchant who was to become a prominent figure in women's movement, led the group. These women demanded the right to bear arms, in order to defend France, and wanted to practice arms drills among themselves. The Assembly applauded, but did not take any further action. Another well-known activist, Théroigne de Mericourt, gave an enthusiastic speech on March 25 in which she claimed women's right to participate in the war effort by forming female militias. In fact, the arms struggle is recognized by some historians as the birth of the feminine *sans-culotterie,* a popular and radical movement of women who posited that bearing arms was an act of citizenship and patriotism (Godineau 1998, 109). This question was also central in the creation of the biggest and most radical women's club, the Society of Revolutionary Republican Women, which brought together women who proclaimed themselves guardians of the nation in May 1793.

The presence of a few women fighters, such as the Fernig sisters, integrated among the men in the revolutionary armies—tolerated even after the April 1793 law forbidding this practice—seemed to cause less of a problem than these "Amazon battalions," as many contemporaries called them. The latter were either not taken seriously nor perceived as a real threat. Indeed, during the French Revolution, the main ideology concerning women's role called on Rousseau's conception of women as naturally suited to remaining within the private-domestic sphere where they could serve the Republic as good mothers and virtuous spouses (Landes 1988, 204). As a consequence, revolutionary authorities proposed that women should only head families during the absence of a husband away fighting for the nation. In contrast, some women protesters proposed that men should be responsible for external defense beyond the borders of the revolutionary while women should be charged with internal defense. The right to bear arms, in this perspective, became a necessity.

These kinds of demands were not only radical in terms of leading women into the public sphere; they also, according to revolutionary men, challenged gender boundaries. Even if men appreciated women's patriotism, they resisted it since the gender transgression it represented was too important to be overlooked. The right to bear arms was seen as an insult to the physical superiority and fashionable difference between men and women, because armed women, for reasons of comfort and gender subversion, often dressed like men and wore male symbols, such as the red cap of liberty. Consequently, the question of women's right to bear arms strongly influenced the National Assembly's decision to prohibit women's political clubs in October 1793. The deputy Fabre d'Eglantine, in a speech against women meeting in female clubs, and therefore against the political implication of women itself, told the Assembly that if women "ask for the red cap [of liberty], [t]hey will not rest there; they will soon demand a belt with pistols [. . .]. These societies [of women] are not at all composed of mothers, daughters, and sisters of families [. . .] but rather of adventuresses, female knights-errant, emancipated girls, and amazons" (Eglantine 1996, 135–136). The next day, October 30, 1793, women's clubs were abolished, a decision that significantly weakened women's protest.

According to Catherine Marand-Fouquet, the war question contributed, through the revolutionary search for male heroism, to reaffirm gender boundaries, indirectly leading women to return home and to abandon concrete political participation. War also raised the specter of depopulation, causing a rise in birth rate that served to further confine women to their traditional roles (Fouquet 1989, 161). In fact, the most positive influence of the war question on women's political awareness might have been the creation of female networks, because the struggle for the right to bear arms allowed women to "fight" together.

—Eve-Marie Lampron

See also China, Women and the Communist Revolution; Cuban Revolution, Women in the; Fernig, Félicitè, and Fernig, Théophile; Germany, Revolution of 1918–1919, Women in the

References and Further Reading

d'Eglantine, Fabre. 1996. "Discussion of Women's Political Clubs and Their Suppression, 29–30 October 1793" pp. 135–138 in *The French Revolution and Human Rights: A Brief Documentary History.* Translated and edited by Lynn Hunt. Boston/New York: Bedford/St. Martin's.

Godineau, Dominique. 1998. *The Women of Paris and Their French Revolution. 1789–1795.* Translated by Katherine Streip. Berkeley: University of California Press.

Landes, Joan. 1988. *Women and the Public Sphere in the Age of the French Revolution.* Ithaca: Cornell University.

Marand-Fouquet, Catherine. 1989. *La femme au temps de la Révolution* [Woman at the Time of the Revolution]. Paris: Stock/Laurence Pernoud.

Friang, Brigitte (1924–)

Well-known French journalist, one of the few war correspondents in the world, male or female, to have covered both phases of the Vietnam war. Brigitte Friang, who was still a high school student when France was invaded by Hitler's army on May 10, 1940, joined the French Resistance. She participated in decoding aerial operations transmissions and later, as a trained parachutist, she was assigned to organize parachuting missions in western France. When her mentor Pierre Brossolette, one of General Charles de Gaulle's top assistants, was arrested by the Gestapo in 1944, Friang attempted to organize his escape, was wounded and then arrested, tortured, and deported to the Ravensbrück concentration camp. The experience is narrated in her book *Regarde-toi qui meures: 1943–1945* (Look at Yourself Dying) (1970), and also in the final episode of André Malraux's *Antimémoirs* (1967). It led to Friang becoming the youngest receiver of the military title of Cavalier of the Legion of Honor.

After World War II Friang became a press attachée and a close collaborator of Malraux, then de Gaulle's minister of information and later minister of cultural affairs. Working as a reporter for ORTF (the French state-owned radio and television), she covered the Indochina war, where she was frequently parachuted on operations with the Expeditionary Forces of the French Union. In 1954 Friang covered the Battle of Dien-Bien-Phu, fought between Viet Minh and the French, the battle that ended the French involvement in Indochina and led to the partition of Vietnam into North and South. In 1956 she reported on the Suez Crisis. In 1967 she accompanied the Israeli troops in Sinai during the Six-Day War, fought against Egypt, Jordan, and Syria. During the American war in Vietnam, Friang was captured twice by the Viet Cong, but not harmed. Early in 1968 she was on the streets of Saigon, covering the Tet Offensive by the North Vietnamese Army and the National Liberation Front against the Nationalist Army and the United States. In May 1968, with the students' uprising, Friang showed support for the liberalization of information in France and was consequently fired from ORTF. With Malraux in the early 1970s, she supported the cause of Bangladesh in the war with Pakistan, which was backed by the United States and China.

As a writer, Friang's work includes *Les Fleurs du Ciel* (Parachutes and Petticoats, 1955), about the Indochina war, the two volumes of *Regarde-tois qui meures* (Look You who Die): *L'Ordre de la nuit* (The Order of the Night) and *La guerre n'a pas de fin* (War Never Ends), *La Mousson de la liberté: Vietnam, du colonialsime au stalinisme* (The Monsoon of Liberty: Vietnam from Colonialism to Stalinism) (1976), *Un autre Malraux* (Another Malraux) (1977), *Petit tour autour de Malraux* (A Small Tour around Malraux) (2001), the novel *Comme un verger durant l'hiver* (Like an Orchard during Winter) (1978), and *Marche autant que tu pourras* (March on as long as You Can) (2004).

—*Georgia Tres*

See also Leroy, Catherine

References and Further Reading

Collins Weitz, Margaret. 1995. *Sisters in the Resistance: How Women Fought to Free France, 1940–1945*. New York: Wiley.

Frontier Soldiers, U.S., Wives of

Wives of United States soldiers stationed in the western frontier lands of the United States. During the nineteenth century, and especially after the Civil War, the United States Army patrolled the trans-Mississippi West in an effort to keep the peace between the region's Native American inhabitants and increasing numbers of white settlers hoping for a fresh start. Regiments of horse cavalry and infantry troops, divided into companies, were dispersed to far-flung posts in Texas, the Northern or Southern Plains, or the desert southwest. Posts were isolated and poorly provisioned; soldiers and officers agreed that the women who accompanied the troops were an essential element of garrison life.

In the nineteenth century laundresses were the only women officially recognized as part of the frontier army. Each company was authorized four laundresses, who received rations and meager pay. They made extra money by washing for officers, with whom they negotiated payment privately. Many laundresses also cooked or cleaned for officers, nursed women during childbirth, or baked pies and cakes and sold them. The laundresses lived on "soapsuds row," a squalid section of quarters on the edge of the post. Some earned extra money through occasional prostitution, but most were married to enlisted men. No woman could remain on a frontier post for long without receiving numerous marriage proposals. The exception to this rule was African American women working for white companies. However, African American women employed by companies in the "colored" regiments found many admirers. Enlisted men valued the presence of the laundresses, married or not. A short-lived mutiny of Company A of the 38th U.S. Colored Infantry occurred when a black laundress was accused of theft and expelled from Fort Cummings. In another case, a laundress known to be an excellent housekeeper and cook informally "married" several soldiers in succession, providing each with a well-run and cheerful home. Upon her death it was found that she was actually a man; her husband at the time committed suicide in humiliation, but the others admitted that she had been such a superb partner that they had overlooked the small detail.

Soldiers had good reason to value their hardworking wives; the women could earn more than a soldier's monthly pay through washing, cooking, and nursing. Many enlisted couples saved thousands of dollars, enabling them to leave the army and buy a business or farm. One sergeant's wife, suspicious of banks, traveled east with $3,000 in cash plastered onto her legs and covered with several layers of oilskin.

Officers also brought their wives to frontier posts when they could, but generally less than half the officers at any given post were accompanied by wives. Some unaccompanied officers left their wives with relatives in the east, while others were not married. The considerable cost of transporting a wife, children, and belongings to a frontier post was borne by the officer himself, and there were no special quarters for married officers. A family with a large number of children could be "ranked out" or ousted from its quarters by a superior officer, even a bachelor officer; the "ranked out" family would in turn rank another family out, and the shift could affect all the officers on post.

Officers' wives did not work for pay, but they did function as the link to home and civilization for the officers, and probably for many enlisted men. They moved from post to post with their husbands, improvising furniture, rugs, and curtains from boxes and empty flour bags. They organized dinner parties and dances, holiday festivities and outings, church choirs, and literary societies; they saw their job as maintaining community life for their husbands and the other officers and men. There were usually less than half a dozen officers' wives on a post, so any woman who refused to participate in social activities was considered to be letting down not only her husband but the entire group. Officers' wives did not socialize with enlisted wives, but they did interact with them as employers and other capacities. An officer's wife helped the frugal sergeant's wife secure her money where it would not be stolen. Another officer's wife described the drowning of a sergeant in a flash flood; from the riverbank, the man's wife and children witnessed his death. The few officers' wives took charge of the bereaved widow until she could be escorted home.

Officers' wives in the nineteenth century produced a great deal of written material, letters, diaries, memoirs, describing their experiences, much of which is held in archives today. While the officers' wives reveal typical nineteenth century prejudices of class, race, religion, and culture, they also provide a glimpse into a lost world of danger, beauty, adventure, and close community. Enlisted wives have not left so much material, but that which exists shows a similar enjoyment of life and a recognition that despite the considerable hardship involved, army life had much to offer courageous women.

—Anni P. Baker

See also Duston, Hannah; Ward, Nancy; Winema; Winnemucca, Sarah

References and Further Reading

Eales, Anne Bruner. 1996. *Army Wives on the American Frontier: Living by the Bugles.* Boulder: Johnson.

Nacy, Michele J. 2000. *Members of the Regiment: Army Officers' Wives on the Western Frontier, 1865–1890.* Westport, CT: Greenwood.

Stallard, Patricia. 1978. *Glittering Misery: Dependents of the Indian Fighting Army.* San Rafael, CA: Presidio.

Fuld, Bracha (1926–1946)

Jewish resistance fighter, who died helping Jewish refugees enter Palestine in 1946. Barbara (Bracha[h]) Fuld immigrated to Palestine from Berlin, Germany, in June 1939. Her father had committed suicide after Kristallnacht, but she was met at Haifa by her mother, who had preceded her.

She entered Balfour High School where she engaged in sports, joined one of the youth organizations, danced, and hiked. At the start of World War II Palestine was a League of Nations Mandate governed by the British. When Nazi General Erwin Rommel's Afrika Corps threatened Egypt the Palmach was established May 16, 1941, as an elite ready reserve of the Haganah, a clandestine Jewish self-defense force formed in 1920. The members would work for 14 days each month on a kibbutz and then take military training for 10 days. Between 1941 and 1943 the British and the Palmach worked together in assaults on Vichy dominated Lebanon and Syria. After graduation Bracha Fuld joined the Palmach. She was sent to an officers' course for training. At age eighteen she was made an officer and put in charge of instructing Jewish women soldiers. Eventually she led her own platoons and commanded several military detachments.

After World War II the British, fearing Arab opposition, sought to prevent the many thousands of the survivors of the Holocaust from immigrating to Palestine. The Jews revolted. From 1945 to mid-1946 the Palmach worked with the Irgun in raids, robberies, and other assaults on British military and civilian establishments. Bracha fought with the Palmach in a raid on the German colony of Sarona outside of Joppa (now the Kirya in Tel Aviv). From 1946 the Palmach sought to aid Jewish immigration to Palestine.

On March 27, 1946, the *Wingate* with 250 illegal Jewish immigrants on board was to arrive from Italy. To keep the British from interfering with the illegal immigrants thousands of people came to provide cover. Bracha Fuld and her squad tried to protect a road the illegal immigrants would use. However, the squad encountered a British tank unit. In the exchange of fire Bracha was badly wounded and died in a hospital shortly afterward.

Her funeral was attended by many people in Tel Aviv. Six months after she died a ship for transporting illegal immigrants was named for her, the S. S. *Bracha Fuld.* Also Bracha Fuld Street in Tel Aviv was named in her honor.

—Andrew Jackson Waskey

See also Bruskina, Masha; Fittko, Lisa; Grossman, Chaika; Israeli Military, Women in the; Kempner, Vitka; Korczak, Rozka; Landau, Emilia; Reik, Haviva; Senesh, Hannah

References and Further Reading

Gal, Sari. 1999. *Bracha Fuld*. Tel-Aviv: Sifriat Poalim Publishing House (in Hebrew).

Segev, Tom. 2000. *One Palestine Complete: Jews and Arabs Under the British Mandate*. NY: Henry Holt.

Gundersen, Joan R. 1996.*To Be Useful to the World: Women in Revolutionary America 1740–1790*. New York: Twayne Press.

Young, Alfred F. 1999. *The Shoemaker and the Tea Party*. Boston: Beacon Press.

Fulton, Sarah Bradlee (1740–1835)

"Mother of the Boston Tea Party." Sarah Fulton is credited with having helped to organize the protest against the Tea Act, which took place in 1773. Born in Dorchester, Massachusetts, in 1740, the fourth daughter of twelve children of Samuel Bradlee and Mary Andrews, Sarah Bradlee married John Fulton in 1762. While the couple was visiting her brother Nathaniel in Boston in December 1773, Fulton and her husband participated in the Tea Party. Participants in the event, who included Sarah's husband and four of her brothers, met at her brother's home. Mrs. Fulton and her sister in law painted the men's faces and put feathers in their hair to resemble Mohawk Indians. The women also welcomed the party back into the Bradlee home after they had dumped tea into Boston Harbor, helped them to clean paint off their faces and destroyed evidence of their activities. Fulton later served as a nurse during the siege of Boston and secretly carried a message to George Washington who was waiting outside the city. The mother of ten children, Fulton died in 1835.

—*Megan Elias*

See also American Revolution, Role of Women in the

References and Further Reading

Claghorn, Charles E. 1991. *Women Patriots of the American Revolution: A Biographical Dictionary*. Metuchen, NJ, and London: The Scarecrow Press.

Fulvia (d. 40 B.C.)

Mark Antony's wife, who played a direct role in military events. Fulvia was one of several women who played very active roles in the series of civil wars that ended the Roman Republic. As the wife of Mark Antony during the second triumvirate she was her husband's most important agent in Italy, trying to halt the spreading authority of the rival triumvir Octavian (the future Augustus Caesar). Like Cleopatra VII of Egypt and unlike Octavian's sister Octavia (both of whom later married Mark Antony), Fulvia played an active military role, even appearing on battlefields as her husband's representative. Fulvia's vilification by Roman historians shows both the triumph of Augustus' propaganda and the deep repugnance felt by many Romans toward women who thus forgot their proper place.

Fulvia became politically active when married to her first husband, the radical politician Publius Clodius, and after his assassination it was her pleas to the Roman mob that won condemnation of his murderers. Her second husband, Gaius Scribonius Curio, was also a politician. After Julius Caesar was assassinated (43 B.C.), Fulvia's third husband, Caesar's loyal supporter Mark Antony, became effective co-ruler of Rome alongside Caesar's heir Octavian. The relationship between the two was soon strained, and Antony could count on the loyalty of few people outside his immediate family. Thus Fulvia was raised to an unofficial lieutenancy. Antony clearly trusted her; Cicero waspishly reports that Fulvia completely dominated her husband. Cicero was far from impartial because Fulvia had been responsible for his exile from Rome after

Fulvia, who contributed significantly to Roman politics as the wife of her third husband, Mark Antony. Painting by Nicolas Andre Monsiau (1754–1837). (Réunion des Musées Nationaux/Art Resource)

he had defended the murderer of her first husband. Fulvia responded to Cicero's barbed wit in kind. When Cicero was killed by Antony's troops at the end of 43, his head was given to Fulvia and she celebrated by driving her hairpins through his tongue. Still, Cicero's denunciations reveal how much Romans hated the notion of being commanded by a woman, or female public involvement in political affairs.

In 42 B.C. Antony went to the eastern part of the empire in a division of power with Octavian; he left Fulvia to look after his interests in Italy. As Octavian's authority in Italy became more and more threatening, the pro-Antony faction responded—Lucius Antonius, Antony's brother, stirred up a rebellion against Octavian. Although Fulvia opposed this policy as untimely, she rallied to the younger Antony. Fulvia raised troops and then tried to rally them for battle by appearing before them, along with her children by Antony. The ensuing Perusine War went badly; most of the Antonine troops refused to fight.

Octavian and Antony made peace in 41 and both sides found it convenient to make Fulvia the scapegoat. Octavian's memoirs of the Perusine War gave all the blame to Fulvia, while Antony, by this time enjoying an affair with Cleopatra of Egypt, also accused her of rashness. Fulvia raised troops to reinforce Antony in the East; they met in Greece where Antony welcomed the warriors but coldly ordered Fulvia home. Fulvia died soon after, according to some sources, of a broken heart.

—*Phyllis G. Jestice*

See also Roman Women and War

References and Further Reading

Barrett, Anthony. 2002. *Livia: First Lady of Imperial Rome.* New Haven, CT: Yale University.

Bauman, Richard A. 1992.*Women and Politics in Ancient Rome.* London: Routledge.

Furse, Lady Katherine Symonds (1875–1952)

Director of the first Voluntary Aid Detachment (VAD) sent to France during World War II, director of the whole Voluntary Aid Detachment Department in London, and director of the Women's Royal Naval Services (WRNS). Katherine Furse was born Katherine Symonds on November 25, 1875, in Clifton near Bristol. As a child she lived in Davos, Switzerland, and Italy. Her father, John Addington Symonds, a historian, who suffered from tuberculosis, moved his family to Switzerland in search of a better climate. Katherine had intended to become a nurse, but married the artist Charles Wellington Furse in 1900. His death from tuberculosis four years later left her with two small children.

In 1909, Furse joined the Red Cross VAD. When World War I broke out she headed the first VAD unit sent to France. She and her women set up a Rest Station at Boulogne. Her administrative ability led to her appointment in 1915 as director of the VAD home office in London. Under Furse's leadership the ranks of VAD expanded rapidly and by the end of the war numbered 90,000. In 1916 she was named commander-in-chief of the VAD and in 1917 she was honored with the Dame Grand Cross Order of the British Empire.

Furse instituted pay for VAD women, but dissatisfied with the limitations imposed upon her, as head of the VAD, and its women, she resigned in 1917. She was then asked by the British Admiralty to organize a female service for the navy. In November 1917 she was appointed director of the Women's Royal Naval service (WRNS or WRENS) and remained its director until the WRNS was demobilized in 1919. The British Navy was the first of the British services to accept women. In the WRNS women served as cooks, clerks, wireless operators, encipherers, and electricians. The success of the WRNS led to the formation of the Women's Auxiliary Army Corps (WAAC) and the Women's Royal Air Force.

After the war Furse worked for a travel agency in Switzerland. Her skill in skiing and her popularization of skiing among British tourists led to her presidency of the Ladies' Ski Club. She founded the Association of WRENS, became the leader of the Sea Rangers, and served as the head of the World Association of Girl Guides and Girl Scouts. She died in London on November 25, 1952.

—Bernard Cook

See also Great Britain, Women in Service during World War I; Great Britain, Women in Service during World War II; Great Britain, Women's Royal Naval Service, Reorganization before World War II; Inglis, Elsie, and the Scottish Women's Hospitals; Stobart, Mabel

References and Further Reading

Furse, Katherine. 1940. *Hearts and Pomegranates: The Story of Forty-five Years, 1874–1920*. London: Peter Davies.

G

Galla Placidia (ca. 390–450)

Daughter of the Roman emperor Theodosius taken hostage by the Visigoths. Galla Placidia exemplifies the use of important women as political plunder in warfare. Like many women in that position, however, Galla Placidia succeeded in using her role as pawn to the advantage of the Roman Empire and her own family.

Galla Placidia was the daughter of Emperor Theodosius the Great (379–395) and his second wife Galla. With Theodosius's death, the western empire fell to Galla Placidia's half-brother Honorius, who disastrously misjudged the demands of his Visigothic allies and provoked a Germanic invasion of the Italian peninsula. The Visigoths tried for years to force the emperor to make a more favorable treaty and finally resorted to sacking the city of Rome in August 410. At some point in the process, the Visigoths captured the princess Galla Placidia, who certainly witnessed the sack of Rome and may have been living in the city at the time of the attack.

The Visigoths took Galla Placidia as a hostage. They treated her well, and she was able to influence her captors to make peace with the Romans and settle down as federates in Gaul. Apparently to confirm this new treaty, Galla Placidia married the Gothic king Athaulf. That was not the end of her political utility. She was soon widowed and given back to the Romans as a condition of a peace treaty in 416. Once she was safely in Roman hands, her brother Honorius arranged Galla Placidia's marriage as a reward to the victorious general Constantius, cementing a political deal through which Constantius soon became coemperor with Honorius.

Galla Placidia was not allowed to play an independent political role until she was well into her thirties. In 425, her six-year-old son became Emperor Valentinian III, and Galla Placidia ruled the western empire as his regent until 437. During that period, an important part of her duty was an increasingly desperate effort to deal with growing pressure from the Germans. The Vandals invaded Roman North Africa in 429, and other Germanic peoples began to settle in Roman territory. Galla Placidia and her councilors took the only possible course, paying the Germans to fight against each other. It was not a great age in Roman military history.

Still, Galla Placidia's career is instructive. For the most part she was a political pawn, but her marriages demonstrate how women could serve as a vital link in creating peace both internally and externally during the later Roman Empire. When she finally reached a position of authority in the state, Galla Placidia's response did not differ from that of male members of the imperial family—a deepening financial crisis made any significant military response to the German invaders impossible.

—*Phyllis G. Jestice*

See also Roman Women and War

References and Further Reading

Holum, Kenneth G. 1982. *Theodosian Empresses.* Berkeley: University of California.

Oost, Stewart. 1968. *Galla Placidia Augusta.* Chicago: University of Chicago.

Gandhi, Indira (1917–1984)

Indian politician, first female prime minister of the world's largest democracy, who, during her tenure, was one of the most powerful women in the world. Indira Priyadarshini Nehru was born on November 10, 1917, the only child of Pandit Jawaharlal Nehru (1889–1964), a Kashmiri brahman, and the lower-caste and uneducated Kamala Kaul in Allahabad, Uttar Pradesh province, in India. The precocious, insecure, shy, yet iron-willed child was tenacious in her beliefs and reputedly developed a Joan of Arc complex in her youth. She was raised by various family members because her father was often jailed for his independence activities. Her mother was ill with tuberculosis and died in 1936.

Gandhi attended schools in India and Switzerland. Always an indifferent student, her postsecondary education at Oxford University in England ended when she failed her Latin exam twice and refused to try a third time. Gandhi went against tradition and chose her own husband. She married Feroze Gandhi (no relation to Mahatma Gandhi) (1912–1960), a Parsi, in 1942. The newlyweds were arrested that year for subversive activity. Gandhi served nine months. Her later paranoid attitude toward any opposition has been attributed to this experience. The couple had two sons, Rajiv Gandhi (1944–1991) and Sanjay Gandhi (1946–1980), but they were living separate lives long before her husband's death in 1960.

Indira Gandhi's father, Nehru, became the first Indian prime minister when the country gained its independence from Britain in 1947, and he served in that capacity until his death in 1964. Indira Gandhi had served as his hostess during his lengthy term as prime minister, so she was well acquainted with the intricacies of India's politics. She had also met global political leaders with whom she forged positive relationships. When Nehru died in 1964, Gandhi was under enormous pressure to serve as a politician because she was recognized as a lucid thinker and brilliant strategist. She succumbed to these pressures because she firmly believed it was her duty as Nehru's daughter to uphold his secular and inclusive ideal of India.

Gandhi was expected to become a passive puppet in the patriarchal political system, but her strong-willed actions surprised local, national, and international leaders. Following the death of her father, she served as minister of information and broadcasting in the government of Prime Minister Lal Bahdur Shastri. When Shastri died in 1966 of an unexpected heart attack, Indira Gandhi won the leadership role in the party and became prime minister. During her tenure as prime minister, Gandhi waged political war with her ministers. To centralize her own authority, she allowed them little power.

Gandhi's disagreements with the Indian National Congress (INC) party leaders, known as the Syndicate, led her to establish a new independent Congress party in 1969, under her leadership, known as the Congress O. Gandhi and her new party won landslide victories in the 1971 elections.

As prime minister, Gandhi immediately waged war on India's poverty. Like her father, she firmly believed that the British Empire caused and perpetuated the poverty in India to the advantage of Britain. In 1972, she claimed that poverty was "the greatest polluter" during her address at the first UN World Environmental Conference in Stockholm. She greatly improved the lives of the poor masses, and they unquestioningly supported all her endeavors wholeheartedly.

Gandhi was one of the first political leaders to attempt to link developmental concerns with environmental issues. She instigated protection of India's coastal environment. She also established a Protect the Tiger campaign. Hunters would no longer be allowed to shoot tigers, which were to be preserved in the wild. Gandhi's Green Revolution focused on improving India's food problems through increased grain production and the diversification of crops throughout India. These steps were intended to eliminate India's traditional dependence on foreign grain imports. Their success led her Congress Party to sweep many states in the 1972 state elections.

Determined to show that India was a modern, technologically advanced nation, Gandhi shocked the world with India's nuclear program. India's first underground nuclear test was on May 18, 1974, at Pikharan Rajashan. She asserted that the program was strictly meant for peaceful purposes. Gandhi also nationalized the banking system, a move strongly criticized by Indian economists but lauded by the masses. Her motive was to eliminate the massive corruption and fraud. She became extremely unpopular with Indian's 278 princes when she abruptly canceled their antiquated Privy Purse payments, which, in reality, were state-paid subsidies. By eliminating these payments, Gandhi saved the Exchequer at least $6 million a year, which was diverted to more needy elements of the economy. Conversely, her empathy with the poor increased her popularity.

Gandhi involved India in the cold war when she initiated the nine-month interstate war with neighboring Pakistan, India's enemy since partition in 1947–1948. Her involvement was instrumental in East Pakistan seceding from the rest of Pakistan, which lay more than 1,000 miles to the west. Pakistan, however, had the support of the United States under Richard Nixon, who despised Gandhi. Despite her nonaligned foreign policy, she received support from the Soviet Union and was willing to confront Nixon. Nixon sent the aircraft carrier, USS *Enterprise,* to intimidate India, but it arrived too late; Gandhi had already won the war. This successful venture allowed for the formation of the independent Republic of Bangladesh, created from East Pakistan, and cemented closer ties with the Soviet Union.

A personality cult emerged around Gandhi. Despite her popularity with the masses and her triumphs, her socialist opponents repeatedly accused Gandhi of electoral fraud and procedural violations in the 1971 elections. In June 1975, the High Court of Allahabad found her guilty of election fraud. In response, she waged war against her opposition. Rather than accepting the requisite loss of her seat for a six-year term, at the behest of her controversial son Sanjay, she utilized Article 352 of the Constitution to declare a State of Emergency. Gandhi thereby garnered astonishing powers and ended democracy in India. She cracked down on any type of opposition and imprisoned dissidents. She muzzled the free press by cutting off its electricity. State legislatures were suspended. Civil liberties were completely abolished. Gandhi used the dominance of her party in parliament to enact harsh bills and amendments to the constitution without debate. Her imperious style of governance was encouraged by Sanjay, who urged her to play India's societal, religious, and political groups against one another. Sanjay used the State of Emergency to enrich himself. He was also in charge of the large-scale sterilization program for women who had more than two children.

The Emergency lasted nineteen months. In 1977, Gandhi, due to increasing unrest and continued opposition from her political opponents, called an election. In March 1977, the parliamentary elections favored the opposition Janata Party (the People's Front Party), a coalition of four parties headed by Moraji Desai (1896–1995), which gained 295 seats. The Congress Party won only 125 seats, and Gandhi lost hers. She then left the Congress Party and broke with tradition to appeal openly to the Indian people. She received considerable support to establish her own Congress (I) ("I" for Indira) Party on January 2, 1978. The new government had her arrested, but, perhaps because of her popular support, she was only jailed for a short time.

In the 1980 election, Gandhi regained her seat and once again became prime minister, but she was assassinated as a result of her conflict with militant Sikhs, led by Jarnail Singh Bhindranwale and supported by Pakistan. Bhindranwale's aim was to create an independent state called Khalistan, which would be supported by Pakistan. He took control of the Sikhs' holiest shrine, the Harmindar Sahib (Golden Temple), at Amritsar on June 6, 1984. The government saw this as a terrorist act and ordered Operation Blue Star, commanded by Major General Kuldip Singh Brar of the 9th Infantry Division, to drive Bhindranwale and his supporters from the shrine. The militants refused to leave. The resulting clash caused the deaths of 83 soldiers and 493 occupiers; scores more were injured. This episode was followed by Operation Woodrose, a mopping-up operation in which hundreds of Sikhs were killed. This last operation clearly violated human rights. The Sikhs' rage knew no bounds. Two of Gandhi's bodyguards, Beant Singh and the newly appointed Satwant Singh, both Sikhs, assassinated her at her compound on October 31, 1984. Her body was riddled with 25 bullets. Beant Sing was shot down at the assassination site, and Satwant Singh was executed in 1988. Gandhi's death caused anti-Sikh riots in New Delhi, in which some 3,000 Sikhs were burned or hacked to death.

Gandhi was succeeded by her son Rajiv. He was assassinated on May 21, 1991, by a female Tamil terrorist who opposed his policy toward the conflict in Sri Lanka. His widow, Sonia (1946–), then became the leader of the Congress Party.

—*Annette Richardson*

See also Kashmir, Conflict in, Women and

References and Further Reading

Ali, Tariq. 1985. *An Indian Dynasty: The Story of the Nehru-Gandhi Family.* New York: G. P. Putnam.

Bhatia, Vinod. 1987. *Indira Gandhi and Indo-Soviet Relations.* New Delhi: Panchsheel.

Dhar, P. N. 2003. *Indira Gandhi, the "Emergency," and Indian Democracy.* New Delhi: Rupa, 2003.

Gandhi, Indira. 1985. *Letters to an American Friend 1950–1984.* San Diego, CA: Harcourt Brace Jovanovich.

Mistry, Rohinton. 1997. *A Fine Balance.* Toronto: M&S.

Moraes, Dom. 1980. *Indira Gandhi.* Boston: Little, Brown.

Vasudev, Uma. 2003. *Indira Gandhi: Courage under Fire.* New Delhi: Rupa.

Garibaldi, Anita (1821–1849)

Heroine of republican movements in South America and Italy who fought alongside her husband Giuseppe Garibaldi. Anita Garibaldi was born Ana Maria de Jesus Ribeiro da Silva on August 30, 1821, in Morrinhos, Santa Catarina, Brazil. Her father was a herdsman, and her mother worked as a household servant. Two of Anita's young brothers were given away due to the poverty of the family and died of fever soon afterward. In 1834, Anita's father died as a result of an accident at work. The following year Anita migrated with her mother to the seaport of Laguna. After Anita successfully resisted an attempted rape, her worried mother convinced her to marry a local shoemaker, who turned out to be an abusive drunkard. In 1835, republicans known as *farrapos* ("ragamuffins") in Brazil's southernmost province of Rio Grande do Sul broke with the Brazilian Empire and proclaimed an independent nation, which they were able to maintain for a decade. Anita's husband went off with Brazil's imperial cavalry in May 1839. Two months later, the farrapos took Laguna, and Anita met Giuseppe Garibaldi, who had joined the farrapos in Brazil after a failed plot to create a unified, republican Italy caused him to flee his homeland in 1834. For the rest of her life, Anita remained with Garibaldi as he fought for political democracy and republican ideals.

Anita accompanied Garibaldi when he sailed northward to raid Brazilian shipping in October 1839. Upon returning to Laguna, the raiders met a Brazilian warship. Despite pleas to stay below, Anita took a musket and fought the Brazilian imperial forces. After the Brazilian government sent reinforcements to retake Santa Catarina, Garibaldi and Anita retreated overland southward with the farrapos to Rio Grande do Sul. In December 1839, Anita participated in the Battle of Santa Vitória, where she helped transport and nurse the wounded. In January 1840, Anita was in charge of munitions during the Battle of Curitibanos. She was captured but managed to escape. She rejoined Garibaldi after traveling through hostile territory for four days without food. During the Battle of São José do Norte in July 1840, Anita, eight months pregnant, commanded the cavalry. In 1841, Anita and Garibaldi decided to leave Rio Grande do Sul for Montevideo, Uruguay, which was in the midst of a civil war. Anita organized women in Montevideo to build fortifications, distribute food, and raise money. She married Garibaldi after learning of the death of her husband in 1842, the same year Garibaldi became a commander in the Uruguayan navy and assisted Uruguayans who opposed the Argentine dictator Juan Manuel de Rosas.

In December 1847, Anita sailed for Italy with the couple's three children to stay with her mother-in-law in the city of Nice. Garibaldi and his legionaries soon followed his wife across the Atlantic to continue the struggle for Italian unification. Anita helped her husband's cause through recruiting activities and arranging weapons procurement. Garibaldi's dream of a Roman Republic was established in February 1849, but Pope Pius IX called upon Austrian, French, Spanish, Neapolitan, and Tuscan troops to restore him to power. Anita joined Garibaldi in Rome to defend the republic. In July 1849, she cut her hair, donned men's clothes, and retreated with Garibaldi and 4,000 volunteers following the republic's collapse. Delirious with fever and six months pregnant, Anita was carried by her husband to a farm near the city of Ravenna in the Mandriole Valley, where she died on August 4, 1849. Today her body rests atop the Janiculum Hill overlooking Rome at the foot of a large bronze equestrian monument to her memory designed by sculptor Mario Rutelli in 1932. The Brazilian city where Anita Garibaldi was born is now named in her honor.

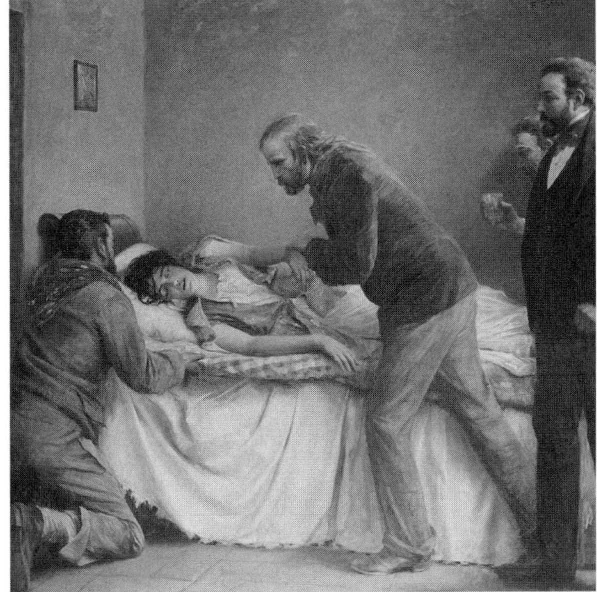

Death of Anita Garibaldi, *by Fabio Fabbi (1861–1946). (Scala/Art Resource)*

—David M. Carletta

See also Sicilian Revolutions of 1820 and 1848, Women and the

References and Further Reading

Sergio, Lisa. 1969. *I Am My Beloved: The Life of Anita Garibaldi.* New York: Weybright and Talley.

Valerio, Anthony. 2001. *Anita Garibaldi: A Biography.* Westport, CT: Praeger.

Gellhorn, Martha (1908–1998)

American war correspondent. Martha Gellhorn was married to Ernest Hemingway for just over five years, from November 1940 to December 1945. Both of them had peripatetic personalities and were drawn to dangerous adventures, whether reporting from the front lines in war zones or pursuing exotic game in the remote corners of the world. In addition, she was already a highly regarded journalist and fiction writer and understood what committed writing required. Yet perhaps because they were so similar in personality, their marriage was as volatile as it was short-lived. Although Gellhorn has not completely transcended her footnote status as the third and least compatible of Hemingway's four wives, her own career was too long and too consistently productive to be ignored. In the last quarter-century, critics have begun to recognize how substantive her literary achievement has been. In both her nonfiction and fiction, Gellhorn provided a perspective on human conflict remarkable for its consistent clarity and commitment to truth.

Born in St. Louis, Missouri, Gellhorn attended Bryn Mawr College. She began her writing career with the *New Republic,* and during the Great Depression, she traveled extensively throughout the United States, reporting on the ways in which the economic crisis had affected the lives of ordinary Americans. Her experiences inspired the four novellas included in *The Trouble I've Seen* (1936), a well-received collection that established her as a writer of fiction who understood and honored the distinctions between reportage and fiction, even fiction presented in the style of documentary realism. In 1937, *Colliers* hired Gellhorn to report on the Spanish Civil War, demonstrating considerable confidence in her abilities at a time when there were few female war correspondents and when she was still untested in that role. Although her sympathies were clearly with Spain's republican forces, she was able to report credibly on their excesses and on their tactical and moral failures.

Gellhorn subsequently reported for *Colliers* on the Russo-Finnish War, on the Nazi Blitz against London and other British cities, on the Normandy landings, and on the Communists' victory over the Nationalists in the Chinese civil war. For the *Atlantic Monthly,* she covered the trial of Adolf Eichmann in Israel. In the late 1960s, she reported for the British newspaper *The Guardian* on the escalating U.S. involvement in Vietnam and on the recurring conflict between Arabs and Israelis. She subsequently reported from Nicaragua on the conflict between the Sandinistas and the Contras. Her war reporting was collected in *The Face of War,* originally published in 1959 and updated in 1986. The collection permits a critical appraisal of the scope, the vivid immediacy, and the moral engagement of her reportage.

Gellhorn's peacetime reporting has been collected in *The View from the Ground* (1986) and her travel writing, along with reminiscences of her marriage to Hemingway, in *Travels with Myself and Another* (1978). Gellhorn's fiction includes *A Stricken Field* (1940), *The Heart of Another* (1941), *Liana* (1944), *The Wine of Astonishment* (1948), and *The Honeyed Peace* (1953). Her novellas have been collected in *The Short Novels of Martha Gellhorn* (1991) and *The Novellas of Martha Gellhorn* (1993).

—*Martin Kich*

See also Lederer, Edie; Schuyler, Philippa; Tomara, Sonia; Trotta, Liz; Watts, Jean

References and Further Reading

Deibler, William E. 2001. "Dateline: D-Day: Ernest Hemingway Reported on Ernest Hemingway Martha Gellhorn Reported on the War Both Were Searching for the Truth." *North Dakota Quarterly* 68 (spring-summer): 295–302.

Horwell, Veronica. (1998). "Martha Gellhorn: A Witness to Our World at War" *Brick* 59 (spring): 53–56.

Lassner, Phyllis. 1998. "'Camp Follower of Catastrophe': Martha Gellhorn's World War II Challenge to the Modernist War." *Modern Fiction Studies* 44 (fall): 792–812.

McLoughlin, Kate. 2004. "Bringing War Home: Martha Gellhorn's Second World War Correspondence." *Symbiosis: A Journal of Anglo-American Literary Relations* 8 (October): 156–164.

Spanier, Sandra Whipple. 2002. "Rivalry, Romance, and War Reporters: Martha Gellhorn's *Love Goes to Press* and the *Collier's* Files." *Hemingway and Women: Female Critics and the Female Voice,* edited by Lawrence R. Broer and Gloria Holland, 256–275. Tuscaloosa: University of Alabama Press.

Germany, Armed Forces (Wehrmacht), World War II Atrocities of

Atrocities committed by the German military during World War II indiscriminately against men and women, who, particularly in the east, were objectified and dehumanized. For decades historians maintained that the German armed forces during World War II, collectively called the *Wehrmacht,* were simple soldiers who had the misfortune of fighting for a criminal regime. Historians tended to separate the Wehrmacht from the specialized units that accompanied it into battle such as the SS, the Secret Police (Gestapo), and the infamous police battalions responsible for murdering entire Jewish communities on the eastern front.

Soon after the war, memoirs from leading German generals seeking to distance themselves from the Nazi regime flooded the publishing market. U.S. and British historians tended to rely on these accounts and portrayed the Wehrmacht as an honorable institution that was hijacked by a clique of criminals. One of the underlying reasons for this sympathetic portrayal was the cold war. The perceived threat from the Soviet Union necessitated that West Germany become a full partner in the defense of western Europe. Denigrating the Wehrmacht, many of whose generals were needed to rebuild the new German military (now called the *Bundeswehr*), was counterproductive. There was also a sense that the Nuremburg Trials properly identified and punished those responsible for Nazi Germany's crimes during the war. Too many historians accepted the notion that the Wehrmacht was not involved in the widespread atrocities committed against civilians and soldiers. For the most part, these atrocities occurred on the eastern front against the Soviet people, specifically Jews.

By the mid-1980s historians started to delve further into Wehrmacht activities on the eastern front and quickly learned that regular army units were intimately involved in committing atrocities. The Wehrmacht supported the Nazi regime's goal of racially reordering Europe and conquering *Lebensraum* (living space) for Germany in the East. Every organ of the German government was given a role in accomplishing this task, including the Wehrmacht. In 1934 all officers and enlisted men of the Wehrmacht personally swore a loyalty oath to Adolf Hitler. Most did so enthusiastically because they considered Hitler an advocate of military spending and saw a chance to return the military to greatness. The oath bound the Wehrmacht tightly to the Nazi regime and ensured its participation in every phase of Hitler's plan to destroy European Jewry and dismantle what he called Judeo-Bolshevism in the Soviet Union. Even without the Wehrmacht's ideological affinity for National Socialism, the German military already had a past record of committing atrocities against civilians during World War I, specifically in Belgium and parts of eastern Europe. Most of the incidents during World War I were isolated, but this was not the case during World War II. Mass executions, population removals, poor treatment of prisoners, and the use of slave labor were Wehrmacht policies handed down from generals to subordinates in an organized fashion.

The Wehrmacht prepared for a different sort of war against the Soviet Union years before the conflict began. According to Nazi leadership, the future war against Poland and the Soviet Union was to be one of annihilation. Beginning with the invasion of Poland in September 1939, the

Wehrmacht carried with it into battle orders from Hitler to liquidate the Polish intelligentsia so that they would not threaten the German settlement of Polish territory. The Wehrmacht applied broad definitions of who could be considered a partisan and treated large numbers of civilians as legitimate military targets. This definition included Jews, who by virtue of being Jewish were considered automatic threats to the Wehrmacht. Most people identified as partisans were executed, a task shared by the Wehrmacht, the SS, the Gestapo, and police battalions created to occupy territory after the Wehrmacht moved forward. Although many Wehrmacht generals disapproved of their soldiers participating in executions and otherwise enforcing a harsh occupation (mostly for reasons of limited resources), evidence shows that Wehrmacht units were used interchangeably with the SS to execute Jews, Polish clergy, and intellectuals.

Once Germany invaded the Soviet Union in July 1941, the Wehrmacht was already experienced at fighting a war of racial annihilation. The Wehrmacht had to guard against disorder in the ranks while still fulfilling its ugly task of killing large numbers of civilians. Letters and films taken by Wehrmacht soldiers at the front reveal that daily life on the eastern front involved treating civilians and enemy soldiers alike as subhumans worthy of extreme treatment. One of the more infamous Wehrmacht policies was to execute a large number of citizens for every Wehrmacht soldier killed by partisans or resistance fighters. This policy applied to all of Germany's occupied territories, but it was enforced more regularly in the East. For example, if 5 soldiers were killed by partisans, the Wehrmacht might kill 500 civilians from the town where the partisans allegedly lived. Such policies typified the Wehrmacht's conduct on the eastern front in particular, especially because it regarded the Soviet people, not just the military, as a dangerous enemy.

Although the Wehrmacht did not specifically target women when committing atrocities, it had no qualms about executing women and children during reprisals for actions taken against its soldiers. Films taken by Wehrmacht soldiers show soldiers putting nooses around the necks of Russian women accused of spying and attaching signs labeling them "Jewish cows" or other insults. Men and women had different experiences in the ghettos and concentration camps erected by other organs of the National Socialist state, but the Wehrmacht's atrocities were characterized by their speed, brutality, and indifference to artificialities such as gender. The Wehrmacht viewed entire populations as enemies and treated them accordingly.

—*Brian E. Crim*

See also Einsatzgruppen; Holocaust and Jewish Women

References and Further Reading

Bartov, Omer. 1992. "The Conduct of War: Soldiers and the Barbarization of Warfare." *The Journal of Modern History* 64:32–45.

———. 1992. *Hitler's Army: Soldiers, Nazis, and War in the Third Reich.* New York: Oxford University Press.

Forster, Jurgen. 1981. "The Wehrmacht and the War of Extermination against the Soviet Union." *Yad Vashem Studies* 14:7–33.

Rossino, Alexander B. 2003. *Hitler Strikes Poland: Blitzkrieg, Ideology, and Atrocity.* Lawrence: University Press of Kansas.

Germany, Peasants' War

See Peasant's War

Germany, Revolution of 1918–1919, Women in the

Role of women in the German Revolution and the gains made by women as a result of the establishment of the Weimar Republic (1919–

1933). As a result of the German Revolution of 1918–1919, women enjoyed more political freedom than ever before in German history: they went from possessing no political power in the Wilhelminian monarchy to helping form a new republican government in which they could vote and hold political office. Nevertheless, their overall participation and influence was minimal in comparison to men's roles in and sway on the revolution. Women held few leadership positions during the rebellion and thus were often in no position to influence major political decisions. Those who were able to play important roles frequently found their policies opposed by male colleagues. Women's responsibilities in political parties were often limited to issues such as social welfare and education, which deeply concerned many women but left them marginalized in the political process. Many female activists blamed feminine passivity and years of patriarchy for the failure of women to engage more in the political process. On the other hand, in a reaction to the horrors of World War I, many advocates of the women's movement believed that female, motherly nature could better combat violence than the male disposition. Women needed to become more politically active to ensure that a war such as World War I did not occur again.

Women in centrist and conservative political parties and groups sought suffrage and supported the Weimar National Assembly of January 1919 and the Weimar Republic that was born from it. Women in leftist parties supported the workers' and soldiers' councils that were formed in 1917 and 1918 along the Soviet model and that, for the most part, demanded the economic, political, and social democratization of Germany. Indeed, many women espoused the construction of councils to educate women politically because they had historically been excluded from the political process. These women's councils were either unpopular or never truly materialized. Unfortunately, participation of women in the workers' and soldiers' councils was rare.

The most politically active woman in the revolution was Rosa Luxemburg. Along with Karl Liebknecht, she led the Sparticist movement and Communist Party (KPD) during the revolution until her murder by Freikorps troops in January 1919. Although not deeply involved in revolutionary events because of health problems, Clara Zetkin of the Independent Socialist Party (USPD) and later the KPD was one of the theoretical leaders of the women's movement. She believed that only a radical Marxist upheaval of society would bring all human beings egalitarianism and, thus, all women true equality. Another important leftist women leader was Käte Duncker, who, along with Rosa Luxemburg, was one of two female members of the thirteen-member Sparticist Central Committee. Other prominent women to support the council movement, but not considered as leftist as Luxemburg, Zetkin, and Duncker, were Toni Sender who was a member of the USPD and active in Frankfurt am Main during the revolution and Anita Augspurg and Lida Gustava Heymann who were members of the Council Congress in Bavaria.

Many female members of the centrist Social Democratic Party (SPD), of the conservative German Democratic Party (DDP), and of bourgeois women's groups hailed democratic reforms that led to the creation of the Weimar Republic as the true revolution that had occurred in Germany. Luise Zietz and Marie Juchacz were both Social Democratic delegates at the Weimar National Assembly. Juchacz was the first woman to speak at the assembly in February 1919 and thus the first women ever to address a German parliament. Marianne Weber, the wife of Max Weber, became a member of the Baden National Assembly as a German Democrat, and Helene Lange and Minna Cauer, both long-time activists in the women's movement, became members of the DDP in 1918. Getrud Bäumer, the chairperson from 1910 until 1918 of the largest women's organization at the time, the League of German Women, supported the National Assembly as a means to combat the chaos that the revolution and World War I had introduced in Germany.

World War I was a catalyst for the revolution. During the war, women first began to experience economic and political freedoms. In factories they replaced men who were drafted to fight and, as a result, began working in sectors of the workforce in which employers had not previously engaged them. The length and loss of the war, hunger and even starvation, long workdays, sole responsibility for raising children, and war-related deaths of family members led women to strike for better working conditions, higher wages, an end to the war, and political freedoms. They believed that through these sacrifices they had earned rights such as suffrage and political office.

Indeed, the Weimar Constitution guaranteed women suffrage under articles 17 and 22, and article 109 ensured legal and social equality with men. Other freedoms for women that resulted from the revolution were the lifting of the statutory celibacy for all female civil servants, their ability to become judges and jurors, and the payment of wages during pregnancy. Unfortunately, many of the freedoms gained by women during the revolution and the Weimar Republic were revoked during the world economic crisis in 1929 and by the National Socialist government after 1933.

—Chad Wallo

See also Luxemburg, Rosa

References and Further Reading

Arendt, Hans-Peter, and Peter Kuhlbrodt. 1988. "Die Proletarische Frauenbewegung in der Novemberrevolution 1918/19" [Proletarian women's movement in the November Revolution]. *Beiträge zur Geschichte der Arbeiterbewegung* 30, no. 6: 761–773.

Grebing, Helga. 1994. *Frauen in der deutschen Revolution 1918/19* [Women in the German Revolution]. Heidelberg: Stiftung Reichspräsident-Friedrich-Ebert-Gedenkstätte.

Hervé, Florence. 1983. "Novemberrevolution und Nachkriegskrise 1918–1923." In *Geschichte der deutschen Frauenbewegung* [History of the German women's movement], edited by Florence Hervé, 119–128. Cologne: PahlßRugenstein.

Germany, Special Action Groups

See Einsatzgruppen

Germany, Women and the Home Front, World War I

Impact of World War I on German women. The role of German women in World War I was characterized by increased participation in the economy, active involvement in the wartime political unrest, and the struggle to survive as food, clothing, and heat became scarce.

For German women, World War I was an introduction into a new kind of warfare that depended as much on the home front as it did the battlefronts. The role of women in the economic, political, and military planning of the German nation underwent tremendous changes. Women replaced conscripted men, producing the goods of war, keeping production going and releasing valuable reserves to the military. Government propaganda focused on women because they were the principle home-front population during the war. Women were the main consumers of German goods, and their support was necessary to keep the economy strong.

One way that women coped with the deprivations of the war was through participation in the activities of social organizations. Social organizations served as a source of comfort and camaraderie for women and played a vital role in mobilizing the women on the home front. Gertrud Bäumer asked the nearly 600,000 members of the Federation of German Women's Associations (BDF) to put aside their demands for suffrage and for greater access to education and state employment in the name of national solidarity. BDF members worked in soup kitchens and hospital wards, tended to the rising number of orphans, and knitted woolen clothing for the troops at the front (Herwig 1997, 35). The largest German nursing movement, the Vaterlandische Frauenverein (Union of Women of the Fatherland), known as the Kaiserin's (Empress's) army, had 3,000 branches and 800,000 members in 1914, and in all there were more than 6,300 bodies of nurses with 1.1 million members (Strachan 2001, 109).

The expanded presence of women in the workforce during the war is often noted as one of the significant results of the war. After the first military actions of the war proved indecisive, German society was mobilized for total war. The need for more soldiers meant that many men were conscripted from important industrial and manufacturing jobs. To replace them, the German government called upon women to enter the workforce. Some women answered that call. Machine shops recruited over 400,000 women, and ammunitions plants recruited 600,000 women. At the Krupp works, where no women were employed before the war, 30,000 women were added to a workforce of 80,000 men by 1918 (Herwig 1997, 294).

Although it is true that the number of women entering the workforce for the first time did grow substantially, this was not a departure from prewar trends (Daniel 1997, 37). What did change was where women worked. A large portion of the women who entered the armaments and industrial workforces were already employed at the start of the war, many within the textile and luxury goods industries. When it became apparent that the war would not be short, the production of textiles and luxury goods were reduced or banned in favor of increased production of goods necessary for the war. As much as 40 percent of the women who had worked in the textile industry in 1914 were relocated to more important industries.

The drives for conscription often met with substandard results, largely due to the handling of wartime benefits and aid. The German state faced a conundrum: the financial support of the wives of German soldiers at the front undermined efforts to mobilize German women to work. Women assisted by the government found it economically beneficial to remain unemployed or to work from the home. The government's attempts to save money by decreasing aid to women who worked only increased their incentives to stay home and watch the family.

Horrible work conditions also undermined government efforts to increase female employment. Women who entered the workforce for the first time often experienced hostility or apathy. Men resented women being in the workplace. Women were constantly reminded that they were there only temporarily and that they were too weak to do good work, and they were denied technical training. The new types of work that women undertook were often difficult and dangerous. Work environments were not safe, and hunger and extremely long shifts made the new workers more susceptible to accidents. In the final analysis, given the horrible atmosphere women faced, the hostility of employers and coworkers, and the lack of progress made in women's place in the workforce, there was no true emancipation of female German workers during World War I.

Because women made up the majority of the home-front population, they bore the brunt of the economic deprivations caused by the war and the blockade. The task of procuring food for themselves and their families was made difficult by long lines, constant shortages, war profiteering, hoarding, and government propaganda that often blamed women for the problems. The Allied blockade of the German coast and the trade embargo on the continent were quickly felt on the German home front. Germany had imported a large part of its food before the war, and many shortages appeared during the first winter. For women, this meant that it became increasingly difficult to find enough food for themselves and their families. Particularly among the lower and lower middle classes, everyday food staples such as bread and potatoes became unattainable or unaffordable. In an effort to calm the growing protests over food shortages, the Imperial Grain Authority (established in November 1914) issued ration cards for bread in January 1915, while setting a price ceiling for potatoes (Davis 2000, 47). The attempt to use rationing to quell the crisis was ineffectual. Complaints of unfairly dispersed rations and the lack of adequate supplies to meet the minimum rations of the population doomed the system. The only thing rationing accomplished was to further place the blame for food shortages on the frivolousness of women.

The hunger women felt in 1914 only worsened in the coming years. In 1916, early frosts spoiled the potato harvest, leaving many women undernourished and scrambling to stretch their rations to feed the family. Turnips, a vegetable of poor nutritive value and even less taste, was used to replace the potato. It was that hated food that gave its name to the brutal winter of 1916. The Turnip Winter, which saw temperatures dip below –25 degrees Fahrenheit, was a low point for many on the home front. Many women survived on diets just above starvation level. Increased work and longer shifts made queuing up in food lines even more difficult and aggravating. Lack of fuel and clothing exacerbated the poor diets, making the last years of the war extremely miserable for women in Germany (Davis 2000, 180–187).

Throughout the war, government propaganda was an important part of the relationship between women and the state. Propaganda was used to mobilize German society and to extol women to support the war effort. Women often faced hostile and disparaging expositions as well. The government blamed the food shortages of 1914 on the improvidence of German women. They were seen negatively by many of the men at the front who bemoaned the luxury in which women lived (Herwig 1997, 265). In short, women were often viewed as the culprits for the many problems on the home front.

The struggle to survive made women an important source of discontent during the war. Although some women did take part in the social and political revolts that occurred during the war, they played a far more important role in the numerous food riots that plagued the German government. For the most part, these riots were small incidents of outraged and desperate women storming food depots, shops, and food lines. As the war dragged on, however, rioters began to link calls for food (particularly bread) with calls for peace, putting the government in a difficult position. They had to stop the riots without resorting to violence or creating a backlash on the home front or the warfront. The last thing the government needed was word getting to the frontline soldiers that their wives, sisters, mothers, and daughters were being repressed. The resolution of those protests, many times in favor of the women, tended to exacerbate the situation, as it showed women that this was a possible way to get food (Davis 2000, 2). The government was never able to overcome food shortages during the war, and shortages and food riots continued to be paramount issues on the home front.

—*Christopher Griffin*

See also Germany, Revolution of 1918–1919, Women in the; Kollwitz, Kathe; Luxemburg, Rosa

References and Further Reading

Daniel, Ute. 1997. *The War from Within: German Working-Class Women in the First World War.* Translated from the German by Margareta Reis. Oxford and New York: Berg.

Davis, Belinda J. 2000. *Home Fires Burning: Food, Politics, and Everyday Life in World War I Berlin.* Chapel Hill and London: University of North Carolina Press.

Herwig, Holger H. 1997. *The First World War: Germany and Austria-Hungary, 1914–1918.* New York: St. Martin's Press.

Strachan, Hew. 2001. *To Arms.* Vol. 1 of *The First World War.* New York: Oxford University Press.

Germany, Women and the Home Front, World War II

Impact of World War II on German women. During World War II, German women actively participated in the war through social organizations, employment, and survival on the home front. Many women supported the regime and its war. Some opposed and resisted it. But all women in Germany bore the brunt of the hardships that beset the home front, including food and material shortages, destruction caused by air raids, grief caused by losses of loved ones on the warfronts, and the retributive actions taken by invading armies.

German women constituted the majority of the home-front population during World War II and were the principle target of many of the Nazi regime's domestic policy initiatives. Adolf Hitler, chancellor of the Third Reich, was adamant that during the war, women would not be the source of difficulties on the home front that they had been during World War I. His policies on state support for mothers and wives of soldiers were implemented to achieve dual purposes: to keep women (and consequently their husbands) content and to transform German womanhood into the Nazi ideal.

Although Germany had been one of the most progressive feminist societies during the early twentieth century, women generally acquiesced to Hitler's desires. Many women experienced the implementation of Nazi gender policies not as aggression against women but as a welcome return to traditional values (Gellately 2001, 10–11). The elevation and reverence of motherhood showed the regime's antifeminism was not inherently antiwoman. Some Nazi party officials did not hide their hostility toward women. Their insulting rhetoric was often discounted, however, either as exceptional in an otherwise agreeable party platform or because the impassioned speeches of the true leader of the Nazi Party, Adolf Hitler, made clear his sympathy for the plight of women (Koonz 1987, 58–61). Many women found comfort in the ideals of the Nazi Party that relegated women's lives to the private sphere of *Kinder, Kirche, Küche* (children, church, kitchen).

Although the Nazi ideal was for women to get married and create large families, many women were unable to do so. The overall surplus of women in Germany and the lack of available men on the home front meant that many German women were single during the war. Most of these women, especially those from the lower classes, were employed before and during the war. The state targeted those who had escaped employment for recruiting drives, with limited success.

Prior to the war, married women were encouraged to leave the workforce to start or expand families. The government gave financial support based on family size. To women in low-paying jobs, with working husbands, significant government assistance in exchange for unemployment was a good deal. The success of the program has often been debated. Although many married women left the labor force, the overall percentage of women employed in Germany was far higher than in Great Britain or the United States (Gellately 2001, 151).

During the war, unemployed married women who did not have children often created a great deal of resentment among those who were forcibly employed. Women of the lower class, even those with young children, could not afford to live off government benefits. Following long hours of work, working women had to stand in long lines for their rations, while unemployed women were able to get the choicest provisions. Most of those unemployed, childless women had the financial means not to work, giving the resentment clear class undertones. Attempts to recruit those women were largely unsuccessful, in part because the Nazi leadership refused to make employment compulsory (Noakes and Pridham 2000, 316–325).

Rather than force married women and mothers into employment, the Nazi regime imported millions of prisoners of war and slave laborers from conquered and satellite nations. Extensive efforts were made to prevent foreign workers from defiling the German women who shared common workspace. The vast majority of the Gestapo's manpower was directed at controlling foreign workers and preventing relationships with German women (Gellately 2001, 152). As the war dragged on and times became more desperate, some women did form sexual relationships with non-German men. Many of the denunciations made against women to the Gestapo involved charges of sexual relations with foreigners (Gellately 2001, 197).

Many women found an outlet for their creativity and leadership through work in Nazi social organizations. The umbrella organization for women was the National Socialist Frauenschaft/Deutsches Frauenwerk (Women's Organization/Women's Work, NSF/DFW). Led by Gertrud Scholtz-Klink, the NSF/DFW acted as a policing organization for women, its main task to indoctrinate, train, control, and organize German women for the needs of the state. Although part of the Nazi Party apparatus, the NSF/DFW did not provide women with avenues to influence political decisions. The leaders within the organizations were given power to operate within the sphere of women but were always subordinate to the command of the male-dominated party. Despite the lack of real power, women participated in the programs of the antifeminist Nazi state in far greater numbers than in the Weimar Republic, which had first enfranchised them (Grunberger 1995, 258). For the most part, women found that the organizations served as support networks, gave them activities to feel useful in the war effort, and provided social benefits for the community.

The situation on the home front never approached the desperation experienced during World War I. Although shortages were felt, women did not suffer from the starvation and disease women had to cope with from 1914 to 1918. In part, this was due to prewar preparation for a wartime economy. It was also due to the importations of millions of prisoners of war, slave labor, and trade with satellite nations, which was far greater than it had been during World War I. Yet the black market was just as strong in 1945 as it had been in 1918. An extensive bartering network existed between the rural and urban areas. Urban women were able to exchange goods that were scarce in the country for food. In this way, many women were able to make ends meet throughout the war (Stephenson 2001, 99).

German women were active among the resistance movements of the war. Sophie Scholl is perhaps the best-known female resister, famous for her actions as part of the White Rose movement in Munich. Another famous act of resistance, the Rosenstrasse Protest in Berlin in 1943, was made up of several hundred German women protesting the arrest of their Jewish husbands. Many women also participated in underground resistance movements, providing food, shelter, and aid to conspirators and even taking over the operations of resistance movements after the men had been arrested. The Gestapo watched the wives of known conspirators closely; many were harassed, interrogated, or arrested. Many wives of the conspirators in the July 1944 bomb plot were arrested.

Woman of non-Aryan descent suffered through a harsh existence during the war. Those of targeted social and ethnic groups were not spared the brutality of the Holocaust. Jewish women suffered under tremendous strain as they worked to support and feed their families while warding off the hopelessness of their existence. Eventually, those who were not protected as privileged or intermarried Jews were deported to concentration camps. They were separated from their families during the roundups and rarely saw them again. Even those who were protected from the Holocaust had to suffer meek existences, isolated from society. Women of other repressed groups, such as Jehovah's Witnesses, Roma and Sinti, and the handicapped suffered fates similar to the men.

As the tide of the war turned against Germany, the home front came under increasing strain. The Allies incessantly bombed Germany from 1942 onward. Many women were killed in air raids, many were made homeless, and many were forced to relocate to the interior. Yet even as the air attacks of the Allies penetrated farther into Germany, a greater fear loomed on the horizon: the Red Army. Stories about the Soviet military forces' inhumanity and barbarity toward women had filtered into Germany during the war. Joseph Goebbels's propaganda machine created some of the stories to dehumanize the Soviets. Much of it came from soldiers returning from the front, refugees, and news reports. In late 1944 and early 1945, German woman braced themselves for the Soviet onslaught. What occurred barely eclipsed the worst predictions as the Soviet army raped millions of German women in East Prussia and Berlin (Beevor 2002, 410). Tens of thousands of women died from the attacks or committed suicide.

—*Christopher Griffin*

See also Forced Labor, Nazi Germany; Harnack-Fish, Mildred; Holocaust and Jewish Women; Jehovah's Witnesses in Nazi Germany; Kuckhoff, Greta; Rape: Red Army in World War II; Roma/Sinti; Rosenstrasse and Intermarriage of Jews and German Gentiles; Scholl, Sophie; Scholtz-Klink, Gertrud; Schulze-Boysen, Libertas

References and Further Reading

Beevor, Anthony. 2002. *The Fall of Berlin.* New York: Viking Penguin.

Gellately, Robert. 2001. *Backing Hitler: Consent and Coercion in Nazi Germany.* New York: Oxford University Press.

Grunberger, Richard. 1995. *The 12-Year Reich: A Social History of Nazi Germany 1933–1945.* New York: Da Capo Press.

Koonz, Claudia. 1987. *Mothers in the Fatherland: Women, the Family, and Nazi Politics.* New York: St. Martin's Press.

Noakes, Jeremy, and Geoffrey Pridham. 2000. *Nazism: 1919–1945.* 4 vols., 5th ed. Exeter, England: Exeter University Press.

Stephenson, Jill. 2001. *Women in Nazi Germany.* London: Pearson Education.

Ghesquière, Virginie (ca. 1755–1854)

Soldier in the French army between 1806 and 1812. Virginie Ghesquière served in the French army during the First French Empire (1804–1814) of Napoleon Bonaparte and is one of the first French women to become a member of the French Legion of Honor.

Ghesquière had a brother who was a soldier in Napoleon's army. When he fell in battle in 1806, Ghesquière, disguised as a man, took his place as a soldier in his old regiment, the 27th Line regiment. She participated in various campaigns and fought in the Peninsular War under the command of General Jean-Andoche Junot, taking part in the invasion of Portugal in 1807.

Ghesquière was distinguished many times for bravery and devotion in her military career. She was eventually promoted to the rank of sergeant. Six years after having joined the army, when she was wounded in battle in 1812, her gender was discovered. She was immediately dismissed. Nevertheless, for her contribution in the Napoleonic Wars, Ghesquière was awarded upon dismissal what is now recognized as the French Legion of Honor—and by Napoleon himself. This highest French national order had been created by Bonaparte while he was First Consul of France (1799–1804) and was approved by the General Assembly on May 19, 1802. It is believed that Napoleon did not intend for women to receive the award. The exclusion of women was not addressed in the statutes of the order, however, and there is no officially recorded mention anywhere that women should have been excluded. In fact, Napoleon had already decorated women for heroic behavior in the Italian Campaign of 1796–1797. Later he continued to award women with Legion of Honor insignia but without any official written record. Only recently has there been public effort to acknowledge these women as legitimate *chevalièrs* of the French Legion of Honor.

At the time of Ghesquière's dismissal from the army, an article about the discovery of her gender was published in the October 31, 1812, issue of *Journal de l'Empire.* This article is said to have led to the composition and subsequent dissemination of a popular song about her exploits. This song seems to be the source of her nickname, *jolie sergent* ("pretty sergeant"). Ghesquière's year of birth is unknown, but she is believed to have been almost 100 years old when she passed away in 1854.

—Georgia Tres

See also Agustina de Aragón; Fernig, Félicité, and Fernig, Théophile; Great Britain, Women in Service in the Seventeenth, Eighteenth, and Early Nineteenth Centuries; Plater, Emilia

References and Further Reading

Déon-Beeière, Danièle. 2002. *Les femmes et la Légion d'Honneur: Depuis sa creation* [Women of the Legion of Honor since its creation]. Paris: Les Éditions de l'Officine.

Gierczak, Emilia (1925–1945)

Polish soldier in the all-women's Emilia Plater Independent Women's Battalion in World War II. Second Lieutenant Emilia Gierczak (called Elka) distinguished herself during the fighting on the Pomeranian Rampart and was killed while leading an assault group in Kolobrzeg (formerly Kolberg) in Pomerania. She was a platoon commander of the 10th Infantry Regiment of the Polish army formed in the Soviet Union. She served in the Emilia Plater Independent Women's Battalion, initially subordinated to Tadeusz Kosciuszko 1st Division, which was created in the Soviet Union in 1943. She was among the battalion of women soldiers trained at the Infantry Officers' School in Riazan to command companies and platoons of the new Polish army. Women were selected for officer training because of the drastic shortage of Polish male officers, in part caused by the Soviet massacres of Polish prisoners of war in the Kozel'sk, Starobel'sk, and Ostashkov camps, as well as the unsuitability for officer training of many of the male recruits of the Polish army.

Polish patriotism was an important element in Gierczak's upbringing. It was assumed that Gierczak's parents (Jozef and Leontyna) had named her Emilia because the name was made famous by the legendary Emilia Plater, a leader in the 1830–1831 Polish uprising against Russian rule whose death was romanticized by the great nineteenth-century Polish poet Adam Mickiewicz in his famous poem, "Death of a Colonel."

An eyewitness to Gierczak's death on March 17, 1945, wrote, "She was charged with a difficult task—to capture a stoutly defended building. She could have waited until it got dark to do this, but she didn't want anyone to think that she was afraid. . . . She was never to learn that the mission was accomplished, for she was hit in the forehead as she moved up to embolden her men, who had earlier gone to ground, by stirring them to action by her personal example. So the devil himself took possession of the platoon! Henceforward, no obstacle could deter the men from avenging the death of their woman-commander!" (Jagielski 1979, 14–15).

Gierczak's memorabilia, including her last letter to her mother, are on display in the Military Museum in Kolobrzeg, a seaside resort and port on the Baltic formerly known by its German name, Kolberg. A street in Kolobrzeg as well as a number of schools and Polish scouting organizations have been named after Gierczak.

—Kazimiera J. Cottam

See also Polish Independent Women's Battalion, Emilia Plater

References and Further Reading

Cottam, K[azimiera] Jean. 1986. "Veterans of Polish Women's Combat Battalion Hold a Reunion." *Minerva: Quarterly Report on Women and the Military* 4, no. 4 (winter): 1–7.

———. Kazimiera J[ean]. 2003. "Gierczak, Emilia." In *Amazons to Fighter Pilots,* Vol. 1, edited by Reina Pennington, 184. Westport, CT: Greenwood Press.

Jagielski, B. 1979. "Bylo to w Kolobrzegu ..." [This happened in Kolobrzeg]. *Zolnierz Polski* 10 (March 11): 14–15.

Gillars, Mildred Elizabeth

See "Axis Sally"

Gizycki, Krystyna Skarbek

See Granville, Christine

Goldstein, Vida (1869–1949)

Teacher, journalist, and peace campaigner. Vida Goldstein is the most noted Australian suffragette. Born in Portland, Victoria, in 1869, one of five children, Vida Goldstein completed her education at Presbyterian Ladies College and decided afterward to dedicate her life to social issues and peace. Editor of the *Women's Sphere* (1900–1905), she emerged on the Australian political scene by the turn of the century and became the first woman in the British Empire to campaign for a legislative body. Goldstein was a candidate for the Victoria Senate from 1903 to 1917. Although she was never elected, her several electoral campaigns received noteworthy press attention. A pioneer feminist and delegate from Australasia to the International Woman Suffrage Conference (Washington, D.C., 1902), Goldstein contributed to the foundation of many women's organizations including the National Council of Women. Politically independent, Goldstein was the militant figure of the Women's Political Association, which, although not Marxist, opposed imperialism, and propagated her ideas in *The Women Voter,* a magazine later frequently censured by the authorities for its antimilitaristic views. A passionate pacifist despite verbal insults and physical intimidations, Goldstein was chairperson of the Australian Peace Alliance (APA). During World War I, she founded a major peace movement, the Women's Peace Army (WPA) on July 15, 1915, with the famous mottos "I Didn't Raise My Son to Be a Soldier" and "We War against War." On October 21, 1916, a WPA anticonscription demonstration attracted 80,000 people to a rally in the heart of Melbourne. Following World War I, Goldstein participated in the Women's International Peace Conference at Zurich (1919). During the interwar years, then well recognized as a devoted Christian Socialist, she incessantly promoted the cause of complete disarmament and advocated the pursuit of better living standards. Her final campaign was an antinuclear meeting in Melbourne in the summer of 1946. She died at age 80 in 1949 in South Yarra (Melbourne). A tree was planted in the grounds of the Victorian Parliament to honor her accomplishments.

—*Jérôme Dorvidal*

See also Moore, Eleanor May; Street, Jessie

References and Further Reading

Bomford, Janette M. 1994. *That Dangerous and Persuasive Woman.* Melbourne: Melbourne University Press.

Daniels, Kay, and Mary Murnane. 1980. *Uphill All the Way: Documentary History of Women in Australia.* Brisbane, Australia: University of Queensland Press.

Gonne, Maud (1865–1953)

Irish political activist and polemicist, founder of Inghínidhe na hEireann (Daughters of Erin), campaigner for social justice, and inspirational figure for Irish nationalists. Maud Gonne was born in Surrey, England, the daughter of Colonel Thomas Gonne and Edith Cooke. Her father was part of the British forces in Ireland, yet Gonne's autobiography, *A Servant of the Queen,* described him as unconventional, favoring Irish self-government. Edith Cooke died in 1871, and in 1886, after her father's death, Gonne inherited sufficient wealth to live independently. Suffering from incipient tuberculosis, she went to France to recuperate, met the politician Lucien Millevoye, and began a "passionate alliance," working jointly for Irish freedom and the regaining of Alsace and Lorraine for France. Their son Georges died in infancy; Iseult, born in 1894, was referred to in public as Gonne's niece. Although Gonne discovered her sex debarred her from membership of Irish nationalist organizations, male leaders recognized her beauty and wealth as assets. She was sent to Donegal in 1891 to campaign against peasant evictions. She had been introduced to John O'Leary, veteran of the 1848 Young Ireland rebellion and a supporter of the use of physical force. She met the poet William Butler Yeats in 1899 and remained his muse for decades while spurning marriage. They worked together campaigning for political prisoner release, commemoration of the 1798 United Irish Rising, and developing a National Literary Society. Her paper, *L'Irlande libre* (Free Ireland, 1897–1898), carried her polemic on Queen Victoria, "The Famine Queen." The Boer War against British domination in South Africa (1899–1901) provided the opportunity to mobilize anti-British sentiment in Ireland, and Gonne helped found the Transvaal Committee. Inghínidhe na hEireann, formed in April 1900, provided women with the opportunity for political involvement. Gonne broke with Millevoye in 1900, and on meeting John MacBride, who was applauded for his role in leading the Irish fight against the British in South Africa, decided to marry. In 1903, after converting to Catholicism, she married MacBride in Paris. Their son, Séan, was born in 1904, but she filed for divorce in 1905, returning only intermittently to Ireland. Inghínidhe published *Bean na hEireann* (Woman of Ireland, 1908–1911) and campaigned for free school meals. During World War I, Gonne and Iseult, exiled in France, nursed the wounded. On May 5, 1916, MacBride was executed as a leader of the Easter Rising, and in 1918 Gonne returned to Ireland. Arrested by the British and imprisoned for six months, she supported Sinn Féin ("We Ourselves"—the Irish Republican party devoted to the independence of all of Ireland) during the War of Independence while Séan joined the Irish Republican Army. During the Civil War, she helped form the Women's Prisoners Defence League, protesting against the government's repression of dissent. Imprisoned in Kilmainham Jail in April 1923, she won release after going on a hunger strike. She opposed the Irish Free State for the rest of her life, continuing to support political prisoners and women's rights.

—Margaret Ward

See also Ireland, Easter Rising of 1916; Ireland, War of Independence

References and Further Reading

Steele, Karen. 2004. *Maud Gonne's Irish Nationalist Writings 1895–1946.* Dublin: Irish Academic Press.

Ward, Margaret. 1990. *Maud Gonne: Ireland's Joan of Arc.* London: Pandora.

Grajales Coelho, Mariana

See Grajales Cuello, Mariana

Grajales Cuello (also Coelho), Mariana (1808–1893)

Revolutionary Cuban mother. Called the *Generala Mambisa* (Rebel General), Mariana Grajales sacrificed her husband, ten sons, and two daughters, whom she had prepared to the fight for Cuban independence from Spain. Grajales was born in Santiago de Cuba, a rural eastern province where tobacco and sugar plantations predominated. Her parents, José Grajales and Teresa Cuello, were mulattos who had free status. Despite the advantages of legal freedom Grajales grew up suffering from the indignities of racism, colonialism, and extreme poverty. Grajales was committed to throwing off the yoke of cultural oppression and racial discrimination that plagued the Spanish colony; she married the like-minded Fructuoso Regueyferos, who helped her from the beginning to raise their four sons with strong revolutionary ideals. Widowed at the age of thirty-two, three years later she married Marcos Maceo, a Venezuelan immigrant of mixed race. At that time, a new representative of the Spanish Empire, Capitán General Leopoldo O'Donnell, arrived on the island and began to employ a new degree of violence and repression. The already tenuous existence of the Grajales-Maceo family was threatened when immigrants of color were ordered to leave Cuba. When groups of rebels began to gather in the jungles and swamps to commence guerrilla warfare in 1868, Mariana Grajales and Marcos Maceo led their entire young family to join the uprising. Grajales lived with the rebels, sharing the horrors and deprivations of war with her husband and children. Throughout she maintained a steadfast and unselfish patriotism, exemplified in her exhortation to her youngest boy at the graveside of his brother: "And you, stand up tall; it is already time that you should fight for your country" (Sierra n.d.). All but one of the Grajales family died during the struggle for independence, including the famed war hero Antonio Maceo. For her heroic words and actions Grajales is revered as the first Cuban woman revolutionary and an icon of the ideal self-sacrificing mother. When the popular uprising against Cuban dictator Fulgencio Batista commenced in the 1950s, fifteen-year-old Teté Puebla gathered with other women to form a fighting unit inspired by the historical icon, and thus, the first all-woman platoon of the Cuban Revolution was born—the Mariana Grajales platoon.

—Sara E. Cooper

See also Cuban Revolution, Women and the

References and Further Reading

Balán, María Elena. "Mariana Grajales, Madre mayor de Cuba," Cuba Web, http://www.nnc.cubaweb.cu/historia/historia27.htm (accessed September 21, 2004).

Puebla, Teté. 2003. *Marianas in Combat: Tete Puebla and the Mariana Grajales Women's Platoon in Cuba's Revolutionary War, 1956–58.* New York: Pathfinder.

Ramos, Raul. "Mariana Grajales," Cuba Web, http://www.ain.cubaweb.cu/mujer/mariana.htm (accessed September 21, 2004).

Sierra, J. A. n.d. "The Antonio Maceo Timeline," History of Cuba.com, http://www.historyofcuba.com/history/mactime1.htm (accessed September 21, 2004).

Granville, Christine, pseud. (Krystyna Skarbek Gizycki) (1915–1952)

British secret agent during World War II. Born in Mlodziesyn, Poland, on May 1, 1915, Krystyna Skarbek was the daughter of a count who was a wealthy banker and his Jewish wife. Skarbek and her husband, Jerzy Gizycki, a Polish diplomat, were in Africa when the Germans invaded Poland in 1939. They went to England where, under the name Christine Granville, she

Christine Granville. (Keystone/Hulton Archive/Getty Images)

joined the British Special Operations Executive (SOE). One of the earliest agents to work for the SOE, Granville brought information to the Polish resistance against the Nazi occupation during World War II, and she helped set up escape routes for British prisoners of war to get from Poland to Athens and then to Britain (Binney 2002, 5). Although her native country did not recognize her contributions, the British government awarded her the George Medal and the Order of the British Empire (OBE). From France, Granville received the Croix de Guerre (Forty and Forty 1997, 156).

Granville was noted for her resourcefulness, resilience, and bravery. To distribute needed information to Polish resisters, she skied from Hungary over the Tatras Mountains into Poland. When she returned from these trips, Granville also brought out intelligence for the British. On one trip back to her homeland, she tried to convince her widowed mother to leave Poland, but her mother refused. Later she found out the Nazis had captured her mother, and she never saw or heard from her again (Forty and Forty 1997, 155).

On her last trip into Poland in 1941, Granville and her colleague and companion Andrew Kowerski were arrested by the Hungarian police and handed over to the Gestapo for interrogation. They were soon released after she feigned tuberculosis, which she achieved by biting her tongue so that she seemed to be coughing blood. Granville and Kowerski were freed in part because of a sympathetic and convinced doctor but also because the authorities hoped they would lead them to their underground network, which did not happen (Binney 2002, 64).

Granville, who made her way back to England after her escape, was parachuted into occupied France on July 6, 1944. She was sent to the Jockey Network, headed by Francis Cammaerts, as a replacement for Cecily Lefort, who had been arrested. Granville was discharged in 1945, and soon afterward she became a British citizen. In 1951, Granville took a job as a stewardess on the *Rauhine,* sailing on its maiden voyage to Australia (Forty and Forty 1997, 156). On this ship, she met Dennis George Muldowney, a man who became obsessed with her and murdered her on June 15, 1952.

—Heather E. Ostman

See also Lefort, Cecily; Poland, Resistance during World War II, Women and

References and Further Reading

Binney, Marcus. 2002. *The Women Who Lived for Danger: The Women Agents of SOE in the Second World War.* London: Hodder and Stoughton.

Forty, George, and Anne Forty. 1997. *Women War Heroines.* London: Arms and Armour Press.

Great Britain, Women, Social Impact of World War I on

World War I as a watershed in the achievement of female equality in England. Women's activities in the war effort, both as civilians and military auxiliaries, brought about a significant improvement in their political status as well as their overall position in British society. Prior to 1914, the women who worked, mostly from the lower classes, were employed in the sweated trades, as shop assistants, or in domestic service. There they faced long hours and low wages. Meanwhile few middle- or upper-class women worked, and those who did found jobs as governesses, nurses, or teachers. Also, a number joined in philanthropic enterprises.

This is not say that important changes were not taking place. Educational opportunities had increased, and universities had become available. Even Oxford and Cambridge had women's colleges, although they refused to grant the students university degrees. In addition, women were voting in local elections, and some were serving in office. By far the most significant development before World War I was the emergence of the movement for women's suffrage. Two important groups had emerged: the Suffragists (National Union of Women's Suffrage Societies—NUWSS), led by Mrs. Henry Fawcett, who followed a gradualist approach, and the Suffragettes (Women's Social and Political Union—WSPU), led primarily by Emmeline Pankhurst and her daughter Christabel, who stood for a much more militant approach that often resulted in violence, injury, and vandalism. Such actions increased dramatically until the beginning of the war, as the government of Herbert Asquith took no action to deal with the suffrage question and reacted with growing severity against those advocating the vote for women.

At the outset of hostilities, the WSPU announced an important shift in its policy, declaring a moratorium on its agitation for the vote and giving complete support to the war effort. This caused a rift among the Pankhurst family as daughter Sylvia embraced pacifism and put her energies into fighting poverty in the east end of London. Moreover the NUWSS, although also committing itself to the military, continued to advocate women's suffrage. While many women were ready to volunteer, the government at first showed little interest. Asquith tried to maintain the status quo. For example, when the Scottish doctor Elsie Inglis suggested initiating an ambulance service, she was told to "go home and be quiet."

Some women, however, did organize nursing or charitable groups. Among the factors that led to women's involvement in the national war effort was the crisis in the munitions industry, which occurred in 1915 with the revelation that the men in the front were facing a shortage of shells. This led to the establishment of the ministry of munitions and the call for women to take up work in the factories. Great numbers of women, called *munitionettes,* were employed in a variety of jobs manufacturing arms. They demonstrated their abilities and capacities for the job and earned better wages than had been available to women before the war. The work was tough and frequently unhealthy, and their male counterparts often responded with anger at the apparent threat to men's jobs. At the beginning of 1916, conscription was introduced, creating many more opportunities for women in the workforce. Consequently, they moved into areas such as transportation, taking up positions as drivers of cars, buses, and trucks. In addition, they were employed as gas fitters, postal workers, and police. Women also entered the world of commerce and became a larger presence in education. Other women joined the so-called Land Army, taking the places of men who had been called up from the agricultural sector. These diverse occupations attracted women from a wide range of social classes, giving many their first work experience.

Women also performed military or paramilitary functions. The Women's Army Auxiliary Corps (WAAC), the Women's Royal Naval

Service (WRNS), and the Women's Auxiliary Air Force (WAAF) were organized to serve in support capacities such as driving, communications, and clerical duties. In addition, there were the women who served as doctors or nurses, both at home and on the continent. The VADs (Voluntary Aid Detachments) also helped out in hospitals, catering and housekeeping. The service of these women and the women war workers as well as the continued support of British women for the war effort convinced many of those who had earlier opposed granting women the franchise to commit themselves to granting it after the war. Indeed, women were allowed to vote in the December 1918 parliamentary election.

In social terms, the war raised significant issues concerning women. In the first place there were the large number of war babies, which were the cause of comment and anxiety. Reflecting the nature of the conflict and the frequent venues where men and women were brought together, this increase of births promoted responses from welfare agencies, but, at the same time, others praised this development as providing replacements for the men dying at the front. The question of war babies is directly related to the changes that had taken place in women's living conditions and sexual attitudes. In the new situation, girls often left their parents' home and lived in close proximity to the factories where they worked. The result was a greater sense of confidence as well as permissiveness, especially because the men they met might be killed shortly afterward. The "new woman" was therefore a blend of independence and sexual freedom. Manifestations of this can be seen in the short skirts worn for factory work or the trousers and boots they wore for agricultural work.

The end of the war meant the end of employment for many women. There was a strong feeling that the returning soldiers should have priority in employment and that women did not need to work and should be mothers, supported by their husbands. Women who were dismissed were provided with a donation to cushion their loss of work, but it was only a temporary relief. It was argued that many women were using these donations to live off the public purse and were not looking for new jobs as was expected. Part of the problem was that these jobs were often in the sweated trades and domestic service, which women had left to enter war employment. Many women refused to go back into service, even though there was an effort to make these jobs more attractive. It is instructive that following the war, there were fewer women in domestic service than before. Women continued their presence in office employment, however.

The sum of women's experience in World War I had many positive aspects. The fact that women obtained the franchise is evidence of a change in their image and status in British society. No longer could it be argued that women were incapable of holding their own and contributing in demonstrable ways to the national effort. At the same time, the mind-set of women underwent a substantial transformation. They became aware of their own skills and potential. Despite the disappointment of the postwar period, they retained confidence, pride, and a sense of accomplishment. The new woman, like the genie, could not be put back in the bottle.

—Marc L. Schwarz

See also Fawcett, Millicent; Great Britain, Women in Service during World War I; Inglis, Elsie, and the Scottish Women's Hospitals; Pankhurst Family: Emmeline, Christabel, E. Sylvia, and Adela Pankhurst

References and Further Reading

Braybon, Gail. 1981. *Women Workers in the First World War.* London: Routledge.

Braybon, Gail, and Penny Summerfield. 1987. *Out of the Cage: Women's Experiences in Two World Wars.* London: Routledge.

Marwick, Arthur. 1965. *The Deluge.* Boston: Little, Brown.

———. 1977. *Women at War 1914–1918.* London. Fontana.

Great Britain, Women in Service during World War I

Pioneering role in military service played by British women in World War I. During World War I, women in Great Britain heeded the same patriotic call to arms as the British men did, assisting the armed forces in many capacities. Although few women officially engaged in combat, thousands of women served on or near the front lines as nurses, ambulance drivers, gas-mask instructors, and mechanics, and thousands more worked behind the front lines as munitions workers, fund-raisers, seamstresses, laundresses, and spies. By 1917, an immense manpower shortage forced Britain to become the first country in the war to bring women into formal military service with the creation of three female auxiliary units, the Women's Auxiliary Army Corps (WAAC), the Women's Royal Air Force (WRAF), and the Women's Royal Naval Service (WRNS, referred to as the Wrens). By 1918, the three voluntary organizations boasted 25,000 recruits, and by the end of the war, more than 100,000 women had joined.

When Great Britain declared war against Germany on August 4, 1914, thousands of women eagerly looked for ways they could help in the war effort. For many, nursing was the obvious choice and, at first, the only legitimate and acceptable occupation for women in the military. Caring for the sick and wounded was a long-honored role for women, and female nurses had served officially in the British army since the Boer War in the early twentieth century. By the end of the war, more than 23,000 nurses had served in the British military, assisted by another 15,000 women who served as nurses' aides. In the hospitals closest to the battle lines, nurses were accorded responsibilities far surpassing their normal duties, anesthetizing patients and conducting minor surgery.

Volunteer organizations such as the Women's Volunteer Force and the Women's Emergency Corps appealed to thousands more women who wished to protect their children and other noncombatants from a potential German invasion. The Women's Legion, a unit established to cook and provide transportation assistance to the armed forces, probably provided the most practical assistance to the armed forces. Many women served as ambulance drivers and maintenance workers, conveying injured soldiers and supplies between the front and the hospitals behind the front lines. A few women who could muster great resources assisted the wounded in other ways; an example is the duchess of Sutherland, who set up a hospital for wounded soldiers at Dunkirk.

On the home front, many women heeded Chancellor of the Exchequer David Lloyd George's War Service for Women campaign, a program initiated by George and suffragist Emmeline Pankhurst in 1915 to persuade women to work in factories, particularly in the munitions industry, by appealing to their sense of patriotism. Government propaganda referred to women war workers as "100,000 Joans of Arc," applauding their patriotic selflessness. Many women wore badges that proclaimed themselves "Mothers who make munitions," suggesting that a sense of patriotic maternalism helped them reconcile doing work traditionally done by men. Female munitions workers generally worked twelve-hour shifts, making less pay than men but more than the amount women received in other industries. Women in war plants had to face many hazards, not the least of which was the possibility of being bombed by German planes. Many women worked with dangerous chemicals such as TNT, which yellowed the skin and caused the workers to be dubbed "Canary Girls." Other women working in airplane factories had to work with dangerous varnish that covered airplanes. Overall, accidental explosions and toxic chemicals in the war plants brought about the deaths of several hundred female workers.

Many women wanted to take up arms and fight for their nation despite the disapproval of the general public. Some women argued as May Bateman did in 1916 that women had the obligation to assume some of the burden and hardship of combat. Generally, however, the public

Press Accounts of British Women in War Service in World War I

"England is very proud of the pluck, endurance, and determination of her munition girls—The twenty-six women who were killed and thirty wounded in that explosion in a North of England factory on Tuesday night had, like thousands of other munition workers, faced the possibility of that fate hourly, and probably faced it with jest. Yet knowing that, and realizing their kinship with the men who keep their souls unshaken in the trenches, we may marvel at the courage, and above all the perfect discipline, which after the disaster kept the other girls in the factory unperturbably at their work.

"It fits in with stories one hears from all the deadliest departments of the factories, where, as is well known, the girls, breathing in danger as they work, are reluctant to abandon the task at the end of the term prescribed. Zeppelin nights in some places have put a very hard strain on the nerves of these girls, who in some factories have spent hours waiting in black darkness, knowing that at any moment a bomb may explode the munitions piled beside them. One hears thrilling stories of what happens during those hours—there was, for instance, the singer working in a canteen who for two hours sang away the horror of the night. . . . The girls have come through the ordeal without panic or collapse. They should all have medals for their war service, with special bars for Zeppelin night service."

—*Manchester Guardian,* December 8, 1916.

"It is quite impossible to keep pace with all the new incarnations of women in war-time—bus-conductress, ticket-collector, lift-girl, club waitress, post-woman, bank clerk, motor-driver, farm-labourer, guide, munition maker. There is nothing new in the function of ministering angel: the myriad nurses in hospital here or abroad are only carrying out, though in greater numbers than ever before, what has always been woman's mission. But whenever he sees one of these new citizens, or hears fresh stories of their address and ability, Mr. Punch is proud and delighted. Perhaps in the past, even in the present, he may have been, or even still is, a little given to chaff Englishwomen for some of their foibles, and even their aspirations. But he never doubted how splendid they were at heart; he never for a moment supposed they would be anything but ready and keen when the hour of need struck."

—*Punch Magazine,* June 1916.

was scandalized by the notion of women in combat. Women serving as nurses, laundresses, and canteen organizers were viewed as a vital, if unfortunate, necessity of war. Women as combatants evoked multiple objections that displayed the inflamed but hardly unified opinions on the subject. Some traditionalists believed that fighting was a man's duty and that women had no place in conflict. Many believed that a woman's place was at home, tending to her hearth and children. Others questioned whether women could deal with the reality of the battleground. Some were concerned with the moral implications of women fighting next to men under such stressful conditions. Some public commentators were concerned that if women served in the military, this might give them grounds for full citizenship—most significantly, the right to vote. Others were simply suspicious of women who tried to act like men, questioning their sexuality and their innate womanhood. The concern of women dressing as soldiers was first seen in the outrage over the military-style khaki uniforms favored by women in the volunteer service organizations. Such garb was seen as posturing and as such was an affront to the male soldiers' valor and the dignity of the nation. The marchioness of Londonderry, the founder of the

Women's Legion and the colonel-in-chief of the Women's Volunteer Reserve, addressed the concern of the moralists by assuring her opponents that the women in her organization would not mimic male soldiers or behave in a masculine fashion but rather would perform their duties solely to help men return to active service in an unselfish act of patriotism.

The only officially recognized female combatant from Britain was Flora Sandes, a middle-class woman seeking the excitement of war. A week after the war began, Sandes joined St. John's Ambulance brigade and went to Serbia as a nurse but later found combat more to her liking, finishing her service as a decorated sergeant in the Serbian army.

The vicious reality of war and the rising death toll gradually softened the harsh public stance against women serving in the military. In 1917, the British government finally accepted the recommendation of the female leader of the Voluntary Aid Detachment (VAD) for women to officially staff administrative jobs held by men wherever possible, enabling more able-bodied men to fight on the front lines. This led to the creation of the three auxiliary women's units designed to support the army, air force, and the navy. Each unit was to be led by a female commander and follow a hierarchical military-style authority, but the ranks were purposefully different from those held by men. Women did not receive their commissions from the king as the men in command did. Female officers held the title of "administrators," noncommissioned officers were "forewomen" or "assistant forewomen," and enlisted women were "workers."

The first of the three auxiliary units, the WAAC, was established in early 1917 with the idea that women would work in the canteens, serve as clerks and telephone operators, and instruct civilians and soldiers in the use of the gas mask. Any British woman who was eighteen was eligible for service and could be sent abroad at age twenty. Typically, applicants had to present personal recommendations and undergo a medical examination by a board of female physicians before being allowed to serve. Recruits had to sign a contract understanding that they had to obey military authority and were subject to fines and imprisonment if they violated the terms of their enlistment. Before being shipped to their units, most received several weeks of intensive military training even though they were not expected to engage in combat or even to bear arms. Although the WAACs wore military-style uniforms and held different ranks, the women were not saluted, they were tried in civil courts rather than military tribunals for infractions, and generally they were not treated as real soldiers in the Royal Army.

The WRNS was established in November 1917. The terms of service and other regulations were drafted by three women, Dame Katharine Furse, Tilla Wallace, and Edith Crowdy, who had been invited by the first lord of the admiralty to develop a "Naval Organization of Women." The Wrens served as paymasters, coders and decoders, telegraphists, signalers, and draughtsmen as well as other positions that released able-bodied seamen to active service. Among their myriad duties, they fitted depth charges, washed life-belts, and manned listening stations.

The WRAF was the third women's auxiliary unit to be created. Since 1917, women had served in all-female companies in the Royal Flying Corps. Women in these units lived at home to diminish the threat of improper behavior between men and women and to keep operational costs down. In 1918, the Royal Flying Corps and the Royal Naval Air Service combined to create the Royal Air Force, from which the Auxiliary Women's Royal Air Force emerged. Most of the recruits were enlisted to occupations such as mechanics, radio operators, parachute packers, armorers, cooks, and nurses, but there were no female pilots.

In one of the more unusual occupations during the war, hundreds of women were employed by the British War Office as intelligence workers, ranging from adolescent Girl Guides to octogenarian grandmothers, often entrusted with secret reports issued by Military Intelligence 5, Counterespionage (MI5) in London.

British Voluntary Aid Detachments (VADs) stand with their ambulances along the British western front. (Underwood and Underwood/Corbis)

Few female spies seem to have been killed during the war, but those who died in the line of duty quickly became martyrs for the cause. One of the most famous spy-martyrs was Edith Cavell, a nurse who secretly helped Allied soldiers escape occupied Belgium until her capture and death by a German firing squad in 1915. Propagandists used the image of an innocent nurse murdered by Germans as a way to illustrate the alleged atrocities by Germans in Belgium. Other women, such as Muriel Doyrell-Browning, were employed as linguists for the War Office and wrote subversive propaganda dropped in Germany and other enemy-occupied territories.

The official involvement of women in the war effort brought about a dramatic shift in public opinion. Following the creation of WAAC, women who wore sharply turned uniforms became more respected, as the uniform came to represent efficiency, service, and patriotic duty. By 1918, women who were not in uniform, whether in the volunteer organizations or in the auxiliary units, began to be criticized and mocked by the popular press as unpatriotic "slackers."

No matter how accepted the sight of women in military uniforms became, the message for women was that this was a temporary arrangement borne out of the extremities of war. When the male soldiers returned home at the end of the war, most women were displaced from their jobs and forced to return to women's work or to no paid work at all. Many disillusioned soldiers resented the women, whom they believed had usurped men's traditional jobs, and many of the women's accomplishments and skills were ignored. Ultimately, the women who served in the war, whether in the auxiliary units, the volunteer units, or the war plants, during World War I all helped pioneer the way for future generations of women who would come to hold vital positions of genuine military authority in all of the royal armed forces.

—*Susanna Calkins*

See also Cavell, Edith Louisa; Furse, Lady Katherine Symonds; Great Britain, Women's Royal Naval Service, Reorganization before World War II; Inglis, Elsie, and the Scottish Women's Hospitals; Sandes, Flora

References and Further Reading

Braybon, Gail. 1998. "Women, War, and Work." In *World War I: A History*, edited by Hew Strachan, 149–162. Oxford and New York: Oxford University Press.

Fletcher, M. H. 1989. *A History of the Women's Royal Naval Service*. Annapolis, MD: Naval Institute Press.

Gould, Jenny. 1987. "Women's Military Services in First World War Britain." In *Behind the Lines: Gender and the Two World Wars,* edited by Margaret Randoph Higonnet, 119. New Haven, CT: Yale University Press.

Grayzel, Susan R. 1999. *Women's Identities at War: Gender, Motherhood, and Politics in Britain and France during the First World War.* Chapel Hill: University of North Carolina Press.

Heyman, Neil M. 2002. *Daily Life during World War I.* Westport, CT: Greenwood Press.

Higonnet, Margaret R., ed. 1999. *Lines of Fire: Women Writers of World War I.* New York: Penguin Putnam.

Proctor, Tammy M. 2003. *Female Intelligence: Women and Espionage in the First World War.* New York and London: New York University Press.

Pyecroft, Susan. 1994. "British Working Women and the First World War." *Historian* 56 (1994): 699–711.

GREAT BRITAIN, WOMEN IN SERVICE DURING WORLD WAR II

The direct mobilization of British women in the war effort during World War II. In addition to work in war-related industry, civil defense, and the Home Guard, women contributed substantially to the British war effort in World War II by enlisting in the auxiliary organizations set up by each branch of the armed services. Hundreds of thousands of British women made crucial contributions to British victory in a surprisingly wide range of capacities. Their wartime experience led many to hope for greater equality in the postwar era, even while encountering problems with contemporary assumptions about gender roles.

In 1939, the Royal Navy revived the Women's Royal Navy Service (WRNS), an auxiliary service that had first been established in late 1917 but disbanded after the end of World War I. Members of the WRNS (known informally as Wrens) occupied a wide variety of shore-based duties to free up their male colleagues for duty at sea. Wrens took on roles such as telegraph, radio, and telephone operators; couriers; meteorologists; supply clerks; cooks; radar operators; censors; signalers; and intelligence officers. The WRNS reached peak strength in 1944 with 73,500 women serving in almost all theaters of the war in which Britain was involved. The total personnel of the Royal Navy in 1944 numbered 863,500 including the WRNS, which means that women accounted for 8.5 percent of the Royal Navy complement in 1944 (Roskill 1966, 22). Although the vast majority served on shore, a small number served on Motor Torpedo Boat patrols. Auxiliary status notwithstanding, service in the WRNS could be hazardous. Twenty-two Wrens lost their lives when the SS *Aguila* was sunk by a German submarine on August 12, 1941, on a voyage from Liverpool to Gibraltar. Nurses serving the Royal Navy were organized into Queen Alexandra's Royal Navy Nursing Service.

In 1939, the Royal Air Force (RAF) established the Women's Auxiliary Air Force (WAAF). The WAAF was the successor to the Women's Royal Air Force, which had been formed in 1918 but disbanded in 1920. The WAAF reached peak strength of 181,835 in July 1943 (Beauman 1971, 284). As with the Wrens, women in the WAAF performed a remarkable range of duties, including work as aircraft mechanics, and served in all theaters of the war. Women working as nurses for the RAF were organized into the Princess Mary's RAF Nursing Service. Women also served as pilots with the Air Transport Auxiliary (ATA), flying aircraft from factories to RAF bases. The ATA remained a civilian organization throughout the war, however.

The WAAF also employed women in tasks specific to the needs of an air force. Photographic interpretation was a particularly valued service. In 1958, one such interpreter, Constance Babington Smith, published a memoir, *Evidence in Camera: The Story of Photographic Intelligence in World War Two,* that dramatically detailed British efforts to locate and identify the launch sites for German V1 and V2 rockets in 1944. In addition, photographic interpreters worked to assess the results of the Allied strategic bombing campaign over Germany during the war. Members of the WAAF performed a variety of other highly secret and demanding technical jobs during the war. For example, women played a key role in the Y-service, the name given to the interception of enemy radio and telephone messages. The Y-service members were grouped into the signal corps of each branch of the armed services. Women worked in RAF headquarters as radar plotters. One of the most distinctive and enduring images of World War II shows WAAF radar plotters with croupier rakes, plotting the location of aircraft on a vast map of the British Isles during the climactic stages of the Battle of Britain in 1940.

In 1938, the British army established the Auxiliary Territorial Service (ATS), the successor to the Women's Army Auxiliary Corps of World War I. Army nurses served with either the Queen Alexandra's Imperial Nursing Service or with the Territorial Army Nursing Service. The ATS reached peak strength of 214,420 in 1943 (Terry 1988, 135). Women in the ATS served as drivers, communications workers, postal workers, military police, and ammunition inspectors. Women served in no fewer than eighty trades and occupations in the ATS alone. Considerable numbers served in direct combat roles as members of antiaircraft gun crews. By 1943, almost one in four members of the ATS worked on antiaircraft gun crews (Saywell 1985, 12). They loaded the guns, fused the shells, and tracked enemy aircraft, but on direct order from Prime Minister Winston Churchill, they were not allowed to fire the guns on the dubious grounds that they might not be able to live with the knowledge that they had caused the death of an enemy. According to thinking about gender roles at the time, women had to be limited to noncombat, supportive roles.

Enlistment in the ATS, WRNS, and WAAF during the first two years of the war was voluntary, but the need for more women recruits in the auxiliary services and war industry led the British government to pass the National Service (No. 2) Act of December 18, 1941. Under this act, unmarried women between the ages of twenty and thirty were conscripted, but they could choose between the auxiliary services and work in war industry or war-related occupations. Those who opted for the auxiliary services (about one-quarter of the total) would not be posted to combat areas unless they requested it. A further shortage of female recruits in 1942 prompted the government to send all eligible women born between 1920 and 1921 to the auxiliary services, unless engaged in crucial war work.

Service in the auxiliary forces, especially the ATS and WAAF, was not always popular with recruits. Poor housing conditions, drab uniforms, and unfounded accusations about the morality and character of women in the auxiliary forces had a negative impact on morale. Some members of the public believed that women were taking jobs that should have gone to men. In 1941, members of the ATS and the WAAF were given full military status. This is sometimes seen as a step toward equality, and there is some validity to that view; but the major reason for this step appears to have been the desire to bring the ATS and the WAAF under codes of military discipline (especially court martial) to discourage desertion. Previously nothing could prevent members of the ATS or WAAF from simply walking away from their jobs. The consequences could be serious, especially if the recruit in question was a highly trained radar plotter. The WRNS stayed exempt from full military status and remained the most popular of the auxiliary forces, possibly because large numbers of WRNS could live at home and commute daily to work.

In 1907, the British army organized the volunteer First Aid Nursing Yeomanry (FANY), a specialized civilian nursing organization designed to provide medical aid to soldiers under fire. FANY was reorganized as the Motor Transport Service in 1938, but it continued to be known as FANY and tended to attract women from aristocratic backgrounds. When the Special Operations Executive (SOE) came looking for female agents to be parachuted into occupied Europe, FANY provided the largest numbers of recruits. At least some SOE agents also had to be trained in the use of explosives. Recruiting from FANY, an ostensibly civilian organization, evaded armed service prohibition on women as combatants. The SOE, along with the technology of the war, placed women in range of enemy bombing, blurring the distinction between combatant and noncombatant roles. The SOE parachuted fifty female agents into occupied Europe, including twenty-four from FANY and fourteen from WAAF. Fifteen of the fifty were captured by the Germans, all but three of whom were tortured and executed or died in concentration camps. Some agents disappeared after their drops and were never heard from again (Beauman 1971, 222).

Women in Britain's three auxiliary services (exclusive of the SOE) suffered 1,486 casualties from enemy action (killed, wounded, missing, and prisoners of war) during the war. The three services reported a total of 624 fatalities, about half of whom were in the ATS and army nursing services (Mellor 1972, 838). By 1944, women comprised slightly more than 10 percent of the personnel of the British armed forces (Goldman and Stites 1982, 36). A total of 640,000 women served in Britain's auxiliary services during the war (Mellor 1972, 830). All three of the auxiliary services continued in the postwar era, a reflection of the value of the work they performed. The total peak strength of the nursing services in 1944 numbered 19,000 (Mellor 1972, 833).

Most of the women who entered the three auxiliary services during World War II came from middle- or upper-class families. Mass Observation, Britain's foremost social research and polling organization of the 1940s, reported that many of the women serving in the WRNS, ATS, and WAAF wanted to travel abroad after the war ended and showed little desire to marry and raise families. Mass Observation also reported that service women expressed the hope that they would be able to compete with men on an equal basis for jobs in the postwar world. The expectations of service women contrasted with those of women working in industry, who anticipated much less in the way of equality for women after the war.

Many of the positions given to women in the auxiliary services—in fact, the very use of the term *auxiliary*—reflected contemporary assumptions about the nurturing, supportive role of women. Strict efforts were made to ensure that women's roles were defined as noncombatant. Accordingly throughout the war women were paid less than their male counterparts on the grounds that they were serving in a noncombat role. Women crewed antiaircraft guns, often came under enemy fire, or fell victim to enemy bombing but still were seen as noncombatants. Assumptions about gender also slotted many women in radar operations on the grounds that their heightened sensitivities made them more suitable for work with delicate electronics.

The widespread presence of women in the services led, perhaps inevitably, to accusations of impropriety from those with more traditional views of gender roles. Women in industry also had to struggle against similar prejudice. Members of the WAAF and the ATS seem to have borne the brunt of the hostility, with members of the ATS, for example, scorned as "officer's groundsheets." The Wrens escaped the worst opprobrium, probably because many lived at home and were assumed to remain under parental discipline. Anger directed at ATS and WAAF members may have partially caused the problems with desertion, which in turn led to the imposition of military discipline on the ATS and WAAF in 1941. Criticism of service women was expressed by both men and women, military and civilian alike. Anxiety was also expressed about stationing women outside the British Isles, where it was alleged that morals were lower than in Britain. The critics had absolutely no solid evidence to support their views;, army statistics showed that rates of sexually transmitted diseases and pregnancies were much lower among service women than among women of the same age groups who were not in the services (Goldman and Stites 1982, 32). Ill-founded criticisms of armed forces women, however, hinted at the long struggle for equality faced by women in the postwar world.

—Paul W. Doerr

See also Atkins, Vera H.; Granville, Christine, pseud.; Great Britain, Women in Service during World War I; Hall, Virginia; Khan, Noor Inayat; Stark, Dame Freya; Szabo, Violette; Wake, Nancy; Witherington, Pearl

References and Further Reading

Beauman, Katharine Bentley. 1971. *Partners in Blue: The Story of the Women's Service with the Royal Air Force.* London: Hutchinson.

Fletcher, M. H. 1989. *The WRNS: A History of the Royal Naval Service.* Annapolis, MD: Naval Institute Press.

Goldman, Nancy Loring, and Richard Stites. 1982. "Great Britain and the World Wars." In *Female Soldiers—Combatants or Noncombatants? Historical and Contemporary Perspectives,* edited by Nancy Loring Goldman, 21–45. Westport, CT: Greenwood.

Goodman, Philomena. 2002. *Women, Sexuality and War.* Basingstoke, England: Palgrave.

Mellor, W. Franklin, ed. 1972. *Casualties and Medical Statistics.* London: Her Majesty's Stationery Office.

Roskill, S. W. 1966. *White Ensign: The British Navy at War, 1939–1945.* Annapolis, MD: United States Naval Institute.

Saywell, Shelley. 1985. *Women in War: From World War Two to El Salvador.* Harmondsworth, England: Penguin.

Smith, Constance Babington. 1958. *Evidence in Camera: The Story of Photographic Intelligence in World War Two.* London: Chatto and Windus.

Terry, Roy. 1988. *Women in Khaki: The Story of the British Woman Soldier.* London: Columbus.

GREAT BRITAIN, WOMEN IN SERVICE IN THE SEVENTEENTH, EIGHTEENTH, AND EARLY NINETEENTH CENTURIES

British female combatants in the early modern period. Women occasionally accompanied their husbands in the British army and served as auxiliaries. This even occurred on ships of the Royal Navy. Wives and mistresses of officers and even prostitutes sailed with the British navy. In both the army and navy, accompanying women were frequently drawn into battle as bearers of ammunition, as providers of drink or medical assistance, or as actual combatants. A number of women also disguised themselves as men and served in the army and navy. Although some of the stories might well have been inventions, many seem to be legitimate.

Christian "Kit" Cavanagh (Davies), often referred to as Mother Ross, fought as a dragoon in the Royal Scots Greys at Ramillies in 1706 during the War of Spanish Succession. Davies, who

Hannah Snell, who disguised herself as a man and served as an English soldier. (MPI/Getty Images)

had served with the regiment for four years disguised as a man, was wounded in the battle. She was released from service. She was awarded a pension, however, and when she died in 1739, she was buried with military honors at Chelsea Hospital.

Phoebe Hessel (1713–1821) was born in Stepney in March 1713. There are two versions of how she entered the British army. According to one account, Phoebe's father, a soldier, disguised his young daughter as a boy after the death of her mother and brought her along with him to the British army, where she became a fife player. The other version has Phoebe disguising herself to join her lover, Samuel Golding, in the military. She served with the 5th regiment of Foot (the Northumberland Fusiliers) in the Caribbean and Europe. She fought at the Battle of Fontenoy in 1745 and was seriously wounded in the arm by a bayonet. After recovering, she left the army and moved to Plymouth where she married Golding and bore nine children. After Golding's death, she moved to Brighton and married Thomas Hessel. Following Hessel's death, she became a street vendor. In 1808, Prince George, the prince regent, awarded her a pension of half a guinea a week. Her military service is recorded on her gravestone in St. Nicholas's Churchyard in Brighton.

Hannah Snell, dressed as a man and calling herself James Grey, joined the marines in 1747. She sailed on the *Swallow* to India and was sent ashore against the French at Ponicherry. She was severely wounded, but after a year of recuperation, she sailed again. In 1750, she revealed her true identity to her fellow marines. She was released with a pension and died in 1791.

The *Navy Chronicle* in 1807 reported that a woman had served as a boatswain's mate on a man-of-war for twenty years under the assumed name of Tom Bowling. In another case, a young black woman, born in Edinburgh, joined the British navy in 1804 under the name William Brown. She became captain of the foretop on the 110-gun *Queen Charlotte* before her sex was discovered in 1815.

—Bernard Cook

See also Snell, Hannah; Talbot, Mary Anne

References and Further Reading

Gribble, Francis. 1917. *Women and War.* New York: E. P. Dutton.

Jones, David E. 1997. *Women Warriors: A History.* Washington, DC: Brassey's.

Lucas, Susan. 2004. "'Jane Tars': The Women of the Royal Navy," Admiral Lord Nelson and His Navy, http://www.aboutnelson.co.uk/30janetars.htm (accessed March 14, 2004).

Stark, Suzanne J. 1996. *Female Tars: Women aboard Ship in the Age of Sail.* Annapolis, MD: Naval Institute.

Great Britain, Women on the Home Front during World War II

Role of women in Great Britain during World War II. When World War II began in 1939, the British government called on the complete mobilization of every citizen and resource. Just as men were called to arms, women were called to support the military, to help defend the nation from invasion, and, most important, to "keep the home fires burning." As the men of Great Britain entered into the armed services in record numbers, the defense and preservation of the home front fell largely to women.

From the outset of the war, women contributed to the war effort in a variety of ways. While some women were on or near the front lines, serving in the Women's Royal Naval Service (WRNS) or in the Women's Auxiliary Air Force (WAAF), the majority of Britain's women were involved in the war on the home front. Some women knitted, sewed, or rolled bandages in the Women's Volunteer Service (WVS). Others volunteered in the Home Guard, an organization originally known as the Local Defense Volunteers that had formed in May 1940 to help civilians prepare for foreign invasion. But women's most visible contribution to the war effort occurred in the plants and factories. Less visible but even more pervasive was women's assumption of the role of heads of their households when their fathers, husbands, and brothers left for war.

Women's involvement in the war effort had profound social, economic, gender-role, and military implications. Many women who had been gainfully employed at the outset of the war suddenly found themselves out of work, as certain consumer industries that produced textiles, clothing, and shoes were deemed nonessential by Prime Minister Winston Churchill's Coalition Government. Others found the factories and plants where they worked suddenly became producers of war goods such as airplanes, tanks, uniforms, and munitions, meaning that women often had to learn new skills quickly or face unemployment. Women in reserved occupations, such as switchboard operation, were not allowed to leave their work even if they wanted to volunteer for a more heroic occupation, such as nursing or engineering.

With so many men at war, injured, or deceased, Great Britain faced a serious labor shortage. To counteract this problem, women were conscripted to duty through a series of legislative acts, including the National Service Act (1941), the Restoration of Employment Order (1941), and the Employment of Women Order (1942). These measures ensured that every British woman between the ages of eighteen and forty could be conscripted by the government into service. Enforcement of these acts caused great social dislocation and the disruption of social networks, especially for young unmarried women who were considered more mobile by the government. Married women, by contrast, were designated nonmobile and were less affected by the enforcement of these acts.

These laws forced women into supportive and supplementary positions, usually filling positions held by men, although with less status and pay. Under these acts, single women often became dilutees in industry, meaning that they would take over a man's work responsibilities to free him for soldiering duty or for more skilled tasks. Other women became Land Girls—young women conscripted to work on farms and in agriculture to augment the labor of experienced farmers and agricultural laborers. Other women assisted firefighters, demolition or rescue workers, or worked switchboards in government offices. For many women, these measures meant a reconstruction of their feminine identity as they reinvented themselves as new, capable workers able to take on tasks they never would have imagined they could do before the war.

The government also authorized the deployment of women in the Auxiliary Territorial Service (ATS) and the Auxiliary Military Service

(AMS). In this capacity, women could participate in the creation and servicing of military weapons but were generally constrained from actually using them. Deferring to the recommendation of Caroline Hasket, a well-known authority on women's labor, General Sir Frederick Pile, the commander of Britain's antiaircraft defenses, convinced the government that women under his command could serve as height finders, radio locators, and radar operators but should not be exposed to open combat. Indeed, women were officially banned from bearing arms and shooting weapons—a prohibition deeply resented by many women impatient with their noncombatant support positions.

Women who worked in the factories often found the work difficult, tiresome, and dirty. Although the pay in factories was often better than what could be made as seamstresses, laundresses, or other menial jobs, many women were hard-pressed to stay motivated when they could perceive little connection between the drudgery of their factory work and the war effort. After the first flush of patriotic enthusiasm had paled, many women began to quit their factory and plant jobs and seek out either less strenuous work near their homes or more glamorous, heroic work that took them closer to the war. Some factory and plant managers sought to motivate and retain their employees by showing patriotic films or bringing in army or navy personnel to praise them for their commitment to the war effort. Other managers encouraged singing, reinforcing the bonds of community and friendship that many female workers shared in the factories. A handful even sponsored competitions in which the winners could see firsthand the ships or planes that they helped produce. Most factories simply played "Music While You Work," a BBC program that provided light background music that helped alleviate the tedium of war work.

To further encourage women to stay involved in the war effort, the government even produced a film that celebrated women's involvement. Endorsed by the Ministry of Information, the film *Millions Like Us,* released in 1943, told the story of a young woman in a factory who was employed to make aircraft components. Through the course of the film, she experienced both the valor of war work and the terrible reality of war. All the while, she was buoyed by the female solidarity that surrounded her and the knowledge that her work was vital to winning the war.

Inspiration for women came in other forms as well. In 1943, the War Artists Advisory Committee commissioned the British artist Dame Laura Knight to create heroic images of the women who worked in factories. She focused on Ruby Loftus, a highly skilled technician charged with screwing the breech ring of the Bofors gun. The images Knight rendered were produced in postcard form and distributed to factories across Britain. Like the legendary Rosie the Riveter, the tireless heroine of U.S. factories, heroic images of staunch, hardworking women were used as propaganda to stimulate patriotic feelings and to encourage women to work valiantly for the soldiers in their own lives and for their country.

The National Togetherness campaign stressed the idea that the daughters of nobles were sweating alongside the daughters of refuse collectors and shopkeepers. In reality, while women often formed tight social networks, a worker's position in the factory, and thus the friendships she formed, often reflected her class and background. Upper-class women with family connections were often able to negotiate jobs with better salaries, titles, and responsibilities than women who lacked such connections. Londoners and other city dwellers often did not get on well with women from the farms and rural communities. In general, the nuances of class and social distinctions were keenly observed in the factories and plants, and the social networks that were forged during work hours often extended into the outside community after the workday was done.

The war also changed leisure and courtship patterns for women. In many ways, finding a husband remained a woman's most important job, a plight made harder by the vicissitudes of war. Dancing, cinema-going, and pub crawls were popular leisure activities for single women in search of a husband because the war had disrupted long-standing courtship venues such as the evening walkabout and social clubs. Younger, unmarried women from all classes and social backgrounds began to frequent pubs—to the chagrin of the general public. These activities offered women a measure of independence that they had not had prior to the war.

After 1945, women virtually vanished from the factories and plants when the men returned home. Women relinquished their positions—some gratefully, others with resentment and anger—as men reclaimed their jobs and reasserted their dominance and authority in the plants, factories, and other civilian occupations.

—*Susanna Calkins*

See also Great Britain, Women in Service during World War II; Great Britain, Women's Royal Naval Service, Reorganization before World War II; Rosie the Riveter

References and Further Reading

Braybon, Gail, and Penny Summerfield. 1987. *Out of the Cage: Women's Experiences in Two World Wars.* London and New York: Pandora.

Connelly, Mark. 2004. *We Can Take It! Britain and the Memory of the Second World War.* London and New York: Pearson.

De Groot, Gerard J. 1997. "'I Love the Scent of Cordite in Your Hair'": Gender Dynamics in Mixed Anti-Aircraft Batteries during the Second World War." *History* 82, no. 165: 73–92.

Langhamer, Claire. 2003. "'A public house is for all classes, men and women alike': Women, Leisure and Drink in Second World War England." *Women's History Review* 12, no. 3: 423–443.

Summerfield, Penny. 1998. *Reconstructing Women's Wartime Lives: Discourse and Subjectivity in Oral Histories of the Second World War.* Manchester and New York: Manchester Press.

Great Britain, Women's Royal Naval Service (WRNS), Reorganization before World War II

Reorganization of the British Women's Royal Naval Service (WRNS) on the eve of World War II. The decision to reorganize the British WRNS, which had been disbanded after World War I, was made on November 22, 1938. Dame Katherine Furse, who had overseen the formation and direction of the WRNS in World War I, declined to accept the directorship. She deferred to youth, and Mrs. Vera Laughton Matthews was offered the post at the end of March 1939. Her deputy was E. M. (Angela) Goodenough, at that time the chief woman official at the admiralty.

Recruits were required to be British citizens with British-born parents. The age limits at first were from eighteen to forty-five but were later expanded to seventeen and a half to fifty. The first tasks allotted to the women were office work, motor transport, cooking, and general duties. Volunteers were accepted, trained, and put in uniform and service with the outbreak of the war.

The director was determined that women, given training, were capable of performing most shore duties. Objections were raised, but eventually the need for women prevailed. Numbers and job categories expanded dramatically with the demands of the war. By the end of 1940, there were 10,000 WRNS officers and ranks. Some of the new categories were radio technicians, aircraft mechanics, torpedo servicers and handlers, and harbor-boat crews. By the end of 1942, there were 1,801 WRNS officers and 36,554 ranks serving on the British islands and 952 officers and ranks serving overseas. By September 1944, there were 74,635 officers and ranks serving in 50 branches of duty with 90 job categories. In January 1941, the first WRNS were dispatched to Singapore. Eventually WRENS were stationed in South and East Africa, the Middle East, Australia, India, Ceylon, and Hong Kong.

The WRNS had suffered their first wartime casualty in World War I when Josephine Carr was lost in the torpedoing of the mail steamer *Leinster* on the Irish Sea in October 1918. The first WRNS casualties of World War II were suffered on September 14, 1940, when 10 WRNS were killed when their boarding house at Lee on Solent in Northern Ireland was hit by a German bomb. The first WRNS contingent sent to Gibraltar was lost en route on August 19, 1941, when the SS *Aguila* was torpedoed. Twelve cipher officers, ten radio operators, and a nurse lost their lives. In December, forty WRNS successfully crossed the Mediterranean in the first convoy to cross the sea from Gibraltar through the Suez. After they transferred to another ship for Colombo, however, it was torpedoed, and thirty-eight WRNS were lost.

After World War II, the WRNS was not disbanded as it had been after World War I. On February 1, 1946, the WRNS became part of the Royal Navy. In November 1946, Dame Vera Laughton Matthews, the director who had overseen the rebirth and the development of the service, was succeeded by Dame Jocelyn Wollcombe. In the 1970s, the WRNS came under the Naval Discipline Act, and the Queen's Commission was given to WRNS officers. Closer integration of the WRNS with the Royal Navy continued in the 1980s. Women received the same training as men for shore support. Female personnel competed with their male counterparts for posts aboard ships in refit and for shore support for seagoing units, and during the Falklands War, WRNSs took over operations cells. Women also served at sea with helicopter units for brief postings and as part of Royal Marine postings to Northern Ireland.

—*Bernard Cook*

See also Furse, Lady Katherine Symonds; Great Britain, Women in Service during World War I

References and Further Reading

Fletcher, Marjorie H. 1989. *The WRNS: A History of the Women's Royal Naval Service.* Annapolis, MD: Naval Institute.

Mason, Ursula Stuart. 1977. *The Wrens 1917–1977: A History of the Women's Royal Naval Service.* Reading, England: Educational Explorers.

Greece, Resistance during World War II, Women and

Role of women during the German, Italian, and Bulgarian occupation of Greece during World War II. During World War II and Nazi occupation (1941–1944), Greek women entered the public sphere en masse for the first time. Most of them joined the resistance through the military and political organizations of the Ethniko Apeleftherotiko Metopo (EAM; National Liberation Front). This was a coalition of many parties, in which the Communist Party of Greece played a dominant role. Women formed the majority of Ethniki Allilegyi (EA; National Solidarity), and young girls formed some 45 percent of Eniaias Panelladikis Organosis Neon (EPON; United Panhellenic Organization of Youth) strength. In EAM's military branch, Ellinikos Laikos Apeleftherotikos Stratos (ELAS; Greek People's Liberation Army), women were crucial in its auxiliary services but not in its fighting units (Vervenioti 1994, 186–192, 226–232, 307–311). The gender division of labor existing in society was clearly reproduced in the resistance movement.

Nevertheless, war and the triple occupation (German, Italian, and Bulgarian) gave women the opportunity to act as historical subjects and gain self-respect and self-confidence through their resistance activities. For teenage girls in particular, who had not yet completely accepted traditional gender roles, the radical spirit of the resistance and the difficulties of the struggle provided opportunities for initiatives and activities that had been unavailable in peacetime.

Before the war, nobody disputed that a woman's place was in the home and that her destiny was to marry and to bring up children.

The prerequisite for a good marriage was a hardworking, healthy, modest, and above all moral and honorable girl. Her morality and honor depended on her virginity and the absence of any kind of relationships with men outside the family. Father, brother, and husband had to protect a woman's honor by controlling where she went and what she did because her purity affected their honor and that of the family.

The economic and social changes that had begun between the wars and accelerated after 1941 breached the ideology of the patriarchal family. During occupation, the loss of property either in the city because of famine and the black market or in the countryside because of antiguerrilla reprisals, together with a general uncertainty about the future, weakened the role of the family. Dowries were lost and with them the prospect of a traditional marriage settlement. The inability of men to protect their womenfolk also weakened their control over them. This was one of the factors that allowed women to organize in the resistance and to enter the public sphere.

Wartime resistance was explicitly linked to demands for social reform and the creation of a new society in which there would be gender equality. Inside EAM's military or political organizations, women were treated not only as women but as human beings as well. Moreover, the resistance itself, for reasons of its own organizational growth and ideology, came to encompass some of the functions formerly attributed to the family. The honor of EAM or the Communist Party depended on the moral behavior of its members. For the partisans of ELAS, who were the basic defenders of the nation's honor, any love affair was forbidden—even glancing at or walking with a woman. Inside the political organizations, relationships were also under the control of the leadership. All these restrictions functioned positively for the massive development of the resistance movement. In the resistance, there was considerably more gender equality than in the traditional family and society. Even today, resistance women believe that in EAM or the Communist Party, there was no discrimination between men and women.

The spring of 1943 was a turning point for the Greek resistance and especially for women's participation in it. Before that, the main social problem was famine; women's action against it was more or less an extension of their gender role—for instance, they ran soup kitchens. In March 1943, ELAS liberated the first city in the countryside, and Free Greece started expanding rapidly, mainly in the mountains. In Athens, the capital, five mass demonstrations took place from March to July 1943 in which women's presence was impressive. In the last one, a tank crushed an eighteen-year-old girl.

After Italy's surrender in September 1943, ELAS was able to arm itself with Italian guns. The German occupation forces reacted with brutal operations against the partisans, however. By the end of occupation, the Germans, as a reprisal for sheltering partisans, had destroyed totally or partially one-third of Greek villages. During this bloody period, women's largest and most dynamic participation in the resistance took place. EAM utilized women's mobilizations and demonstrations. In addition, in ELAS Exemplary Women's Platoons were founded, in which women undertook risky and traditionally male tasks.

The resistance movement proclaimed its support for women's rights. It granted women the right to vote in local elections, which took place in Free Greece, as well as in the general elections for its parliament, the National Council. Five women were elected, but only three attended its sessions, which were held at a mountain village in spring 1944. Despite the massive presence of women in resistance, they made up only 3 percent of the National Council (Vervenioti 2000, 103–118).

Women's massive participation in the resistance did not gain them political rights immediately after the war, as was the case in Italy and France. The new society, People's Democracy, which was expected by EAM members and supporters, did not become a reality. Liberation was followed by a bloody civil war in which the Right was victorious.

—*Anastasia (Tasoula) Vervenioti*

See also Greek Civil War, Women in the

References and Further Reading

Flaiser, Hagen. 1987. *Stemma kai Svastika. I Ellada tis Katohis kai tis Antistasis 1941–1944* [Crown and swastika: Occupation and resistance in Greece], Vol. 2. Athens: Papazisis.

Mazower, Mark. 1993. *Inside Hitler's Greece: The Experience of Occupation, 1941–1944.* New Haven, CT, and England: Yale University Press.

Vervenioti, Tasoula. 1994. *I gynaika tis Antistasis. I eisodos ton gynaikon stin Politiki* [Resistance's woman: Women's entrance into politics]. Athens: Odysseas.

———. 1999. "Les résistantes grecques et le Front National de Libération (EAM). Le militantisme féminin et ses contraintes (1941–1944)" [Greek resistance and the National Liberation Front (EAM): Female militancy and its limits (1941–1944)]. In *La résistance et les Européens du Sud* [The resistance and southern Europeans], edited by Jean-Marie Guillon and Robert Mencherini, 61–72. Paris: L' Harmattan.

———. 2000. "The Adventure of Women's Suffrage in Greece." In *When the War Was Over: Women, War, and Peace in Europe, 1940–1956,* edited by Claire Duchen and Irene Bandhauer-Schoffmann, 103–118. London and New York: Leicester University.

GREECE, WOMEN AND FEMALE IMAGERY IN GREEK WARFARE

Greece itself is female. Female imagery is rooted both in ancient times and in Christianity—from the ancient Greek goddess of wisdom and peace, Minerva, who fought against Neptune and gained Athens (the capital of Greece), to the Virgin Mary. Most of all, Greece's imagery is a female warrior fighting for justice: liberty. The national anthem of Greece, written by the poet Dionysius Solomos (1798–1857), is titled *Anthem for Liberty;* in it, Greece and liberty are almost the same entity—a woman. Greece's feminine character is divided into two: one glorious and heroic, the other suffers. In poetry, songs, and painting, Greece appears either as a pretty young woman dressed in white or as an older woman dressed in black. The images coexist in work representative of war. As for Greek women, they look like Greece: they are glorious fighters or those who support the fighters and mourn their loss.

In the imagery of the Greek Revolution of 1821–1828 that led to the founding of the Greek state, Greece is dressed in white when she is leading the fighters—her sons or her brothers—into glorious battles; when in distress, she is dressed in black and is usually desperately alone. In the *Anthem for Liberty,* Greece went alone to the Great Powers asking for help and came back alone; all doors were closed. In fact, Greece is a little country surrounding by foreign nations, most of whom have at times been hostile. Its origin, alphabet, and language differ from those of its neighbors: to the east the Turks are Muslim, and to the north its neighbors are Christian Slavs and Bulgarians and Muslim Albanians. Thus, all Greeks, men and women, have at times had to fight. Kostis Palamas (1862–1943), one of the best-known and best-loved Greek poets of the twentieth century, wrote in "Daughter of Limnos" that it is not shameful when a woman leads male fighters because in ancient times there were militant goddesses, and Nike, the goddess of victory, was a virgin.

There are many popular songs about the women of Souli, the Souliotisses, who fought for their freedom in the prerevolutionary years. Many of the heroines of the Greek Revolution are depicted in paintings. In their portraits,

Manto Mavrogenous is well dressed and pretty, as is Bouboulina, forty-five years old with six children. Manto Mavrogenous appears with a rose in her hair, and Bouboulina is armed and determined in her ship; her right hand is pointing or indicating an order (*Historia tou Ellinikiou Ethnous,* 282). This glorious and heroic imagery is accompanied—as always—by one who suffers. In Eugene Delacroix's *Massacre of Chios,* there are three women in the foreground: one dead, a young one leaning at the shoulder of a man, and an older woman who looks anxious and terrified (*Historia tou Ellinikou Ethnous,* 245). In other paintings, Turks slaughter women who hold their children in their arms, trying to protect them.

In the 1940s, Greece was afflicted with war and occupation. The participation of women during this crucial period was frequent and of vital importance to mother Greece. During the Albanian war (1940–1941) when the Greeks fought Benito Mussolini's fascist Italy, the women of Mountain Pindos carried ammunitions to the soldiers because there were no roads and no mules or donkeys. They were depicted in the paintings of both well-known and unknown artists (Baharian and Antaios 1986, 29, 41). At the same time, the singer Sofia Vembo—known as the singer of Victory—sang the still-popular song "Go on Children of Greece Who Fight for Us on the Mountains."

During Nazi occupation (1941–1944) in one of the most famous songs of the Greek resistance, a partisan says, "My mother, sweet Greece, the partisans of the National Liberation Front would light for you the candle of honor and freedom" (*To antartiko tragoudi,* 43). The honor of Greece was lost because of occupation. The only way for Greece to regain its dignity and accordingly for the Greek people to be honored was to fight for their country's liberation. At this point, it was socially acceptable for women to join both the civilian and the armed resistance. Although Greek women had no political rights, it was acceptable during the occupation for them to enter the public arena and participate in demonstrations and battles against occupied forces. Greece was in danger, and all Greek people—men and women—had to fight for its and, consequently, their own freedom.

Following World War II, during the Greek Civil War (1946–1949), the children of mother Greece were deeply divided. The right wing accused left-wing women of being dishonorable and prostitutes because their main focus was on political issues rather than solely on their families. When left-wing women stood in front of the firing squad, they sang the same song that Souliotisses had sung a hundred years earlier: "a fish could not live on land nor a flower on sea and Souliotisses could not live without freedom" (Papadouka 1981, 79). These women believed that they were fighting for their country's liberation from English and U.S. occupation, and they were determined as they faced execution to prove that they were real Greek women, real daughters of Greece.

—Anastasia (Tasoula) Vervenioti

See also Greek Civil War, Women in the; Greek Revolution, Women and the

References and Further Reading

Baharian, Asantour, and Petros Antaios. 1986. *Eikastikes Martyries ston polemo, stin Katohi kai stin Antistasi* [Painting in war, occupation and resistance]. Athens: Ministry of Culture.

Historia tou Ellinikou Ethnous. I elliniki epanastasi kai i idrysi tou ellinikou kratous (1821–1832) [History of the Greek nation: The Greek Revolution and the establishment of the Greek state (1821–1832)]. 1975. Vol. IB. Athens: Ekdotiki Athinon.

Papadouka, Olympia. 1981. *Gynaikeis Fylakes Averof* [Women's prisons]. Athens: Autoedition.

Polylas, Iakovos. 1955. *Dionysiou Solomoy Apanta ta evriskomena* [Complete works of Dionisiou Solomou]. Athens: Editions Mari.

To antartiko tragoudi [Partisan's songs]. 1986. 5th ed. Athens: Editions Mnimi.

Greek Civil War, Women in the

The role of women in the Greek Civil War (1946–1949) and its subsequent impact on women. A civil war is fought not only between soldiers on the battlefield but with civilians as both combatants and targets; women are crucial to establishing its specific form and agenda. The Greek Civil War was fought between the left and the right in the aftermath of World War II and in the context of the cold war. The left was supported by the Soviet bloc and the right by the British and, from 1947, the United States. Although Greek women only had the legal status of minors, their presence at military and political levels was crucial for both sides.

As for the left, at the military level, women constituted half of the Democratic Army of Greece (DAG) dominated by the Communist Party; 30 percent of its fighters and 70 percent of its personnel in support services were women (Zahariadi 1949, 258–263). The political involvement of left-wing women is self-evident; for the first time in Greek history, women were executed by fellow Greeks—members of the right-wing government. At the end of the armed conflict, almost 5,000 women, some with their children, were in a camp for exiles, which had been established especially for women on the island of Trikeri (*Syllogos* 1996). In addition, the Central Women's Prison in Athens was overcrowded, and the government established local women's prisons in many other cities.

The leader of the right-wing women was Queen Fredericka. She established a fund and initiated an international campaign to rescue children—and hence the nation—from the Communists, who were transporting children from Greece to Soviet bloc countries. The Commissioned Ladies of the Queen's Fund affected public opinion. Their campaign for children's salvation changed the political climate of the UN meetings and altered public opinion on behalf of the official Greek government, which had been castigated for its policy of executions. Whereas on the left, women were bona-fide fighters, the structure of the government's army as well as the right-wing ideology of national-mindedness relegated women to knitting sweaters for the soldiers.

Just as periods of social upheaval and crisis often act as vehicles for the expansion of women's roles, so does their ending force women back into their traditional roles. This process of forced domestication was especially painful in postwar Greece in view of the role of women in the resistance. During World War II, as a result of the occupation of Greece by Nazi Germany, Italy, and Bulgaria, Greek women entered into the public sphere en masse through the National Liberation Front, which was dominated by the Communist Party. The end of World War II and the defeat of fascism had given rise to hopes for a better world in which women would obtain equality, but Greek women were not granted political rights as they were in Italy and France. In the first year following the end of the war, the resistance vision of a new society was still vivid. Women's unions were mushrooming all over the country. Women Communists and the feminist League for Women's Rights, which had struggled for the vote since the 1920s, founded the largest ever women's federation in Greece. For a short period of time, all women's unions cooperated to demand the right to vote.

In 1946, Greece had signed the UN Charter. Thus, gender equality had theoretically become Greek law. That very year, however, due to the civil war, the League of Greek Women Scientists, as well as other women's unions, adopted the view of right-wing politicians that women should not yet be given suffrage. In a civil war, nobody can remain neutral; the women's unions had to choose sides. In 1947, the right-wing Greek government dissolved the left-wing women's unions because they were sympathetic to the Communist Party, which was outlawed.

In 1948, the country was deeply divided; there were two governments and two armies. In October, women DAG fighters established their own organization, but the next year the left was defeated by the right. Near the end of 1948, the United Nations asked the official Greek government to send a delegate to the Commission on the Status of Women. The women's unions took advantage of this and established a Coordination Committee of Seven Cooperating Unions and started demanding the vote for women. The civil war placed a crucial dilemma before the feminist League for Women's Rights, which had to choose a side; ultimately it joined the right-wing women's coalition. U.S. influence was clearly crucial in making the link between the right wing and the women's movement. The newest of the seven unions, founded in 1948, was the Greek Federation of Women's Unions, the Greek branch of the U.S. General Federation of Women's Clubs. Lina Tsaldari, widow of a former prime minister and a commissioned lady of the Queen's Fund, was its president. She was appointed as the Greek government's delegate to the UN Commission on the Status of Women.

The tactic of right-wing women's unions differed from their opponents. They did not demonstrate, petition, or hold public meetings as the left-wing unions had done to demand suffrage. They exploited the power of the male members of their family, usually ministers or bankers, and visited the ministers or the leaders of the political parties to exert pressure. They also cooperated with the local and state authorities who, because of the civil war, were hostile to the left wing. Right-wing women could register to vote more easily, and thus the leadership of right-wing women provided a new electorate for right-wing politicians.

The paradox is that right-wing women demanded the right to vote and the right to occupy political office, but at the same time they insisted that a woman's place was in the home. Lina Tsaldari stated that the vote was a "national duty" and that "a woman's first duty is to her family." She made it clear that Greek women were not like those women who "rejected everything Greek and everything womanly"—that is, the left-wing women who were exiled or imprisoned (Vervenioti 2002, 115–126). Tsaldari did not argue for equality but for difference. She argued that a woman is first a woman and then a citizen; not only did she invoke nature and the difference between the sexes but, by implication, also right-wing women's difference from the so-called other women—the women of the left wing. This difference-based feminism fit perfectly within a nationalist framework, making it an acceptable part of its ideology.

Finally, in the general election of February 19, 1956, Greek women participated on equal terms with men. Two women were elected: the left-wing Vasso Thanassekou and Lina Tsaldari. Tsaldari became the first woman minister in Greece, serving as minister of social welfare, while left wing women's leaders were imprisoned or exiled. The Greek Civil War overrode common gender identity and even gender interests.

—Anastasia (Tasoula) Vervenioti

See also Greece, Women and Female Imagery in Greek Warfare

References and Further Reading

Duchen, Claire, and Irene Bandhauer-Schoffmann. 2000. *When the War Was Over: Women, War and Peace in Europe, 1940–1956*. London and New York: Leicester University.

Mazower, Mark. 2000. *After the War Was Over. Reconstructing the Family, Nation and State in Greece, 1943–1960*. Princeton, NJ, and Oxford, England: Princeton University.

"Syllogos politikon exoriston gynaikon" [Union of politically exiled women]. 1996. In *Gynaikes exoristes sta stratopeda tou emfyliou* [Women in exile during the Civil War]. Athens: Kastaniotis.

Vervenioti, Tasoula. 2002. "Charity and Nationalism: The Greek Civil War and the Entrance of Right-Wing Women into Politics." In *Right-Wing Women: From Conservatives to Extremists around the World,* edited by Paola Bacchetta and Margaret Power, 115–126. New York and London: Routledge.

Zahariadi, Roula. 1949. "I 1 Panelladiki Syndiaskepi tis P.D.E.G." [The first pan-Hellenic meeting of democratic women]. In *Dimocratikos Stratos* [Democratic army], Vol. 4: 258–263.

Greek Revolution, Women and the

Role of women in the Greek Revolution against the Ottoman Empire (1821–1830). Women participated in the Greek Revolution not only as mothers, wives, or sisters of fighters, but as fighters themselves. There were women members or followers of the *Filiki Etaireia* organization (the Society of Friends) that organized the revolution, women members of solidarity committees, and an unknown number of women who participated in battles, both on land and at sea. Women from other European countries supported the revolution through the Philhellenist movement. Among them were the wife of the poet Percy Bysshe Shelley and the daughter-in-law of Johann Wolfgang von Goethe.

Although many Greek women in mountain villages knew how to use a weapon, there were two areas, Souli and Mani, where women used weapons not only to defend themselves but also to fight against their enemies. In the prerevolution period, Ali Pasha of Joannina in northwest Greece attacked the villages of Souli (1792–1804). Its inhabitants, orthodox Albanians, strongly resisted, and women played an important role. Their example was a vital inspiration for women's participation in the Greek Revolution because their heroism was widely known through popular songs. According to one song, Moscho led 300 armed women to win the battle of Kiafa in 1792, and Despo, her daughters, daughters-in-laws, and grandchildren, fortified in a castle, fought against Muslim Albanians. In December 1803, when Despo realized that they would be captured, she blew up the castle. Moreover, after Souli's defeat, 22 women and their children singing and dancing a song of liberty threw themselves in a gorge; they preferred to die rather than be arrested and raped by their enemies.

Mani is located in southern Greece, near ancient Sparta. Mani's women participated in battles in separate units. In 1826, Turk and Egyptian forces blocked and attacked the villages of Mani, where many had sought refuge. The whole population strongly resisted, but of the 1,500 Greek combatants in the crucial battle, 1,000 were women.

Nevertheless, Laskarina Bouboulina and Manto Maurogenous, the most famous women fighters of the Greek Revolution, were not from mountain villages but islands. Bouboulina was from Spetses. She was a forty-five-year-old widow and had six children, three from her first marriage and three from her second. Both of her husbands were ship owners, and both had died during sea battles against Algerian corsairs. Bouboulina, from the beginning of the revolution, armed ships and participated in naval sieges as well as on horseback in battles on land. Three of her sons, the youngest only twelve years old, followed her. The eldest was killed during battle. Bouboulina, in addition to fighting and serving as a leader of the revolution, supported it financially. She was killed in 1825 not by Turks but by members of another Greek family. One of her sons had kidnapped the girl he loved, and the girl's family shot Bouboulina, thinking that she was responsible for the abduction.

Manto Mayrogenous was born in Trieste, but during the revolution, she lived on her home island of Myconos. She sold all her property, even her jewelry, and contributed the money to the needs of the revolutionary struggle. She wrote letters addressed to the women of Paris and Great Britain seeking their support for the Greek Revolution. She also fought on land and sea and was known by the honorary title of lieutenant general. She twice defended Myconos successfully: in 1822, when 200 Algerian corsairs attacked it and in 1824 when the Egyptian navy assaulted the island. Her personal life was not as successful. She was in love with Prince Dimitrios Ipsilandis, a leader of the revolution, but while he was absent, some masked men kidnapped her and took her to Myconos. The prince never sought her return, and Manto denounced him to the National Assembly. She insisted that because he had taken her virginity, he should marry her. He did not respond. She was disowned by her mother and sister and died in poverty during an epidemic in 1840.

The Massacre at Chios, *by Eugene Delacroix (1798–1863). (Scala/Art Resource)*

Apart from Bouboulina and Manto, thousands of Greek women were involved in the revolution. As part of the unarmed civilian population, they faced starvation, capture, enslavement, rape, and death. During battles or sieges, many women supported the fighters by building fortifications; transporting guns, ammunition, food, and water; looking after the wounded; and even using the guns of their dead husbands or sons and fighting the enemy to avenge their death. There are many reported cases of young girls who participated in battles dressed as men or who followed their lovers in battles. Because of her beauty, loyalty, and courage, the lover of Captain Georgios Karaiskaki obtained the privilege of participating in military counsels. Women also played leading roles in committees that sheltered refugees and orphans and collected material support for the revolution. A famous case is that of Psorokostaina, a woman beggar who donated the only penny she had to the revolution. Psorokostaina has become a byword in Greece, symbolic of the fact that even poor Greeks support those in need.

—*Anastasia (Tasoula) Vervenioti*

See also Greece, Women and Female Imagery in Greek Warfare

References and Further Reading

Historia tou Ellinikou Ethnous. I elliniki epanastasi kai i idrysi tou ellinikou kratous (1821–1832) [History of the Greek nation: The Greek Revolution and the establishment of the Greek state (1821–1832)]. 1975. Vol. IB. Athens: Ekdotiki Athinon.

Xiradaki, Koula. 1995. *Gynaikes tou '21. Prosfores, iroismoi kai thysies* [Women of 1821: Offerings, heroism and sacrifices]. Athens and Joannina: Dodoni.

Greek Women and War in Antiquity

A few notable exceptions to the largely passive role of Greek women. Despite their own legends of ferocious women warriors, ancient Greek military practice did not lend itself to the direct involvement of women. By the seventh century B.C., a fighting system had evolved that depended almost exclusively on a citizen militia whose fighters, the hoplites, wore heavy armor and marched in tight ranks. This fighting method depended on bodily strength to wield shield and spear and left almost no scope for personal fighting skill in which a woman's quickness could compensate for her lack of muscle. The hoplite ranks were also a club exclusive to citizens—that is, men with voting rights with sufficient means to arm themselves. Greek women did not have political rights and thus would automatically have been rejected from their city's armies, along with foreigners and the poor. Legends of Amazons, hordes of wild females who fought Greece's primal heroes, should be taken as tales of dangerous cultural inversion rather than as historical fact. The main deity of war, Athena, was female, and she played a uniquely powerful role thanks in large part to her position as both the emanation of Zeus's will and as a virgin. We can presume that at least some Greek women bore arms in a last desperate defense of their homes when their male defenders lay dead, but in general, the work of Greek women was to support male military endeavor rather than to fight.

Nowhere was this supporting role clearer than in Sparta. The Spartan upper class was militarized to an astonishing degree; the men had no occupation but war, and their training was conducted with iron rigor from age seven. Spartan women were recognized as playing a vital role in this military machine. They were trained to a high standard of physical fitness so that they could bear healthy soldiers for Sparta. Spartan women were the only females of ancient Greece to receive an education as a matter of course. This was done so the women could conduct the vital early training of Spartan warriors. Men lived in barracks until age thirty and after that still spent most of their time with their units, so Spartan women also played an extraordinary economic role, running their households and family estates so that the men could devote themselves to war. These upper-class Spartan women also embodied the patriotism of the state. Collections of Spartan women's sayings (almost the only female voices we have from ancient Greece) include praise of sons who died bravely, bitter rebukes of cowards, and even murder of sons who failed in courage.

In the rest of archaic and classical Greece, women were unlikely to assume an important economic position during wars because their men were rarely off fighting for more than a few days at a time, battling near neighbors in a single afternoon battle. Women were expected to be patriotic but passive.

Most women who appear in a Greek military context were first and foremost victims. An important reason for Greek men to fight was to protect their women, an important form of wealth much coveted by invaders. The *Iliad* includes Andromache's moving plaint at the harsh fate of a woman whose man has been killed and her city taken. She was taken captive and forced to labor for and give pleasure to her city's enemies. Accounts recovered from thirteenth-century B.C. Pylos show that this was not simply literary hyperbole; ration lists included, among palace servants, groups of women from a series of towns and villages along the Asia Minor coast, clearly captured in raids. Enslavement of the losers in war continued throughout the ancient world, mostly women and children because they were easier to handle than men and because their skills, especially as weavers, were valuable.

A number of Greek cities had heroine cults of sacrificial virgins who died for the good of their city. For example, there is a legend of a prophecy that Athens would win a war if somebody would commit suicide for the sake of the city. The virgin Aglauros did so by jumping off a cliff, and Athens honored her with a shrine. Rarely did these victims have actual dealings with the enemy, but the city of Naxos honored a woman named Polykrite who was captured in war and forced to become the enemy commander's concubine. She passed secret information on to her family, and the city was able to win its freedom, although Polykrite was killed in the process.

It is only when the democracies of the classical period gave way to Hellenistic monarchies that a few women came to play a more active role in war. In a hereditary system, soldiers, loyal to a royal leader, would also extend their devotion to the king's female kin. This principle was already clear in the wars of succession that followed the death of Alexander the Great in 323 B.C. At one stage, to the astonishment of most Greeks, two royal women tried to rally troops to support the claims of their male puppets. Olympias, Alexander's mother, sought to protect the rights of his minor son, while Eurydice, granddaughter of Philip II of Macedon, fought to support the claim of Alexander's mentally retarded half-brother Arridaios, to whom she was married. Both Olympias and Eurydice appeared on the battlefield to inspire their troops.

Olympias was robed as a priestess, while Eurydice, who very unusually had been trained in arms, wore Macedonian armor and seems to have intended to fight. The Macedonian soldiers rallied to Olympias, however, and both Eurydice and her husband were captured and soon killed.

The Greek historian Polybius and the apocryphal 3 Maccabees in the Old Testament both tell that Queen Arsinoë of Egypt (c. 224–c. 203 B.C.) played a decisive role in the Fourth Syrian War between Egypt and Syria. Still a young girl, Arsinoë was brought to the front before the Battle of Raphia (217) where she rallied the demoralized Egyptian troops, weeping and urging them to fight for their wives and children. Doubtless charmed by such a royal appeal, the Egyptians then won the day.

The only Hellenistic woman known to have taken command in the field was Cleopatra VII (69–30 B.C.), the last Ptolemaic queen of Egypt. Cleopatra assumed this military role because she was a ruling queen instead of sharing her power with a male. Early in her career, Cleopatra's brother/husband Ptolemy XIII drove her from Alexandria. She raised troops and won Julius Caesar's assistance to gain control. On a larger scale, Cleopatra joined up with the Roman triumvir Mark Antony a decade later, first as his mistress and then as his wife. Full-scale civil war broke out between Antony and his rival Octavian in 32 B.C., and Cleopatra provided a fleet to support Antony, which she commanded herself. She was present at the Battle of Actium in September of 31. Most accounts simply report that the queen fled with her contingent, but because her ships had masts and sails on board (which they would not have had for a fight), it seems much more likely that she was making a planned effort to break out with Antony's war chest to continue the war in Egypt. In Egypt Cleopatra was unable to rally an army against Octavian and soon committed suicide.

—*Phyllis G. Jestice*

See also Amazons; Cleopatra VII, Queen of Egypt

References and Further Reading

Brule, Pierre. 2003. *Women of Ancient Greece.* Edinburgh: Edinburgh University.

Larson, Jennifer. 1995. *Greek Heroine Cults.* Madison: University of Wisconsin.

Pomeroy, Sarah B. 1984. *Women in Hellenistic Egypt.* New York: Schocken.

———. 2002. *Spartan Women.* Oxford, England: Oxford University Press.

Greene, Catharine Littlefield (Caty) (1755–1814)

The wife of the American Revolutionary War general Nathanael Greene, who accompanied her husband during numerous wartime campaigns and after his death successfully petitioned the U.S. government for reimbursement of the personal debts he incurred to supply his troops.

Catharine "Caty" or "Kitty" Littlefield married Nathanael Greene in 1774, one year before General George Washington appointed him brigadier general in the Continental Army. Catharine initially remained in her home state of Rhode Island at the start of the war but soon joined her husband at camp. Confident, pretty, and witty, she became renowned for her social graces and enjoyed the acquaintance of such preeminent Revolutionary figures as Henry Knox, Alexander Hamilton, and the Marquis de Lafayette, as well as the close friendship of Martha Washington and Lucy Knox.

Catharine gave birth to four children during the war years, yet spending much of the year at camp, she chose camp life and the company of her husband over a more isolated domestic life. Her children on occasion would accompany her, but they were more often left in the care of family in Rhode Island. Catharine cheered spirits during the bleak winters at Valley Forge and Middlebrook, nursed the sick and wounded in South Carolina, and took part in dances, balls, and quilting circles that maintained gentility amid hardship.

In 1780, Nathanael took command of the southern troops, and he supplied them by any means available, even using his personal credit. He incurred debt that weighed heavily on the Greene family in the years following the war. In 1785, two years after the war's end, Nathanael was unable to support the family in New England, and they moved south to a plantation land near Savannah that had been granted to Greene by South Carolina and Georgia in thanks for his service. He died of a stroke less than a year later.

After Nathanael's death, Catharine submitted an indemnity petition to the government for reimbursement of his wartime debts. She received private encouragement from President Washington and personally presented her case to the U.S. Treasury Department in 1791. The next year, Congress approved an award of $47,000 to be paid to her in installments. Later in life, she married Phineas Miller and was instrumental in supporting Eli Whitney's invention of the cotton gin.

—*Kristen L. Rouse*

See also American Revolution, Role of Women in the

References and Further Reading

Stegeman, John F., and Janet A. Stegeman. 1985. *Caty: A Biography of Catharine Littlefield Greene.* Athens: University of Georgia Press.

Greenhow, Rose O'Neale (1814–1864)

Confederate socialite and spy ringleader during the American Civil War. Rose O'Neale was born in 1814 at Tobacco Landing, Maryland. She was orphaned in 1817 when her father, a planter, was murdered by one of his slaves. Generously

Confederate spy Rose O'Neal Greenhow with her daughter in the courtyard of the Old Capitol Prison in Washington, D.C., ca. 1862. (Library of Congress)

dowered, she moved in the social circle of her sister-in-law Dolley Madison and married Dr. Robert Greenhow, a medical doctor, lawyer, and linguist in 1835. Between 1848 and 1852, the pair and their children traveled to Mexico City and San Francisco on assignment for the State Department. Greenhow died in 1854 after a fall in San Francisco, and the widowed Rose returned to Washington, D.C., with her children. There she wielded significant influence as a society hostess and maintained contact with powerful politicians including James Buchanan and Henry Clay.

Rose Greenhow continued to hold dinner parties as the political atmosphere grew more charged in the late 1850s, ending with the election of Abraham Lincoln with whom she had no influence. Greenhow was an outspoken secessionist and clashed with her niece, Stephen Douglas's wife Adele, and her son-in-law, Treadwell Moore, a Union army officer. When war was declared, Rose was the paid agent of

Confederate Woman Spy

Charleston, Virginia, November 14, 1862

"These females have generally descended from the high and dignified spheres of the social circle and domestic fireside, and metamorphosed themselves into the shape and status of politicians, columniators [*sic*] and traducers of their country and its flag. Nor does the picture end here. It is from these females, who have played the successful scouts and spies, that the rebel leaders have gathered their best information. These women, practicing a deception on our own generals, sometimes in the guise of ladies and again in the disguise of the rustic, have been permitted to pass our lines, visit our camps, and those of the first named have been feted by our officers. It is unnecessary to individualise instances of this kind in passing the subject. I will only mention the names of Belle Boyd and Mrs. Greenhow as heading the list of one hundred female rebels who have made for themselves infamous reputations. I have an instance fresh to my mind which was related to me recently by an officer of worth, who told me of a case in which one of our two star generals was deceived most egregiously by one of these female rebel adepts. He was enchanted, as it were, by her personal beauty, her volubility of language and innocent manner. She was allowed the liberty of the camp for several days; but suddenly she was non est inventus [not to be found]. She gained the information she came for, and her departure was as mysterious as her advent."

—*Peoria Morning Mail,* November 21, 1862, p. 2, c. 2, http://www.uttyler.edu/vbetts/Peoria_mail.htm (accessed January 23, 2006).

Colonel Thomas Jordan, adjutant-general to General P. T. Beauregard, and acted as his source of information in Washington. Through her social contacts, she reported dissension in Lincoln's cabinet, organization plans for the army, and provided copies of military maps of railroads and the defenses of Washington. Her most valuable coup, however, was providing advance warning that the federal army planned to cut the rail lines at Manassas Gap, giving enough warning for reinforcements to aid the Confederates at the First Battle of Bull Run.

Greenhow visited Confederate prisoners in Washington, providing clothing, food, and money, and she gathered information on federal troop positions and their conditions in the field. She also charmed the blueprints for a new line of naval gunboats from naval officers who had been guests at her social events. She never modulated her vociferous hostility toward Lincoln or the North, despite running an extensive, if haphazard, network of informants and messengers. Because of her indiscretions, Detective Allan Pinkerton arrested her on August 23, 1861, and placed her under house arrest. She thwarted her captors by burning the most incriminating of the materials in her possession, but without her, the spy ring unraveled, and the Pinkertons caught many Confederate spies.

Greenhow behaved so belligerently that she was moved to the Old Capitol Prison in January 1862 and was kept there until she was tried by the U.S. Commission for the Trial of State Prisoners. The Commission found little for which she could be legitimately charged with treason. Instead, she was sent south to Richmond, where Jefferson Davis greeted her as a heroine. Her exploits convinced the federal government that southern women were not misguided patriots but potentially devastating enemy agents, and the increased vigilance of Union agents led to the subsequent capture of spies such as Belle Boyd. Davis sent Greenhow to England in 1863 to publish her memoirs of imprisonment and raise support for the Confederacy. While there she met Queen Victoria and Napoleon III and Empress Eugenie of France, but she could gain little real support from them or their nations.

With profits in gold from the sales of her book, Rose returned to the Confederacy onboard the *Condor,* which ran aground off of Wilmington, North Carolina. She insisted on being rowed to a nearby fort rather than waiting onboard for rescue. She drowned on October 1, 1864, due to the weight of the gold sewn into her clothes. She was buried with full honors of the Confederacy, and her grave is still maintained by the Daughters of the Confederacy.

Margaret Sankey

See also Baker, E. H.; Boyd, Isabelle; Civil War, American, and Women; Moon, Lottie, and Moon, Ginnie; Tubman, Harriet

References and Further Reading

Burger, Nash K. 1967. *Confederate Spy: Rose O'Neale Greenhow.* New York: Franklin Watts.

Greenhow, Rose O'Neale. 1863. *My Imprisonment and the First Year of Abolition Rule in Washington.* London: R. Bentley.

Ross, Ishbel. 1954. *Rebel Rose.* New York: Harper.

Grenadier Squaw

See Nonhelema

Grese, Irma (1923–1945)

Youngest Nazi concentration camp guard executed for war crimes. Irma Grese was the most notorious of the 3,500 female concentration and death camp guards (Brown 1996, 6–7). Grese was born on October 7, 1923, into a farming family in Wrechem in Mecklenburg. Her father was either an agricultural worker or a small farmer. Grese left school at fifteen. After working as a farm laborer, as a clerk, and at a hospital, Grese, who had joined a Nazi youth organization, the League of German Girls (*Bund deutscher Mäde*), was assigned by the Labor Exchange to train as a female guard at Ravensbrück, the concentration camp for women. She was transferred to the Auschwitz-Birkenau death camp in March 1943. Grese went home to visit her father before heading east. Her arrival in an SS uniform provoked a violent reaction from her father, and she never visited her family again. In the fall of 1943, she was promoted to the SS rank of Oberaufseherin, or senior supervisor, the second-highest female SS rank, and became an overseer of the female prisoners in the camp's Lager C. At Auschwitz, Grese reputedly became the mistress of Dr. Josef Mangele (Hart 1982, 93). In January 1945, when Auschwitz was evacuated as the Russians approached, Grese was reassigned to Ravensbrück, and she was transferred to the Bergen-Belsen concentration camp in March 1945. After the British liberated Bergen-Belsen on April 15, Grese was arrested and subsequently condemned to death with two other women and eight men at the Belsen Trial conducted at Lüneberg. At the trial, she was accused of torturing prisoners by former inmates of the camps where she had served, arbitrarily shooting or setting her vicious dogs on prisoners and selecting prisoners for the gas chamber. Grese, Elisabeth Volkenrath, Juana Bormann, and the eight men condemned at Lüneberg were hung at the Hamelin jail in Westphalia on December 13, 1945.

—Bernard Cook

See also Braunsteiner, Hermine; Holocaust and Jewish Women; Koch, Ilse

References and Further Reading

Brown, D. P. 1996. *The Beautiful Beast: The Life and Crimes of SS-Aufseherin Irma Grese.* Ventura, CA: Golden West.

Hart, Kitty. 1982. *Return to Auschwitz.* New York: Atheneum.

Manvell, Roger, and Heinrich Fraenkel. 1967. *The Incomparable Crime: Mass Extermination in the Twentieth Century: The Legacy of Guilt.* New York: G. P. Putnam.

Phillips, Raymond. 1949. *The Trial of Josef Kramer and Forty-four Others.* London: William Hodge.

Grizodubova, Valentina Stepanovna (1910–1993)

The sole woman commanding officer of a men's wing during World War II and one of the few Soviet women to attain the rank of full colonel. Born in Khar'kov (currently Kharkiv) on January 31, 1910, the daughter of an aircraft designer, Valentina Grizodubova graduated from Penza Flying Club (1929), Kharkiv Flying School, and Advanced Flying School in Tula (1933). She mastered many types of aircraft, setting seven world records. On September 24–25, 1938, Grizodubova flew nonstop from Moscow to the Pacific (6,450 km) aboard an ANT-37 named Rodina (Homeland). Grizodubova failed to reach the final destination, the airfield in Komsomol'sk on the Amur River. Running out of fuel, she was forced to belly land. (The crew suspected that their mechanics failed to refill the tanks after testing Rodina on the ground.) For this pioneer flight, she, her copilot Polina Osipenko (1907–1939), and navigator Marina Raskova (1912–1943) were awarded Hero of the Soviet Union, the highest Soviet military decoration. They were the first Soviet women to be thus honored.

In May 1942, Grizodubova was appointed commanding officer of the 101st Long-Range Air Regiment (renamed the 31st Krasnosel'sky Guards Bomber Regiment in 1944) and successfully demonstrated the suitability of the Li-2 (modified DC-3) for use as a night bomber. In June 1942, she led her unit in delivering supplies to the blockaded Leningrad. She was noted for flying more than her male colleagues and sometimes monitored her pilots' performance as copilot. Because of her intervention, her superior, a troublesome general, was demoted.

In September 1942, her unit was placed at the disposal of Central Partisan Headquarters. Overcoming dense enemy flak and engaging enemy fighters, her aircrews flew more than 1,850 supply missions (Cottam 1998, 7) and on their way back evacuated wounded partisans and children. In 1943, Grizodubova prevailed on her superiors not to decrease the frequency of these flights.

She flew about 200 wartime missions, spent 18,000 hours in the air (Cottam 1998, 8–9), and was awarded many prestigious military decorations. A senior official of civil aviation after the war, Grizodubova also served on the executive of several veterans' organizations, assisting numerous former prisoner-of-war camp inmates who were persecuted by Soviet authorities. As a member of the Soviet parliament, she courageously criticized Stalin's reign of terror.

—*Kazimiera J. Cottam*

See also Soviet Union, Women in the Armed Forces

References and Further Reading

Cottam, Kazimiera J. 1998. *Women in War and Resistance.* Nepean, Canada: New Military Publishing.

———. 2003. "Grizodubova, Valentina Stepanovna." In *Amazons to Fighter Pilots,* edited by Reina Pennington, Vol. 1, 186–188. Westport, CT: Greenwood.

Grossman, Chaika (1919–1996)

Organizer of the Bialystok Ghetto revolt during World War II and active Jewish resistance delegate and courier for various Eastern European ghettos under Nazi control.

At the outbreak of World War II, Chaika Grossman left her native Bialystok, Poland, for Vilna, Lithuania, to help organize Zionist youth group (*Hashomer Hatzair*) refugees who were fleeing the advancing Germans. When Vilna also fell to the Nazis, Grossman hid her Jewish identity and used falsified papers to move back and forth between the city and the Vilna ghetto where she consulted with other underground leaders and was named leader of the effort to organize the Bialystok ghetto. She was also responsible for the establishment of communications with the Warsaw ghetto. In Bialystok, she persuaded a number of the ideologically based underground groups to give up their differences and to work together to resist the Nazis. She argued for and received the same cohesion from Warsaw ghetto leaders. While in Warsaw, Grossman also took part in the decision to "carry out one concentrated action at the decisive hour and not to waste our forces in frequent skirmishes" (Grossman 1987, 81). This decision helped to determine the strategy taken by the fighters of the Bialystok underground. Back in Vilna, she was given the order to centralize the political work of the underground and to keep the lines of communication open between Vilna, Bialystok, and Warsaw. In this capacity she made numerous trips across dangerous borders and showed her intelligence, courage, and wit when confronted with the searches and interrogations of the border guards.

Eventually travel became more restricted and liaison activities between the three ghettos more difficult. Grossman then increased her involvement in the local Bialystok underground movement where she was vital to that ghetto's overall defense strategy. One of Grossman's major contributions was her daring rescue of an explosives expert from the Volkovisk concentration camp (Grossman 1987, 156). Explosives, as well as the guns Grossman and her colleagues smuggled into the ghetto, were vital for the coming revolt.

The revolt began on August 16, 1942, when the Nazis began a liquidation operation inside the ghetto. During the revolt, Grossman fought alongside her comrades, attempting to create an opening for the ghetto inhabitants to escape. They failed in their attempt, and she was among the few survivors who escaped the ghetto. She continued her underground activities as the leader of a group of couriers and was instrumental in coordinating resistance activities with the forest partisans. Grossman continued her underground activities until the Soviets liberated Bialystok in August 1944.

Grossman was awarded the Polish Government's Grunwald Cross for valor in 1948. That same year, she immigrated to Israel where she eventually became a member of the Israeli parliament and also wrote a book about her involvement in the Bialystok underground.

—*Tracey J. Axelrod*

See also Bruskina, Masha; Fittko, Lisa; Fuld, Bracha; Kempner, Vitka; Korczak, Rozka; Landau, Emilia; Reik, Haviva; Senesh, Hannah

References and Further Reading

Grossman, Chaika. 1987. *The Underground Army: Fighters of the Bialystok Ghetto.* Translated from the Hebrew by Shmuel Beeri. New York: Holocaust Library.

Guatemala, Civil Conflict and Women

The impact of Guatemala's prolonged internal social conflict on women. In 1954, Guatemala entered a bloody era that lasted until the 1990s. Guatemala became a pawn in the cold war but was also immersed in its own extended battles

Activist author Rigoberta Menchú, winner of the 1992 Nobel Peace Prize. (Dorante/Corbis Sygma)

over culture, society, politics, and economics. From 1944 to 1954, Guatemalans enjoyed what is commonly referred to as Ten Years of Spring under Presidents Juan José Arévalo (1944–1950) and Jacobo Arbenz (1950–1954). During that period, the two reformists permitted greater civil liberties including freedom of expression, whether through the press or through political and union organization. Arévalo embarked on an agrarian reform policy, which was continued by Arbenz but was ultimately ended with U.S. intervention. Their plan redistributed fallow lands of large plantations to the poor. This policy infringed on the holdings of the United Fruit Company that had ties to powerful politicians in the Eisenhower administration. Moreover, Arbenz recognized the communist Guatemalan Labor Party (PGT) as a legitimate political entity. With the land reform and communists gaining more governmental positions in Guatemala, the U.S. Central Intelligence Agency organized a group of disillusioned military men to move against Arbenz, who had also been an officer. In June 1954, the United States–backed General Carlos Castillo crossed into Guatemala from Nicaragua and overthrew Arbenz, the democratically elected president.

After the overthrow of Arbenz, Guatemala entered an era of violent repression that continued into the mid-1990s. The military and the landed elite united to roll back many reforms that Arbenz and Arévalo had initiated, particularly in the area of land reform. The Guatemalan army and government resorted to violence to protect business and landholding interests and repress civil society. Increased militarization, fraudulent elections, and the destruction of broad-based activism took a toll, leading to the outbreak of civil war led by left-of-center guerrillas.

In 1962, two ex-military officers influenced by Arbenz formed the Revolutionary Armed Forces (FAR). FAR predominantly comprised middle-class men and women who looked to Cuba as an example. Women mobilized, joining the guerrillas, student groups, unions, peasant collectives, and Catholic organizations. Women protested government-sponsored state violence as well as harsh working conditions, and many women suffered violence. In 1963, young and mature women participated in a teacher's strike that inevitably led to a confrontation with police forces. In 1968, Rogélia Cruz Martínez, a 1950 Miss Guatemala and an activist in the armed opposition, was found dead after being raped, beaten, and mutilated by a right-wing paramilitary group, La Mano Blanco (the White Hand). Other women active in the guerrilla movement were raped and tortured, and some were burned alive.

To combat FAR, the Guatemalan government developed an effective counterinsurgency tactic that ultimately destroyed FAR. In the 1970s, the revolution shifted away from the middle classes to Mayan peasants. The Guerrilla Army of the Poor (EGP), founded by some ex-FAR combatants, and the Organization of People in Arms (ORPA) emerged. Again, women played significant roles in the struggle for indigenous rights and as combatants. In 1978, Mama Maquín led hundreds of peasants in an attempt to regain their lands in Panzos. The army massacred Maquín and more than 100 men, women, and children. One of the most famous Mayan women, who publicly exposed the atrocities taking place in Guatemala, was 1992 Nobel Peace Prize winner Rigoberta Menchú. She documented the systematic genocide of the Guatemalan people by the government and right-wing death squads in her book, *I Rigoberta Menchú*. Like her father, Menchú was a member of the Peasant Unity Committee (CUC). She became an activist due to the general repression within Guatemalan society and the violent repression of opposition by the military.

The violence waged against unionists, students, Mayans, and poor peasants led many, like Menchú, to join the guerrillas. In 1981, with escalating violence, EGP and ORPA united with the PGT as the Guatemalan National Revolutionary Unity, URNG. With the formation of the URNG and the success of the Sandinistas in Nicaragua and the continued civil war in El Salvador, President and General Efrían Ríos Montt received support from the United States for a scorched-earth counterinsurgency campaign that left more than 200,000 people dead and 500,000 displaced. A born-again Christian, Ríos Montt believed he had a mandate from God to bring the end of the civil war though his "beans and guns" policy. He created Self-Defense Patrols to reign in the civilian population by building a civilian network of terror.

The civil war raged through the 1990s. In Guatemala, mothers and spouses of the disappeared organized; however, popular organizations were targeted during the beans and gun campaign of the early 1980s. After a coup ousted Ríos Montt, human rights organizations, such as the Mutual Support Society (GAM), reemerged. GAM was formed by mothers and wives of the disappeared, but violence continued to mark Guatemalan society. In 1984, the body of Rosario Godoy, leader of GAM, who had been raped, tortured, and murdered, was found with the bodies of her brother and her infant son.

Throughout the civil war women endured horrific human rights violations. In 1997, URNG issued a report documenting the war crimes against women. Women were raped, tortured, and killed. At times, their husbands, fathers, and sons were murdered by the military, and the surviving women were forced to serve the soldiers' physical needs—sexual and nonsexual. The URNG argued that women became targets of the military and paramilitaries because they provided the social fabric of the community.

Women continue to be important in Guatemala as the source of community and the keepers of the memories of the disappeared and murdered remains. By the mid-1990s, women also organized to address the needs of returning refugees who had been displaced by the bloody civil war. In 1993, Mayan women formed Mama Maquín for this purpose; however, organizations such as Mama Maquín moved beyond addressing refugees and attempted to become a political force for change in Guatemala. The URNG, transformed into a political party, recognized the significance of women by offering them political parity within its organization.

—*Elaine Carey*

See also Latin America, Women in Guerrilla Movements in

References and Further Reading

Gleijeses, Piero. 1991. *Shattered Hope: The Guatemalan Revolution and the United States.* Princeton, NJ: Princeton.

Menchú, Rigoberta. 1984. *I Rigoberta Menchú: An Indian Woman in Guatemala,* edited by Elisabeth Burgos-Debray, translated by Ann White. New York: Verso.

Stoll, David. 2000. *Rigoberta Menchú and the Story of All Poor Guatemalans.* New York: HarperCollins.

Gulf War (1990–1991), Women and the

American women in the Gulf War and the impact of the war on their role in the U.S. military. From August 1990 to February 1991, the United States led a coalition of nations including Britain, Egypt, France, and Saudi Arabia in armed conflict against Iraq. Encompassing Operation Desert Shield and Operation Desert Storm, the war in the Persian Gulf occurred in response to the Iraqi invasion of Kuwait on August 1, 1990, and the country's subsequent failure to comply with demands of the United Nations for peaceful withdrawal. At peak strength in February 1991, more than 500,000 American troops served in the gulf area. Approximately 7.2 percent, or nearly 41,000, of these deployed forces were women, who then comprised 11 percent of total U.S. active duty military and more than 13 percent of the reserves. Nearly 10 percent of the women deployed to the gulf served in the army; 7 percent in the air force; 4.2 percent in the navy; and 1.5 percent in the marines.

The Gulf War marked the largest deployment of military women in U.S. history, as well as the first major test of the U.S. armed forces since the initiation of the all-volunteer military force in 1973 and the elimination of separate military units for women during the 1970s. The ability of service women to perform their jobs in a major war was still unproven, and the reliability of mixed-gender combat support units in a major war operation was unknown.

Deployment of women to the Persian Gulf raised two critical issues. Contemporary technology and strategies of warfare had eliminated traditional front lines and blurred the distinction between combat and noncombat functions. Yet women had been barred from combat positions in the U.S. Air Force, Marines, and Navy under the 1948 Combat Exclusion Act. The U.S. Army, although not covered by the act, maintained its own regulatory ban on women in combat roles.

Women were assigned to positions according to the Direct Combat Probability Coding System (DCPC) initiated in 1983. Known as the Risk Rule, the DCPC limited women's exposure to direct combat, rating each military job assignment along a continuum. Jobs with low probability of enemy contact were on one end; those of high probability were on the other and were closed to women.

In Operations Desert Shield and Desert Storm, women served as administrators, air traffic controllers, logisticians, engineer equipment mechanics, ammunition technicians, ordnance specialists, communicators, radio operators, drivers, law enforcement specialists, and guards. Women truck drivers hauled supplies and equipment into Kuwait. Some brought enemy prisoners of war (POWs) back to holding facilities. Many flew helicopters and reconnaissance aircraft, manned machine guns, and directed and launched Patriot missiles. Still others served on hospital, supply, oiler, and ammunition ships. Others served as public affairs officers and chaplains. Several women commanded brigade, battalion, company, and platoon units in the combat support and combat service support areas. They endured the same hardships under the same conditions of desert warfare as their male counterparts without special considerations. They were also subjected to combat. Thirteen women were killed in action and thirty-five were wounded. Two women became POWs. Four women marines qualified for and received the Combat Action Ribbons after returning fire from Iraqi troops.

Women's involvement in the Persian Gulf War and extensive media coverage focused public attention on deployed mothers and dual-service couples and prompted public concern for the welfare of children left behind. In February 1991, the Subcommittee on Military Personnel and Compensation of the Committee on Armed Services of the U.S. House of Representative conducted hearings on the impact of Operation Desert Storm on military families, particularly families headed by a single parent or dual-service families. The committee considered whether to pursue gender-neutral legislation defining some exemptions and deferments for parents. Speakers from the Department of Defense opposed all limitations on the ability to deploy soldiers overseas, emphasizing that such legislation jeopardized military readiness and mission fulfillment. Military representatives stressed that laws denying parents the right to serve in the same capacity as nonparents were discriminatory and more likely to affect military women, limiting their jobs assignments, promotions, income, and benefits.

Emphasizing that restrictive legislation would reverse progress toward gender equality and mitigate military effectiveness, military spokespersons articulated the provisions of existing policy on the deployment of single parents and dual-member military couples with minor children. Each military service required such parents to establish family care plans that included all provisions necessary for the care of dependents, including powers of attorney for temporary and long-term guardians, signed financial support documentation, and other requisite legal measures. Regulations required annual review and validation. Personnel were separated from the service if plans failed without possible rectification. Despite the congressional hearings, political pressure to restrict parental deployment was slight, and the armed forces retained existing authority.

A Department of Defense Interim Report to Congress on the conduct of war indicated that women had played a vital part in the theater of operations and acknowledged difficulties in the application of combat restrictions. Between May and November 1991, Congress debated issues concerning women in the armed forces, and in December 1991 President George H.W. Bush signed the National Defense Authorization Act for Fiscal Year 1992 and 1993, which included provisions repealing the combat exclusion law of 1948. The act provided legislative authority to the Department of Defense to restructure policy concerning the role of women in the U.S. armed forces, and throughout the 1990s, the services addressed restrictions on the assignment of women.

—*Lee Ann Ghajar*

See also Cornum, Rhonda; Whittle, Reba Zitella

References and Further Reading

Finlan, Alastair. 2003. *The Gulf War, 1991*. Oxford: Osprey.

Guljamal-Khan(um) (ca. 1836–1919)

An influential leader of Turkmen tribes in the Akhal and Merv area in the late nineteenth century who played an important role in the political and military development in this part of Central Asia. Guljamal-Khan(um) was the third wife of the influential Nurberdy-Khan, the leader of the Teke tribes in the Akhal and Merv areas (contemporary Turkmenistan and northern Iran). She broke with the tradition dominant in Central Asian society of that time that viewed women exclusively as silent housewives who had no political rights or public voice. Gradually she became interested in political and military development, and soon after her marriage to Nurberdy-Khan she became one of the most trusted advisers to her husband.

During the second half of the nineteenth century, Turkmen tribes were deeply divided and were engaged in devastating conflicts with each other and against powerful neighboring states, the Persian Empire and Khiva Khanate. The irregular Turkmen militia fiercely resisted invaders and won several important battles. The better-equipped armies of the Persian Shah and Khiva Khan regularly destroyed Turkmen villages and towns, however, impoverishing the local economy. In the brutal military tradition of that era, the winners often captured civilians along with combatants and sold them in the slave markets as far away as the Middle East and South Asia. In this environment of perpetual war, many Turkmen women abandoned their traditional role as housewives and often became involved in the military campaigns, helping the Turkmen militia by all possible means. In the 1870s and 1880s, the Russian Empire entered the political scene and attempted to establish its control over this part of Central Asia.

Guljamal-Khan(um) entered the Central Asian political arena at a difficult time for the Turkmen tribes because they were exhausted by uneven wars. In 1880, Nurberdy-Khan died, and Guljamal-Khan(um) became the leader of the Teke tribes in the Merv area. In an important battle at Geok Tepe fortress in January 1881, the independent-minded Turkmen tribes were defeated with great losses in military manpower and among the civilian population. Yet the Turkmen tribes refused to surrender and vowed to continue the struggle.

In 1884, the Turkmen elders and tribal leaders organized a gengesh (council) to discuss the Russian advance into the Akhal and Merv areas. They faced the difficult choice of accepting a peace agreement brought by Alikhanov-Avarskii, an officer in czarist service, or continuing the unequal war with great losses to civilian population. The voice of Guljamal-Khan(um) was instrumental in the gengesh's decision to accept the peaceful settlement and Russian control in the region. This ended several decades of wars and instability in the Turkmen land. Guljamal-Khan(um) was among the few women in nineteenth-century Central Asia who received a special award from the Russian emperor.

—Rafis Abazov

See also Kurmanjan-Datkha

References and Further Reading

Abazov, Rafis. 2004. *Historical Dictionary of Turkmenistan.* Lanham, MD, and Oxford, England: Scarecrow Press.

Gundogdyev, Ovez, and Ruslan Muradov. 2000. *Istoriko-kulturnoye naslediye Turkmenistana* [Historical and cultural heritage of Turkmenistan]. Ashgabat, Turkmenistan: UNDP.

Gwynne-Vaughan, Helen (1879–1967)

Botanist, scholar, war activist, and suffrage supporter, who served as the chief controller of Britain's Women's Auxiliary Army Corps (WAAC) and commander of Britain's Women's Royal Air Force (WRAF) in World War I and as major-general of the Auxiliary Territorial Services (ATS) in World War II. Helen Gwynne-Vaughan was the first female professor at Birkbeck College and facilitated the development of the WAAC and the WRAF.

Helen Isabella Charlotte Fraser was born into a Scottish aristocratic family in 1879. She briefly attended Cheltenham Ladies College before entering London University in 1899 to study science. She earned her degree in botany and later joined the Women's Suffrage Society. She became a lecturer at Birkbeck College where she met a colleague, T. G. Gwynne-Vaughan, whom she later married.

Her academic career was interrupted by the outbreak of war in 1914. She undertook voluntary war work through the Red Cross and Volunteer Aid Detachment. Her husband died a year later, and, with her new role as widow, she plunged herself more deeply into public service. The government established the WAAC in 1917. Its function was to have women play an active role in Britain's defense against Germany by serving as clerks, cooks, and the like (Izzard 1969, 134). Gwynne-Vaughan was named the WAAC's chief controller, earning high praise as an efficient administrator and leader. By the fall of 1918, after a scathing government review and shake up in leadership, she had also assumed command of the WRAF. She received commendation again for her work and was named a dame of the British Empire at the end of the war.

She returned to academia by the early 1920s and published several important works, most significantly key studies of the cytology of fungi. When World War II erupted in 1939, she resumed public service, acting as major-general of the ATS. At the conclusion of that conflict, Gwynne-Vaughan, in her early sixties, retired both from civic activism and from her duties at Birkbeck. Now a distinguished professor emeritus, she devoted the last years of her life to the cause of military welfare through her support in the Soldiers', Sailors' and Airmen's Families Association (SSAFA). She died in 1967, leaving most of her estate to Birkbeck to create a scholarship in her husband's name.

—*Rachel Finley-Bowman*

See also Great Britain, Women in Service during World War I; Great Britain, Women in Service during World War II

References and Further Reading

Izzard, Molly. 1969. *A Heroine in Her Time: A Life of Dame Helen Gwynne-Vaughan, 1879–1967.* London: Macmillan

Gypsies

See Roma/Sinti

Haas, Elena (1912/13–1945)

Czech resistance fighter during World War II. In early 1945, near the end of World War II, Elena Haas was leading a group of Czech partisans against a Nazi-controlled airfield near Melnik where the Vltava (Moldau) River joins the Labe (Elbe) River, 18 miles north of Prague. There she was fatally wounded. She was still firing her Sten gun when the fatal shots brought her down.

Elena Haas was twenty-five years old and just beginning her career as a civil engineer when the Nazis invaded Czechoslovakia on March 15, 1938. She eventually joined the Czech Resistance. Her professional skills were valuable for the work of sabotage because she could plan where to place charges for the maximum destructive impact. In September 1944, she led a raid that destroyed an important bridge on the Ohne River between Terezin (Theresienstadt) and its conjunction with the Labe River. In that raid, she had also helped destroy Nazi supplies and ammunition. Aided by a French agent and operatives trained and supplied by the British Special Operations Executive, she killed thirty-five of the enemy.

—*Andrew Jackson Waskey*

See also Senesh, Hannah; Svobod, Maria

References and Further Reading

Lande, D. A. 2000. *Resistance! Occupied Europe and Its Defiance of Hitler.* Osceola, WI: MBI.

Truby, J. David. 1977. *Women at War: A Deadly Species.* Boulder, CO: Paladin.

Hall, Virginia (1906–1982)

British special agent during World War II and the only female civilian to receive the Distinguished Service Cross as well as Member of the British Empire. Virginia Hall was born in Baltimore, Maryland, on April 6, 1906. She attended Radcliffe and Barnard Colleges from 1924 to 1926. She was a talented linguist and could speak French, Italian, and German fluently. In 1931, Hall assumed a clerk's position with the U.S. Embassy in Warsaw, Poland. During the 1930s, she served at various posts in Tallin, Estonia; Vienna, Austria; and Izmir, Turkey. While in Izmir, her shotgun slipped from her grasp during a hunting trip, and she was wounded. One

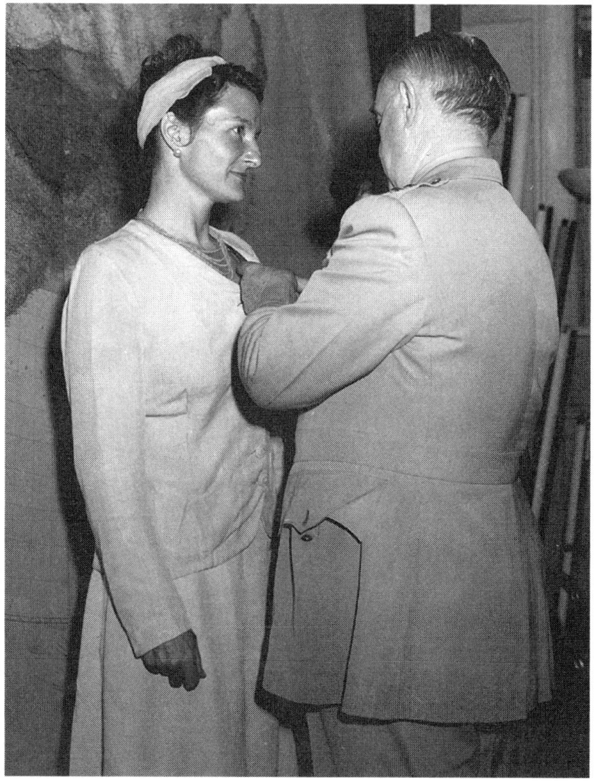

Virginia Hall receives the Distinguished Service Cross from Major General William J. Donovan, founder of the OSS, 1945. (National Archives)

leg was amputated, and she was fitted with an artificial limb; later, her friends in the French underground would call her "the limping lady." Because of a U.S. State Department regulation regarding disabilities, she was forced to resign her position in May 1939.

Hall was living in France when World War II broke out. While in Paris, she joined the French Ambulance Service Unit as a private second class. The fall of France in June 1940 caused her to flee to England. There, while working as a code clerk for the military attaché in the U.S. Embassy, she was recruited by the British Special Operations Executive (SOE). Her fluency in French enabled her to set up resistance networks in Vichy, France, beginning in August 1941. Using the code name Marie, Hall posed as a reporter for the *New York Post.* In early 1942, she moved to Lyons. She established contact with the French underground and began assisting in the return to England of escaped prisoners and downed U.S. aircrews. When the United States entered the war, she was listed as an enemy alien. Hall was forced to conduct business secretly from numerous bistros and restaurants.

In the aftermath of the invasion of North Africa in November 1942, thousands of German troops poured into Vichy. Hall managed to escape to Spain. After a few months, she returned to England where the SOE trained her as a wireless operator. She was then transferred to the American Office of Strategic Services. In 1944, operating under the code name Diane, Hall returned to the Haute-Loire region of central France. She worked setting up sabotage and guerrilla groups and supplying them with money, arms, and rations. Several weeks prior to D-Day, disguised as a peasant and with heavy clothing to hide her limp, she reported on German troop movements. The Gestapo hierarchy regarded her as the most dangerous allied agent in France. Despite her precarious situation, she informed the Allies that the German General Staff had relocated its headquarters to LePuy. In the final days of the German occupation of France, Hall's teams destroyed four bridges, derailed several freight trains headed for Germany, downed key telephone lines, killed more than 150 enemy soldiers, and captured more than 500 prisoners. At the conclusion of the war, she received the American Distinguished Service Cross as well as recognition as a Member of the British Empire.

In 1951, Hall began work for the Central Intelligence Agency in Washington, D.C. She became an intelligence analyst on French paramilitary affairs. She was one of the first women operations officers in the new Office of the Deputy Director of Plans. During her CIA career, which ended when she retired in 1966, Hall accepted several overseas assignments. Regarded as one of the true heroines of World War II, Hall died in Rockville, Maryland, on July 12, 1982.

—Charles F. Howlett

See also Atkins, Vera H.

References and Further Reading

Binney, Marcus. 2003. *The Women Who Lived for Danger: The Agents of the Special Operations Executive.* New York: HarperCollins.

Collins-Weitz, Margaret. 1995. *Sisters in Resistance: How Women Fought to Free France, 1940–1945.* New York: John Wiley and Sons.

Haines, Gerald K. 1994. "Virginia Hall Goillet, Career Intelligence Officer." *Prologue Quarterly of the National Archives* 26 (winter): 249–260.

McIntosh, Elizabeth. 1999. *Sisterhood of Spies.* New York: Dell.

Hamilton, Cicely Marie (1872–1952)

British novelist and playwright who unabashedly called for women to support the war effort during World War I. Cicely Hamilton, through deft and witty illustration, unearthed and displayed the gender inequities that were so embedded in Edwardian cultural norms as to be essentially invisible and thus neither understood nor challenged. Furthermore, she applied these revelatory goals in the course of her eclectic and energetic career, emerging as not only a cultural but a political leader in the women's suffrage movement and other organizations lobbying for the social and political rights of women.

Hamilton was born on June 15, 1872, in Paddington. She was one of four children born to Maud Piers and Cecil Hammill. She appears to have lived with both parents until around age ten, when her mother disappeared from her life under rather mysterious circumstances, which Cicely rarely discussed. Her father was an adamant supporter of the women's suffrage cause. This may well have shaped Hamilton's own views and activism later in life. After her mother's departure, she was raised by foster parents because her father, a member of the Gordon Highlanders, was serving in Egypt. She was educated at Malvern and other private schools in England and Germany and upon graduation served for a short time as a teacher before changing her last name and moving on to acting.

Hamilton's considerable writing talents came to fruition at first primarily because of her lack of success as an actor; after she failed to secure London acting spots, she turned her attentions to writing plays. These grew into a substantial oeuvre, including, in chronological order, *The Traveller Returns, Diana of Dobsons, How the Vote Was Won,* and *A Pageant of Great Women.*

In 1909, she wrote her first and probably most influential work, *Marriage as a Trade.* Hamilton contended that women were socialized to aspire to marriage to gain the success and financial stability of a man rather than to achieve these themselves. She scathingly documented the impact of this process on women's intellects and self-esteem. Other books include *Senlis* (1917), *William, an Englishman* (1919), her autobiography *Life Errant* (1935), *Modern Italy* (1932), *Modern France* (1933), *Modern Russia* (1934), *Modern Ireland as Seen by an Englishwoman* (1936), *Modern England* (1938), *Lament for Democracy* (1940), and *The Englishwoman* (1940).

Hamilton's writing takes on even greater power and legitimacy in the context of the manner in which she put her beliefs into action in her own life. She was a member of numerous feminist activist organizations, including the Women's Social and Political Union (WSPU, which she left over differences with Emma Pankhurst), the Women's Freedom League, the Actresses' Franchise League, and the Women Writers Suffrage League, the latter two of which she was a founder.

The outbreak of World War I raised new questions about the proper—or even possible—roles of women in the public sphere. Unlike many feminist activists, who renounced participation in government projects (especially those associated with the military), Hamilton was one of a group that evidently saw participation in the war effort

Cicely Marie Hamilton on the Mobilization of Women in Total War

"Modern warfare is so monstrous, all-engrossing and complex, that there is a sense, and a very real sense, in which hardly a civilian stands outside it; where the strife is to the death with an equal opponent the non-combatant ceases to exist. No modern nation could fight for its life with its men in uniform only; it must mobilize, nominally or not, every class of its population for a struggle too great and too deadly for the combatant to carry on alone. The 'unfit' who step into the shoes of the fit, the old men who fill the gaps left by their sons, the women who press into fields and workshops—all these keep the fighting line going, and without them the fighting line must fail; and hence, under modern conditions of war, an increasing difficulty in drawing the line that protects the civilian from open attack by the soldier. A munition factory staffed by women, a laboratory where some weakling discovers a chemical compound, may be deadlier instruments of death and destruction than thousands of horses and men. Further, where each party to the strife enlists the services of his entire population—puts forth, in a word, his utmost—the question of national exhaustion looms far larger than it did in the day of the professional soldier and the army running to thousands. Consciously or unconsciously, while the armies are at grips, the civilians of one nation are outstripping, exhausting the other—or are being outstripped and exhausted in the struggle for resources and replenishment. The work and resources of a civilian population have always been an indirect factor in every military situation; but to-day they are a factor direct and declared, to-day the exempt and the women are openly mobilized and enlisted. One sees that this direct intervention of the civilian in warfare must entail a certain loss of his immunity from direct attack and punishment, and that a leader hard pressed or unscrupulous may deem himself entitled to interpret the fundamental maxim enjoining him to cut his enemy's communications in a fashion undreamed by those who framed rules for a conflict confined to the soldier. . . . The German leaders decided at the outset that their war was a war on non-combatants."

—Cicely Hamilton, *Senlis* (London: W. Collins Sons, 1917), 34–36.

as either morally just or politically expedient—and probably both. Hamilton joined the new Scottish Women's Hospitals Committee, which established auxiliary hospitals along the front lines. She helped found the Auxiliary Hospital at Royaumont Abbey on the French front. She personally nursed casualties. In 1917, she joined the Women's Auxiliary Army Corps and under this aegis headed a postal unit in the French theater of operations and performed in theatrical productions for troops serving on the front lines.

After the war Hamilton worked as a journalist, contributing regularly to the *Daily Express, Daily Mail, Daily Mirror,* and the feminist journal *Time and Tide.* Her activist interests expanded to include reproductive rights such as free birth control advice and the right to choose, causes she advocated in her writings. Hamilton died on December 6, 1952.

—*Bethany A. Barratt*

See also Orczy, Baroness Emma; Pankhurst Family: Emmeline, Christabel, E. Sylvia, and Adela Pankhurst Walsh

References and Further Reading

Chothia, Jean. "Cicely Hamilton," *The Literary Encyclopedia,* http://www.litencyc.com/php/speople.php?rec=true&UID=1956 (accessed August 2, 2004).

Whitelaw, Lis. 1990. *The Life and Rebellious Times of Cicely Hamilton: Actress, Writer, Suffragist.* Toronto: Women's Press.
"Women in History of Scots Descent: Cicely Hamilton," *Electric Scotland,* http://www.electricscotland.com/history/women/wih30.htm (accessed August 2, 2004).

Harnack-Fish, Mildred (1902–1943)

American executed by the Nazis for espionage. Mildred Fish was born in Milwaukee, Wisconsin, the daughter of an unambitious and downwardly mobile father of old Yankee stock and a "strong and self-reliant" Christian Scientist mother (Brysac 2000, 24, 22). Mildred entered graduate school at the University of Wisconsin after completing her undergraduate education there. She participated in a progressive discussion group of graduate students and professors sponsored by John Commons. There she met Arvid Harnack, a German with two doctorates who was studying economics at Wisconsin as a Rockefeller Fellow. They married in 1926. Harnack returned to Germany in 1928, where he taught and held the U.S. desk at the Ministry of Economics. Mildred joined him the following year. She began doctoral studies at the University of Berlin, where she briefly taught American literature until she was replaced by a Nazi sympathizer. After completing her doctorate at the University of Giessen in 1941, Mildred taught in the Foreign Policy Institute of the University of Berlin.

In the mid-1930s, the Berlin home of the Harnacks became a gathering place for intellectuals opposed to the Nazi regime. The Harnacks moved from opposition to resistance. They and their associates disseminated critical information and communicated information on the plans of the Nazi regime to Americans and then, after joining the Red Orchestra group led by Harro Schulze-Boysen, to the Russians. The Nazis uncovered the group in August 1942. The Harnacks were arrested on September 7 and were held and interrogated at the Gestapo headquarters on Prinz-Albrecht-Strasse. On December 9, Arvid was sentenced to death, and he was hung on December 22. Mildred was originally sentenced to six years of hard labor, but Hitler refused to accept the sentence. She was tried again in January and sentenced to death. She was beheaded at Plötzensee prison on February 16, 1943.

—Bernard Cook

See also Kuckhoff, Greta; Schulze-Boysen, Libertas

References and Further Reading

Brysac, Shareen Blair. 2000. *Resisting Hitler: Mildred Harnack and the Red Orchestra: The Life and Death of an American Woman in Nazi Germany.* New York: Oxford University Press.

Hart, Nancy (1735–1830)

Heroine of the American Revolution. Nancy Morgan was born in North Carolina. After marrying Benjamin Hart, she and her husband moved to the backcountry of Georgia on the Broad River. An audacious frontier woman, Nancy Hart acted as a spy for the patriots and bested Tories a number of times. Her most noted exploit was the killing of one Tory and the capture of five others who had come to her house demanding food. While they drank, she took their guns. When they realized what was happening, she wounded one and killed another. When her husband arrived, alerted by the gunfire, he suggested shooting the rest. She, however, said that they had boasted of killing a neighbor, Colonel John Dooley, and that they should be

Nancy Morgan Hart capturing British soldiers. (Bettmann/Corbis)

hung. As they died, she reputedly sang "Yankee Doodle." After the death of her husband, she moved to Kentucky where she died in 1830.

—*Bernard Cook*

See also American Revolution, Women and the

References and Further Reading

"Nancy Hart, Revolutionary Heroine," http://smithdray.tripod.com/history/nancyhart.htm (accessed March 5, 2006).

Hart, Nancy (ca. 1841–ca. 1902)

Confederate guerrilla during the American Civil War. Born in the mountains of western Virginia, Nancy Hart became a Confederate guerrilla during the American Civil War. She joined Perry Conley's Moccasin Raiders, serving as a spy and scout for the unofficial regiment. She also led several raids on federal outposts in Virginia.

In 1861, federal troops captured Hart after a skirmish with the Moccasin Raiders. She played on her femininity, convincing the Union soldiers that she was innocent and had no knowledge of Conley's actions. Consequently, they released Hart, who headed back to the guerrilla band with valuable information about the local Home Guards and the movement of federal troops being sent to disband the guerrillas. Throughout the next year, Hart continued to play a part in the guerrilla raids in the area. After Conley's death in the summer of 1862, the Moccasin Raiders disbanded. Hart, who had married a fellow Raider, moved into the mountains near Confederate lines. From her new home, she carried information on Union movements to Confederate officials. Like other female spies, Hart played on her femininity to outsmart the enemy.

Union soldiers saw her as an innocent country girl, not a dangerous enemy operative.

Hart's role in the Confederate army eventually led federal officials to place a price on her head. In June 1862, she was captured in Summersville by Lieutenant Colonel William C. Starr's troops. Because she was a woman, Hart was not held to the stringent rules enforced on other prisoners of war. She was allowed the freedom to walk around the yard under the watchful eye of a guard. Hart took advantage of the freedoms she received as a female prisoner. She flirted with her guard, convincing him to let her hold his gun, and then shot him before fleeing on horseback. In the early morning hours of July 25, 1862, Hart returned to the Union camp accompanied by two hundred Confederate cavalrymen. Hart and the southern soldiers entered the town without opposition, captured Starr and other federal officers as well as a few enlisted men, set fire to three houses, and took mules and horses with them.

Nancy Hart reportedly died in 1902.

—Lisa Tendrich Frank

See also Baker, E. H.; Barton, Clara; Blackwell, Elizabeth; Boyd, Isabelle; Civil War, American, Women Combatants during the; Clayton, Frances; Cushman, Pauline; Dix, Dorothea; Edmonds, Sarah Emma; Etheridge, Anna; Greenhow, Rose O'Neale; Moon, Lottie, and Moon, Ginnie; Tubman, Harriet

References and Further Reading

Leonard, Elizabeth D. 1999. *All the Daring of the Soldier: Women of the Civil War Armies.* New York: W. W. Norton.

Haverfield, Evelina (1867–1920)

Administrator of the Scottish Women's Hospital (SWH) service in Serbia during World War I. The work of Evelina Haverfield in Serbia as well as her direction of the transport section of the SWH unit in Dobrudja during the Romanian campaign in 1916 led the Serbian government to award her posthumously its highest honor, the Order of the White Eagle.

Evelina was the daughter of William Scarlett, the third baron of Abinger, and Helen Magruder, Lady Abinger, at Inverlochy Castle in Scotland. Her unusual youth, filled with outdoor activities, was followed by a rather unconventional life. At nineteen, she married an army officer, Henry Haverfield, twenty years her senior. Their happy marriage of eight years was terminated by his death in 1895 but produced two sons. In 1899, she married another military man, Major John Balguy, but retained her first married name and her separate residence. She accompanied him to South Africa during the Boer War and rode with him on horseback as he supervised the administration of martial law in a large rural area. After ten years, the two separated but did not bother with divorce.

Haverfield played an active role in the suffragette movement before the outbreak of World War I. She was arrested with Emmeline Pankhurst during the Bill of Rights March when they attempted to enter the House of Commons. Her efforts turned to rousing support for the war, which erupted in August 1914. She proposed the formation of a women's volunteer rifle corps to defend Britain's coast against invasion. From this project, several women's organizations were developed to support the war effort, the Women's Emergency Corps, the Women's Volunteer Reserve, and the Women's Reserve Ambulance Corps.

In 1915, Haverfield volunteered to go to Serbia as an administrator of the SWH, founded by Dr. Elsie Inglis, an Edinburgh surgeon. While administering Dr. Edith Holloway's SWH unit near Serbia's northern border, Haverfield was informed that her eldest son had been killed in battle in Mesopotamia.

In the face of an Austrian offensive in October, the unit, staffed by twenty-two Scottish women, was forced to withdraw to Krushevatz in central Serbia. With an Austrian victory imminent, most of the Scottish women decided to leave Serbia. Haverfield and thirty-four other women decided to stay with Inglis and Holloway. After a German unit occupied the town, the Scottish women continued to provide care for wounded Serbian prisoners of war and ill civilians. When rumors spread that the Scottish medical staff would be interned, Haverfield decided to go underground, but before she and two companions were able to carry out their plan, they were detained, shipped to Vienna, and handed over to the Red Cross, which arranged for their return to England.

In England, Haverfield tirelessly promoted the Serbian cause. When asked by Inglis to participate in an SWH effort in support of Serbian soldiers fighting in Romania, Haverfield agreed to head the transport section, consisting of ambulances, trucks, and mobile kitchens all driven and serviced by women. The seventy-five women of this SWH contingent went by ship to Archangel in Russia and then by rail to Dobrudja in Romania. As the Central Powers' troops inexorably advanced, Haverfield and her assistants evacuated wounded Allied troops from the battlefront. For her bravery under fire, she received a Russian military award. When the Romanian front collapsed as Russia was convulsed by revolution, Haverfield returned to England. There she continued to work on behalf of Serbia. She and Flora Sandes garnered contributions to set up canteens and provide clothing for Serbian soldiers. She also organized a Serbian Red Cross Society in Britain to mobilize material assistance for Serbia. Shortly after the armistice, she traveled to Serbia to oversee the distribution of aid. In the summer of 1919, she once again returned to Serbia with some SWH women to set up an orphanage for Serbian war orphans at Baijna Bashta. Her effort was cut short by her death from pneumonia on March 21, 1919.

—Bernard Cook

See also Hodges, Katherine; Hutton, Lady Isabel Galloway; Inglis, Elsie, and the Scottish Women's Hospitals; King, Olive; Sandes, Flora

References and Further Reading

Gaddes, Boyce. 1995. *Evelina: Outward Bound from Inverlochy.* London: Merlin.

———. "The Life of Evelina Haverfield," First World War.com, http://www.firstworldwar.com/features/haverfield_02.htm (accessed October 1, 2003).

"Haw Haw, Lady"

See "Lady Haw Haw"

Helen of Troy

Symbol of women as victims and spoils of war. The subject of Greek legend, Helen of Troy's was "the face that launched a thousand ships"; her abduction sparked the Trojan War (a legendary conflict traditionally dated 1194–1184 B.C.; dated by Greek sources to the twelfth or thirteenth centuries B.C.). She first appears in the works of Homer, who wrote in the eighth century B.C., about four centuries after the accepted time of the war. The Trojan War was almost certainly fought for economic reasons, not to regain a stolen woman. Homer romanticized the conflict, suggesting how Greek honor—in this case the need for vengeance after the theft of a prized possession (Helen)—can provoke war. His sympathetic treatment, however, highlights the role of women as victims and spoils of war.

According to legend, Helen was the daughter of Zeus and Leda. She was given in marriage to Menelaus of Sparta, but there was such fear that her incredible beauty would lead to bloodshed that all the suitors swore to abide by the choice—and to wage war to regain her if somebody stole her from her husband. Sure enough, a problem soon arose. During a wedding celebration among the gods, the goddess Eris (Discord) threw a golden apple into the assembly to be the reward for the most beautiful goddess present. Three goddesses claimed the prize; they turned to the youthful Prince Paris of Troy to act as judge. Each offered a bribe for choosing her. Paris's choice fell on Aphrodite in return for the most beautiful woman in the world—Helen. He soon went to Sparta and, with Aphrodite's help, succeeded in carrying Helen home to Troy.

Menelaus demanded help to regain his bride, and the long siege of Troy began. Thus Helen could easily be blamed for causing a devastating war. Instead, the poet Homer portrayed Helen as a pawn of fate, manipulated by powers beyond her control. She appears in the *Iliad* as a woman of sensibility who is suffering deeply from her position—forced to abandon her husband and live among her people's enemies. Helen remains a pawn to the end. When her lover, Paris, went out to fight, Aphrodite preserved his life, carrying him from the battlefield to his bedchamber and forcing Helen (much against her will) to join him and provide distraction so he would not return to the fight. The only power Helen ever displays is in performing a traditional function of Greek women: she weaves a tapestry that tells the story of the war. In Mycenaean and archaic Greece, such tapestries lauded and preserved the memory of men's prowess on the battlefield. The war ended with the Greeks' successful assault on Troy; Helen was captured and returned to her husband, Menelaus. The tale ends with Helen reinstated in Sparta.

Classical-era Greek writers were less kind to Helen. Euripides in his play *Trojan Women,* for example, condemns her as a slut whose loose morals provoked the war. Such literary treatments suggest how esteem of women had declined since the age of Homer.

—Phyllis G. Jestice

See also Greek Women and War in Antiquity

References and Further Reading

Barber, E. J. W. 1995. *Women's Work: The First 20,000 Years.* New York: Norton.

Homer. 1990. *The Iliad.* Translated by Robert Fagles. London: Penguin.

Pomeroy, Sarah B. 1995. *Goddesses, Whores, Wives, and Slaves: Women in Classical Antiquity.* New York: Schocken.

HELLO GIRLS

American women recruited by the U.S. Army during World War I to work as operators on the army's telephone switchboards in France. Most French telephone operators at the time of World War I spoke little English; therefore General John Pershing, the commander of the American Expeditionary Force, advertised in U.S. newspapers in 1917 for women volunteers for the U.S. Signal Corps. The women had to be single, college graduates, in good health, and fluent in French; 7,000 applied, and 450 were selected to be trained by the American Telephone and Telegraph Company. This initial training was followed by training in military signaling procedures (Sharp, Small, and Somerville 2002, 427).

The first 33 of approximately 200 operators sailed for France in the spring of 1918. In France they were known as the Hello Girls because they invariable answered calls with "hello." Despite the fact that they were sworn in, wore military uniforms, and were subjects to military regulations, they were denied veteran status after the war. The army insisted that they were civilians, who had contracted to work with the army. In 1978, President Jimmy Carter signed legislation that gave them veteran status.

—Bernard Cook

See also United States, Women's Army Auxiliary Corps

References and Further Reading

Sharp, Mike, Steve Small, and Donald Somerville. 2002. *History of World War I: Victory and Defeat.* Vol. 2. New York/London: Marshall Cavendish.

Herero of Namibia, Repression of the

The first example of genocide in the twentieth century. Germany embarked on a program of imperial expansion in 1884. That year, the Germans claimed Namibia, which they called German Southwest Africa. Major Theodor Leutwein, appointed the administrator of the new colony, pitted the indigenous Herero against the Nama (Hottentots). The Herero at first cooperated with the Germans against their traditional rivals but eventually became exasperated by the loss of land to German colonists and rebelled in January 1904. Led by Samuel Maherero, they killed more than150 German soldiers and settlers.

The German government dispatched Lieutenant General Lothar von Trotha, who had led German troops against the Chinese during the Boxer Rebellion and had participated in the repression of resistance in German East Africa. With a force of 10,000, von Trotha mercilessly pushed the rebellious Herero—women and children as well as men—into the Kalahari Desert. Von Trotha then issued his infamous extermination order (*Vernichtungsbefehl*): "Every Herero found within German borders, with or without guns, with or without livestock, will be

First Genocide of the Twentieth Century: The Herero

The 1904 Letter of the Nama Chief Hendrik Witbooi to Major Theodor Leutwein, the German Military Governor of German Southwest Africa

"The German himself . . . introduces laws into the land . . . [which] are entirely impossible, untenable, unbelievable, unbearable, unmerciful and unfeeling. . . . He personally punishes our people at Windhoek and has already beaten people to death for debt. . . . [I]t is not just and right to beat people to death for that. . . . He flogs people in a shameful and cruel manner. We stupid and unintelligent people, for so he thinks us to be, we have never yet punished a human being in such a cruel and improper way for he stretches people on their backs and flogs them on the stomach and even between the legs, be they male or female, so Your Honour can understand that no one can survive such a punishment."

—Independent Media Center of Atlanta,
http://lists.indymedia.org/pipermail/imc-atlanta/2005-May/0515–9u.html
(accessed February 10, 2006).

Order of General Lothar von Trotha on October 2, 1904

"All the Herero must leave the land. If they refuse, then I will force them to do it with the big guns. Any Herero found within German borders, with or without a gun, will be shot. No prisoners will be taken. This is my decision for the Herero people."

—Peace Pledge Union, http://www.ppu.org.uk/genocide/g_namibia1.html
(accessed February 10, 2006).

shot. I will not give shelter to any Herero women or children. They must either return to their people or be shot at" (Tucker 1998). Armed posts were established along the fringe of the desert. Men who attempted to escape or surrender were killed. Women and children were driven back into the desert where water holes had been poisoned.

Despite the extermination order, some Herero survived. The men who were taken alive were confined in labor camps, where they were decimated by overwork, starvation, and disease. Surviving women were reduced to servitude and sex slavery. Only approximately 15,000 of the 80,000 Herero survived.

—Bernard Cook

See also Armenian Holocaust

References and Further Reading

Bebsman, Todd. 1999. "African Tribe Asks Reparations for German Atrocities: Holocaust Seeds Sown in Early 1900s." *Times-Picayune* (New Orleans) (March 21): A26.

Gewald, Jan-Bart. 1999. *Herero Heroes: A Socio-political History of the Herero of Namibia, 1890–1923*. Athens: Ohio University.

Tucker, Neely. 1998. "Seeds of Horror: African Genocide Laid Groundwork for the Holocaust 30 Years Later." *Toronto Star* (April 8): A18.

Hernández Rodríguez del Rey, Melba (1921–)

Cuban revolutionary. Melba Hernández Rodríguez del Rey is one of the two women who participated in the failed 1953 attack on the Moncada Barracks with Fidel Castro. From the province of Cienfuegos in Cuba, Hernández had been prompted to join the revolutionary forces in part due to her early contact with Corina Rodríguez, who had been a rebel in the struggle for Cuban independence (Barreras Ferrán 2001). As a result of her part at Moncada, she, along with Haydée Santamaría, served between six and seven months of jail time and was a witness to torture and brutalities. After her release, Hernández traveled to Mexico, where she continued to work with Fidel Castro to plan the overthrow of Fulgencio Batista, whose coup d'état had placed him in power for a second time. Back in Cuba, Hernández served as a guerrilla fighter in the Third Front of the *Ejército Rebelde* (Rebel Army) until its triumph in 1959. A revolutionary at heart, she was a follower of Eduardo Chibás, founder and leader of the Partido del Pueblo Cubano (Party of the Cuban People) (Hernández 2004). Hernández continued to be active in Cuban domestic and foreign affairs, serving as ambassador to Vietnam and Kampuchea (Cambodia), representative in the National Assembly, member of the Central Committee of the Communist Party, and more recently as vice president of the Cuban Association of the United Nations. She was showered with honors and recognition for her role in the revolution and for her continuing solidarity with the cause. In a 2004 interview published in *Juventud Rebelde,* the key publication for Cuban youth, she applauded her audience "because they have known how to follow with dignity the path that we initiated fifty years ago" (Pérez Sáez 2003). As the sole surviving woman from the Moncada assault, Melba Hernández was for a long time a living hero and source of inspiration for the Cuban people.

—Sara E. Cooper

See also Cuban Revolution, Women in the; Santamaría Cuadrado, Haydée

References and Further Reading

Barreras Ferrán, Ramón. 2001. "La impaciente y apasionada Melba," *Granma Diario* (July 29), http://www.latinamericanstudies.org/cuba/melba.htm (accessed October 28, 2004).

Hernández Serrano, Luis. 2004. "Empezaron otra vida y otro mundo," *Juventud Rebelde Web* (February 20), http://www.jrebelde.cubaweb.cu/2004/enero-marzo/feb-20/empezaron.html (accessed October 28, 2004).

Pérez Sáez, Dora. 2003. "Encuentro feliz," *Juventud Rebelde Web* (July 11), http://www.jrebelde.cubaweb.cu/Archivo/2003/Julio/ 20030711_01_04.html (accessed October 28, 2004).

Vega Belmonte, Belkis, dir. 1996. *Pensar con el corazón: Melba Hernández.* Havana: ICAIC.

Higgins (Hall), Marguerite (1920–1966)

First woman to win the Pulitzer Prize for war correspondence. Marguerite Higgins was born in Hong Kong, but her family returned to the United States when she was three. She received a bachelor's degree from the University of California, Berkeley, and graduated from Columbia University with a master's degree in journalism. Hall reported from the fronts of World War II and those of the cold war and from Korea, the Congo, and Vietnam. Although the *New York Tribune* hired her in 1942 to report the war in Europe, her editor would not send her overseas to London until 1944. In 1945, she moved to mainland Europe, reporting the war from France and later from Germany, and she accompanied the U.S. 7th Army when it entered the Nazi extermination camps of Dachau and Buchenwald. When World War II ended, Higgins covered the Nuremberg War Trials and the cold war tensions between the West and the Soviet Union. In 1947, the *New York Tribune* promoted her to bureau chief in Berlin.

In 1950, the *Tribune* assigned her to Japan and promoted her to Far East bureau chief. When the Korean War broke out, Higgins moved to South Korea, where she reported the fall of its capital, Seoul, to the North Korean army. At this point, the *Tribune* sent Homer Bigart, its top war reporter, to South Korea and ordered Higgins to return to Tokyo because all women reporters were banned from the front line. Refusing to leave, she kept competing with Bigart to get the best stories, a competition for readers that she won because the U.S. public liked her more personal style of reporting. Eventually she persuaded General Douglas MacArthur to allow her to continue her frontline reporting. Marguerite Higgins was with the marines when they landed in Inchon, 200 miles behind the North Korean lines on September 15, 1950.

Higgins wrote a book called *War in Korea,* and it became a best-seller in 1951. She also won the Pulitzer Prize for international reporting that year, and the Associated Press news organization voted her Woman of the Year. In 1952, she married air force Lieutenant General William Hall, and then in 1953, Higgins went to Vietnam to report on the French army's defeat at Dien Bien Phu. During this tour of duty, she narrowly escaped injury while walking alongside photographer Robert Capra. He stepped on a land mine and was killed. In 1955, she published her book *Red Plush and Black Bread,* based on her extensive travels in the Soviet Union. She also covered the civil war in the Congo.

In 1965, Higgins published her book *Our Vietnam Nightmare* in which she used her extensive knowledge of Vietnam to document her concerns about U.S. military involvement in Southeast Asia. While she was on this Vietnam tour, she contracted leishmaniasis, a tropical disease, and returned to the United States. She died on January 3, 1966. She is buried in Section 2 of Arlington National Cemetery in recognition of her record as an outstanding war correspondent.

—*Kathleen Warnes*

See also Chapelle, Dickey; Emerson, Gloria; Fallaci, Oriana; Hull, Peggy; Journalists, American Women, during World War I; Luce, Clare Boothe; Schuyler, Philippa; Trotta, Liz; Watts, Jean

References and Further Reading

Elwood-Akers, Virginia. 1988. *Women War Correspondents in the Vietnam War, 1961–1975.* Metuchen, NJ: Scarecrow.

May, Antoinette. 1985. *Witness to War: A Biography of Marguerite Higgins.* New York: Penguin.

Hiroshima, Nagasaki, and Women

U.S. atomic bombing of Japanese cities and its effects on the women of Japan. In August 1945, U.S. military forces deployed two atomic weapons, each with devastating blast, thermal, and radiation effects, against the Japanese cities of Hiroshima and Nagasaki. The first weapon, which used enriched uranium, had never been tested but was dropped on August 6, 1945, on Hiroshima with no advance warning. Casualty estimates vary, but some 100,000 people died immediately and perhaps another 70,000 over the next five years, most from burns, internal injuries, and excessive exposure to radiation. Survivors of the initial blast and fires, including many women, retreated to suburban areas where makeshift first aid stations were established. Over the next few days, internal injuries and radiation sickness killed hundreds, and the aid stations became burial stations.

The Nagasaki bomb, based on plutonium, was similar to the one tested at Alamogordo, New Mexico, in July 1945. It was dropped on Nagasaki on August 9, 1945. Although this weapon had a considerably greater explosive force than the Hiroshima bomb, it was dropped slightly off target. Nagasaki's lower population density and hilly terrain resulted in fewer total casualties, perhaps 75,000 immediate deaths with an equal number of major injuries.

Casualties in both cities were more prevalent among women than men, largely because of the conscription of males for the war effort, which left more female than male civilians present at the time of the attacks. Both Hiroshima and Nagasaki had strategic value to the Japanese war effort, but each also had a large noncombatant population. In selecting cities as the targets, U.S. officials ensured that there would be a substantial number of female casualties.

The weapons were deployed primarily for their devastating blast effects, but U.S. officials were aware that survivors of the initial explosions would also be subject to radiological effects. After Japan's surrender and its occupation by the United States, U.S. officials decided to study the long-term effects on survivors of their exposure to radiation. Beginning in late 1945, survivors were subjected to blood and bone marrow tests and screened for leukemia and other diseases that might be attributable to radiation exposure. Although few cancers were identified, researchers did learn that a large fraction of male survivors were rendered at least temporarily sterile and that women seemed able to absorb larger radiation doses than men without immediate ill effects.

In 1947, the U.S. government decided to study the genetic effects of radiation exposures. A massive investigation was launched to identify survivors' whereabouts at the time of the explosions to estimate the radiation doses they received. Hundreds of midwives in both cities aided the research by registering and reporting pregnancies, terminations, and live births. Midwives and mothers were crucial to the data-gathering effort, which involved identifying and following the progress of some 76,626 newborns. Analysis of data gathered through 1953 indicated that parents' radiation exposures had no statistically significant influence on the health of children, but controversy surrounded the conclusion. The Japanese data continue to inform contemporary international regulations on radiation exposure limits.

Although it had earlier banned all reports on the atomic weapons, the U.S. occupation force permitted a Peace Restoration Festival to take place at Hiroshima in August 1946. Japanese women played an important role in making the festival an annual event, and in 1949 at the request of female activist Kinko Yamada, a peace rally in Hiroshima called for the elimination of nuclear weapons. The Hiroshima Peace Festival is now regarded as the world's premier demonstration of antinuclear activism.

In 1955, the U.S. government flew several female Hiroshima survivors to the United States, where they underwent reconstructive surgery to repair burn scars suffered during the bombing.

The Hiroshima Maidens, as they were known in U.S. newspapers, stayed with American families while recuperating and became an international symbol of courage and survival.

—Laura M. Calkins

See also Japan, Women and the Home Front, World War II

References and Further Reading

Barker, Rodney. 1985. *The Hiroshima Maidens: A Story of Courage, Compassion, and Survival.* New York: Viking Press.

Kelen, Stephen. 1983. *I Remember Hiroshima.* Sydney: Hale and Iremonger.

Neel, James V. 1990. "The Very Early Years of the ABCC Genetics Program, 1946–1954." *RERF Update* 2, no. 3: 6–9. Available at the Radiation Effects Research Foundation Web site, http://www.rerf.or.jp/eigo/historic/psnacunt/schull.htm (accessed September 13, 2004).

Neel, James V., and William J. Schull. 1991. *The Children of Atomic Bomb Survivors: A Genetic Survey.* Washington, DC: National Academy Press.

Newcombe, Howard B. 1962. "Genetic Effects in Populations, with Special Reference to Studies in Man, Including ABCC Results." *Radiation Research* 16: 531–545.

Schull, William J. 1990. "Role of Japanese Midwives Critical to Birth of Genetic Program." Available at the Radiation Effects Research Foundation Web site, http://www.rerf.or.jp/eigo/historic/psnacunt/schull.htm (accessed September 13, 2004).

Hirsch, Ilse (b. 1922)

Guide for a German assassination team. Ilse Hirsch was born in Hamm, Germany, in 1922. When she was sixteen, she joined the League of Young German Women (Bund der Deutschen Mädchen), the Hitler youth group for female adolescents, and was one of its leaders in Monschau. She was trained for a mission to assassinate Franz Oppenhoff, who had been appointed mayor of Aachen by the Americans after they seized the German city. Hirsch was parachuted with a team of five men, led by SS Lieutenant Herbert Wenzel, to the countryside outside the city. Hirsch, who knew the area, led the team to Oppenhoff's residence where Wenzel and Sepp Leitgeb killed him. During their attempted escape, Hirsch detonated a mine attached to a trip-wire. Leitgeb was killed, and she was badly injured. She was apparently not suspected of participating in the assassination and was able to return home after a lengthy recovery. After the war, Hirsch and the other living perpetrators, with the exception of Wenzel, were eventually apprehended and tried in the Werewolf Trial in Aachen in October 1949. They were found guilty and sentenced to terms ranging from one to four years.

—Bernard Cook

See also Terrorists, Women

References and Further Reading

"Ilse Hirsch," George Duncan's Women of the Third Reich, http://members.iinet.net.au/~gduncan/women.html (accessed January 13, 2004).

Hobby, Oveta Culp (1905–1995)

First director of the U.S. Women's Army Auxiliary Corps (WAAC) and its successor, the Women's Army Corps (WAC). Born on January 19, 1905, in Killeen, Texas, the daughter of lawyer and state legislator Ike W. Culp, she showed an interest in law, parliamentary procedure, and journalism. She served as parliamentarian for the Texas House of Representatives, assisted in codifying Texas banking laws, served as assistant city attorney of Houston, and wrote a textbook on parliamentary procedure, *Mr. Chairman* (1937). In 1931, she married William P. Hobby, publisher of the *Houston Post* and former governor (1917–1921) of Texas. At

Oveta Culp Hobby. (Dwight D. Eisenhower Library)

the *Houston Post,* she advanced from research editor in 1931 to executive vice president in 1938. Hobby was the mother of a ten-year-old son and a five-year-old daughter when she took the position as director of the WAAC in 1942.

As chief of the Women's Interests Section of the War Department's Bureau of Public Relations (1941–1942), Oveta Culp Hobby was instrumental in planning a women's corps. On May 14, 1942, Congress established the Women's Army Auxiliary Corps, and on May 16, Hobby took the oath of office as its director, holding the relative rank of colonel.

Director Hobby prepared WAAC regulations to govern enlistment, training, uniforms, pay, promotion, and a code of conduct for the noncombatant women's service. WAAC recruiting surpassed initial goals, and by March 1943, five WAAC training centers were in operation. Hobby had to confront a slanderous campaign against the reputation of the WAAC in the spring of 1943, however, which slowed women's enlistment. Most likely begun by men in the army who were hostile toward the WAAC, the slander spread unfounded scurrilous jokes and gossip about the women's moral character and behavior. Another problem she encountered was that because Congress did not grant WAAC members military status as an integral part of the U.S. Army, the auxiliaries were not eligible to receive veterans' benefits, which especially affected auxiliaries stationed overseas. After much congressional debate, on July 1, 1943, President Franklin D. Roosevelt signed the bill to establish the Women's Army Corps in the U.S. Army. Colonel Hobby retained responsibility for preparing WAC plans and policies and overseeing training and discipline.

When Congress dropped auxiliary status and created the Women's Army Corps on July 1, 1943, Director Hobby took the oath of office on July 5 as a colonel in the U.S. Army. Having completed her mission to organize and administer a women's corps, Colonel Hobby resigned as director of the Women's Army Corps in July 1945. On July 12, 1945, Westray Battle Boyce, Hobby's deputy since May, assumed directorship of the WAC.

In January 1945, Hobby was awarded the Distinguished Service Medal. The citation praising her contributions to the war effort stated, "Without the guidance of precedents in United States military history to assist her, Colonel Hobby established sound initial policies, planned and supervised the selection of officers and the preparation of regulations. The soundness of basic plans and policies promulgated is evidenced by the outstanding success of the Women's Army Corps, composed of nearly 100,000 women and comprising an essential and integral part of the Army" (Treadwell 1954, 721).

Oveta Culp Hobby returned to Houston to resume her career at the *Post,* interrupted only when she returned to Washington to serve as the first secretary of the Department of Health, Education, and Welfare from 1953 to 1955. She died on August 16, 1995, in Houston.

—*Sharon Ritenour Stevens*

See also United States, Women's Army Auxiliary Corps

References and Further Reading

Morden, Bettie J. 1990. *The Women's Army Corps, 1945–1978*. Washington, DC: U.S. Government Printing Office.

Treadwell, Mattie E. 1954. *The Women's Army Corps,* a volume in the *United States Army in World War II*. Washington, DC: U.S. Government Printing Office.

Hobhouse, Emily (1860–1926)

English humanitarian and pacifist who opposed the South African (Anglo-Boer) War and condemned British treatment of Afrikaner women and children in concentration camps in the Orange Free State and the Transvaal.

Emily Hobhouse was born in Liskeard on April 9, 1860, and grew up in the tiny village of St. Ive in eastern Cornwall. Her father was an Anglican priest, but both her father's and her mother's families were prominent in politics. After the death of her mother, she cared for her ill father until his death in 1895. Hobhouse then became more active in social work and political reform, traveling to the United States to do welfare work among the Cornish miners in Minnesota. In 1898, Hobhouse returned to England and worked for the Women's Industrial Committee and became adept at investigating social problems. She and her brother, Leonard Hobhouse, were both members of the Adult Suffrage Society, which promoted universal suffrage. Like many radical liberals, she opposed the Boer War. In 1899, as secretary for the South African Conciliation Committee, she lobbied the British government and organized mass

Emily Hobhouse's Condemnation of British Policy during the Boer War

Corroboration by an American Historian

"[A]s the guerrilla campaign replaced conventional warfare, Gen. Horatio Herbert Kitchner, the British commander in chief, adopted a strategy targeting women and children. . . . Kitchner's strategy of land clearance was designed to deny the Boer enemy the refuge and resupply provided by their families. He did this by burning down their farmhouses, killing their livestock, and carrying the homeless civilians to concentration camps. . . . There is no evidence of deliberate cruelty: those in charge of the camps did the best they could under the circumstances. But the end result was the death of more than twenty-six thousand women and children. Since the entire population of the two Boer states was less than four hundred thousand, these deaths represented a catastrophic loss. *Genocide* is not too harsh a word."

—Linda Grant De Pauw, *Battle Cries and Lullabies: Women in War from Pre-History to the Present* (Norman: University of Oklahoma, 1998), 194. Reprinted by permission of the publisher.

Protest of the Boer Government, November 21, 1901

"With indignation the Government and the people were surprised with the policy followed by the British military authorities in removing the families of burghers from their dwellings. This removal took place in the most uncivilized and barbarous manner, while such action is moreover in conflict with all up to the present acknowledged rules of civilized warfare. The families were put out of their houses under compulsion, and in many instances by force, which [the houses] were destroyed and burnt with everything in them—such as bedding, clothes, furniture, and food; and these families, meetings protesting the war. The following year, she founded the South African Women and Children Distress Fund to raise money for British and Afrikaner families that had lost homes and livelihoods in the war.

Hobhouse traveled to South Africa in December 1900 with relief supplies and to see the camps firsthand. Although Lord Kitchener placed severe restrictions on her movements, she did visit several camps around Bloemfontein. Here she witnessed appalling suffering caused by the lack of adequate water, rations, sanitary facilities, medical supplies, and shelter. Hobhouse was particularly moved by the plight of the thousands of undernourished children who were dying of treatable, but untreated, illnesses, such as typhus and dysentery. When British officials seemed unable or unwilling to take action, Hobhouse returned to England to plead her case directly to the British people and government. Despite fierce opposition from prowar factions, she goaded Parliament into debating her report on the camps, addressed public meetings, and raised relief funds. Hobhouse's efforts forced the government to appoint a women's committee headed by Millicent Fawcett to travel to South Africa and investigate the camps, but Hobhouse was denied a place on it. The committee's February 1902 report essentially vindicated Hobhouse and led to some improvements.

In October 1901, Hobhouse returned to South Africa but was refused leave to come ashore in Cape Town; after five days, she was

among whom were many aged ones, pregnant women, and children of very tender years, were removed in open trolleys [exposed] for weeks to rain, severe cold wind, and terrible heat . . . with the result that many of them became very ill, and some of them died shortly after their arrival in the women's camps."

S. W. Burger, Acting State President
F. W. Reitz, State Secretary

—Emily Hobhouse, *The Brunt of the War and Where It Fell* (London: Methuen, 1902), 107.

Hobhouse's Report

"I had seen families swept close to the railway line near Warrenton and Fourteen Streams. I had seen saw a crowded train crawl the whole long day into Kimberley—the people, old and young, packed in open trucks under a cruel sun—kept at the station building without food until late at night, brought up at midnight to bare tents, where, groping in the dark, they sought their bundles and lay down, finding no preparation, no food or drink. I had seen them in crowds by railway sides in bitter cold, in streaming rain, hungry, sick, dying, and dead. I have seen these patient people packed in train-loads for Bethulie and elsewhere, and I never doubted but that every countrywoman of mine, had they seen and known, would have felt as I did, great sympathy with their forlorn condition and a desire to alleviate it.

"Never before have women and children been so warred against. England by the hands of Lord Roberts and Lord Kitchener, adopted the policy of Spain [in Cuba], while improving upon her methods. She has placed her seal upon an odious system. Is it to be a precedent for future wars, or is it to be denounced . . . by every humane person of every creed and every tongue, denounced as a 'method of Barbarism' which must never be resorted to again—the whole cruel sequence of the burning, the eviction, the rendering destitute, the deporting, and finally reconcentrating of the non-combatants of the country, with no previous preparation for their sustenance?"

—Emily Hobhouse, *The Brunt of the War and Where It Fell* (London: Methuen, 1902), 122 and 317–318.

deported back to England. In poor health, she learned of the Afrikaner surrender in the Treaty of Vereeninging in May 1902 while recuperating in Savoy, France. Determined to effect rehabilitation and reconciliation, Hobhouse went to South Africa in 1905 to teach spinning, weaving, and lace making to women and girls, eventually establishing twenty-eight schools in the Free State and Transvaal. Ill health forced her to return to Europe in 1908 and also prevented her from attending the December 1913 ceremony in Bloemfontein unveiling the Women's Monument commemorating the 26,000 women and children who died in the concentration camps.

Hobhouse took up the antiwar cause again in 1914, protesting World War I. Following the war, she organized a relief effort that provided food for tens of thousands of starving European women and children. Hobhouse died on May 23, 1926. She is remembered as the Angel of Love by Afrikaner women. Her ashes are buried at the Women's Monument in Bloemfontein.

—Roger B. Beck

See also Fawcett, Millicent

References and Further Reading

Balme, Jennifer H. 1994. *To Love One's Enemies: The Life and Work of Emily Hobhouse.* Cobble Hill, Canada: Hobhouse Trust.

Beer, Frank H. 2003. *Emily Hobhouse: The Angel of Love.* Cornwall, England: Charaton Books.

Reenen, Rykie van. 1984. *Emily Hobhouse: Boer War Letters.* Cape Town: Human and Rousseau.

Roberts, Brian. 1991. *Those Bloody Women: Three Heroines of the Boer War.* London: John Murray.

Hodges, Katherine (1888–1982)

Ambulance driver for the Scottish Women's Hospitals (SWH), Young Men's Christian Association (YMCA), and Hackett-Lowther Unit during World War I; recipient of the Medal of St. George, Order of St. Stanislav, and Croix de Guerre for her contributions.

Katherine Hodges joined the SWH Transport Unit headed to Russia in July 1916. Hodges's unit provided medical care for the First Division of the Serbian army stationed in Romania. As an ambulance driver, Hodges transported wounded soldiers from the front lines to field hospitals. The transport unit also evacuated SWH hospitals during their frequent retreats.

In January 1917, Hodges joined a medical unit sponsored by the Union of Zemstva. She served as an ambulance driver as well as a nurse on the Galician front. Hodges returned to Britain in the summer of 1917 due to the heightening revolutionary activity in Russia and personality conflicts with the administration of the unit.

During her stay in Britain, she served as a YMCA driver in London until leaving for France with the Hackett-Lowther Unit in January 1918. As part of the unit, Hodges became a paid solider in the French army, where she served as a driver until the armistice. The Hackett-Lowther Unit was the only group of women officially working on the front lines.

During World War II, Hodges worked as a driver with the London Auxiliary Ambulance Service during the blitz. After the war, she served as a headquarters officer with the British Red Cross Society until 1968.

—Barbara Penny Kanner

See also Haverfield, Evelina; Hutton, Lady Isabel Galloway; Inglis, Elsie, and the Scottish Women's Hospitals; King, Olive; Sandes, Flora

References and Further Reading

Cahill, Audrey Fawcett. 1999. *Between the Lines: Letters and Diaries from Elsie Inglis's Russian Unit.* Edinburgh, Cambridge, and Durham, United Kingdom: Pentland Press.

Hoge, Jane Currie Blaikie (1811–1890)

Civilian worker during the American Civil War in the Northwestern Sanitary Commission. Jane Currie Blaikie was born in Philadelphia on July 31, 1811. She attended Young's Ladies' College in Philadelphia and married Abraham Hoge, a merchant. In 1848, they moved to Chicago.

In 1861, fifty-year-old Jane Hoge assumed, with Mary Livermore, the management of the Northwestern Sanitary Commission branch based in Chicago. She would hold the post throughout the Civil War. She was already an experienced leader of women's charitable organizations and probably more prepared for the responsibility than any other woman living in Chicago. Her outspoken demeanor, emboldened by her conviction that the war relief effort needed an efficient mother's perspective, served the commission well.

Hoge's wartime job drew her further into public life than she had previously ventured. She traveled, made speeches, raised large amounts of money, worked with both civilians and military personnel, helped manage the commission's daily business deals, and organized the myriad donated supplies destined for the western armies. Along with Livermore and a number of clubwomen, she planned and implemented the Northwestern Soldier's Fair in 1863, which earned almost $100,000. Although men in the commission had initially remained on the sidelines, by 1865 they made up the fair's managing board, although they retained Hoge and Livermore.

In the course of Hoge's wartime career, she met and corresponded with Abraham Lincoln. Whether she was nursing a wounded enlisted man in an army hospital, chairing a fair board in Chicago, or corresponding with the nation's president, however, she was quintessentially a mother who did her work on a national stage. She was a woman who believed her patriotic and divinely sanctioned wartime duty was to work.

In 1867, Hoge published her war memoir, *The Boys in Blue,* which heaped praise on the enlisted men and became one of the earliest accounts of the war. With the exception of this foray into the broader public world, the postwar Hoge resumed her role as a well-known and respected regional mother. The skills she had learned while immersed in the Sanitary Commission and its work enhanced the activities that she took up after the war. In the late 1860s, for example, she helped to establish Chicago's Home for the Friendless, a refuge for needy children and women. In 1871, she played a key role in launching the Evanston College for Ladies, and she served for more than a decade on the Women's Presbyterian Board of Foreign Missions for the Northwest.

Unlike her associate Mary Livermore, Hoge did not parlay her wartime experiences into a gainful career for herself. Moreover, she never joined the ranks of suffragists. More self-assured than Livermore had been but possessing less postwar energy, Hoge used her skills and reputation garnered from the war years to continue leading in women's work. For the remainder of her life, she was a regionally respected advocate of women who knew how to get big jobs done. She died in Chicago on August 26, 1890.

—Nancy Driscol Engle

See also Baker, E. H.; Barton, Clara; Blackwell, Elizabeth; Boyd, Isabelle; Civil War, American, and Women; Clayton, Frances; Cushman, Pauline; Dix, Dorothea; Edmonds, Sarah Emma; Etheridge, Anna; Greenhow, Rose O'Neale; Hart, Nancy; Livermore, Mary Ashton Rice; Moon, Lottie, and Moon, Ginnie; Tubman, Harriet

References and Further Reading

Brockett, Linus P., and Marcy C. Vaughn. 1867. *Woman's Work in the Civil War: A Record of Heroism, Patriotism and Patience.* Introduction by Henry W. Bellows. Philadelphia: Zeigler, McCurdy.

Henshaw, Sarah Edwards. 1868. *Our Branch and Its Tributaries: Being a History of the Northwestern Sanitary Commission and Its Auxiliaries during the War of Rebellion.* Chicago: Alfred L. Sewell.

Hoge, Jane (Mrs. A. H.). 1867. *The Boys in Blue, or Heroes of the "Rank and File."* Introduction by Thomas E. Eddy. New York: E. B. Treat.

Livermore, Mary A. 1889. *My Story of the War: A Woman's Narrative of Four Years Personal Experience as Nurse in the Union Army.* Hartford, CT: A. D. Worthington.

Holocaust and Jewish Women

Fate of Jewish women during the Holocaust. The National Socialist state did everything in its power to destroy European Jewry, female and male. More women than men died during the Holocaust, however, revealing that both race and gender played important roles. From the initial period of ghettoization, when most European Jews were crammed into small and filthy quarters in several Eastern European cities, to the horrific world of the concentration and extermination camps, Jewish women suffered unique abuses at the hands of perpetrators. Jewish women also learned to survive in the ghettos and camps in ways that men could not.

The roots of women's strength and leadership during the Holocaust stem from their involvement in the youth movements popular in Europe before World War II. Many of the groups with a large Jewish membership were socialist and stressed sexual equality, preparing many young women to assume leadership roles during times of crisis. German Jewish women organized self-help groups after anti-Semitic laws passed in Germany stripped Jews of civil rights and economic security. Nevertheless, several sociocultural factors contributed to the higher death rate of women during the Holocaust. Unwilling to leave their families, especially older relatives and small children, fewer women emigrated to safer countries than men. Women were also less likely to convert or marry non-Jews than Jewish men. This meant that women were less likely to have Christian spouses to protect them during the forced movement of Jews to the ghettos and eventually the camps. Finally, men naturally assumed official leadership positions and made decisions that benefited them.

In 1939, the Nazis decreed that the Jewish communities in occupied territories be administered by a Jewish Council of Elders. The councils, although entirely male in composition, employed female secretaries, many of whom were influential behind the scenes and active in the underground. Dr. Dietl Orenstein, the only woman to be named to a council, led an 11,000-

The Nazi View of Women

"It was the Nazi view of all women as cell-bearers that condemned the Jewish ones. Even within the lowest life-form—the anti-race—women ranked lower still, for spawning it. In Hitler's cliché, 'Every child that a woman brings into the world is a battle, a battle waged for the existence of her people.' Because women in their biology held history, one gestating Jewish mother posed a greater threat than any fighting man. To be a father to a child had no impact on selection. To be a mother in fact or in future—that was the final sentence."

—Mary Lowenthal Felstiner, *To Paint Her Life: Charlotte Salomon in the Nazi Era* (Berkeley: University of California Press, 1997), 207.

Selection process at Auschwitz concentration camp, Poland, ca. 1944. A German soldier stands with Jewish prisoners, identified by the yellow stars sewn on their coats. (Imagno/Getty Images)

woman-strong Women's Employment Service in Theresienstadt, the one concentration camp open to international inspection. The unique female labor service managed multiple industries and ensured that the women of this unusual concentration camp were fed properly until the camp was liquidated in the final months of World War II. In most ghettos, however, the Jewish councils decided that able-bodied men should be given the best chance for survival. Consequently, young men received the lion's share of the ghetto's food and resources. After the Nazis dissolved the ghettos in the autumn of 1942, the fragile Jewish communal structures disappeared, and voluntary, informal communities took their place. It was under these desperate conditions that women demonstrated strength and adaptability while facing what many scholars believe to have been even greater hardship than male inmates.

Women had proved themselves resourceful in the ghettos, and those lucky enough to flee the German invasion were valuable assets in the partisan movements in the occupied Soviet Union. Only a small percentage of women escaped the concentration camps. Female inmates were subjected to gender-specific burdens and cruelties but also created valuable relationships and adapted to the merciless environment. Almost every female survivor described being humiliated when first arriving at the camp. Women were stripped nude before SS personnel and male inmates alike. Pregnant women and women with small children were often killed within minutes of arriving at the camp. The German goal was the annihilation of the Jewish people but not before extracting hard labor from them. Children were nothing but burdens in the German scheme. The Germans reserved one of their most infamous cruelties for women with small children. Those women who could work in the camps were forced to witness their children's murder. All Jews were dehumanized before being exterminated or worked to death, but women suffered exceptional brutality at the hands of perpetrators.

Significantly, women used their traditional gender roles and biology to survive. Women demonstrated a greater biological resistance to starvation, were more aware of the importance of hygiene in the camps, and tended to form social groups more easily than men. Women sent to some of the larger camps became camp sisters, small groups of unrelated inmates who formed quasi-family ties and maintained a group identity in most aspects of camp life. These women had similar schooling and tended to come from the same cities or regions. As in the ghettos, food sharing was the key to survival. The extended family of camp sisters reserved most of the collected food for the young and sick. The SS did not appoint women to the internal administration of the camps, which would have ensured them a source of food and some preferential treatment. Female inmates were forced to pool their resources and maintain a strong network. Women were also forced to use sex as a commodity. Both male inmates and SS personnel traded food for sex. Given the German need for labor, the absence of women in official leadership positions, and the burdens pregnancy and motherhood placed on female inmates, it is not surprising women's survival rate was much lower than men's.

Jewish women suffered primarily for being Jews but were treated with exceptional cruelty for being women. Women also had unique strengths that facilitated their survival in the ghettos and camps. They were socially conditioned to act as mothers and protectors for other inmates, even when the inmates were unrelated. Women were generally more religious than men and were compelled to freely assist strangers. Finally, one of the ironies of the Holocaust was that so-called women's work, such as preparing food, cleaning, and caring for the sick, was the only meaningful labor during such a trying time. By surviving and helping others to survive, Jewish women practiced a form of nonviolent resistance. The Holocaust claimed a diverse group of victims representing dozens of nationalities, but more than half of the 6 million victims that perished in the Holocaust were women.

—Brian E. Crim

See also Bruskina, Masha; Fittko, Lisa; Frank, Anne; Fuld, Bracha; Grossman, Chaika; Kempner, Vitka; Korczak, Rozka; Landau, Emilia; Ravensbrück; Reik, Haviva; Rosenstrasse and Intermarriage of Jews and German Gentiles; Senesh, Hannah

References and Further Reading

Baumel, Judith Tydor. 1995. "Social Interaction among Jewish Women in the Crisis during the Holocaust: A Case Study." *Gender and History* 7: 64–84.

Kremer, Lillian. 1999. *Women's Holocaust Writing: Memory and Imagination.* Lincoln: University of Nebraska.

Ofer, Dalia, and Lenore J. Weitzman, eds. 1998. *Women in the Holocaust.* New Haven, CT: Yale University.

Ritvo, Roger, and Diane Plotkin, eds. 1998. *Sisters in Sorrow: Voices of Care in the Holocaust.* College Station: Texas A&M University.

Hughan, Jessie Wallace (1875–1955)

A major figure in the war resistance movement in the United States between the two world wars and the founder and driving force behind the War Resisters League during its formative years.

Jessie Wallace Hughan was born in Brooklyn in 1875. She was educated at the Unitarian Northfield Seminary in Massachusetts and graduated from Barnard College in 1898. Influenced by Henry George's single tax theory, Hughan studied economics at Columbia University, receiving her master's in 1899 and her doctorate in 1910. Her growing interest in socialism led her doctoral adviser to suggest that she attend socialist meetings to deepen her understanding of the topic. In 1907, she joined the Socialist Party, serving in several party offices. Between 1915 and 1924, she was the party's candidate for a number of city, state, and national offices. Although unsuccessful in each political campaign, Hughan consistently insisted that the roots of modern war and economic oppression were located within the capitalist system.

While completing her doctorate, Hughan began her teaching career at schools in Naugatuck, Connecticut, and White Plains, New York. In the early 1900s, she returned to New York City where she began her long career in the employ of the city's public school system. She taught in a number of high schools throughout the city, primarily in Brooklyn. In the 1920s, she was in charge of the English Department at Textile High School. She retired in 1945.

A learned and respected teacher, her politics prevented her employment as a college professor. Still, she managed to publish a number of books and articles related to socialist ideas and war. In 1911, her dissertation was published as *The Present Status of Socialism in America*. In 1916, she published *The Socialism of Today*, along with William English Walling and J. G. Phelps Stokes. These works were followed by *A Study of International Government* (1923), *What Is Socialism* (1928), *If We Should Be Invaded: Facing a Fantastic Hypothesis* (1940), and *Three Decades of War Resistance* (1942). In her writings, she offered compelling arguments in favor of socialist opposition to war as well as a strong defense of pacifism.

It was during World War I that Hughan began her lifelong dedication to pacifism. She initiated her personal struggle against war by establishing an organization for war opponents who had no traditional religious basis for their pacifist beliefs. Hughan joined Frances Witherspoon and Tracy Mygatt in forming a number of peace groups linking pacifism, Christianity, and socialist politics. Unlike other opponents of war, Hughan intellectually developed a sophisticated socialist-pacifist position. Prior to U.S. military intervention in World War I, she challenged prowar socialists, such as Graham Stokes. In 1915, she organized the Anti-Enlistment League. Operating out of her apartment, the league managed to enroll 3,500 men who signed a declaration against military enlistment. The league had hoped to gain enough signatures to prove the war's unpopularity and convince the Wilson administration not to become involved. Government pressure, along with seizure of the organization's files, quickly led to its demise, however. Because her antiwar activity preceded the nation's 1917 declaration of war, Hughan was not fired like other antiwar New York schoolteachers. Yet she was the victim of numerous attacks for her antiwar stance. In 1919, during the Red Scare, the Lusk Committee of the New York Legislature called on her to testify regarding her loyalty. The committee denied her the Certificate of Character and Loyalty because she had deliberately added the following words to the state's teacher's loyalty oath: "This obedience being qualified always by dictates of conscience" (Kennedy 1999, 39). That same year, the Senate Judiciary Committee, headed by Lee Overman, received a list of some sixty-two eminent citizens who were labeled as dangerous radicals. Among the names submitted were Jane Addams, Lillian D. Wald, Oswald Garrision Villard, and Hughan.

After the war, Hughan led a campaign to organize an active war resistance movement in the United States. In 1923, she successfully managed to secure approval from the peace groups Fellowship of Reconciliation, Women's Peace Society, and Women's Peace Union to endorse the creation of the War Resisters League (WRL). For years, she spearheaded the organization from her apartment in Brooklyn.

During the 1920s, she signed up numerous war resisters, delivered many speeches, and wrote pamphlets and tracts on the use of active nonviolence. She also organized various public protests against war and militarism, including some New York "NO More War" parades. In 1938, she helped found the United Pacifist Committee, a group created for the purpose of coordinating peace education and conscientious objectors. In 1940, after World War II began in Europe, she worked to defeat the conscription bill and established the Pacifist Teachers League when New York teachers were requested to register young men for the draft. She was one of the first war protestors to criticize the government's establishment of the Civilian Public Service Camps in which conscientious objectors who accepted civilian conscript labor worked without wages. During World War II, she persuaded the WRL to support all objectors to war, regardless of their feelings about conscription. She continued heading the league as secretary until 1945, when she became its honorary secretary. She continued serving on the WRL's executive committee until her death in her Manhattan apartment in 1955.

—*Charles F. Howlett*

See also Balch, Emily Green; McDowell, Mary Stone

References and Further Reading

Early, Frances H. 1995. "Revolutionary Pacifism and War Resistance: Jessie Wallace Hughan's 'War against War.'" In *Peace and Change* (July): 307–328.

———. 1997. *A World without War: How U.S. Feminists and Pacifists Resisted World War I.* Syracuse, NY: Syracuse University Press.

Hughan, Jessie Wallace. 1923. *A Study of International Government.* New York: Thomas and Crowell.

Kennedy, Kathleen. 1999. *Disloyal Mothers and Scurrilous Citizens: Women and Subversion during World War I.* Bloomington: Indiana University.

Hull, Peggy, pseud. (Deuell, Henrietta Eleanor Goodnough) (1889–1967)

The first female journalist accredited by the U.S. War Department and a founder of the Overseas Press Club. Henrietta Eleanor Goodnough was born in Kansas in 1889. An active child who always wanted to be somebody, Goodnough started her journalism career in Junction City, Kansas. She next worked in Denver, San Francisco, and Hawaii. She later moved to Minneapolis, changing her byline at this time to Peggy Hull.

In 1916, Hull moved to Cleveland to write an advertising column while running a shopping service. Wishing to report on the activities of the Ohio National Guard, she joined the Women's Auxiliary of the Guard when General John J. Pershing and his troops were being sent to the Mexican border. Hull traveled to Texas ahead of the unit as a freelancer and simultaneously pursued a busy social life. Once in Texas, she was hired by an El Paso newspaper. She accompanied the 20,000 men of the Tenth Division on a fifteen-day march in New Mexico, and in February 1917 she rode out to meet the soldiers, managing to be filmed riding with Pershing at the head of troops.

When the United States entered World War I in April 1917, the *El Paso Morning Times* agreed to send her to France, but the War Department did not consider the paper large enough to warrant an accredited reporter. She sailed anyway in June 1917, writing stories on her experiences while her acquaintance with Pershing helped her get access to the troops. As the articles she sent back to the United States gained popularity, other reporters complained, and she was recalled. In the summer of 1918, she was accredited and authorized to travel with the American Expeditionary Forces to Siberia, sponsored by the Newspaper Enterprise Association (NEA) and the *Cleveland* (Ohio) *Press.*

Peggy Hull. (Library of Congress)

Next Hull worked in Shanghai and was there in January 1932 when the city was attacked by the Japanese. She wrote about the Japanese attack on China for the *New York Daily News*. She was again accredited during World War II for the Pacific theater reporting from Hawaii, Guam, and other islands. She was awarded the U.S. Navy Commendation for her service writing about the ordinary day-to-day lives of the soldiers.

Hull was married to George Hull, John Kinley, and Harvey Deuell; the first two marriages ended in divorce and the third with the death of Deuell. She spent the last several years of her life in California and died of breast cancer on June 19, 1967.

—*Katherine Burger Johnson*

See also Chapelle, Dickey; Emerson, Gloria; Fallaci, Oriana; Higgins, Marguerite; Journalists, American Women, during World War I; Luce, Clare Boothe; Schuyler, Philippa; Trotta, Liz; Watts, Jean

References and Further Reading

Smith, Wilda M., and Eleanor A. Bogart. 1991. *The Wars of Peggy Hull: The Life and Times of a War Correspondent.* El Paso: Texas Western Press.

Hutton, Lady Isabel Galloway (née Isabel Emslie) (1887–1960)

Doctor and officer with the Scottish Women's Hospitals (SWH) in France and Serbia during World War I. Hutton received the Serbian Order of the White Eagle for her services.

After being turned away by the Royal Army Medical Corps, Dr. Isabel Hutton (née Emslie), a trained psychiatrist, accepted the position of assistant medical officer and pathologist with the SWH in 1915. Her unit, the Girton and Newnham Unit, established a tent hospital in Troyes, France. The members of her unit were sent to Ghevgeli, Serbia, in November 1915, where they worked for a few weeks until retreating to Salonika, Greece, in December 1915. Hutton was in the same SWH unit as Olive King and was also a friend of Flora Sandes.

In summer 1918, she was appointed as the chief medical officer of an SWH unit at Ostrovo, Greece, which moved to Vranja, Serbia, in October 1918. Her unit, although equipped with limited resources and staff, treated both the military and Serbian civilians. Her hospital remained in Vranja until October 1919. Hutton helped to establish local hospitals to replace the SWH hospital before it closed. She then assumed command over another unit in Belgrade. After her service with the SWH in Serbia ended in June 1920, Hutton worked briefly with Lady Muriel Paget's Child Welfare Scheme in the

Crimea. There she assumed the role of commanding medical officer at a hospital in Sebastopol. However, the hospital's work was cut short by the Russian Civil War. The Bolshevik advance in November 1920 forced the hospital to evacuate to Constantinople where Hutton led a campaign to assist Russian refugees.

During World War II, Hutton was stationed in India with her husband, Lord Hutton. There she directed the Indian Red Cross Welfare Service and chaired the Ladies' Advisory Committee of the Auxiliary Nursing Service.

—*Barbara Penny Kanner*

See also Haverfield, Evelina; Hodges, Katherine; Inglis, Elsie, and the Scottish Women's Hospitals; King, Olive; Sandes, Flora

References and Further Reading

Hutton, Isabel. 1928. *With a Women's Unit in Serbia, Salonika and Sebastopol.* London: Williams and Norgate.

Kanner, Barbara Penny. 1997. *Women in Context.* New York: G. K. Hall.

I

Ibárruri, Dolores (La Pasionaria) (1895–1989)

Symbol of antifascist Spanish womanhood both during and after the Spanish Civil War (1936–1939). A committed member of the Spanish Communist Party, Dolores Ibárruri opposed nationalist forces led by General Francisco Franco and supported the republic, the existing government. Following the 1939 defeat of the republican forces, Ibárruri went into exile and continued to struggle for an end to the Franco dictatorship. She is known as *La Pasionaria* because of her fiery, eloquent oratory in defense of the republic and the Communist movement.

Dolores Ibárruri was born to a family of modest means in the northern Basque region of Spain. She grew up at a time when the mining, iron, steel, and textile industries were developing in the region. These industries created new sources of employment and transformed peasants into workers. Many of these workers joined working-class movements and identified with the ideals and demands of the Communist Party (CP) that were gaining popularity in Spain. Ibárruri joined the CP in the 1920s, and from that time she dedicated her life to the party and to building a world based on Communist ideals. She rose rapidly in the ranks of the CP. In 1930, she was elected to the central committee, the main leadership body of the party. In 1932, she headed the party's Women's Commission. What catapulted her to national prominence and international renown, however, was her role in the Spanish Civil War.

During the civil war, Ibárruri distinguished herself through her stirring speeches in defense of the republic and in opposition to the forces of General Francisco Franco. Following the June 1936 revolt of the Franco forces, she took to the airwaves of Madrid and uttered her famous call to the Spanish people: "No pasarán!" (They shall not pass) and coined the heroic phrase, "It is better to die on your feet than live on your knees" (Thomas 1961, 140). For most of the war, she did not call on Spanish women to renounce their roles as mothers and take up arms. Instead, she urged the mothers of Spain to support their sons who were fighting for the republic.

When the republican forces lost the war in 1939, she went into exile but not inactivity. In 1942, she was elected secretary general of the Communist Party. After Franco's death in 1975, she returned to Spain and was elected as a deputy in the parliament. She published numerous books, including her autobiography, *Memorias de Dolores Ibárruri.*

Her affective life was not as successful as her political life, perhaps because she usually prioritized the latter. Her marriage to Julián Ruiz, a leader in the Communist Party, was not a happy one. Three of her daughters died in infancy, and her son died at the siege of Stalingrad. The CP disapproved of her relationship with a male Communist Party member seventeen years her junior, and when the party asked her to end the relationship, she did.

—*Margaret Power*

See also Spanish Civil War, Women and the

References and Further Reading

García-Nieto Paris, Carmen, ed. 1992. *El único camino.* Madrid: Editorial Castalia, Instituto de la Mujer.

Ibárruri, Dolores. 1985. *Memorias de Dolores Ibárruri.* Barcelona: Planeta.

Thomas, Hugh. 1961. *The Spanish Civil War.* New York: Harper.

IL-2

See Pilots of IL-2

India to 1857, Women Warriors in

Dramatic role of women warriors in Indian history. When Alexander the Great moved on India in 326 B.C., he was challenged at the Battle of Hydaspes by King Porus. One of Porus's commanders was reputedly a woman, Masaga. Masaga was not the first woman warrior from the subcontinent celebrated in Indian tradition and legend. Two centuries earlier, Nayanika was the queen and military leader of the Satavahana Empire located in the south central portion of today's India. The practice of women serving as warriors was strong and persistent in the south. The Nayars of Malabar consistently maintained a small force of women fighters. Sugala of Sri Lanka is remembered as "Sugala the rebel queen fearless" (Jones 1997, 42). In 1240, Raziyya, the female ruler of Delhi, was killed in battle. Queen Karnavatti of Chitor, at the end of a long defensive effort, is said to have had a great fire set. She "exhorted her maidens and the wives and daughters of the citizens to be of good cheer, for it was better to die by the hands of their brethren than to become the slaves and mistresses of their enemies" (Pool 1954, 73–74). Attired in her armor, she walked into the fire to avoid capitulation and capture. Her example was then voluntarily followed by her female officers and 13,000 females from the besieged city (Pool 1954, 73). Karnavatti thus imitated Princess Korumdevi of Aureent, who, upon the death of her beloved husband in single combat, severed her right arm bearing her marriage jewels and sent it to her father-in-law, before immolating herself on a funeral pyre.

Queen Durgautti (Durgawati) of Gurrah (Gondwana) in Hindustan was a remarkable military figure. She successfully led 1,500 war elephants and 6,000 horsemen against Asaf Khan, a Mogul. In a 1564 rematch, Asaf Khan added artillery to his retinue. When Durgautti's son was killed, her forces wavered. Durgautti, enraged, charged forward on her war elephant. Her valor rallied her forces against the Muslims, but she was reputedly struck in the eye by an arrow. She broke off the staff and continued her attack until she was struck by another arrow. Unwilling to be taken alive by the enemy, Durgautti ordered her driver to kill her. He was unwilling to kill his commander, so she took a dagger and killed herself. In the early seventeenth century, Durgautti's valor was replicated in Queen Nur Jehan, who went into battle against Mohabat Khan. Recklessly charging the enemy on the back of her war elephant, she poured down arrows with deadly effect. The battle, however, was lost when her driver was killed and her wounded elephant bolted.

Rani of Jhansi, Lakshimi Bai, who opposed the British and was killed in battle in 1858. Watercolor from Kalighat, India. (Victoria and Albert Museum/Art Resource)

During the early eighteenth century, women of the Maratha caste fought enthusiastically against the Mogul Aurangzeb and then the British. Tarabai confounded the efforts of both Aurangzeb and a usurper who was sent by Aurangzeb's successor Azim Shag to undermine her rule. A contemporary who observed Tarabai in battle recounted, "Tara Bae did wonders that day, and was admired by all beholders, and men found it difficult to believe that the strong arm which sent them reeling from the saddle was that of a lady" (Pool 1954, 147).

Postindependence India celebrated a number of Indian women warriors who fought against the British in the nineteenth century. Kittur Rani Chennamma (1778–1829) fought the British, who had rejected her choice of an adopted son as successor in Belgaum in Karnataka. She fought but was defeated and died a prisoner in Bailhongal Fort. Lakshmi Bai, rani of Jhansi (1834–1858), after the death of her only son, also wished to have an adopted son succeed to the throne. The British, who wished to annex Jhansi to the British-controlled Raj, objected. Lakshmi Bai fought courageously but was killed in battle on June 18, 1858. Rani Avantibai fought the British when they refused to allow her to succeed her husband as the ruler of Ramgarh. In the midst of a battle on March 20, 1858, when the defeat of her forces seemed inevitable, she killed herself with her sword.

Hazrat Mahal, the Muslim regent of Oudh, was a formidable opponent of the British. For a year in 1857, the army she led prevented the British from taking the city of Lucknow. A contemporary British reporter, W. H. Russell, offered his assessment of her, which can be generalized into a broader view of Asian women who resisted the European imperialists. He wrote that Hazrat Mahal was "one of those tigress women, more virile than their husbands, who when finding themselves in a position to gratify their lust for power, have played a considerable part in Oriental history" (Salmonson 1991, 5).

—Bernard Cook

See also Lakshmi Bai and Sepoy Rebellion

References and Further Reading

Great Women of India, http://www.geocities.com/dakshina_kan_pa/art31/women1.htm (accessed March 24, 2004).

Jones, David E. 1997. *Women Warriors: A History.* Washington, DC: Brassey's.

Pool, John J. 1954. *Famous Women of India.* Calcutta: Susil-Gupta.

Salmonson, Amanda. 1991. *Encyclopedia of Amazons.* New York: Paragon House.

Inglis, Elsie (1864–1917), and the Scottish Women's Hospitals

Pioneering doctor and suffragist, founder of the Scottish Women's Hospitals (SWH), an organization that evolved from within the suffrage movement and provided medical assistance in Europe, particularly in Serbia, during World War I. Elsie Inglis was born in India in 1863. Her family moved to Edinburgh after her father retired in 1878. She was one of the first women in Scotland to study medicine. She moved to London and taught at the New Hospital for Women, a teaching hospital run by women for women, which had been established by another pioneer, Elizabeth Garrett Anderson, the first English woman doctor (unless one counts Dr. "James" Barry). When Inglis returned to Edinburgh, she followed Anderson's example and established a women's hospital with an all-female staff. By now a committed and dedicated suffragist and member of the National Union of Women's Suffrage Societies (NUWSS), Inglis was an important force behind the setting up of

Dr. Elsie Inglis

"My good lady, go home and sit still."

Quote from British War Office Official to Dr. Elsie Inglis when she proposed to send a field hospital totally staffed by women to the battle front.

—Monica Krippner,
The Quality of Mercy: Women at War, Serbia 1915–18
(London: David and Charles, 1980), 30.

Ambulance Drivers of the Scottish Women's Hospitals on the Serbian Front

"Miss Bedford, who had joined at Ostrovo with Dr. Cooper from Australia, was in charge of the cars, and a hard worker she proved. Owing to her great efforts to keep the cars on the road by begging or borrowing spare parts from all and sundry, she became known among the M.T. [motor transport] as far down as Salonika way as 'Miss Spare Parts,' and I fancy she earned the cognomen all right.

" . . . The road up to Gornicevo was an extraordinary track to take an ambulance car, even a Ford one, when we first made its acquaintance. And, mind you, all the ambulances were driven by the girl chauffeurs. After leaving Ostrovo village the tracks run . . . along the north edge of Lake Ostrovo, nearly two miles of deep sand furrowed by some dozen or more deep parallel ruts which went in and out of deeper holes and gullies in which the car more often than not stuck and had to be pushed out by main force. You could take your choice between the pairs of ruts, but whichever pair you picked out invariably appeared the worst. Then the climb up the mountain by the rocky track began, and though subsequently improved it remained a rocky track for most of the way, plentifully bestrewn with boulders and projecting rocky masses. In many places two cars could only just pass on the track with little to spare, and as the journey was usually made midst innumerable transport, horses, mules, carts, ammunition caissons, often with teams of eight horses, men mounted and afoot, and cars of all sorts and conditions in long convoys, the arduous nature of the journey can be dimly imagined. The cars boiled, literally boiled, going up, and for this reason alone had to be stopped several times to cool down; and the boiling usually upset the oiling, and the cars wouldn't restart. But if going up was a difficult and appallingly bumpy business, the coming down was worse. No Ford car brakes which are necessarily a new organization, the Scottish Women's Suffrage Federation (SWSF), and she took on the role of honorary secretary.

In 1914 when war broke out in Europe, Inglis offered her services and that of her trained staff as medical units on the western front. She was told by the War Office "to go home and be still." Far from taking the advice, Inglis formed the SWH with financial assistance from a number of organizations, in particular, the NUWSS. The suffragists were determined to show the British government and society in general that women, too, had a valuable contribution to make to the war effort. Having been denied a role with the British army, Inglis redirected her offer of help to the French and Serbian governments. Both governments accepted the offer, and three months later the SWH dispatched an all-female medical unit to Royaumont Abbey, 35 kilometers north of Paris, the first such unit ever to be sent to a war zone. The abbey, owned by Jules Edouard Goüin, was temporarily given over to the SWH, which established a 200-bed auxiliary hospital. It was in Serbia, however, that the SWH had its greatest impact and where it developed its strongest loyalties.

light would hold on these mountainous tracks. The cars bumped down, now heeling over on one side, now on the other, as wheels jolted over great masses of rock or boulders it was impossible to avoid, and on the steep slopes on many a journey the reverse was the only method of preventing the car taking charge when the brakes became functionless—and this with two badly wounded men on the stretchers behind. . . .

"I should never have thought it possible that cars could negotiate such tracks. . . . We got into the habit of carrying a few heavy rocks on the foot-board. As soon as the car stopped the passenger had to hop out, seize the biggest piece of rock, and get it under the wheel of the slowly slipping car. . . . This, be it remembered, with a steep slope or precipice to go over if the driver failed to keep an open eye backwards, or the passenger was not smart enough with his props. . . . That we did not have serious accidents is due as much as anything to the skillful driving and extraordinary coolness of the girl drivers.

" . . . An ambulance going up to the dressing station got off its wheels on a large rock mass and fell over on its side. Riddell, of the R.A.M.C., who was with the driver, Miss Green, was shot out and rolled down the slope, being pulled up by a rock. He picked himself up, gave himself a shake, and finding he was not dead, climbed up to see what had happened to car and girl. The car lay on its side, the wheels still revolving, and the girl still clinging to her wheel, also lying on her side. The engine was stopped, the driver hauled out and stood on her feet, and the first thing those two did was to swear at each other because, though each had a camera, neither had thought of taking a photograph before she had been hauled out!

" . . . On the way back the driver came across an ambulance which had broken down. After spending some time in futile efforts to start it she offered to take over the wounded—luckily there were only two—but she already had three. Night had fallen long before she restarted, and she was alone. Her drive down that mountain track was very nervy work. But she stuck to it and eventually got back to the camp at 11 P.M. She had brought down seven wounded men that day (the ambulances only hold two lying-down cases or three sitting), and brought them down the Drina. It was a marvelous plucky feat. Her name is Miss Wardel."

—E. P. Stebbing, *At the Serbian Front in Macedonia*
(London: John Lane, The Bodley Head, 1917),
Pages 151, 158–159, 160, 162–163, 165.

The role of the independent SWH in Serbia during the war was curious and unique. SWH medical units effectively attached themselves to the Serbian army; some medical personnel remained with the army for most of the war and during many of the major campaigns, including the retreat through Albania and the return to the Salonica front in 1916. The first SWH medical units arrived in Serbia at the end of December 1914 and set up a surgical hospital in the historic city of Kragujevatz. The most immediate and pressing concerns for the SWH were not injuries from the battlefields but a typhus epidemic that swept through Serbia and killed tens of thousands. The exact number of deaths is unknown, but Inglis claimed that "of the 425 doctors in Serbia, 125 died of the disease, and two-thirds of the remainder had it" (Inglis 2000, 264). The SWH organizing committee quickly dispatched urgently needed medical supplies and personnel. It took three months to bring the typhus under control, and in that time 12 members of the SWH became ill and 3 died from the highly infectious disease. In addition to Kragujevatz, 2 other medical hospitals were established by the SWH at Valjevo and Mladenovatz.

By the spring of 1915, Inglis herself was in Serbia. The three SWH establishments were functioning well, and further help had been extended by the SWH, which was now providing medical units to staff Serbian hospitals as well as staffing frontline dressing stations and field hospitals. In anticipation of an expected renewed campaign by the enemy Inglis ensured that all of the units were capable of performing surgical work. From October 1915, what followed was a complex story of advances by the Germans, Austrians, and Bulgarians, desperate retreats by the Serbians, notably through Albania, and the steadfast support of the SWH medical units throughout. Members of the SWH joined with the Serbian army and the vast numbers of ordinary Serbs fleeing in the face of enemy occupation through the frozen mountains of Albania, the SWH providing as much medical support along the way as they could. Two medical units headed by Dr. Holloway and Inglis were in the Serbian hospital in Kragujevatz when the Germans arrived and took over the town. They established a camp for Serbian prisoners of war near the hospital, and those who were wounded were hospitalized by the SWH. As the injured Serbians recovered, the services of the SWH doctors and nurses were no longer required, so the German arrested them and took them to enemy-controlled Belgrade. Eventually through the offices of the U.S. ambassador, all the medical staff were released and sent back to Britain.

In 1917, Inglis and seventy-five other seasoned veterans once more returned to provide medical support to the Serbian army, this time on the eastern front. The Russian Revolution in 1917 caused the withdrawal of the Russian army from the war and left the remnants of the Serbian army exposed and almost friendless. Through the efforts of Inglis, the British government was persuaded to evacuate the Serbian soldiers to England. Inglis had become seriously ill but would not leave for home ahead of the Serbian troops. When they were evacuated from Archangel on board British naval ships, she joined them on the journey. Sadly, notwithstanding the attentions of doctors, she died one day after arriving back in Newcastle-upon-Tyne in November 1917.

Despite losing their inspirational leader, the women of the SWH continued their dedicated work until the end of the war. During the hostilities, fourteen SWH medical units had operated in seven countries, but it was the Serbian people with whom a special bond was formed. After the war, members of the SWH helped in the recovery of the country through personal service and fund-raising efforts. In memory of Inglis's life and work, the Elsie Inglis Memorial Maternity Hospital was opened in 1925 in Edinburgh using the surplus funds from the SWH. It remained part of the Scottish health system until it closed in 1988.

—*Susan R. Allan*

See also Haverfield, Evelina; Hodges, Katherine; Hutton, Lady Isabel Galloway; King, Olive; Sandes, Flora; Stobart, Mabel

References and Further Reading

Inglis, Elsie. 2000. "The Tragedy of Serbia." In *Women's Writing of the First World War: An Anthology*, edited by Angela K. Smith, 262–270. Manchester, England: Manchester University Press.

Leneman, Leah. 1994. *In the Service of Life: The Story of Elsie Inglis and the Scottish Women's Hospitals.* Edinburgh: Mercat.

McLaren, Eva Shaw, ed. 1919. *History of the Scottish Women's Hospitals.* London: Hodder and Stoughton.

Ross, Ishobel, 1988. *Little Grey Partridge: First World War Diary of Ishobel Ross Who Served with the Scottish Women's Hospital's Unit in Serbia.* Aberdeen, Scotland: University Press.

International Congress of Women: Antiwar Protest of Women in World War I

Effort of women opponents of war to mobilize opposition to war during World War I. The year 1915 was not a terribly propitious moment to organize an international women's peace movement. For nearly nine months, Europeans had been locked in a murderous war that had already left hundreds of thousands of men dead on the battlefields. On both sides of enemy lines, governments demanded that their citizens rally behind the fatherland. Women, who in most of Europe and North America had little say in political matters, were expected to contribute morally and economically to the war effort. In belligerent countries, freedom of speech was or soon would be seriously curtailed. The fight for women's rights was put on the back burner.

None of these hurdles prevented Dr. Aletta Jacobs, a prominent Dutch suffragist, from appealing to feminists from across Europe and North America to gather together at The Hague to protest the war raging around them. Her invitation was not always well received. Neither the Russian nor the French suffrage societies elected to send any delegates. The French were particularly strident in their refusal, asking, "How would it be possible for us, given the current conditions, to meet with the women of enemy countries? . . . Have they disavowed the political crimes of their governments?" (Report of the International Congress of Women, 28 April–1 May, 1915, The Hague, WILPF, WHC). Women from other countries struggled to obtain the visas necessary to travel. For three days, the British government prevented the U.S. delegation from crossing the English Channel, nearly causing them to miss the meeting altogether. Despite these hurdles, on April 28, 1915, an International Congress of Women convened; 1,136 delegates from 12 nations, neutral and belligerent, were in attendance (Bussey and Tims 1980, 19).

The participants ensured that both women's rights and international peace would remain the core objectives of the congress. Indeed, the delegates saw the two as inextricably intertwined, as they explained, "The International Congress of Women is convinced that one of the strongest forces for the prevention of war will be the combined influence of women of all countries. But as women can only make their influence effective if they have equal political rights with men, this Congress declares that it is the duty of women of all countries to work with all their force for their political enfranchisement" (cited in Alonso 1993, 68). To promote these ends, the congress founded a new organization, the International Committee of Women for Permanent Peace (ICWPP), and it elected the prominent U.S. social activist Jane Addams as its first international president. The congress also agreed to send envoys to meet with the leaders of the major European governments to pressure them into publicizing their terms for peace. Finally, the delegates insisted that women should have a voice when it came to drawing up an eventual peace treaty, and they agreed to reconvene wherever and whenever such a settlement was to be drafted.

For the remaining years of World War I, members of the ICWPP struggled to carry out their pacifist and feminist agenda in a persistently hostile environment. The organization's envoys did gain an audience with many of the major belligerent and neutral powers. President Woodrow Wilson of the United States was reported to have been particularly impressed by the resolutions brought to him by Jane Addams (Bussey and Tims 1980, 21). In the meantime, members returned to their respective nations and attempted to build support for a negotiated settlement to the war. In the United States, the Women's Peace Party, founded in 1915, took up the charge, although the U.S. entry into the war led to divisions in the organization, particularly over the appropriateness of women's war relief work. English members concentrated their efforts on pacifist education in cooperation with other liberal pacifist organizations in their country. In Germany ICWPP members marked the second anniversary of the 1915 congress by sending the Kaiser a declaration of war aims and a call for peace without annexation.

French suffrage societies had declined to send any delegates to The Hague in 1915, but almost as soon as the congress ended, several prominent feminists, including the labor activist Gabrielle Duchêne, broke with the mainstream and founded a French section of the ICWPP. Before the end of the year, the group published a pamphlet titled *An Urgent Duty for Women* asking their female compatriots, "Does our responsibility end with charitable activity and hero worship? . . . Can we truly answer that we are not interested in the future and that the war will end of its own accord?" (*Un Devoir urgent pour les femmes*). The brochure went on to demand that members of the French legislature make known their terms for peace. The police responded by confiscating the French section's papers and threatening those members who did not keep silent with imprisonment.

When World War I ended in November 1918, the leadership of the ICWPP began to prepare for a second international meeting. The decision of the Allied powers to base the peace conference in Paris posed a dilemma. For the ICWPP to follow through with its original plan to meet concurrently with the peace talks would mean that Central European members would not be able to attend. The organization therefore located the conference in neutral Switzerland. Delegates from sixteen nations gathered in Zurich from May 12 to 19, 1919. Great Britain, Germany, and the United States were represented in the largest numbers. Although the French government refused to issue visas to ICWPP members, two French women managed to cross the border. A third French delegate, Jeanne Mélin from the war-torn region of the Ardennes, secured a visa just in time to arrive for the last day of the congress. By coincidence, she walked into the hall just as one of the German delegates, Lida Gustav Heymann, was addressing the gathering. The delegates greeted the unexpected arrival of the French woman with a resounding ovation, and Heymann spontaneously grabbed a bouquet of flowers from the stage to offer to her French counterpart. Mélin took the podium and responded, "I, a French woman of an invaded country affirm that we women never wanted a war that was possible only because we were denied our political rights and continued only because we did not have the power to stop it. I offer my hand to my German sisters; together we will work, henceforth, not against man, but for him" (Compte rendue de la Conférence Internationale des Femmes, WILPF, WHC). Deeply moved, the entire delegation of women rose in response, pledging to work tirelessly against war.

Before adjourning the delegates at the Zurich congress passed a series of resolutions opposing the ongoing blockade of Germany, protesting against the injustices of the Versailles Treaty, offering their qualified support to a new League of Nations, and laying the foundations for a permanent women's international peace organization, henceforth to be known by the name Women's International League for Peace and Freedom (WILPF). The WILPF, which continues to exist today, became the most enduring legacy of women's peace activism during World War I.

—*Mona L. Siegel*

See also Addams, Jane; Balch, Emily Green; International Manifesto of Women

References and Further Reading

Alonso, Harriet Hyman. 1993. *Peace as a Women's Issue: A History of the U.S. Movement for World Peace and Women's Rights.* Syracuse, NY: Syracuse University.

Bussey, Gertrude, and Margaret Tims. 1980. *Pioneers for Peace: Women's International League for Peace and Freedom, 1915–1965.* Geneva: WILPF, 1980.

Section française du Comité International des Femmes pour la Paix Permanente. 1985. *Un Devoir urgent pour les femmes.* Reprinted in *Le Mouvement ouvrier français contre la guerre.* Vol. 2, *L'Opposition des femmes, 1914–1918.* Paris: Edition Edhis, 1985.

Women's International League for Peace and Freedom Papers, Western Historical Collections, Norlin Library, University of Colorado, Boulder (cited as WILPF, WHC).

International Manifesto of Women (1915)

Proposal for peace issued by the International Congress of Women (ICW) at The Hague, Netherlands, in April 1915. Representing the views of 1,200 women from 12 countries, the International Manifesto of Women called on the governments of Europe and the president of the United States, Woodrow Wilson, to negotiate a democratic and nonviolent end to World War I. The manifesto, created by Aletta Jacobs (Netherlands), Chrystal Macmillan (Great Britain), Rosika Schwimmer (Austria-Hungary), Emily G. Balch (United States), and Jane Addams (United States), proposed a permanent peace settlement based on principles of justice, democracy, and international cooperation; offered guidelines for diplomatic negotiations among hostile nations; and endorsed political equality for women in all nations.

The ICW convened to protest the horror and destruction caused by warfare, especially for women. The manifesto first commiserated with those who suffered under the burden of war and then identified common ideals of justice and autonomy on which a peace settlement could rest. According to the manifesto, a conference of neutral nations was needed to mediate between belligerent nations to facilitate a peaceful end to international hostilities.

The manifesto further delineated five principles of permanent peace, resolving that (1) nationality and the people's right to self-government must be respected; (2) governments must agree to bring disputes among nations to international arbitration and conciliation; (3) governments of all nations must agree to bring great social, economic, and moral pressure against any country that ignores international arbitration and conciliation and resorts to war; (4) foreign politics must be placed under democratic control, on the premise that war does not come from the masses but rather from small groups pursuing specific interests; and (5) women in all countries must have political equality (through both suffrage and active participation in government), on the premise that women do not seek war.

For countries to achieve the goal of international cooperation, the manifesto recommended that a Society of Nations create a permanent International Court of Justice to interpret treaty rights and the law of nations. A permanent International Conference would be convened regularly to enforce principles of equity, justice, and good will and to offer practical suggestions to maintain cooperation among nations. A permanent Council of Conciliation and Investigation would settle international issues resulting from expanding commercial and economic interests. The ICW further advocated the general disarmament of nations, open trade among nations, the abolition of all secret treaties, and the education of all children worldwide. Finally, the manifesto demanded that women be included at the peace conference and in all subsequent diplomatic conferences to avert the threat of war.

The ICW sent two delegations to visit leaders of neutral and belligerent nations, including England, Germany, Austria-Hungary, Italy, France, Sweden, Denmark, Russia, the Netherlands, and Switzerland. Jane Addams, the first president of the International Committee of Women for Permanent Peace and future Noble Peace Prize laureate, visited President Wilson six times in 1915 to persuade him to mediate peace, a futile effort given that the United States entered the war in 1917. Nevertheless, the manifesto's guidelines for peace and diplomacy may have helped shape Wilson's Fourteen Points (including the construction of the League of Nations) and the terms of the postwar peace settlement.

—*Susanna Calkins*

See also Addams Jane; Balch, Emily Green; International Congress of Women: Antiwar Protest of Women in World War I

References and Further Reading

Addams, Jane, Emily G. Balch, and Alice Hamilton. 2003. *Women at the Hague: The International Peace Congress of 1915*. Amherst, MA: Humanity Books.

Alonso, Harriet Hyman. 1995. "Nobel Peace Laureates, Jane Addams and Emily Greene Balch: Two Women of the Women's International League for Peace and Freedom." In *Journal of Women's History* 7: 6–26.

Iran-Iraq War and Gulf War, Impact on Women of Iraq

Impact of two twentieth-century conflicts on Iraqi women. From 1979 to 2003 Saddam Hussein influenced the lives of Iraqi women through his actions, dictates, and policies. The Iran-Iraq War (1980–1988) compelled women to leave their kitchens to take jobs in the public arena left vacant by the hundreds of thousands of Iraqi men who went off to war. During the Gulf War (1990–1991), Iraqi women supported their country by taking part in political, social, and military actions. Iraq's women were particularly affected by the sanctions imposed on their country by the United Nations following the Gulf War. Throughout all of this, Hussein tried to establish his own popular cult by targeting Iraq's women for support.

The Hussein regime afforded rights and opportunities to Iraqi women seldom seen in the Middle East, such as the right to vote and gender equality in the workplace. The Iraqi government launched an aggressive literacy campaign targeting rural women. Furthermore, all education (through college) was paid for by the state, and thus university degrees became the rule not the exception for Iraq's women. The government encouraged women who needed or sought specialized training or degrees not offered in Iraq to seek and obtain scholarships and grants to attend school abroad. Unlike women in Saudi Arabia and other Gulf states who were segregated from men throughout their academic careers, Iraqi men and women learned side by side from elementary school through their university training. With education came employment. With more and more Iraqi women during the Hussein regime gaining college degrees and obtaining employment, Iraqi women started to postpone marriages until their middle to late twenties. Furthermore, family sizes tended to be much smaller among educated Iraqi women. Finally, the *abaiya,* or veil, became almost extinct among Iraq's women (Ward 1990, A13).

Hussein successfully created a personality cult in the hearts and minds of many Iraqi women, such as Sagidah al-Mousawi, who referred to the Iraqi leader not as a mere leader but rather as a member of the family: "He is a friend and a model, a dear house, a son. Saddam is a heart, a lighted candle, a memory, a tear, a land and people, pure water and roses. Saddam is all of Iraq" (Sachs 1990b, A1).

At a solidarity meeting in Baghdad sponsored by the Iraqi Women's Federation in October 1990, the Iraqi poet Sagidah al-Mousawi proclaimed, "Saddam is an era that overshadows all other eras. Saddam is like a river that flows with goodness between fire and light. Saddam is our key to paradise" (Sachs 1990a). Her poetry emphasizes the decades-long secularization and modernization campaigns of the Baath government in general and Saddam Hussein in particular in which gender barriers to education, employment, and salary discrimination came to an end and Iraqi women enjoyed benefits such as state-supported maternity and child health care.

Hussein routinely praised women in his speeches, rarely even using the word *women* without some qualifier such as beloved, honored, noble, or martyr. A physical example of Hussein's enshrinement of women was the Martyrs Museum. One of the exhibits was called "The Martyr Bride of Mendela," a woman who allegedly died (along with her husband) on her wedding night when her house was blown up by an Iranian missile attack in the 1980s. Her wedding dress and shoes were part of the display along with other personal possessions. A statue of the woman had her rising presumably to heaven with arms outstretched (Sachs 1990b, A1).

Before Hussein took power in 1979, the Iraqi government had a history of spending its petrodollars on social programs and on the infrastructure of Iraq's major cities, such as Baghdad. Even though there were intermittent material shortages during the eight years of warfare between Iran and Iraq, most Iraqis seemed to be happy. According to Manal Yunis, head of the General Union of Iraqi Women (GUIW), "The kind of experience we have had here, with services and a higher standard of living, isn't like the shah's modernization. We haven't built up our industrial base while neglecting our human resources" (Ibrahim 1984).

The wars propelled many Iraqi women into the public sector workforce. According to Yunis, approximately 70 percent of women living in Baghdad were working in industries such as banking, airlines, and even the government (Ibrahim 1984). The GUIW, which was also known as the General Federation of Iraqi Women, was established by the Baath Party shortly after it took over Iraq in the late 1960s and had been controlled by the government ever since. Publicly the GUIW supported the war because it saw it as an opportunity for Iraq's women to gain economic equality. By 1985, women made up approximately 30 percent of Iraq's workforce in the public sector. Before the Hussein government outlawed sex discrimination in education and employment, women comprised only 7 percent of the public workforce (*Seattle Times* 1985). According to Suhaila Khazal, a 28-year-old bottling factory worker in Basra, she not only enjoyed the opportunity to work outside of the home during the 8-year war, but she had no plans to give up her job once the war was over. For her and many other Iraqi women, the Iran-Iraq War provided them with the opportunity to become equal members of Iraqi society not only by working in the public sector but also by showing Iraq's men that women were as patriotic and capable as men: "There are no differences between men and women in this factory," Khazal said, adding that her coworkers did not "treat me any differently just because I'm a woman" (*Seattle Times* 1985).

War was not always portrayed as a blessing for women, however. In 1985 at the United Nations Decade for Women conference in Nairobi, Kenya, Iraqi women called on their Iranian counterparts to help bring an end to the war, arguing that war was a gender-specific agent. The GUIW leader, Manal Yunis, said that "the woman is the first loser in war. . . . The woman is the first beneficiary of security and stability"

("Different Roles Seen" 1985, 10). According to her neighbors in the urban, upscale Baghdad neighborhood of Yarmouk, Yunis possibly fled the country seventy-two hours before the U.S. forces entered Baghdad in 2003, possibly because of her ties to the Baath Party (Shahin 2003, 18).

Some Iraqi women, such as Suhayla Salman, Aliya Talib, and Lutifiya al-Dulaymi, did manage to protest the war through state-sponsored publications. For example, Salman rejected the genderization of the war in which Hussein asked Iraqi women to produce at least five children each, calling those who did Patriotic Mothers. Talib's articles satirized Iraqi notions of the aggressive male and passive female by alluding that these outdated belief systems both allowed the war to begin and prevented a peaceful end. In her 1988 novel *Seeds of Fire,* the pro-Baathist al-Dulaymi suggested that at the heart of Iraqi experience beats a totalitarian society in which women are second-class citizens (Cooke 1995, 159–160). Nevertheless, women who lost a son in the war were honored with the title Martyr Mothers and were routinely given gifts and praise from government officials. The Iraqi government institutionalized the ultimate sacrifices of women by giving the wife or mother of every soldier killed in the Iran-Iraq war a house, a car, and a pension for the rest of her life (Sachs 1990b, A1).

Iraqi women performed many roles during the Gulf War. They were also severely affected by the popular uprising that came on the heels of the United States–led victory in 1991. Women, just like men, were mobilized before the Iraqi invasion of Kuwait in the summer of 1990. Technically, all positions in the Iraqi military were open to women, including combat roles; however, there is no evidence to suggest that Iraqi women took part in the actual invasion force. Hussein called them the *mujahedat,* or female holy warriors. In a national radio address shortly after Iraq invaded Kuwait, Hussein, who referred to Iraqi women as "glorious," called on women to do their part to support the war effort by conserving food and energy. Shortly thereafter, some Iraqi women began protesting in front of the U.S. embassy in Baghdad, carrying signs that read "We are with you, Saddam, until the very last drop of blood!" (Chong 1990, 28A).

Iraqi men were drafted into the army while women were volunteers. None of the volunteers were trained in combat arms; however, some of the volunteers created their own home guard units. Nevertheless, many Iraqi women saw it as their patriotic duty to send their sons into the conflict—even women who had lost sons in the Iran-Iraq War, such as Najiba Elias Toma. Toma's youngest son died during the early stages of the Iran-Iraq War, and even though her eldest son completed his military service one year before the Iraqi invasion of Kuwait, she supported his return to active duty. "He's defending his country," she said (Sachs 1990b, A1).

Four months after the Iraqi invasion, some Iraqi women began seeking a peaceful end to the conflict. On December 27, they carried signs denouncing the United Nations sanctions in general and U.S. President George H.W. Bush's decision in particular to prohibit a small flotilla of humanitarian aid from reaching Iraq. The ship, the *Ibn Khaldun,* departed Algiers carrying sugar, rice, milk, and medical supplies as well as 250 female peace activists from all over the world. The delivery was organized by the Arab Women's Union. The protests in front of the U.S. embassy were an almost daily occurrence for weeks. Thousands upon thousands of Iraqi women marched, carrying signs that read "Yes for Peace, No for War" and "Saddam's Iraq Will Burn Bush and His Filthy Gang" (Reuters 1990).

Iraqi women in exile were divided with regard to the Gulf War. "I will never defend Hussein as long as I live," reported one Iraqi exile living in London during the war. Many Iraqi women living in Great Britain told stories of the regime's brutality against Christians, Shiites, Kurds, and anyone who spoke out against the regime. Many others questioned the reaction of the United States to the Iraqi invasion of Kuwait. A woman named Parwin, a Kurdish Iraqi from Suleymania, asked why the world did nothing to stop the

Israeli treatment of Palestinians while it is willing to come to Kuwait's rescue? She also believed that both the Israeli and Iraqi governments should be tried for crimes against humanity for their equally brutal and inhumane treatment of people. Other Iraqi women living in exile were concerned that the United States–led attacks were destroying Iraq's history through the bombing of sites such as the Defense Ministry and the National Museum (Hazelton 1991, 32).

Shortly after the end of hostilities, President Bush openly called for the people of Iraq to rise up and rid their country of Saddam Hussein and his regime. Many did. In southern Iraq, anti-Baathists launched a rebellion, but there was no support from the United States or any member of the coalition that pushed the Iraqi army out of Kuwait. In late March 1991, the Iraqi government initiated a counteroffensive. The Iraqi army massacred a large number of women and children in and around the southern Iraqi city of Suk as-Shuyukh. An unknown number of women became the heads of their households when the army began rounding up and killing all males over the age of fifteen.

The United Nations–imposed sanctions against Iraq (such as prohibitions on the importation of food, medicine, and technology) between 1990 and 2003 had particularly negative effects upon Iraq's women. More Iraqi women than ever before had become de facto heads of households when their husbands or fathers left in search of work overseas. Consequently, the divorce rate increased. Prior to 1990, rural women were making great strides in education and were entering the workforce. The Iran-Iraq War in particular was the springboard for rural women to leave behind the economic realities of the countryside. Because inflation outstripped the government's capacity to pay its civil servants, however, women began leaving their state jobs and returning to the family farms. In 1999, the female civil servants' monthly salary was approximately one-tenth of the price of a new pair of dress shoes (Halliday 1999, 34). For many Iraqi women who had already sold their possessions—homes, land, furniture, clothes, and books—the only source of income, the only way to put food on the table, was through prostitution.

Professional women were also pushed out of their positions to make room for men. Many were able to obtain work in sweatshops. Younger women all but gave up the dream of getting married. Instead, they had to work to help support their nuclear families. As a result of the sanctions, the Iraqi government ended its decades-long subsidies for education, health care, and the support of children, thus placing additional responsibility on Iraq's women. Mothers became their children's teachers as schoolteachers quit their jobs, and illiteracy increased.

Even though the sanctions devastated the country and Hussein's regime became more brutal and repressive as the 1990s wore on, many women nonetheless feared that the end of the Hussein era would mark the end of their equality in Iraqi society. Many secular Iraqi women who enjoyed decades of gender equality in education and employment feared losing those rights if the Shiite majority were to establish a government in Iraq modeled after the theocracy of Iran.

—Jim Ross-Nazzal

See also Islamic Resistance Movements, Women and

References and Further Reading

Chong, Linda. 1990. "Women Bear Burden of Iraqi Mobilization." *Dallas Morning News* (August 18): 28A.

Cooke, Miriam. 1995. "Arab Women Arab Wars." In *Reconstructing Gender in the Middle East: Tradition, Identity, and Power,* edited by Fatma Gocek and Shiva Balaghi, 144–166. New York: Columbia University Press.

"Different Roles Seen for Women in War at UN Conference." 1985. *Globe and Mail* (July 24): 10.

Halliday, Denis. 1999. "The Impact of the UN Sanctions on the People of Iraq." *Journal of Palestine Studies* 28, no. 2 (winter): 29–37.

Hazelton, Fran. 1991. "Gulf War Brings Glimmer of Hope for Exiled Iraqi Women Living in Britain." *The Guardian* (February 12): 32.
Ibrahim, Youssef M. 1984. "The Mideast War: Iraqis Scoff at Notion They Are on the Ropes in Conflict with Iran." *Wall Street Journal* (May 2): 1.
Reuters. 1990. "Iraqi Women, Children Protest at Boarding of 'Peace Boat.'" (December 27).
Sachs, Susan. 1990a. "In Iraq, Women in Step with Men." *Newsday* (October 30): 13.
———. 1990b. "Iraqi Women Sing Praises of Saddam, the Man Who Gave Them Freedom." *Newsday* (October 30): A1.
Seattle Times. 1985. "War Takes Iraq Women from Home to Factory." (April 14): A8.
Shahin, Mariam. 2003. "Snapshots from Iraq." *Middle East Journal* (June): 18.
Ward, Olivia. 1990. "Saddam's Iraq Gave Women Better Lot." *Toronto Star* (August 20), A13.

Ireland, Easter Rising of 1916

An armed uprising against British rule over Ireland, organized by the nationalist Irish Volunteers and the trade-union-based Irish Citizen Army (ICA). These amalgamated to fight jointly as the Irish Republican Army. Occurring at the height of World War I, the Easter Rising was intended to take advantage of British preoccupation with trench warfare in Europe and was aimed at ensuring the right of Ireland to be included as one of the so-called small nations whose independence would be decided in the peace negotiations at the end of war.

The insurgents held out for 6 days, surrendering to prevent further loss of life. An estimated 426 people were killed, of whom 230 were civilians, and 3,000 were injured. Although women participated, they did so in smaller numbers than the men. Almost 200 are reckoned to have contributed in some way to the rising, but numbers are difficult to calculate because many left their outposts before the final surrender. Seventy-seven women are listed as subsequently imprisoned by the British.

Prior to the rising, as a result of a countermanding order that attempted to cancel plans for rebellion, women played a vital role in traveling around the countryside, carrying new orders that resulted in a smaller group of insurgents marching out one day later than originally planned in some country areas as well as Dublin. Testimony from such couriers as Nora and Ina Connolly, daughters of James Connolly, commander of the ICA, provides evidence of women's commitment to armed rebellion and to the difficult circumstances in which they were forced to operate.

Women from Cumann na mBan (Council of Women), the women's section of the Irish Volunteers, and women members of the Irish Citizen Army were part of the personnel in the outposts of commandeered buildings that ringed the city of Dublin, acting as cooks, nurses, and messengers between outposts. Cumann na mBan women were not given the mobilization orders issued to the volunteers, and women had to negotiate individual entry to the outposts. They were refused entry to Boland's Mill, commanded by Eamon de Valera, future president of Ireland. In contrast, the Citizen Army women had equality of treatment within their organization and marched to their allotted positions with their male comrades. The ICA contingent that unsuccessfully attempted to take over Dublin Castle included ten men and nine women. Countess Constance Markievicz was a lieutenant with the ICA, and Dr. Kathleen Lynn was its medical officer.

The Proclamation of the Republic, read out by Patrick Pearse at the start of the rising, guaranteed equal citizenship for women and men, thereby enabling female insurgents to argue for equal rights in combat. Citizen Army member Margaret Skinnider, a schoolteacher from Glasgow, sustained serious injuries as a consequence of her participation in an attack on a sniper position. One woman, Margaretta Keogh of Cumann na mBan, was shot dead while helping the wounded at the South Dublin Union outpost. Cumann na mBan member Elizabeth O'Farrell delivered the final message of surrender, risking death by gunfire when first leaving the General Post Office (GPO) headquarters to carry a white handkerchief to the nearby British barricades. Winifred Carney, Connolly's secretary in the GPO, refused to leave the building when the other women left before the final surrender. In Jacob's Biscuit Factory on Bishop Street, one of the six positions seized by the rebels, Maire nic Shiubhlaigh provided evidence that the women left because their commander, Thomas McDonagh, felt it would upset the men to see women arrested.

Women unconnected to nationalist organizations also contributed to the rising. The suffragist leader Hanna Sheehy Skeffington (whose uncle, Father Sheehy, acted as confessor to the GPO insurgents) carried messages for the leadership on the second day. She had been informed that she would be a member of a civil government, which the leadership intended would come into existence if the rising managed to sustain itself. Members of the Irish Women's Franchise League carried in food supplies to the outpost occupied by Markievicz. After Frank Sheehy Skeffington was arrested and executed by British troops while attempting to organize a citizen's militia to stop the wide-scale looting he feared would discredit the ideals of the rising, his widow spent months in a crusade to force the British prime minister to hold an inquiry into the circumstances of her husband's death. She then joined other bereaved women in touring the United States in an effort to gain support for the Irish cause.

After surrender, only five women were detained for lengthy periods. All were Citizen Army members. Markievicz had her death sentence commuted to life imprisonment because of her sex. She was released in June 1917, one of the last prisoners to win release. Dr. Lynn was deported to England, where she worked as a doctor until granted permission to return to Ireland in August.

Initially, the rising was deeply unpopular among the Irish people, few of whom understood the motivations of the insurgents. Some 85,000 Irish men had enlisted in the British army, and the "separation women," who with the post office closed found themselves deprived of the allowances paid to them as wives of men fighting in World War I, hurled abuse at the defeated rebels being marched to prison. The execution of 16 leaders and the work of the bereaved female relatives in holding memorial masses and supporting the released prisoners did much to change public opinion. Grace Gifford married her fiancé, Joseph Plunkett, minutes before his execution in Kilmainham Jail. Kathleen Clarke, whose husband Tom was first signatory to the proclamation, had charge of the remaining funds of the conspirators. She immediately disbursed relief to those who had lost their family breadwinner and helped to reestablish a political network. A newly resurgent nationalist Ireland ensured that British attempts to impose conscription were resisted. Women were at the forefront of opposition. They formed a new group, the League of Women Delegates, to ensure that they would be effectively represented in the future reorganization of nationalist forces. When the Sinn Fein (the Irish Republican independence party; the term means "we ourselves") Convention was staged in October 1917, the league succeeded in having four women elected to its executive, all of whom had some connection with the rising.

—Margaret Ward

See also Markievicz, Countess Constance

References and Further Reading

McCoole, Sinead. 2003. *No Ordinary Women, Irish Female Activists in the Revolutionary Years 1900–1923*. Dublin: O'Brien.

Taillon, Ruth. 1996. *When History Was Made, the Women of 1916*. Belfast: Beyond the Pale.

Ward, Margaret. [1983] 1995. *Unmanageable Revolutionaries: Women and Irish Nationalism*. London: Pluto.

Ireland, War of Independence

A guerrilla war between the Irish Republican Army and the British forces in Ireland that resulted in the independence of the south of Ireland. The War of Independence began on January 21, 1919, and continued until a truce was declared on July 11, 1921. Two events on January 21 encapsulated the dual nature of the war: the secessionist Irish parliament, Dáil Eireann, had its inaugural meeting in Dublin, and two members of the Royal Irish Constabulary were shot by Irish Volunteers in an ambush at Soloheadbeg, County Tipperary. As physical resistance to British rule increased, politicians were forced into hiding and large parts of the country were declared by the British government to be under martial law, allowing for arbitrary arrest and imprisonment.

The strategy of the Irish party Sinn Fein (the party for an independent Irish republic; the term means "we ourselves") was to supplant British authority in Ireland through the creation of its own Irish institutions. In December 1918, following the ending of World War I, the British government had called elections in Britain and Ireland. It was the first occasion when women could vote and stand for office, and the imprisoned Constance Markievicz became the first woman to be elected to Westminster. Nationalists had been arrested for alleged involvement in a German plot, and Markievicz was imprisoned in England, together with Maud Gonne MacBride and Kathleen Clarke, both of whom had husbands executed by the British because of their involvement in the Easter Rising. The elected Sinn Fein members boycotted the British Parliament in favor of a new Irish assembly. Markievicz became minister for labor. Dáil Eireann courts were created, and many women served as judges in this underground network. Cumann na mBan, the women's auxiliary organization of the Irish Republican Army, developed in strength, with 600 branches located throughout Ireland. They provided essential support for both Dáil Eireann and the guerrilla fighters of the Irish Republican Army, who operated in locally based flying columns. Cumann na mBan squads provided safe houses, carried food and clothing to men hiding in hillsides, transported weaponry, scouted for targets, undertook intelligence work, and formed guards of honor at funeral processions.

In late 1919, all nationalist organizations were declared illegal, meetings were forbidden, and the dangers of opposing British rule intensified. In March 1920, the British brought in reinforcements, known as Black and Tans because of the motley nature of their uniforms. They began a reign of terror, burning down houses and workplaces and assassinating leading political figures, sometimes in front of their wives. That year, British forces killed 203 people, including 6 women and 12 children, outside of the casualties of combat, and almost 50,000 homes were raided. The U.S. Commission into Conditions in Ireland heard evidence from witnesses in 1920 and 1921. Their conclusion was that the "sanctity of the family home was violated" by the activities of the British forces (Ward 1983, 143). In December 1920, the U.S. Committee for Relief in Ireland organized fund-raising, and the White Cross organization was formed in Ireland to help the 100,000 people who had been left destitute. Nationalist women formed the backbone of the organization, which was headed by Aine Ceannt, another widow of one of the leaders of the 1916 rising.

Women were elected to local government positions in 1920, and in elections to the Second Dáil in 1921, six women were returned: Markievicz; Kate O'Callaghan, whose murdered husband had been a mayor of Limerick; Mary MacSwiney, sister of Terence, the Lord Mayor of Cork who died after a lengthy hunger strike; Kathleen Clarke; Margaret Pearse, mother of Patrick Pearse; and Dr. Ada English.

Intelligence was a vital part of the war effort. Michael Collins, who combined roles of adjutant general of the volunteers, director of intelligence, and minister of finance, used women as couriers and as spies within the British administration in Dublin Castle. Women were also in-

Sinn Fein Standing Committee, March 1922. Left to right, front row: *Mrs. Ceanant, Mr. E. Duggan, Dr. Kathleen Lynn, Arthur Griffiths, Eamon De Valera, Michael Collins, Harry Boland, Mrs. Sheehy Skeffington.* Middle row: *Mrs. Wyse Power, George Lyons, Farrell Figgis, Mr. Murnaghan, Mr. A. Stack, and Dr. Dillon.* Top row: *Sean Milroy, Walter Cole, Sean MacCaoilte, P. O'Hanrahan, P. O'Keefe. (Bettmann/Corbis)*

valuable in the production of the underground Sinn Fein paper, the *Irish Bulletin,* which defied censorship laws in providing information to the foreign press relating to the war. Around 50 women were imprisoned during this period, comparatively few when measured against the male figure of 4,000. This reflected the nature of their work and the difficulties in getting evidence for conviction. Many were untried prisoners. After the truce, 40 women still remained in detention in Mountjoy Jail, although some prominent political figures, including Countess Markievicz (rearrested in April 1921 and sentenced to 2 years of hard labor on the charge of having organized the nationalist boy-scout movement, Fianna Eireann, in 1909), had been released so that they could participate in peace talks. Four women, including Linda Kearns, serving a 10-year sentence for driving a car full of IRA men and weaponry, escaped on October 31 by climbing over the prison wall with a rope ladder. They remained in hiding until the signing of the treaty in December 1921.

No women were included among the Dáil delegates chosen to negotiate terms with the British government, although Lily O'Brennan, sister of Aine Ceannt, former secretary of Cumann na mBan, was a secretary for the Irish delegation. The final terms did not give Ireland the status of a republic, requiring members of the Dáil to take an oath of allegiance to the British monarchy and confirming the exclusion of six counties of Ulster from the settlement. Cumann na mBan was the first organization to declare its opposition. All six female deputies also opposed the treaty, which was accepted by the Dáil in January 1922. A subsequent motion introduced by Kate O'Callaghan to enfranchise women between the ages of 21 and 30 was defeated before the country voted on the issue. This symbolized the nature of the new Free State in some antitreaty quarters. A provisional government, opposed by many IRA and Cumann na mBan members, was formed, but irreconcilable differences led to the subsequent civil war between 1922 and 1923. In that period, more than 400 women were imprisoned, an indication both of their activities and of the greater understanding of the former comrades of their capabilities.

—Margaret Ward

See also Devlin, Bernadette; Gonne, Maud; Ireland, Easter Rising of 1916; Markievicz, Countess Constance

References and Further Reading

Litton, Helen, ed. 1991. *Kathleen Clarke, Revolutionary Woman.* Dublin: O'Brien.

McCoole, Sinead. 2003. *No Ordinary Women, Irish Female Activists in the Revolutionary Years 1900–1923.* Dublin: O'Brien.

Ward, Margaret. [1983] 1995. *Unmanageable Revolutionaries: Women and Irish Nationalism.* London: Pluto.

Islamic Resistance Movements, Women and

Role of Muslim women in violent resistance. Middle Eastern women have only recently entered what has traditionally been seen as the male arena of suicide bombing. This is a result, in part, of Islamic resistance movements' successful recruitment efforts that have developed in the wake of the end of Europe's colonial dominance during the second half of the twentieth century. In addition, it is necessary to consider Israel's position in the Middle East to understand the expanded role of women in combat, especially as suicide bombers.

Unlike the Free Officers, the Palestine Liberation Organization, or the Kurdish People's Union, which are secular-nationalist movements, many groups associated with post–World War II Islamic resurgence are religiously based in both ideology and in mass support. They have been spurred on by the success of the Iranian revolution of 1979 and are usually attempting to remove non-Islamic governments or occupying powers to establish Islamic governments of their own design.

Even non-Islamic-based groups, such as al-Fatah and the al-Aqsa Martyr's Brigade, have publicly embraced Islamic phraseology. In fact, many Islamic groups work within the social, political, and economic structures established by non-Islamic groups (Victor 2003, 64). Women have recently become active in many of the Islamic resistance movements such as Hezballah, Hamas, and Islamic Jihad as well as Islamic-inspired groups such as the al-Aqsa Martyr's Brigade.

On January 27, 2002, Wafa Idris did not show up for work at the local Red Crescent office. Instead she met with members of the al-Aqsa Martyr's Brigade who had built a bomb for her to carry into an Israeli shoe store later that day. The twenty-six-year-old college graduate and refugee camp resident blew herself up in a Jerusalem shopping center, killing one Israeli citizen and wounding over 130 others. Idris was the forty-seventh suicide bomber and the first woman to blow herself up in the name of defending her country (Victor 2003, 20).

During the second Intifada (al-Aqsa Intifada), which began in September 2002 (the first Intifada lasted from 1987 to August 1993), Hamas leadership issued statements calling on all women to be properly covered when they went out in public and to refrain from taking part in violent demonstrations. The majority of Palestinian women rejected the call for more modest dress, but some did adhere to the call. These women also began to participate in individual, sporadic, and uncoordinated attacks against Israeli soldiers, known as *jihad fardi* (personal initiative attacks). A Palestinian woman wearing the *jihab,* for example, would be able to hide a knife or a gun and either use it herself or pass it along to a man. According to Mohammad Dahalan, the onetime head of Yasser Arafat's West

Bank security force, "the leaders of the various factions also realized that as long as women were dressed in the proper attire, they could be used more effectively to penetrate security and transport weapons" (Victor 2003, 14).

Although it is difficult to measure, women in general sympathized with Hamas (Abdo 1999, 49). One woman in particular, Darine Abu Aisha, was such a staunch supporter that she blew herself up at the Maccabim checkpoint near Jerusalem on February 27, 2002, under the auspices of that Islamic movement (Victor 2003, 97). According to the videotape she left behind, she became a suicide bomber in part because of the abuse she had witnessed and experienced under Israeli occupation. For example, when she acted as an interpreter at a checkpoint for another woman who was trying to take her dying baby to the hospital, the Israeli soldiers would not allow the mother to pass until Abu Aisha kissed a man in the crowd (Victor 2003, 107). The same day that Abu Aisha took her own life, the religious leader of Hamas, Sheik Yassin, issued a decree permitting women to participate in suicide attacks and stated that those who did would receive special blessings in heaven (Victor 2003, 110).

Women have always been targeted for recruitment into the various Palestinian resistance movements (Sayigh 1996, 148). The roles that women performed in organizations such as the PLO had traditionally been limited to support, however, such as marching in protest parades or running orphanages or aid stations. According to the Palestinian leader Hanan Ashwari, women's inequality in Arab society is directly linked to the failure of liberation movements. A Palestinian female social worker said she could "feel guilty if [she] asked for more rights as a woman at a time like this [under Israeli occupation]" (Sayigh 1985, 191). This could help to explain the interest, active roles, and the development of women suicide bombers in some Islamic movements.

Whatever the reasons or justifications, many Palestinian schoolgirls seem more than merely willing to commit suicide and murder to further the Palestinian cause. For example, when a group of six-year-old girls at a Jabaliya refugee camp school were asked who wanted to be martyrs, every girl raised her hand. One schoolgirl said if she became a martyr, she would be given everything she wanted in heaven. Another said she was willing to become a suicide bomber "to kill the Jewish . . . and to live near our God," while a third child believed she would win immortality: "We never die. The Jewish die but we live forever" (Victor 2003, 185). She was alluding to the fact that posters of suicide bombers hang near mosques, at marketplaces, and throughout the streets of refugee camps. Both Hamas and the Islamic Jihad host summer camps in Gaza where children are taught verses from the Koran that glorify martyrdom. Armed with plastic guns and explosives, the children and adults practice suicide bomb attacks (Victor 2003, 186).

In 2003, Tuha Aziz, a twelve-year-old girl, said that she was willing and even training to become a female suicide bomber. According to Aziz, her parents knew of their daughter's goal and even supported it. "They are proud of us all because they know it is the only way to conquer the Jews and have a homeland" (Victor 2003, 189). If Tuha makes it to fifteen, she can join the Women for Wafa Idris Martyr's Brigade, whose volunteers hope that their names will live on forever in songs and poems if they are able to become suicide bombers like their idol, Wafa Idris (Victor 2003, 191).

The women who join Islamic-based resistance movements have much in common. First, they all have at least some college education. Second, they grew up in one of the refugee camps. Third, they have at least one family member abused (usually to death) by the established power authority. Fourth, they usually believe that the established, nonreligious nationalist organizations (such as the PLO) have failed to secure a better life for the people.

—Jim Ross-Nazzal

See also Arab-Israeli Wars; Ashwari, Hanan; Terrorists, Women

References and Further Reading

Abdo, Nahla. 1999. "Gender and Politics under the Palestinian Authority." *Journal of Palestine Studies* 28, no. 2 (winter): 38–51.

Ahmed, Leila. 1992. *Women and Gender in Islam.* New Haven, CT: Yale University Press.

Badran, Margot. 1995. *Feminists, Islam, and Nation.* Princeton, NJ: Princeton University Press.

Saad-Ghorayed, Amal. 2002. *Hizbu'llah: Politics and Religion.* London: Pluto.

Sayigh, Rosemary. 1985. "Encounters with Palestinian Women under Occupation." In *Women and the Family in the Middle East: New Voices of Change,* edited by Elizabeth Warmock Fernea, 191–208. Austin: University of Texas Press.

———. 1996. "Researching Gender in a Palestinian Camp: Political, Theoretical, and Methodological Problems." In *Gendering the Middle East,* edited by Deniz Kandiyoti, 145–167. Syracuse, NY: Syracuse University Press.

Victor, Barbara. 2003. *Army of Roses: Inside the World of Palestinian Women Suicide Bombers.* Emmaus, PA: Rodale.

Israeli Military, Women in the

The changing role of women in the Israeli military. The place of women in Israel's armed forces has changed substantially since 1948. Although women always performed a critical role in the Israeli military, few of these soldiers resembled the Hollywood stereotype of machine gun–armed beauty queens.

In the decades before Israel's declaration of independence on May 14, 1948, women served in many of the semiofficial and underground organizations that protected the growing Jewish community in Palestine including Hashomer, Hagana, Irgun, and Palmach. Other women stood guard duty at kibbutzim and isolated communities. Women remained a minority in these military units and generally served in noncombat positions. Only the Palmach, which had a socialist and egalitarian ethos, included a significant number of female fighters and even a few female officers. Several Jewish women died in combat in the increasingly violent years before Israeli statehood. It is likely that the first two Jewish women to die in combat in Palestine did so in 1920 while defending the settlement of Tel Hai. Eight male members of Hashomer died fighting alongside them.

More than 12,000 women served in military units in Israel's War of Independence (1947–1949), and 114 of them died in combat, representing 2.8 percent of Jewish combat fatalities (Gal 1986, 46). Many distinguished themselves, among them Netiva Ben Yehuda, a Palmach fighter who earned a reputation among Arabs as the Blonde Devil for her deadly accuracy as a sniper. Despite the soldiers' generally good combat performance, Jewish leaders began pulling women out of combat positions in mid-1948 after Arab soldiers raped, mutilated, and murdered a captured Hagana woman. By the end of the war, only a handful of women remained in combat positions. Most served in rear areas performing administrative or technical duties.

After the war, Israel reorganized its various military organizations into the Israeli Defense Force (IDF). The government established universal conscription for Israel's Jewish citizens, and Israel remains the only nation to conscript women. The length of mandatory service has varied over time depending on the nation's security situation. Generally, men served for about 3 years and women for 21 months, although married women, women with children, and those from observant Orthodox families received draft exemptions, as have women from the Druze community and other minority communities that agreed to conscription. Women who qualified and volunteered to become officers served an additional 9 months. After their mandatory term of service, both men and women serve in the reserves, but women's reserve commitment ends with their first pregnancy or at age 34 (changed to 38 in 2001). Because of these exemptions and because for most of its history the IDF did not conscript all women (because of the limited number of positions in which they were allowed to serve), only about 60 percent of Israeli women served in the military compared with 90 percent of men. Following legal changes in the 1990s, the percentage of women serving rose to 70 percent (Gal 1986, 32; van Creveld 1998, 263). Surveys continue to show that even without conscription, the majority of these women would volunteer for military service.

The fear of losing women in combat combined with pressure from Israel's religious political parties and immigrants from Arab nations, who generally retained a traditional view of women's place in society, led the government to systematically restrict women from combat and near-combat positions. In the 1950s, the IDF assigned many women as teachers to help new immigrants learn Hebrew and adjust to life in Israel. An effort to train women as pilots ended before the 1956 war. Nonetheless, a female pilot flew one of the planes that dropped paratroopers over the Mitla Pass in the 1956 war, and other women served close to the front lines. By the early 1960s, however, women only served in rear areas. Occasional efforts to restore them to flight or near-combat duties failed.

Until 2001, women served in the IDF as part of the Women's Corps (Chel Nashim), the Hebrew abbreviation for which (Chen) translates roughly as *charm* or *grace*. Chen trained women and men in separate camps. After training, the IDF assigned them to various military units. These women functioned normally within the military chain of command, but each battalion or similarly sized military unit had a Chen officer who oversaw the accommodation and treatment of the women in that unit. This dual chain of command further isolated women from the predominantly male army. With only limited opportunities for advancement, few women attained the rank of colonel.

Historically, women accounted for about 10 percent of Israel's active duty forces, and virtually all units, including elite airborne and other specialized combat units, contained some women, usually in clerical or medical positions (Gal 1986, 48–49). A unique Israeli position for female soldiers is the company clerk, a special aide who assists the commander with administrative tasks but who also helps raise troop morale by arranging social activities and even baking cookies for the soldiers. In many ways, the company clerks function as surrogate mothers for the young soldiers. Commanders expect them to add homey touches to military life. While restricting women from combat, the IDF steadily opened new military specializations to women, particularly after the 1973 war when it began assigning women as arms, artillery, and tank instructors. In addition to medical specialties, many women worked in communications, intelligence, radar, air traffic control, computers, and electronics, but almost half of them still served as clerks and secretaries.

The IDF's policy in the 1960s and 1970s was to evacuate women from the front lines before combat began, but this sometimes proved impossible. Three women died in the surprise Arab attacks that began the 1973 war. The IDF prohibited women from entering Lebanon during the first two months of Israel's 1982 invasion and occupation. Afterward, the women joined their units in the field, but for several years, the high command expected them to return to Israel each night. Despite their exclusion from combat service in the IDF, the government allowed women to perform their mandatory military service in paramilitary forces such as the Chiba auxiliary police unit that assists police in security and counterterrorism patrols. Other women chose to serve in the Border Police (MaGav), another well-armed paramilitary force that offered more opportunities for women. The MaGav remains more integrated and egalitarian than the IDF, with numerous coed platoons, and a few platoons composed almost entirely of women. Armed with M-16s, machine guns, and light mortars, MaGav units have proved of critical importance in protecting Jewish neighborhoods and responding to suicide attacks. MaGav instruction is completely coed, and women serve as snipers and in elite units without any gender restriction.

Many Israeli women resented their second-class status in the military, especially because military service in Israel is highly regarded and often a path for upward mobility. Their efforts steadily forced open more occupational specialties to women, and in the 1990s, several lawsuits opened the door even further to full female participation in the military. In 1995, Israel's Supreme Court ruled that the IDF had to allow Alice Miller, an immigrant from South Africa with a pilot's license, to apply for pilot training in the Israeli Air Force. Although Miller failed the entrance exam, other women have graduated from flight school. Further legal challenges opened up other positions for women. On January 10, 2000, Israel's parliament amended the military service law to give women equal access to all military positions unless the nature of the job specifically prevents their service. If they wish to serve in combat units, women must serve the same three-year initial term of service as men do and accept an obligation in the reserves through the age of forty-three. Many women have chosen to do so. By the end of 2001, women held combat positions in artillery, air defense, combat engineers, several border patrol units, and in the air force as both fixed-wing and helicopter pilots.

Following the onset of the suicide bombings of the Second Intifada, the IDF began assigning female soldiers to guard Jewish communities. One of them, Corporal Keren Ya'akobi, died in combat guarding a Jewish settlement near Hebron on December 12, 2002. Recently, Israel created coed combat units, most notably the Karakal (Hebrew for "wildcat") Brigade. Women outnumber men in several of the Karakal's companies. This unit patrols the Jordanian border to prevent drug smuggling and terrorist infiltration and has distinguished itself in several small skirmishes. The IDF continues to open new positions to women and current plans include expanding options for women in the reserves.

—*Stephen K. Stein*

See also Fuld, Bracha

References and Further Reading

Gal, Reuven. 1986. *A Portrait of the Israeli Soldier.* Westport, CT: Greenwood.

Kiesling, Eugenia C. 2001. "Armed but Not Dangerous: Women in the Israeli Military." *War in History* 8, no. 1 (January): 99–100.

Official Web site of Israeli Defense Force: http://www.idf.il/ (accessed September 28, 2004).

Schiff, Zeev. 1986. *A History of the Israeli Army, 1874 to the Present.* New York: Macmillan.

Van Creveld, Martin. 1998. *The Sword and the Olive: A Critical History of the Israeli Defense Force.* New York: Public Affairs.

ITALY, WOMEN IN THE RESISTANCE DURING WORLD WAR II

Role of women in the antifascist and anti-Nazi resistance in Italy during World War II. In 1943, the Italian Resistance came to life when the Fascist Grand Council removed Benito Mussolini from power in July. Women, who constituted 105,000 out of a total 250,000 Italian partisans, struggled against fascism by caring for Resistance fighters, assisting Jews, acting as messengers, and fighting. Approximately 4,600 women were arrested; 2,750 were deported to German concentration camps; and 623 died at the hands of Italian fascists or the Germans. After the war, 17 were awarded the gold medal of valor (De Grazia 1992; Slaughter 1997).

To understand the role of women in the Resistance, one must first understand the Resistance itself. In 1943, there were two competing governments in Italy, the monarchical government under the new premier, Marshal Pietro Badoglio, that had fled to southern Italy, and the German occupiers, who reimposed Mussolini in northern Italy in the puppet Italian Social Republic. As the Allies advanced north, political parties banned by Mussolini in the 1920s—the Communist Party, the Socialists, and the Christian Democrats—and the new Action Party began to form independent Resistance units, which were tied together by the National Committee for the Liberation of Northern Italy.

Italian leftists had fought against fascism during the Spanish Civil War (1936–1939). Within Italy, World War II, Mussolini's alliance with Adolf Hitler, and the behavior of the Germans in Italy, especially after the deposition of Mussolini, created a "crisis of conscience" (Slaughter 1997) that affected women as well as men. In November 1943, the Women's Defense Groups formed in Milan as a component of the National Committee for the Liberation of Northern Italy. Although much of women's participation tended to be grassroots mobilization, women's groups such as the Union of Italian Catholic Women, Union of Italian Women, Women's Movement of Christian Democracy, and Center of Italian Women helped to institutionalize and to legitimize women's political activity. The size of Italy's Resistance movement and the massive involvement of women in it were unique in the Western European theater. Traditional roles of women in predominantly Catholic Italy as nurturers and the anchors of their families and communities ironically served as a catalyst for women's involvement. Nevertheless, women, "unlike the men, for whom this was prescribed behavior" (Slaughter 1997, 70), had to make a very personal decision to take up the cause and to fight. They resisted not only fascism but social and religious stereotypes that had confined them to the private sphere. The complex role of women in the Resistance was at once a means of enacting their own citizenship while also remaining true to traditional family and religious values. Their roles as mothers, wives, and sisters undeniably affected their decisions to join their male counterparts in the fight for their country. By participating in the Resistance, they felt they were fulfilling their rightful place in society. Their participation was not so much for the state but for the family unit. Preserving community was something they had always done. Even the closeness of the big city blocks huddled around piazzas lent itself to the virtues of intuition, shrewdness, protectiveness, and other qualities of community ascribed to women in society (De Grazia, 1992).

By virtue of being female, Italian women performed crucial jobs in the Resistance. Former partisan Giovanna Zangrandi noted that while male partisans met secretly in participants' homes, women were there in the kitchen. The women provided clothing, food, and medical supplies during the clandestine meetings. The most important role of women in the Resistance was communication and information. The ironic underestimation of women served as a natural disguise for collecting and moving munitions, supplies, and information essential to the cause. Given that they were underestimated by the establishment, women were natural choices to become *staffette,* or messengers. A seemingly pregnant woman would not be suspected of stuffing her clothes with pamphlets, Resistance newspapers, or even weapons. Male fascists did not hesitate to discuss politics and their plans in front of "uninterested" or "frivolous" women (Slaughter 1997). "The *staffetta* on her bicycle became the symbolic heroine [of the Resistance], fearlessly passing Nazi and Fascist checkpoints or eluding pursuit and capture" (Slaughter 1997, 53). Some 35,000 women participated as *staffette.*

Women who participated in the Resistance also served with the fighters, the partisans. The women partisans were guides, cooks, and clothes menders for mountain brigades. They also served as combatants and held formal rank. Most, however, were consigned to segregated quarters and were assigned functions ranging from "sabotage and single-strike activity to serving as auxiliaries for the Brigades, to recruiting, education and defending [their homes and neighborhoods]" (Slaughter 1997, 57).

Although some women participated in combat, they were primarily valued for and even relegated to gender-specific roles. Scholars analyzing the Resistance in Italy and other countries, such as Yugoslavia, note that there is a difference between "togetherness in combat" and "equality of roles." Gender differences held during the Resistance because "customary activities like food

Italian resistance fighters who helped South African troops in Pistoia locate German snipers. (Hulton-Deutsch Collection/Corbis)

shopping and child care and feminine stereotypes of weakness and flirtation either hid or supported partisan activity" (Slaughter 1997, 53).

Women joined the original Women's Defense Groups to help in the Resistance and organize for women's emancipation, but emancipation took a backseat to the more urgent issue of war. The participation of women in the Italian Resistance during World War II affected female emancipation in Italy. Women were granted the right to vote after the war. In addition, the 1948 Italian constitution not only declared Italy to be a democratic republic "founded on work," it also guaranteed equal rights to all regardless of "sex, race, religion, political opinion, or personal and social conditions."

—Marcie L. Hinton

See also France, Resistance during World War II, Women and; Greece, Resistance during World War II, Women and; Norway, Resistance Movement during World War II, Women and

References and Further Reading

De Grazia, Victoria. 1992. *How Fascism Ruled Women: Italy, 1922–1945.* Berkeley: University of California Press.

Slaughter, Jane. 1997. *Women and the Italian Resistance, 1943–1945.* Denver, CO: Arden Press.

Vigano, Renata. 1999. *Partisan Wedding: Stories by Renata Vigano.* Translated by Suzanne Branciforte. Columbia: University of Missouri Press.

Wilhelm, Maria de Blasio. 1988. *The Other Italy: Italian Resistance in World War II.* London: W. W. Norton.

Italy, Women on the Home Front and in the Services during World War I

The role of women in Italy during World War I. When Italy entered World War I on May 24, 1915, it fought the Austrians and Germans in the mountainous region of the southern Tyrol and along the Isonzo River. Despite the emigration of more than 2.5 million in the late nineteenth and early twentieth centuries, Italy mobilized more than 5 million of its nearly 9 million men between the ages of 18 and 65.

Intellectual middle-class women were among those who vociferously advocated Italian intervention in the war as early as the autumn of 1914. The *Fede nuova* (New Faith) was a review devoted to promulgating the principles of Giuseppe Mazzini, the apostle of Italian nationalism, and had as its president Signora Alvina Albini Tondi. Along with Virginia Pincellotti Pace, a journalist and poet, and Professor Theresa Labriola of the University of Rome, Tondi formed the National Committee for Italian Intervention. In December 1917, it called on Italian women to support the war effort in any way they could. Its appeal was echoed by the National Woman Suffrage Federation.

The women of Italy were called on to support the war effort in many ways. Yet female workers in the armaments factories and other war industries were, in comparison to their allies, appallingly paid and labored under horrible conditions. As industrial cities grew to accommodate the influx of workers, overcrowding became a problem. Food shortages eventually led to strikes, often fronted by women, for whom the threat to send strikers to the front held no real terror. Peasant women, on the other hand, whose lives were traditionally harsh, were actually less affected by the food shortages that plagued their urban sisters. While they had to take up the work their men left behind including public transactions, many peasant families benefited from the increased inflation that allowed them to pay off their debts to absentee landowners. Women in Perugia were praised for yielding a better harvest in 1916–1917 than had been reaped in the preceding year.

Women also went to work in offices, asylums, and hospitals. They were employed as railroad ticket agents, street sweepers, conductors on street cars, and telegraph operators. The Italian gas mask was said to have been devised by a woman from Bologna. In Verona, 80 refugee women in workrooms and 1,000 women in their homes produced more than 19,000 field tents and 125,000 articles of clothing for soldiers (Wannamaker 1923, 35). One workroom in Milan sent 43,000 garments to the front in the first 2 years (Wannamaker 1923, 31). In Palermo, Messina, and Como, female telephone operators alternated their regular work with making garments.

Women of the middle and upper classes organized voluntary work. The Citizen Relief Committees dealt with various needs from soldiers' clothes to the distribution of milk to needy children. The first state provisions for the war needy were instituted in May 1915 for the families of recalled servicemen and were later extended to all draftees.

The Central Bureau of News was established by Countess Lina Cavazza in Bologna in May 1915 and ultimately employed 25,000 women who sent messages from the wounded soldiers to their families (Wannamaker 1923, 36). These aristocratic women visitors also delivered sweets and collected information for the News Bureau. The *Ufficio Notizie Militari* (Office of Military News) was another female-managed conduit for the interchange and distribution of news between soldiers and their families. Other women managed rest houses and canteens for soldiers. One, the *Casa del Soldato* (Soldiers' Home) in Genoa, was founded and maintained exclusively by the women's association *Pro Patria*.

The professional nurse was a new phenomenon in Italy, the first school for training opening only in 1908. Like women elsewhere, however, Italian women were eager to enroll once war was declared. In one Milan school, the enrollment was 54 in 1913–1914 but 704 in 1914–1915. By 1917, the Red Cross in Italy had 10,000 nurses, 600 of whom served in the war zone. Nine died of disease contracted during their service, and it was reported in one contemporary memoir that 15 Italian nurses had volunteered to permit grafts from their skin for the treatment of wounded men (Wannamaker 1923, 39).

In the mountainous terrain of the Italian front, women were essential in the work of clearing the roads of snow and in carrying materials and food to the soldiers. They also transported concrete and wire for the trenches. Some were decorated for their bravery. Maria Brighenti was posthumously awarded the Gold Medal of Military Valor for having nursed the wounded during a siege at Tarhuna in July 1915. Her remains were not found until 1924. Maria Boso was awarded the Silver Medal of Civic Virtue for having helped her soldier brother in the Austrian army escape to Italy. She was captured by the Austrians and died in prison.

The thousands of ordinary widows and grieving mothers were venerated in national mourning organized by the patriotic Associazione Madri e Vedove dei Caduti in Guerra (Association of Mothers and Widows of the Fallen), founded in Milan in 1917. The new woman, who may have felt energized by the possibilities of wartime employment, was, by contrast, subject to a conservative backlash. New opportunities, experienced mainly by urban middle-class women, were short-lived.

—*Jane Potter*

See also France, World War II, Women and the Home Front; Germany, Women and the Home Front, World War II; Great Britain, Women on the Home Front during World War II; Soviet Union, Women and the Home Front during World War II; United States, Home Front during World War II

References and Further Reading

Adamson, Walter L. 1999. "The Impact of World War I on Italian Political Culture." In *European Culture in the Great War: The Arts, Entertainment, and Propaganda, 1914–1918*, edited by Aviel Roshwald and Richard Stites, 308–329. Cambridge: Cambridge University Press.

Cotillo, Salvatore A. 1922. *Italy during the World War.* Boston: Christopher Publishing House.

Fédération Interalliée des Anciens Combattants. 1934. *Femina Patriae Defensor: Woman in the Service of Her Country.* Paris, Limoges, and Nancy: Charles-Lavauzelle.

Strachan, Hew, ed. 1998. *The Oxford Illustrated History of the First World War.* Oxford, England: Oxford University Press.

Wannamaker, Odin D. 1923. *With Italy in Her Final War of Liberation.* New York: F. H. Revell.

J

Japan, Women and the Home Front, World War II

Effort of the Japanese government to win the active support of Japanese women during World War II. During World War II, the Japanese government attempted to reinforce national patriotism and popular support for its ambitious expansionist efforts not only among the military but also among civilians by building the home front. National patriotism and support were especially important for the government as Japan's military campaign in China and Southeast Asia during World War II stretched the human and economic resources of the country to its limits. Japanese women became the primary target for the political propaganda and social and economic engineering by the country's leaders. This campaign brought about significant changes in the social status of Japanese women.

In the Meiji era (1868–1912) women were traditionally viewed as a part of the "family system." They were discouraged from active participation in public and political life and were expected to conform to the image of "Good wife and wise mother," silently obeying fathers and, after marriage, husbands. This situation changed slightly in the 1920s and 1930s as rapid urbanization, modernization, and the development of mass education had an effect on Japanese women. For the first time in Japanese history women became workers in secondary and tertiary industries. They gained some degree of economic and social independence, and they were able to actively participate in the public life. For example, in 1930 the number of working women increased to approximately 28 percent of the total labor force in the industrial sector of the country (Ohasato 1996, 53).

During this period the concept of a "modern girl" or a "career girl" emerged in the country. For many young women in Japan, this concept often implied a professional woman who had independent income, who could voice her opinion in public, who wore western clothes, and who spent time at coffee shops, restaurants, movie theaters, or dance halls. At that time Japanese women started their own organizations, such as the Greater Japan Young Women's Association (1927), the Foundation of Mother's Day (1928), the All-Japan Women's Economic Convention (1929), the Greater Japan Allied Women's Society (1931), and the Greater Japan National Defense Women's Association (1932). These organizations, however, were relatively small and often remained under the strict control of various government agencies.

In 1937 the Japanese government began its occupation of China and in 1940 sent its military forces to different parts of Southeast Asia. In December 1941 it attacked the United States at Pearl Harbor. These military campaigns consumed enormous human and economic resources and immediately led to a sharp increase in hardship and poverty in Japanese society. Labor productivity in the war industries was low compared with the United States. The workforce of Japan therefore had to be shifted to war industry more dramatically than in the United States. In addition, mass conscription of peasants and farm workers led to a significant drop in agricultural production. This caused a shortage of food as well as consumer goods.

Most Japanese experienced shortages of food, clothing, and housing. In 1940 the government introduced the rationing of rice, sugar, matches, and many other products. For example, an adult received 345 grams (12.17 ounces) of rice per day. Annual consumption of rice decreased from 160.8 kilograms (354.5 pounds) per person in 1940 to 122.1 kilograms (269.2 pounds) in 1945; consumption of sugar decreased from 13.54 kilograms (29.85 pounds) per person in 1940 to 0.64 kilograms (1.41 pounds) per person in 1945 (Ohasato 1996, 354–355).

In order to justify spending and to build up domestic support for the war, the government launched a massive propaganda campaign between 1941 and 1943. In December 1941 the war in China and the Pacific was proclaimed to be the "Greater East Asia War." This was portrayed as a battle against the immoral and imperialistic West and in defense of the colonized people of Asia.

It was, however, the strategic bombing of Japanese cities and major industrial centers from the autumn of 1944 through August 1945 that brought the war directly to the door of ordinary Japanese people. According to the U.S. Strategic Bombing Survey, *The Effects of Strategic Bombing on Japan's War Economy*, the strategic bombing impacted 66 cities, where between 25 and 90 percent of the houses, public buildings, and other facilities were destroyed. Urban residents experienced the destruction of housing and the collapse of food distribution. Many civilians were evacuated from large industrial cities to towns and villages. This negatively affected the morale of ordinary citizens throughout the country.

The home front actions included large media campaigns and strict control over the patriotism of the mass media publications. It also promoted hard work by all civilians in order to help the military. Journalists were encouraged to write only positive articles about military actions and about popular support of the government among the Japanese people, including the contribution of women to the eventual victory. This propaganda campaign changed the image of Japanese women in mass media because they were portrayed not only as important contributors to the family system but also as responsible members of the society who contributed significantly to the home front. Any publications that were suspected of pessimism or criticism of the Japanese government were censored, and there were dire consequences for the authors.

In order to broaden popular support, government agencies created several large organizations that eventually enrolled all Japanese citizens from schoolchildren to pensioners. This campaign included creating mass women's organizations for the first time in Japanese history. It was during World War II when a large class of working women emerged in Japan, significantly changing the social fabric of Japanese society. Japanese authorities understood these changes, and in 1942 they created the Dainihon Fujin Kai (Greater Japan Women's Association) by merging the Aikoku Fujin Kai (Patriotic Women's Association) with other groups (Kurihara 2001, 305). Upon reaching the age of 21, every Japanese woman was encouraged to join the newly unified organization, and by 1943 its membership had grown to 19 million. The Greater Japan Women's Association members organized various public actions, such as fund-raisers, collected such personal items as gold jewelry and clothes, and performed various duties at military hospitals and elsewhere.

With more than 7 million Japanese men in active military duty at the end of World War II, Japanese women replaced them in factories, farms, and offices. In 1941 the Japanese government introduced the *Kokumin Kinrou Houkoku Kyouryoku Rei* (Ordinance for Cooperation with the National Patriotic Labor Corps) that obliged every single woman between the ages of 14 and 25 to start labor service within 30 days. In addition, in August 1944 the *Joshi Teishintai Kinrou Rei* (Women's Volunteer Labor Corps Work Ordinances) was introduced, mobilizing all women between the ages of 12 and 39 to engage in various public works (Momose 1990, 305). Yet the Japanese government refused to conscript women to fight even during the most difficult period of the war. Nevertheless, in June 1945 the government enacted the *Kokumi Giyu Heieiki Hou* (Volunteer Army Military Service Code). According to the code, Japanese women were organized into a Kokumin Giyu Sentou Tai (National Volunteer Army Combat Corps). The war ended, however, before Japanese women engaged in fighting (Momose 1990, 270–271).

All the actions on the home front were vigorously enforced and helped to mobilize economic and social resources for the war. The organizations often propagated extreme nationalist sentiments and anticolonial feelings. After the Japanese capitulation in 1945, however, the propaganda machine of the home front and all militant public organizations were dismantled. But the changes of the era continued to shape social and economic development in Japan for decades.

—Kazuo Ota and Rafis Abazov

See also France, World War II, Women and the Home Front; Germany, Women and the Home Front, World War II; Great Britain, Women on the Home Front during World War II; Korea, Women and the Home Front, World War II; Soviet Union, Women and the Home Front during World War II; United States, Home Front during World War II

References and Further Reading

Bernstein, Gail Lee. 1991. *Recreating Japanese Women, 1600–1945.* Berkeley: University of California.

Dower, John W. 1999. *Embracing Defeat: Japan in the Wake of World War II.* New York and London: W. W. Norton.

Goldstein, Joshua S. 2001. *War and Gender: How Gender Shapes the War System and Vice Versa.* Cambridge, England: Cambridge University.

Hane, Mikiso. 1988. *Reflections on the Way to the Gallows: Rebel Women in Pre-War Japan.* Berkeley: University of California.

Haruko, Taya Cook, and Theodore F. Cook. 1993. *Japan at War: An Oral History.* New York: New Press.

Kurihara, Rumi. 2001. *Nihon-gata Minsyusyugi* [Japanese-Style Democracy]. Tokyo: Nihon Klezai Hyouronsha.

McClain, L. James. 2002. *Japan: A Modern History.* New York and London: W. W. Norton.

Momose, Takashi. 1990. Jiten Showa Senzen-ki no Hinon Seido to Jittai [Systems and the Realities]. In *Encyclopedia Japan.* Edited by Takashi Ito. Tokyo: Yoshikawa Kobunkan.

Ohasato, Katsuma. 1996. *Hundred-Year Statistics of the Japanese Economy.* Tokyo: Bank of Japan, Statistics Department.

Pauer, Erich. 1999. *Japan's War Economy.* Routledge Studies in the Growth Economies of Asia, 21. London: Routledge.

Toland, John. 2003. *The Rising Sun: The Decline and Fall of the Japanese Empire, 1936–1945.* Modern Library War Series. New York: Random House.

Wakakuwa, Midori. 2001. *Sensou ga tsukuru josei-zou* [Women's Image Made by War]. Tokyo: Chikuma Shobo Publishing Co., Ltd.

Japan, Women Warriors in Ancient and Medieval Japan

Role of women as rulers and fighters in ancient Japan. The great Japanese epic, *Heike Monogatari* (Tale of the Heike), celebrates many women warriors. The *naginata,* a heavy blade on the end of a staff, was their favored weapon. If the naginata were to fail, female samurai carried a *kai-ken* (a long dagger) for last-ditch defense or, if capture seemed inevitable, for ritual suicide.

According to Japanese tradition, in the fourth century A.D., Empress Jingo-Kogo, although pregnant, led her forces in a victorious campaign against Korea. The medieval warrior Lady Yatsushiro also reputedly went into battle while pregnant, mounted on horseback and accompanied by her attack-wolf, Nokaze. The most renowned female warrior of medieval Japan, however, was Tomoe Gozen. Among her legendary exploits was the presentation of the head of the shogun Uchida Iyeyoshi to her husband, Miyamoto Musashi. Gozen decapitated Iyeyoshi in hand-to-hand combat. She also single-handedly defended a bridge against a multitude of attackers using only her naginata. Other legends assert that after the defeat of her husband, Gozen fled with his severed head and cast herself into the sea in order to prevent her husband from being dishonored, to avoid the dishonor of possible capture, and to die with him.

Among the many women warriors recorded in Japanese history are: Masaki Hojo (1157–1225), the widow of the first Minamoto shogun; Koman, a late sixteenth- and early seventeenth-century warrior; Fujinoye, who defended Takadachi Castle in 1189 by blocking the stairs with her naginata; and Hangaku, the daughter of a samurai, who rained down deadly arrows on the attackers of Echigo Castle in 1201. Dressed in men's clothing, Hangaku mounted the tower of the castle and "all those who came to attack her were shot down by her arrows which pierced them either in their chests or their heads. Their horses were killed and their shields were broken into pieces from their arms." An archer finally avoided her by circling to the rear of the castle and, undetected by Hangaku, was able to wound her with an arrow. The shogun Yoriye described her while in captivity as "fearless as a man and beautiful as a flower" (Beard 1953, 72–73).

Inazo Nitobe, a nineteenth-century commentator on the samurai Bushido, wrote,

> Young girls . . . were trained to repress their feelings, to indurate their nerves, to manipulate weapons—especially the long-handled sword called *nagi-nata,* so as to be able to hold their own against unexpected odds. . . . [A] woman owning no suzerain of her own, formed her own body-guard. With her weapon she guarded her personal sanctity. . . . Girls, when they reached womanhood, were presented with dirks (*kai-ken,* pocket poniards), which might be directed to the bosom of their assailants, or, if advisable, to their own. . . . Her own weapon lay always in her bosom. It was a disgrace to her not to know the proper way in which she had to perpetrate self-destruction. (Nitobe 1979, 89–90)

Nitobe, however, cautioned that "masculinity" was not the Bushido ideal for women. He saw no contradiction between being a warrior and being feminine. He asserted that central to the code was self-sacrificing service and that for women this was primarily to home and family. For a woman, he wrote, "the domestic utility of her warlike training was in the education of her sons" (Nitobe 1979, 89–90).

—Bernard Cook

See also China to 1911, Women Warriors in; India to 1857, Women Warriors in; Vietnam, Women in War and Resistance before 1954

References and Further Reading

BBC (British Broadcasting Corporation). "Miyamoto Musashi and Tomoe Gozen—Samurai Warriors." http://www.bbc.co.uk/dna/h2g2/alabaster/A681004 (accessed March 30, 2004).

Beard, Mary Ritter. 1953. *The Force of Women in Japanese History.* Washington, DC: Public Affairs Press.

Jones, David E. 1997. *Women Warriors: A History.* Washington, DC: Brassey's.

Nitobe, Inazo. 1979 (1899). *Bushido: The Warrior's Code.* Compiled and edited by Charles Lucas. Burbank, CA: Ohara Publications.

Japanese Interned in U.S. Camps

Removal of over 112,000 Japanese, including both resident aliens and U.S. citizens, from the West Coast of the United States during the early stages of the U.S. involvement in World War II. Japanese on the U.S. West Coast were interned in concentration camps following the Japanese attack on the U.S. territory of Hawaii at Pearl Harbor on December 7, 1941. The United States declared war on Japan following the attack, and the U.S. government saw a possible threat from the Japanese population in the United States. To meet this threat, all Japanese were interned in U.S. camps for the duration of the war. More than 70,000 of these Japanese were American-born and were citizens of the United States. Their U.S. citizenship and the rights entitled to them did not exclude them from internment during wartime. Many families were left with only a female head of the household instead of the usual male because the Federal Bureau of Investigation (FBI) arrested many male Japanese American leaders after the Pearl Harbor attack. There were fifteen assembly centers located in California, Washington State, Oregon, and Arizona. The Japanese internees remained at the assembly centers for up to 100 days before being sent to relocation centers managed by the Department of the Interior's War Relocation Authority (WRA). Over 112,000 Japanese were distributed among 10 locations: 2 centers each in California, Arizona, and Arkansas and 1 each in Idaho, Wyoming, Colorado, and Utah. In addition to the relocation centers, some suspect aliens of Japanese ancestry were sent to internment camps managed by the Department of Justice. There were four Department of Justice internment camps, located in New Mexico, North Dakota, Texas, and Montana. These centers were prison camps for Japanese community leaders, Shinto priests, and teachers from Japanese-language schools. The Department of Justice internment camps housed both men and women. The Texas camp housed female Japanese noncitizens. There were also two citizen isolation camps in Utah and Arizona housing Japanese Americans who were regarded as troublemakers in the relocation centers. Starting in 1943, some of the Japanese internees were granted leave. Those who were not eligible for leave remained in the camps until the end of World War II.

On February 19, 1942, President Franklin Roosevelt signed Executive Order 9066 that allowed the U.S. War Department to supervise the evacuation of the Japanese population from the West Coast. General John DeWitt of the War Department issued Public Proclamation I, which created military areas in California, Oregon, Arizona, and Washington. In these areas, enemy aliens, who included Japanese aliens and citizens of Japanese ancestry, were required to register with the U.S. government. At first, there was a voluntary program allowing Japanese to resettle outside of the military zones. This voluntary program was terminated after the War Department received complaints from the states where the Japanese resettled. On March 11, 1942, General DeWitt created the Wartime Civil Control Authority (WCCA), which took full control of the mass evacuation of Japanese from the West Coast. On March 18, 1942, President Roosevelt signed Executive Order 9102 creating the WRA. The WRA assisted people who were evacuated by the military. Beginning in March 1942, fifteen assembly centers were established to process the Japanese evacuees. The U.S. government posted evacuation notices in Japanese American communities ordering Japanese families to report to the control centers. Each family received a number after registration. These families had only a few weeks to take care of their personal matters before evacuation. Many lost a great deal of their possessions. At the end of March 1942, the evacuation to assembly centers started. By August 7, 1942, the evacuation was completed.

Beginning August 10, 1942, Japanese evacuees were interned in relocation centers. The residents of the relocation centers were divided into three groups. The first group included the elderly and those born in Japan. Most of them came to the United States in the 1910s. The second group was composed of those who were born in the United States and had U.S. citizenship. This group was more pro-American. The third group included Japanese born in the United States but who had received some education in Japan. This group was more pro-Japan. Living quarters in the relocation centers resembled military housing. The camps were patrolled by armed guards and were surrounded by barbed wire and watchtowers. Each barrack was 20 feet by 100 to 120 feet with no interior walls. Wood and tarpaper were used to construct the barracks. Each barrack was partitioned into 4 to 6 rooms of approximately 500 square feet. One family was assigned to each room. A block contained 12 to 14 barracks. Each block had a mess hall, recreation hall, bathroom, shower, and laundry. The barracks themselves did not have cooking and plumbing facilities. The residents of the centers could participate in activities such as movies and baseball. The menus of all relocation centers were based on a ration cost that allowed no more than forty-five cents per person per day. The centers provided only basic elementary through high school education. Some died while they were interned: Some were shot trying to escape; some died of poor medical care and the trauma of incarceration.

On February 8, 1943, internees of all relocation centers could register to receive leave clearance. Only a small number of the internees, however, were actually eligible for release from the camps. Those released could not resettle on the West Coast. Those in the group labeled as disloyal to the United States were not eligible to leave the camps until after the war ended.

On December 17, 1944, the War Department revoked the West Coast mass exclusion orders against Americans with Japanese ancestry. On December 18, 1944, the WRA announced that it would close all relocation centers before the end of 1945, and its program would be terminated on June 30, 1946. In January 1945, the army lifted the West Coast ban prohibiting those Japanese released from the camps from resettling on the West Coast. On August 15, 1945, Japan surrendered and the war between the United States and Japan ended. On September 4, 1945, the Western Defense Command issued the Public Proclamation 24, which revoked all individual exclusion orders and military restrictions against persons of Japanese ancestry. On December 1, 1945, with the exception of the relocation center at Tule Lake, California, all Japanese relocation centers were closed. On February 23, 1946, the last group of Japanese repatriates left Tule Lake and sailed to Japan. On June 30, 1946, the United States government officially terminated the WRA. In 1988, President George H.W. Bush issued an apology to the Japanese Americans for the internment and offered $20,000 to each of the families of the interned.

—*Edy M. Parsons*

See also Holocaust and Jewish Women; Jehovah's Witnesses in Nazi Germany; Roma/Sinti; Trauma and Brutalization Unleashed by World War I

References and Further Reading

Daniels, Roger, Sandra C. Taylor, and Harry H. L. Kitano. 1986. *Japanese Americans: From Relocation to Redress.* Salt Lake City: University of Utah.

Myer, Dillon S. 1971. *Uprooted Americans.* Tucson: The University of Arizona.

Ng, Wendy. 2002. *Japanese American Internment during World War II.* Westport, CT: Greenwood.

Smith, Page. 1995. *Democracy on Trial: The Japanese American Evacuation and Relocation in World War II.* New York: Simon and Schuster.

Jeanne d'Arc

See Joan of Arc

Jehovah's Witnesses in Nazi Germany

Banning and persecution of Jehovah's Witnesses as a rival ideology after Hitler came to power. Jehovah's Witnesses refused to swear allegiance to secular governments or to fight in their armies. The refusal to subject themselves unquestioningly to the state led to arrests. Nevertheless, they continued to meet and to distribute literature smuggled into Germany from Switzerland. In 1936 at a convention held in Lucerne, Switzerland, the Jehovah's Witnesses condemned the Nazi regime and denounced its persecution of the Jews. By 1939 approximately 6,000 Jehovah's Witnesses were imprisoned. The Nazis broke up the group's families, sending their children to orphanages. After 1939 most active Witnesses, female as well as male, were sent to concentration camps where they were marked with purple triangles inscribed with a "B" for *Bibelforscher* (Bible researcher). There are various estimates for the number of Witnesses who died in concentration camps. The *1974 Yearbook of Jehovah's Witnesses* states that of the 6,019 who were arrested, 2,000 were sent to concentration camps. In addition to these German Witnesses, approximately 700 to 800 non-German Witnesses, predominantly from the Netherlands and Austria, were sent to concentration camps. There 838 Witnesses died; of these, 203 were executed (Watch Tower Bible and Tract Society of New York 1973, 212). Other sources set the number of Jehovah's Witnesses who died in the camps at between 2,500 and 5,000.

Among those who died was Helene Gotthold (1896–1944), who was condemned to death with five other Witnesses for holding illegal meetings and undermining the morale of the nation. She was guillotined at the Plötzenzee Prison on December 8, 1944.

—*Bernard Cook*

See also Holocaust and Jewish Women; Roma/Sinti

References and Further Reading

Friedman, Ina R. 1990. *Other Victims: First Person Stories of Non-Jews Persecuted by the Nazis.* Boston: Houghton Mifflin.

King, Christine. 1990. Jehovah's Witnesses under Nazism. In *Mosaic of Victims: Non-Jews Murdered and Persecuted by the Nazis.* Edited by Michael Berenbaum. New York: New York University.

United States Holocaust Memorial Museum. n.d. *Jehovah's Witnesses.* Washington, DC: United States Holocaust Museum.

Watch Tower Bible and Tract Society of New York. 1973. *1974 Yearbook of Jehovah's Witnesses.* Brooklyn: Watch Tower Bible and Tract Society.

Jewish Women of Antiquity and War

Jewish women victims, survivors, patriots, and leaders in antiquity. In the ancient Near East the battlefield was almost exclusively the province of men, whose upper-body strength made them more efficient than women with the weapons of the age—chariots, spears, slings, axes, and swords. Women were not trained to fight and, except for camp followers, were expected to stay at home during times of war. War was the men's realm, to the point that the ultimate humiliation for a man was to die at the hands of a woman. This was the fate of the Canaanite Sisera, the Assyrian Holofernes, and the Shechemite Abimelech. Abimelech, after realizing that he had received a mortal blow from a millstone hurled by a woman, asked his armor-bearer to "draw your sword and dispatch me, lest they say of me that a woman killed me," thereby unsuccessfully trying to avoid the stigma of death at a woman's hands (Judges 9:50–55).

Nevertheless, women played important roles especially in the earliest military history of Israel as the state was being established. They almost completely vanish from a military context after the state was created. Women not only had the burden of waiting for their sons or husbands to return from battle (poignantly described in Judges 5) but also had to ensure the survival of households, farms, and businesses in the absence of their menfolk. Women could also be the reason for war, either because a family was insulted by an attack on their female members or, more simply, because women comprised an important part of the plunder from any war. Finally, a few exceptional women played central roles in early Jewish victories.

One of the Hebrews' earliest recorded victories was against the people of Shechem around 1500 B.C. The casus belli was a woman named Dinah who was raped by the prince of Shechem. Her outraged brothers were determined to get revenge, and although the prince and all of his men made the exceptional restitution of being circumcised so the prince could marry Dinah, the brothers slaughtered the Shechemites (taking advantage of their weakness after surgery). Thus, the family honor was restored. Dinah's feelings were not recorded; she was family property to be guarded. The need to defend women was especially important because, in an age with little portable wealth, women were the most valuable "livestock" an army could win. Israelite women were enslaved after victories, and the Israelites themselves assumed that a victorious warrior would bring home a few new handmaidens as his share of the spoils.

Although women did not bear weapons, they were regarded as patriotic and resourceful, sometimes using physical seduction to save their people. The Philistine Delilah was regarded as evil for discovering the secret of Samson's strength and betraying him (Judges 16), but when the Israelite women Jael and Judith seduced enemy generals to save their people, they won praise. Jael gained access to the Canaanite Sisera's tent and drove a tent peg through his head as he slept, after which she cut off his head in triumph. The Canaanites, shocked to see Sisera's head hanging from the wall of the town they were attacking, were easily defeated (Judges 4). Probably inspired by this early account is the story of Judith, a folktale written toward the end of the second century B.C. The book of Judith tells that the Assyrian general Holofernes besieged the town of Bethulia. The Jews began to despair, but the wise widow Judith (whose name is simply a feminine form of the word "Jew") presented a plan. Over the next several days she seduced Holofernes and when the time was ripe got him drunk and chopped off his head with his own sword. Again, the disheartened enemy was easily defeated.

The only true military heroine of ancient Israel, however, was Deborah, a twelfth-century B.C. prophet and the only female judge of the Israelites in the period before the monarchy. Her story is told in Judges 4–5. When Israel was savaged by Canaanite attacks, Deborah sent for the tribal leader Barak and instructed him to muster troops. Barak, however, refused to lead the army unless Deborah accompanied them to battle. She did so, although Deborah did not wield weapons or give commands. Nevertheless, according to the book of Judges 5, she was responsible for victory because to reward her faithfulness God sent a heavy rain that bogged down the massive Canaanite chariot force, making it possible for the Israelite infantry to triumph.

Deborah's victory song is one of the oldest texts in the Hebrew scriptures, perhaps nearly as old as the events it describes. It seems likely that such songs of triumph (another is attributed to Miriam after pharaoh's forces were destroyed in the Red Sea) were more typical of women's roles during ancient Israelite wars than Deborah's leadership. Israelite women celebrated in song the victories won by the Israelite men with the aid of God. The account of Deborah in the book of Judges was important to the Hebrews as evidence that God could use anyone, even a woman, to give victory to his people.

—Phyllis G. Jestice

See also Greek Women and War in Antiquity; Israeli Military, Women in the; Spartan Women

References and Further Reading:

Barquist, Jon L. 1992. *Reclaiming Her Story: The Witness of Women in the Old Testament.* St. Louis: Chalice.

Herzog, Chaim, and Mordechai Gichon. 1978. *Battles of the Bible.* New York: Random House.

Nowell, Irene. 1997. *Women in the Old Testament.* Collegeville, MN: Liturgical Press.

Joan of Arc (Jeanne d'Arc) (ca. 1412–1431)

French patriot-warrior. Born in Domrémy, France, probably in 1412, Joan was one of five children of Jacques and Isabelle d'Arc, relatively prosperous peasant farmers. Joan evidenced a deep piety as a child but was surrounded by the political and military crisis of the Hundred Years' War. In the late 1420s Joan began to reveal to family members that Saints Michael, Catherine, and Margaret had appeared to her with two extraordinary charges: first, free the city of Orleans from English siege, and second, see the dauphin Charles crowned king of France at Rheims. At the time, the fulfillment of either charge seemed extremely unlikely as the French army was reeling from defeats by Henry V, France was enduring a humiliating peace, and more than half of the country was occupied by the English. The French court itself was paralyzed by factional fighting and rebellious powerful nobles.

Through a family connection, Joan arranged to meet a regional French commander, Robert de Baudricourt, in nearby Valcouleurs. De Baudricourt, not totally convinced of Joan's mission, passed her on to the Duke of Lorraine, Charles II, whom Joan met at Nancy. Taking careful notice of Joan's growing reputation and popular rumors supporting her cause, the duke arranged for Joan to meet the dauphin Charles. Traveling to this meeting, Joan adopted men's clothing to better cross the countryside in safety, a mode of dress she would continue the rest of her life. At Chinon Joan famously identified the dauphin after he had disguised himself and mingled with a crowd of nobles, and she impressed Charles with her calling. After close examination by the dauphin's mother-in-law, Yolande of Aragon, and leading theologians, Joan was found to be a devout virgin. After Charles outfitted her with armor, Joan's voices directed her to a sword concealed at the monastery of St. Catherine de Fierbois. She was then allowed to raise an army for the relief of the besieged Orleans.

Joan, adept at riding and sword handling, attracted an army of 10,000 to 12,000 men and led them to Orleans. They arrived in late April 1429. The army entered Orleans during a diversionary ruse on St. Loup Boulevard in which Joan used her position on the walls to provoke an English attack. At Orleans she began to show great military talent, including a profound understanding of the use of cannon, something that many noble commanders resisted. The army had high morale and, when led by Joan, was willing to undertake high-casualty frontal attacks on English bastions. By May 8 Joan had forced the English to abandon the siege of Orleans and letters circulated in Europe comparing Joan to Alexander the Great and Charles Martel. With morale still high during the early summer of 1429, Joan pursued the English through their garrisons in the Loire Valley, eventually drawing the remaining English field army into battle at Patay on June 18. Throughout the campaign Joan won the obedience and adoration of the army and the surrounding population, who believed that by driving out the English, she was doing the work of God. Amazingly, Joan was able to discipline the army, preventing them from the usual looting and molesting of civilians. Joan also insisted on sending each enemy garrison written declarations of war and offering good terms of surrender.

Joan's accomplishments during the summer of 1429 paved the way for the dauphin Charles to march on Rheims, the traditional coronation site of French kings, and have himself crowned with Joan at his side. Once this was accomplished, however, Charles began to find Joan inconvenient and politically embarrassing. She insisted on moral reform of the French court, famous for adultery and underhanded dealing, and resisted Charles's inclination to deal with Burgundy through diplomacy rather than further fighting. Also, Joan had accomplished her two-part mission and received no further spiritual directives. The English, resentful of having been defeated by a female commoner, painted Joan in their dispatches as a whore and a witch, further embarrassing the French court. Charles allowed Joan to besiege Paris, still occupied by the English, but gave her little support, and in August 1429 Charles ordered her away from the city empty-handed.

Following the advice of men resentful of Joan's influence, including Georges de Tremoille, Charles stripped away her important supporters, most crucially sending Jean, the Duke of Alencon back to his home. Joan was then sent to the upper Loire valley with a much smaller, badly supplied army to fight the mercenary Captain Perrinet Gressart. Not surprisingly, the high number of casualties suffered during Joan's attacks on Burgundian fortifications soon wore out her army, which was not resupplied. Although Charles ennobled Joan in December 1429 and granted her a coat of arms, she was being set up for failure. Extremely frustrated, Joan wrote a threatening letter to the Hussite rebels of Bohemia, perhaps a hint that she considered campaigning outside of France.

In late winter of 1430 Joan disobeyed the king and traveled to Compiègne, which had been given to the Burgundians by treaty. Although she reached the city and began to prepare tactics for its defense, voices revealed to her that she would be captured. Joan was taken prisoner during a sortie from Compiègne on March 23, 1430. She was cut off by a large number of Burgundians and prevented from returning to the city, the gates of which had been locked. The Burgundians, after displaying Joan as a prisoner, sold her to the English, who promptly tried her for heresy, a rationalization of their defeat at her hands. Treated badly and probably raped and beaten in prison, Joan confessed but then recanted the charges. The French did nothing to intervene, and she was burned as a heretic in the Rouen marketplace on May 30, 1431.

French court writer Christine de Pizan wrote in 1429 of Joan's victory at Orleans and her presence at the coronation of Charles, and she became a popular folk hero in France, as well as the archetype of female military leaders. Joan has been studied as a military leader, a breaker of medieval gender roles, a peasant revolutionary, and a religious fanatic. In 1920, to popular acclaim, the Roman Catholic Church made her a saint.

—Margaret Sankey

See also De Pizan, Christine

References and Further Reading

Blaetz, Robin. 2001. *Visions of the Maid.* Charlottesville: University of Virginia.

Devries, Kelly. 1999. *Joan of Arc: A Military Leader.* Thrupp, Stroud, UK: Sutton.

Pernoud, Regine. 1982. *Joan of Arc by Herself and Her Witnesses.* Trans. Edward Hyams. New York: Stein and Day.

Johnson, Amy (1903–1941)

British military shuttle pilot during World War II. Amy Johnson was born to working-class parents in England in 1903. After attending school in Sheffield, she developed a passion for flying. Johnson was working as a typist when she joined the London Aeroplane Club, but she quickly turned flying into more than a hobby. Johnson became the first British Air Ministry–certified female engineer and earned a strong reputation as a long-distance endurance flyer. From the time she received her pilot's license in 1928 until her untimely death as a pilot for the British Air Transportation Authority in 1941, Johnson's life revolved around flying.

Johnson's war experience began in 1940 when she volunteered as a pilot delivering military aircraft from factories to various air bases. Her last delivery on January 5, 1941, is shrouded in mystery. She left Blackpool in a twin-engine Airspeed Oxford, planning to fly a route to Kidlington Airbase in Oxfordshire in the Thames Estuary. The flight should have taken only 90 minutes, but she was not spotted for 4 hours and strayed more than 70 miles (112.7 km) off course. There were clouds and icy weather, but no one can definitively confirm these as the reason for her delay and aborted flight. Johnson was spotted parachuting from her plane near the aircraft carrier HMS *Haslemere*. The ship attempted to rescue her, but she disappeared into the icy waters of the North Sea. Lieutenant Commander Walter Fletcher entered the water to save her, but he also was quickly immobilized by the cold and later died. Some historians suggest that the aviatrix was pulled under the water and killed by the ship's propellers, but this is impossible to verify because her body was never recovered.

Johnson is remembered for her bravery during World War II but also for her aviation records. Her round-trip flight from Japan to Moscow and her 1932 round-trip flight to Cape Town were popularly documented long-distance endurance flights. Johnson held the women's record for her solo flight from London to Cape Town in 1936. In 1930 she became the first woman to fly solo from England to Australia. Her attempts to set solo flight records were highly popular in England where the press called her "Queen of the Air." She was made a Commander of the British Empire (CBE) by King George VI. *Jason,* the De Havilland Gipsy Moth airplane used in her attempt to break the solo female endurance record from England to Australia, is now on display in the flight gallery at London's Science Museum. There is a museum devoted to Amy Johnson's life in her birthplace of Hull, England. A significant number of her papers were purchased in 1987 for the aviation collection at Wright State University in Ohio.

—Pamela Lee Gray

See also United States, Women Airforce Service Pilots; United States, Women's Auxiliary Ferrying Squadron; United States, Women's Flying Training Detachment

References and Further Reading

Adams, Jean, and Margaret Kimball, in collaboration with Jeanette Eaton. 1942. *Heroines of the Sky.* New York: Doubleday.

Gillies, Midge. 2004. *Amy Johnson: Queen of the Air.* London: Orion.

Gower, Pauline. 1938. *Women with Wings.* London: John Long.

Luff, David. 2002. *Amy Johnson: Enigma in the Sky.* Wilshire, UK: Crowood Press.

Jongh, Andrée (Dédée) de

See De Jongh, Andrée (DéDée)

Journalists, American Women, during World War I

American women who wrote about World War I from the areas of combat in Europe. It is difficult to establish the exact number of American women who covered the war in Europe. Frequently, the only woman mentioned is Henrietta Eleanor Goodnough, writing as Peggy Hull, who was accredited by the U.S. War Department to cover the expeditionary forces. Hull, an experienced reporter, received sponsorship from the Newspaper Enterprise Association (NEA) for travel to France and was able to use previous friendships with Generals John J. Pershing and Peyton C. March to obtain formal credentials. Hull was the first and only "official" female war correspondent, but there were many other American women who wrote about the war for newspaper and magazine readers in the United States.

There were over twenty different American female journalists and writers who reported on World War I. Some of these names are well-known writers, but others are less famous, and little is known about them. Several wrote mainly about the revolution in Russia rather than the fighting on the western front. Some were purportedly affiliated with individual newspapers or large news organizations. These include Bessie Beatty (*San Francisco Bulletin*); Andrea Beaumont (*New York American*); Louise Bryant (the Bell Syndicate); Rheta Childe Dorr (*New York Evening Mail*); Cecil Dorrian (*Newark Evening News*); Mildred Farwell (*Chicago Tribune*); Peggy Hull (*El Paso Times, Chicago Tribune,* and the NEA); Winifred Black, writing as Annie Laurie (*San Francisco Examiner*); Mary Boyle O'Reilly (the NEA); Sigrid Schultz (*Chicago Tribune*); Eunice Tietjens (*Daily News*); and Sophie Treadwell (*San Francisco Bulletin*).

Many other female fiction and nonfiction authors were writing stories and articles about the war for popular periodicals or women's magazines. Among them were Mabel Potter Daggett (*Pictorial Review*); Corra Harris (*Saturday Evening Post*); Mary Roberts Rinehart (*Saturday Evening Post*); Clara Savage (*Good Housekeeping*); and Edith Wharton (*Scribner's*). Women were also credited as photographic correspondents for *Leslie's Magazine*. Among them were Florence Harper, Helen Johns Kirtland, and Alice Rohe. Other well-known women writers, such as Mildred Aldrich, Madeleine Zabriski Doty, Inez Haynes Irwin, Elizabeth Shepley Sergeant, and Mary Heaton Vorse, were either living in or visiting Europe and wrote about the war for readers in the United States.

These women came from all over the United States, traveled to the war zone for a variety of reasons, and wrote for many different types of readers. Most were not considered war correspondents at the time because they lacked official credentials from the U.S. government. But if the criterion for determining one's status as a war correspondent is writing about being in or near a war zone, then all these women qualify.

—*Katherine Burger Johnson*

See also Beatty, Bessie; Hull, Peggy

References and Further Reading

Crozier, Emmet. 1959. *American Reporters on the Western Front, 1914–1918*. New York: Oxford University Press.

Desmond, Robert W. 1988. *Windows on the World: The Information Process in a Changing Society, 1900–1920*. Iowa City: University of Iowa Press.

Edwards, Julia. 1988. *Women of the World: The Great Foreign Correspondents*. New York: Ivy Books.

Emery, Michael. 1995. *On the Front Lines: Following America's Foreign Correspondents across the Twentieth Century*. Washington, DC: American University Press.

Schilpp, Madelon Golden, and Sharon M. Murphy. 1983. *Great Women of the Press*. Carbondale: Southern Illinois University Press.

JOYCE, MARGARET CAIRNS

See "Lady Haw Haw"

JUNGE, GERTRAUD (TRAUDL) (1920–2002)

A personal secretary of Hitler from 1943 until his death in April 1945. Gertraud (Traudl) Humps was born in Munich to the daughter of an army officer and her husband, a master brewer. Humps aspired to become a dancer but needing work and seeking influential support for

Adolf Hitler's secretary, Traudl Junge, walks to a waiting car with her new husband, SS officer and Hitler aide Hans Junge, Berlin, 1943. (Pictorial Parade/Getty Images)

her aspirations, she applied for a secretarial job at the Reichs Chancellery. She was personally hired by Hitler. In December 1943, at the age of 22, she became the youngest of Hitler's secretaries. In 1943 she married an aide to Hitler, Hans Junge, who was killed at Normandy. On July 20, 1944, Traudl Junge was at Hitler's headquarters at Rastenburg when Lieutenant-Colonel Count Klaus von Staufenberg's bomb exploded in the July 20, 1944, attempt to assassinate Hitler. In January 1945 Junge moved with Hitler's staff into an underground bunker in Berlin. Junge took down Hitler's final testament before he committed suicide. After being captured, Junge was held first by the Russians and then by the Americans. She was interrogated and spent six months in prison. After her release Junge worked as a secretary.

Filmmakers Andre Heller and Othmar Schmiderer interviewed Junge before her death and produced an intriguing documentary that delved into what has been called "the banality of evil." Junge demonstrated a great sense of guilt for what she should have known. Despite this, Efraim Zuroff, the director of the Simon Wiesenthal Center's Israel office, has said, "Her story reflects the blind loyalty of far too many Germans whose allegiance to Hitler and the Nazi party enabled the implementation of the final solution" (Hooper 2002).

—Bernard Cook

See also Germany, Women and the Home Front, World War II

References and Further Reading

Hooper, John. "Traudl Junge: She Shared Hitler's Bunker, but Claimed Ignorance of the Holocaust," *The Guardian*, February 14, 2002.

Junge, Gertraud. 1989. *Derniers témoins du bunker* [Last Witnesses in the Bunker]. Trans. Jan Dalley, ed. Pierre Galante and Eugène Silianoff. London: Sidgwick and Jackson.

———. 2004. *Until the Final Hour: Hitler's Last Secretary* [*Bis zur letzten Stunde*]. Ed. Melissa Müller, trans. Anthea Bell. New York: Arcade.

K

Kashmir, Conflict in, Women and

Site of tension and conflict between India and Pakistan since their independence in 1947. More than 4 million Muslims live in Kashmir, a region that has been governed by India but claimed by Pakistan since the partition of British India in 1947. The roots of the conflict are somewhat arcane. Muslims have long been in the majority in Kashmir, but the population also includes large minorities of Hindus, Sikhs, and Buddhists. At the time of partition, the state was ruled by a Hindu maharaja who initially thought he might be able to assert Kashmir's independence. When Muslim forces marched on the capital to protect the Muslim majority's right to become part of Pakistan, the maharaja called on the Indian army to protect his own ancestral right to determine Kashmir's future. The relatively dormant conflict intensified again in the late 1980s, and between 25,000 and 80,000 combatants and civilians have been killed since that time (Crittenden 1998). In 2005 approximately 100,000 Indian troops were stationed in the region to combat the Muslim insurgency that has extended over almost a half-century. The violence has severely impacted the tourist industry that has been the focal point of the region's economic development. Beyond the calculable physical and material costs, the conflict has taken a tremendous toll on the mental health of the population, psychologically traumatizing many of those who are most vulnerable—women, children, and the aged.

A five-year study by Human Rights Watch has documented the use of rape and other attacks on women as a means of terrorizing both the Muslim and Indian populations of Kashmir (Fife 1995). Muslim insurgents have used the threat of violence, in particular rape, both to coerce Muslim villagers into providing material support and to erode Hindu villagers' confidence that their military could protect them (Moore and Anderson 1995). In the ostensibly less reactionary cities of the region Muslim extremists have also been responsible for the shootings of young Muslim women who have worn pants in public (Farrell 2000). Because the insurgents have made it impossible for government agencies to deliver family-planning services, there has been an increase in "back street" and self-induced abortions among women of all ethnicities. The region's hospitals have been incapable of keeping up with the manifold demands on facilities, staff, and medical resources. Women suffering from botched abortions have often chosen to die rather than face the stigma of seeking whatever treatment might be available (Goldenberg 1995).

On the other side of the conflict, the Indian army has been accused of everything from ignoring random atrocities committed against the Muslim population to secretly endorsing such terror tactics—an integral part of their overall strategy against the insurgents. Moreover, the Indian press has been reluctant to report atrocities, including rapes, committed by Indian troops, fearing that any acknowledgment of these incidents will undermine the Indian claim to Kashmir and provide the Muslim insurgents with ready propaganda (Moore and Anderson 1995). The Indian government and press have, however, publicized fact-finding visits to the region by Indian groups such as the Women's Guild of Service, which has sought to provide medical services and vocational training to Kashmiri widows.

The conflict has lasted for so long that even the most remote parts of the region have been affected by the violence. According to a report in *The Independent* written by Tim McGirk and Mukhtiar Kupwara, 800 Indian soldiers allegedly surrounded the isolated Muslim village of Kunan Poshpura on the night of February 23, 1991. After compelling all of the men in the village to leave their homes and putting them under armed guard in a nearby field, the remaining Indian soldiers systematically went from house to house, gang-raping the women of the village. More than 60 women claimed to have been raped, some by 6 or more soldiers. One woman who was 9 months pregnant claimed that she had been gang-raped and then kicked in the abdomen by one of her attackers. Four days later, her full-term baby boy was born with a broken arm. In response to escalating rumors about the incident, the Indian government formally denied the allegations, dismissing them as flagrant propaganda. The report in *The Independent,* however, emphasizes that the Indian government responded slowly to the allegations, as if hoping the reports of the atrocities would attract minimal attention and eventually disappear under the almost constant accounts of violence in the region.

—Martin Kich

See also East Timor, Abuse of Women during War; Tamils, Women and the Conflict in Sri Lanka

References and Further Reading

Baldauf, Scott. "Peace, on Women's Terms." *Christian Science Monitor,* June 13, 2001.

Crittenden, Jules. "Despair in Kashmir: A Vale of Tears—In Kashmir Rivers of Blood Flow through a Lost Paradise." *Boston Herald,* August 31, 1998.

Dhar, Aarti. "India: 'Healing Touch' for Jammu and Kashmir Widows." *Hindu,* June 21, 2000.

Farrell, Stephen. "Taliban-Style Terror Comes to Kashmir." *Times* (London), June 3, 2000.

Fife, Robert. "Rape Used as a Tactic in War; Human Rights Watch." *Toronto Sun,* September 4, 1995.

Goldenberg, Suzanne. "Kashmiri Hospital Patients Pay the Price of Uprising against Indian Rule." *Guardian* ([London), September 9, 1995.

McGirk, Tim, and Mukhtiar Kupwara. "Indian Villagers Tell of Mass Rape by Soldiers." *Independent* (London), March 19, 1991.

Mishra, Pankaj. "Pride and Blood in Kashmir." *New York Times,* March 22, 2000.

Moore, Molly, and John Ward Anderson. "Kashmir in Flames: Why India Hides from the Truth." *Washington Post,* May 21, 1995.

Kea, Salaria (1917–1990)

The only African American nurse among the medical volunteers with the Abraham Lincoln Battalion during the Spanish Civil War. Salaria Kea was born in Georgia in 1917. Her father was killed when she was three months old, and after the remarriage of her mother, Salaria and her three brothers were raised by family friends in Akron, Ohio. Despite the fact that her brothers had to leave school at an early age, Salaria's foster family was inspired by her academic ability and athletic talent and was able to keep her in school. In secondary school she was determined to play basketball despite racial prejudice and gained a transfer to another school, which accepted her right to play on an integrated team.

Salaria trained as a nurse at the Harlem Hospital in New York. It was there she became involved in civil rights protests and developed an interest in international politics as a result of the Italian invasion of Ethiopia. She organized the shipment of medical supplies to the beleaguered Ethiopians. When the Spanish Civil War erupted in July 1936, she decided to serve in Spain with the Second American Medical Unit. Salaria Kea was the only African American among the forty-eight nurses in the group. The unit set up a base hospital at Villa Paz near Madrid. Kea also served near the front at Teruel. She was captured by the Nationalists but escaped after seven weeks and rejoined her unit. Kea was later seriously wounded in a bombardment, which necessitated her return to the United States.

After she recovered, Kea volunteered to serve in France as a nurse with the United States Army Nurse Corps during World War II. After the war she married John O'Reilly, an Irishman.

—Bernard Cook

See also Nurses, U.S. Army Nurse Corps in World War II; Spanish Civil War, Women and the; Thurstan, Violetta

References and Further Reading

Adie, Kate. 2003. *Corsets to Camouflage: Women and War.* Published in association with The Imperial War Museum, London. London: Hodder and Stoughton.

Endres, Kathleen. 2004. "Salaria Kea O'Reilly." Akron Women's History. http://www3.uakron.edu/scholcomm/womenshistory/oreilly_k.htm (accessed November 29, 2004).

Kempner, Vitka (1920–)

Jewish partisan who fought the Nazis during World War II. Born in the Polish town of Kalisch in 1920, Vitka Kempner fled Poland following the German conquest in 1939. Arriving in Vilna, Lithuania, after an arduous journey on foot, Kempner linked up with fellow members of *HaShomer HaTzair* (the Young Guard), a Zionist youth organization. They helped her find work and a roommate, Ruzka Korczak, another refugee from Poland. Following the German invasion of the Soviet Union and conquest of Lithuania, both Kempner and Korczak joined an underground resistance movement organized by Abba Kovner, a Young Guard leader. Kovner built his organization, the *Fareynigte Partizaner Organizatsie* (FPO; United Partisan Organization) into one of the largest and most effective Jewish partisan units of the war.

Kempner, who bleached her hair blond and could pass as non-Jewish, became one of the FPO's most important scouts and spies. She frequently traveled from the Vilna ghetto, where the Germans had ordered all Jews confined, past German patrols to nearby forests to meet with various partisan units. She helped smuggle weapons into the ghetto and led an FPO team on one of its first missions, the successful demolition of a German train as it crossed a bridge. As the Germans slowly deported Jews from the ghetto to labor and death camps, Kempner helped Kovner smuggle more and more partisans out of Vilna and into the nearby forests. She led the last group out of Vilna on the night of September 23–24, 1943, shortly before the Germans massacred the ghetto's remaining inhabitants. Operating from bases in the forests, Kempner and the FPO continued to conduct sabotage operations against the Germans for the next year, blowing up trains and bridges, cutting telephone lines, and supplying the Soviet army with important intelligence. The FPO also rescued several hundred Jews from labor camps.

After the war, Kovner and 50 other partisans, including 8 women, formed a new organization, *Nakam* (Hebrew for revenge), to avenge the Holocaust. The Jewish leadership in Palestine opposed extrajudicial revenge and blocked

Nakam's attempts to smuggle large quantities of poison into Europe to use against Allied-held Nazi prisoners. Kovner persevered, and Nakam operatives sought out targets in Europe and manufactured poison on their own. Kempner coordinated part of this operation from Paris and decided to focus on the Nuremberg camp, where the Allies held 30,000 Nazi and SS prisoners. Nakam operatives poisoned the camp's bread shipment with arsenic in April 1946. Several thousand prisoners became seriously ill and more than 100 died over the next few months as a direct result of arsenic poisoning (Cohen 2000, 212). Afterward, Kempner smuggled the plot's participants into Palestine, where she married Abba Kovner. Along with several other former partisans, they settled in Kibbutz Ein Hahoresh.

—*Stephen K. Stein*

See also Korczak, Rozka; Landau, Emilia

References and Further Reading

Arad, Yitzhak. 1982. *Ghetto in Flames: The Struggle and Destruction of the Jews in Vilna in the Holocaust.* New York: Holocaust Library.

Bar-Zohar, Michael. 1967. *The Avengers.* New York: Hawthorne Books.

Cohen, Rich. 2000. *The Avengers: A Jewish War Story.* New York: Alfred A. Knopf.

Levin, Dov. 1985. *Fighting Back: Lithuanian Jewry's Armed Resistance to the Nazis, 1941–1945.* Translated by Moshe Kohn and Dina Cohen. New York and London: Holmes and Meier.

KHAN, NOOR INAYAT (1914–1944)

British secret agent during World War II. Noor Inayat Khan (Madeleine), was one of the first group of 40 female radio operators assigned by British Special Operations Executive (SOE) to work with the resistance movement in France. She enlisted in the Women's Auxiliary Air Force (WAAF) in November 1940. She was the first woman sent to France, not as a courier but as a wireless operator. Noor was captured, held for nearly a year, and was executed by the Germans at Dachau concentration camp.

Khan, also known as Princess Noor-un-nisa, was a descendent of the Indian spiritual and political leader Tipu Sultan and Christian Science founder Mary Baker Eddy. Her father was a Sufi leader from a mystic Islamic sect who moved his family to Russia at the invitation of Czar Nicholas. Noor was born in the Kremlin in 1914 and later moved with her family to Suresnes, near Paris. After graduation from the Sorbonne, Khan was employed as a writer for Radio Parks but left France with her mother and siblings following the German invasion.

Radio communications were essential to the French Underground movement. The British used radio to organize the delivery of supplies, weapons, and funds by parachute drop and boat. Radio operation required months of training. The Germans had sophisticated radio detection equipment, and operators were frequently able to work only a few months before capture.

With her fluency in French, Khan was an invaluable operative. She had trained as a nurse but later joined the SOE when her oldest brother enlisted in the Royal Air Force. Within a week of her June 1943 arrival in France, three important agents were betrayed, leaving Khan as the only Paris radio contact. Because of the extreme danger, she was ordered to return, but Khan continued to send messages. She was captured and tortured after only three and a half months in the field. She managed to escape twice but was recaptured each time. Khan was transferred to Pforzheim and held in solitary confinement until she was moved, with fellow SOE radio operator Yolande Beekman and two SOE couriers, Eliane Plewman and Madeleine Damerment, to the Dachau concentration camp. All four were shot on September 11, 1944. Khan was posthumously awarded the

George Cross and the Croix de Guerre (Gold Cross) and was designated as the first woman saint of the Sufi religious order.

—Pamela Lee Gray

See also Atkins, Vera H.; Beekman, Yolande; Damerment, Madeleine; Plewman, Eliane

References and Further Reading

Binney, Marcus. 2003. *The Women Who Lived for Danger: The Agents of the Special Operations Executive.* New York: HarperCollins.

Fuller, Jean Overton. 1952. *Madeleine.* London: Gollancz.

King, Olive (1885–1958)

Driver with the Scottish Women's Hospitals (SWH) in France and Serbia; sergeant with the Serbian army; administrator of the Australian–Serbian Canteens. Olive King, who was born in Sydney, Australia, in 1885, was the daughter of a wealthy philanthropist, Sir George Kelso King. She attended finishing schools in Germany and Switzerland, where she became fluent in French and German. Olive was an avid athlete, and after she returned to Australia, her father purchased a large touring car for her, and she developed a passion for rally driving. Following an adventurous trip to Mexico financed by her father (who was anxious to get her away from a supposedly "fortune-hunting" boyfriend), Olive moved to England to manage the household of her sister Sunny, who was pregnant for the third time.

When World War I broke out, Olive decided to put her driving skills to work as an ambulance driver. In May 1915 King bought an ambulance and joined the Girton and Newnham Unit of the SWH, stationed first in Troyes, France, then in the Balkans. The SWH unit established a tent hospital in Ghevgeli, Serbia, but after a few weeks was forced to retreat to Salonika, Greece.

In 1916 King left the SWH for the Serbian army and served as a driver attached to the Medical Service Headquarters in Salonika. Her duties included transporting officers and supplies to the front. While in Salonika she had short-lived romances with Captain Milan Yovitchitch, the Serbian liaison officer to the British army, and a fellow army driver.

She worked closely with the men in her garage, who were usually hungry. This inspired King to establish a canteen for those who were not allowed to use the Allied canteen. With the help of her father, who established a fund in Sydney, Australia, between 1918 and 1920 King and her staff organized and ran more than ten canteens in locations throughout Serbia including Belgrade, Nish, Baja, Kragujevats, Kraljevo, Vinkovici, Bord, and Skoplje. Although King came down with malaria and had difficulty in securing transportation and supplies, her canteens provided comfort and affordable food to soldiers and civilians. When the canteens closed, King donated the remainder of the fund to Belgrade University for the establishment of an institute of anthropology, sociology, and economics.

During World War II, King again volunteered to be an ambulance driver, but, to her disappointment, she was rejected because of her age. She did, however, serve as an examiner at the De Havilland aircraft factory in Mascot, Australia, before returning to England to care for her ill sister. Olive King received the Serbian Gold Medal for Zealous Service and the Silver Bravery Medal. King died in Australia in 1958.

—Barbara Penny Kanner

See also Hutton, Lady Isabel Galloway; Inglis, Elsie, and the Scottish Women's Hospitals; Sandes, Flora

References and Further Reading

De Vries, Susanna. 2004. *Heroic Australian Women in War.* Sydney: HarperCollins.

King, Hazel, ed. 1986. *One Woman at War: Letters of Olive King, 1915–1920.* Melbourne: Melbourne University Press.

Kirchner, Johanna (1899–1944)

German anti-Nazi resister. Johanna Kirchner was born in Frankfurt on April 24, 1889. Her family was aligned with the Social Democratic party. Kirchner joined the Socialist youth organization when she was fourteen and the Social Democratic party when she was eighteen. In 1913 she married Karl Kirschner, a metal worker turned journalist and Social Democratic party secretary. She worked for the party's Workers' Welfare Organization in Frankfurt and served as a party press officer. Her opposition to the Nazis forced her to seek safety in France, first in the French-occupied Saar region and then in France proper, where she worked as a cook and servant. Kirchner continued her political and welfare work, however, organizing refuge for people fleeing the Nazi regime and maintaining contact with the internal resistance in Germany.

With the outbreak of the war, Kirchner was temporarily interned as a German national by the French. Friends in France secured her release, but with the German victory, the Vichy government handed her over to the Nazis. Following interrogation by the Gestapo, she was sentenced to ten years of imprisonment. New proceedings in April 1944 produced a death sentence after a mere half hour, and Kirchner was executed at Plötzenzee Prison on June 9, 1944.

—Bernard Cook

See also Buch, Eva Maria; Fittko, Lisa; Harnack-Fish, Mildred; Kuckhoff, Greta; Monte, Hilda; Niederkirchner, Käthe; Schulze-Boysen, Libertas

References and Further Reading

Leber, Annedore. 1994. *Conscience in Revolt: Sixty-Four Stories of Resistance in Germany, 1933–1945*. Boulder, CO: Westview.

Kleeck, Mary van

See Van Kleeck, Mary

Knocker, Elsie

See T'Serclaes, Baroness Elizabeth de

Koch, Ilse (1906–1967)

The wife of Karl Otto Koch, the commandant of the Sachsenhausen and Buchenwald concentration camps. The inmates of Buchenwald called Koch the "Witch of Buchenwald" (Manvell and Fraenkel 1967, 84). Ilse Köhler was born in Dresden on September 22, 1906. She worked as a secretary and typist in Berlin and joined the Nazi party in 1932. She had been Karl Koch's mistress and in 1936 married him in a Nazi ceremony. She went with him when he was transferred from Sachsenhausen to Buchenwald in 1937. Both were promiscuous sexual sadists. Ilse Koch collected lampshades made from the tanned skin of prisoners and even had a handbag covered with tanned tattooed skin. She had a riding hall constructed at the camp by slave laborers for her personal pleasure. She and her husband were charged by the SS with embezzlement and were arrested. Though she was released, he was executed by the Nazi regime in April 1945.

After the war Ilse Koch was tried by an American military court. She avoided a death sentence because she was pregnant. She was, however, sentenced to life imprisonment, but the sentence was subsequently reduced and she was released. In 1949 Koch was charged with multiple murders. She was rearrested by the West German government, was tried, and was sentenced to life imprisonment. On September 1, 1967, she hung herself in her cell in the Aichach Prison in Bavaria.

—Bernard Cook

See also Bilien, Valentina; Grese, Irma; Plavsic, Biljana

References and Further Reading

Manvell, Roger, and Heinrich Fraenkel. 1967. *Incomparable Crime: Mass Extermination in the Twentieth Century: The Legacy of Guilt.* New York: G. P. Putnam's Sons.

Shirer, William L. 1990. *Rise and Fall of the Third Reich: A History of Nazi Germany.* New York: Simon and Schuster.

KOLLONTAI, ALEXANDRA (1872–1952)

Russian revolutionary. The 1917 Revolution in Russia not only ushered millions of workers and peasants onto the historical stage, it also advanced a whole layer of representatives of the socialist intelligentsia—bearers of the revolution's political consciousness—who had imbibed the international traditions of European social democracy. Women played an important role in this milieu. The Bolshevik seizure of power in 1917 and the ensuing communist regime, however, have often been portrayed as a man's revolution, with women as bystanders or even victims.

Though women, protesting shortages of food and fuel on International Women's Day on March 8, 1917, in Petrograd, played a central role in the disturbances that triggered the fall of the monarchy, few women stand out as leading figures in the revolution. An exception is Alexandra Kollontai. The daughter of a Russian general, she was born Alexandra Domontovich in Ukraine in 1872. The family moved to St. Petersburg, but Alexandra was not allowed to go to school as her parents were worried that she would meet "undesirable elements." In 1893 Alexandra, to escape the domination of her parents, married an engineer, Vladimir Kollontai. She gave birth to a son but left her husband after three years of marriage. Alexandra Kollontai worked for a number of educational charities. This involved visiting people living in extreme poverty. It was at this time that she became interested in Marxism. During the 1896 strike of textile workers in St. Petersburg, Kollontai organized collections for the strikers. She also began writing articles for political journals about the plight of industrial workers in Russia. In August 1896 Kollontai left Russia and became a student of labor history at the University of Zurich. There she became a committed Marxist and joined the Russian Social Democratic Labor Party.

On her return to Russia, Kollontai, whose mother was from Finland, began to take a keen interest in the Finnish struggle for independence. She helped workers in Finland organize themselves into trade unions and wrote articles about the struggle between the Finnish people and the Russian autocracy. Her book, *The State of the Working Class in Finland,* was published in 1903.

When Lenin and his followers, the Bolsheviks, broke with the Mensheviks in 1903, Kollontai found it difficult to choose between the two. Kollontai eventually decided to not join either group and instead offered her services to both factions. After witnessing Bloody Sunday, Kollontai concentrated on establishing a trade union movement in Russia. She was particularly active in helping to organize female workers and arranged special meetings and clubs for them.

Kollontai became increasingly concerned about the dictatorial attitudes of Vladimir Lenin and the Bolsheviks, and in 1906 she joined the Mensheviks. Two years later she was

Alexandra (Aleksandra Mikhailovna) Kollontai. (Hulton Archive/Getty Images)

forced to flee Russia after her pamphlet, *Finland and Socialism,* was published. Her call for an armed insurrection upset Russian authorities, and to avoid arrest, she went to live in Germany. In 1915 Kollontai joined the Bolsheviks. She returned to Russia following the February 1917 Revolution and participated in the Bolshevik October Revolution. Although her relations with Lenin were not cordial, she was appointed commissar for social welfare in the male-dominated Bolshevik administration. She clashed with Lenin and was marginalized after identifying with dissident Bolsheviks. She was posted abroad from 1923 until 1945. Kollontai survived the Stalinist purges and died on March 9, 1952.

—*Olivier Buirette*

See also Russian Revolution and Women

References and Further Reading

Figes, Orlando, and Boris Kolonitskii. 1999. *Interpreting the Russian Revolution: The Language and Symbols of 1917.* New Haven, CT: Yale University.

Fitzpatrick, Sheila, and Yuri Slezkine. 2000. *In the Shadow of Revolution: Life Stories of Russian Women from 1917 to the Second World War.* Princeton, NJ: Princeton University Press.

McDermid, Jane, and Anna Hillyar. 2004. *Midwives of the Revolution: Female Bolsheviks and Women Workers in 1917.* Athens: Ohio University.

Spartacus Web. "Russian Revolution." http://www.spartacus.schoolnet.co.uk/LRUSsimulation.htm (accessed March 26, 2004).

World Socialist Website. http://www.wsws.org/articles/2003/jul2003/sedv-j01.shtml (accessed March 26, 2004).

Kollwitz, Kathe (1867–1944)

German artist whose works illustrated the suffering caused by poverty and war. Kathe Kollwitz (née Schmidt) was born in Königsberg, Prussia, in 1867. As a young graphic artist, Kollwitz, who attended the School for Women Artists in Berlin and the Academy of Arts in Munich, unequivocally depicted her concerns for oppressed victims in anguished portrayals of poverty, unemployment, and hunger. In 1891 she married Karl Kollwitz, a physician who ran a clinic for the needy in one of Berlin's most impoverished neighborhoods. As Kollwitz worked alongside her husband, she became even more moved by the exploitation of the poor. Initially committed to revolution as a means of attacking societal ills, Kollwitz earned her artistic reputation for depictions of historical events such as the revolt of Silesian weavers in 1844, first exhibited as *The Weavers' Rebellion* in 1898, and for her series, *The Peasant War,* based on an unsuccessful uprising of sixteenth-century peasants. Completed in 1908, *The Peasant War* earned her a year's study in Italy.

Between 1908 and 1943, Kollwitz recorded her thoughts in journals, which were published in 1955. Although her entries for August 1914 revealed a mother's fear that her two sons might enlist in the military, they also indicated that she was so swayed by the rhetoric of sacrifice that she persuaded her husband that their second-born son, Peter, was doing his duty to Germany by volunteering. Although her diaries record overwhelming expressions of grief after Peter was killed on the western front in October 1914, they also include her avowal to keep the faith. Inspired by Goethe's philosophical statement that "seed for the planting must not be ground," Kollwitz was determined to cultivate her own artistic talent to achieve what Peter, an aspiring artist, might have accomplished himself. In 1916 she also completed the first of eighty-four self-portraits (Kearns 1976, 135).

By 1918, distressed by the huge numbers of young German men who had been killed and appalled by the devastating effect of war on human lives, Kollwitz concluded that her son and others had sacrificed their lives for hollow and meaningless ideals. Hence, she refuted poet Richard Dehmel's appeal for all fit men to volunteer in order to save Germany's honor. She published an open letter in a socialist daily, pleading that "no more should die" (Friedrichsmeyer 1989, 213). Kollwitz's etchings and lithographs had routinely demonstrated a deep and abiding compassion for the suffering of mothers and children. After the war, however, she realized these figures were the primary victims of social injustice and warfare, and they became the major focus of her work. When asked to create a memorial to the memory of Karl Liebknecht, the leader of the German Communist Party who was murdered in 1919, Kollwitz reluctantly agreed. Although she had abandoned her belief in revolution and violence as a means of achieving social justice, she had applauded his antiwar stance. The memorial, Gedankblah für Karl Liebknecht (Memorial for Karl Liebknecht), the first of many woodcuts, emphasized the workers filing past Liebknecht's bier rather than the revolutionary figure himself.

Although Kollwitz never joined any movements, she produced several posters for the International Workers Aid organization and offered the Women's International League for Peace and Freedom some of her lithographs. In 1924 she created her most famous poster, *Never Again War,* which depicted a young German raising his arm to protest the call-to-arms. Kollwitz also completed a series of woodcuts entitled *War,* which portrayed women speaking forcefully of the need for peace. In 1931 she unveiled a pair of sculptures titled *Mourning Parents,* modeled on herself and her husband, Karl. Begun in 1916 as a memorial to Peter, who was killed and buried in Flanders, the work now paid tribute to all victims of war. The memorial was placed in the military cemetery at Vladslo, a few miles north of Ypres, in Belgium.

Kollwitz signed a manifesto that called for the parties of the left to unite against the Nazis. She paid a price, however, for this political gesture. When Hitler rose to power in 1933, the Nazis forced her to resign her position as the first woman elected to the Prussian Academy of Arts. They also took away her teaching position and her studio space and, after 1936, forbade her to exhibit her works, which they classified as "degenerate" (Klein 1975, 119). When the Gestapo, after hearing an interview they deemed incriminating, threatened to imprison the Kollwitzes in a concentration camp, the couple vowed to commit suicide rather than capitulate. The artist was once again overwhelmed with grief when her grandson, Peter, was killed while fighting for the German army in 1942. She was further devastated when her house was bombed in 1943. By 1944 Kollwitz had begun to call herself a pacifist, admonishing that pacifism did not consist of passive waiting but "hard, hard work" (Kollwitz 1955, 183–184). Moreover, in her last lithograph, *Seeds for the Sowing,* Kollwitz stressed that the image of a physically powerful mother enclosing and protecting her children in her arms was not just encouraging an end to war but also demanding it. Kollwitz died at Moritzburg four months before the end of World War II.

—Donna Coates

See also Trauma and Brutalization Unleashed by World War I

References and Further Reading

Friedrichsmeyer, Sara. 1989. "Seeds for the Sowing": The Diary of Kathe Kollwitz. Pages 205–282 in *Arms and the Woman: War, Gender, and Literary Representation.* Edited by Helen M. Cooper, Adrienne Auslander Munich, and Susan Merrill Squier. Chapel Hill: University of North Carolina Press.

Hinz, Renate, ed. 1981 *Kathe Kollwitz: Graphics, Posters, Drawings.* New York: Pantheon.

Kearns, Martha. 1976. *Kathe Kollwitz: Woman and Artist.* New York: Feminist Press.

Klein, Mina C., and H. Arthur Klein. 1975. *Kathe Kollwitz: Life in Art.* New York: Schocken.

Kollwitz, Kathe. 1955. *The Diary and Letters of Kathe Kollwitz.* Edited by Hans Kollwitz. Chicago: Henry Regnery.

Korczak, Rozka (1921–1988)

Jewish partisan who fought the Nazis during World War II. Born in Bielsko, Poland, in 1921, Rozka Korczak moved with her family to the small village of Plosk, where she attended the public school and experienced fierce anti-Jewish bigotry. As a teenager, she joined HaShomer HaTzair (the Young Guard), a Zionist youth organization. She fled Poland following the German conquest in 1939 and made her way on foot to Vilna, Lithuania. There she joined other members of the Young Guard, who helped her find work and a roommate, Vitka Kempner, another refugee from Poland. Following the German invasion of the Soviet Union and the conquest of Lithuania, both Korczak and Kempner joined an underground resistance movement organized by Abba Kovner, a Young Guard leader. Kovner built his organization, the Fareynigte Partizaner Organizatsie (FPO; United Partisan Organization), into one of the largest and most effective Jewish partisan units of the war.

Operating from the Vilna ghetto, where the Germans had ordered Jews confined, Korczak and fellow members of the FPO smuggled food and other supplies into the area. As the Germans slowly deported Jews from the ghetto to work and death camps, Korczak and other FPO members tried to convince residents to fight back against the Nazis. Some ghetto residents took up arms and joined the FPO, but most refused and insisted that resistance would simply provoke even harsher Nazi reprisals. In small groups, Kovner smuggled his partisans out of the ghetto and into the nearby Rudninkai Forest, where they set up camp and operated as saboteurs against the German army. Korczak was among the first to leave the ghetto. She distinguished herself in sabotage operations and emerged as one of the FPO's most important leaders. She led several raids against the Germans, and Kovner, with whom she had formed a close relationship, placed her in charge of the partisans' camp.

The FPO fought alongside the Soviet army to liberate Vilna in July 1944, but afterward the Soviets ordered the Jewish partisan units to disperse. Korczak and other FPO members turned their efforts toward helping Jewish refugees left starving and homeless by the war. Korczak helped smuggle some of the refugees past the British blockade and into Palestine, arriving there herself on December 12, 1944. She was among the first eyewitnesses to report to Jewish leaders on the severity of the Holocaust, and from Palestine she continued to help smuggle Jewish refugees into the country. Along with Kovner, Kempner, and other former partisans, she settled in Kibbutz Ein Hahoresh in 1946. She remained active in the kibbutz movement and Holocaust education until her death in 1988.

—Stephen K. Stein

See also Kempner, Vitka; Landau, Emilia

References and Further Reading

Arad, Yitzhak. 1982. *Ghetto in Flames: The Struggle and Destruction of the Jews in Vilna in the Holocaust.* New York: Holocaust Library.

Cohen, Rich. 2000. *The Avengers: A Jewish War Story.* New York: Alfred A. Knopf.

Levin, Dov. 1985. *Fighting Back: Lithuanian Jewry's Armed Resistance to the Nazis, 1941–1945.* Translated by Moshe Kohn and Dina Cohen. New York and London: Holmes and Meier.

Korea: Comfort Women

Korean sex slaves of the Japanese military. During World War II the Japanese military enslaved some 200,000 women from occupied territories, forcing them to serve as comfort women in brothels operated and used by military personnel. The term *comfort women* derives from the common Japanese euphemism for brothels—comfort stations. Although substantial numbers of these women were Chinese, Taiwanese, and Filipino, the largest number came from Korea, which had been under Japanese control since the conclusion of the first Sino-Japanese War in the late nineteenth century. Three-quarters of these comfort women died during the course of the war, and a substantial percentage of the survivors succumbed soon after due to the consequences of their enslavement—chronic malnourishment, communicable diseases, and severe psychological disorders that led to institutionalization or suicide (Pollitt 2001). Thus, despite the large numbers of women subjected to this type of enslavement, relatively few survived long enough to bring the crimes against them to the attention of the world. Indeed, because of the stigma attached to prostitution, whether forced or not, those women who did survive relatively intact often wished to conceal their victimization in order to salvage what they could of their lives. Given that their patriarchal societies typically stigmatized the victims of rape, the comfort women could not have expected to be regarded with sympathy.

In the early 1990s, however, as the fiftieth anniversaries of the beginning and end of World War II occasioned a renewed interest in the events of that era, some of the surviving comfort women began to come forward, tell their personal stories, and demand a formal apology and compensation from the Japanese government. Having reconstructed their lives in the aftermath of the war, these women were now becoming elderly and recognized that the record of the atrocities committed against them might disappear entirely with their deaths if they did not speak out. Paradoxically, the Japanese government's long-standing reluctance to acknowledge any specific atrocities committed by the Japanese military during the war actually served to bring more attention to the almost forgotten enslavement of the comfort women. Moreover, some reactionary political elements in Japan provoked outrage by asserting that the comfort women had been volunteers, and the sense of outrage was compounded when this lie made its way into a very popular Japanese history published in comic-book form. Developments in the intervening decades—the women's rights movement, the postwar independence movements in the non-Western world, the development of a postcolonial consciousness, and the continual reminders of the war criminals who had escaped judgment before the tribunals of the immediate postwar years—all served to create sympathy for the comfort women, not only because of the crimes committed against them but also because of the long delay in bringing their oppressors to justice. The comfort women, called *halmoni* in Korean, eventually formed an organization, the Korean Council for the Women Drafted for Sexual Slavery in Japan, in order to share and create a documentary record of their experiences; to create a clearinghouse for information, contacts, and services of use to the membership; and to assist with legal and journalistic inquiries. By the late 1990s there were about 150 surviving comfort women in Korea.

The Japanese government has long claimed that its $500 million reparation payment to South Korea in 1965, when the two nations normalized relations, included any compensation due to the comfort women (*The Economist,* October 10, 1998). In 1995 Japanese Prime Minister Tomiichi Muayama expressed his great personal regret at the enslavement of the comfort women, but he stopped short of offering a formal government apology. Likewise, although he established a fund to compensate these women, the compensation was loosely defined and the fund was to be sustained by voluntary contributions from Japanese corporations, not by monies allocated from the Japanese government. The sense that these were at best half-measures was reinforced by a Japanese appeals court decision to overturn an almost token award made to three of the comfort women; the three had brought a civil case against former Japanese officers who had run the brothels in which the women had been forced to work. When the women attempted to use the U.S. Alien Tort Claims Act—which allows foreigners to use U.S. courts to sue for compensation for human rights violations—the cases were derailed by the intervention of the U.S. State Department, which pointed out that treaties between the United States and Japan precluded claims for damages resulting from the war. Again, there was a great show of sympathy for the comfort women but very little actual action on their behalf. Internationally, the most positive, concrete result of the comfort women's testimony and the increased activism on their behalf has been the pointed judicial attention paid by international courts to crimes against women in subsequent conflicts such as those in Bosnia and Rwanda.

In Korea itself, however, the government has established a fund to support the former comfort women, now largely elderly and retired. A residence called the House of Sharing, intended for those women who can no longer rely on family support, has been built adjacent to the Memorial Hall for Comfort Women, a multipurpose facility that is part memorial, part museum, part art gallery, and part educational center. In the past decade, several noteworthy novels have explored the lives of the comfort women: Nora Okja Keller's *Comfort Woman* (1997); Chang-Rae Lee's *A Gesture Life* (1999); and Therese Park's *A Gift of the Emperor* (1997).

—Martin Kich

See also Korea, Women and the Home Front, World War II

References and Further Reading

The Economist. 1996. "Cold Comfort." May 18: 36–37.

———. 1998. "Squid, Remorse, and Unpop Music." October 10: 38–39.

Hirofumi, Hayashi. 1998. Japanese Comfort Women in Southeast Asia. *Japan Forum* 10 (September):211–219.

Piper, Nicola. 2001. Transnational Women's Activism in Japan and Korea: The Unresolved Issue of Military Sexual Slavery. *Global Networks* 1 (April):155–170.

Pollitt, Katha. 2001. Subject to Debate. *Nation,* June 11:10.

Shanahan, Noreen. 1999. The Fifty-Year Search for Justice. *Herizons* 12 (Winter):15–17.

———. 1999. Kim Soon-duk. *New Internationalist* 312 (May):34–35.

Stetz, Margaret D., and Bonnie B. C. Oh, eds. 2001. *Legacies of the Comfort Women of World War II.* Armonk, NY: M. E. Sharpe.

Tanaka, Toshiyuki. 2002. *Japan's Comfort Women: Sexual Slavery and Prostitution during World War II and the U.S. Occupation.* London: Routledge.

Yoshiaki, Yoshimi. 2000. *Comfort Women: Sexual Slavery in the Japanese Military during World War II.* New York: Columbia.

Korea, Women and the Home Front, World War II

Numerous changes for women on the Korean Peninsula were brought about by World War II. Prior to the onset of the war, Confucianism's rigid hierarchical order of human relationships largely restricted women's roles in Korea to that of wife and mother. Japanese colonial policy (1910–1945), in conjunction with manpower shortages caused by military conscription, created a breakdown in the Confucian value system as women were increasingly recruited to work in factories and fields. Grinding rural poverty and a desire to help support their families forced growing numbers of impoverished young women with little or no formal education to migrate to Seoul in search of employment. This migration laid the foundation for changes that would reverberate throughout Korea in the coming decades.

Patriarchal Korean society was put under extreme pressure by the Japanese colonial administration during World War II as imperial policies sought to exploit every available resource on the Korean Peninsula. As acute manpower shortages brought about by military conscription devastated the economy, women were viewed as an exploitable and inexpensive labor supply. Workers were needed to replace men forcibly transferred to Japan's mines and factories to support the Japanese war effort. In an effort to fully mobilize Korean society, the Japanese colonial administration established the Women's Volunteer Labor Corp in 1944 as a means of providing cheap labor for Japanese factories in Korea and Japan.

Not all women chose to conform to the rigid patriarchal social system that defined a woman's place in society. Some decided to go underground to fight the Japanese occupation while other activists fled Korea in order to join overseas independence movements. Some women had also gained access to education.

Under Japanese educational policy, Korean children were indoctrinated to become subjects of the emperor. Nevertheless, increasing numbers of parents, inspired by the ideas of modernization and Korean national liberation, began sending their daughters to school. By the start of World War II some women had entered the education mainstream. During the war, however, Japan's mass military mobilization forced many Korean women to quit their studies to work in service industries and factories to support the war effort.

It was also during World War II that thousands of Korean women were forcibly conscripted and shipped throughout Asia as "comfort women" to service the sexual needs of Japanese troops. As far back as the 1920s, Japanese agents recruited Korean women with promises of jobs abroad. Once separated from their families, the women were forced into prostitution. It became commonplace for Korean women to be abducted and sold to pay debts or forced to become sex slaves for the Japanese military. Following Japan's defeat, Korean comfort women were either deserted or detained in allied POW camps; some never returned home.

—Keith A. Leitich

See also Korea: Comfort Women

References and Further Reading

Cho, Kyung Won. 1994. Overcoming Confucian Barriers: Changing Educational Opportunities for Women in Korea. In *Women of Japan and Korea: Continuity and Change.* Edited by Joyce Gelb and Marian Lief Palley. Philadelphia: Temple.

Hicks, George. 1995. *The Comfort Women: Japan's Brutal Regime of Enforced Prostitution in the Second War.* New York: W. W. Norton.

Lee, Hyo-Chae, and Joo-Sook Kim. 1979. *The Status of Korean Women.* Seoul: Ehwa Women's University.

Park, Yong-Ock. 1977. The Women's Modernization Movement in Korea. In *Virtues in Conflict: Tradition and the Korean Woman Today.* Edited by Sandra Mattielli. Seoul: Royal Asiatic Society, Korea Branch/Samhwa.

Korean War, American Women and the

The mobilization of American women necessitated by the Korean War (1950–1953). In June 1950, when the Korean War began, 22,000 women were serving in the U.S. armed forces as a result of the Women's Armed Services Integration Act of 1948. Of this number, nurses comprised 7,000. The remainder served in the ranks of the Women's Army Corps (WAC), Women Accepted for Voluntary Emergency Service (WAVES; or Navy Women's Reserve), Women Marines, and Women in the Air Force (WAF). As the U.S. government moved more men to the front, women again assumed vacated clerical and administrative, engineering, and technical positions.

Before recruiting began in earnest, 1,600 servicewomen of the Organized Reserve Corps (which in 1952 became known as the U.S. Army Reserve) returned to the Army Nurse Corps, Women's Medical Specialist Corps, and the WAC. A total of 640 military nurses served in Korea (540 from the army, 50 from the navy, and 50 from the air force). Seventy percent of the

Korean War (1950–1953)

American Army Nurses

"Army nurses were the first American women to be dispatched with the Armed Forces to the combat zone. A unit assigned to a mobile surgical hospital arrived here July 5 (1950), less than 10 days after hostilities began. Now with more than 300 nurses in the combat zone, they are providing expert surgical and bedside care in every hospital to which wounded are evacuated."

—John P Wooden, "Background on Army Nurses in Korea," Department of the Army, Office of the Surgeon General, Technical Information Office, February 12, 1951, Record Group 112, Office of the Surgeon General, U.S. Medical Department (AMEDD) Records 1947–1961, HD 211 (Nurses) Korea, National Archives and Records Administration, College Park, MD.

"As in the case of other early acute military shortages, we didn't have nearly enough nurses to go around. Anesthetists, like 1st Lieutenant Katherine Wilson, Wanesboroo, Va., were obliged to serve as many as six operating tables simultaneously and at times worked until they themselves were nearly anesthetized by the fumes."

—SFC Doug Du Bois, "Angels of Mercy," *Stars and Stripes,* October 14, 1950.

Margaret Zane's Notebook

Zane, assistant chief nurse of the first MASH unit, had served in Europe during World War II and was then assistant operating room supervisor at the Walter Reed Hospital, Washington, D.C. In 1950, she was transferred overseas, assigned to a hospital in Korea.

" . . . based on World War II experience, [n]inety percent of fatal casualties occurred on the front line because the critically wounded could not receive immediate surgical treatment. Therefore it seemed logical to set up a hospital unit mobile enough to render this service on division level reasonably safe from the fighting. Some authorities debated sending female nurses with this type of unit on the grounds that it was a rough and rugged existence and the girls couldn't take it."

army nurses were attached to Mobile Army Surgical Hospital (MASH) Units. In the United States, 120,000 military servicewomen served during the war, primarily as clerks and administrators.

In 1950, 629 WAC personnel served in the Far East Command (FEC) Headquarters. By 1951 their numbers had increased to 2,600. Women were able to rise in the ranks and to move into arenas formerly occupied only by men. Women were ward masters in military hospitals in Japan and senior noncommissioned officers (NCOs) in motor pools, mess halls, and post offices. Women could be found in administration, in communications, and in intelligence. They worked as censors, interpreters, draftsmen, weather personnel, and even aides-de-camp.

The Army Nurse Corps (ANC) numbered 3,450 in 1950. By 1951 it had grown to 5,397 women, the majority of these being World War II veterans. Five hundred and forty nurses volunteered to serve in Korea. One, Captain Viola McConnell of the U.S. Military Advisory Group/Republic of Korea (USMAG/ROK), assisted in the evacuation of 700 Americans from

October 1950

"They ran into their first brush with death at the hands of the enemy when their unit, attached to the 7th Division, was ordered to move to Pusan on October 7 by convoy. Twice during the 326-mile trip over rugged mountain roadways, the motorcade was attacked by North Koreans, who had been bypassed by American troops. At 3 A.M. in the pitch dark of a single-file mountain pass, a battalion of Reds opened up on the 1,000-yard-long line of vehicles composed of medics, signalmen and other service troops. The nurses scrambled into a roadside ditch, while the battle flared all about them. . . . All through the night they huddled together for warmth in the cold roadside pit as machine guns and rifles hammered. Tracers penciled lines in the night overhead and ricochets screamed from hillside rock. The siege lasted nearly 12 hours and then a mile further [the siege] reoccurred."

—Tom A. Hamrick,
"The Lucky 13: Army Nurses in Korea Bring Medical Aid and Morale to Frontlines,"
Pacific Stars and Stripes, clipping in Zane's notebook.

November 1951

"Our hospital was the last to evacuate Hungnan. It was not a happy farewell when the soldiers escorted us to the beach. Just before our LCM pulled away, one dewy-eyed youth cried out, 'Everything seemed all right as long as the nurses were here.'"

—Captain Margaret Zane (later Fleming), Report on Nursing Aspects in Korea,
Army Nurse Corps, November 1951, Collection no. 1925, Margaret (Zane) Fleming Collection,
Gift of Frances Zane, Women in Military Service for America Memorial Foundation, Inc.

American Teacher Working for the U.S. Air Force

" . . . working in Korea with the fellows fighting there proved to be the ultimate experience of my lifetime. When I first arrived at Air Base K-13, four or five USO girls were also assigned there but, within 6 weeks, they were removed. . . . Then I was the only woman on a base of 5,000 men."

—Ann B. Zoss (later Roberts), teacher in the GED-Educational Center,
as told to Kathleen Vander-Boom, March 26, 2000,
Women in Military Service for America Memorial Foundation Archives.

Seoul. For her actions, McConnell received a Bronze Star and the Oak Leaf Cluster.

Four days after U.S. troops joined United Nations forces, 57 female nurses arrived in Korea. Twelve army nurses in the first MASH unit moved out on July 8, 1950, to the front line at Taejon. One month later, over 100 army nurses were stationed near the front lines within Korea, positions they would occupy throughout the war. Three African American nurses served in Korea: Lt. Martha E. Cleveland and Lt. Nancy Greene Peace were posted at the 11th Evacuation Hospital, and Lt. Evelyn Decker served with the 8055th MASH. Still others served in hospitals in Japan and Hawaii.

MASH nurses also adopted the protective clothing of the male soldiers for whom they were caring. Combat boots, fatigues, and steel helmets replaced more traditional nursing uniforms, and the women lived in tents like other military personnel. Amazingly, despite their proximity to battles, not a single army nurse died in Korea.

At the beginning of the war, the navy's WAVES hoped to enlist 1,000 officers and 10,000 servicewomen in their ranks. That initial goal was not met. To increase their numbers, Captain Joy Bright Hancock implemented a voluntary recall. When that failed to provide the desired numbers, an involuntary recall followed. It was the first time in American history that women, as well as their male counterparts, were called up, voluntarily or not. To further add to the ranks, unreasonable deterrents were eliminated. The ban against married women serving was dropped; additionally, the age of enlistment was lowered to eighteen, following the successful 1948 model of the army and air force. As a result, WAVES numbers went from 3,239 in 1950 to a high of 9,466 in November 1952.

Recruited WAVES were sent to a six-week training program, initially held at the Great Lakes Training Center; in October 1951, the program moved to the Naval Training Center in Bainbridge, Maryland. Petty officer leadership schools were established at San Diego and Bainbridge, Georgia, in 1953, while officer candidates trained at Officer Indoctrination Unit (W) at Newport, Rhode Island. Finally, a Reserve Officer Candidate (ROC) Program began at the Great Lakes Training Center.

The Navy Nurse Corps consisted of 1,921 women when the Korean War broke out in June 1950. It peaked at 3,405 in November 1951, but only 2,600 remained at the end of the war. The growth included an involuntary recall of 926 navy nurses. The Navy Nurse Corps also recruited and commissioned civilian nurses. Captain Winnie Gibson oversaw the Nurse Corps, which served in 126 stations in the United States; at 25 foreign stations; on 8 Military Sea Transport Service (MSTS) ships; in 3 MSTS ports; in 15 civilian schools; and on 3 hospital ships. In fact, thirty-five percent of the U.S. battle casualties from the Korean War were evacuated directly to the USS *Consolation,* USS *Haven,* and USS *Repose.* In August 1950, a fourth ship, the USS *Benevolence,* was accidentally rammed and sank before leaving port. One nurse died as a result.

The women's auxiliary unit of the U.S. Coast Guard, the SPARs (*Semper Paratus*—Always Ready), had been demobilized in 1946. The unit began recruiting again in late 1949, and by 1950 200 former SPARs had voluntarily reenlisted. They served mostly in U.S. territory. The Air Force Nurse Corps was involved in the evacuation of approximately 350,000 patients during the course of the war. Within the marines, many of the 2,787 women in the corps earned entry to a broader range of occupational specialties than did those in other branches of military service.

In all, the navy lost twelve nurses as well as eighteen enlisted WAVES. Eleven navy nurses were killed when their plane crashed on takeoff from Kwaejon Island, and another one died as a result of the sinking of the USS *Benevolence.* The deaths of the WAVES were also not combat related. Three nurses received the Bronze Star, six the Commendation Ribbon, and ninety the Navy Unit Commendation. In addition, U.S. Army Major Genevieve Smith died in a plane crash in transit to her post as chief nurse in Korea. Three air force nurses also died.

Prior to 1950 American women had a limited presence in Korea, primarily as missionaries. During the war, women were captured, marched, and treated as brutally as their male soldier counterparts. Nellie Dyer from North Little Rock, Arkansas, and Helen Rosser, from Atlanta, Georgia, were held as POWs along with members of the 24th Infantry Division.

While most servicewomen were confined to traditional or "female" jobs, the Korean War afforded a unique opportunity for a few civilian women to break the mold. Anna Rosenberg had been a political consultant and labor relations expert, working for President Roosevelt as his personal observer during World War II. Building on her career as one of the first women to hold various directorial posts in the U.S. government, Rosenberg was appointed assistant secretary of defense for manpower and personnel in 1950. During her tenure she oversaw all defense department policies and created the Defense Advisory Committee on Women in the Services (DACOWITS), a committee of fifty professional women (chaired by Mary Lord) that aggressively recruited women for military service. Rosenberg, a lifelong civil rights and women's suffrage advocate, also effectively integrated formerly segregated African American and white troops into cohesive combat units. For her service, Anna Rosenberg received the Department of Defense's Exceptional Civilian Award in 1953.

The war provided unique opportunities for both U.S. civilian women and women in the military, who were now an integral part of the armed forces. Marguerite "Maggie" Higgins, a reporter for the *New York Herald Tribune,* had the distinction of being the only female war correspondent during the Korean War. Margaret Bourke-White, a photographer with World War II experience, was sent by *Life* magazine in the spring of 1951 to photograph bomber planes belonging to the Strategic Air Command in Korea. Bourke-White was the first woman to fly in a B-47 jet, and she subsequently accompanied South Korean police as they moved against guerrilla fighters.

—*Sarah Hilgendorff List*

See also Bourke-White, Margaret; Higgins, Marguerite

References and Further Reading

Godson, Susan H. 2001. *Serving Proudly: A History of Women in the U.S. Navy.* Annapolis, MD: Naval Institute Press.

Goldberg, Vicki. 1987. *Margaret Bourke-White: A Biography.* Reading, MA: Addison-Wesley.

Higgins, Marguerite. 1951. *War in Korea: The Report of a Woman Combat Correspondent.* Garden City, NY: Doubleday.

"1950s." Women in Military Service for America Memorial. http://www.womensmemorial.org (accessed January 21, 2005).

Korean War, Women and the

The roles of women during the Korean War (1950–1953). Not only were women indiscriminate victims of offensives and counteroffensives, they were also active participants in the war effort. Women from all sides of the conflict filled essential noncombat support roles, from nurses and caregivers to supply clerks and corpsmen as well as communication technicians and intelligence analysts, to help alleviate labor shortages.

South Korean women were not only refugees during the Korean War, they were also active participants in the South Korean war effort. Korean women served in a variety of capacities and filled medical support occupations, such as surgeons, nurses, and dentists, that were in short supply due to the need for active duty troops. In the U.N. forces under U.S. military command, women from the United States, Australia, Canada, and Britain played a variety of subordinate roles: from logistical and administrative posts to nurses and healthcare providers in hospitals and Mobile Army Surgical Hospital (MASH) units. In contrast with their southern counterparts, women in North

An American military nurse stands over wounded soldiers before directing the medical service technicians to load the soldiers on the military medical aircraft, 1953. (Genevieve Naylor/Corbis)

Korea were fully integrated in the military, serving in guerrilla units alongside their male counterparts as well as serving in military support roles.

Freed from the constraints of the Yi Dynasty and Japanese occupation, women in South Korea had made gains in education and were increasingly entering the workforce. The 1948 constitution had given women equality with men. The onset of the Korean War changed the status of women in South Korea. Not only did women who were trained at the Republic of Korea's army medical field school serve in the Republic of Korea Women's Army Corp (ROKWAC) as surgeons, nurses, and dentists, they were employed by war industries. As the need for servicewomen increased, more and more Korean women enlisted, and some trained to serve as officers in the ROKWAC. Recruits were given basic military training and then assigned to units as needed. As the war continued, women were given specialized training and were attached to specialized units.

The greatest need for non-Korean servicewomen in Korea during the war was for nurses. Between 500 and 600 female U.S. Army Nurse Corp personnel served in the war zone supporting troops during combat operations. In addition, several thousand women worked in hospitals in the Far East Command during the Korean War. By the end of the war, over 120,000 women were on active duty serving as administrative aids, stenographers, and translators to release male soldiers for combat duty. There were also women from other countries—Australia, Belgium, Canada, Denmark, France, Great Britain, Greece, Italy, the Netherlands, Norway, Sweden, Thailand, and Turkey—who served during the Korean War. Like their American counterparts, a majority of these women served as nurses in hospitals.

Women in North Korea were on a different footing than their southern counterparts. Following the consolidation of his control, Premier Kim Il Sung (president after 1972) promoted gender equality through the incorporation of equal rights in the North Korean constitution. North Korean women became members of the Worker-and-Peasant Red Guard or joined political organizations for women.

By the beginning of the Korean War women were integrated into the ranks of the North Korean military. Women aided in transporting supplies to the front as well as other logistical tasks. Female soldiers served not only in traditional support roles but as frontline troops alongside their male counterparts. North Korean women frequently posed as refugees to infiltrate enemy lines to gather intelligence or to inflict casualties on unsuspecting U.N. forces. In addition, women fought with guerrilla units in the South, engaging in hit-and-run operations as well as sabotage.

—Keith A. Leitich

See also Korean War, American Women and the

References and Further Reading

Jancar, Barbara Wolfe. 1978. *Women under Communism.* Baltimore: Johns Hopkins University Press.

Lee, Hyo-Chae, and Joo-Sook Kim. 1979. *The Status of Korean Women.* Seoul: Ehwa Women's University Press.

Lee, Young Moo. 1980. Birth of the Korean Army, 1945–1950: Evaluation of the Role of the United States Occupation Forces. Pages 639–656 in *Korea and World Affairs.* Vol. 4. Seoul: Research Center for Peace and Reunification.

Kuckhoff, Greta (1902–1981)

Member of the anti-Nazi *Rote Kapelle* (Red Chorus) resistance group in Germany. Greta Lorke was born in Frankfurt on December 14, 1902. She studied in Germany at the University of Berlin under Werner Sombart and Max Weber before attending the University of Wisconsin. There she was part of John Commons's social-discussion group, the "Friday-niters," and met Avrid Harnack and Mildred Fish, Harnack's future wife. After returning to Germany, she taught English and worked as a translator. She married Adam Kuckhoff in January 1937 and had a son.

She introduced the Harnacks to Harro and Libertas Schulze-Boysen in 1940. After the Nazis discovered Schulze-Boysen's espionage network, Greta Kuckhoff was arrested on September 9, 1942. She was sentenced to die, but the sentence was commuted to ten years of imprisonment. She was freed by the Soviets when they took control of Berlin. She remained in East Germany and became director of the Notenbank.

—*Bernard Cook*

See also Harnack-Fish, Mildred; Schulze-Boysen, Libertas

References and Further Reading

Brysac, Shareen Blair. 2000. *Resisting Hitler: Mildred Harnack and the Red Orchestra: The Life and Death of an American Woman in Nazi Germany.* New York: Oxford University.

Kuckhoff, Greta. 1974. *Vom Rosenkranz zur Roten Kapelle: Ein Lebensbericht* [From Roseranz to the Rote Kapelle: An Account of My Life]. Frankfurt: Röderberg-Verlag.

Kuczynski, Ursula (aka Werner, Ruth [Sonja]) (1907–2000)

Secret agent of the Soviet intelligence service. Ursula Kuczynski was born on May 15, 1907, in Germany. In the mid-1920s Kuczynski joined the German communist party and was recruited by the Soviet intelligence service. Her code name was Ruth (or Sonja) Werner. After initial espionage training Kuczynski was sent to China where she became acquainted with Dr. Richard Sorge, who later became one of Stalin's top spies during World War II. From the mid-1930s she served as an intelligence officer in several European countries including Britain and Switzerland. She was supported by her father, brother, and husband, who were all engaged in Soviet intelligence work. During World War II Kuczynski helped the Soviet war effort by providing military intelligence. She was part of the worldwide Soviet spy network that helped Stalin obtain the scientific information needed for development of the Soviet atomic bomb. It seems that Kuczynski lost contact with her Soviet handlers after the end of the war, but she turned up in the newly established communist (East) German Democratic Republic in 1950, where she took a position within the state-run propaganda apparatus. By the mid-1950s she was engaged in a new career as a freelance author. Kuczynski not only wrote about her professional experience as a spy and intelligence handler but also published several children's books. She may not have been active within the East German intelligence service, but she was looked upon as a role model for young communist intelligence officers. When East Germany collapsed in 1989–1990, she was already well into her eighties but was still engaged in party work within the reformed communist party. She died on July 7, 2000.

Ursula Kuczynski was remarkable for her own career in intelligence and politics, but that was true for other members of her family as well, especially for her brother Jürgen Kuczynski (1904–1997). Jürgen worked for the Soviet intelligence service within Western intelligence agencies during World War II. He later became one of the most important German historians of economic history. The secret careers of the Kuczynski family still need to be addressed in more detail by historical research because current information relies heavily on communist propaganda publications.

—Oliver Benjamin Hemmerle

See also Harnack-Fish, Mildred; Niederkirchner, Käthe; Rosenberg, Ethel

References and Further Reading

Kuczynski, Jürgen. 1975. *Memoiren* [Memoirs]. Berlin (Ost): Aufbau.

Sagasser, Joachim, ed. 1982. *Auskünfte über Ruth Werner zum 75. Geburtstag.* [About Ruth Werner on Her 75th Birthday]. Berlin (Ost): Neues Leben.

Werner, Ruth. 1978. *Sonjas Rapport* [Sonja's Report]. Berlin: Neues Leben.

KUFRIN, MILKA (1921–)

Yugoslav partisan. The daughter of Catholic peasants in Croatia, Milka Kufrin was encouraged by her parents to attend school. Although her father had been active in the Croatian Peasant Party, as a student at the Faculty of Agriculture at the University of Zagreb, Milka joined the Communist Youth Organization. Because she was the daughter of peasants, in 1940 Kufrin was sent to the suburbs of Zagreb to work with young peasants.

When Kufrin volunteered for military service following the German invasion of Yugoslavia and the organization of the Partisan resistance, her request was refused. When she persisted, she was sent in October 1941 to join a unit of partisans at Kordun about seventy miles from Zagreb.

In 1942 Kufrin was assigned the task of sabotaging the Zagreb–Riejka railroad line. For nearly eight months she went out every night and set explosives along the heavily guarded line. Following the war she was proclaimed a national hero by the Yugoslav communist government.

—Bernard Cook

See also Durova, Nadezhda Andreyevna; Makarova, Tat'iana Petrovna, and Belik, Vera Luk'ianovna; Milosavljevic, Danica

References and Further Reading

Jancar-Webster, Barbara. 1990. *Women and Revolution in Yugoslavia, 1941–1945.* Denver, CO: Arden.

KURMANJAN-DATKHA (CA. 1811–1907)

An influential leader of Kyrgyz tribes in the Pamiro-Alay area in the second half of the nineteenth century. Kurmanjan played an important role in the political and military development in this part of Central Asia. She grew up in the highlands of Kyrgyzstan and received no formal education. In 1832 she married Alymbek-Datkha, the leader of the Kyrgyz tribes in the highlands of Pamiro-Alay (now southern Kyrgyzstan).

At that time, the Kyrgyz tribes were involved in a devastating war against the powerful Kokand Khanate, a regional power in the Fergana valley of Central Asia that attempted to establish its control over all of the land populated by Kyrgyz tribes. The irregular Kyrgyz militia from Pamiro-Alay was involved in domestic conflicts within the Kokand Khanate and its numerous military campaigns against its neighbors. In the brutal military tradition of that era, the winners often took no prisoners, killing entire military regiments. In this environment of perpetual war, many Kyrgyz women had no choice but to become the breadwinners in their families, assuming the difficult duties of highland animal husbandry and often helping men in military campaigns against enemies.

Kurmanjan entered the Central Asian political arena in an unusual way. She broke the traditional perception dominant in Central Asian society at the time that viewed women exclusively as silent housewives who had no political rights or public voice. She became interested in political and military developments and, soon after her marriage, became one of her husband's most trusted advisers. In 1862 Kokand troops killed Alymbek-Datkha and threatened the Kyrgyz tribes who had been under his leadership. Under these circumstances Kyrgyz tribal leaders accepted Kurmanjan as the Datkha, the leader of their tribes (called Kurmanjan Mamatbai-Kyzy, or Alay Queen, by Russian officers in the region). She consolidated the Kyrgyz tribes and revived military morale among the militiamen. She also began an active search for allies in the fight against the Kokand Khanate.

In 1864 Kurmanjan-Datkha contacted the commander of the Russian Imperial troops. She led intense negotiations with the Russian military officials and diplomats as well as consultations among other Kyrgyz tribes. Meanwhile, the Kokand Khanate was defeated by the Russian troops, and in 1876 it was abolished by the Russian colonial authorities, ending several decades of wars and instability in the region. After several years of talks Kurmanjan-Datkha peacefully accepted the Russian Empire's protectorate over the tribes under her leadership. Her son Abdyldabek, however, actively resisted the Russian advance in this area and fought against the Imperial troops. The Russian officers in the region often called her "Alay Queen." She became the only woman in nineteenth-century Central Asia who was awarded the military rank of colonel in the Russian Imperial Army.

In post-Soviet Kyrgyzstan she was promoted as the symbol of the liberal attitudes of traditional Kyrgyz society toward women. Many streets, schools, and charity organizations were named after her.

—Rafis Abazov

See also Guljamal-Khan(um)

References and Further Reading

Abazov, Rafis. 2004. *Historical Dictionary of Kyrgyzstan.* Lanham, MD: Scarecrow Press.

Akayev, Askar. 2003. *Kyrgyz Statehood and the National Epos "Manas."* New York: Global Scholarly Publications.

Kakeev, Askar, and Vladimir Ploskikh, eds. 2002. *Tsarina of the Mountains: Kurmanjan and Her Times.* Bishkek, Kyrgyzstan: Ilim.